MARKS &
SPENCER

ENGLISH RUGBY

PLAYER BY PLAYER

A compilation of every player ever to have played for England

WRITTEN BY
STUART FARMER, PAUL MORGAN, NICK LODGE & ADAM HATHAWAY

This Edition first published in the UK by Green Umbrella Publishing exclusively for Marks and Spencer p.l.c.

www.marksandspencer.com

Publishers Jules Gammond, Vanessa Gardner

Printed and bound in Italy

ISBN 978-1-905828-16-6

The abbreviations in Appearances refer to the country England played against, eg Fj is Fiji and A is Australia. The asterisk denotes that the player was captain in that match. The number next to a country, eg Ar2 denotes the number of times England played against a country in that year. The (r) next to a country, eg Fj(r) denotes that the player came on as a replacement.

TION

When England played Scotland in 1871, those 40 players on duty (yes, it was 20-a-side in those days) would have had no idea what they were starting, and over 136 years later more than 1250 players have followed them into the England shirt. Well, 1285 to be precise, and I know because this book's renowned statistician, Stuart Farmer, has counted each and every one in, and out!

It was about time that those 1285 players – up to the end of the 2007 RBS Six Nations – were placed in one book and I am indebted to the publishers for bringing this project to fruition.

As editor of the world's best-selling rugby magazine, Rugby World, it is almost impossible to find all these players in one place, at one time, so, if nothing else, this book will provide me with an invaluable research resource.

The stories of the great players from the incredible Ronnie Poulton-Palmer and Wavell Wakefield, through Eric Evans and on to the incomparable Martin Johnson, have been fascinating for me to discover. Most of the players featured deserve books all to themselves and many have been the subject of biographies and autobiographies.

But it was crucial that every player, from Johnson to those who only represented England once, was included in all their glory. Each one has achieved a dream of playing international rugby. It happens to so few people that the honour must be treasured. We have listed every player but were only able to profile in detail a small percentage of those who have played for England since 1871.

No book of this nature can make it onto the shelves without a great deal of blood, sweat and yes, sometimes tears. Without Stuart the book clearly couldn't have got close to getting off the ground. I am also grateful for the contributions from Barry Newcombe, Adam Hathaway and Nick Lodge, the Green Umbrella design team, and Jane Pamenter, our proof-reader, who officially has the patience of a saint.

Things were also made all the more exciting by the arrival of Elodie May into the Morgan household as we moved into a crucial stage of the book's production. So this book must be dedicated to her and her wonderful mother, Jo. Perhaps one day Elodie will appear in the women's version of this book?

I hope, therefore, you enjoy this book as much as the team has enjoyed putting it together. We are all rugby nuts and are fascinated by the rich history of the game, which I believe cannot be matched by any other sport.

If you have any suggestions for future tomes or any comments please direct them to me at Rugby World Magazine.

As with all books of this type the odd omission and inaccuracy may appear. If any reader has any further information, which may be of use, would they please contact me at the email address below.

Yours in rugby

Paul Morgan, Editor
Paul_morgan@ipcmedia.com

A

Rob Andrew

AARVOLD, Carl Douglas, KBE
ABBOTT, Stuart Richard D, MBE
ACKFORD, Paul John
ADAMS, Alan Augustus
ADAMS, Frank Reginald
ADEBAYO, Adedayo Adeyemi
ADEY, Garry John
ADKINS, Stanley John
AGAR, Albert Eustace
ALCOCK, Arnold
ALDERSON, Frederick Hodgson Rudd
ALEXANDER, Harry
ALEXANDER, William
ALLEN, Anthony Owen
ALLISON, Dennis Fenwick
ALLPORT, Alfred
ANDERSON, Stanley Watson
ANDERSON, William Francis
ANDERTON, Charles
ANDREW, Christopher Robert, MBE
APPLEFORD, Geoff N
ARCHER, Garath Stuart
ARCHER, Herbert
ARMSTRONG, Reginald, OBE
ARTHUR, Terence Gordon
ASHBY, Roland Clive
ASHCROFT, Alan
ASHCROFT, Alec Hutchinson
ASHFORD, William, OBE
ASHWORTH, Abel
ASKEW, John Garbutt
ASLETT, Alfred Rimbault
ASSINDER, Eric Walter
ASTON, Randolph Littleton
AUTY, Joseph Richard

Sir Carl Douglas AARVOLD, KBE

Born: 7 June 1907 in Hartlepool
Died: 17 March 1991 in West Humble, Surrey
Educated: Durham School
Clubs: Cambridge University (7), Headingley (4), West Hartlepool, Durham County, Blackheath (5)
Position: Wing (8), Centre (8)
Debut: 7 Jan 1928 v Australia (Twickenham). Number: 628
Last game: 21 Jan 1933 (capt) v Wales (Twickenham)
Caps: 16 (W:9, D:1, L:6). As captain: 7 (W:2, L:5)
Scoring: 4T, 12 Pts
Appearances: 1928:A,W,I,F,S, 1929:W,I,F, 1931:W,S*,F*, 1932:SA*,W*,I*,S*, 1933:W*
Honours: Grand Slam 1928

Described by eminent rugby historian John Griffiths as "the senior gentleman of England rugby internationals", Sir Carl Aarvold made a big impact on pre-war rugby in the 1920s and 1930s.

Of Norwegian heritage Sir Carl took to the game of rugby remarkably quickly and within two years of arriving at Cambridge University he was playing for England.

Aarvold appeared in one of the game's most memorable pictures, Captains Courageous rugby print, which in 1928 showed some of the leading players in the world game.

He was only 20 when he was part of the 1928 Grand Slam winning side – under Ronald Cove-Smith – and a star of the British and Irish Lions tour to New Zealand in 1930.

Born in Hartlepool, Aarvold made a big impact on The Lions, scoring two tries – one from 40 metres – as the Lions went down 13-10 in an epic second Test on the 1930 tour, in Christchurch.

Aarvold's feat for the Lions in New Zealand – where he was also captain for the first Test – has never been bettered. Two Welshmen – Malcolm Price (1959) and Gerald Davies (1971) – joined Aarvold in the two-try club but no one has outdone him.

The 1930 Lions won the first Test 6-3 so Aarvold became the first Lions captain to beat the All Blacks, a feat not matched until 29 years later.

After his England debut Aarvold missed just seven of England's next 22 matches, leading the side in his last six appearances.

"Aarvold was regarded by those lucky enough to have seen him in action as one of the greatest midfield-backs ever to play in New Zealand," was how Peter Jackson remembers him in his Lions of England.

"Elegant was the adjective most used to capture the essence of a player whose four Varsity matches for Cambridge from 1925 to 1928 resulted in four wins for the Light Blues, Aarvold appearing in the first three in different positions: at centre, full-back and wing."

After 16 Tests for England and four with the Lions, Sir Carl retired in 1933 at just 26, called to The Bar, and away from the fields of England.

An officer in the Royal Artillery, Sir Carl, had a distinguished war record and in 1945 received the OBE.

Educated at Durham School, he was a man who excelled at a number of sports, playing rugby for Headingley, West Hartlepool and Blackheath. Sir Carl was also president of the Lawn Tennis Association. The LTA even named their most prestigious award after him. He also served on the British Boxing Board of Control and became a seven-handicap golfer.

He wasn't knighted for services to rugby, unlike Sir Clive Woodward many decades later, but for his work in the legal profession in a career that saw him become Recorder of London.

Sir Carl was from a bygone rugby era, barely recognisable today. "A true Corinthian from an era when sport was played for the love of the game, and not much else," Jackson added.

Stuart Richard D ABBOTT, MBE

Born: 3 June 1978 in Cape Town, South Africa
Educated: Bishop's College, Diocesan College
Clubs: Stellenbosch University (SA), Griffons (SA), Western Province (SA), Leicester, Stormers (SA), Wasps (9), Harlequins
Position: Centre (6), Replacement (3)
Debut: 23 Aug 2003 v Wales (Cardiff) - 1T, 5 Pts. Number: 1248
Last game: 17 Jun 2006 (rep) v Australia (Melbourne)
Caps: 9 (W:5, L:4)
Scoring: 2T, 10 Pts
Appearances: 2003:W,F,Sm,U,W(r), 2004:NZ1(r),NZ2, 2006:I,A2(r)
Honours: RWC Winner 2003

Stuart Abbott

Paul Ackford

Paul John ACKFORD

Born: 26 February 1958 in Hanover, West Germany
Educated: Plymouth College
Clubs: Kent University, Cambridge University, Plymouth, Rosslyn Park, Metropolitan Police, Harlequins (22)
Position: Lock (22), Bench (1)
Debut: 5 Nov 1988 v Australia (Twickenham). Number: 1128
Last game: 2 Nov 1991 v Australia (Twickenham)
Caps: 22 (W:16, D:1, L:5)
Scoring: 1T, 4 Pts
Appearances: 1988:A, 1989:S,I,F,W,R,Fj, 1990:I,F,W,S,Ar, 1991:W,S,I,F,A,NZ,It,F,S,A
Honours: Grand Slam 1991

According to team-mate Jeremy Guscott, former police officer Paul Ackford was the best lock he'd ever seen. Ackford was a late developer, only joining the England fray at the age of 30, almost 10 years after appearing as an England B international, when a postgraduate at Cambridge, also earning a Blue the same season.

At 6'7" his presence in the lineout, combined with assured handling skills and a big match temperament, made him an asset to any side, especially his club, Harlequins.

When he finally broke into the England team in 1988, after impressing for London Division against Australia, he immediately formed a formidable partnership with fellow policeman Wade Dooley.

His impact with England was duly noted and he was selected for the 1989 Lions tour of Australia where he played in all three Tests, driving his forwards to Test victory, and ultimate success.

Despite, or maybe because of, his Herculean size and strength, Ackford has also gone down in union folklore for a bizarre incident in 1990 against Argentina when he was knocked out by a punch from 18-year-old Federico Mendez, leaving the field with his knees visibly buckling. It seems the harder they come, the harder they really do fall.

His consistency and commitment made him an England regular for the next two seasons, where he played an integral role in the 1991 Grand Slam. His too short international career came to an end following England's 12-6 defeat at the hands of the Australians in the 1991 World Cup final, and he now works as a journalist for The Sunday Telegraph.

Australia international David Campese paid Ackford the ultimate compliment when he said: "This guy was tough and durable, a real workhorse in the pack. It's just a shame he was a Pom and not an Aussie."

Alan Augustus ADAMS

Born: 8 May 1883 in Greymouth, New Zealand
Died: 28 July 1963 in Greymouth, New Zealand
Educated: Auckland GS
Clubs: Otago University, Otago (NZ), South Island (NZ), London University, London Hospital (1)
Position: Centre (1)
Debut: 3 Mar 1910 v France (Parc des Princes). Number: 500
Caps: 1 (W:1, L:0)
Scoring: 0 Pts
Appearances: 1910:F
Honours: Championship: 1910

Adedayo Adebayo

Frank Reginald ADAMS

Born: 1853
Died: 1932
Educated: Wellington College
Clubs: Richmond (7)
Position: Forward (7)
Debut: 15 Feb 1875 v Ireland (The Oval). Number: 57
Last game: 24 Mar 1879 (capt) v Ireland (The Oval) - 1T, 1 Pt
Caps: 7 (W:4, D:3, L:0). As captain: 2 (W:1, D:1, L:0)
Scoring: 2T, 2 Pts
Appearances: 1875:I,S, 1876:S, 1877:I, 1878:S, 1879:S*,I*

Adedayo Adeyemi ADEBAYO

Born: 30 November 1970 in Ibadan, Nigeria
Educated: Kelly College
Clubs: Swansea University, Bath (6), Parma (IT)
Position: Wing (6)
Debut: 23 Nov 1996 v Italy (Twickenham). Number: 1166
Last game: 22 Mar 1998 v Scotland (Murrayfield)
Caps: 6 (W:3, D:1, L:2)
Scoring: 2T, 10 Pts
Appearances: 1996:It, 1997:Ar1,Ar2,A,NZ1, 1998:S

Garry John ADEY

Born: 13 June 1945 in Loughborough
Educated: Humphrey Perkins GS, Loughborough TC
Clubs: Loughborough Town, Leicester (2)
Position: No 8 (2)
Debut: 6 Mar 1976 v Ireland (Twickenham). Number: 1041
Last game: 20 Mar 1976 v France (Parc des Princes)
Caps: 2 (W:0, L:2)
Scoring: 0 Pts
Appearances: 1976:I,F

Stanley John (Akker) ADKINS

Born: 2 June 1922 in Coventry
Died: 2 January 1992 in Coventry
Educated: Stoke School
Clubs: Stoke Old Boys, Army, Combined Services, Coventry (7)
Position: Lock (5), No 8 (2)
Debut: 11 Feb 1950 v Ireland (Twickenham). Number: 808
Last game: 21 Mar 1953 v Scotland (Twickenham) - 1T, 3 Pts
Caps: 7 (W:4, D:1, L:2)
Scoring: 1T, 3 Pts
Appearances: 1950:I,F,S, 1953:W,I,F,S
Honours: Championship: 1953

Albert Eustace AGAR

Born: 12 November 1923 in Hartlepool
Educated: West Hartlepool GS
Clubs: Hartlepool Rovers, Durham City, Lloyds Bank, Harlequins (7)
Position: Centre (7)
Debut: 5 Jan 1952 v South Africa (Twickenham) Number: 826
Last game: 14 Feb 1953 v Ireland (Lansdowne Road)
Caps: 7 (W:4, D:1, L:2)
Scoring: 1T, 1DG, 6 Pts
Appearances: 1952:SA,W,S,I,F, 1953:W,I
Honours: Championship: 1953

Arnold ALCOCK

Born: 18 August 1882 in Woolstanton, Staffs
Died: 7 November 1973 in Gloucester
Educated: Newcastle-under-Lyne HS
Clubs: Manchester University, Guy's Hospital (1), Richmond, Blackheath
Position: Hooker (1)
Debut: 8 Dec 1906 v South Africa (Crystal Palace). Number: 436
Caps: 1 (W:0, D:1, L:0)
Scoring: 0 Pts
Appearances: 1906:SA

Frederick Hodgson Rudd ALDERSON

Born: 27 June 1867 in Hartford, Northumberland
Died: 18 February 1925 in Hartlepool
Educated: Durham School
Clubs: Oxford University, Hartlepool Rovers (6), Blackheath
Position: Three-quarter (6)
Debut: 3 Jan 1891 (capt) v Wales (Newport) - 2C, 4 Pts. Number: 222
Last game: 7 Jan 1893 v Wales (Cardiff)
Caps: 6 (W:4, L:2). As captain: 5 (W:4, L:1)
Scoring: 1T, 4C, 11 Pts
Appearances: 1891:W*,I*,S*, 1892:W*,S*, 1893:W
Honours: Championship: 1892 (capt)

Harry ALEXANDER

Born: 6 January 1879 in Birkenhead
Died: Killed in action in 1915 in Hulluch, France
Educated: Brombrough School, Uppingham School
Clubs: Cambridge University, Birkenhead Park (7), Richmond
Position: Forward (7)
Debut: 3 Feb 1900 v Ireland (Richmond) - 1C, 2 Pts. Number: 352
Last game: 8 Feb 1902 v Ireland (Leicester)
Caps: 7 (W:2, D:1, L:4). As captain: 1 (W:0, L:1)
Scoring: 2C, 1PG, 7 Pts
Appearances: 1900:I,S, 1901:W,I,S, 1902:W*,I

William ALEXANDER

Born: 6 October 1905
Clubs: Northern (1)
Position: Wing (1)
Debut: 2 Apr 1927 v France (Stade Colombes). Number: 624
Caps: 1 (W:0, L:1)
Scoring: 0 Pts
Appearances: 1927:F

Anthony Allen

Anthony Owen ALLEN

Born: 1 September 1986 in Southampton
Educated: Clayesmore School, Millfield School
Clubs: Gloucester (2)
Position: Centre (2)
Debut: 5 Nov 2006 v New Zealand (Twickenham). Number: 1274
Last game: 11 Nov 2006 v Argentina (Twickenham)
Caps: 2 (W:0, L:2)
Scoring: 0 Pts
Appearances: 2006:NZ,Ar

Dennis Fenwick ALLISON

Born: 20 April 1931 in Tynemouth
Educated: Dame Allan's School
Clubs: Durham University, Northern, Coventry (7)
Position: Full-back (7)
Debut: 21 Jan 1956 v Wales (Twickenham) - 1PG, 3 Pts. Number: 860
Last game: 15 Mar 1958 v Scotland (Murrayfield)
Caps: 7 (W:3, D:2, L:2)
Scoring: 5PG, 15 Pts
Appearances: 1956:W,I,S,F, 1957:W, 1958:W,S
Honours: Championship: 1957, 1958

Alfred ALLPORT

Born: 12 September 1867 in Brixton
Died: 2 May 1949 in Maidenhead
Educated: London International College
Clubs: Guys Hospital, Blackheath (5)
Position: Forward (5)
Debut: 2 Jan 1892 v Wales (Blackheath). Number: 234
Last game: 17 Mar 1894 v Scotland (Raeburn Place)
Caps: 5 (W:3, L:2)
Scoring: 0 Pts
Appearances: 1892:W, 1893:I, 1894:W,I,S
Honours: Championship: 1892

Stanley Watson ANDERSON

Born: 5 August 1871 in Walsend, Tynemouth
Died: 12 February 1942 in Alnwick, Northumberland
Clubs: Rockcliff (1)
Position: Wing (1)
Debut: 4 Feb 1899 v Ireland (Lansdowne Road). Number: 332
Caps: 1 (W:0, L:1)
Scoring: 0 Pts
Appearances: 1899:I

William Francis ANDERSON

Born: 1945 in Ormskirk
Clubs: Orrell (1)
Position: Prop (1)
Debut: 6 Jan 1973 v New Zealand (Twickenham). Number: 1016
Caps: 1 (W:0, L:1)
Scoring: 0 Pts
Appearances: 1973:NZ

Charles ANDERTON

Born: c 1868
Died: c 1959
Clubs: Manchester Free Wanderers (1)
Position: Forward (1)
Debut: 16 Feb 1889 v New Zealand Natives (Blackheath). Number: 197
Caps: 1 (W:1, L:0)
Scoring: 0 Pts
Appearances: 1889:M

Christopher Robert (Rob) ANDREW, MBE

Born: 18 February 1963 in Richmond, Yorks
Educated: Barnard Castle School
Clubs: Cambridge University, Middlesbrough, Nottingham (9), Gordon (AU), Wasps (56), Toulouse (FR,5), Newcastle (1)
Position: Fly-half (68), Full-back (1), Replacement (2), Bench (9)
Debut: 5 Jan 1985 v Romania (Twickenham) - 4PG, 2DG, 18 Pts. Number: 1100
Last game: 15 Mar 1997 (rep) v Wales (Cardiff)
Caps: 71 (W:50, D:2, L:19). As captain: 2 (W:2, L:0)
Scoring: 2T, 33C, 86PG, 21DG, 396 Pts
Appearances: 1985:R,F,S,I,W, 1986:W,S,I,F, 1987:I,F,W,J(r),US, 1988:S,I,I,A1,A2,Fj,A, 1989:S,I,F,W,R*,Fj, 1990:I,F,W,S,Ar, 1991:W,S,I,F,Fj,A,NZ,It,US,F,S,A, 1992:S,I,F,W,C,SA, 1993:F,W,NZ, 1994:S,I,F,W,SA1,SA2,R,C, 1995:I,F,W,S,Ar,It*,A,NZ,F, 1997:W(r)
Honours: Grand Slam: 1991, 1992, 1995

One of England's greatest fly-halves, Rob Andrew, had a great kicking talent, which helped him to become one of his country's highest points scorers, despite the fact that he only became England's regular dead-ball expert in 1994. Astonishingly he took 55 internationals to reach 151 points, but only 15 games to score a further 245. Who knows how many points he would have scored had he been the regular kicker from the beginning?

Although a very talented cricketer who captained Cambridge University, scoring a ton against Notts in 1984, and playing for Yorkshire's 2nd XI, he made his debut for England against Romania in 1985, scoring 18 of England's 22 points.

Rob Andrew

Andrew took a while to build consistency into his game but by 1989, he was the regular England fly-half, captaining England and receiving a late call-up to The Lions squad that won in Australia.

In 1993 he claimed The Lions No 10 shirt for himself.

Under Will Carling, Andrew became a Grand Slam winner three times – 1991, 1992 and 1995, as well as suffering the agony of losing a World Cup final in 1991.

Andrew's career was defined by him winning a running battle with Bath's Stuart Barnes for the England No 10 shirt.

Although he came in for a great deal of criticism as a 'kicking fly-half' he played a crucial role in the most successful period in English rugby history.

Coach Geoff Cooke constructed one of the most destructive packs the game had ever seen and they needed a fly-half – like Andrew – to play to their strengths.

The 1993-94 season was pivotal in his abilities as a goal-kicker. Andrew completely rebuilt his kicking technique, took on permanent kicking duties for England and went on a record-breaking scoring spree.

Seven times he scored more than 20 points in a game, and nine times he scored all of England's points.

He also became the first Englishman to utilise every method of scoring in beating South Africa in 1994 – a try, a drop goal, five penalties and two conversions.

Andrew's tally of 30 points against Canada in 1994 was at the time the highest in a single match and his tally of 71 caps is still a record for an English fly-half.

No profile of a modern rugby great would be complete without a World Cup moment.

With the scores tied in the quarter-final against Australia and going into the second minute of injury time, 40 yards from the posts, Andrew saw his sweet drop goal sail beautifully between the uprights to give England victory – perhaps this was at the back of Jonny Wilkinson's mind eight years later.

England and Andrew failed to capitalise on that win over Australia in 1995 and they were beaten by a Jonah Lomu-inspired NZ in the semis, to finally finish fourth.

In 1995, when the game turned professional, he left Wasps – whom he joined from Nottingham – to become player and director of rugby at Newcastle Falcons, where he oversaw the development of many young players, most notably Wilkinson.

In the 1997-98 season Andrew – as player-coach – led Newcastle to the first Premiership title in England, and then to two English Cup victories.

In 2006 Andrew ended his association with Newcastle to become the RFU's Elite Rugby Director, where one of his first jobs was to sack Andy Robinson as England coach and appoint Brian Ashton.

Geoff Appleford

Geoff N APPLEFORD

Born: 26 September 1977 in Dundee, South Africa
Educated: Dundee HS, Martitzburg College
Clubs: Natal (SA), Pumas (SA), London Irish (1), Northampton
Position: Centre (1)
Debut: 22 Jun 2002 v Argentina (Buenos Aires). Number: 1239
Caps: 1 (W:1, L:0)
Scoring: 0 Pts
Appearances: 2002:Ar

Garath Stuart ARCHER

Born: 15 December 1974 in Durham
Educated: Durham School
Clubs: Westoe, Durham City, Bristol (7), Newcastle (14)
Position: Lock (21), Bench (2)
Debut: 2 Mar 1996 v Scotland (Murrayfield). Number: 1165
Last game: 2 Apr 2000 v Scotland (Murrayfield)
Caps: 21 (W:13, D:2, L:6)
Scoring: 0 Pts. Discipline - Sin bins: 1
Appearances: 1996:S,I, 1997:A,NZ1,SA,NZ2, 1998:F,W,S,I,A,NZ1,H,It, 1999:Tg,Fj, 2000:I,F,W,It,S
Honours: Championship: 1996, 2000

Herbert ARCHER

Born: August 1883 in Bridgwater
Died: 26 December 1946 in West Penrith, Cornwall
Educated: Blundell's School
Clubs: Guys Hospital (3), Bridgwater & Albion
Position: No 8 (3)
Debut: 16 Jan 1909 v Wales (Cardiff). Number: 467
Last game: 13 Feb 1909 v Ireland (Lansdowne Road)
Caps: 3 (W:2, L:1)
Scoring: 0 Pts
Appearances: 1909:W,F,I

Reginald (Rex) ARMSTRONG, OBE

Born: 6 December 1897 in Newcastle-upon-Tyne
Died: 17 February 1968 in Morpeth
Educated: Newcastle College of Medicine
Clubs: Durham University, Northern (1)
Position: Prop (1)
Debut: 17 Jan 1925 v Wales (Twickenham) - 1PG, 3 Pts. Number: 598
Caps: 1 (W:1, L:0)
Scoring: 1PG, 3 Pts
Appearances: 1925:W

Garath Archer

Terence Gordon ARTHUR
Born: 5 September 1940 in Hartlepool
Educated: West Hartlepool GS
Clubs: West Hartlepool, Manchester University, Cambridge University, Wasps (2), Moseley, Waterloo
Position: Centre (2)
Debut: 15 Jan 1966 v Wales (Twickenham). Number: 936
Last game: 12 Feb 1966 v Ireland (Twickenham)
Caps: 2 (W:0, D:1, L:1)
Scoring: 0 Pts
Appearances: 1966:W,I

Roland Clive (Clive) ASHBY
Born: 24 January 1937 in Mozambique
Educated: RGS High Wycombe, Harper Adams Agricultural College
Clubs: Wasps (3)
Position: Scrum-half (3)
Debut: 12 Feb 1966 v Ireland (Twickenham). Number: 942
Last game: 7 Jan 1967 v Australia (Twickenham) - 1T, 3 Pts
Caps: 3 (W:0, D:1, L:2)
Scoring: 1T, 3 Pts
Appearances: 1966:I,F, 1967:A

Alan (Ned) ASHCROFT
Born: 21 August 1930 in St Helens
Educated: Cowley GS
Clubs: RAF, St Helens, Waterloo (16)
Position: No 8 (16)
Debut: 21 Jan 1956 v Wales (Twickenham). Number: 861
Last game: 21 Mar 1959 v Scotland (Twickenham)
Caps: 16 (W:10, D:4, L:2)
Scoring: 1T, 3 Pts
Appearances: 1956:W,I,S,F, 1957:W,I,F,S, 1958:W,A,I,F,S, 1959:I,F,S
Honours: Grand Slam: 1957. Championship: 1958

Alec Hutchinson ASHCROFT
Born: 18 October 1887 in West Derby
Died: 18 April 1963 in Bath
Educated: Birkenhead Institute
Clubs: Cambridge University (1), Birkenhead Park, Blackheath, Edinburgh Wanderers
Position: Fly-half (1)
Debut: 9 Jan 1909 v Australia (Blackheath). Number: 472
Caps: 1 (W:0, L:1)
Scoring: 0 Pts
Appearances: 1909:A

William ASHFORD, OBE
Born: 18 December 1871
Died: 1 January 1954 in Topsham, Devon
Clubs: St Thomas's Hospital, Richmond (3), Exeter (1)
Position: Forward (4)
Debut: 9 Jan 1897 v Wales (Newport). Number: 297
Last game: 2 Apr 1898 v Wales (Blackheath)
Caps: 4 (W:1, D:1, L:2)
Scoring: 0 Pts
Appearances: 1897:W,I, 1898:S,W

Abel ASHWORTH
Born: Second quarter 1864 in Ashton
Died: 10 January 1938 in Oldham
Clubs: Oldham (1), Rochdale Hornets
Position: Forward (1)
Debut: 6 Feb 1892 v Ireland (Manchester). Number: 242
Caps: 1 (W:1, L:0)
Scoring: 0 Pts
Appearances: 1892:I
Honours: Championship: 1892

John Garbutt ASKEW
Born: 2 September 1908 in Gateshead
Died: 31 August 1942 in Stannington, Morpeth
Educated: Durham School
Clubs: Durham School, Durham City, Cambridge University (3)
Position: Full-back (3)
Debut: 18 Jan 1930 v Wales (Cardiff). Number: 653
Last game: 22 Feb 1930 v France (Twickenham)
Caps: 3 (W:2, L:1)
Scoring: 0 Pts
Appearances: 1930:W,I,F
Honours: Championship: 1930

Alfred Rimbault ASLETT
Born: 14 January 1901
Died: May 1980 in Cowfold
Educated: Clifton College
Clubs: RMC Sandhurst, Blackheath, Lansdowne, Richmond (6), King's Own Royal Regt, Army
Position: Centre (6)
Debut: 16 Jan 1926 v Wales (Cardiff). Number: 605
Last game: 1 Apr 1929 v France (Stade Colombes)
Caps: 6 (W:2, D:1, L:3)
Scoring: 2T, 6 Pts
Appearances: 1926:W,I,F,S, 1929:S,F

Eric Walter ASSINDER
Born: 29 August 1888 in King's Norton
Died: 11 October 1974 in Stratford-on-Avon
Educated: King Edward's School
Clubs: Old Edwardians (2)
Position: Centre (2)
Debut: 9 Jan 1909 v Australia (Blackheath). Number: 473
Last game: 16 Jan 1909 v Wales (Cardiff)
Caps: 2 (W:0, L:2)
Scoring: 0 Pts
Appearances: 1909:A,W

Randolph Littleton ASTON
Born: 6 September 1869 in Kensington
Died: 3 November 1930 in Salisbury
Educated: Cheltenham College, Tonbridge School
Clubs: Cambridge University (2), Blackheath
Position: Three-quarter (2)
Debut: 1 Mar 1890 v Scotland (Raeburn Place). Number: 217
Last game: 15 Mar 1890 v Ireland (Blackheath)
Caps: 2 (W:2, L:0)
Scoring: 0 Pts
Appearances: 1890:S,I

Joseph Richard (Dick) AUTY
Born: 19 August 1910 in Batley, Yorks
Died: 7 June 1995 in Leeds
Educated: Mill Hill School
Clubs: Old Millhillians, Batley, Headingley (1), Leicester
Position: Fly-half (1)
Debut: 16 Mar 1935 v Scotland (Murrayfield). Number: 722
Caps: 1 (W:0, L:1)
Scoring: 0 Pts
Appearances: 1935:S

Bill Beaumont

B

BACK, Neil Antony, MBE
BAILEY, Mark David
BAINBRIDGE, Stephen
BAKER, Douglas George Santley
BAKER, Edward Morgan
BAKER, Hiatt Cowles
BALSHAW, Iain Robert, MBE
BANCE, John Forsyth
BARKLEY, Oliver John
BARLEY, Bryan
BARNES, Stuart
BARON, James Henry
BARR, Robert John
BARRETT, Edward Ivo Medhurst
BARRINGTON, Thomas James Mountstevens
BARTLETT, Jasper Twining
BARTLETT, Richard Michael
BARTON, John
BATCHELOR, Tremlett Brewer
BATES, Stephen Michael
BATESON, Alfred Hardy
BATESON, Harold Dingwall
BATSON, Thomas
BATTEN, John Maxwell
BAUME, John Lea
BAXENDELL, Joshua John Neill
BAXTER, James
BAYFIELD, Martin Christopher
BAZLEY, Reginald Charles
BEAL, Nicholas David
BEAUMONT, William Blackledge, OBE
BEDFORD, Harry
BEDFORD, Lawrence Leslie
BEER, Ian David Stafford
BEESE, Michael Christopher
BEIM, Thomas David
BELL, Duncan Stuart Crampton
BELL, Frederick James
BELL, Henry
BELL, John Lowthian
BELL, Peter Joseph
BELL, Robert William
BENDON, Gordon John
BENNETT, Norman Osborn
BENNETT, William Neil
BENNETTS, Barzillai Beckerleg, MBE
BENTLEY, John
BENTLEY, John Edmund
BENTON, Scott
BERRIDGE, Michael John
BERRY, Henry
BERRY, John
BERRY, Joseph Thomas Wade
BESWICK, Edmund
BIGGS, John Maundy
BIRKETT, John Guy Giberne
BIRKETT, Louis
BIRKETT, Reginald Halsey
BISHOP, Colin Charles
BLACK, Brian Henry
BLACKLOCK, Joseph H
BLAKEWAY, Phillip John
BLAKISTON, Arthur Frederick
BLATHERWICK, Thomas
BODY, James Alfred
BOLTON, Charles Arthur
BOLTON, Reginald, MBE
BOLTON, Wilfred Nash, OBE
BONAVENTURA, Maurice Sydney
BOND, Anthony Matthew
BONHAM-CARTER, Sir Edgar, KCMG
BONSOR, Frederick
BOOBBYER, Brian
BOOTH, Lewis Alfred
BORTHWICK, Stephen William
BOTTING, Ian James
BOUGHTON, Harold John
BOYLAN, Francis
BOYLE, Cecil William
BOYLE, Stephen Brent
BRACKEN, Kyran Paul Patrick, MBE
BRADBY, Matthew Seymour, MBE
BRADLEY, Robert
BRADSHAW, Harry
BRAIN, Stephen Edward
BRAITHWAITE, John
BRETTARGH, Arthur T
BREWER, J
BRIGGS, Arthur
BRINN, Alan
BROADLEY, Thomas
BROMET, William Ernest
BROOK, Peter Watts Pitt
BROOKE, Terence John
BROOKS, Frederick George
BROOKS, Marshall Jones
BROPHY, Thomas John
BROUGH, James Wasdale
BROUGHAM, Henry
BROWN, Alan Arthur
BROWN, Alexander Thomas
BROWN, Leonard Graham
BROWN, Spencer Peter
BROWN, Thomas William
BRUNTON, Joseph
BRUTTON, Ernest Bartholomew
BRYDEN, Charles Cowper
BRYDEN, Henry Anderson
BUCKINGHAM, Ralph Arthur
BUCKNALL, Anthony Launce
BUCKTON, John Richard
BUDD, Arthur
BUDWORTH, Richard Tom Dutton
BULL, Arthur Gilbert
BULLOUGH, Edward
BULPITT, Michael Philip
BULTEEL, A J
BUNTING, William Louis
BURLAND, Donald William
BURNS, Benjamin Henry
BURTON, George William
BURTON, Hyde Clarke
BURTON, Michael Alan
BUSH, James Arthur
BUTCHER, Christopher John Simon
BUTCHER, Walter Vincent
BUTLER, Arthur Geoffrey
BUTLER, Peter Edward
BUTTERFIELD, Jeffrey
BYRNE, Francis Alban
BYRNE, James Frederick

Neil Antony BACK, MBE

Born: 16 January 1969 in Coventry
Educated: Woodlands School
Clubs: Earlsdon, Barkers Butts, Nottingham, Leicester (66)
Position: Flanker (63), Replacement (3), Bench (4)
Debut: 5 Feb 1994 v Scotland (Murrayfield). Number: 1152
Last game: 22 Nov 2003 v Australia (Sydney)
Caps: 66 (W:52, D:1, L:13). As captain: 4 (W:4, L:0)
Scoring: 16T, 1DG, 83 Pts. Discipline - Sin bins: 1
Appearances: 1994:S,I, 1995:Ar(r),It,Sm, 1997:NZ1(r),SA,NZ2, 1998:F,W,S,I,H,It,A,SA, 1999:S,I,F,W,A,US,C,It,NZ,Fj,SA, 2000:I,F,W,It,S,SA1,SA2,A,Ar,SA, 2001:W,It,S,F,I,A*,R*,SA, 2002:S,I,F,W*,It*,NZ(r),A,SA, 2003:F,W,S,I,NZ,A,F,Geo,SA,Sm,W,F,A
Honours: RWC Winner: 2003. Championship: 2000, 2001, 2003

A master of controlling the ball in a rolling maul, a defensive guru and another pivotal player in the World Cup-winning team of 2003, Neil Back almost didn't measure up to the job, literally. They say size doesn't matter, but Back was initially considered, at 5'10", too small for international rugby union.

He had already changed position at 18, from scrum-half, in order to follow in the footsteps of hero Jean-Pierre Rives as a world-class flanker. Now he needed to prove himself again.

And prove himself he did, making his England debut against Scotland in 1994, going on to win Championships in 2000 and 2001 and a Grand Slam in 2003.

With such a wilful streak, it's not surprising that Back has courted controversy during his career. In 1996 after losing the Pilkington Cup Final with Leicester, he pushed over the referee Steve Lander, earning himself a six-month ban. In 2002, as Leicester beat Munster to retain the Heineken Cup, Back swatted the ball from Peter Stringer's hand in the dying minutes and allowed Leicester to clear, and win 15-9.

"In a way I wish I hadn't done it," Back admitted afterwards. "I must be honest, because I don't like people thinking I'm a cheat. I don't think I'm a cheat, but this has undoubtedly tarnished my reputation and that is disappointing. I'd hope people would evaluate me over my career and not just label me for one incident."

However, it is this kind of passion and competitiveness that fed his game, and his ferocious tackling and unrivalled fitness helped to make him an England regular and earned him the RFU player of the year in 1998, and, along with fellow back-rowers Dallaglio and Richard Hill, he became part of the most-capped back row in the history of the game.

Between 1999 and 2002 Back enjoyed phenomenal success with his club, Leicester, winning four successive Zurich Premiership titles, and coming out as top try scorer with 16 in 1999, perfecting the rolling maul strategy that proved so effective with England.

His bullish temperament, allied to his fitness, made him famously vow never to retire from international rugby.

Although he did finally retire from the England set-up after the 2004 Six Nations, he was, at 36, selected for his third Lions tour a year later, becoming the oldest ever British and Irish Lion in the process.

"Neil has rewritten the openside flanker book of playing the game," said Leicester chief executive and former England captain, Peter Wheeler.

"He put fitness levels to a much higher degree and people have caught up now, as they often do when someone sets a new standard. "I think there was a huge amount of prejudice because of his size. "That was a time in professional rugby when people were getting bigger and stronger and some selectors felt you had to be a certain height in the back row to be able to play."He was not only quick to the breakdown, he was always able to carry on movements, carry on attacks because of his ball-playing skills and his great strength in taking the ball off the opposition."

Eventually though players have to submit to time, and after 339 games and a phenomenal 125 tries for Leicester Tigers, Back is now working as their technical director, first team defensive coach and academy and reserve team coach, where he has already claimed an A-League title.

Neil Back

Mark Bailey

Mark David BAILEY
Born: 21 November 1960 in Castleford
Educated: Ipswich School
Clubs: Durham University, Cambridge University, Ipswich, Bedford, Wasps (7)
Position: Wing (6), Replacement (1), Bench (5)
Debut: 2 Jun 1984 v South Africa (Port Elizabeth). Number: 1088
Last game: 17 Mar 1990 (rep) v Scotland (Murrayfield)
Caps: 7 (W:4, L:3)
Scoring: 1T, 4 Pts
Appearances: 1984:SA1,SA2, 1987:US, 1989:Fj, 90:I,F,S(r)

Stephen (Steve) BAINBRIDGE
Born: 7 October 1956 in Newcastle-upon-Tyne
Educated: John Marlay School, Alsager College
Clubs: Gosforth (11), Fylde (7)
Position: Lock (18)
Debut: 20 Feb 1982 v France (Parc des Princes). Number: 1076
Last game: 3 Jun 1987 v United States (Sydney)
Caps: 18 (W:7, D:1, L:10)
Scoring: 0 Pts
Appearances: 1982:F,W, 1983:F,W,S,I,NZ, 1984:S,I,F,W, 1985:NZ1,NZ2, 1987:F,W,S,J,US

Douglas George Santley (Doug) BAKER
Born: 29 November 1929 in Las Palmas, Canary Islands
Educated: Merchant Taylors' School
Clubs: Oxford University, Old Merchant Taylors' (4)
Position: Fly-half (4)
Debut: 22 Jan 1955 v Wales (Cardiff). Number: 849
Last game: 19 Mar 1955 v Scotland (Twickenham)
Caps: 4 (W:1, D:1, L:2)
Scoring: 0 Pts
Appearances: 1955:W,I,F,S

Steve Bainbridge

Edward Morgan BAKER
Born: 12 August 1874
Died: 25 November 1940 in Winchester
Educated: Denstone College
Clubs: Oxford University (7), Moseley, Blackheath, Wolverhampton, Burton
Position: Centre (4), Wing (3)
Debut: 5 Jan 1895 v Wales (Swansea). Number: 272
Last game: 9 Jan 1897 v Wales (Newport)
Caps: 7 (W:3, L:4)
Scoring: 0 Pts
Appearances: 1895:W,I,S, 1896:W,I,S, 1897:W

Hiatt Cowles BAKER
Born: 30 June 1863 in Clifton
Died: 19 September 1934 in Almondsbury, Bristol
Educated: Rugby School
Clubs: Clifton (1)
Position: Forward (1)
Debut: 8 Jan 1887 v Wales (Llanelli). Number: 186
Caps: 1 (W:0, D:1, L:0)
Scoring: 0 Pts
Appearances: 1887:W

Iain Robert BALSHAW, MBE
Born: 14 April 1979 in Blackburn
Educated: Stonyhurst College
Clubs: Bath (22), Leeds (4), Gloucester (3)
Position: Full-back (17), Wing (3), Replacement (9), Bench (3)
Debut: 5 Feb 2000 (rep) v Ireland (Twickenham). Number: 1217
Last game: 10 Feb 2007 v Italy (Twickenham)
Caps: 29 (W:21, L:8)
Scoring: 13T, 65 Pts
Appearances: 2000:I(r),F(r),It(r),S(r),A(r),Ar,SA(r), 2001:W,It,S,F,I, 2002:S(r),I(r), 2003:F,F,Sm,U,A(r), 2004:It,S,I, 2005:It,S, 2006:A1,A2,NZ,Ar, 2007:It
Honours: RWC Winner: 2003. Championship: 2000, 2001

Iain Balshaw

John Forsyth BANCE
Born: 15 January 1925 in Kingsclere
Educated: Radley College
Clubs: Cambridge University, Bedford (1)
Position: Lock (1)
Debut: 20 Mar 1954 v Scotland (Murrayfield). Number: 839
Caps: 1 (W:1, L:0)
Scoring: 0 Pts
Appearances: 1954:S

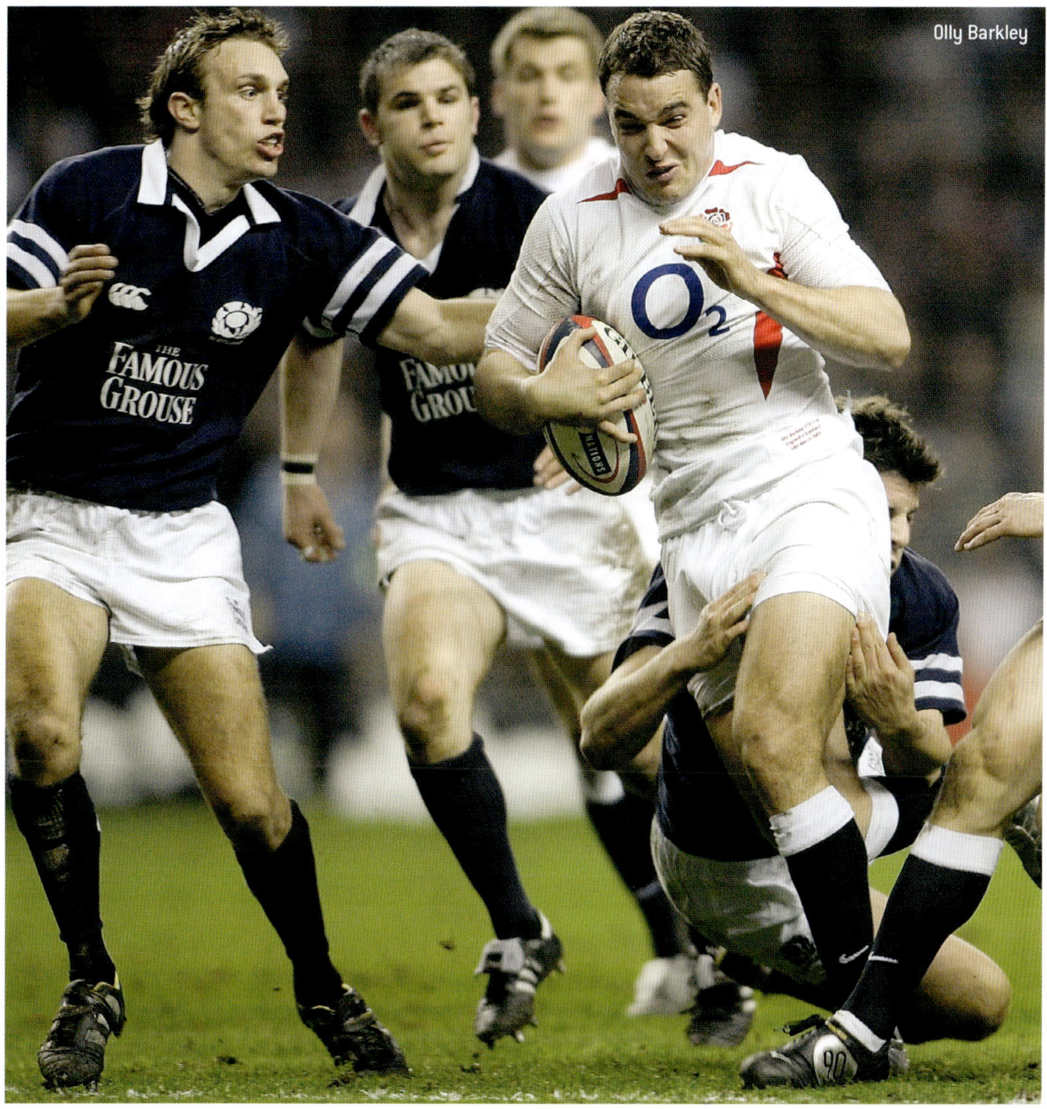
Olly Barkley

Bryan Barley

Oliver John (Olly) BARKLEY
Born: 28 November 1981 in Hammersmith
Educated: Colston's School
Clubs: Bath (16), Marist (NZ)
Position: Centre (4), Fly-half (3), Replacement (9), Bench (3)
Debut: 16 Jun 2001 (rep) v United States (San Francisco). Number: 1231
Last game: 17 Jun 2006 (rep) v Australia (Melbourne)
Caps: 16 (W:7, L:9)
Scoring: 1T, 4C, 9PG, 40 Pts
Appearances: 2001:US(r), 2004:It(r),I(r),W,F,NZ2(r),A(r), 2005:W(r),F,I,It,S,A(r),Sm(r), 2006:A1,A2(r)

Bryan BARLEY
Born: 4 January 1960 in Wakefield
Educated: Normanton GS
Clubs: Leeds University, Wakefield (7), Sandal
Position: Centre (7), Bench (5)
Debut: 18 Feb 1984 v Ireland (Twickenham). Number: 1083
Last game: 16 Jun 1988 v Fiji (Suva) - 1T, 4 Pts
Caps: 7 (W:2, L:5)
Scoring: 1T, 4 Pts
Appearances: 1984:I,F,W,A, 1988:A1,A2,Fj

Stuart BARNES
Born: 22 November 1962 in Grays, Essex
Educated: Bassaleg College
Clubs: Oxford University, Newport, Bristol (2), Bath (8)
Position: Fly-half (6), Replacement (4), Bench (23)
Debut: 3 Nov 1984 v Australia (Twickenham) - 1PG, 3 Pts. Number: 1095
Last game: 20 Mar 1993 v Ireland (Lansdowne Road)
Caps: 10 (W:3, L:7)
Scoring: 5C, 7PG, 1DG, 34 Pts
Appearances: 1984:A, 1985:R(r),NZ1,NZ2, 1986:S(r),F(r), 1987:I(r), 1988:Fj, 1993:S,I

James Henry BARON
Born: 28 August 1874 in Micklethwaite
Died: 2 December 1942 in Bingley
Educated: Bingley School
Clubs: Bingley (3)
Position: Forward (3)
Debut: 14 Mar 1896 v Scotland (Glasgow). Number: 290
Last game: 6 Feb 1897 v Ireland (Lansdowne Road)
Caps: 3 (W:0, L:3)
Scoring: 0 Pts
Appearances: 1896:S, 1897:W,I

Robert John (Bobby) BARR
Born: 26 May 1907 in Blisworth
Died: 22 September 1975 in Great Oxendon
Educated: Stamford School
Clubs: Westleigh, Leicester (3)
Position: Full-back (3)
Debut: 2 Jan 1932 v South Africa (Twickenham). Number: 684
Last game: 13 Feb 1932 v Ireland (Lansdowne Road)
Caps: 3 (W:1, L:2)
Scoring: 1C, 2 Pts
Appearances: 1932:SA,W,I

Edward Ivo Medhurst BARRETT
Born: 22 June 1879 in Churt, Frensham, Surrey
Died: 10 July 1950 in Boscombe
Educated: Cheltenham College
Clubs: RMC Sandhurst, Lennox (1), Army
Position: Centre (1)
Debut: 21 Mar 1903 v Scotland (Richmond). Number: 391
Caps: 1 (W:0, L:1)
Scoring: 0 Pts
Appearances: 1903:S

Steve Bates

Jos Baxendell

Thomas James Mountstevens BARRINGTON
Born: 8 July 1908 in Bridgwater
Died: 6 September 1973 in Taunton
Educated: Wrekin College
Clubs: Bridgwater & Albion, Harlequins, Richmond, Bristol (2)
Position: Fly-half (2)
Debut: 17 Jan 1931 v Wales (Twickenham). Number: 667
Last game: 14 Feb 1931 v Ireland (Twickenham)
Caps: 2 (W:0, D:1, L:1)
Scoring: 0 Pts
Appearances: 1931:W,I

Jasper Twining BARTLETT
Born: 17 October 1924 in Birmingham
Died: 16 January 1969 in Liverpool
Educated: Birkenhead Institute
Clubs: Liverpool University, Northern University, Combined University, Waterloo (1), Army, Combined Services
Position: Lock (1)
Debut: 20 Jan 1951 v Wales (Swansea). Number: 811
Caps: 1 (W:0, L:1)
Scoring: 0 Pts
Appearances: 1951:W

Richard Michael (Ricky) BARTLETT
Born: 13 February 1929 in Kingston
Died: 6 March 1984 in Liss, Hants
Educated: Stowe School
Clubs: Cambridge University, Harlequins (7)
Position: Fly-half (7)
Debut: 19 Jan 1957 v Wales (Cardiff). Number: 869
Last game: 15 Mar 1958 v Scotland (Murrayfield)
Caps: 7 (W:6, D:1, L:0)
Scoring: 0 Pts
Appearances: 1957:W,I,F,S, 1958:I,F,S
Honours: Grand Slam: 1957. Championship: 1958

John BARTON
Born: 19 March 1943
Educated: Caludon Castle School
Clubs: Coventry (4)
Position: Lock (4), Bench (3)
Debut: 11 Feb 1967 v Ireland (Lansdowne Road). Number: 953
Last game: 26 Feb 1972 v France (Stade Colombes)
Caps: 4 (W:1, L:3)
Scoring: 2T, 6 Pts
Appearances: 1967:I,F,W, 1972:F

Tremlett Brewer BATCHELOR
Born: 22 June 1884 in Wirral
Died: 21 December 1966 in Liverpool
Educated: Rugby School
Clubs: Oxford University (1), London Hospital, Richmond
Position: Wing (1)
Debut: 5 Jan 1907 v France (Richmond). Number: 438
Caps: 1 (W:1, L:0)
Scoring: 0 Pts
Appearances: 1907:F

Stephen Michael (Steve) BATES
Born: 4 March 1963 in Merthyr Tydfil, Wales
Educated: West London Institute
Clubs: Welwyn GC, Wasps (1), Newcastle
Position: Scrum-half (1), Bench (20)
Debut: 13 May 1989 v Romania (Bucharest). Number: 1132
Caps: 1 (W:1, L:0)
Scoring: 0 Pts
Appearances: 1989:R

Alfred Hardy BATESON
Born: 10 August 1901 in Otley, Yorks
Died: 21 February 1982 in Scarborough
Educated: Bramley School
Clubs: Otley (4)
Position: Prop (4)
Debut: 18 Jan 1930 v Wales (Cardiff). Number: 654
Last game: 15 Mar 1930 v Scotland (Twickenham)
Caps: 4 (W:2, D:1, L:1)
Scoring: 0 Pts
Appearances: 1930:W,I,F,S
Honours: Championship: 1930

Martin Bayfield

Harold Dingwall BATESON
Born: 2 May 1855 in Liverpool
Died: 29 October 1927 in Liverpool
Educated: Rugby School
Clubs: Oxford University, Blackheath, Liverpool (1)
Position: Forward (1)
Debut: 24 Mar 1879 v Ireland (The Oval). Number: 117
Caps: 1 (W:1, L:0)
Scoring: 0 Pts
Appearances: 1879:I

Thomas BATSON
Born: Second quarter 1846 in Ross
Died: 5 February 1933 in Battersea
Educated: Sydney College
Clubs: Oxford University, Blackheath (3)
Position: Forward (3)
Debut: 5 Feb 1872 v Scotland (The Oval). Number: 21
Last game: 15 Feb 1875 v Ireland (The Oval)
Caps: 3 (W:3, L:0)
Scoring: 0 Pts
Appearances: 1872:S, 1874:S, 1875:I

John Maxwell BATTEN
Born: 28 February 1853 in Almora, Kumaon, India
Died: 15 October 1917 in St Albans
Educated: Haileybury & ISC
Clubs: Cambridge University (1)
Position: Full-back (1)
Debut: 23 Feb 1874 v Scotland (The Oval). Number: 45
Caps: 1 (W:1, L:0)
Scoring: 0 Pts
Appearances: 1874:S

John Lea BAUME
Born: 18 July 1920 in Dewsbury
Educated: Ashville College Harrogate
Clubs: Northern (1), Headingley, Harrogate, Royal Northumberland Fusiliers, Army, Combined Services
Position: Prop (1)
Debut: 18 Mar 1950 v Scotland (Murrayfield). Number: 810
Caps: 1 (W:0, L:1)
Scoring: 0 Pts
Appearances: 1950:S

Joshua John Neill (Jos) BAXENDELL
Born: 3 December 1972 in Manchester
Educated: King's School Macclesfield
Clubs: Sheffield Hallam University, Wilmslow, Sheffield, Sale (2)
Position: Centre (2)
Debut: 27 Jun 1998 v New Zealand (Auckland). Number: 1206
Last game: 4 Jul 1998 v South Africa (Cape Town)
Caps: 2 (W:0, L:2)
Scoring: 0 Pts
Appearances: 1998:NZ2,SA

James (Bim) BAXTER
Born: 8 June 1870
Died: 4 July 1940 in Rock Ferry, Cheshire
Educated: Liverpool Institute
Clubs: Birkenhead Park (3)
Position: Forward (3)
Debut: 6 Jan 1900 v Wales (Gloucester). Number: 341
Last game: 10 Mar 1900 v Scotland (Inverleith)
Caps: 3 (W:1, D:1, L:1)
Scoring: 0 Pts
Appearances: 1900:W,I,S

Martin Christopher BAYFIELD
Born: 21 December 1966 in Bedford
Educated: Bedford School
Clubs: Bedford, Northampton (31), Metropolitan Police
Position: Lock (31)
Debut: 20 Jul 1991 v Fiji (Suva). Number: 1142
Last game: 3 Feb 1996 v Wales (Twickenham)
Caps: 31 (W:22, L:9)
Scoring: 0 Pts
Appearances: 1991:Fj,A, 1992:S,I,F,W,C,SA, 1993:F,W,S,I, 1994:S,I,SA1,SA2,R,C, 1995:I,F,W,S,Ar,It,A,NZ,F,SA,Sm, 1996:F,W
Honours: Grand Slam: 1992, 1995. Championship: 1996

Reginald Charles BAZLEY
Born: 15 December 1929 in Barrow-in-Furness
Educated: Barrow GS
Clubs: Liverpool University, Waterloo (10), Royal Engineers, Army, Combined Services
Position: Wing (10)
Debut: 29 Mar 1952 v Ireland (Twickenham). Number: 832
Last game: 19 Mar 1955 v Scotland (Twickenham)
Caps: 10 (W:6, D:2, L:2)
Scoring: 2T, 6 Pts
Appearances: 1952:I,F, 1953:W,I,F,S, 1955:W,I,F,S
Honours: Championship: 1953

Nicholas David (Nick) BEAL
Born: 2 December 1970 in Howden, York
Educated: RGS High Wycombe
Clubs: High Wycombe, Northampton (15)
Position: Wing (3), Full-back (3), Centre (3), Replacement (6), Bench (5)
Debut: 14 Dec 1996 v Argentina (Twickenham). Number: 1173
Last game: 24 Oct 1999 v South Africa (Stade de France)
Caps: 15 (W:9, L:6)
Scoring: 3T, 15 Pts. Discipline - Cautions: 1
Appearances: 1996:Ar, 1997:A, 1998:NZ1,NZ2,SA, 1999:H(r),SA,S,F(r),A(r),C(r),It(r),Tg(r),Fj,SA

Nick Beal

Bill Beaumont

William Blackledge (Bill) BEAUMONT, OBE

Born: 9 March 1952 in Preston
Educated: Ellesmere College
Clubs: Fylde (34)
Position: Lock (33), Replacement (1), Bench (1)
Debut: 18 Jan 1975 v Ireland (Lansdowne Road). Number: 1025
Last game: 16 Jan 1982 (capt) v Scotland (Murrayfield)
Caps: 34 (W:14, D:3, L:17). As captain: 21 (W:11, D:2, L:8)
Scoring: 0 Pts
Appearances: 1975:I,A1(r),A2, 1976:A,W,S,I,F, 1977:S,I,F,W, 1978:F*,W*,S*,I*,NZ*, 1979:S,I*,F*,W*,NZ*, 1980:I*,F*,W*,S*, 1981:W*,S*,I*,F*,Ar1*,Ar2*, 1982:A*,S*
Honours: Grand Slam: 1980 (capt)

England has been blessed with inspirational leaders over the last 30 years, none more so than Bill Beaumont, who possessed an innate ability to motivate a team with simple common sense, a friendly demeanour and example-setting performances.

Beaumont, who was a one-club man with Fylde, made his England debut in 1975, coming in at the last minute for the injured Roger Uttley.

Within a year, his power around the park coupled with the ability to take clean lineout possession made him a first choice. He was called up halfway through the 1977 Lions tour of New Zealand, and quickly became one of the discoveries of the series, forming a strong second-row partnership with Gordon Brown.

He took on the England captaincy in 1978, and the 1979-80 season saw him written into history books as one of rugby union's iconic skippers, captaining his country a total of 21 times.

Early in that season he conceived the strategy that enabled the North of England to overcome the All Blacks, a victory some consider to be the most satisfying of any English divisional side.

He ended the season – in which he also led Lancashire to the County Championship title – being carried off the pitch on the shoulders of his team-mates as the 1980 Grand Slam celebrations began, England's first since 1957.

That clean sweep with England led him to become the Lions captain that same year, the first Englishman to receive the honour for 50 years.

Later that year his career was celebrated on the television show 'This is Your Life' and he was awarded an OBE in 1982.

A head injury – in the County Championship final – prematurely brought his career to an end in 1982, but he continued his role as an inspirational leader, this time on television as a captain on 'A Question of Sport', where he became one of the few household names to emerge from the sport.

Currently a member of the International Rugby Board, he managed the British and Irish Lions tour of New Zealand in 2005.

In 2007 his status in the English game was reflected when the country's County Championship competition was renamed the Bill Beaumont Cup.

Harry BEDFORD

Born: 1866 in Gildersome
Died: January 1929 in Leeds
Clubs: Morley (3)
Position: Forward (3)
Debut: 16 Feb 1889 v New Zealand Natives (Blackheath) - 2T, 2 Pts. Number: 198
Last game: 15 Mar 1890 v Ireland (Blackheath)
Caps: 3 (W:3, L:0)
Scoring: 2T, 2 Pts
Appearances: 1889:M, 1890:S,I

Lawrence Leslie BEDFORD

Born: 11 February 1903 in Leeds
Died: 25 November 1963 in Harewood, Leeds
Clubs: Headingley (2)
Position: Full-back (2)
Debut: 17 Jan 1931 v Wales (Twickenham). Number: 668
Last game: 14 Feb 1931 v Ireland (Twickenham)
Caps: 2 (W:0, D:1, L:1)
Scoring: 0 Pts
Appearances: 1931:W,I

Ian David Stafford BEER

Born: 28 April 1931 in Croydon
Educated: Whitgift School
Clubs: Cambridge University, Harlequins (2), Bath
Position: No 8 (2)
Debut: 26 Feb 1955 v France (Twickenham). Number: 855
Last game: 19 Mar 1955 v Scotland (Twickenham) - 1T, 3 Pts
Caps: 2 (W:1, L:1)
Scoring: 1T, 3 Pts
Appearances: 1955:F,S

Michael Christopher BEESE

Born: 8 October 1948 in Bristol
Educated: Keynsham School
Clubs: Liverpool (3)
Position: Centre (3), Bench (1)
Debut: 15 Jan 1972 v Wales (Twickenham). Number: 1002
Last game: 26 Feb 1972 v France (Stade Colombes) - 1T, 4 Pts
Caps: 3 (W:0, L:3)
Scoring: 1T, 4 Pts
Appearances: 1972:W,I,F

Thomas David (Tom) BEIM

Born: 11 December 1975 in Frimley
Educated: Cheltenham College
Clubs: Gloucester, Hamiltons (SA), Sale (2), Viadana (IT), Birmingham
Position: Wing (1), Replacement (1)
Debut: 20 Jun 1998 (rep) v New Zealand (Dunedin) - 1T, 5 Pts. Number: 1204
Last game: 27 Jun 1998 v New Zealand (Auckland)
Caps: 2 (W:0, L:2)
Scoring: 1T, 5 Pts
Appearances: 1998:NZ1(r),NZ2

Duncan Stuart Crampton BELL

Born: 1 October 1974 in King's Lynn
Educated: Katherine Lady Berkeley's School, Colston's School
Clubs: Ebbw Vale, Sale, Pontypridd, Bath (2)
Position: Prop (1), Replacement (1), Bench (1)
Debut: 12 Mar 2005 (rep) v Italy (Twickenham). Number: 1262
Last game: 19 Mar 2005 v Scotland (Twickenham)
Caps: 2 (W:2, L:0)
Scoring: 0 Pts
Appearances: 2005:It(r),S

Frederick James (Fred) BELL

Born: 3 August 1876 in Cullercoates
Died: 7 September 1947 in Whitley Bay
Clubs: Northern (1), Hunslet RL
Position: Forward (1)
Debut: 6 Jan 1900 v Wales (Gloucester). Number: 342
Caps: 1 (W:0, L:1)
Scoring: 0 Pts
Appearances: 1900:W

Henry BELL

Born: First quarter 1859 in Liverpool
Died: 20 September 1935 in Marylebone
Educated: Liverpool Institute
Clubs: New Brighton (1)
Position: Forward (1)
Debut: 4 Feb 1884 v Ireland (Lansdowne Road). Number: 163
Caps: 1 (W:1, L:0)
Scoring: 0 Pts
Appearances: 1884:I
Honours: Championship: 1884

John Lowthian BELL

Born: Second quarter 1853 in Newcastle-upon-Tyne
Died: 16 December 1916 in Christchurch
Clubs: Darlington (1)
Position: Half-Back (1)
Debut: 11 Mar 1878 v Ireland (Lansdowne Road). Number: 102
Caps: 1 (W:1, L:0)
Scoring: 0 Pts
Appearances: 1878:I

Tom Beim

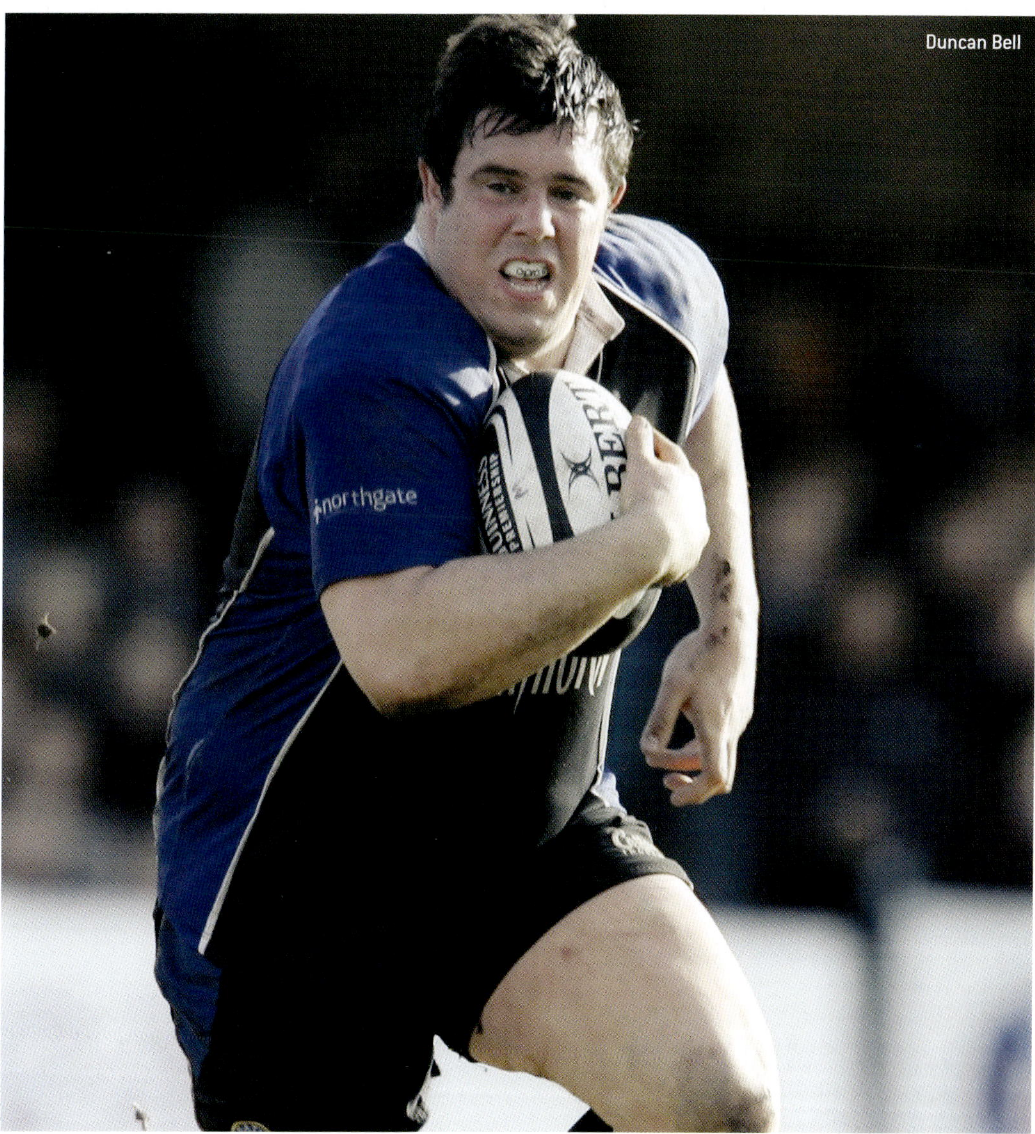

Duncan Bell

John Bentley

Peter Joseph BELL
Born: 28 April 1937 in Wandsworth
Educated: Caterham College, Cirencester Agricultural College
Clubs: Cranbrook, Ashford, Blackheath (4), Bay of Plenty (NZ)
Position: Flanker (4)
Debut: 20 Jan 1968 v Wales (Twickenham). Number: 962
Last game: 16 Mar 1968 v Scotland (Murrayfield)
Caps: 4 (W:1, D:2, L:1)
Scoring: 0 Pts
Appearances: 1968:W,I,F,S

Robert William BELL
Born: 19 December 1875 in Newcastle-upon-Tyne
Died: 9 June 1940 in Newcastle-upon-Tyne
Educated: Uppingham School
Clubs: Cambridge University (3), Northern, Blackheath
Position: Forward (3)
Debut: 6 Jan 1900 v Wales (Gloucester). Number: 343
Last game: 10 Mar 1900 v Scotland (Inverleith)
Caps: 3 (W:1, D:1, L:1)
Scoring: 0 Pts
Appearances: 1900:W,I,S

Gordon John BENDON
Born: 9 April 1929 in Lambeth
Educated: King's College Wimbledon
Clubs: RAF, Wasps (4)
Position: Prop (4)
Debut: 17 Jan 1959 v Wales (Cardiff). Number: 878
Last game: 21 Mar 1959 v Scotland (Twickenham)
Caps: 4 (W:1, D:2, L:1)
Scoring: 0 Pts
Appearances: 1959:W,I,F,S

Norman Osborn (Billy) BENNETT
Born: 21 September 1922 in Putney
Died: 7 July 2005 in Dinkley, Blackburn
Educated: Epsom College
Clubs: St Mary's Hospital (3), United Services (4), Waterloo
Position: Centre (7)
Debut: 18 Jan 1947 v Wales (Cardiff). Number: 753
Last game: 20 Mar 1948 v Scotland (Murrayfield)
Caps: 7 (W:3, D:1, L:3)
Scoring: 1T, 3 Pts
Appearances: 1947:W,S,F, 1948:A,W,I,S

William Neil BENNETT
Born: 20 April 1951 in Ramsey, Isle of Man
Educated: Tiffin School
Clubs: Bedford (3), Colwyn Bay, London Welsh (4)
Position: Fly-half (6), Replacement (1), Bench (1)
Debut: 15 Mar 1975 v Scotland (Twickenham) - 1PG, 3 Pts. Number: 1027
Last game: 17 Mar 1979 v Wales (Cardiff) - 1PG, 3 Pts
Caps: 7 (W:2, D:1, L:4)
Scoring: 2T, 5PG, 23 Pts
Appearances: 1975:S,A1, 1976:S(r), 1979:S,I,F,W

Barzillai Beckerleg (Barrie) BENNETTS, MBE
Born: 14 July 1883 in Penzance
Died: 26 July 1958 in Alverton, Penzance
Educated: Bridgend College
Clubs: Penzance (2), Devonport Albion, Redruth, Richmond
Position: Wing (2)
Debut: 9 Jan 1909 v Australia (Blackheath). Number: 474
Last game: 16 Jan 1909 v Wales (Cardiff)
Caps: 2 (W:0, L:2)
Scoring: 0 Pts
Appearances: 1909:A,W

John BENTLEY
Born: 5 September 1966 in Dewsbury
Educated: Heckmondwicke GS
Clubs: Cleckheaton, Otley, Sale (2), Leeds RL, Rotherham, Newcastle (2)
Position: Wing (4)
Debut: 23 Apr 1988 v Ireland (Lansdowne Road). Number: 1124
Last game: 29 Nov 1997 v South Africa (Twickenham)
Caps: 4 (W:1, L:3)
Scoring: 1T, 4 Pts
Appearances: 1988:I,A1, 1997:A,SA

John Edmund BENTLEY
Born: c 1847
Died: 12 December 1913 in West Hampstead
Educated: Tonbridge School
Clubs: Gipsies (2)
Position: Half-Back (2)
Debut: 27 Mar 1871 v Scotland (Raeburn Place). Number: 1
Last game: 5 Feb 1872 v Scotland (The Oval)
Caps: 2 (W:1, L:1)
Scoring: 0 Pts
Appearances: 1871:S, 1872:S

Scott BENTON
Born: 8 September 1974 in Bradford
Educated: Morley HS
Clubs: Morley, Gloucester (1), Leeds, Sale, Orrell
Position: Scrum-half (1), Bench (5)
Debut: 6 Jun 1998 v Australia (Brisbane). Number: 1195
Caps: 1 (W:0, L:1)
Scoring: 0 Pts
Appearances: 1998:A

Scott Benton

Michael John (Mike) BERRIDGE
Born: 28 February 1923 in Huntingdon
Died: 2 October 1973 in Oundle
Educated: King's School
Clubs: Peterborough, Northampton (2), Leicester
Position: Prop (2)
Debut: 15 Jan 1949 v Wales (Cardiff). Number: 787
Last game: 12 Feb 1949 v Ireland (Lansdowne Road)
Caps: 2 (W:0, L:2)
Scoring: 0 Pts
Appearances: 1949:W,I

Henry BERRY
Born: 8 January 1883 in Gloucester
Died: Killed in action in 1915 in Festubert, France
Educated: St Mark's School
Clubs: Gloucester (4), Gloucestershire Regt, Army
Position: Forward (4)
Debut: 15 Jan 1910 v Wales (Twickenham). Number: 492
Last game: 19 Mar 1910 v Scotland (Inverleith) - 1T, 3 Pts
Caps: 4 (W:3, D:1, L:0)
Scoring: 2T, 6 Pts
Appearances: 1910:W,I,F,S
Honours: Championship: 1910

John BERRY
Born: 25 September 1866 in Fellside
Died: 10 May 1930 in Manchester
Clubs: Tyldesley (3)
Position: Half-Back (3)
Debut: 3 Jan 1891 v Wales (Newport). Number: 223
Last game: 7 Mar 1891 v Scotland (Richmond)
Caps: 3 (W:2, L:1)
Scoring: 0 Pts
Appearances: 1891:W,I,S

Joseph Thomas Wade (Tom) BERRY
Born: 17 July 1911 in Slawston
Died: 1 July 1993 in Market Harborough
Educated: Eastbourne College
Clubs: Market Harborough, Leicester (3)
Position: Flanker (3)
Debut: 21 Jan 1939 v Wales (Twickenham). Number: 743
Last game: 18 Mar 1939 v Scotland (Murrayfield)
Caps: 3 (W:2, L:1)
Scoring: 0 Pts
Appearances: 1939:W,I,S

Edmund (Teddy) BESWICK
Born: Third quarter 1858 in Penrith
Died: 23 January 1911 in Salford
Clubs: Swinton (2)
Position: Three-quarter (2)
Debut: 6 Feb 1882 v Ireland (Lansdowne Road). Number: 140
Last game: 4 Mar 1882 v Scotland (Manchester)
Caps: 2 (W:0, D:1, L:1)
Scoring: 0 Pts
Appearances: 1882:I,S

John Maundy BIGGS
Born: Third quarter 1855 in Reading
Died: 3 June 1935 in Barnstaple
Educated: University College School
Clubs: University College Hospital (2), Wasps
Position: Forward (2)
Debut: 4 Mar 1878 v Scotland (The Oval). Number: 95
Last game: 24 Mar 1879 v Ireland (The Oval)
Caps: 2 (W:1, D:1, L:0)
Scoring: 0 Pts
Appearances: 1878:S, 1879:I

John Guy Giberne BIRKETT
Born: 27 December 1884 in Richmond
Died: 16 October 1967 in Cuckfield
Educated: Haileybury & ISC
Clubs: Brighton, Harlequins (21)
Position: Centre (21)
Debut: 17 Mar 1906 v Scotland (Inverleith). Number: 431
Last game: 8 Apr 1912 v France (Parc des Princes) - 1T, 3 Pts
Caps: 21 (W:12, D:2, L:7). As captain: 5 (W:2, L:3)
Scoring: 10T, 1DG, 34 Pts
Appearances: 1906:S,F,SA, 1907:F,W,S, 1908:F,W*,I,S, 1910:W,I,S*, 1911:W*,F*,I*,S, 1912:W,I,S,F
Honours: Championship: 1910

Louis BIRKETT
Born: 1 January 1853 in St Saviour
Died: 11 April 1943 in Barnstaple
Educated: Haileybury & ISC
Clubs: Clapham Rovers (3)
Position: Full-back (3)
Debut: 8 Mar 1875 v Scotland (Raeburn Place). Number: 66
Last game: 5 Mar 1877 v Scotland (Raeburn Place)
Caps: 3 (W:1, D:1, L:1)
Scoring: 0 Pts
Appearances: 1875:S, 1877:I,S

Reginald Halsey BIRKETT
Born: 28 March 1849 in London
Died: 30 June 1898 in Kingston
Educated: Lancing College
Clubs: Clapham Rovers (4)
Position: Forward (2), Three-quarter (2)
Debut: 27 Mar 1871 v Scotland (Raeburn Place) - 1T, 1 Pt. Number: 2
Last game: 5 Feb 1877 v Ireland (The Oval)
Caps: 4 (W:2, D:1, L:1)
Scoring: 1T, 1 Pt
Appearances: 1871:S, 1875:S, 1876:S, 1877:I

Colin Charles BISHOP

Born: 5 October 1903 in Hampstead
Died: 4 March 1980 in Winchester
Educated: University College School
Clubs: Cambridge University, Blackheath (1)
Position: Fly-half (1)
Debut: 2 Apr 1927 v France (Stade Colombes). Number: 625
Caps: 1 (W:0, L:1)
Scoring: 0 Pts
Appearances: 1927:F

Brian Henry BLACK

Born: 27 May 1907 in South Africa
Died: Killed in action in 1940 in Chilmark,Wilts
Educated: St Andrew's School
Clubs: Oxford University (4), Blackheath (6)
Position: Lock (8), No 8 (2)
Debut: 18 Jan 1930 v Wales (Cardiff) - 1C, 1PG, 5 Pts. Number: 655
Last game: 21 Jan 1933 v Wales (Twickenham)
Caps: 10 (W:3, D:2, L:5)
Scoring: 2T, 6C, 4PG, 30 Pts
Appearances: 1930:W,I,F,S, 1931:W,I,S,F, 1932:S, 1933:W
Honours: Championship: 1930

Joseph H BLACKLOCK

Born: 20 October 1878 in South Shields
Died: 28 June 1945 in Wigton
Clubs: Aspatria (2)
Position: Forward (2)
Debut: 5 Feb 1898 v Ireland (Richmond). Number: 312
Last game: 4 Feb 1899 v Ireland (Lansdowne Road)
Caps: 2 (W:0, L:2)
Scoring: 0 Pts
Appearances: 1898:I, 1899:I

Phillip John (Phil) BLAKEWAY

Born: 31 December 1950 in Cheltenham
Educated: Sherborne Park School
Clubs: Cheltenham, Gloucester (19), Moseley
Position: Prop (19), Bench (2)
Debut: 19 Jan 1980 v Ireland (Twickenham). Number: 1061
Last game: 30 Mar 1985 v Ireland (Lansdowne Road)
Caps: 19 (W:11, D:1, L:7)
Scoring: 0 Pts
Appearances: 1980:I,F,W,S, 1981:W,S,I,F, 1982:I,F,W, 1984:I,F,W,SA1, 1985:R,F,S,I
Honours: Grand Slam: 1980

One of the key coaching mantras in modern-day rugby is that it is the tight five, and particularly the front row, that win matches at every level.

So when England won their first Grand Slam in 23 years, back in 1980, although Bill Beaumont took the plaudits, great praise must be reserved for the tight-head prop and scrummaging cornerstone of that side, Phil Blakeway.

"It was a pleasure to play in that pack," Blakeway recalls. "We could have beaten anyone that year. I remember coming off the day we did it at Murrayfield, elated that the pain in my ribs could now die down but also for all the others who, unlike me, the new boy, had all suffered badly in the past from England's haphazard selection policies."

A Gloucester legend, Blakeway certainly found it hard to end his career, Sinatra-like, continually coming back from retirement to the game he loved.

Like many props he endured an injury-ravaged career, but seemed to come back stronger from every knock, although injury did end his only Lions tour of 1980.

Against South Wales Police – in 1978 – he broke his neck and two years later in the Grand Slam decider against France he broke his rib cage. He not only played on in that game but also in the two Tests that followed.

A sporting all-rounder, Blakeway was a junior modern pentathlon champion.

"Blakeway was neither dirty nor demonstrative. Nor was he a giant. But he had matchless technical nous and cunning," was how The Sunday Times rugby correspondent Stephen Jones remembers him. "He was able to hold his opponent in an uncomfortable position so that the enemy could not transfer their weight."

In 1985 Blakeway's international retirement seriously weakened the England pack but it wasn't the first occasion on which he had declared time on his career. He also retired in 1980 and 1982, but in 1985 a trapped nerve in the neck was enough to end his England career.

In 1992 with the game hurtling towards professionalism and Blakeway having coached at Berry Hill he made a comeback, moving to Moseley with Mike Teague.

Playing club rugby at 41, something that would be unheard of in the current era he explained his reasons for yet another comeback: "Keeping old age at bay is one reason for playing again. "More seriously, I thoroughly enjoy the game and was pleased Moseley asked me to help in whatever capacity I could. It would not have mattered whether that was propping for one of the lower teams or coaching the colts. I am now doing both."

In 1997 he had settled down to become a fruit and vegetable farmer at Tewkesbury, and even became a financial advisor, arranging a mortgage for another famous son of Gloucester, Phil Vickery.

His book, the aptly titled Rubbing Shoulders (Stanley Paul, £8.95) told the story of his life.

Phil Blakeway (Left) with Peter Wheeler and Colin Smart

Arthur Frederick BLAKISTON
Born: 16 June 1892 in West Derby
Died: 31 January 1974 in Salisbury
Educated: Bedford School
Clubs: Cambridge University, Northampton (7), Blackheath (1), Liverpool (9)
Position: Flanker (11), Lock (6)
Debut: 20 Mar 1920 v Scotland (Twickenham). Number: 564
Last game: 13 Apr 1925 v France (Stade Colombes)
Caps: 17 (W:13, D:1, L:3)
Scoring: 2T, 6 Pts
Appearances: 1920:S, 1921:W,I,S,F, 1922:W, 1923:S,F, 1924:W,I,F,S, 1925:NZ,W,I,S,F
Honours: Grand Slam: 1923, 1924. Championship: 1921

Thomas BLATHERWICK
Born: 25 December 1855
Died: 29 January 1940 in Bucklow
Educated: Epsom College
Clubs: Manchester (1)
Position: Forward (1)
Debut: 11 Mar 1878 v Ireland (Lansdowne Road). Number: 103
Caps: 1 (W:1, L:0)
Scoring: 0 Pts
Appearances: 1878:I

James Alfred BODY
Born: Third quarter 1846 in Tenterden, Kent
Died: 9 September 1929 in Manitoba, Canada
Educated: Tonbridge School
Clubs: Gipsies (2)
Position: Forward (2)
Debut: 5 Feb 1872 v Scotland (The Oval). Number: 22
Last game: 3 Mar 1873 v Scotland (Glasgow)
Caps: 2 (W:1, D:1, L:0)
Scoring: 0 Pts
Appearances: 1872:S, 1873:S

Charles Arthur BOLTON
Born: 3 January 1882 in Kensington
Died: 23 November 1963 in Eastbourne
Educated: Marlborough School
Clubs: Oxford University, Manchester Regt, United Services Portsmouth (1)
Position: Flanker (1)
Debut: 30 Jan 1909 v France (Leicester). Number: 484
Caps: 1 (W:1, L:0)
Scoring: 0 Pts
Appearances: 1909:F

Reginald BOLTON, MBE
Born: 20 November 1909 in Prescot
Educated: Queen Elizabeth GS
Clubs: London University, Wakefield (1), University College Hospital, Harlequins (4)
Position: Flanker (5)
Debut: 21 Jan 1933 v Wales (Twickenham). Number: 698
Last game: 12 Feb 1938 v Ireland (Lansdowne Road) - 1T, 3 Pts
Caps: 5 (W:3, L:2)
Scoring: 2T, 6 Pts
Appearances: 1933:W, 1936:S, 1937:S, 1938:W,I
Honours: Championship: 1937

Wilfred Nash BOLTON, OBE
Born: 14 September 1862 in Ireland
Died: 12 August 1930 in Contrexeville, France
Clubs: RNA Gosport, Wiltshire Regt, Blackheath (11)
Position: Three-quarter (11)
Debut: 6 Feb 1882 v Ireland (Lansdowne Road) - 1T, 1 Pt. Number: 141
Last game: 5 Mar 1887 v Scotland (Manchester)
Caps: 11 (W:7, D:2, L:2)
Scoring: 6T, 2C, 10 Pts
Appearances: 1882:I,S, 1883:W,I,S, 1884:W,I,S, 1885:I, 1887:I,S
Honours: Championship: 1883, 1884

Maurice Sydney BONAVENTURA
Born: 28 April 1902
Died: 14 July 1992 in Lewes
Educated: Cranleigh School
Clubs: Hon Artillery Company, Lensbury, Blackheath (1)
Position: Prop (1)
Debut: 17 Jan 1931 v Wales (Twickenham). Number: 669
Caps: 1 (W:0, D:1, L:0)
Scoring: 0 Pts
Appearances: 1931:W

Tony Bond

Anthony Matthew (Tony) BOND
Born: 3 August 1953 in Urmston, Manchester
Educated: Wellacre County School
Clubs: Sale (6)
Position: Centre (6), Bench (5)
Debut: 25 Nov 1978 v New Zealand (Twickenham).
Number: 1054
Last game: 6 Feb 1982 v Ireland (Twickenham)
Caps: 6 (W:1, D:1, L:4)
Scoring: 0 Pts
Appearances: 1978:NZ, 1979:S,I,NZ, 1980:I, 1982:I
Honours: Championship: 1980

Sir Edgar BONHAM-CARTER, KCMG
Born: 2 April 1870 in Kensington
Died: 24 April 1956 in Alton, Hants
Educated: Clifton College
Clubs: Oxford University (1), Blackheath
Position: Forward (1)
Debut: 7 Mar 1891 v Scotland (Richmond).
Number: 232
Caps: 1 (W:0, L:1)
Scoring: 0 Pts
Appearances: 1891:S

Frederick (Fred) BONSOR
Born: 1865
Died: February 1932
Clubs: Bradford (6)
Position: Half-Back (6)
Debut: 2 Jan 1886 v Wales (Blackheath).
Number: 176
Last game: 16 Feb 1889 (capt) v New Zealand Natives (Blackheath)
Caps: 6 (W:3, D:3, L:0). As captain: 1 (W:1, L:0)
Scoring: 0 Pts
Appearances: 1886:W,I,S, 1887:W,S, 1889:M*

Brian BOOBBYER
Born: 25 February 1928 in Ealing
Educated: Uppingham School
Clubs: Oxford University (6), Rosslyn Park (3)
Position: Centre (9)
Debut: 21 Jan 1950 v Wales (Twickenham).
Number: 800
Last game: 5 Apr 1952 v France (Stade Colombes)
Caps: 9 (W:4, L:5)
Scoring: 2T, 6 Pts
Appearances: 1950:W,I,F,S, 1951:W,F, 1952:S,I,F

Lewis Alfred BOOTH
Born: 26 September 1909 in Horsforth, Leeds
Died: Killed in action in 1942
Educated: Giggleswick School
Clubs: Headingley (7), Bohemians, RAF
Position: Wing (7)
Debut: 21 Jan 1933 v Wales (Twickenham).
Number: 699
Last game: 16 Mar 1935 v Scotland (Murrayfield) - 1T, 3 Pts
Caps: 7 (W:3, D:1, L:3)
Scoring: 3T, 9 Pts
Appearances: 1933:W,I,S, 1934:S, 1935:W,I,S
Honours: Championship: 1934

Steve Borthwick

Stephen William (Steve) BORTHWICK

Born: 12 October 1979 in Carlisle
Educated: Hutton GS
Clubs: Bath University, Preston Grasshoppers, Bath (27)
Position: Lock (19), Replacement (8), Bench (7)
Debut: 7 Apr 2001 v France (Twickenham). Number: 1222
Last game: 18 Mar 2006 v Ireland (Twickenham) - 1T, 5 Pts
Caps: 27 (W:15, L:12)
Scoring: 1T, 5 Pts
Appearances: 2001:F,C1,C2(r),US,R, 2003:A(r),W(r),F, 2004:I,F(r),NZ1(r),NZ2,A,C,SA,A, 2005:W(r),It(r),S(r),A,NZ,Sm, 2006:W,It,S,F,I
Honours: Championship: 2001

Ian James BOTTING

Born: 18 May 1922 in Dunedin, New Zealand
Died: 9 July 1980 in Merivale, Christchurch, New Zealand
Educated: Christ's School
Clubs: Otago University (NZ), Otago (NZ), Oxford University (2), RAF, Blackheath, Leicester
Position: Wing (2)
Debut: 21 Jan 1950 v Wales (Twickenham). Number: 801
Last game: 11 Feb 1950 v Ireland (Twickenham)
Caps: 2 (W:1, L:1)
Scoring: 0 Pts
Appearances: 1950:W,I

Kyran Bracken

Harold John BOUGHTON

Born: 7 September 1910 in Gloucester
Died: 1986
Clubs: Gloucester (3)
Position: Full-back (3)
Debut: 19 Jan 1935 v Wales (Twickenham) - 1PG, 3 Pts. Number: 712
Last game: 16 Mar 1935 v Scotland (Murrayfield)
Caps: 3 (W:1, D:1, L:1)
Scoring: 1C, 4PG, 14 Pts
Appearances: 1935:W,I,S

Francis (Patsy) BOYLAN

Born: Third quarter 1878 in Hartlepool
Died: 3 February 1938 in Kingston-upon-Hull
Clubs: Hartlepool Rovers (4), Hull KR RL
Position: Forward (4)
Debut: 1 Jan 1908 v France (Stade Colombes). Number: 452
Last game: 21 Mar 1908 v Scotland (Inverleith)
Caps: 4 (W:2, L:2)
Scoring: 0 Pts
Appearances: 1908:F,W,I,S

Cecil William BOYLE

Born: 16 March 1853 in St George's Hospital, London
Died: Killed in action in 1900 in Boshof, South Africa
Educated: Clifton College
Clubs: Oxford University (1)
Position: Half-Back (1)
Debut: 3 Mar 1873 v Scotland (Glasgow). Number: 35
Caps: 1 (W:0, D:1, L:0)
Scoring: 0 Pts
Appearances: 1873:S

Stephen Brent BOYLE

Born: 9 August 1953 in Warrington
Educated: Sir Thomas Rich's GS
Clubs: Gloucester (3), Moseley
Position: Lock (3)
Debut: 5 Feb 1983 v Wales (Cardiff). Number: 1077
Last game: 19 Mar 1983 v Ireland (Lansdowne Road)
Caps: 3 (W:0, D:1, L:2)
Scoring: 0 Pts
Appearances: 1983:W,S,I

Kyran Paul Patrick BRACKEN, MBE

Born: 22 November 1971 in Dublin, Ireland
Educated: Stonyhurst College
Clubs: Bristol University, Waterloo, Bristol (11), Saracens (40)
Position: Scrum-half (38), Replacement (13), Bench (16)
Debut: 27 Nov 1993 v New Zealand (Twickenham). Number: 1150
Last game: 16 Nov 2003 (rep) v France (Sydney)
Caps: 51 (W:40, D:2, L:9). As captain: 3 (W:3, L:0)
Scoring: 3T, 15 Pts
Appearances: 1993:NZ, 1994:S,I,C, 1995:I,F,W,S,It,Sm(r),SA, 1996:It(r), 1997:Ar1,Ar2,A,NZ1,NZ2, 1998:F,W, 1999:S(r),I,F,A, 2000:SA1,SA2,A,2001:It(r),S(r),F(r),C1*,C2*,US*,I(r),A,R(r), SA, 2002:S,I,F,W,It, 2003:W,I t(r),I(r),NZ,A,F,SA,U(r),W(r),F(r)
Honours: RWC Winner: 2003. Grand Slam: 1995.
Championship: 2001, 2003

Matthew Seymour BRADBY, MBE
Born: 25 March 1899 in Rugby
Died: 11 June 1963 near Shatterbury
Educated: Rugby School
Clubs: RNEC Keyham, Cambridge University, United Services (2), Royal Navy
Position: Centre (2)
Debut: 11 Feb 1922 v Ireland (Lansdowne Road). Number: 573
Last game: 25 Feb 1922 v France (Twickenham)
Caps: 2 (W:1, D:1, L:0)
Scoring: 0 Pts
Appearances: 1922:I,F

Robert BRADLEY
Born: Details unknown
Died: Details unknown
Clubs: West Hartlepool (1)
Position: Forward (1)
Debut: 10 Jan 1903 v Wales (Swansea). Number: 383
Caps: 1 (W:0, L:1)
Scoring: 0 Pts
Appearances: 1903:W

Harry BRADSHAW
Born: 17 April 1868 in Bramley, Leeds
Died: 31 December 1910 in Halifax
Clubs: Bramley (7), Leeds RL
Position: Forward (7)
Debut: 5 Mar 1892 v Scotland (Raeburn Place). Number: 246
Last game: 17 Mar 1894 v Scotland (Raeburn Place)
Caps: 7 (W:3, L:4)
Scoring: 2T, 5 Pts
Appearances: 1892:S, 1893:W,I,S, 1894:W,I,S
Honours: Championship: 1892

Stephen Edward (Steve) BRAIN
Born: 11 November 1954 in Moseley
Educated: Harold Malley School
Clubs: Moseley, Coventry (13), Rugby
Position: Hooker (12), Replacement (1)
Debut: 9 Jun 1984 v South Africa (Johannesburg). Number: 1093
Last game: 15 Mar 1986 v France (Parc des Princes)
Caps: 13 (W:4, D:1, L:8)
Scoring: 0 Pts
Appearances: 1984:SA2,A(r), 1985:R,F,S,I,W,NZ1,NZ2, 1986:W,S,I,F

John (Jacky) BRAITHWAITE
Born: 21 April 1873 in Leeds
Died: 14 November 1915 in West Humberstone, Leicester
Clubs: Holbeck, Vulcan Rovers, Leicester (1), Nottingham
Position: Scrum-half (1)
Debut: 2 Dec 1905 v New Zealand (Crystal Palace). Number: 413
Caps: 1 (W:0, L:1)
Scoring: 0 Pts
Appearances: 1905:NZ

Arthur T BRETTARGH
Born: 22 December 1877 in Egremont, Cheshire
Died: May 1954 in Croydon
Educated: Liverpool College
Clubs: Liverpool Old Boys (8)
Position: Centre (8)
Debut: 6 Jan 1900 v Wales (Gloucester). Number: 344
Last game: 18 Mar 1905 v Scotland (Richmond)
Caps: 8 (W:1, D:1, L:6)
Scoring: 1T, 3 Pts
Appearances: 1900:W, 1903:I,S, 1904:W,I,S, 1905:I,S

Steve Brain

Alan Brinn

J BREWER
Born: Details unknown
Died: Details unknown
Clubs: Gipsies (1)
Position: Forward (1)
Debut: 13 Dec 1875 v Ireland (Dublin). Number: 69
Caps: 1 (W:1, L:0)
Scoring: 0 Pts
Appearances: 1875:I

Arthur (Spafty) BRIGGS
Born: 1869
Died: 18 August 1943 in Bradford
Clubs: Otley, Bradford (3)
Position: Half-Back (3)
Debut: 2 Jan 1892 v Wales (Blackheath). Number: 235
Last game: 5 Mar 1892 v Scotland (Raeburn Place)
Caps: 3 (W:3, L:0)
Scoring: 0 Pts
Appearances: 1892:W,I,S
Honours: Championship: 1892

Alan BRINN
Born: 21 July 1940 in Ystrad, Rhondda, Wales
Educated: RGS High Wycombe
Clubs: Gloucester (3)
Position: Lock (3)
Debut: 15 Jan 1972 v Wales (Twickenham). Number: 1003
Last game: 18 Mar 1972 v Scotland (Murrayfield)
Caps: 3 (W:0, L:3)
Scoring: 0 Pts
Appearances: 1972:W,I,S

Thomas (Tom) BROADLEY
Born: 18 August 1871 in Bingley
Died: 26 November 1950 in Bradford
Clubs: Bingley (6), Bradford
Position: Forward (6)
Debut: 7 Jan 1893 v Wales (Cardiff). Number: 249
Last game: 14 Mar 1896 v Scotland (Glasgow)
Caps: 6 (W:1, L:5)
Scoring: 0 Pts
Appearances: 1893:W,S, 1894:W,I,S, 1896:S

William Ernest BROMET
Born: 17 May 1868 in Tadcaster
Died: 23 January 1949 in Winchester
Educated: Richmond School
Clubs: Oxford University, Tadcaster (5), Richmond (7)
Position: Forward (12)
Debut: 3 Jan 1891 v Wales (Newport). Number: 224
Last game: 1 Feb 1896 v Ireland (Leeds)
Caps: 12 (W:8, L:4)
Scoring: 1T, 2 Pts
Appearances: 1891:W,I, 1892:W,I,S, 1893:W,I,S, 1895:W,I,S, 1896:I
Honours: Championship: 1892

Peter Watts Pitt BROOK
Born: 21 September 1906 in Thornton Heath
Died: 6 August 1992 in Bristol
Educated: Whitgift School
Clubs: Cambridge University (1), Harlequins, Bristol
Position: Flanker (2), No 8 (1)
Debut: 15 Mar 1930 v Scotland (Twickenham). Number: 663
Last game: 21 Mar 1936 v Scotland (Twickenham)
Caps: 3 (W:1, D:1, L:1)
Scoring: 0 Pts
Appearances: 1930:S, 1931:F, 1936:S
Honours: Championship: 1930

Terence John BROOKE
Born: 8 October 1940 in north-east Surrey
Educated: Purley County GS, Battersea College
Clubs: Richmond (2)
Position: Centre (2)
Debut: 24 Feb 1968 v France (Stade Colombes). Number: 970
Last game: 16 Mar 1968 v Scotland (Murrayfield)
Caps: 2 (W:1, L:1)
Scoring: 0 Pts
Appearances: 1968:F,S

Frederick George (Freddie) BROOKS
Born: 1 May 1883 in Cape Town, South Africa
Died: September 1947 in South Africa
Educated: Bedford GS
Clubs: Bedford (1), Rhodesia
Position: Wing (1)
Debut: 8 Dec 1906 v South Africa (Crystal Palace) - 1T, 3 Pts. Number: 437
Caps: 1 (W:0, D:1, L:0)
Scoring: 1T, 3 Pts
Appearances: 1906:SA

Marshall Jones BROOKS
Born: 30 May 1855 in Haslingden, Lancs
Died: 5 January 1944 in Tarporley, Cheshire
Educated: Rugby School
Clubs: Oxford University (1)
Position: Full-back (1)
Debut: 23 Feb 1874 v Scotland (The Oval). Number: 46
Caps: 1 (W:1, L:0)
Scoring: 0 Pts
Appearances: 1874:S

Thomas John BROPHY
Born: 8 July 1942 in Liverpool
Educated: Westpark GS
Clubs: Liverpool University, Loughborough College, Liverpool (8)
Position: Fly-half (8)
Debut: 8 Feb 1964 v Ireland (Twickenham). Number: 923
Last game: 26 Feb 1966 v France (Stade Colombes)
Caps: 8 (W:1, D:1, L:6)
Scoring: 0 Pts
Appearances: 1964:I,F,S, 1965:W,I, 1966:W,I,F

James Wasdale (Jim) BROUGH
Born: 5 November 1903 in Silloth
Died: 16 September 1986 in Workington
Educated: Silloth School
Clubs: Silloth (2), Leeds RL
Position: Full-back (2)
Debut: 3 Jan 1925 v New Zealand (Twickenham). Number: 594
Last game: 17 Jan 1925 v Wales (Twickenham)
Caps: 2 (W:1, L:1)
Scoring: 0 Pts
Appearances: 1925:NZ,W

Henry BROUGHAM
Born: 8 July 1888 in Wellington College
Died: 18 February 1923 in La Croix, France
Educated: Wellington College
Clubs: Oxford University, Harlequins (4)
Position: Wing (4)
Debut: 20 Jan 1912 v Wales (Twickenham) - 1T, 3 Pts. Number: 517
Last game: 8 Apr 1912 v France (Parc des Princes) - 1T, 3 Pts
Caps: 4 (W:3, L:1)
Scoring: 3T, 9 Pts
Appearances: 1912:W,I,S,F

Alan Arthur BROWN
Born: 28 August 1911 in St Helens
Died: August 1987 in Honiton
Educated: Cowley GS, Carnegie College
Clubs: St Luke's, Exeter University, Exeter (1)
Position: Flanker (1)
Debut: 19 Mar 1938 v Scotland (Twickenham). Number: 742
Caps: 1 (W:0, L:1)
Scoring: 0 Pts
Appearances: 1938:S

Alexander Thomas (Alex) BROWN
Born 17 May 1979 in Bristol
Educated: Colston's School
Clubs: Bath, Pontypool, Bristol, Gloucester (1)
Position: Lock (1)
Debut: 11 Jun 2006 v Australia (Sydney). Number: 1269
Caps: 1 (W:0, L:1)
Scoring: 0 Pts
Appearances: 2006:A1

Leonard Graham (Bruno) BROWN
Born: 6 September 1888 in Brisbane, Australia
Died: 23 May 1950 in Charing Cross
Educated: Brisbane GS
Clubs: Queensland (AU), Oxford University (1), London Hospital (4), Blackheath (5)
Position: Prop (18)
Debut: 21 Jan 1911 v Wales (Swansea). Number: 511
Last game: 21 Jan 1922 (capt) v Wales (Cardiff)
Caps: 18 (W:14, L:4). As captain: 1 (W:0, L:1)
Scoring: 4T, 12 Pts
Appearances: 1911:W,F,I,S, 1913:SA,W,F,I,S, 1914:W,I,S,F, 1921:W,I,S,F, 1922:W*
Honours: Grand Slam: 1913, 1914, 1921

Alex Brown

Spencer Peter BROWN
Born: 11 July 1973 in Eton
Educated: Weaver's School
Clubs: Deal Wanderers, Richmond (2), Bristol, Bedford, Rugby, Nottingham
Position: Wing (2)
Debut: 6 Jun 1998 v Australia (Brisbane).
Number: 1196
Last game: 4 Jul 1998 v South Africa (Cape Town)
Caps: 2 (W:0, L:2)
Scoring: 0 Pts
Appearances: 1998:A,SA

Thomas William BROWN
Born: Third quarter 1907 in Bristol
Died: 14 May 1961 in Bristol
Educated: Colston's School
Clubs: Bristol University, Bristol (9)
Position: Full-back (9)
Debut: 17 Mar 1928 v Scotland (Twickenham).
Number: 636
Last game: 18 Mar 1933 v Scotland (Murrayfield)
Caps: 9 (W:5, L:4)
Scoring: 0 Pts
Appearances: 1928:S, 1929:W,I,S,F, 1932:S, 1933:W,I,S
Honours: Championship: 1928

Joseph BRUNTON
Born: 21 August 1888 in Tynemouth
Died: 18 September 1971 in Hammersmith, London
Clubs: North Durham (3), Rockcliff, Army
Position: Lock (3)
Debut: 17 Jan 1914 v Wales (Twickenham).
Number: 535
Last game: 21 Mar 1914 v Scotland (Inverleith)
Caps: 3 (W:3, L:0)
Scoring: 0 Pts
Appearances: 1914:W,I,S
Honours: Championship: 1914

Ernest Bartholomew (Rev) BRUTTON
Born: 29 July 1864 in Tynemouth
Died: 19 April 1922 in Aylesbeare, Devon
Educated: Durham School
Clubs: Cambridge University (1)
Position: Three-quarter (1)
Debut: 13 Mar 1886 v Scotland (Raeburn Place).
Number: 185
Caps: 1 (W:0, D:1, L:0)
Scoring: 0 Pts
Appearances: 1886:S

Spencer Brown

Charles Cowper BRYDEN
Born: 16 June 1852 in Banbury
Died: 20 February 1941 in Poole
Educated: Cheltenham College
Clubs: Clapham Rovers (2)
Position: Forward (2)
Debut: 13 Dec 1875 v Ireland (Dublin).
Number: 70
Last game: 5 Mar 1877 v Scotland (Raeburn Place)
Caps: 2 (W:1, L:1)
Scoring: 0 Pts
Appearances: 1875:I, 1877:S

Henry Anderson BRYDEN
Born: 3 May 1854 in Banbury
Died: 23 September 1937 in Parkstone, Dorset
Educated: Cheltenham College
Clubs: Clapham Rovers (1)
Position: Forward (1)
Debut: 23 Feb 1874 v Scotland (The Oval).
Number: 47
Caps: 1 (W:1, L:0)
Scoring: 0 Pts
Appearances: 1874:S

Ralph Arthur BUCKINGHAM
Born: 15 January 1907 in Blaby
Died: 10 April 1988 in Stoneygate, Leicester
Educated: Stoneygate School, Rossall School
Clubs: Stoneygate, Leicester (1)
Position: Centre (1)
Debut: 2 Apr 1927 v France (Stade Colombes).
Number: 626
Caps: 1 (W:0, L:1)
Scoring: 0 Pts
Appearances: 1927:F

Tony Bucknall

Anthony Launce (Tony) BUCKNALL
Born: 7 June 1945 in Torquay
Educated: Ampleforth College
Clubs: Oxford University, Richmond (10)
Position: Flanker (10)
Debut: 20 Dec 1969 v South Africa (Twickenham). Number: 978
Last game: 27 Mar 1971 v Scotland (Murrayfield)
Caps: 10 (W:3, D:1, L:6). As captain:1 (W:0, L:1)
Scoring: 0 Pts
Appearances: 1969:SA, 1970:I,W,S,F, 1971:W*,I,F,S,S

John Richard BUCKTON
Born: 22 December 1961 in Hull
Clubs: Hull & ER, Marist Old Boys (NZ), Saracens (3)
Position: Centre (2), Replacement (1), Bench (2)
Debut: 5 Nov 1988 (rep) v Australia (Twickenham). Number: 1131
Last game: 4 Aug 1990 v Argentina (Buenos Aires)
Caps: 3 (W:2, L:1)
Scoring: 0 Pts
Appearances: 1988:A(r), 1990:Ar1,Ar2

Arthur (Jimmy) BUDD
Born: 14 October 1853 in Bristol
Died: 27 August 1899 in London
Educated: Clifton College
Clubs: Cambridge University, St Bart's Hospital, Blackheath (5)
Position: Forward (5)
Debut: 11 Mar 1878 v Ireland (Lansdowne Road). Number: 104
Last game: 19 Mar 1881 v Scotland (Raeburn Place)
Caps: 5 (W:3, D:2, L:0)
Scoring: 1T, 1 Pt
Appearances: 1878:I, 1879:S,I, 1881:W,S

Richard Tom Dutton BUDWORTH
Born: 17 October 1867 in Grensted Hall, Essex
Died: 7 December 1937 in London
Educated: Christ's School
Clubs: Oxford University, Blackheath (3), London Welsh
Position: Forward (3)
Debut: 15 Feb 1890 v Wales (Dewsbury). Number: 209
Last game: 7 Mar 1891 v Scotland (Richmond)
Caps: 3 (W:1, L:2)
Scoring: 1T, 1 Pt
Appearances: 1890:W, 1891:W,S

Arthur Gilbert BULL
Born: Third quarter 1890 in Newport Pagnell
Died: 15 March 1963 in Chandlers Ford
Educated: Bedford Modern School
Clubs: Old Bedford Moderns, Bedford, Northampton (1), Leicester
Position: Prop (1)
Debut: 17 Jan 1914 v Wales (Twickenham). Number: 536
Caps: 1 (W:1, L:0)
Scoring: 0 Pts
Appearances: 1914:W
Honours: Championship: 1914

Edward BULLOUGH
Born: 17 December 1866 in Wigan
Died: 6 July 1934 in Manchester South
Clubs: Wigan (3)
Position: Forward (3)
Debut: 2 Jan 1892 v Wales (Blackheath). Number: 236
Last game: 5 Mar 1892 v Scotland (Raeburn Place)
Caps: 3 (W:3, L:0)
Scoring: 0 Pts
Appearances: 1892:W,I,S
Honours: Championship: 1892

Michael Philip (Mike) BULPITT
Born: 12 April 1944 in Richmond, Yorks
Educated: Berkhamsted School
Clubs: Chelmsford, Osterley, Blackheath (1)
Position: Wing (1)
Debut: 21 Mar 1970 v Scotland (Murrayfield). Number: 985
Caps: 1 (W:0, L:1)
Scoring: 0 Pts
Appearances: 1970:S

A J BULTEEL
Born: Details unknown
Died: Details unknown
Clubs: Manchester (1)
Position: Forward (1)
Debut: 13 Dec 1875 v Ireland (Dublin). Number: 71
Caps: 1 (W:1, L:0)
Scoring: 0 Pts
Appearances: 1875:I

William Louis BUNTING
Born: 9 August 1874 in Daventry
Died: 15 October 1947 in Odiham, Hants
Educated: Bromsgrove School
Clubs: Cambridge University, Richmond (6), Moseley (3)
Position: Centre (9)
Debut: 6 Feb 1897 v Ireland (Lansdowne Road). Number: 306
Last game: 9 Mar 1901 (capt) v Scotland (Blackheath)
Caps: 9 (W:2, D:2, L:5). As captain: 2 (W:0, L:2)
Scoring: 0 Pts
Appearances: 1897:I,S, 1898:I,S,W, 1899:S, 1900:S, 1901:I*,S*

Donald William BURLAND
Born: 22 January 1908 in Bristol
Died: 26 January 1976 in St Austell
Clubs: Bristol (8)
Position: Centre (8)
Debut: 17 Jan 1931 v Wales (Twickenham) - 1T, 1C, 5 Pts. Number: 670
Last game: 18 Mar 1933 v Scotland (Murrayfield)
Caps: 8 (W:3, D:1, L:4)
Scoring: 3T, 4C, 2PG, 23 Pts
Appearances: 1931:W,I,F, 1932:I,S, 1933:W,I,S

Benjamin Henry BURNS
Born: 28 May 1848 in Scotland
Died: 3 June 1932
Educated: Smeston's School
Clubs: St Andrew's University, Edinburgh Academy, Blackheath (1)
Position: Forward (1)
Debut: 27 Mar 1871 v Scotland (Raeburn Place). Number: 3
Caps: 1 (W:0, L:1)
Scoring: 0 Pts
Appearances: 1871:S

George William BURTON
Born: 29 August 1855 in Wakefield
Died: 17 September 1890 in West Hampstead
Educated: Winchester College
Clubs: Blackheath (6)
Position: Forward (6)
Debut: 10 Mar 1879 v Scotland (Raeburn Place) - 1T, 1 Pt. Number: 110
Last game: 19 Mar 1881 v Scotland (Raeburn Place)
Caps: 6 (W:4, D:2, L:0)
Scoring: 6T, 6 Pts
Appearances: 1879:S,I, 1880:S, 1881:I,W,S

Mike Burton

Hyde Clarke BURTON
Born: 10 June 1898 in Bishop's Stortford
Died: 27 January 1990 in Brighton
Clubs: RNEC Keyham, Royal Navy, Bishops Stortford, Richmond (1)
Position: Wing (1)
Debut: 16 Jan 1926 v Wales (Cardiff). Number: 606
Caps: 1 (W:0, D:1, L:0)
Scoring: 0 Pts
Appearances: 1926:W

Michael Alan (Mike) BURTON
Born: 18 December 1945 in Maidenhead
Educated: Longlevens School
Clubs: Gloucester (17)
Position: Prop (17), Bench (8)
Debut: 15 Jan 1972 v Wales (Twickenham). Number: 1004
Last game: 4 Feb 1978 v Wales (Twickenham)
Caps: 17 (W:4, D:1, L:12)
Scoring: 0 Pts. Discipline - Sent off: 1
Appearances: 1972:W,I,F,S,SA, 1974:F,W, 1975:S,A1,A2, 1976:A,W,S,I,F, 1978:F,W

James Arthur BUSH

Born: 28 July 1850 in Cawnpore, India
Died: 21 September 1924 in Clevedon, Somerset
Educated: Clifton College
Clubs: Clifton (5), Gloucester
Position: Forward (5)
Debut: 5 Feb 1872 v Scotland (The Oval). Number: 23
Last game: 6 Mar 1876 v Scotland (The Oval)
Caps: 5 (W:3, D:2, L:0)
Scoring: 0 Pts
Appearances: 1872:S, 1873:S, 1875:S,I, 1876:S

Chris Butcher

Christopher John Simon (Chris) BUTCHER

Born: 19 August 1960 in Karachi, Pakistan
Educated: St Peter's School
Clubs: Harlequins (3)
Position: No 8 (3)
Debut: 2 Jun 1984 v South Africa (Port Elizabeth). Number: 1089
Last game: 3 Nov 1984 v Australia (Twickenham)
Caps: 3 (W:0, L:3)
Scoring: 0 Pts
Appearances: 1984:SA1,SA2,A

Walter Vincent BUTCHER

Born: 2 February 1878 in Tooting Graveney, Surrey
Died: 16 August 1957 in Bexhill
Educated: Carlisle GS
Clubs: Streatham (1), Bristol (6), Gloucester
Position: Scrum-half (4), Half-Back (2), Fly-half (1)
Debut: 21 Mar 1903 v Scotland (Richmond). Number: 392
Last game: 18 Mar 1905 v Scotland (Richmond)
Caps: 7 (W:1, D:1, L:5)
Scoring: 0 Pts
Appearances: 1903:S, 1904:W,I,S, 1905:W,I,S

Arthur Geoffrey BUTLER

Born: 30 September 1914 in Oxford
Educated: Royal Henley GS
Clubs: Henley, Harlequins (2)
Position: Wing (2)
Debut: 16 Jan 1937 v Wales (Twickenham). Number: 728
Last game: 13 Feb 1937 v Ireland (Twickenham) - 1T, 3 Pts
Caps: 2 (W:2, L:0)
Scoring: 1T, 3 Pts
Appearances: 1937:W,I
Honours: Championship: 1937

Peter Edward BUTLER

Born: 23 June 1951 in Gloucester
Educated: Crypt GS
Clubs: Gloucester (2)
Position: Full-back (2)
Debut: 24 May 1975 v Australia (Sydney Cricket Ground) - 1C, 1PG, 5 Pts. Number: 1028
Last game: 20 Mar 1976 v France (Parc des Princes) - 1C, 1PG, 5 Pts
Caps: 2 (W:0, L:2)
Scoring: 2C, 2PG, 10 Pts
Appearances: 1975:A1, 1976:F

Jeffrey (Jeff) BUTTERFIELD

Born: 9 August 1929 in Heckmondwike
Died: 30 April 2004 in Wicken, Bucks
Educated: Cleckheaton GS
Clubs: Cleckheaton, Loughborough College, Northampton (28)
Position: Centre (28)
Debut: 28 Feb 1953 v France (Twickenham) - 1T, 3 Pts. Number: 835
Last game: 21 Mar 1959 (capt) v Scotland (Twickenham)
Caps: 28 (W:16, D:5, L:7). As captain: 4 (W:1, D:2, L:1)
Scoring: 5T, 15 Pts
Appearances: 1953:F,S, 1954:W,NZ,I,S,F, 1955:W,I,F,S, 1956:W,I,S,F, 1957:W,I,F,S, 1958:W,A,I,F,S, 1959:W*,I*,F*,S*
Honours - Grand Slam: 1957. Championship: 1953, 1958

When Jeff Butterfield finally made his way into the England team there was no dropping the centre from the West Riding and such was his influence on the side he played in a record 28 successive Tests from 1953 to 1959.

That side was one of England's best, picking up a Grand Slam in 1957 – their first for 29 years – and his England career gave Butterfield the springboard to go on two tours with the British and Irish Lions, starring on the 1955 trip to South Africa.

Born in Yorkshire, Butterfield was influenced greatly by rugby league, and became a player committed to the philosophy of expansive rugby, so sought after in the modern era.

He was an impressive athlete and swimmer at Cleckheaton grammar school. A student at Loughborough, and later a games master, his rugby career blossomed at Northampton, where he made 227 appearances. The County Championship was also a key development tool for players of that era, Butterfield representing Yorkshire 54 times, captaining the county from 1951 to 1958.

On the world stage he made his reputation with the 1955 Lions as they drew their series 2-2 in South Africa, ensuring that Butterfield wouldn't be far from selection in any all-time England team. Butterfield scored a try in three of the four Test matches.

In tandem with Wales' Cliff Morgan, Butterfield was often untouchable. David Frost, writing in The Guardian summed up Butterfield's brilliance.

"The clue to Jeff Butterfield's rugby success was the suppleness of his hips. He could take a pass impeccably, facing the passer, and then, with his legs moving inwards but his body facing outwards, give a perfect pass to the man outside him," said Frost.

"When his opponents had grown accustomed to this then classical style, he would effortlessly use his hips again to swerve outside his immediate opponent. He was the ideal centre three-quarter.

"But his individual skills and consistency made him one of England's greatest players."

Paul Stephens, in The Independent added: "Where others used brawn and power, Butterfield relied on subtlety and sublime handling skills. Quite simply, he was the prince of centres, not only in England but throughout the British Isles."

A modest man, Butterfield – who formed a potent centre partnership with WPC Davies – was made England captain for the Five Nations Championship in 1959.

His vision was legendary and Frank Sykes, who played outside him at Northampton, once said to him: "Jeff, for God's sake let me do a bit towards scoring some of the tries occasionally."

An arthritic hip did not stop him playing club rugby into the early 1960s.

After his playing days were over Butterfield was involved in the development of one of the first coaching manuals produced by the RFU.

Butterfield was given the job of preparing the section on back play. "The ball", he once said, "should be caressed, not hurled around like a weapon."

Towards the end of his life Butterfield – and his wife Barbara, were the hosts at The Rugby Club in Hallam Street, central London.

Francis Alban BYRNE

Born: Second quarter 1873 in Aston, Birmingham
Died: 1950 in Nairobi, Kenya
Clubs: Moseley (1)
Position: Wing (1)
Debut: 9 Jan 1897 v Wales (Newport). Number: 298
Caps: 1 (W:0, L:1)
Scoring: 0 Pts
Appearances: 1897:W

James Frederick (Fred) BYRNE

Born: 19 June 1871 in Penns, Birmingham
Died: 10 May 1954 in Edgbaston
Educated: Downside School
Clubs: Moseley (13)
Position: Full-back (13)
Debut: 6 Jan 1894 v Wales (Birkenhead Park). Number: 261
Last game: 4 Feb 1899 v Ireland (Lansdowne Road)
Caps: 13 (W:4, D:1, L:8). As captain: 3 (W:1, D:1, L:1)
Scoring: 2C, 4PG, 2DG, 24 Pts
Appearances: 1894:W,I,S, 1895:I,S, 1896:I, 1897:W,I,S, 1898:I*,S*,W*, 1899:I

Jeff Butterfield

Will Carling

C

CAIN, John Joseph
CALLARD, Jonathan Edward Brooks
CAMPBELL, David Alfred
CANDLER, Peter Laurence
CANNELL, Lewis Bernard
CAPLAN, David William Nigel
CARDUS, Richard Michael
CAREY, Godfrey Mohun
CARLETON, John
CARLING, William David Charles, OBE
CARPENTER, Alfred Denzel
CARPENTER, John MacGregor Kendall, CBE
CARR, Robert Stanley Leonard
CARTWRIGHT, Vincent Henry
CATCHESIDE, Howard Carston, OBE
CATT, Michael John, MBE
CATTELL, Richard Henry Burdon
CAVE, John Watkins
CAVE, William Thomas Charles
CHALLIS, Robert
CHAMBERS, Ernest Leonard
CHANTRILL, Bevan Stanislaw
CHAPMAN, Charles Edward
CHAPMAN, Dominic Edward
CHAPMAN, Frederick Ernest
CHEESMAN, William Inkersole
CHESTON, Ernest Constantine
CHILCOTT, Gareth James
CHRISTOPHERS, Philip Derek
CHRISTOPHERSON, Percy
CHUTER, George Scala
CLARK, Charles William Henry
CLARKE, Allan James
CLARKE, Benjamin Bevan
CLARKE, Simon John Scott
CLAYTON, John Henry
CLEMENTS, Jeffrey E Woodward
CLEVELAND, Sir Charles Raitt, KBE
CLIBBON, William George
CLOUGH, Francis John
COATES, Charles Hutton
COATES, Vincent Hope Middleton
COBBY, William
COCKERHAM, Arthur
COCKERILL, Richard
CODLING, Alexander John
COHEN, Ben Christopher , MBE
COLCLOUGH, Maurice John
COLEY, Eric, OBE
COLLINS, Philip John
COLLINS, William Edward, CMG
CONSIDINE, Stanley George Ulick
CONWAY, Geoffrey Seymour
COOK, John Gilbert
COOK, Peter William
COOKE, David Alexander
COOKE, David Howard
COOKE, Paul
COOP, Thomas
COOPER, John Graham
COOPER, Martin John
COOPPER, Sydney Frank
CORBETT, Leonard James
CORLESS, Barry James
CORRY, Martin Edward, MBE
COTTON, Francis Edward
COULMAN, Michael John
COULSON, Thomas John
COURT, Edward Darlington
COVERDALE, Harry
COWLING, Robin James
COWMAN, Alan Richard
COX, Norman Simpson
CRANMER, Peter
CREED, Roger Norman
CRIDLAN, Arthur Gordon
CROMPTON, Charles Arthur
CROSSE, Charles William
CUETO, Mark John
CUMBERLEGE, Barry Stephenson, OBE
CUMMING, Sir Duncan Cameron, KBE
CUNLIFFE, Foster Lionel
CURREY, Frederick Innes
CURRIE, John David
CUSANI, David Anthony
CUSWORTH, Leslie

John Joseph CAIN
Born: 12 June 1920 in West Derby
Educated: St Mary's College
Clubs: Waterloo (1)
Position: Flanker (1)
Debut: 21 Jan 1950 v Wales (Twickenham). Number: 802
Caps: 1 (W:0, L:1)
Scoring: 0 Pts
Appearances: 1950:W

Jonathan Edward Brooks (Jon) CALLARD
Born: 1 January 1966 in Leicester
Educated: Bassaleg College, St Paul's College
Clubs: Newport, St Mary's College, Bath (5)
Position: Full-back (5), Bench (18)
Debut: 27 Nov 1993 v New Zealand (Twickenham) - 4PG, 12 Pts. Number: 1151
Last game: 18 Nov 1995 v South Africa (Twickenham) - 3PG, 9 Pts
Caps: 5 (W:3, L:2)
Scoring: 3C, 21PG, 69 Pts
Appearances: 1993:NZ, 1994:S,I, 1995:Sm,SA

Jon Callard

David Alfred CAMPBELL
Born: 1915 in Adelong, NSW, Australia
Died: 1982
Educated: King's School
Clubs: Cambridge University (2)
Position: Flanker (2)
Debut: 16 Jan 1937 v Wales (Twickenham). Number: 729
Last game: 13 Feb 1937 v Ireland (Twickenham)
Caps: 2 (W:2, L:0)
Scoring: 0 Pts
Appearances: 1937:W,I
Honours: Championship: 1937

Peter Laurence CANDLER
Born: 28 January 1914 in Exeter
Died: 27 November 1991 in Natal, South Africa
Educated: Sherborne School
Clubs: Cambridge University (1), St Bart's Hospital (9), Richmond
Position: Fly-half (6), Centre (4)
Debut: 19 Jan 1935 v Wales (Twickenham). Number: 713
Last game: 19 Mar 1938 v Scotland (Twickenham)
Caps: 10 (W:5, D:2, L:3)
Scoring: 2T, 6 Pts
Appearances: 1935:W, 1936:NZ,W,I,S, 1937:W,I,S, 1938:W,S
Honours: Championship: 1937

Lewis Bernard CANNELL
Born: 10 June 1926 in Coventry
Died: March 2003
Educated: Northampton GS
Clubs: Northampton (1), Oxford University (8), St Mary's Hospital (10), RAF
Position: Centre (19)
Debut: 29 Mar 1948 v France (Stade Colombes). Number: 784
Last game: 9 Feb 1957 v Ireland (Lansdowne Road)
Caps: 19 (W:9, D:1, L:9)
Scoring: 2T, 6 Pts
Appearances: 1948:F, 1949:W,I,F,S, 1950:W,I,F,S, 1952:SA,W, 1953:W,I,F, 1956:I,S,F, 1957:W,I
Honours: Championship: 1953, 1957

David William Nigel CAPLAN
Born: 5 April 1954 in Leeds
Educated: Leeds GS
Clubs: Newcastle University, Oxford University, Headingley (2)
Position: Full-back (2)
Debut: 4 Mar 1978 v Scotland (Murrayfield). Number: 1052
Last game: 18 Mar 1978 v Ireland (Twickenham)
Caps: 2 (W:2, L:0)
Scoring: 0 Pts
Appearances: 1978:S,I

Richard Michael CARDUS
Born: 23 May 1956 in Leeds
Educated: Foxwood School
Clubs: Roundhay (2), Wasps
Position: Centre (2)
Debut: 3 Mar 1979 v France (Twickenham). Number: 1056
Last game: 17 Mar 1979 v Wales (Cardiff)
Caps: 2 (W:1, L:1)
Scoring: 0 Pts
Appearances: 1979:F,W

Godfrey Mohun CAREY
Born: 17 August 1872 in St Peterport, Guernsey
Died: 18 December 1927 in Sherborne
Educated: Sherborne School
Clubs: Oxford University (3), Blackheath (2)
Position: Forward (5)
Debut: 5 Jan 1895 v Wales (Swansea) - 1T, 3 Pts. Number: 273
Last game: 1 Feb 1896 v Ireland (Leeds)
Caps: 5 (W:3, L:2)
Scoring: 1T, 3 Pts
Appearances: 1895:W,I,S, 1896:W,I

John Carleton

John CARLETON
Born: 24 November 1955 in Orrell
Educated: Upholland GS, Chester College
Clubs: Orrell (26)
Position: Wing (26)
Debut: 24 Nov 1979 v New Zealand (Twickenham). Number: 1058
Last game: 3 Nov 1984 v Australia (Twickenham)
Caps: 26 (W:12, D:3, L:11)
Scoring: 7T, 28 Pts
Appearances: 1979:NZ, 1980:I,F,W,S, 1981:W,S,I,F,Ar1,Ar2, 1982:A,S,I,F,W, 1983:F,W,S,I,NZ, 1984:S,I,F,W,A
Honours: Grand Slam: 1980

William David Charles (Will) CARLING, OBE

Born: 12 December 1965 in Bradford-on-Avon
Educated: Sedbergh School
Clubs: RMA Sandhurst, Durham University (4), Harlequins (68)
Position: Centre (72)
Debut: 16 Jan 1988 v France (Parc des Princes). Number: 1120
Last game: 15 Mar 1997 v Wales (Cardiff)
Caps: 72 (W:53, D:1, L:18). As captain: 59 (W:44, D:1, L:14)
Scoring: 12T, 54 Pts
Appearances: 1988:F,W,S,I,I,A2,Fj,A*, 1989:S*,I*,F*,W*,Fj*, 1990:I*,F*,W*,S*,Ar1*,Ar2*,Ar*, 1991:W*,S*,I*,F*,Fj*,A*,NZ*,It*,US*,F*,S*,A*, 1992:S*,I*,F*,W*,C*,SA*, 1993:F*,W*,S*,I*,NZ*, 1994:S*,I*,F*,W*,SA1*,SA2*,R*,C*, 1995:I*,F*,W*,S*,Ar*,Sm*,A*,NZ*,F*,SA*,Sm*, 1996:F*,W*,S*,I*,It,Ar, 1997:S,I,F,W
Honours: Grand Slam: 1991 (capt), 1992 (capt), 1995 (capt). Championship: 1996 (capt)

Like politics or religion everyone has an opinion (and usually a heartfelt one) on England's most successful post-war captain, Will Carling.

The most professional skipper the game had ever seen, said some; a player barely worth his place in the side, said others.

But what you couldn't deny was his ability to get results. In his 59 Tests as England captain the side won 44 times!

The Harlequins centre heralded a new era for English rugby when he became England's youngest skipper for 57 years – in 1988 – coming into a national side stung by a poor World Cup performance 12 months before. His first game as captain was a 28-19 victory over Australia and he never looked back.

England hadn't won a Grand Slam since 1980 but when Carling played his last game – in 1997 – England had three Grand Slams and a Championship in the trophy cabinet at Twickenham and they had made one final (1991) and one semi-final (1995) of the Rugby World Cup.

A solid centre at the Quins with whom he won the Pilkington Cup in 1988 and 1991, it was his leadership qualities that made him such an asset on the pitch. He is credited with restoring a winning mentality to a talented but under-performing team, his record of 44 wins from 59 games as skipper speaks for itself. And when the final whistle signalled England's first Grand Slam for 11 years, in 1991, Carling was carried from the field by his team.

His influence within the England set-up and the respect he commanded from his team was in evidence when, after publicly branding the RFU Council "57 old farts", in an off the cuff remark in a television interview, he was stripped of his captaincy, only to be reinstated when the team refused to play under anyone else.

Carling always put his duties as captain ahead of everything else and there was often a feeling that he played within himself.

His final season for England – 1997 – saw him play some of his best rugby under the captaincy of Phil de Glanville, and perhaps gave spectators a glimpse of what he could have been had he been able to focus more on his game.

Peter Brook, the president of the Rugby Football Union, said: "His contribution to England as a player, and through his record number of appearances as captain, was immense."

Colin Herridge, the former RFU committee man and Harlequins stalwart called him – in The Independent – a "national treasure", while Geoff Cooke, who handed him the England captaincy added: "Making him captain was the best rugby selection I ever took."

He made an ill-fated return to the Harlequins first team in 1999, after 13 months out of the game, with injury finally forcing him to retire in 2000.

Still the holder of the records for most internationals at centre and most consecutive internationals with 44, he was awarded the OBE in 1992.

Will Carling

Alfred Denzel CARPENTER

Born: 23 July 1900 in Mitcheldean
Died: 18 April 1974 in Gloucester
Clubs: Cinderford, Gloucester (1), RAF
Position: Prop (1)
Debut: 2 Jan 1932 v South Africa (Twickenham). Number: 685
Caps: 1 (W:0, L:1)
Scoring: 0 Pts
Appearances: 1932:SA

John MacGregor Kendall CARPENTER, CBE

Born: 25 September 1925 in Cardiff, Wales
Died: 24 May 1990 in Wellington, Somerset
Educated: Truro School
Clubs: Oxford University (8), Penzance & Newlyn (7), Bath (8)
Position: No 8 (18), Prop (5)
Debut: 12 Feb 1949 v Ireland (Lansdowne Road). Number: 796
Last game: 10 Apr 1954 v France (Stade Colombes)
Caps: 23 (W:12, D:1, L:10). As captain: 3 (W:1, L:2)
Scoring: 1T, 3 Pts
Appearances: 1949:I,F,S, 1950:W,I,F,S, 1951:I*,F*,S*, 1952:SA,W,S,I,F, 1953:W,I,F,S, 1954:W,NZ,I,F
Honours: Championship: 1953

Robert Stanley Leonard CARR

Born: 11 July 1917 in Backlow
Died: c 1977
Educated: Cranleigh School
Clubs: Old Cranleighans (3), Manchester, Moseley
Position: Wing (3)
Debut: 21 Jan 1939 v Wales (Twickenham). Number: 744
Last game: 18 Mar 1939 v Scotland (Murrayfield)
Caps: 3 (W:2, L:1)
Scoring: 0 Pts
Appearances: 1939:W,I,S

Vincent Henry CARTWRIGHT

Born: 10 September 1882 in The Park, Nottingham
Died: 25 November 1965 in Loughborough
Educated: Rugby School
Clubs: Oxford University (8), Nottingham (6), Harlequins
Position: Forward (14)
Debut: 10 Jan 1903 v Wales (Swansea). Number: 384
Last game: 8 Dec 1906 (capt) v South Africa (Crystal Palace)
Caps: 14 (W:2, D:2, L:10). As captain: 6 (W:2, D:1, L:3)
Scoring: 4C, 8 Pts
Appearances: 1903:W,I,S, 1904:W,S, 1905:W,I,S,NZ*, 1906:W*,I*,S*,F*,SA*

Howard Carston (Carston) CATCHESIDE, OBE

Born: 18 August 1899 in Sunderland
Died: 10 May 1987 in Wandworth
Educated: Oundle School
Clubs: Percy Park (8)
Position: Wing (6), Full-back (2)
Debut: 19 Jan 1924 v Wales (Swansea) - 2T, 6 Pts. Number: 586
Last game: 19 Mar 1927 v Scotland (Murrayfield)
Caps: 8 (W:5, D:1, L:2)
Scoring: 6T, 18 Pts
Appearances: 1924:W,I,F,S, 1926:W,I, 1927:I,S
Honours: Grand Slam: 1924

Mike Catt

Michael John (Mike) CATT, MBE

Born: 17 September 1971 in Port Elizabeth, South Africa
Educated: Grey College
Clubs: Eastern Province (SA), Bath (65), London Irish (2)
Position: Centre (24), Full-back (15), Fly-half (14), Wing (1) Replacement (13), Bench (13)
Debut: 19 Mar 1994 (rep) v Wales (Twickenham). Number: 1154
Last game: 17 Jun 2006 v Australia (Melbourne)
Caps: 67 (W:46, D:1, L:20)
Scoring: 7T, 16C, 22PG, 3DG, 142 Pts
Appearances: 1994:W(r),C(r), 1995:I,F,W,S,Ar,It,Sm,A,NZ,F,SA,Sm, 1996:F,W,S,I,It,Ar, 1997:W,Ar1,A,A,NZ1,SA, 1998:F,W(r),I,A(r),SA, 1999:S,F,W,A,C(r),Tg(r),Fj,SA(r), 2000:I,F,W,It,S,SA1,SA2,A,Ar, 2001:W,It,S,F,I,A,R(r),SA, 2003:Sm(r),U,W(r),F,A(r), 2004:W(r),F(r),NZ1,A, 2006:A1,A2
Honours: RWC Winner: 2003. Grand Slam: 1995. Outright Championship: 1996, 2000, 2001

When Mike Catt led England to their Six Nations triumph against France in 2007 – in his 36th year – he became the oldest captain at Twickenham for more than three-quarters of a century.

Recalled six years after his last start in the Championship, South Africa-born Catt inspired his side to a 26-18 victory.

In the team alongside him that day was Shane Geraghty, the London Irish starlet who was just seven when Catt made his England debut, back in 1994, again against Wales.

Before he ran out at Twickenham in March 2007, England had only had three older skippers than Catt – Sam Tucker (1931), Eric Evans (1958) and Dorian West (2003).

But Catt – the 15th-oldest player ever to appear in an England shirt – has always been the sort of player to buck the trend, to think the unthinkable.

In American sport almost every team has a 'go-to' player. The man you reach for when your side is in trouble.

Well in the recent history of English rugby that man has been Mike Catt.

Born in Port Elizabeth, South Africa, Catt was the man who England turned to in the mid-1990s to fill a number of different positions; full-back, centre, outside-half and wing.

And in the 2003 World Cup when England were struggling to overcome a spirited Welsh side in the quarter-finals it was Catt who stepped forward with a virtuoso performance to keep England in the competition.

England trailed 10-3 at half time but the introduction of Catt at the break brought an experienced head into England's midfield and they finally got home 28-17 as Catt appeared as a calming influence alongside Jonny Wilkinson.

He had a less auspicious 1995 World Cup – his first – where most people remember him being run over by Jonah Lomu, as England lost to New Zealand in the semi-finals. He ended up as a bit-part player in 1999.

Most people thought Catt had played his last match when he kicked the ball into touch to signal England's World Cup win in 2003.

But he never retired, never wanting to give up the thrill of international rugby after starting his Test career in the amateur era.

England coach Brian Ashton had no doubts about Catt, saying: "He is a player with a wide range of skills, and he is a talismanic figure in many ways. He is very good at talking to players and is extremely knowledgeable about the game.

"He has never been a 'what if' man – he's a free thinker.

"I think he is a natural athlete, with a triathlete's base to his physicality. He will be just as fit when he is 45, as he is now."

The key reason why Catt enjoyed such an illustrious Indian summer was his decision to move club after England's World Cup win in 2003.

Catt moved to London Irish where coach Brian Smith gave him the responsibility that he revelled in, making him captain and allowing Catt to have key input into his training schedule.

He delighted everyone at London Irish with his performances inspiring them to third place in the Guinness Premiership in 2006 and a place in the Heineken Cup.

"We obviously do our best to take care of him, but Mike is a remarkable athlete. He knows the game so well and is so skilful. His distribution and kicking game are without peer," said Smith.

London Irish may have been where he was rejuvenated but it was at Bath where he made his name.

He had joined Bath in 1992 as understudy to Stuart Barnes and his many accolades include being Premiership player of the year in 2001.

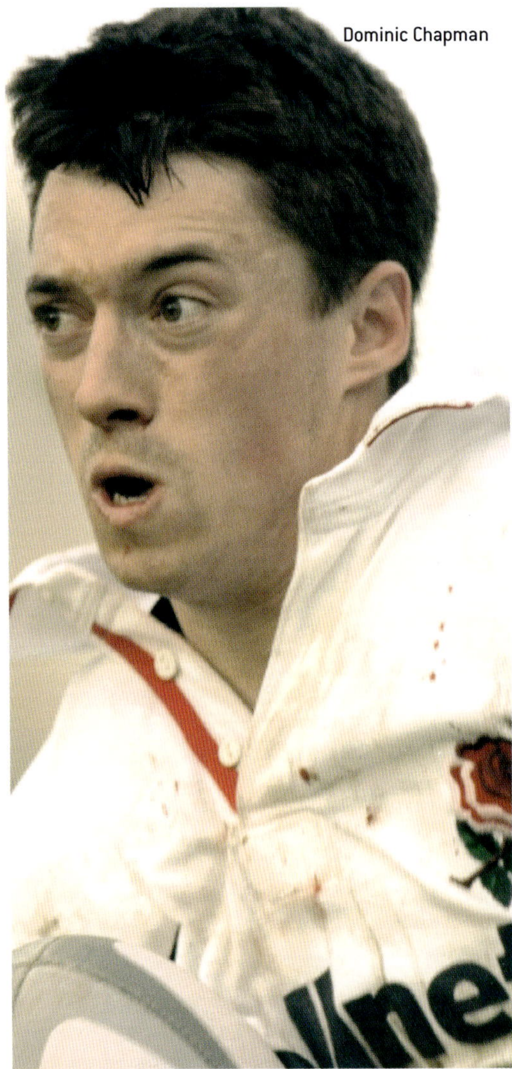
Dominic Chapman

Richard Henry Burdon CATTELL
Born: 23 March 1871 in Erdington
Died: 19 July 1948 in Fakenham
Educated: Trinity College
Clubs: Oxford University, Moseley (4), Blackheath (3)
Position: Fly-half (7)
Debut: 5 Jan 1895 v Wales (Swansea). Number: 274
Last game: 6 Jan 1900 (capt) v Wales (Gloucester)
Caps: 7 (W:3, L:4). As captain: 1 (W:0, L:1)
Scoring: 2T, 6 Pts
Appearances: 1895:W,I,S, 1896:W,I,S, 1900:W*

John Watkins CAVE
Born: 5 February 1867 in Surbiton
Died: 4 December 1949 in Wokingham
Educated: Wellington College
Clubs: Cambridge University (1), Richmond
Position: Forward (1)
Debut: 16 Feb 1889 v New Zealand Natives (Blackheath). Number: 199
Caps: 1 (W:1, L:0)
Scoring: 0 Pts
Appearances: 1889:M

William Thomas Charles CAVE
Born: 24 November 1882 in Croydon
Died: Details unknown
Educated: Tonbridge School
Clubs: Cambridge University, Blackheath (1)
Position: Forward (1)
Debut: 14 Jan 1905 v Wales (Cardiff). Number: 393
Caps: 1 (W:0, L:1)
Scoring: 0 Pts
Appearances: 1905:W

Robert (Bob) CHALLIS
Born: 9 March 1932 in Long Ashton
Died: 12 May 2000
Educated: Cathedral School
Clubs: Bristol (3)
Position: Full-back (3)
Debut: 9 Feb 1957 v Ireland (Lansdowne Road) - 1PG, 3 Pts. Number: 870
Last game: 16 Mar 1957 v Scotland (Twickenham) - 2C, 1PG, 7 Pts
Caps: 3 (W:3, L:0)
Scoring: 2C, 2PG, 10 Pts
Appearances: 1957:I,F,S
Honours: Championship: 1957

Ernest Leonard CHAMBERS
Born: 24 July 1882 in Hackney
Died: 23 November 1946 in Cheam
Educated: Bedford GS
Clubs: Cambridge University, Blackheath, Bedford (3)
Position: Forward (3)
Debut: 1 Jan 1908 v France (Stade Colombes). Number: 453
Last game: 12 Feb 1910 v Ireland (Twickenham)
Caps: 3 (W:2, D:1, L:0)
Scoring: 0 Pts
Appearances: 1908:F, 1910:W,I
Honours: Championship: 1910

Bevan Stanislaw CHANTRILL
Born: 11 February 1897 in Barton Regis
Died: Details unknown
Educated: Bristol GS
Clubs: Clifton, RAF, Bristol (4), Richmond, Manchester, Rosslyn Park, Gloucester
Position: Full-back (4)
Debut: 19 Jan 1924 v Wales (Swansea). Number: 587
Last game: 15 Mar 1924 v Scotland (Twickenham)
Caps: 4 (W:4, L:0)
Scoring: 0 Pts
Appearances: 1924:W,I,F,S
Honours: Grand Slam: 1924

Charles Edward CHAPMAN
Born: 26 August 1860 in Bourn, Lincs
Died: 23 August 1901 in Horncastle
Educated: Trent College, St Paul's School
Clubs: Cambridge University (1), Eden Wanderers, Trojans
Position: Three-quarter (1)
Debut: 5 Jan 1884 v Wales (Leeds). Number: 160
Caps: 1 (W:1, L:0)
Scoring: 0 Pts
Appearances: 1884:W
Honours - Championship: 1884

Dominic Edward CHAPMAN
Born: 7 March 1976 in Kingston
Clubs: Esher, Harlequins, Richmond (1), Bracknell
Position: Replacement Wing (1)
Debut: 6 Jun 1998 (rep) v Australia (Brisbane). Number: 1201
Caps: 1 (W:0, L:1)
Scoring: 0 Pts
Appearances: 1998:A(r)

Frederick Ernest (Fred) CHAPMAN
Born: Third quarter 1887 in South Shields
Died: 8 May 1938 in Hartlepool
Educated: South Shields HS
Clubs: Durham University, Westoe (5), Hartlepool Rovers (2)
Position: Wing (5), Centre (2)
Debut: 15 Jan 1910 v Wales (Twickenham) - 1T, 1C, 1PG, 8 Pts. Number: 471
Last game: 14 Feb 1914 v Ireland (Twickenham) - 1C, 2 Pts
Caps: 7 (W:6, D:1, L:0)
Scoring: 1T, 7C, 1PG, 20 Pts
Appearances: 1910:W,I,F,S, 1912:W, 1914:W,I
Honours: Championship: 1910, 1914

William Inkersole CHEESMAN
Born: 20 June 1889 in Pancras
Died: 20 November 1969 in Swindon
Educated: Merchant Taylors' School
Clubs: Old Merchant Taylors' (4), Oxford University
Position: Scrum-half (4)
Debut: 4 Jan 1913 v South Africa (Twickenham). Number: 525
Last game: 8 Feb 1913 v Ireland (Lansdowne Road)
Caps: 4 (W:3, L:1)
Scoring: 0 Pts
Appearances: 1913:SA,W,F,I
Honours: Championship: 1913

Ernest Constantine CHESTON

Born: 24 October 1848 in Hackney
Died: 9 July 1918 in Eastly
Educated: Haileybury & ISC
Clubs: Oxford University, Law Club (1), Richmond (4)
Position: Forward (5)
Debut: 3 Mar 1873 v Scotland (Glasgow). Number: 36
Last game: 6 Mar 1876 v Scotland (The Oval)
Caps: 5 (W:3, D:2, L:0)
Scoring: 1T, 1 Pt
Appearances: 1873:S, 1874:S, 1875:I,S, 1876:S

Gareth Chilcott

Phil Christophers

Gareth James (Coochie) CHILCOTT

Born: 20 November 1956 in Bristol
Educated: Aditon Park School
Clubs: Old Redcliffians, Bath (14)
Position: Prop (10), Replacement (4), Bench (11)
Debut: 3 Nov 1984 v Australia (Twickenham). Number: 1096
Last game: 13 May 1989 v Romania (Bucharest)
Caps: 14 (W:8, L:6)
Scoring: 0 Pts
Appearances: 1984:A, 1986:I,F, 1987:F(r),W,J,US,W(r), 1988:I(r),Fj, 1989:I(r),F,W,R

Philip Derek (Phil) CHRISTOPHERS

Born: 16 June 1980 in Heidelberg, West Germany
Educated: RGS Lancaster
Clubs: RG Heidelberg (GER), Leicester, Brive (FR), Bristol (3), Leeds, Castres (FR)
Position: Wing (2), Replacement (1), Bench (1)
Debut: 22 Jun 2002 v Argentina (Buenos Aires) - 1T, 5 Pts. Number: 1240
Last game: 22 Feb 2003 (rep) v Wales (Cardiff)
Caps: 3 (W:3, L:0)
Scoring: 1T, 5 Pts. Discipline - Sin bins: 1
Appearances: 2002:Ar,SA, 2003:W(r)
Honours: Championship: 2003

Percy CHRISTOPHERSON

Born: 31 March 1866 in Kidbrooke, Blackheath
Died: 4 May 1921 in Elham, Kent
Educated: Bedford GS, Marlborough College
Clubs: Oxford University, Blackheath (2)
Position: Three-quarter (2)
Debut: 3 Jan 1891 v Wales (Newport) - 2T, 2 Pts. Number: 225
Last game: 7 Mar 1891 v Scotland (Richmond)
Caps: 2 (W:1, L:1)
Scoring: 2T, 2 Pts
Appearances: 1891:W,S

George Scala CHUTER

Born: 9 July 1976 in Greenwich
Educated: Trinity School
Clubs: Old Midwhitgiftians, Saracens, Leicester (9)
Position: Hooker (7), Replacement (2), Bench (1)
Debut: 11 Jun 2006 (rep) v Australia (Sydney). Number: 1272
Last game: 24 Feb 2007 v Ireland (Croke Park)
Caps: 9 (W:3, L:6)
Scoring: 1T, 5 Pts
Appearances: 2006:A1(r),A2,NZ,Ar,SA1,SA2(r), 2007:S,It,I

George Chuter

Charles William Henry CLARK
Born: 19 March 1857 in West Derby
Died: 11 May 1943 in Battersea
Educated: Rugby School
Clubs: Liverpool (1)
Position: Half-Back (1)
Debut: 13 Dec 1875 v Ireland (Dublin) - 1T, 1 Pt. Number: 72
Caps: 1 (W:1, L:0)
Scoring: 1T, 1 Pt
Appearances: 1875:I

Allan James CLARKE
Born: 21 February 1913 in Coventry
Died: 25 September 1975 in Coventry
Clubs: Coventry (6)
Position: Lock (6)
Debut: 19 Jan 1935 v Wales (Twickenham). Number: 714
Last game: 8 Feb 1936 v Ireland (Lansdowne Road)
Caps: 6 (W:2, D:2, L:2)
Scoring: 0 Pts
Appearances: 1935:W,I,S, 1936:NZ,W,I

Benjamin Bevan (Ben) CLARKE
Born: 15 April 1968 in Bishop's Stortford
Educated: Bishop's Stortford College
Clubs: Bishop's Stortford, Saracens, Bath (28), Richmond (12), Worcester
Position: Flanker (23), No 8 (13), Replacement (4), Bench (3)
Debut: 14 Nov 1992 v South Africa (Twickenham). Number: 1147
Last game: 26 Jun 1999 (rep) v Australia (Sydney)
Caps: 40 (W:26, L:14)
Scoring: 3T, 15 Pts. Discipline - Cautions: 1
Appearances: 1992:SA, 1993:F,W,S,I,NZ, 1994:S,F,W,SA1,SA2,R,C, 1995:I,F,W,S,Ar,It,A,NZ,F,SA,Sm, 1996:F,W,S,I,Ar(r), 1997:W,Ar1,Ar2,A(r), 1998:A(r),NZ1,NZ2,SA, H,It, 1999:A(r)
Honours: Grand Slam: 1995. Championship: 1996

Ben Clarke

Simon John Scott CLARKE
Born: 2 April 1938 in Westcliff
Educated: Wellington College
Clubs: Cambridge University (9), Royal Navy, Bath, Yokohama (JP), Blackheath (4)
Position: Scrum-half (13)
Debut: 19 Jan 1963 v Wales (Cardiff). Number: 908
Last game: 20 Mar 1965 v Scotland (Twickenham)
Caps: 13 (W:4, D:3, L:6)
Scoring: 1T, 3 Pts
Appearances: 1963:W,I,F,S,NZ1,NZ2,A, 1964:NZ,W,I, 1965:I,F,S
Honours: Championship: 1963

John Henry CLAYTON
Born: 24 August 1848 in Liverpool
Died: 21 March 1924 in London
Educated: Rugby School
Clubs: Liverpool (1)
Position: Forward (1)
Debut: 27 Mar 1871 v Scotland (Raeburn Place). Number: 4
Caps: 1 (W:0, L:1)
Scoring: 0 Pts
Appearances: 1871:S

Jeff E Woodward CLEMENTS
Born: 18 August 1932 in Wincanton
Died: 4 October 1986 in France
Educated: Cranleigh School
Clubs: Old Cranleighans (3), Cambridge University, Royal Navy, Devonport Services
Position: Flanker (3)
Debut: 14 Feb 1959 v Ireland (Lansdowne Road). Number: 884
Last game: 21 Mar 1959 v Scotland (Twickenham)
Caps: 3 (W:1, D:2, L:0)
Scoring: 0 Pts
Appearances: 1959:I,F,S

Sir Charles Raitt CLEVELAND, KBE
Born: 2 November 1866 in Bombay, India
Died: 17 January 1929 in London
Educated: Christ's College
Clubs: Oxford University (2), Blackheath
Position: Forward (2)
Debut: 8 Jan 1887 v Wales (Llanelli). Number: 187
Last game: 5 Mar 1887 v Scotland (Manchester)
Caps: 2 (W:0, D:2, L:0)
Scoring: 0 Pts
Appearances: 1887:W,S

William George CLIBBON
Born: Second quarter 1862 in North Aylesford
Died: Details unknown
Clubs: Richmond (6)
Position: Forward (6)
Debut: 2 Jan 1886 v Wales (Blackheath). Number: 177
Last game: 5 Mar 1887 v Scotland (Manchester)
Caps: 6 (W:2, D:3, L:1)
Scoring: 0 Pts
Appearances: 1886:W,I,S, 1887:W,I,S

Jeff Clements

Francis John (Fran) CLOUGH
Born: 1 November 1962 in Wigan
Educated: St John Rigby College
Clubs: Durham University, Cambridge University, Orrell (4), Wasps, Bedford
Position: Centre (3), Replacement (1), Bench (3)
Debut: 1 Mar 1986 v Ireland (Twickenham). Number: 1113
Last game: 3 Jun 1987 v United States (Sydney)
Caps: 4 (W:3, L:1)
Scoring: 0 Pts
Appearances: 1986:I,F, 1987:J(r),US

Charles Hutton COATES
Born: 4 May 1857 in Lambeth
Died: 15 February 1922 in Boscombe, Hants
Educated: Christ's College
Clubs: Cambridge University (1), Leeds (1), Yorkshire Wanderers (1), Bishop Auckland
Position: Forward (3)
Debut: 28 Feb 1880 v Scotland (Manchester)
Number: 128
Last game: 4 Mar 1882 v Scotland (Manchester)
Caps: 3 (W:1, D:1, L:1)
Scoring: 0 Pts
Appearances: 1880:S, 1881:S, 1882:S

Richard Cockerill

Vincent Hope Middleton COATES
Born: 18 May 1889
Died: 14 November 1934 in Maidenhead
Educated: Haileybury & ISC
Clubs: Cambridge University, Bridgwater, Bath (5), Leicester, Richmond
Position: Wing (5)
Debut: 4 Jan 1913 v South Africa (Twickenham).
Number: 526
Last game: 15 Mar 1913 v Scotland (Twickenham)
Caps: 5 (W:4, L:1)
Scoring: 6T, 18 Pts
Appearances: 1913:SA,W,F,I,S
Honours: Grand Slam: 1913

William COBBY
Born: 5 July 1877 in Swine, Hull
Died: 15 January 1957 in Holderness
Educated: Uppingham School
Clubs: Cambridge University, Hull (1), Castleford
Position: Forward (1)
Debut: 6 Jan 1900 v Wales (Gloucester).
Number: 345
Caps: 1 (W:0, L:1)
Scoring: 0 Pts
Appearances: 1900:W

Arthur COCKERHAM
Born: First quarter 1876 in Bradford
Died: Details unknown
Clubs: Bradford Olicana (1), Manningham RL
Position: Forward (1)
Debut: 6 Jan 1900 v Wales (Gloucester).
Number: 346
Caps: 1 (W:0, L:1)
Scoring: 0 Pts
Appearances: 1900:W

Richard COCKERILL
Born: 16 December 1970 in Rugby
Educated: Harris CofE School
Clubs: Newbold, Coventry, Leicester (27), Montferrand (FR)
Position: Hooker (22), Replacement (5), Bench (3)
Debut: 31 May 1997 (rep) v Argentina (Buenos Aires).
Number: 1183
Last game: 20 Oct 1999 (rep) v Fiji (Twickenham)
Caps: 27 (W:14, D:2, L:11)
Scoring: 3T, 15 Pts. Discipline - Cautions: 1
Appearances: 1997:Ar1(r),Ar2,A(r),NZ1,SA,NZ2, 1998:W,S,I,A,NZ1,NZ2,SA,H,It,A,SA, 1999:S,I,F,W,A,C(r),It,NZ,Tg(r),Fj(r)

Alexander John (Alex) CODLING
Born: 25 September 1973 in Lewisham
Clubs: Wasps, Blackheath, Richmond, Bedford, Neath, Harlequins (1), Saracens, Northampton, Montpellier (FR)
Position: Lock (1)
Debut: 22 Jun 2002 v Argentina (Buenos Aires).
Number: 1241
Caps: 1 (W:1, L:0)
Scoring: 0 Pts
Appearances: 2002:Ar

Alex Codling

Ben Christopher COHEN, MBE

Born: 14 September 1978 in Northampton
Educated: Kingsthorpe School
Clubs: Northampton Old Scouts, Northampton (57)
Position: Wing (54), Replacement (3), Bench (5)
Debut: 5 Feb 2000 v Ireland (Twickenham) - 2T, 10 Pts.
Number: 1215
Last game: 25 Nov 2006 v South Africa (Twickenham)
Caps: 57 (W:40, L:17)
Scoring: 31T, 155 Pts
Appearances: 2000:I,F,W,It,S,SA2,Ar,SA, 2001:W,It,S,F,R, 2002:S,I,F,W,It,NZ,A,SA, 2003:F,W,S,I,NZ,A,F,F,Geo,SA,Sm,W,F,A, 2004:It,S,I,W,F,NZ1,NZ2,A,C(r),A(r), 2005:F(r),A,NZ, 2006:W,It,S,F,I,NZ,Ar,SA1,SA2
Honours: RWC Winner: 2003. Championship: 2000, 2001, 2003

The perfect modern wing, Ben Cohen stands second only to Rory Underwood in a list of all-time England try scorers, putting him in the top 10 all-time England points scorers.

He made his debut for home town club Northampton in 1997, having played for Northampton Old Scouts RFC from the age of 12.

Three years later his dynamic wing play earned him an England call-up, scoring two tries against Ireland in 2000, in one of the most spectacular England debuts of the professional era. That season was capped with a Heineken Cup medal as Northampton beat Munster 9-8.

In 2001 he was in the British and Irish Lions squad to take on Australia, but didn't feature in any of the Tests. Despite this, he became a fixture in the England team over the next couple of years, rewarding the selectors with some spectacular tries and not afraid to add his considerable presence to the defence.

Ben Cohen

Great moments include the 2002 autumn internationals when he scored twice against Australia and put in the try-saving tackle that led to England's win over the All Blacks.

"He's got power as well as pace. Once he feels the opposition breathing down his neck, he simply slips up a gear and streaks clear," said former Wales legend Jonathan Davies.

In 2003 he put in some sparkling performances as he played his part in England's World Cup triumph, completing a remarkable family double – his uncle, George Cohen, won a football World Cup winner's medal with England in 1966.

Ben suffered relegation from the Guinness Premiership – with Northampton – in 2007 as they went down on the final day of the season, and turned down the chance to go on England's summer tour to South Africa in 2007 to spend more time with his family.

Maurice John COLCLOUGH

Born: 2 September 1953 in Oxford
Died: 27 January 2006
Educated: Duke of York School
Clubs: Liverpool University, Angouleme (FR,16), Wasps (5), Poitiers (FR), Swansea (4), Liverpool
Position: Lock (25), Bench (1)
Debut: 4 Mar 1978 v Scotland (Murrayfield).
Number: 1053
Last game: 15 Mar 1986 v France (Parc des Princes)
Caps: 25 (W:14, D:1, L:10)
Scoring: 1T, 4 Pts
Appearances: 1978:S,I, 1979:NZ, 1980:F,W,S, 1981:W,S,I,F, 1982:A,S,I,F,W, 1983:F,NZ, 1984:S,I,F,W, 1986:W,S,I,F
Honours: Championship: 1980

As one of the locks in England's Grand Slam winning side of 1980 Maurice Colclough was hardly known for his try-scoring exploits but in 1983 he bulldozed over the line for one of the most famous tries in English rugby history and his only one in an international match.

Colclough played 25 times for England between 1978 and 1986 and apart from his role in the Grand Slam side he will always be remembered as the man who scored England's try in an epic 15-9 win over the All Blacks in 1983.

Shorn of the majority of their all-conquering side of 1980 England were skippered by Leicester hooker Peter Wheeler but came into the game more in hope than expectation.

They hadn't beaten the All Blacks at Twickenham since 1936, but that record was changed by Colclough storming over from a lineout.

Legend has it that Wheeler even inflicted a new moniker on Colclough afterwards calling him "the Marquis de Colclough", referring to Prince Obolensky, the last Englishman to score tries to beat the All Blacks – at the home of English rugby – 47 years earlier.

Wheeler also recalled Colclough's influence in the Grand Slam side. "There was one scrum which I regarded as the best I've ever been a part of. It took place near Scotland's line and Billy called for a double shove," said Wheeler the England hooker.

"I can still recall the feeling as we surged forward, like a supercharged car in overdrive. It was an uncommon experience. Occasionally it happened at the end of a club game, but you don't expect that surge in the early stages of an international."

Born in Oxford Colclough was educated at the Duke of York's Royal Military School, Dover, and Liverpool University,

Maurice Colclough

playing for Liverpool RFC.

Earlier in his rugby career he played for Kent and London Schools, Sussex and Lancashire and for London against Argentina and New Zealand. On his two Lions tours, to South Africa and New Zealand, he played in all eight Tests.

Colclough made his debut for England in a 15-0 win over Scotland in 1978 having taken over from veteran lock Nigel Horton in the second row, and also played in a victory over Ireland, finally sealing his place in the side for the Grand Slam season of 1980.

A convivial figure in English rugby Colclough was one of the first Englishmen to play in France, where he captained the Angouleme club. He later played for Wasps and Swansea.

Colclough was also something of a practical joker and terrific company. In one legendary incident he fooled his team-mate Colin Smart into drinking aftershave following a victory over France!

Unfortunately Smart ended up in hospital but lived to tell the tale! Scrum-half Steve Smith was later observed to say: "Colin was in a bad way, but his breath smelt lovely."

Bill Beaumont was England's captain in 1980 and Colclough's second-row partner. He said: "Maurice was a powerful and very athletic rugby player who made a massive contribution to the clubs he played for, to his country and to the Lions. He had a huge heart and will be greatly missed."

Colclough died in 2006, aged 52, after a long battle against a brain tumour.

Eric COLEY, OBE

Born: 23 July 1903 in Northampton
Died: 3 May 1957 in Northampton
Educated: Northampton Town & County School
Clubs: Northampton (2), Army
Position: No 8 (2)
Debut: 1 Apr 1929 v France (Stade Colombes). Number: 648
Last game: 16 Jan 1932 v Wales (Swansea) - 1T, 3 Pts
Caps: 2 (W:1, L:1)
Scoring: 1T, 3 Pts
Appearances: 1929:F, 1932:W

Philip John COLLINS

Born: 4 November 1928 in Redruth
Clubs: Camborne (3)
Position: Full-back (3)
Debut: 15 Mar 1952 v Scotland (Murrayfield). Number: 831
Last game: 5 Apr 1952 v France (Stade Colombes)
Caps: 3 (W:3, L:0)
Scoring: 0 Pts
Appearances: 1952:S,I,F

William Edward COLLINS, CMG

Born: 14 October 1853 in Monghyr, India
Died: 11 August 1934 in Wellington, New Zealand
Educated: Cheltenham College
Clubs: Old Cheltonians (2), St George's Hospital (3), Oxford University
Position: Half-Back (5)
Debut: 23 Feb 1874 v Scotland (The Oval). Number: 48
Last game: 6 Mar 1876 v Scotland (The Oval) - 1T, 1 Pt
Caps: 5 (W:4, D:1, L:0)
Scoring: 1T, 1 Pt
Appearances: 1874:S, 1875:I,S,I, 1876:S

Stanley George Ulick CONSIDINE

Born: 11 August 1901 in Bilasur, India
Died: 31 August 1950 in Bath
Educated: Blundell's School
Clubs: Bath (1)
Position: Wing (1)
Debut: 13 Apr 1925 v France (Stade Colombes). Number: 604
Caps: 1 (W:1, L:0)
Scoring: 0 Pts
Appearances: 1925:F

Geoffrey Seymour CONWAY

Born: 15 November 1897 in Cardiff, Wales
Died: Details unknown
Educated: Fettes School
Clubs: Cambridge University (8), Rugby (9), Harlequins, Hartlepool Rovers (1), Manchester, Blackheath
Position: No 8 (10), Lock (8)
Debut: 31 Jan 1920 v France (Twickenham). Number: 556
Last game: 15 Jan 1927 v Wales (Twickenham)
Caps: 18 (W:15, D:1, L:2)
Scoring: 1T, 11C, 25 Pts
Appearances: 1920:F,I,S, 1921:F, 1922:W,I,F,S, 1923:W,I,S,F, 1924:W,I,F,S, 1925:NZ, 1927:W
Honours: Grand Slam: 1923, 1924. Championship: 1921

John Gilbert COOK

Born: 16 May 1911 in Houghton Regis, Beds
Died: 10 September 1979 in Overstrand, Norfolk
Educated: Bedford School
Clubs: Bedford (1)
Position: Flanker (1)
Debut: 20 Mar 1937 v Scotland (Murrayfield). Number: 735
Caps: 1 (W:1, L:0)
Scoring: 0 Pts
Appearances: 1937:S
Honours: Championship: 1937

Peter William COOK

Born: 8 January 1943 in High Wycombe
Educated: Dulwich College
Clubs: Richmond (2)
Position: Wing (2)
Debut: 13 Feb 1965 v Ireland (Lansdowne Road). Number: 934
Last game: 27 Feb 1965 v France (Twickenham)
Caps: 2 (W:1, L:1)
Scoring: 0 Pts
Appearances: 1965:I,F

David Alexander COOKE

Born: 10 February 1949 in Malta
Educated: Gravesend GS
Clubs: Harlequins (4)
Position: Centre (4), Bench (1)
Debut: 17 Jan 1976 v Wales (Twickenham). Number: 1039
Last game: 20 Mar 1976 v France (Parc des Princes)
Caps: 4 (W:0, L:4)
Scoring: 0 Pts
Appearances: 1976:W,S,I,F

Martin Cooper

David Howard COOKE

Born: 19 November 1955 in Brisbane, Australia
Educated: Haileybury & ISC, NE London Poly
Clubs: Harlequins (12)
Position: Flanker (12), Bench (3)
Debut: 17 Jan 1981 v Wales (Cardiff). Number: 1063
Last game: 8 Jun 1985 v New Zealand (Wellington)
Caps: 12 (W:5, D:1, L:6)
Scoring: 0 Pts
Appearances: 1981:W,S,I,F, 1984:I, 1985:R,F,S,I,W,NZ1,NZ2

Paul COOKE

Born: 18 December 1916 in Marylebone
Died: Killed in action in 1940 in Calais, France
Educated: St Edward's School
Clubs: Oxford University, Richmond (2)
Position: Scrum-half (2)
Debut: 21 Jan 1939 v Wales (Twickenham). Number: 745
Last game: 11 Feb 1939 v Ireland (Twickenham)
Caps: 2 (W:1, L:1)
Scoring: 0 Pts
Appearances: 1939:W,I

Thomas COOP

Born: 10 March 1863 in Tottington, Lancs
Died: 16 April 1929 in Bucklow
Clubs: Leigh (1)
Position: Full-back (1)
Debut: 5 Mar 1892 v Scotland (Raeburn Place). Number: 247
Caps: 1 (W:1, L:0)
Scoring: 0 Pts
Appearances: 1892:S
Honours: Championship: 1892

John Graham COOPER

Born: 3 June 1881 in Birmingham
Died: 26 October 1965 in Canada
Educated: Aston GS
Clubs: Moseley (2)
Position: Forward (2)
Debut: 9 Jan 1909 v Australia (Blackheath). Number: 475
Last game: 16 Jan 1909 v Wales (Cardiff)
Caps: 2 (W:0, L:2)
Scoring: 0 Pts
Appearances: 1909:A,W

Martin John COOPER

Born: 23 April 1948 in Burton-upon-Trent
Educated: Burton-on-Trent GS, Wednesfield School
Clubs: Moseley (11)
Position: Fly-half (10), Replacement (1), Bench (9)
Debut: 24 Feb 1973 v France (Twickenham). Number: 1020
Last game: 5 Mar 1977 v Wales (Cardiff)
Caps: 11 (W:6, L:5)
Scoring: 1T, 4 Pts
Appearances: 1973:F,S,NZ(r), 1975:F,W, 1976:A,W, 1977:S,I,F,W

Sydney Frank COOPPER

Born: October 1878 in Hoo
Died: 16 January 1961 in Truro
Clubs: RNEC Keyham, Blackheath (7)
Position: Wing (7)
Debut: 6 Jan 1900 v Wales (Gloucester). Number: 347
Last game: 12 Jan 1907 v Wales (Swansea)
Caps: 7 (W:1, L:6)
Scoring: 2T, 6 Pts
Appearances: 1900:W, 1902:W,I, 1905:W,I,S, 1907:W

Leonard James CORBETT

Born: 12 May 1897 in Bristol
Died: 26 January 1983 in Taunton
Educated: Fairfield School
Clubs: Bristol (16), Gloucester
Position: Centre (16)
Debut: 28 Mar 1921 v France (Stade Colombes). Number: 570
Last game: 2 Apr 1927 (capt) v France (Stade Colombes)
Caps: 16 (W:11, D:1, L:4). As captain: 4 (W:2, L:2)
Scoring: 3T, 1PG, 1GM, 15 Pts
Appearances: 1921:F, 1923:W,I, 1924:W,I,F,S, 1925:NZ,W,I,S,F, 1927:W*,I*,S*,F*
Honours: Grand Slam: 1924. Championship: 1921, 1923

Barry Corless

Barry James CORLESS

Born: 7 November 1945 in Booton, Norfolk
Educated: Wymondham College
Clubs: Coventry (2), Moseley (8)
Position: Centre (9), Replacement (1)
Debut: 3 Jan 1976 v Australia (Twickenham) - 1T, 4 Pts. Number: 1036
Last game: 18 Mar 1978 v Ireland (Twickenham)
Caps: 10 (W:5, L:5)
Scoring: 1T, 4 Pts
Appearances: 1976:A,I(r), 1977:S,I,F,W, 1978:F,W,S,I

Martin Edward CORRY, MBE

Born: 12 October 1973 in Birmingham
Educated: Tunbridge Wells GS, Newcastle Poly
Clubs: Newcastle-Gosforth, Bristol (2), Leicester (50)
Position: No 8 (24), Flanker (8), Lock (1), Replacement (19), Bench (13)
Debut: 31 May 1997 v Argentina (Buenos Aires). Number: 1177
Last game: 24 Feb 2007 v Ireland (Croke Park)
Caps: 52 (W:32, L:20). As captain: 14 (W:7, L:7)
Scoring: 4T, 20 Pts
Appearances: 1997:Ar1,Ar2, 1998:H,It,SA(r), 1999:F(r),A,C(r),It(r),NZ(r),SA(r), 2000:I(r),F(r),W(r),It(r),S(r),Ar(r),SA(r), 2001:W(r),It(r),F(r),C1,I, 2002:F(r),W(r), 2003:W,F,F,U, 2004:A(r),C,SA,A, 2005:F,I ,It*,S*,A*,NZ*,Sm*, 2006:W*,It*,S*,F*,I*,NZ*,Ar*,SA1*,SA2*, 2007:S,It,I
Honours: RWC Winner: 2003. Outright Championship: 2000, 2001

Martin Corry became England's 119th captain in 2005 and his record of skippering the Red Rose 14 times is only bettered by Will Carling, Martin Johnson, Lawrence Dallaglio and Bill Beaumont.

He was however unfortunate enough to captain England during one of the worst periods in their history, as they dropped down the world rankings following their Rugby World Cup win in 2003.

A thumb injury to Jason Robinson gave Corry his chance midway through the 2005 RBS Six Nations.

His attitude as a grafter endears him to friends and enemies alike.

"Corry is one of the most admirable blokes you could meet. He's honest, polite, and dependable, without side or ego. He's a yeoman Englishman, probably a rustic son of the soil if he had another life, all depth, substance, ruggedness and simplicity," according to Mick Cleary in The Daily Telegraph.

Modest to a fault Corry adds: "The highlight of the championship, not to mention my entire career, was leading the team out for the first time against Italy."

Having started playing rugby in the mini section at Tunbridge Wells RFC, Corry started his club career at Newcastle Gosforth before a spell at Bristol, moving to Leicester in 1997 and being an integral part of the most successful period in the club's history. Champions of England in four successive seasons from 1999-2000 and European champions (twice!) to boot, Corry was a central figure, specialising in the hard yards.

Alongside him through that incredible run was Martin Johnson, his training partner.

"Coz does things on the field that are inspirational so I knew he would be the main contender to be England captain," said Johnson.

"I saw him in the physio's room after he dislocated his left elbow against Gloucester. All he wanted to do was get back on the field again. He didn't want to give away a grimace, didn't want any of the boys to see him in pain. That's the kind of bloke he is."

Corry earned his international reputation as a super sub, joining the 2001 Lions as a mid-tour replacement and going straight into the team for the first Test.

"The first Lions Test in 2001 in Brisbane is my most

Martin Corry

memorable sporting moment," said Corry. "I was not initially picked for the squad but came on as a late replacement. Running out in that stadium, and seeing three-quarters of the spectators wearing red shirts, was mind-blowing.

"The atmosphere in the stadium was magnificent, and we defeated Australia with a great performance."

Corry was the perfect Lions player finally playing in all three Tests in 2001 and repeating the feat in New Zealand four years later.

A great season in 2004-05, confirmed with his Zurich Premiership and PRA Player of the Season award, led to the England captaincy.

He was succeeded by Phil Vickery as captain for the 2007 Six Nations, but maintained his place in the team, to add to his 50-plus caps.

Corry's England career was rejuvenated in 2007 when coach Brian Ashton decided to move him from No 8 to the second row during the RBS Six Nations. This change helped England to their best win since lifting the World Cup almost three and a half years earlier when they beat France at Twickenham. He was awarded an MBE in 2004 after the World Cup triumph.

Fran Cotton

Francis Edward (Fran) COTTON

Born: 3 January 1947 in Wigan
Educated: Newton-le-Willows GS
Clubs: Liverpool, Loughborough College (7), Coventry (7), Sale (17)
Position: Prop (31), Bench (2)
Debut: 20 Mar 1971 v Scotland (Twickenham). Number: 997
Last game: 17 Jan 1981 v Wales (Cardiff)
Caps: 31 (W:13, L:18). As captain: 3 (W:0, L:3)
Scoring: 1T, 4 Pts
Appearances: 1971:S,S,P, 1973:W,I,F,S,NZ,A, 1974:S,I, 1975:I*,F*,W*, 1976:A,W,S,I,F, 1977:S,I,F,W, 1978:S,I, 1979:NZ, 1980:I,F,W,S, 1981:W
Honours: Grand Slam: 1980

The piano shifters – as some people like to call the front five forwards – rarely get as much praise as the piano players in the backs but one who left an indelible mark on the English game was prop Fran Cotton.

The son of a former rugby league player, Cotton honed his craft in a struggling England team of the 1970s before harnessing his awesome power to help claim a Grand Slam in 1980.

Cotton – who played for Coventry and Sale – finally represented England 31 times, which was a record for a prop, captaining them on three occasions.

Lancastrian Cotton was not only a star on England duty but cemented his fearsome reputation with world-class displays for the British and Irish Lions.

A seven-Test Lions tally for the 6ft 2in Cotton is impressive for a prop and especially as he was one of the rocks on which the 1974 prospered in South Africa.

His versatility took him to the loosehead side in South Africa and three years later – when the Lions came calling again – he switched to the tighthead for the trip to New Zealand.

His third Lions tour – in 1980 – was cut short by a health scare. Initially heart problems were feared but although they were allayed the injury still took him out of the tour.

Cotton was the subject of one of sport's most famous images, The Muddy Man, when Colorsport's Colin Elsey caught Cotton, covered in mud at a lineout on the 1977 Lions tour of New Zealand.

Cotton – who has done a lot of work for charity since retiring through the Wooden Spoon Society – made an all-time, worldwide, Test team selected by legendary television commentator Bill McLaren.

"England and British Lions bulwark who was solid in the scrummage, quick to breakdowns and a strong leader," said McLaren.

Like so many players of that time Cotton was banned from rugby union after writing his autobiography and thereby in the eyes of rugby's rulers classing himself as a professional.

That didn't however dim his commitment to England and the Lions and in the same year he made two huge contributions to rugby in the northern hemisphere.

He was a streetwise manager of the 1997 Lions, doing much to help their 2-1 series win in South Africa and in the same year – as part of the RFU hierarchy – was a key figure in the appointment of Clive Woodward as England coach.

In 2005 Cotton resigned his positions within the RFU to concentrate on his business interests.

After his decision became public RFU president Malcolm Phillips described him as "one of the icons of the game".

Phillips added: "Fran has been a dedicated servant to rugby union through a successful playing career, his management of the Lions and as an administrator."

Cotton again backed Woodward – in 2006 – to become the RFU's Elite Rugby Director – but Rob Andrew beat the England former coach to the job.

Along with another former England captain, Steve Smith, Cotton opened Cotton Traders in 1987. The business has grown to achieve a turnover in excess of £50 million a year, with over 600 employees across the UK and many more employed worldwide by its suppliers.

Michael John (Mike) COULMAN
Born: 6 May 1944 in Stafford
Educated: Risingbrook School
Clubs: Moseley (9), British Police, Salford RL
Position: Prop (9)
Debut: 7 Jan 1967 v Australia (Twickenham). Number: 949
Last game: 16 Mar 1968 v Scotland (Murrayfield) - 1T, 3 Pts
Caps: 9 (W:3, D:2, L:4)
Scoring: 1T, 3 Pts
Appearances: 1967:A,I,F,S,W, 1968:W,I,F,S

Thomas John COULSON
Born: 31 December 1896
Died: 26 March 1948 in Meriden
Clubs: Gloucester, Coventry (3)
Position: No 8 (3)
Debut: 15 Jan 1927 v Wales (Twickenham). Number: 615
Last game: 21 Jan 1928 v Wales (Swansea)
Caps: 3 (W:3, L:0)
Scoring: 0 Pts
Appearances: 1927:W, 1928:A,W
Honours: Championship: 1928

Edward Darlington COURT
Born: 22 June 1862 in Northwich
Died: 3 April 1935 in Cheltenham
Educated: Rugby School
Clubs: Oxford University, Blackheath (1)
Position: Forward (1)
Debut: 3 Jan 1885 v Wales (Swansea). Number: 169
Caps: 1 (W:1, L:0)
Scoring: 0 Pts
Appearances: 1885:W

Harry COVERDALE
Born: 22 March 1889 in Hartlepool
Died: 29 October 1965 in South Africa
Educated: Rossall School
Clubs: Hartlepool Rovers, Blackheath (4)
Position: Fly-half (4)
Debut: 3 Mar 1910 v France (Parc des Princes). Number: 501
Last game: 17 Jan 1920 v Wales (Swansea)
Caps: 4 (W:3, L:1)
Scoring: 1DG, 4 Pts
Appearances: 1910:F, 1912:I,F, 1920:W
Honours: Championship: 1910

Robin James COWLING
Born: 24 March 1944 in Ipswich
Educated: Sidcot School
Clubs: Gloucester, Leicester (8)
Position: Prop (8), Bench (3)
Debut: 15 Jan 1977 v Scotland (Twickenham). Number: 1044
Last game: 17 Feb 1979 v Ireland (Lansdowne Road)
Caps: 8 (W:2, D:1, L:5)
Scoring: 0 Pts
Appearances: 1977:S,I,F,W, 1978:F,NZ, 1979:S,I

Alan Richard (Dick) COWMAN
Born: 18 March 1949 in Workington
Educated: Workington GS
Clubs: Newcastle University, Loughborough College (3), Coventry (2)
Position: Fly-half (5), Bench (4)
Debut: 20 Mar 1971 v Scotland (Twickenham). Number: 998
Last game: 10 Feb 1973 v Ireland (Lansdowne Road)
Caps: 5 (W:0, L:5)
Scoring: 2DG, 6 Pts
Appearances: 1971:S,S,P, 1973:W,I

Norman Simpson COX
Born: 3 September 1877 in Sunderland
Died: 29 March 1930 in Sunderland
Educated: Repton School
Clubs: Sunderland (1)
Position: Centre (1)
Debut: 9 Mar 1901 v Scotland (Blackheath). Number: 367
Caps: 1 (W:0, L:1)
Scoring: 0 Pts
Appearances: 1901:S

Mark Cueto

Peter CRANMER
Born: 10 September 1914 in Acocks Green, Birmingham
Died: 29 May 1994 in Sussex
Educated: St Edward's School
Clubs: Oxford University (5), Richmond (8), Moseley (3)
Position: Centre (15), Wing (1)
Debut: 20 Jan 1934 v Wales (Cardiff). Number: 704
Last game: 19 Mar 1938 v Scotland (Twickenham)
Caps: 16 (W:10, D:2, L:4). As captain: 2 (W:1, L:1)
Scoring: 1T, 1PG, 2DG, 14 Pts
Appearances: 1934:W,I,S, 1935:W,I,S, 1936:NZ,W,I,S, 1937:W,I,S, 1938:W*,I*,S
Honours: Championship: 1934, 1937

Roger Norman CREED
Born: 19 November 1945 in Solihull
Educated: Solihull GS
Clubs: Old Sillhillians, Moseley, Coventry (1)
Position: Flanker (1)
Debut: 17 Apr 1971 v Presidents XV (Twickenham). Number: 1000
Caps: 1 (W:0, L:1)
Scoring: 0 Pts
Appearances: 1971:P

Arthur Gordon CRIDLAN
Born: 9 July 1909 in Ealing
Died: 1993 in Exeter
Educated: Uppingham School
Clubs: Oxford University, Blackheath (3)
Position: Flanker (3)
Debut: 19 Jan 1935 v Wales (Twickenham). Number: 715
Last game: 16 Mar 1935 v Scotland (Murrayfield)
Caps: 3 (W:1, D:1, L:1)
Scoring: 0 Pts
Appearances: 1935:W,I,S

Charles Arthur CROMPTON
Born: 21 October 1848
Died: 6 July 1875 in Bengal, India
Educated: Cheltenham College
Clubs: RMA Woodwich, Royal Engineers, Blackheath (1)
Position: Forward (1)
Debut: 27 Mar 1871 v Scotland (Raeburn Place). Number: 5
Caps: 1 (W:0, L:1)
Scoring: 0 Pts
Appearances: 1871:S

John Currie

Charles William CROSSE
Born: 13 June 1854 in Bushey, Herts
Died: 28 May 1905 in Paris, France
Educated: Rugby School
Clubs: RMC Sandhurst, King's Dragoon Guards, Oxford University (2)
Position: Forward (2)
Debut: 23 Feb 1874 v Scotland (The Oval). Number: 49
Last game: 15 Feb 1875 v Ireland (The Oval)
Caps: 2 (W:2, L:0)
Scoring: 0 Pts
Appearances: 1874:S, 1875:I

Mark John CUETO
Born: 26 December 1979 in Workington
Educated: St Thomas More School
Clubs: Altrincham Kersal, Sale (18)
Position: Wing (18)
Debut: 13 Nov 2004 v Canada (Twickenham) - 2T, 10 Pts. Number: 1255
Last game: 25 Nov 2006 v South Africa (Twickenham) - 1T, 5 Pts
Caps: 18 (W:9, L:9)
Scoring: 13T, 65 Pts
Appearances: 2004:C,SA,A, 2005:W,F,I,It,S,A,NZ,Sm, 2006:W,It,S,F,I,SA1,SA2

Barry Stephenson CUMBERLEGE, OBE
Born: 5 June 1891 in Newcastle-upon-Tyne
Died: 22 September 1970 in Sandgate, Folkestone
Educated: Durham School
Clubs: Cambridge University, Blackheath (8)
Position: Full-back (8)
Debut: 17 Jan 1920 v Wales (Swansea). Number: 545
Last game: 21 Jan 1922 v Wales (Cardiff)
Caps: 8 (W:6, L:2)
Scoring: 1C, 2 Pts
Appearances: 1920:W,I,S, 1921:W,I,S,F, 1922:W
Honours: Grand Slam: 1921

Sir Duncan Cameron CUMMING, KBE
Born: 10 August 1903 in Blackburn
Died: 10 December 1979 in Wandsworth
Educated: Giggleswick School
Clubs: Cambridge University (2), Blackheath
Position: No 8 (2)
Debut: 21 Mar 1925 v Scotland (Murrayfield). Number: 603
Last game: 13 Apr 1925 v France (Stade Colombes)
Caps: 2 (W:1, L:1)
Scoring: 0 Pts
Appearances: 1925:S,F

Foster Lionel CUNLIFFE
Born: 20 April 1854 in Llanfyllin, Wales
Died: 15 April 1927 in Cuckfield
Educated: Rugby School
Clubs: RMA Woolwich (1), Royal Artillery
Position: Forward (1)
Debut: 23 Feb 1874 v Scotland (The Oval). Number: 50
Caps: 1 (W:1, L:0)
Scoring: 0 Pts
Appearances: 1874:S

Frederick Innes CURREY

Born: 3 May 1849
Died: 18 December 1896 in Marylebone
Educated: Marlborough School
Clubs: Marlborough Nomads (1)
Position: Forward (1)
Debut: 5 Feb 1872 v Scotland (The Oval). Number: 24
Caps: 1 (W:1, L:0)
Scoring: 0 Pts
Appearances: 1872:S

John David (Muscles) CURRIE

Born: 3 May 1932 in Clifton
Died: 8 December 1990 in Leicester
Educated: Bristol GS
Clubs: Oxford University (13), Harlequins (9), Bristol (3)
Position: Lock (25)
Debut: 21 Jan 1956 v Wales (Twickenham). Number: 862
Last game: 24 Feb 1962 v France (Stade Colombes)
Caps: 25 (W:14, D:6, L:5)
Scoring: 2C, 4PG, 16 Pts
Appearances: 1956:W,I,S,F, 1957:W,I,F,S, 1958:W,A,I,F,S, 1959:W,I,F,S, 1960:W,I,F,S, 1961:SA, 1962:W,I,F
Honours: Grand Slam: 1957. Championship: 1958

David Anthony CUSANI

Born: 16 July 1959 in Wigan
Educated: St John Rigby College
Clubs: Wigan, Liverpool St Helens, Orrell (1)
Position: Lock (1)
Debut: 7 Feb 1987 v Ireland (Lansdowne Road). Number: 1115
Caps: 1 (W:0, L:1)
Scoring: 0 Pts
Appearances: 1987:I

Leslie (Les) CUSWORTH

Born: 3 July 1954 in Normanton
Educated: Normanton GS, West Midlands College
Clubs: Birmingham University, Wakefield, Moseley, Leicester (12)
Position: Fly-half (12), Bench (5)
Debut: 24 Nov 1979 v New Zealand (Twickenham). Number: 1059
Last game: 6 Feb 1988 v Wales (Twickenham)
Caps: 12 (W:4, D:1, L:7)
Scoring: 4DG, 12 Pts
Appearances: 1979:NZ, 1982:F,W, 1983:F,W,NZ, 1984:S,I,F,W, 1988:F,W

Les Cusworth

Les Cusworth could do no wrong for Leicester where his mercurial play at fly-half was a huge factor in the club's successes but England never looked upon him quite so warmly because he won just 12 caps in a nine-year period.

For most of his time as a serious challenger for an England place Cusworth was forced to be in stop-go mode. He started off for England in the 1979 match against New Zealand when the All Blacks squeezed home 10-9 at Twickenham and Cusworth did not fire as well as everyone at Leicester knew he could.

He gained a measure of revenge against New Zealand in the autumn of 1983 when England gained their first win at home over New Zealand since 1936. In 1984 he played in all the Championship matches but it was a poor year for the English team with only one win, against Ireland at Twickenham. The following year Rob Andrew took over the No 10 shirt and Cusworth was not called upon again until 1988 when he played against France and Wales.

Cusworth's club career continued at a high level with a sequence of quality performances over the years that made him one of the legends at Welford Road. He was a quick thinker and quick mover and those two qualities alone meant he was valuable to Leicester's ambitious game planning. Strategically he was a fine kicker.

When he stopped playing he spent time coaching at Worcester and also worked at Rugby School. In October 2006 he returned to prominence in the world game when he was appointed director of rugby for Argentina who are one of the most quickly improving countries in the rugby world. As part of the World Cup build up, Cusworth came back to Leicester with his Argentine squad and in a special match Argentina beat Leicester 41-21. Cusworth enjoyed coming back home.

"I live in Buenos Aires now but I still have lots of friends in Leicester," he said.

Cusworth used the trip to lay some foundations for the World Cup. Argentina, as he pointed out, do not have the benefit of playing in either the Six Nations or the Tri-Nations, but what may help his squad come competition time is the fact that so many Argentine players are now with European clubs and playing professionally.

Cusworth will have an army of Leicester supporters for this South American venture into the next World Cup and there will be huge interest in seeing whether Cusworth can lay the groundwork for his men to move into the highest echelons of the world game.

D

Matt Dawson

D'AGUILAR, Francis Burton Grant
DALLAGLIO, Lawrence Bruno Nero, MBE
DALTON, Timothy J
DANBY, Thompson
DANIELL, John
DARBY, Arthur John Lovett
DAVENPORT, Alfred
DAVEY, James
DAVEY, Richard Frank
DAVIDSON, James
DAVIDSON, Joseph
DAVIES, Geoffrey Huw
DAVIES, Harry Patrick
DAVIES, Vivian Gordon
DAVIES, William John Abbott, OBE
DAVIES, William Philip Cathcart
DAVIS, Alec Michael
DAWE, Richard Graham Reed
DAWSON, Ernest Frederick
DAWSON, Matthew James Sutherland, MBE
DAY, Harold Lindsay Vernon
DEACON, Louis Paul
DEAN, Geoffrey John
DEE, John MacKenzie
DE GLANVILLE, Philip Ranulph
DEVITT, Sir Thomas Gordon
DEWHURST, John Henry, MBE
DE WINTON, Robert Francis Chippiani
DIBBLE, Robert
DICKS, John
DILLON, Edward Wentworth
DINGLE, Arthur James
DIPROSE, Anthony James
DIXON, Peter John
DOBBS, George Eric Burroughs
DOBLE, Samuel Arthur
DOBSON, Denys Douglas
DOBSON, Thomas Hyde
DODGE, Paul William
DONNELLY, Martin Paterson
DOOLEY, Wade Anthony
DOVEY, Beverley Alfred
DOWN, Percy John
DOWSON, Aubrey Osler
DRAKE-LEE, Nicholas James
DUCKETT, Horace
DUCKHAM, David John, MBE
DUDGEON, Herbert William
DUGDALE, John Marshall
DUN, Andrew Frederick
DUNCAN, Robert Francis Hugh
DUNCOMBE, Nicholas Steven
DUNKLEY, Philip Edward
DUTHIE, James
DYSON, John William

Francis Burton Grant D'AGUILAR

Born: 11 December 1849
Died: 24 July 1896 in Bath
Educated: Cheltenham College
Clubs: RMA Woodwich, Royal Engineers (1), Army
Position: Forward (1)
Debut: 5 Feb 1872 v Scotland (The Oval) - 1T, 1 Pt
Number: 25
Caps: 1 (W:1, L:0)
Scoring: 1T, 1 Pt
Appearances: 1872:S

Lawrence Bruno Nero DALLAGLIO, MBE

Born: 10 August 1972 in Shepherd's Bush
Educated: Ampleforth College
Clubs: Wasps (77)
Position: No 8 (46), Flanker (22), Replacement (9), Bench (1)
Debut: 18 Nov 1995 (rep) v South Africa (Twickenham). Number: 1161
Last game: 12 Mar 2006 (rep) v France (Stade de France)
Caps: 77 (W:55, D:2, L:20). As captain: 22 (W:10, D:2, L:10)
Scoring: 16T, 80 Pts. Discipline - Sin bins: 2
Appearances: 1995:SA(r),Sm, 1996:F,W,S,I,It,Ar, 1997:S,I,F,A,A*,NZ1*,SA*,NZ2*, 1998:F*,W*,S*,I*,A*,SA*, 1999:S*,I*,F*,W*,US,C,It,NZ,Tg,Fj,SA, 2000:I,F,W,It,S,SA1,SA2,A,Ar,SA, 2001:W,It,S,F, 2002:It(r),NZ,A(r),SA(r), 2003:F(r),W,It,S,I,NZ,A,Geo,SA,Sm,U,W,F,A, 2004:It*,S*,I*,W*,F*,NZ1*,NZ2*,A, 2006:W(r),It(r),S(r),F(r)
Honours: RWC Winner: 2003. Grand Slam: 2003. Championship: 1996, 2000, 2001

Lawrence Dallaglio

'We Don't Need Another Hero' sang Lawrence Dallaglio as a member of Tina Turner's backing choir in 1985. Wasps and England fans would beg to differ, as over the course of his career coming to an end he became a world class No 8, and a man to turn to when the going got tough.

Had he chosen to take his father's Italian nationality over the Red Rose at 18 it could have been so different, but by 1993 he was winning the World Cup 7s with England, playing alongside Matt Dawson and Tim Rodber.

Dallaglio and Dawson remain the only two players to have won the World Cup at Sevens and in the 15-a-side code.

The 1996-97 season was a breakthrough campaign for Dallaglio, leading Wasps to the first fully professional English title, following the departure of Rob Andrew, and making his England debut against South Africa. He played his first 23 games as a flanker, before turning to No 8.

A natural leader, Dallaglio was appointed England captain by new coach Clive Woodward in 1997, after a Lions series victory (2-1) in South Africa that established his place in the world game.

But his tenure as England captain was dogged by injury and controversy, and he was forced to resign the captaincy in the run-up to the 1999 World Cup after an off-field sting by a British tabloid newspaper. Martin Johnson took over, but Dallaglio remained a massive presence in the back row alongside Neil Back and Richard Hill.

It is a testament to both his resilience and his ability that he bounced back, regaining the Wasps (and later England) captaincy in 2000, and capturing the Tetley's Bitter Cup.

In 2001, as part of the Lions squad, he suffered a career-threatening knee injury, only to again come back fitter and stronger to become an integral member of England's Grand Slam and World Cup-winning teams, scoring highly on the tackle count and yardage, and for which he was awarded the MBE.

Dallaglio completed his rehabilitation in 2004 when he regained the England captaincy with Martin Johnson's retirement, although he led a less successful Six Nations campaign. Injury struck again to hamper appearances for both England and the Lions in 2005, and by 2007 it was unlikely that he would add to his 73 caps and 15 tries for England.

Dallaglio – who was educated at Ampleforth College – has been a hugely influential figure not just for country but also for club.

Between 2003 and 2005 Wasps dominated the Premiership, winning the title three times, and in 2004 they also conquered Europe, beating Toulouse in the last minute of the Heineken Cup final.

"Lawrence has been not only an outstanding player for England but a great captain," said Woodward.

"Lawrence was my first captain when I took over the role in September 1997 and he has always been an important and valued member of the squad."

Ian McGeechan, his Lions coach in 1997 added: "Lawrence was one of the central personalities in England's success over the last seven years.

"I found him a very good player to work with. He had a great attitude to the game and a good understanding of it and I always found him very easy to talk to.

"There is no doubt the consistency of his performance within a core group of players that England have fielded over the last few years was instrumental to their success."

Huw Davies

Timothy J DALTON
Born: 2 September 1940 in Warwick
Educated: Warwick School
Clubs: Kenilworth, Coventry (1), Rugby
Position: Replacement Wing (1), Bench (2)
Debut: 15 Mar 1969 (rep) v Scotland (Twickenham). Number: 976
Caps: 1 (W:1, L:0)
Scoring: 0 Pts
Appearances: 1969:S(r)

Thompson (Tom) DANBY
Born: 10 August 1926 in Trimdon, Durham
Educated: Barnard Castle School, St John's College
Clubs: Durham City, Gosport, Harlequins (1), Army
Position: Wing (1)
Debut: 15 Jan 1949 v Wales (Cardiff). Number: 788
Caps: 1 (W:0, L:1)
Scoring: 0 Pts
Appearances: 1949:W

John DANIELL
Born: 12 December 1878 in Bath
Died: 24 January 1963 in Holway, Somerset
Educated: Clifton College
Clubs: Richmond (5), Cambridge University (2)
Position: Forward (7)
Debut: 7 Jan 1899 v Wales (Swansea). Number: 326
Last game: 19 Mar 1904 (capt) v Scotland (Inverleith)
Caps: 7 (W:4, D:1, L:2). As captain: 6 (W:4, D:1, L:1)
Scoring: 0 Pts
Appearances: 1899:W, 1900:I*,S*, 1902:I*,S*, 1904:I*,S*

Arthur John Lovett DARBY
Born: 9 January 1876 in Chester
Died: 15 January 1960 in Dartmouth
Educated: Cheltenham College
Clubs: Cambridge University (1), Sorbonne (FR), Birkenhead Park, Richmond
Position: Forward (1)
Debut: 4 Feb 1899 v Ireland (Lansdowne Road). Number: 333
Caps: 1 (W:0, L:1)
Scoring: 0 Pts
Appearances: 1899:I

Alfred DAVENPORT
Born: 5 May 1849
Died: 2 April 1932 in Abingdon
Educated: Rugby School
Clubs: Oxford University, Ravenscourt Park (1)
Position: Forward (1)
Debut: 27 Mar 1871 v Scotland (Raeburn Place). Number: 6
Caps: 1 (W:0, L:1)
Scoring: 0 Pts
Appearances: 1871:S

James (Maffer) DAVEY
Born: 25 December 1880 in Redruth
Died: 21 October 1951 in Redruth
Educated: Trewirgie School Cornwall
Clubs: Redruth (2), Coventry
Position: Fly-half (2)
Debut: 21 Mar 1908 v Scotland (Inverleith). Number: 462
Last game: 16 Jan 1909 v Wales (Cardiff)
Caps: 2 (W:0, L:2)
Scoring: 0 Pts
Appearances: 1908:S, 1909:W

Richard Frank DAVEY
Born: 22 September 1905 in Paddington
Died: 24 May 1983 in Bexhill
Educated: Wellington College
Clubs: Teignmouth, Wanstead, Leytonstone (1), Exeter
Position: Flanker (1)
Debut: 17 Jan 1931 v Wales (Twickenham). Number: 671
Caps: 1 (W:0, D:1, L:0)
Scoring: 0 Pts
Appearances: 1931:W

James DAVIDSON
Born: 28 December 1868
Died: 23 December 1945 in North Northumberland
Clubs: Aspatria (5)
Position: Forward (5)
Debut: 13 Mar 1897 v Scotland (Manchester). Number: 310
Last game: 11 Mar 1899 v Scotland (Blackheath)
Caps: 5 (W:2, D:1, L:2)
Scoring: 0 Pts
Appearances: 1897:S, 1898:S,W, 1899:I,S

Joseph DAVIDSON
Born: 5 October 1878 in Chester-le-Street
Died: 8 October 1910 in Wigton
Clubs: Aspatria (2)
Position: Forward (2)
Debut: 7 Jan 1899 v Wales (Swansea). Number: 327
Last game: 11 Mar 1899 v Scotland (Blackheath)
Caps: 2 (W:0, L:2)
Scoring: 0 Pts
Appearances: 1899:W,S

Geoffrey Huw (Huw) DAVIES
Born: 18 February 1959 in Eastbourne
Educated: King Edward VI School
Clubs: UWIST, Cambridge University (8), Wasps (10), Coventry (3)
Position: Fly-half (8), Full-back (6), Centre (6), Replacement (1), Bench (11)
Debut: 21 Feb 1981 v Scotland (Twickenham) - 1T, 4 Pts. Number: 1065
Last game: 15 Mar 1986 v France (Parc des Princes)
Caps: 21 (W:7, D:3, L:11)
Scoring: 4T, 16 Pts
Appearances: 1981:S,I,F,Ar1,Ar2, 1982:A,S,I, 1983:F,W,S, 1984:S,SA1,SA2, 1985:R(r),NZ1,NZ2, 1986:W,S,I,F

Harry Patrick DAVIES
Born: 17 March 1903 in Stockport
Died: 21 February 1979 in Ware, Herts
Educated: Denstone College
Clubs: Manchester, Sale (1)
Position: Flanker (1)
Debut: 12 Feb 1927 v Ireland (Twickenham). Number: 620
Caps: 1 (W:1, L:0)
Scoring: 0 Pts
Appearances: 1927:I

Vivian Gordon DAVIES
Born: 22 January 1899 in Bromley
Died: Killed in action in 1941 in Wandsworth
Educated: Marlborough School
Clubs: Harlequins (2)
Position: Fly-half (1), Centre (1)
Debut: 21 Jan 1922 v Wales (Cardiff). Number: 571
Last game: 3 Jan 1925 v New Zealand (Twickenham)
Caps: 2 (W:0, L:2)
Scoring: 0 Pts
Appearances: 1922:W, 1925:NZ

William John Abbott (Dave) DAVIES, OBE
Born: 21 June 1890 in Pembroke, Wales
Died: 26 April 1967 in Richmond
Educated: RNEC Keyham
Clubs: RNC Greenwich, United Services, Royal Navy (22)
Position: Fly-half (22)
Debut: 4 Jan 1913 v South Africa (Twickenham). Number: 527
Last game: 2 Apr 1923 (capt) v France (Stade Colombes) - 1DG, 4 Pts
Caps: 22 (W:20, D:1, L:1). As captain: 11 (W:10, D:1, L:0)
Scoring: 4T, 3DG, 24 Pts
Appearances: 1913:SA,W,F,I,S, 1914:I,S,F, 1920:F,I,S, 1921:W*,I*,S*,F*, 1922:I*,F*,S*, 1923:W*,I*,S*,F*
Honours: Grand Slam: 1913, 1921 (capt), 1923 (capt). **Championship:** 1914

William Philip Cathcart DAVIES
Born: 6 August 1928 in Abberley, Worcs
Educated: Denstone College
Clubs: Cambridge University, Cheltenham, Harlequins (11)
Position: Centre (9), Wing (2)
Debut: 21 Mar 1953 v Scotland (Twickenham). Number: 837
Last game: 18 Jan 1958 v Wales (Twickenham)
Caps: 11 (W:5, D:2, L:4)
Scoring: 1T, 3 Pts
Appearances: 1953:S, 1954:NZ,I, 1955:W,I,F,S, 1956:W, 1957:F,S, 1958:W
Honours: Championship: 1953, 1957, 1958

Alec Michael (Mike) DAVIS
Born: 23 January 1942 in Lichfield
Educated: Torquay GS, St Luke's College
Clubs: Torquay Athletic (10), Royal Navy, Devonport Services (1), United Services (1), Harlequins (4)
Position: Lock (16), Bench (4)
Debut: 19 Jan 1963 v Wales (Cardiff). Number: 909
Last game: 21 Mar 1970 v Scotland (Murrayfield)
Caps: 16 (W:5, D:2, L:9)
Scoring: 0 Pts
Appearances: 1963:W,I,S,NZ1,NZ2, 1964:NZ,W,I,F,S, 1966:W, 1967:A, 1969:SA, 1970:I,W,S
Honours: Championship: 1963

Richard Graham Reed (Graham) DAWE
Born: 4 September 1959 in Tavistock
Educated: Tavistock School
Clubs: Launceston, Bath (5), Sale, Plymouth
Position: Hooker (5), Bench (33)
Debut: 7 Feb 1987 v Ireland (Lansdowne Road). Number: 1116
Last game: 4 Jun 1995 v Samoa (Durban)
Caps: 5 (W:2, L:3)
Scoring: 0 Pts
Appearances: 1987:I,F,W,US, 1995:Sm

Devon born and bred, Graham Dawe was one of the game's real hard men and set an unenviable England record for the number of times he sat on the bench. He laughs at suggestions he used to psyche himself up before games by head-butting walls, but does not deny it.

He began his playing career with Launceston in 1978

Graham Dawe

before beginning the regular 300-mile round trip to train and play for Bath from his farm in Devon.

Playing under Jack Rowell, though, it was well worth it, as Bath went on to dominate rugby union in the Eighties and early Nineties.

Between 1984 and 1994, Bath won four John Player Cups in a row between 1984 and 1987, the Courage League Championship four times, and the Pilkington Cup four times.

Dawe's England tally of five caps hides his level of involvement in the national set-up. His nine-year battle with Brian Moore for the position of hooker is the stuff of legends. At a time when replacements weren't allowed except for injuries, Dawe sat on the bench more than 30 times.

He got his chance in the 1987 Five Nations against Ireland, but couldn't displace Moore on a regular basis.

He was one of the five England players singled out after the famous Battle of Cardiff in 1987, when a series of brawls marred the game between England and Wales. In the first five minutes, lock Wade Dooley took out his opposite number Bob Norster during a lineout and war broke out between the opposing forwards.

Along with fellow Bath team-mates, Richard Hill and Gareth Chilcott, Dawe was immediately dropped from the team, but even Moore sympathised with his rival.

"At least Wade had hit someone,' he wrote in his autobiography. "Dawe had done nothing. He seemed to be guilty by association.

"I thought I was a better player. I was desperate to play for England but I felt very sorry for Dawe. He never deserved to lose a Test jersey on those grounds. I would have commiserated with him at the time. Unfortunately, we were not talking."

His commitment to Bath – and rugby in general – is legendary. "I can't abide players who turn up and train and can't wait for the end of the session," he said in The Independent. "It's like people who can't wait for retirement. What's the point of living? You want players to turn up for training who are determined to improve themselves, even if it's only by 0.01 per cent."

He played his fifth and final game for England in a 1995 World Cup game against Western Samoa, running out 44-22 winners.

Despite is commitment to Devon he played 40 times for Cornwall and was a key player when they won the County Championship in 1991 against Yorkshire, 40,000 fans following them to Twickenham.

Dawe – who is a farmer – has gone on to some success as a coach, firstly at Sale, and then in 1999 he moved to Plymouth Albion where he is currently chairman of rugby.

He has since led them from Jewson League Two (South) through National League Division Two to National League Division One.

Not content with coaching success, he will occasionally roll back the years and appear for his beloved Devon, well past his 45th birthday!

Matt Dawson

Ernest Frederick DAWSON

Born: 10 May 1858
Died: 7 April 1904 in Hampstead, London
Clubs: Royal Indian Eng College (1), Richmond
Position: Forward (1)
Debut: 11 Mar 1878 v Ireland (Lansdowne Road). Number: 105
Caps: 1 (W:1, L:0)
Scoring: 0 Pts
Appearances: 1878:I

Matthew James Sutherland (Matt) DAWSON, MBE

Born: 31 October 1972 in Birkenhead
Educated: RGS High Wycombe, Mount St Mary's College
Clubs: Marlow, Northampton (65), Wasps (12)
Position: Scrum-half (55), Replacement (22), Bench (3)
Debut: 16 Dec 1995 v Samoa (Twickenham). Number: 1162
Last game: 18 Mar 2006 (rep) v Ireland (Twickenham)
Caps: 77 (W:51, D:1, L:25). As captain: 9 (W:4, L:5)
Scoring: 16T, 6C, 3PG, 101 Pts
Appearances: 1995:Sm, 1996:F,W,S,I, 1997:A,SA,NZ2(r), 1998:W(r),S,I,NZ1*,NZ2*,SA*,H,It, A,SA, 1999:S,F(r),W,A(r),US,C,It,NZ,Tg,Fj(r),SA, 2000:I*,F*,W*,It*,S*,A(r),Ar,SA, 2001:W,It,S,F,I*, 2002:W(r),It(r),NZ,A,SA, 2003:It,S,I,A(r),F(r),Geo,Sm,W,F,A, 2004:It(r),S(r),I,W,F,NZ1,NZ2(r),A(r), 2005:W,F(r),I(r),It(r),S(r),A,NZ, 2006:W(r),It(r),S(r),F,I(r)
Honours: RWC Winner: 2003. Championship: 1996, 2000 (capt), 2001 (capt), 2003

England's most-capped scrum-half with 77 appearances (nine as captain), Matt Dawson's unorthodox style, trademark 'sniping runs' around the scrum and use of the 'tap and go' penalty technique to score tries, played a significant role in making England a real force in world rugby at the beginning of the 21st century.

Dawson was a lynchpin of the England World Cup-winning team and supplied the pass with which Jonny Wilkinson made history.

With high profile television appearances as a ballroom dancer (Strictly Come Dancing runner-up 2006) and a chef (Celebrity Masterchef winner 2006), it is unsurprising that Matt was a bit of a sporting all-rounder at school. He played cricket for Buckinghamshire U-18s and appeared as a winger for Chelsea Schoolboys, before choosing the oval-shaped ball.

He made his debut for Northampton as a teenager in 1991, and in 1993 he was winning the World Cup 7s with England, playing alongside Lawrence Dallaglio and Tim Rodber. Dallaglio and Dawson remain the only two players to have won the World Cup Sevens and 15-a-side version.

He entered the international arena in 1995 against the Western Samoans, and made further strides a couple of years later on his first Lions tour to South Africa.

Starting as third choice scrum-half behind Robert Howley and Austin Healey, injury and good form saw him make the starting line-up. He scored a stunning solo try in his first Test, and the series was won 2-1.

Towards the end of a career which also included a Grand Slam in 2003, two further Six Nations titles and two Premiership titles with Wasps, whom he joined in 2004, Dawson began to focus on a career in the media, and followed in the footsteps of several rugby legends when he became a captain on 'A Question of Sport' in 2004.

Since his retirement in 2006 he has also been working as a BBC summariser.

Harold Lindsay Vernon DAY

Born: 12 August 1898 in Darjeeling, India
Died: 15 June 1972 in Hadley Wood
Educated: Bedford Modern School
Clubs: Royal Artillery, Army, Leicester (4)
Position: Wing (4)
Debut: 17 Jan 1920 v Wales (Swansea) - 1T, 1C, 5 Pts. Number: 546
Last game: 20 Mar 1926 v Scotland (Twickenham)
Caps: 4 (W:0, D:1, L:3)
Scoring: 2T, 2C, 2PG, 16 Pts
Appearances: 1920:W, 1922:W,F, 1926:S

Louis Paul DEACON

Born: 7 October 1980 in Leicester
Educated: Ratcliffe College Leicester
Clubs: Wigston, Syston, Leicester (6)
Position: Lock (5), Replacement (1), Bench (2)
Debut: 26 Nov 2005 v Samoa (Twickenham). Number: 1265
Last game: 24 Feb 2007 v Ireland (Croke Park)
Caps: 6 (W:3, L:3)
Scoring: 0 Pts
Appearances: 2005:Sm, 2006:A1,A2(r), 2007:S,It,I

Louis Deacon

Geoffrey John (Tinny) DEAN

Born: 12 November 1909 in Lewisham
Died: 12 December 1995 in Poole
Educated: Rugby School
Clubs: Cambridge University, Royal Tank Regt, Army, Harlequins (1)
Position: Scrum-half (1)
Debut: 14 Feb 1931 v Ireland (Twickenham). Number: 675
Caps: 1 (W:0, L:1)
Scoring: 0 Pts
Appearances: 1931:I

John MacKenzie DEE

Born: 22 October 1938 in Hartlepool
Educated: Henry Smith GS
Clubs: Hartlepool Rovers (2)
Position: Wing (1), Centre (1)
Debut: 17 Mar 1962 v Scotland (Murrayfield). Number: 904
Last game: 25 May 1963 v New Zealand (Auckland)
Caps: 2 (W:0, D:1, L:1)
Scoring: 0 Pts
Appearances: 1962:S, 1963:NZ1

Philip Ranulph (Phil) DE GLANVILLE

Born: 1 October 1968 in Loughborough
Educated: Bryanston School
Clubs: Oxford University, Bath (38)
Position: Centre (26), Replacement (12), Bench (17)
Debut: 14 Nov 1992 (rep) v South Africa (Twickenham). Number: 1148
Last game: 24 Oct 1999 v South Africa (Stade de France)
Caps: 38 (W:24, D:2, L:12). As captain: 8 (W:5, L:3)
Scoring: 8T, 40 Pts
Appearances: 1992:SA(r), 1993:W(r),NZ, 1994:S,I,F,W,SA1,SA2,C(r), 1995:Ar(r),It,Sm,SA(r), 1996:W(r),I(r),It*, 1997:S*,I*,F*,W*,Ar1*,Ar2*,A*,A,NZ1,NZ2, 1998:W(r),S(r),I(r),A,SA, 1999:A(r),US,It,NZ,Fj(r),SA
Honours: Championship: 1996

Phil De Glanville

Sir Thomas Gordon DEVITT
Born: 27 December 1902 in Bishopsgate, Surrey
Died: 23 December 1995 in Colchester
Educated: Sherborne School
Clubs: Cambridge University (2), Blackheath (2), Seaforth Highlanders, Army
Position: Wing (4)
Debut: 13 Feb 1926 v Ireland (Lansdowne Road). Number: 611
Last game: 21 Jan 1928 v Wales (Swansea)
Caps: 4 (W:3, L:1)
Scoring: 0 Pts
Appearances: 1926:I,F, 1928:A,W
Honours: Championship: 1928

John Henry DEWHURST, MBE
Born: 27 December 1863 in Skipton, Yorks
Died: 22 April 1947 in Gosport
Educated: Mill Hill School
Clubs: Cambridge University (2), Richmond (2), St Thomas's Hospital
Position: Forward (4)
Debut: 8 Jan 1887 v Wales (Llanelli). Number: 188
Last game: 15 Feb 1890 v Wales (Dewsbury)
Caps: 4 (W:0, D:2, L:2)
Scoring: 0 Pts
Appearances: 1887:W,I,S, 1890:W

Robert Francis Chippiani DE WINTON
Born: 9 September 1868 in Hay
Died: 14 March 1923 in Porterville, CA, USA
Educated: Summer Fields School, Marlborough College
Clubs: Marlborough Nomads, Oxford University, Blackheath (1)
Position: Half-Back (1)
Debut: 7 Jan 1893 v Wales (Cardiff). Number: 250
Caps: 1 (W:0, L:1)
Scoring: 0 Pts
Appearances: 1893:W

Robert DIBBLE
Born: Third quarter 1882 in Bridgwater
Died: Third quarter 1963 in Bournemouth
Clubs: Bridgwater & Albion (16), Newport (3)
Position: Forward (19)
Debut: 17 Mar 1906 v Scotland (Inverleith). Number: 432
Last game: 16 Mar 1912 (capt) v Scotland (Inverleith)
Caps: 19 (W:11, D:1, L:7). As captain: 7 (W:4, L:3)
Scoring: 0 Pts
Appearances: 1906:S,F,SA, 1908:F,W,I,S, 1909:A,W*,F*,I*,S*, 1910:S, 1911:W,F,S, 1912:W*,I*,S*
Honours: Championship: 1910

John DICKS
Born: 12 September 1912 in Mears Ashby, Northants
Died: Second quarter 1981 in Northampton
Educated: Northampton GS
Clubs: Wellingborough, Northampton (8)
Position: Lock (6), Prop (1), No 8 (1)
Debut: 20 Jan 1934 v Wales (Cardiff). Number: 705
Last game: 13 Feb 1937 v Ireland (Twickenham)
Caps: 8 (W:6, D:1, L:1)
Scoring: 0 Pts
Appearances: 1934:W,I,S, 1935:W,I,S, 1936:S, 1937:I
Honours: Championship: 1934, 1937

Tony Diprose

Edward Wentworth DILLON
Born: 15 February 1881 in Penge, Kent
Died: 20 April 1941 in Totteridge, Herts
Educated: Rugby School
Clubs: Oxford University, Harlequins (3), Blackheath (1)
Position: Centre (4)
Debut: 9 Jan 1904 v Wales (Leicester). Number: 396
Last game: 14 Jan 1905 v Wales (Cardiff)
Caps: 4 (W:1, D:1, L:2)
Scoring: 0 Pts
Appearances: 1904:W,I,S, 1905:W

Arthur James DINGLE
Born: Third quarter 1891 in Hetton-le-Hole, Durham
Died: Killed in action in 1915 in Gallipoli, Turkey
Educated: Durham School
Clubs: Oxford University, Hartlepool Rovers (3), Richmond
Position: Wing (2), Centre (1)
Debut: 8 Feb 1913 v Ireland (Lansdowne Road). Number: 532
Last game: 13 Apr 1914 v France (Stade Colombes)
Caps: 3 (W:3, L:0)
Scoring: 0 Pts
Appearances: 1913:I, 1914:S,F
Honours: Championship: 1913, 1914

Anthony James (Tony) DIPROSE
Born: 22 September 1972 in Orsett, Essex
Educated: Campion School
Clubs: Loughborough University, Saracens (10), Harlequins
Position: No 8 (8), Replacement (2), Bench (2)
Debut: 31 May 1997 v Argentina (Buenos Aires) - 1T, 5 Pts. Number: 1178
Last game: 4 Jul 1998 v South Africa (Cape Town)
Caps: 10 (W:4, D:1, L:5). As captain: 1 (W:0, L:1)
Scoring: 1T, 5 Pts
Appearances: 1997:Ar1,Ar2,A,NZ1, 1998:W(r),S(r),I,A*,NZ2,SA

Peter John DIXON
Born: 30 April 1944 in Keighley, Yorks
Educated: St Bees School Cumbria
Clubs: Durham University, Oxford University, Harlequins (5), Gosforth (17)
Position: Flanker (21), No 8 (1), Bench (7)
Debut: 17 Apr 1971 v Presidents XV (Twickenham). Number: 1001
Last game: 25 Nov 1978 v New Zealand (Twickenham)
Caps: 22 (W:7, D:1, L:14). As captain: 2 (W:0, L:2)
Scoring: 4T, 16 Pts
Appearances: 1971:P, 1972:W,I,F*,S*, 1973:I,F,S, 1974:S,I,F,W, 1975:I, 1976:F, 1977:S,I,F,W, 1978:F,S,I,NZ

It says a great deal about the back-row skills of Peter Dixon that he was chosen to tour with the 1971 British Lions in New Zealand before he made any appearances for England. His selection for the Lions said a great deal as well about the skill of the selectors. Dixon played in three of the four Tests in New Zealand and missed a clean sweep of appearances because of injury.

Dixon started to play rugby in the north of England and came toprominence through Workington and Durham University. He spent four years at Oxford University from 1967 and in 1971 was chosen for England for the first time when he played at No 8 against an overseas team at Twickenham in a special match to celebrate the Centenary of the Rugby Football Union. The match was lost 28-11 but Dixon, having already spent the summer with the Lions in New Zealand, was on his way domestically as well.

Dixon played for England in all games in the 1972 championship and was captain for the third and fourth matches against France and Scotland. But it was a bleak year for England; for the first time in their history they lost all four matches in the championship.

In 1973 Dixon played three matches in the championship and scored two tries against Scotland. He had also played alongside Tony Neary and Andy Ripley in the back row for a record total of 12 times by the end of 1973,and had extended that record to 17 by 1975.

Dixon played his last full championship in 1977 and in three games in 1978. His final game in an England shirt was against New Zealand in the autumn of 1978 but there was no question that Dixon looked an absolute certainty to play against the All Blacks once more a year later. Dixon had played a significant part in the memorable 21-9 win by the North of England against New Zealand at Otley and it was expected that he would be a definite starter against the All Blacks a week later. But Dixon, one of five England captains in the North team, was not chosen and decided to stand down from representative rugby. It was one hell of a way to say goodbye, as his big mate Roger Uttley put it.

Dixon's top club rugby was with Harlequins and Gosforth and he played a great deal of football in the north east, where he still lives. Uttley rates Dixon as one of the best he has ever been alongside on the pitch.

It was in New Zealand that Dixon's skills are remembered as well. Those who watched at close range the 1971 series between the Lions and the All Blacks knew that the Lions had a special squad with players like Barry John, Gareth Edwards, Mike Gibson and Willie-John McBride anchoring the dramatic Test wins. Dixon fitted perfectly into that company.

In the second Test in Christchurch Dixon was caught in a ruck and was kicked on the head. The cut was deep enough to require five stitches, which was one piece of bad news for Dixon that day. The Lions also lost the Test and Dixon was to miss the third Test, which the Lions won, and return for the fourth at Auckland, which was drawn, 14-all.

The climax to that tour is regarded as one of the most nerve-racking days in international rugby. Dixon was not an original choice for the match but was promoted when the Welsh flanker Derek Quinnell developed fluid on the knee. The Lions were 8-3 down playing into the wind in the first half and hoped they could hold that score until half-time. But in fact they were level at the break through a try by Dixon, the only try they scored that day, as it transpired.

An Oxford doctorate in social anthropology, he was considered one of the quiet men of the 1971 Lions except when he was playing his guitar.

Peter Dixon

George Eric Burroughs DOBBS

Born: 21 July 1884
Died: Killed in action in 1917 in Poperinghe, Belgium
Educated: St Stephens School, Shrewsbury School
Clubs: RMA Woolwich, Royal Engineers, Plymouth Albion, Devonport Albion (2), Llanelli, Army
Position: Flanker (2)
Debut: 13 Jan 1906 v Wales (Richmond). Number: 421
Last game: 10 Feb 1906 v Ireland (Leicester)
Caps: 2 (W:0, L:2)
Scoring: 0 Pts
Appearances: 1906:W,I

Samuel Arthur (Sam) DOBLE

Born: 9 March 1944 in Wolverhampton
Died: 17 September 1977 in Birmingham
Educated: Regis School
Clubs: Moseley (3)
Position: Full-back (3)
Debut: 3 Jun 1972 v South Africa (Johannesburg) - 1C, 4PG, 14 Pts. Number: 1012
Last game: 20 Jan 1973 v Wales (Cardiff) - 2PG, 6 Pts
Caps: 3 (W:1, L:2)
Scoring: 1C, 6PG, 20 Pts
Appearances: 1972:SA, 1973:NZ,W

Denys Douglas DOBSON

Born: 28 October 1880
Died: 10 July 1916 in Ngama, Nyasaland
Educated: Cheltenham College, Newton School
Clubs: Newton Abbot (4), Oxford University (2), Devonport Albion, London Welsh
Position: Forward (6)
Debut: 11 Jan 1902 v Wales (Blackheath) - 1T, 3 Pts. Number: 373
Last game: 21 Mar 1903 v Scotland (Richmond) - 1T, 3 Pts
Caps: 6 (W:2, L:4)
Scoring: 3T, 9 Pts
Appearances: 1902:W,I,S, 1903:W,I,S

Thomas Hyde DOBSON

Born: February 1872 in Bradford
Died: 12 November 1902 in Bradford
Clubs: Bradford (1)
Position: Centre (1)
Debut: 9 Mar 1895 v Scotland (Richmond). Number: 282
Caps: 1 (W:0, L:1)
Scoring: 0 Pts
Appearances: 1895:S

Paul William DODGE

Born: 26 February 1958 in Leicester
Educated: Wreake School
Clubs: Leicester (32)
Position: Centre (32), Bench (1)
Debut: 4 Feb 1978 v Wales (Twickenham). Number: 1049
Last game: 8 Jun 1985 (capt) v New Zealand (Wellington)
Caps: 32 (W:14, D:5, L:13). As captain: 7 (W:2, D:1, L:4)
Scoring: 1T, 1C, 3PG, 15 Pts
Appearances: 1978:W,S,I,NZ, 1979:S,I,F,W, 1980:W,S, 1981:W,S,I,F,Ar1,Ar2, 1982:A,S,F,W, 1983:F,W,S,I,NZ, 1985:R*,F*,S*,I*,W*,NZ1*,NZ2*
Honours: Championship: 1980

Paul Dodge's pedigree and his promise took to the stage when he was 17 and played for Leicester for the first time in the annual post-Christmas match against the Barbarians. That was in 1975 and although Leicester lost, Dodge scored a debut try and, a year later, scored another try against the Barbarians when Leicester gained their revenge against the same opponents.

Dodge's rise to the top continued unchecked and at the age of 19 he made his debut for England at centre in the 1978 match against Wales at Twickenham. Wales won 9-6 for a fourth victory in five visits to Twickenham but did not score a try for the first time in 21 games against England. In that same year Dodge also played against Scotland,

Paul Dodge

Wade Dooley

Ireland and New Zealand.

In 1979 the home championship ended with England suffering their heaviest defeat since 1905 to Wales by 27-3 but the following year England won a Grand Slam to take the championship for the first time in 20 years. Dodge did not make the starting side that season but came in after two games as England surged on for the title. In the deciding game against Scotland Dodge's kick ahead helped wing John Carleton to his hat-trick of tries, the first for 56 years.

Later that summer Dodge, who works in the family book-binding business, went on his first British and Irish Lions tour to South Africa and played in the third and fourth Tests. His England career ended in 1985 when his last match was the 42-15 defeat against New Zealand in Wellington. Dodge, who won 32 caps and captained England eight times, was renowned for the solidity of his midfield play and his long range kicking was always valuable in both attack and defence. He started 437 first team matches for Leicester and has remained with the club as a player development coach and his sons Alex and Ollie have followed him into the Tigers first team.

Martin Paterson (Squib) DONNELLY

Born: 17 October 1917 in Ngaruawahia, New Zealand
Died: 22 October 1999 in Sydney, Australia
Educated: New Plymouth BHS
Clubs: Canterbury University, Oxford University (1), Blackheath
Position: Centre (1)
Debut: 8 Feb 1947 v Ireland (Lansdowne Road). Number: 767
Caps: 1 (W:0, L:1)
Scoring: 0 Pts
Appearances: 1947:I

Wade Anthony DOOLEY

Born: 2 October 1957 in Warrington
Educated: Beaumont Street School
Clubs: Preston Grasshoppers (45), Fylde (10)
Position: Lock (54), Replacement (1), Bench (1)
Debut: 5 Jan 1985 v Romania (Twickenham). Number: 1101
Last game: 20 Mar 1993 v Ireland (Lansdowne Road)
Caps: 55 (W:33, D:2, L:20)
Scoring: 3T, 12 Pts
Appearances: 1985:R,F,S,I,W,NZ2(r), 1986:W,S,I,F, 1987:F,W,A,US,W, 1988:F,W,S,I,I,A1,A2,Fj,A, 1989:S,I,F,W,R,Fj,1990:I,F,W,S,Ar1,Ar2,Ar, 1991:W,S,I,F,NZ,US,F,S,A, 1992:S,I,F,W,C,SA, 1993:W,S,I
Honours: Grand Slam: 1991, 1992

Known throughout the rugby world as The Blackpool Tower, Wade Dooley was an amazingly effective, old school lock-forward.

Dooley, a police officer, formed a formidable partnership with Paul Ackford in England's second row, as the side enjoyed one of the most successful periods in its history.

England had silky backs like Rory Underwood and Jeremy Guscott but if they were going to win honours they also needed the rugged, uncompromising forwards who personified the early 1990s. Dooley – all 6ft 8in of him – was one of the keys to this success.

Dooley was unusual in that he declined the opportunity to play his club rugby at the highest level, instead keeping faith with the Preston Grasshoppers.

This may have led to him having to wait until he was 27 for his first cap, against Romania in 1985. He soon made up for lost time and when he played his last game for England in 1993 he was his country's most-capped second row.

Dooley was as committed to the Red Rose as any player before and after him. "I've never had a problem spurring myself on. Once I stick that old white jersey on, I can't wait to get going," he once said.

Dooley's Lions career came to a premature end when he was the victim of a crass decision by the tour management.

Dooley went home from the 1993 tour for his father's funeral but once he was replaced by Martin Johnson, he was unable to rejoin the tour, leading to him ending his international career, to spend more time with his family.

"The decision not to allow him to return to New Zealand after the death of his father was, in my view, totally insensitive," said England captain Will Carling.

"The New Zealand RU had invited Wade back if he wished. He had 50 England caps, had ruled the lineouts during England's two Grand Slams and World Cup campaign, he had been playing and winning for England for more than seven years. Call me old fashioned on this, but I see these as rather special achievements which deserved sympathetic consideration."

Dooley had happier times with the Lions in 1989 as they won 2-1 in Australia, the lock playing in the last two Tests, both of which were won.

Beverley Alfred DOVEY

Born: 24 October 1938 in Forest of Dean
Educated: Lydney GS
Clubs: Cambridge University, Rosslyn Park (2), Gloucester
Position: Prop (2)
Debut: 19 Jan 1963 v Wales (Cardiff). Number: 910
Last game: 9 Feb 1963 v Ireland (Lansdowne Road)
Caps: 2 (W:1, D:1, L:0)
Scoring: 0 Pts
Appearances: 1963:W,I
Honours: Championship: 1963

Percy John DOWN

Born: 14 October 1882 in Clifton
Died: 29 June 1954 in Weston
Educated: Dr Kemp's School
Clubs: Bristol (1)
Position: Prop (1)
Debut: 9 Jan 1909 v Australia (Blackheath). Number: 468
Caps: 1 (W:0, L:1)
Scoring: 0 Pts
Appearances: 1909:A

Aubrey Osler DOWSON

Born: 10 November 1874 in Stockport
Died: 5 October 1940 in Hanging Langford
Educated: Rugby School
Clubs: Oxford University, Moseley (1), Manchester
Position: Forward (1)
Debut: 11 Mar 1899 v Scotland (Blackheath). Number: 335
Caps: 1 (W:0, L:1)
Scoring: 0 Pts
Appearances: 1899:S

Nicholas James (Nick) DRAKE-LEE

Born: 7 April 1942 in Kettering
Educated: Stonyhurst College
Clubs: Cambridge University (4), Rosslyn Park, Leicester (4), Manchester, Waterloo
Position: Prop (8)
Debut: 19 Jan 1963 v Wales (Cardiff). Number: 911
Last game: 16 Jan 1965 v Wales (Cardiff)
Caps: 8 (W:3, D:2, L:3)
Scoring: 1T, 3 Pts
Appearances: 1963:W,I,F,S, 1964:NZ,W,I, 1965:W
Honours: Championship: 1963

Horace DUCKETT

Born: 11 October 1867 in Thornton, Bradford
Died: 3 March 1939 in Todmorden
Clubs: Bradford (2)
Position: Half-Back (2)
Debut: 4 Feb 1893 v Ireland (Lansdowne Road). Number: 255
Last game: 4 Mar 1893 v Scotland (Headingley)
Caps: 2 (W:1, L:1)
Scoring: 0 Pts
Appearances: 1893:I,S

David John DUCKHAM, MBE

Born: 28 June 1946 in Coventry
Educated: King Henry VIII School
Clubs: Coventry (36), Old Coventrians
Position: Wing (22), Centre (14)
Debut: 8 Feb 1969 v Ireland (Lansdowne Road) - 1T, 3 Pts. Number: 971
Last game: 21 Feb 1976 v Scotland (Murrayfield)
Caps: 36 (W:11, D:2, L:23)
Scoring: 10T, 36 Pts
Appearances: 1969:I,F,S,W,SA, 1970:I,W,S,F, 1971:W,I,F,S,S,P, 1972:W,I,F,S, 1973:NZ,W,I,F,S,NZ,A, 1974:S,I,F,W, 1975:I,F,W, 1976:A,W,S

When England were in one of their darkest periods – in the 1970s – they had one player who could live with the Gods of Welsh and French rugby: David Duckham.

With flowing blond locks, the David Strettle look-a-like, tormented defences across the globe and was one of the few Englishmen who could stand toe-to-toe – in the flair stakes – with the great Welsh players of that era.

When people recall rugby's most famous try, the Gareth Edwards score for the Barbarians against New Zealand in 1973 it is easy to forget Duckham was the sole English back on duty that day.

Duckham's reputation on the world stage was confirmed in 1971 as part of the legendary Lions side that won in New Zealand.

Duckham scored 11 tries on that trip to the Land of the Long White Cloud, six coming in one match, when he played on the right wing against West Coast-Buller and set a record for a visiting player to New Zealand.

His performances clearly caught the eye of the most famous Lions coach of all and Carwyn James picked him for the final three Tests – instead of John Bevan – and he linked up superbly with full-back JPR Williams.

Duckham also found a fan in the legendary television commentator, Bill McLaren

"He was so effective wide out," said McLaren. "He would have scored many more tries if players inside him had used him more. He had a brilliant sidestep; he almost telegraphed it, but still it was devastating.

"He was the archetypal Englishman, blond hair flowing, who would glide away from opponents. He also possessed an aggressive hand-off. He came into his own with the British Isles in 1971 when he scored 11 tries. He showed how brilliant he was for the Barbarians against New Zealand in 1973. In a team of great players, he stood out."

Duckham – who played his club rugby for Old Coventrians and Coventry – made an instant impact on the England team, scoring a spectacular 60-yard try on his debut against Ireland in 1969, when he kicked off his international career in the centre, before moving to the wing.

David Duckham

In that same year – 1969 – England enjoyed one of their greatest days of that period beating South Africa at Twickenham, the first time England had beaten them. But after that England endured some of the worst results in their history, and in those seven years following England failed to win more than two Five Nations games in any one season. Despite that Duckham remained.

For his services to rugby Duckham was awarded the MBE in 1977 and he also wrote an autobiography called Dai for England, as a reference to the way he was affectionately tagged by Welshmen in the 1970s.

Herbert William DUDGEON

Born: Third quarter 1872 in Tynemouth
Died: 4 October 1935 in Cairo, Egypt
Educated: Schooled in Switzerland
Clubs: Durham University, Richmond (7), Northern
Position: Forward (7)
Debut: 13 Mar 1897 v Scotland (Manchester). Number: 311
Last game: 11 Mar 1899 v Scotland (Blackheath)
Caps: 7 (W:2, D:1, L:4)
Scoring: 0 Pts
Appearances: 1897:S, 1898:I,S,W, 1899:W,I,S

John Marshall DUGDALE
Born: 15 October 1851 in Salford
Died: 30 October 1918 in Llanfyllin, Wales
Educated: Rugby School
Clubs: Oxford University, Ravenscourt Park (1)
Position: Forward (1)
Debut: 27 Mar 1871 v Scotland (Raeburn Place).Number: 7
Caps: 1 (W:0, L:1)
Scoring: 0 Pts
Appearances: 1871:S

Andrew Frederick (Andy) DUN
Born: 26 November 1960 in Bristol
Educated: Bristol GS
Clubs: St Bart's Hospital, Bristol, Gloucester, London Scottish, Wasps (1)
Position: Flanker (1)
Debut: 17 Mar 1984 v Wales (Twickenham). Number: 1086
Caps: 1 (W:0, L:1)
Scoring: 0 Pts
Appearances: 1984:W

Nick Duncombe

Robert Francis Hugh DUNCAN
Born: First quarter 1897 in Cardiff, Wales
Died: 19 October 1981 in Henley
Clubs: Cardiff University, Guys Hospital (3)
Position: Prop (3)
Debut: 11 Feb 1922 v Ireland (Lansdowne Road). Number: 574
Last game: 18 Mar 1922 v Scotland (Twickenham)
Caps: 3 (W:2, D:1, L:0)
Scoring: 0 Pts
Appearances: 1922:I,F,S

Nicholas Steven (Nick) DUNCOMBE
Born: 21 January 1982 in Taplow
Died: 14 February 2003 in Lanzarote
Educated: RGS High Wycombe
Clubs: Harlequins (2)
Position: Replacement Scrum-half (2), Bench (1)
Debut: 2 Feb 2002 (rep) v Scotland (Murrayfield). Number: 1237
Last game: 16 Feb 2002 (rep) v Ireland (Twickenham)
Caps: 2 (W:2, L:0)
Scoring: 0 Pts
Appearances: 2002:S(r),I(r)

Philip Edward (Pop) DUNKLEY
Born: 9 August 1904 in Daventry
Died: 17 June 1985 in Doncaster
Clubs: Old Laurentians, Leicester, Harlequins (6), Rugby, Congleton
Position: No 8 (6)
Debut: 14 Feb 1931 v Ireland (Twickenham). Number: 676
Last game: 21 Mar 1936 v Scotland (Twickenham)
Caps: 6 (W:2, D:1, L:3)
Scoring: 0 Pts
Appearances: 1931:I,S, 1936:NZ,W,I,S

James DUTHIE
Born: Second quarter 1881 in Hartlepool
Died: 29 March 1946 in Hartlepool
Clubs: West Hartlepool (1), Winlaton Vulcans
Position: Forward (1)
Debut: 10 Jan 1903 v Wales (Swansea). Number: 385
Caps: 1 (W:0, L:1)
Scoring: 0 Pts
Appearances: 1903:W

John William (Jack) DYSON
Born: 6 September 1866 in Skelmanthorpe
Died: 3 January 1909 in Huddersfield
Clubs: Skelmanthorpe, Huddersfield (4)
Position: Three-quarter (4)
Debut: 1 Mar 1890 v Scotland (Raeburn Place) - 1T, 2 Pts. Number: 218
Last game: 4 Mar 1893 v Scotland (Headingley)
Caps: 4 (W:3, L:1)
Scoring: 1T, 2 Pts
Appearances: 1890:S, 1892:S, 1893:I,S
Honours: Championship: 1892

E

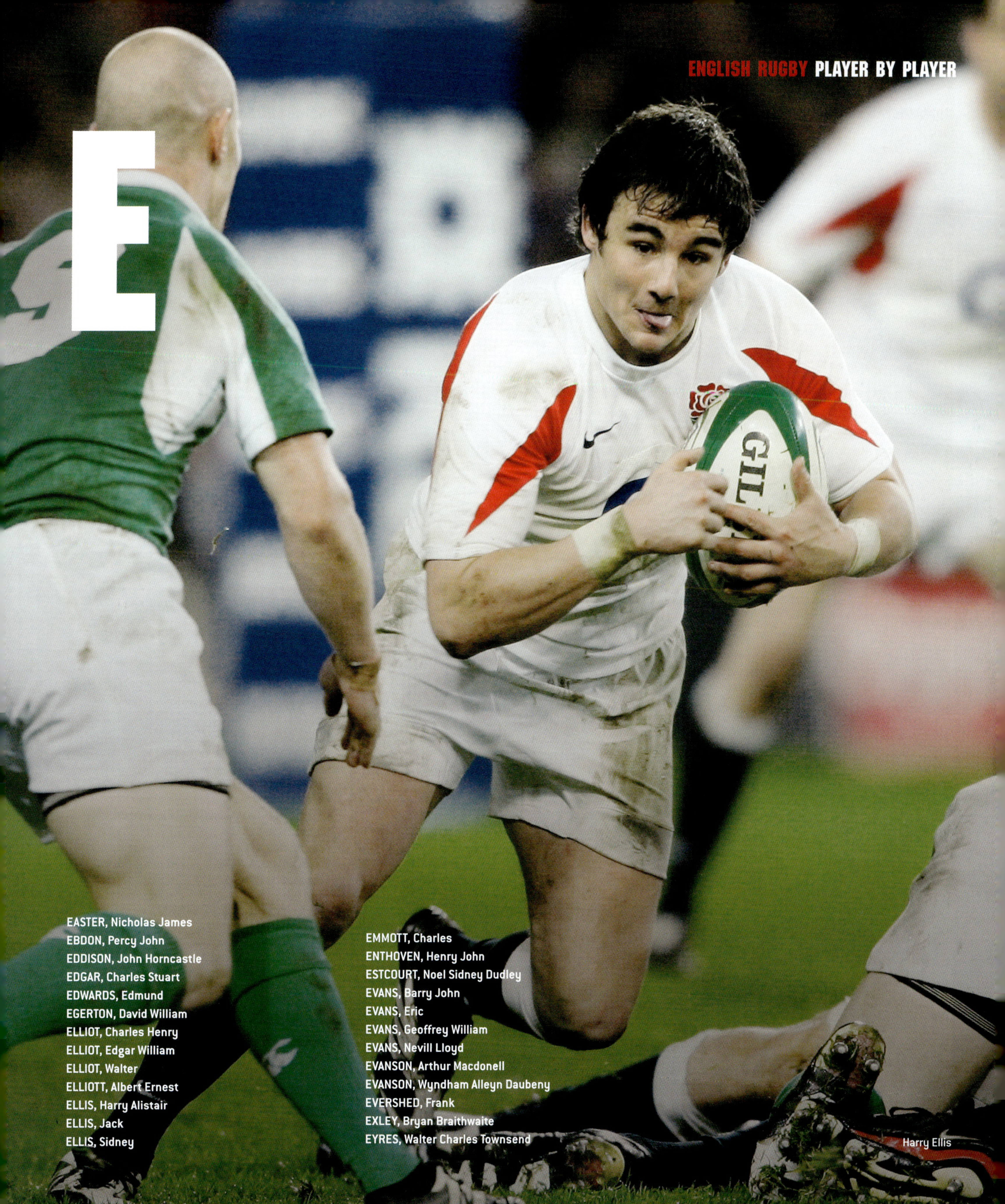

Harry Ellis

Nick Easter

Nicholas James (Nick) EASTER
Born: 15 August 1975 in Epsom
Educated: Dulwich College
Clubs: Villagers (SA), Rosslyn Park, Orrell, Harlequins (1)
Position: Flanker (1)
Debut: 10 Feb 2007 v Italy (Twickenham). Number: 1281
Caps: 1 (W:1, L:0)
Scoring: 0 Pts
Appearances: 2007:It

Percy John EBDON
Born: 16 March 1874 in Milverton, Somerset
Died: 16 February 1943 in Wellington
Clubs: Wellington (2)
Position: Forward (2)
Debut: 9 Jan 1897 v Wales (Newport). Number: 299
Last game: 6 Feb 1897 v Ireland (Lansdowne Road)
Caps: 2 (W:0, L:2)
Scoring: 0 Pts
Appearances: 1897:W,I

John Horncastle EDDISON
Born: 25 August 1888 in Edinburgh, Scotland
Died: 18 November 1982 in Edinburgh
Educated: Ilkley GS, Bromsgrove School
Clubs: Headingley (4)
Position: Forward (4)
Debut: 20 Jan 1912 v Wales (Twickenham). Number: 518
Last game: 8 Apr 1912 v France (Parc des Princes) - 1T, 3 Pts
Caps: 4 (W:3, L:1)
Scoring: 1T, 3 Pts
Appearances: 1912:W,I,S,F

Charles Stuart EDGAR
Born: Second quarter 1877 in West Derby
Died: 26 May 1949 in Chester
Clubs: Birkenhead Park (1)
Position: Forward (1)
Debut: 9 Mar 1901 v Scotland (Blackheath). Number: 368
Caps: 1 (W:0, L:1)
Scoring: 0 Pts
Appearances: 1901:S

Edmund (Reg) EDWARDS
Born: Third quarter 1893 in Newport, Wales
Died: 9 May 1951 in Montreal, Canada
Educated: Preswell School
Clubs: Newport (11)
Position: Prop (11)
Debut: 15 Jan 1921 v Wales (Twickenham). Number: 566
Last game: 3 Jan 1925 v New Zealand (Twickenham)
Caps: 11 (W:8, D:1, L:2)
Scoring: 1T, 3 Pts
Appearances: 1921:W,I,S,F, 1922:W,F, 1923:W, 1924:W,F,S, 1925:NZ
Honours: Grand Slam: 1921. Championship: 1923, 1924

David William EGERTON

Born: 19 October 1961 in Pinner, Middlesex
Educated: Bishop Wordsworth School
Clubs: Loughborough College, Salisbury, Wasps, Bath (7)
Position: No 8 (3), Flanker (2), Replacement (2), Bench (11)
Debut: 23 Apr 1988 v Ireland (Lansdowne Road). Number: 1125
Last game: 4 Aug 1990 (rep) v Argentina (Buenos Aires)
Caps: 7 (W:5, L:2)
Scoring: 1T, 4 Pts
Appearances: 1988:I,A1,Fj(r),A, 1989:Fj, 1990:I,Ar2(r)

Charles Henry ELLIOT

Born: 31 May 1861 in Sunderland
Died: 1 April 1934 in Chard
Educated: Repton School
Clubs: Sunderland (1), Blackheath
Position: Forward (1)
Debut: 2 Jan 1886 v Wales (Blackheath). Number: 178
Caps: 1 (W:1, L:0)
Scoring: 0 Pts
Appearances: 1886:W

Edgar William ELLIOT

Born: 9 July 1878 in Roker, Sunderland
Died: 23 March 1931 in Vancouver, Canada
Educated: Wellington College
Clubs: Sunderland (4)
Position: Wing (4)
Debut: 5 Jan 1901 v Wales (Cardiff). Number: 355
Last game: 9 Jan 1904 v Wales (Leicester) - 2T, 6 Pts
Caps: 4 (W:0, D:1, L:3)
Scoring: 2T, 6 Pts
Appearances: 1901:W,I,S, 1904:W

Walter ELLIOT

Born: 17 February 1910 in Birkenhead
Died: September 1988 in Poole
Educated: HMS Conway
Clubs: RNEC Keyham, United Services (2), Royal Navy (5)
Position: Fly-half (7)
Debut: 13 Feb 1932 v Ireland (Lansdowne Road). Number: 693
Last game: 10 Feb 1934 v Ireland (Lansdowne Road)
Caps: 7 (W:5, L:2)
Scoring: 1T, 3 Pts
Appearances: 1932:I,S, 1933:W,I,S, 1934:W,I
Honours: Championship: 1934

Albert Ernest ELLIOTT

Born: 5 March 1869 in Basset Mount, Southampton
Died: 1 December 1900 in Middelburg, South Africa
Educated: Cheltenham College
Clubs: Cambridge University, St Thomas's Hospital (1)
Position: Forward (1)
Debut: 17 Mar 1894 v Scotland (Raeburn Place). Number: 269
Caps: 1 (W:0, L:1)
Scoring: 0 Pts
Appearances: 1894:S

Harry Alistair ELLIS

Born: 17 May 1982 in Wigston
Educated: Leicester GS, De Montfort University
Clubs: South Leicester, Wigston, Leicester (16)
Position: Scrum-half (12), Replacement (4), Bench (2)
Debut: 20 Nov 2004 (rep) v South Africa (Twickenham). Number: 1259
Last game: 24 Feb 2007 v Ireland (Croke Park)
Caps: 16 (W:8, L:8)
Scoring: 2T, 10 Pts
Appearances: 2004:SA(r),A(r), 2005:W(r),F,I,It,S,Sm, 2006:W,It,S,F(r),I, 2007:S,It,I

Jack ELLIS

Born: 28 October 1912 in Rothwell Haigh, Leeds
Clubs: Wakefield (1)
Position: Scrum-half (1)
Debut: 18 Mar 1939 v Scotland (Murrayfield). Number: 751
Caps: 1 (W:1, L:0)
Scoring: 0 Pts
Appearances: 1939:S

Sidney ELLIS

Born: 13 March 1859 in Lewisham
Died: 1 December 1937 in Croydon
Educated: Dulwich College
Clubs: Faversham, Queen's House (1), Blackheath
Position: Forward (1)
Debut: 30 Jan 1880 v Ireland (Lansdowne Road) - 1T, 1 Pt. Number: 120
Caps: 1 (W:1, L:0)
Scoring: 1T, 1 Pt
Appearances: 1880:I

Charles EMMOTT

Born: First quarter 1869 in Bradford
Died: 10 March 1927 in Saltaire
Clubs: Bradford (1)
Position: Half-Back (1)
Debut: 2 Jan 1892 v Wales (Blackheath). Number: 237
Caps: 1 (W:1, L:0)
Scoring: 0 Pts
Appearances: 1892:W
Honours: Championship: 1892

Harry Ellis

D E F

Jack Ellis

Eric Evans

Henry John ENTHOVEN
Born: 16 March 1855 in Liverpool
Died: Details unknown
Clubs: Richmond (1)
Position: Three-quarter (1)
Debut: 11 Mar 1878 v Ireland (Lansdowne Road). Number: 106
Caps: 1 (W:1, L:0)
Scoring: 0 Pts
Appearances: 1878:I

Noel Sidney Dudley ESTCOURT
Born: 7 January 1929 in Ralolia, Rhodesia
Educated: Plumtree School
Clubs: Rhodesia University, Cambridge University, Blackheath (1)
Position: Full-back (1)
Debut: 19 Mar 1955 v Scotland (Twickenham). Number: 858
Caps: 1 (W:1, L:0)
Scoring: 0 Pts
Appearances: 1955:S

Barry John EVANS
Born: 10 October 1962 in Hinckley
Educated: John Cleveland College
Clubs: Leicester (2), Coventry, Worcester, Market Bosworth
Position: Wing (2)
Debut: 12 Jun 1988 v Australia (Sydney). Number: 1126
Last game: 16 Jun 1988 v Fiji (Suva)
Caps: 2 (W:1, L:1)
Scoring: 0 Pts
Appearances: 1988:A2,Fj

Eric EVANS
Born: 1 February 1921 in Droylsden
Died: 12 January 1991 in Stockport
Clubs: Loughborough College, Sale (30), Old Aldwinians
Position: Hooker (29), Prop (1)
Debut: 3 Jan 1948 v Australia (Twickenham). Number: 775
Last game: 15 Mar 1958 (capt) v Scotland (Murrayfield)
Caps: 30 (W:17, D:3, L:10). As captain: 13 (W:9, D:2, L:2)
Scoring: 5T, 15 Pts
Appearances: 1948:A, 1950:W, 1951:I,F,S, 1952:SA,W,S,I,F, 1953:I,F,S, 1954:W,NZ,I,F, 1956:W*,I*,S*,F*, 1957:W*,I*,F*,S*, 1958:W*,A*,I*,F*,S*
Honours: Grand Slam: 1957 (capt). Championship: 1953, 1958 (capt)

Described in one of the first editions of Rugby World Magazine – in the early 1960s – as "the perfect captain" Eric Evans helped deliver long overdue success to the England rugby team.

When Evans' England started the 1957 Five Nations the Red Rose hadn't won a Grand Slam since 1928 but by the end victories over France, Wales, Scotland and Ireland put them in a group with the immortals. It took England 23 years to equal their feat.

"There are never any stars in a team," said Evans, giving an insight into his philosophy as a captain. "The team itself is the star.

"The worst thing any skipper can do is criticise a man while a game is on. He must encourage all the time, especially if the fellow is not doing well. If things go wrong, the captain must accept some of the blame in the eyes of the players."

Luckily for Evans things didn't go wrong too often in his tenure and he led England for a then record-equalling 13 matches. Under his captaincy England won nine of those 13 games.

A fitness fanatic, Evans captained England on his 37th birthday – in 1958 – even though a few years earlier he had been discarded due to his age by his beloved Lancashire.

First capped at prop – in 1948 against Australia – Evans was moved to hooker where he carved out his international reputation, honing his skills with Sale and Lancashire in a career that started with Old Aldwinians.

But it was his leadership skills that marked him out, the ability to draw the best performances from his players.

"There have been more skilful hookers, more powerful front-row forwards," The Independent's former rugby correspondent Geoffrey Nicholson wrote of Evans, "but there has been no pack leader more capable of keeping his men up to a fine point of concentration for a full 80 minutes, of charging them with his own fury in attack, of refusing to let them give way when they were under pressure.

"This is a quality which is virtually unobservable from the touchline, but the men who played under him acknowledged it, and England's International championships in 1957 and 1958 were largely his doing."

Evans died a few weeks short of his 70th birthday in 1991. His 30 caps on retirement only bettered – at the time – in the history of English rugby by Wavell Wakefield's 31.

In retirement, Evans was a Lancashire selector, and in the late Sixties and early Seventies he was an England selector.

Geoffrey William (Geoff) EVANS
Born: 10 December 1950 in Coventry
Educated: Bablake School
Clubs: Manchester University, Coventry (9)
Position: Centre (8), Replacement (1), Bench (1)
Debut: 18 Mar 1972 v Scotland (Murrayfield). Number: 1011
Last game: 16 Mar 1974 v Wales (Twickenham)
Caps: 9 (W:4, D:1, L:4)
Scoring: 1T, 1DG, 7 Pts
Appearances: 1972:S, 1973:W(r),F,S,NZ, 1974:S,I,F,W

Nevill Lloyd (Barney) EVANS
Born: 16 December 1908 in Lewisham
Educated: Eltham College
Clubs: Royal Naval Eng College Keyham (3), Devonport Services, Combined Services, Royal Navy (2)
Position: Prop (5)
Debut: 16 Jan 1932 v Wales (Swansea). Number: 692
Last game: 11 Feb 1933 v Ireland (Twickenham)
Caps: 5 (W:3, L:2)
Scoring: 0 Pts
Appearances: 1932:W,I,S, 1933:W,I

Arthur Macdonell EVANSON
Born: 15 September 1859 in Llansoy, near Usk, Wales
Died: 31 December 1934 in Dover
Educated: Oundle School
Clubs: Oxford University (3), Richmond (1)
Position: Three-quarter (4)
Debut: 16 Dec 1882 v Wales (Swansea) - 2C, 4 Pts. Number: 149
Last game: 1 Mar 1884 v Scotland (Blackheath)
Caps: 4 (W:4, L:0)
Scoring: 3C, 6 Pts
Appearances: 1883:W,I,S, 1884:S
Honours: Championship: 1883, 1884

Wyndham Alleyn Daubeny EVANSON
Born: Second quarter 1851 in Chepstow, Wales
Died: 30 October 1934 in Uckfield
Educated: St John's School
Clubs: The Owls, Civil Service (1), Richmond (4)
Position: Half-Back (4), Three-quarter (1)
Debut: 8 Mar 1875 v Scotland (Raeburn Place). Number: 67
Last game: 24 Mar 1879 v Ireland (The Oval) - 1T, 1 Pt
Caps: 5 (W:1, D:3, L:1)
Scoring: 1T, 1 Pt
Appearances: 1875:S, 1877:S, 1878:S, 1879:S,I

Frank EVERSHED
Born: 6 September 1866 in Winshill, Staffs
Died: 29 June 1954 in Winshill, Staffs
Educated: Burton-on-Trent GS, Amersham Hall College
Clubs: Oxford University, Burton (6), East Cheam, Blackheath (4)
Position: Forward (10)
Debut: 16 Feb 1889 v New Zealand Natives (Blackheath) - 1T, 1 Pt. Number: 200
Last game: 4 Mar 1893 v Scotland (Headingley)
Caps: 10 (W:7, L:3)
Scoring: 4T, 7 Pts
Appearances: 1889:M, 1890:W,S,I, 1892:W,I,S, 1893:W,I,S
Honours: Championship: 1892

Bryan Braithwaite EXLEY
Born: 30 November 1927 in Wetherby
Educated: Sedbergh School
Clubs: RAF, Headingley (1)
Position: No 8 (1)
Debut: 15 Jan 1949 v Wales (Cardiff). Number: 789
Caps: 1 (W:0, L:1)
Scoring: 0 Pts
Appearances: 1949:W

Walter Charles Townsend (Wallace) EYRES
Born: First quarter 1895 in Barton Regis
Died: Details unknown
Clubs: United Services, Richmond (1), Royal Navy
Position: No 8 (1)
Debut: 12 Feb 1927 v Ireland (Twickenham). Number: 621
Caps: 1 (W:1, L:0)
Scoring: 0 Pts
Appearances: 1927:I

Barney Evans

D E F

F

FAGAN, Arthur Robert St Leger
FAIRBROTHER, Keith Eli
FAITHFULL, Charles Kirke Tindall
FALLAS, Herbert
FARRELL, Andrew, OBE
FEGAN, John Herbert Crangle
FERNANDES, Charles Walker Luis
FIDLER, John Howard
FIDLER, Robert John
FIELD, Edwin
FIELDING, Keith John
FINCH, Richard Tanner
FINLAN, John Frank
FINLINSON, Horace William
FINNEY, Sir Stephen, KBE
FIRTH, Frederick
FLATMAN, David Luke
FLETCHER, Nigel Corbet, OBE
FLETCHER, Thomas
FLETCHER, William Robert Badger
FLOOD, Tobias Gerald
FOOKES, Ernest Faber
FORD, Peter John
FORREST, John William
FORREST, Reginald
FORRESTER, James
FOULDS, Robert Thompson
FOWLER, Frank Dashwood
FOWLER, Howard
FOWLER, R Henry
FOX, Francis Hugh
FRANCIS, Thomas Egerton Seymour, OBE
FRANKCOM, Geoffrey Peter
FRASER, Sir Edward Cleather, KBE
FRASER, George William Frederick
FREAKES, Hubert Dainton
FREEMAN, Harold
FRENCH, Raymond James
FRESHWATER, Perry Thomas
FRY, Henry Arthur
FRY, Thomas William
FULLER, Herbert George

Perry Freshwater

Arthur Robert St Leger FAGAN
Born: 24 November 1862 in Calcutta, India
Died: 15 March 1930 in Highgate
Clubs: Guy's Hospital, United Hospitals (1), Richmond
Position: Three-quarter (1)
Debut: 5 Feb 1887 v Ireland (Lansdowne Road). Number: 194
Caps: 1 (W:0, L:1)
Scoring: 0 Pts
Appearances: 1887:I

Keith Eli FAIRBROTHER
Born: 8 May 1944 in Coventry
Educated: Caludon Castle School
Clubs: Stoke Old Boys, Nuneaton, Coventry (12), Leigh RL
Position: Prop (12), Bench (5)
Debut: 8 Feb 1969 v Ireland (Lansdowne Road). Number: 972
Last game: 27 Feb 1971 v France (Twickenham)
Caps: 12 (W:5, D:1, L:6)
Scoring: 0 Pts
Appearances: 1969:I,F,S,W,SA, 1970:I,W,S,F, 1971:W,I,F

Charles Kirke Tindall (Chubby) FAITHFULL
Born: 6 January 1903 in Fareham
Died: 8 August 1979 in Farnham
Educated: Wellington College
Clubs: Devonport Services, United Services, Halifax, Harlequins (3), Combined Services, Duke of Wellington's Regt, Army
Position: Prop (3)
Debut: 9 Feb 1924 v Ireland (Belfast). Number: 591
Last game: 20 Mar 1926 v Scotland (Twickenham)
Caps: 3 (W:2, L:1)
Scoring: 0 Pts
Appearances: 1924:I, 1926:F,S
Honours: Championship: 1924

Herbert FALLAS
Born: Details unknown
Died: Details unknown
Clubs: Wakefield Trinity (1)
Position: Three-quarter (1)
Debut: 4 Feb 1884 v Ireland (Lansdowne Road). Number: 164
Caps: 1 (W:1, L:0)
Scoring: 0 Pts
Appearances: 1884:I
Honours: Championship: 1884

Andrew (Andy) FARRELL OBE
Born: 30 May 1975 in Wigan
Clubs: Orrell St James RL, Wigan RL, Saracens (3)
Position: Centre (3)
Debut: 3 Feb 2007 v Scotland (Twickenham). Number: 1278
Last game: 24 Feb 2007 v Ireland (Croke Park)
Caps: 3 (W:2, L:1)
Scoring: 0 Pts
Appearances: 2007:S,It,I

After rugby union turned professional in 1995 a number of players who had defected to rugby league returned home. Welsh players like Scott Quinnell, Jonathan Davies, Allan Bateman and Dai Young came back to the 15-a-side code. And once union found its feet as a professional sport the boot was placed on the other foot as union clubs starting arriving at their league rivals with their cheque book open.

In the late 1990s and early 2000s Andy Farrell was quite simply the best rugby league player on the planet. Farrell won everything that British rugby league had to offer and stood above the game for a number of years like a colossus. He was ever present in the Great Britain side from 1993, playing for Wigan in his entire career that brought every domestic honour. In 1996 he became the youngest-ever captain of the British rugby league team at the age of 21 years, four months.

In 2004 Farrell – who is a superb goalkicker – won the rare double of the Golden Boot, awarded to the world's leading player, and Man of Steel, which is awarded to the best player in the British Super League.

Farrell arrived in union – in 2005 – as part of an innovative deal between his club Saracens and the RFU, both contributing to his wages, and with the objective of helping

Andy Farrell

England defend their world title in 2007. But he kicked off his union career with a series of horrendous injuries that kept him out of the game for the first year of his contract.

Those injuries meant that Farrell had to wait until the 2007 Six Nations to make his union debut, in the 42-20 victory over Scotland. But injury struck again before the end of the tournament and although Farrell was able to help his club Saracens revive their Guinness Premiership fortunes he missed the final two rounds of the Six Nations.

The most successful cross-coder, Jonathan Davies, is convinced of Farrell's abilities to play both league and union at the highest level.

"I played with Andy in his first rugby league Test when he was 18 and he was a special player," said Davies. "I have no doubt Andy Farrell will be a success in rugby union because he is a great player.

"He is a very big, talented guy with wonderful handling skills and he is a superb footballer.

"Andy is a great passer, a tremendous kicker and he is in that Lawrence Dallaglio mould – dynamic with the ball in hand as well."

At the start of 2005 he was awarded an OBE in recognition of his services to the 13-man code.

John Herbert Crangle FEGAN

Born: 20 January 1872 in Old Charlton, Kent
Died: 26 July 1949 in Hemel Hempstead
Educated: Blackheath Prep School
Clubs: Cambridge University, Blackheath (3)
Position: Wing (3)
Debut: 5 Jan 1895 v Wales (Swansea). Number: 275
Last game: 9 Mar 1895 v Scotland (Richmond)
Caps: 3 (W:2, L:1)
Scoring: 1T, 3 Pts
Appearances: 1895:W,I,S

Charles Walker Luis FERNANDES

Born: 3 April 1857 in Wakefield
Died: 12 August 1944 in Thirsk, Yorks
Educated: Rossall School
Clubs: Wakefield, Leeds (3)
Position: Forward (3)
Debut: 5 Feb 1881 v Ireland (Manchester). Number: 132
Last game: 19 Mar 1881 v Scotland (Raeburn Place)
Caps: 3 (W:2, D:1, L:0)
Scoring: 1T, 1 Pt
Appearances: 1881:I,W,S

John Howard FIDLER

Born: 16 September 1948 in Cheltenham
Clubs: Cheltenham, Gloucester (4)
Position: Lock (4)
Debut: 30 May 1981 v Argentina (Buenos Aires). Number: 1070
Last game: 9 Jun 1984 v South Africa (Johannesburg)
Caps: 4 (W:1, D:1, L:2)
Scoring: 0 Pts
Appearances: 1981:Ar1,Ar2, 1984:SA1,SA2

Robert John (Rob) FIDLER

Born: 21 September 1974 in Cheltenham
Educated: Cheltenham College
Clubs: Gloucester (2), Bath
Position: Lock (2)
Debut: 27 Jun 1998 v New Zealand (Auckland). Number: 1207
Last game: 4 Jul 1998 v South Africa (Cape Town)
Caps: 2 (W:0, L:2)
Scoring: 0 Pts
Appearances: 1998:NZ2,SA

Rob Fidler

Edwin FIELD

Born: 17 December 1871 in Hampstead
Died: 9 January 1947 in Bromley
Educated: Clifton College
Clubs: Cambridge University, Middlesex Wanderers (2), Richmond
Position: Full-back (2)
Debut: 7 Jan 1893 v Wales (Cardiff). Number: 251
Last game: 4 Feb 1893 v Ireland (Lansdowne Road)
Caps: 2 (W:1, L:1)
Scoring: 0 Pts
Appearances: 1893:W,I

Keith John FIELDING

Born: 8 July 1949 in Birmingham
Educated: King Edward's School
Clubs: Loughborough College (1), Moseley (9)
Position: Wing (10)
Debut: 8 Feb 1969 v Ireland (Lansdowne Road). Number: 973
Last game: 18 Mar 1972 v Scotland (Murrayfield)
Caps: 10 (W:4, L:6)
Scoring: 1T, 3 Pts
Appearances: 1969:I,F,S,SA, 1970:I,F, 1972:W,I,F,S

Richard Tanner FINCH

Born: Third quarter 1857 in Kensington
Died: 12 January 1921 in Seaton
Educated: Sherborne School
Clubs: Cambridge University (1), St George's Hospital, Richmond
Position: Half-Back (1)
Debut: 28 Feb 1880 v Scotland (Manchester). Number: 129
Caps: 1 (W:1, L:0)
Scoring: 0 Pts
Appearances: 1880:S

John Frank FINLAN

Born: 9 September 1941 in Warwick
Educated: Saltley GS
Clubs: Coventry, Moseley (13)
Position: Fly-half (13), Bench (5)
Debut: 11 Feb 1967 v Ireland (Lansdowne Road). Number: 954
Last game: 6 Jan 1973 v New Zealand (Twickenham)
Caps: 13 (W:4, D:2, L:7)
Scoring: 3DG, 9 Pts
Appearances: 1967:I,F,S,W,NZ, 1968:W,I, 1969:I,F,S,W, 1970:F, 1973:NZ

Horace William FINLINSON

Born: 9 June 1871 in Bedford
Died: 31 October 1956 in Bedford
Educated: Bedford Modern School
Clubs: Blair Lodge, Blackheath (3)
Position: Forward (3)
Debut: 5 Jan 1895 v Wales (Swansea). Number: 276
Last game: 9 Mar 1895 v Scotland (Richmond)
Caps: 3 (W:2, L:1)
Scoring: 0 Pts
Appearances: 1895:W,I,S

Sir Stephen FINNEY, KBE
Born: 8 September 1852 in Marylebone
Died: 1 March 1924 in Kensington
Educated: Clifton College
Clubs: Royal Indian Eng College (2)
Position: Half-Back (2)
Debut: 5 Feb 1872 v Scotland (The Oval) - 1T, 1 Pt. Number: 26
Last game: 3 Mar 1873 v Scotland (Glasgow)
Caps: 2 (W:1, D:1, L:0)
Scoring: 1T, 1 Pt
Appearances: 1872:S, 1873:S

Frederick FIRTH
Born: 1870 in Cleckheaton, Yorks
Died: February 1936 in Olneyville, USA
Clubs: Halifax (3)
Position: Wing (3)
Debut: 6 Jan 1894 v Wales (Birkenhead Park). Number: 262
Last game: 17 Mar 1894 v Scotland (Raeburn Place)
Caps: 3 (W:1, L:2)
Scoring: 0 Pts
Appearances: 1894:W,I,S

David Luke FLATMAN
Born: 21 January 1980 in Maidstone
Educated: Dulwich College
Clubs: Saracens (8), Newbury, Bath
Position: Prop (1), Replacement (7), Bench (2)
Debut: 17 Jun 2000 (rep) v South Africa (Pretoria). Number: 1219
Last game: 22 Jun 2002 v Argentina (Buenos Aires)
Caps: 8 (W:7, L:1)
Scoring: 0 Pts
Appearances: 2000:SA1(r),SA2(r),A(r),Ar(r), 2001:F(r),C2(r),US(r), 2002:Ar
Honours: Championship: 2001

Nigel Corbet FLETCHER, OBE
Born: 13 August 1877 in Pancras, London
Died: 21 December 1951 in Hampstead, London
Educated: Merchant Taylors' School
Clubs: Old Merchant Taylors' (4), Cambridge University, University College Hospital
Position: Forward (4)
Debut: 5 Jan 1901 v Wales (Cardiff). Number: 356
Last game: 21 Mar 1903 v Scotland (Richmond)
Caps: 4 (W:0, L:4)
Scoring: 0 Pts
Appearances: 1901:W,I,S, 1903:S

Thomas FLETCHER
Born: 1874 in Seaton, Cumberland
Died: 28 August 1950 in Cockermouth
Educated: Northside School
Clubs: Seaton (1)
Position: Centre (1)
Debut: 9 Jan 1897 v Wales (Newport). Number: 300
Caps: 1 (W:0, L:1)
Scoring: 0 Pts
Appearances: 1897:W

David Flatman

William Robert Badger FLETCHER
Born: 10 December 1851
Died: 20 April 1895 in Kensington
Educated: Marlborough School
Clubs: Marlborough Nomads (2), Oxford University, Blackheath
Position: Forward (2)
Debut: 3 Mar 1873 v Scotland (Glasgow). Number: 37
Last game: 8 Mar 1875 v Scotland (Raeburn Place)
Caps: 2 (W:0, D:2, L:0)
Scoring: 0 Pts
Appearances: 1873:S, 1875:S

Toby Flood

Tobias Gerald (Toby) FLOOD
Born: 8 August 1985 in Morpeth
Educated: King's School
Clubs: Alnwick, Morpeth, Darlington Mowden Park, Newcastle (4)
Position: Replacement Fly-half (4), Bench (2)
Debut: 11 Nov 2006 (rep) v Argentina (Twickenham) - 1PG, 3 Pts. Number: 1277
Last game: 10 Feb 2007 (rep) v Italy (Twickenham)
Caps: 4 (W:2, L:2)
Scoring: 1PG, 3 Pts
Appearances: 2006:Ar(r),SA2(r), 2007:S(r),It(r)

Ernest Faber FOOKES
Born: 31 May 1874 in Waverley, New Zealand
Died: 3 March 1948 in New Plymouth, New Zealand
Educated: New Plymouth BHS (NZ), Owen's College
Clubs: Manchester University, Halifax, Sowerby Bridge (10)
Position: Wing (10)
Debut: 4 Jan 1896 v Wales (Blackheath) - 2T, 6 Pts. Number: 283
Last game: 11 Mar 1899 v Scotland (Blackheath)
Caps: 10 (W:3, L:7)
Scoring: 5T, 15 Pts
Appearances: 1896:W,I,S, 1897:W,I,S, 1898:I,W, 1899:I,S

Peter John FORD

Born: 2 May 1932 in Gloucester
Educated: Central Modern School
Clubs: Gloucester (4), RAF
Position: Flanker (4)
Debut: 18 Jan 1964 v Wales (Twickenham). Number: 921
Last game: 21 Mar 1964 v Scotland (Murrayfield)
Caps: 4 (W:1, D:1, L:2)
Scoring: 0 Pts
Appearances: 1964:W,I,F,S

John William (Jeff) FORREST

Born: Second quarter 1903 in Barnet
Died: 18 March 1963 in Bath
Clubs: United Services, Royal Navy (10), Combined Services
Position: Lock (10)
Debut: 18 Jan 1930 v Wales (Cardiff). Number: 656
Last game: 17 Mar 1934 v Scotland (Twickenham)
Caps: 10 (W:4, D:2, L:4)
Scoring: 1C, 2 Pts
Appearances: 1930:W,I,F,S, 1931:W,I,S,F, 1934:I,S
Honours: Championship: 1930, 1934

Reginald FORREST

Born: 12 May 1878 in Bristol
Died: 11 April 1903 in Minehead
Educated: Christ's School
Clubs: Wellington (2), Blackheath (4), Taunton
Position: Wing (6)
Debut: 7 Jan 1899 v Wales (Swansea). Number: 328
Last game: 21 Mar 1903 v Scotland (Richmond) - 1T, 3 Pts
Caps: 6 (W:2, D:1, L:3)
Scoring: 1T, 3 Pts
Appearances: 1899:W, 1900:S, 1902:I,S, 1903:I,S

James FORRESTER

Born: 9 February 1981 in Oxford
Educated: St Edward's School
Clubs: Bicester, Gloucester (2)
Position: Replacement Back-row (2)
Debut: 5 Feb 2005 (rep) v Wales (Cardiff). Number: 1261
Last game: 26 Nov 2005 (rep) v Samoa (Twickenham)
Caps: 2 (W:1, L:1)
Scoring: 0 Pts
Appearances: 2005:W(r),Sm(r)

Robert Thompson FOULDS

Born: 27 April 1906 in West Derby
Died: 1987 in Uckfield
Educated: King William's School
Clubs: Birmingham, Furness, Moseley, Waterloo (2)
Position: No 8 (2)
Debut: 19 Jan 1929 v Wales (Twickenham). Number: 637
Last game: 9 Feb 1929 v Ireland (Twickenham)
Caps: 2 (W:1, L:1)
Scoring: 0 Pts
Appearances: 1929:W,I

James Forrester

Frank Dashwood FOWLER

Born: 16 August 1855 in Newbury
Died: 14 November 1940 in Newbury
Educated: Cheltenham College
Clubs: Royal Indian Eng College (1), Manchester (1)
Position: No 8 (2)
Debut: 4 Mar 1878 v Scotland (The Oval). Number: 96
Last game: 10 Mar 1879 v Scotland (Raeburn Place)
Caps: 2 (W:0, D:2, L:0)
Scoring: 0 Pts
Appearances: 1878:S, 1879:S

Howard FOWLER

Born: 20 October 1857 in Tottenham
Died: 6 May 1934 in Burnham-on-Sea
Educated: Clifton College
Clubs: Oxford University (1), Walthamstow (2), Blackheath
Position: Forward (3)
Debut: 4 Mar 1878 v Scotland (The Oval). Number: 97
Last game: 19 Mar 1881 v Scotland (Raeburn Place)
Caps: 3 (W:1, D:2, L:0)
Scoring: 0 Pts
Appearances: 1878:S, 1881:W,S

R Henry FOWLER

Born: Details unknown
Died: Details unknown
Clubs: Leeds (1)
Position: Forward (1)
Debut: 5 Feb 1877 v Ireland (The Oval). Number: 87
Caps: 1 (W:1, L:0)
Scoring: 0 Pts
Appearances: 1877:I

Francis Hugh FOX

Born: 12 June 1863 in Wellington
Died: 28 May 1952 in Taunton
Educated: Marlborough School
Clubs: Marlborough Nomads, Wellington (2)
Position: Half-Back (2)
Debut: 15 Feb 1890 v Wales (Dewsbury). Number: 210
Last game: 1 Mar 1890 v Scotland (Raeburn Place)
Caps: 2 (W:1, L:1)
Scoring: 0 Pts
Appearances: 1890:W,S

Thomas Egerton Seymour (Tim) FRANCIS, OBE

Born: 21 November 1902 in Uitenhage, South Africa
Died: 24 February 1969 in Bulawayo, Rhodesia
Educated: Tonbridge School
Clubs: Cambridge University (2), Blackheath (2)
Position: Centre (4)
Debut: 16 Jan 1926 v Wales (Cardiff). Number: 607
Last game: 20 Mar 1926 v Scotland (Twickenham)
Caps: 4 (W:1, D:1, L:2)
Scoring: 4C, 8 Pts
Appearances: 1926:W,I,F,S

Geoffrey Peter FRANKCOM

Born: 5 April 1942 in Bathavon
Educated: King Edward's School
Clubs: Cambridge University (4), Bedford, Headingley, Bath, RAF
Position: Centre (4)
Debut: 16 Jan 1965 v Wales (Cardiff). Number: 927
Last game: 20 Mar 1965 v Scotland (Twickenham)
Caps: 4 (W:1, D:1, L:2)
Scoring: 0 Pts
Appearances: 1965:W,I,F,S

Sir Edward Cleather FRASER, KBE

Born: 1853
Died: 15 October 1927 in Erpingham, Norfolk
Educated: Blackheath Prep School
Clubs: Oxford University (1), Blackheath
Position: Forward (1)
Debut: 15 Feb 1875 v Ireland (The Oval).
Number: 58
Caps: 1 (W:1, L:0)
Scoring: 0 Pts
Appearances: 1875:I

George William Frederick FRASER

Born: 15 September 1877 in Fulham
Died: 20 August 1950 in Clewer Within, Berks
Educated: Godolphin School
Clubs: Richmond (5)
Position: Forward (5)
Debut: 11 Jan 1902 v Wales (Blackheath).
Number: 374
Last game: 14 Feb 1903 v Ireland (Lansdowne Road)
Caps: 5 (W:2, L:3)
Scoring: 0 Pts
Appearances: 1902:W,I,S, 1903:W,I

Hubert Dainton (Trilby) FREAKES

Born: 2 February 1914 in South Africa
Died: Killed in action in March 1942 in North Cotswolds
Educated: Maritzburg College
Clubs: Rhodesia University, Oxford University(3), Harlequins
Position: Full-back (3)
Debut: 15 Jan 1938 v Wales (Cardiff) - 1C, 2 Pts.
Number: 738
Last game: 11 Feb 1939 v Ireland (Twickenham)
Caps: 3 (W:1, L:2)
Scoring: 1C, 2 Pts
Appearances: 1938:W, 1939:W,I

Harold FREEMAN

Born: 15 January 1850
Died: 15 July 1916 in Fitzroy Square, London
Educated: Marlborough School
Clubs: Oxford University, Marlborough Nomads (3)
Position: Three-quarter (3)
Debut: 5 Feb 1872 v Scotland (The Oval) - 1DG, 3 Pts.
Number: 27
Last game: 23 Feb 1874 v Scotland (The Oval) - 1DG, 3 Pts
Caps: 3 (W:2, D:1, L:0)
Scoring: 2DG, 6 Pts
Appearances: 1872:S, 1873:S, 1874:S

Raymond James (Ray) FRENCH

Born: 23 December 1939 in St Helens
Educated: Crowley School
Clubs: Leeds University, St Helens (4), St Helens RL
Position: Lock (4)
Debut: 21 Jan 1961 v Wales (Cardiff).
Number: 895
Last game: 18 Mar 1961 v Scotland (Twickenham)
Caps: 4 (W:1, D:1, L:2)
Scoring: 0 Pts
Appearances: 1961:W,I,F,S

Perry Freshwater

Perry Thomas FRESHWATER

Born: 27 July 1973 in Wellington, New Zealand
Educated: Wellington College
Clubs: Wellington (NZ), Leicester, Coventry, Rugby, Perpignan (FR,7)
Position: Prop (4), Replacement (3)
Debut: 26 Nov 2005 (rep) v Samoa (Twickenham).
Number: 1266
Last game: 24 Feb 2007 v Ireland (Croke Park)
Caps: 7 (W:3, L:4)
Scoring: 0 Pts
Appearances: 2005:Sm(r), 2006:S(r),I(r),Ar, 2007:S,It,I

Henry Arthur FRY

Born: 22 December 1910 in West Derby
Died: 3 November 1977 in Formby, Lancs
Educated: Liverpool College
Clubs: Liverpool (3), Fylde, Waterloo, Rosslyn Park, Army
Position: Flanker (3)
Debut: 20 Jan 1934 v Wales (Cardiff). Number: 706
Last game: 17 Mar 1934 v Scotland (Twickenham)
Caps: 3 (W:3, L:0)
Scoring: 2T, 6 Pts
Appearances: 1934:W,I,S
Honours: Championship: 1934

Thomas William FRY

Born: Third quarter 1859 in Greenwich
Died: In Canada, details unknown
Clubs: Queen's House (3)
Position: Full-back (3)
Debut: 30 Jan 1880 v Ireland (Lansdowne Road).
Number: 121
Last game: 19 Feb 1881 v Wales (Blackheath)
Caps: 3 (W:3, L:0)
Scoring: 1T, 1 Pt
Appearances: 1880:I,S, 1881:W

Herbert George FULLER

Born: 4 October 1856 in Bath
Died: 2 January 1896 in Streatham, London
Educated: Christ's College
Clubs: Cambridge University (6), Bath
Position: Forward (6)
Debut: 6 Feb 1882 v Ireland (Lansdowne Road).
Number: 142
Last game: 5 Jan 1884 v Wales (Leeds)
Caps: 6 (W:4, D:1, L:1)
Scoring: 0 Pts
Appearances: 1882:I,S, 1883:W,I,S, 1884:W
Honours: Championship: 1883, 1884

G

GADNEY, Bernard Cecil
GAMLIN, Herbert Temlett
GARDNER, Ernest Robert
GARDNER, Herbert Prescott
GARFORTH, Darren James
GARNETT, Harry Wharfedale Tennant
GAVINS, Michael Neil
GAY, David John
GENT, David Robert
GENTH, Jacob Schorer M
GEORGE, James Thomas
GERAGHTY, Shane Joseph J
GERRARD, Ronald Anderson
GIBBS, George Anthony
GIBBS, John Clifford
GIBBS, Nigel
GIBLIN, Lyndhurst Falkiner
GIBSON, Arthur Sumner
GIBSON, Charles Osborne Provis
GIBSON, George Ralph
GIBSON, Thomas Alexander
GILBERT, Frederick George
GILBERT, R
GILES, James Leonard
GITTINGS, William John
GLOVER, Peter Bernard
GODFRAY, Reginald Edmund
GODWIN, Herbert O
GOMARSALL, Andrew Charles Thomas, MBE
GOODE, Andrew James
GOTLEY, Anthony Lefroy Henniker
GRAHAM, David
GRAHAM, Harry James
GRAHAM, John Duncan George
GRAY, Arthur
GRAYSON, Paul James, MBE
GREEN, John
GREEN, Joseph Fletcher
GREEN, William Robert
GREENING. Philip Bradley Thomas
GREENSTOCK, Nicholas James Jeremy
GREENWELL, John Henry
GREENWOOD, John Eric
GREENWOOD, John Richard Heaton
GREENWOOD, William John Heaton, MBE
GREG, Walter
GREGORY, Gordon George
GREGORY, John Arthur
GREWCOCK, Daniel Jonathan, MBE
GRYLLS, William Mitchell
GUEST, Richard Heaton
GUILLEMARD, Arthur George
GUMMER, Charles Henry Alexander
GUNNER, Charles Richard
GURDON, Charles
GURDON, Edward Temple
GUSCOTT, Jeremy Clayton, MBE

Jeremy Guscott

Bernard Cecil GADNEY

Born: 16 July 1909 in Oxford
Died: 14 November 2000 in Ipswich
Educated: Dragon School, Stowe College
Clubs: Richmond, Leicester (13), Headingley (1)
Position: Scrum-half (14)
Debut: 13 Feb 1932 v Ireland (Lansdowne Road). Number: 694
Last game: 15 Jan 1938 v Wales (Cardiff)
Caps: 14 (W:9, D:1, L:4). As captain: 8 (W:5, D:1, L:2)
Scoring: 1T, 3 Pts
Appearances: 1932:I,S, 1933:I,S, 1934:W*,I*,S*, 1935:S*, 1936:NZ*,W*,I*,S*, 1937:S, 1938:W
Honours: Championship: 1934 (capt), 1937

In the history of English rugby there have only been six victories over the New Zealand All Blacks and only once have they won in the Land of the Long White Cloud.

The first England v New Zealand game took place in 1905 and 31 years later the first win arrived, 13-0 at Twickenham.

That England side of 1936 was full of heroes, not least their captain Bernard Gadney.

A scrum-half despite his stature (he was 6ft 2in), Gadney was a teacher at Winchester House prep school in Northamptonshire and The Malsis School, playing his club rugby for Leicester.

On that famous day at Twickenham in 1936 Gadney scored a try, sometimes forgotten, as the memories of that match are dominated by Prince Obolensky's length of the field score, a move that was started by Gadney.

Obolensky has taken the headlines ever since – and quite rightly – but Gadney's performance behind his pack impressed. "When England heeled and Gadney smashed away on his own," wrote one correspondent, "we saw that here was a confident, aggressive team, with a captain who knew his own mind and could set his men an example."

He finally won 14 caps for England between 1932 and 1938, captaining them on eight occasions, a run that included the Triple Crown-winning season in 1934.

He was a fitness fanatic and legend has it that Gadney used to jump off the bus to Twickenham 10 stops short and run the rest of the way to the ground.

Gadney was a key figure in the development of the Leicester Tigers – after briefly playing for Richmond – into the world-recognised side it is today. While with Leicester Gadney played 170 games for the club, scoring 63 tries, and was named in the Tigers' "greatest" team of the 20th century.

Leicester chief executive Peter Wheeler added: "He was the first Leicester player to captain England and one of the most influential players ever to wear a Tigers shirt."

Gadney turned down many offers from league clubs to retire from the game in 1938, before taking up post of headmaster at Malsis School.

Gadney's was the first name on the Wall of Fame at Twickenham, and tributes flowed in when he died in November 2000, aged 91.

At that time he was both the oldest surviving England international player and international captain in the world.

Rugby Football Union president Budge Rogers said: "Bernard Gadney was an outstanding scrum-half and England captain. He will be greatly missed."

Bernard Gadney

Herbert Temlett (Octopus) GAMLIN

Born: 12 February 1878 in Wellington, Somerset
Died: 12 July 1937 in Pylford Bridge, Surrey
Educated: Wellington College
Clubs: Wellington, Devonport Albion (11), Blackheath (4)
Position: Full-back (15)
Debut: 7 Jan 1899 v Wales (Swansea). Number: 329
Last game: 19 Mar 1904 v Scotland (Inverleith)
Caps: 15 (W:4, D:2, L:9)
Scoring: 1PG, 3 Pts
Appearances: 1899:W,S, 1900:W,I,S, 1901:S, 1902:W,I,S, 1903:W,I,S, 1904:W,I,S

Ernest Robert GARDNER

Born: 6 October 1886 in Cardiff, Wales
Died: 26 January 1954
Clubs: Devonport Services (9), Royal Navy (1)
Position: Hooker (10)
Debut: 15 Jan 1921 v Wales (Twickenham). Number: 567
Last game: 2 Apr 1923 v France (Stade Colombes)
Caps: 10 (W:8, D:1, L:1)
Scoring: 1T, 3 Pts
Appearances: 1921:W,I,S, 1922:W,I,F, 1923:W,I,S,F
Honours: Grand Slam: 1923. Championship: 1921

Herbert Prescott GARDNER

Born: 1855
Died: 1938 in Australia
Educated: Wellington College
Clubs: Richmond (1)
Position: Forward (1)
Debut: 11 Mar 1878 v Ireland (Lansdowne Road) - 1T, 1 Pt. Number: 107
Caps: 1 (W:1, L:0)
Scoring: 1T, 1 Pt
Appearances: 1878:I

Darren James GARFORTH

Born: 9 April 1966 in Coventry
Educated: Binley Park School
Clubs: Coventry Saracens, Leicester (25), Nuneaton
Position: Prop (20), Replacement (5), Bench (4)
Debut: 15 Mar 1997 (rep) v Wales (Cardiff). Number: 1176
Last game: 18 Mar 2000 v Italy (Rome)
Caps: 25 (W:15, D:1, L:9)
Scoring: 0 Pts
Appearances: 1997:W(r),Ar1,Ar2,A,NZ1,SA,NZ2, 1998:F,W(r),S,I,H,It,A,SA, 1999:S,I,F,W,A,C(r),It(r),NZ(r),Fj, 2000:It
Honours: Championship: 2000

Harry Wharfedale Tennant GARNETT

Born: 16 September 1851 in Otley, Yorks
Died: 27 April 1928 in Wharfedale
Educated: Blackheath Prep School
Clubs: Bradford (1)
Position: Forward (1)
Debut: 5 Mar 1877 v Scotland (Raeburn Place). Number: 92
Caps: 1 (W:0, L:1)
Scoring: 0 Pts
Appearances: 1877:S

Michael Neil (Mike) GAVINS

Born: 14 October 1934 in Leeds
Educated: Roundhay School
Clubs: Old Roundhegians, Leeds University, Loughborough College, Leicester (1), Moseley, Middlesbrough
Position: Full-back (1)
Debut: 21 Jan 1961 v Wales (Cardiff). Number: 896
Caps: 1 (W:0, L:1)
Scoring: 0 Pts
Appearances: 1961:W

David John GAY

Born: 10 March 1948 in Bath
Educated: Oldfield Boys School, Bath Technical College
Clubs: Bath (4), Harlequins
Position: No 8 (4)
Debut: 20 Jan 1968 v Wales (Twickenham). Number: 963
Last game: 16 Mar 1968 v Scotland (Murrayfield)
Caps: 4 (W:1, D:2, L:1)
Scoring: 0 Pts
Appearances: 1968:W,I,F,S

G H I

David Robert (Dai) GENT
Born: 9 January 1883 in Llandovery, Wales
Died: 16 January 1964 in Hellingly, Sussex
Educated: St Paul's College
Clubs: Gloucester (5)
Position: Fly-half (3), Half-Back (2)
Debut: 2 Dec 1905 v New Zealand (Crystal Palace). Number: 414
Last game: 12 Feb 1910 v Ireland (Twickenham)
Caps: 5 (W:1, D:1, L:3)
Scoring: 0 Pts
Appearances: 1905:NZ, 1906:W,I, 1910:W,I
Honours: Championship: 1910

Jacob Schorer M GENTH
Born: Third quarter 1849 in Charlton
Died: Details unknown
Clubs: Manchester (2)
Position: Forward (2)
Debut: 23 Feb 1874 v Scotland (The Oval). Number: 51
Last game: 8 Mar 1875 v Scotland (Raeburn Place)
Caps: 2 (W:1, D:1, L:0)
Scoring: 0 Pts
Appearances: 1874:S, 1875:S

James Thomas GEORGE
Born: 24 August 1918 in Falmouth
Clubs: Falmouth (3)
Position: Lock (3)
Debut: 15 Mar 1947 v Scotland (Twickenham). Number: 768
Last game: 12 Feb 1949 v Ireland (Lansdowne Road)
Caps: 3 (W:2, L:1)
Scoring: 0 Pts
Appearances: 1947:S,F, 1949:I

Shane Joseph J GERAGHTY
Born: 12 August 1986 in Coventry
Educated: Bablake School, Colston's College
Clubs: London Irish (1)
Position: Replacement Fly-half (1)
Debut: 11 Mar 2007 (rep) v France (Twickenham) - 1C, 1P, 5 Pts. Number: 1283
Caps: 1 (W:1, L:0)
Scoring: 1C, 1P, 5 Pts
Appearances: 2007:F(r)

Ronald Anderson GERRARD
Born: 26 January 1912 in Hong Kong
Died: Killed in action in 1943 near Tripoli, Libya
Educated: Taunton School
Clubs: Bath (14)
Position: Centre (14)
Debut: 2 Jan 1932 v South Africa (Twickenham). Number: 686
Last game: 21 Mar 1936 v Scotland (Twickenham)
Caps: 14 (W:8, D:1, L:5)
Scoring: 0 Pts
Appearances: 1932:SA,W,I,S, 1933:W,I,S, 1934:W,I,S, 1936:NZ,W,I,S
Honours: Championship: 1934

Darren Garforth

George Anthony GIBBS
Born: 31 March 1920 in Italy
Educated: Clifton College
Clubs: Bristol (2), Northern
Position: Prop (2)
Debut: 19 Apr 1947 v France (Twickenham). Number: 772
Last game: 14 Feb 1948 v Ireland (Twickenham)
Caps: 2 (W:1, L:1)
Scoring: 0 Pts
Appearances: 1947:F, 1948:I

John Clifford GIBBS
Born: 10 March 1902 in Bromley
Died: 11 January 1998 in Thanet
Educated: Queen's College
Clubs: Harlequins (7)
Position: Wing (7)
Debut: 3 Jan 1925 v New Zealand (Twickenham). Number: 595
Last game: 2 Apr 1927 v France (Stade Colombes)
Caps: 7 (W:4, L:3)
Scoring: 2T, 6 Pts
Appearances: 1925:NZ,W, 1926:F, 1927:W,I,S,F

Nigel GIBBS
Born: 24 September 1922 in Italy
Educated: Clifton College
Clubs: Oxford University, Guildford & Godalming, Bristol, Harlequins (2)
Position: Full-back (2)
Debut: 20 Mar 1954 v Scotland (Murrayfield) - 2C, 4 Pts. Number: 844
Last game: 10 Apr 1954 v France (Stade Colombes)
Caps: 2 (W:1, L:1)
Scoring: 2C, 4 Pts
Appearances: 1954:S,F

Lyndhurst Falkiner GIBLIN
Born: 29 November 1872 in Hobart, Tasmania, Australia
Died: 1 March 1951 in Hobart, Tasmania, Australia
Educated: Hutchin's School
Clubs: London University, Blackheath (2), Cambridge University (1)
Position: Forward (3)
Debut: 4 Jan 1896 v Wales (Blackheath). Number: 284
Last game: 13 Mar 1897 v Scotland (Manchester)
Caps: 3 (W:2, L:1)
Scoring: 0 Pts
Appearances: 1896:W,I, 1897:S

Arthur Sumner GIBSON
Born: 14 July 1844 in New Forest, Hampshire
Died: 23 January 1927 in East Hampstead, Berks
Educated: Marlborough School
Clubs: Oxford University, Manchester (1)
Position: Forward (1)
Debut: 27 Mar 1871 v Scotland (Raeburn Place). Number: 8
Caps: 1 (W:0, L:1)
Scoring: 0 Pts
Appearances: 1871:S

Charles Osborne Provis GIBSON
Born: October 1876 in Newcastle-upon-Tyne
Died: 9 November 1931 in Stocksfield, Northumberland
Educated: Uppingham School
Clubs: Oxford University, Northern (1)
Position: Forward (1)
Debut: 5 Jan 1901 v Wales (Cardiff). Number: 357
Caps: 1 (W:0, L:1)
Scoring: 0 Pts
Appearances: 1901:W

George Ralph GIBSON
Born: March 1878 in Gateshead
Died: October 1939 in Newcastle-upon-Tyne
Educated: Uppingham School
Clubs: Northern (2)
Position: Forward (2)
Debut: 7 Jan 1899 v Wales (Swansea). Number: 330
Last game: 9 Mar 1901 v Scotland (Blackheath)
Caps: 2 (W:0, L:2)
Scoring: 0 Pts
Appearances: 1899:W, 1901:S

Thomas Alexander GIBSON
Born: 30 January 1880 in Gateshead
Died: 27 April 1937
Educated: Uppingham School
Clubs: Cambridge University, Northern (2)
Position: Forward (2)
Debut: 14 Jan 1905 v Wales (Cardiff). Number: 394
Last game: 18 Mar 1905 v Scotland (Richmond)
Caps: 2 (W:0, L:2)
Scoring: 0 Pts
Appearances: 1905:W,S

Frederick George (Fred) GILBERT
Born: First quarter 1884 in Plymouth
Died: 11 December 1964 in Plymouth
Clubs: Devonport Services (2), Royal Navy
Position: Full-back (2)
Debut: 20 Jan 1923 v Wales (Twickenham). Number: 581
Last game: 10 Feb 1923 v Ireland (Leicester)
Caps: 2 (W:2, L:0)
Scoring: 0 Pts
Appearances: 1923:W,I
Honours: Championship: 1923
At almost 39 Fred Gilbert is the oldest player to have represented England.

R GILBERT
Born: Details unknown
Died: Details unknown
Clubs: Devonport Albion (3), Royal Navy
Position: Forward (3)
Debut: 18 Jan 1908 v Wales (Bristol). Number: 459
Last game: 21 Mar 1908 v Scotland (Inverleith)
Caps: 3 (W:1, L:2)
Scoring: 0 Pts
Appearances: 1908:W,I,S

James Leonard (Jimmy) GILES
Born: 5 January 1910 in Coventry
Died: 28 March 1967 in Coventry
Clubs: Coventry (6)
Position: Scrum-half (6)
Debut: 19 Jan 1935 v Wales (Twickenham). Number: 716
Last game: 19 Mar 1938 v Scotland (Twickenham)
Caps: 6 (W:4, D:1, L:1)
Scoring: 2T, 6 Pts
Appearances: 1935:W,I, 1937:W,I, 1938:I,S
Honours: Championship: 1937

Andy Gomarsall

William John GITTINGS
Born: 5 October 1938 in Coventry
Educated: Barker Butts School
Clubs: Barkers Butts, Coventry (1)
Position: Scrum-half (1)
Debut: 4 Nov 1967 v New Zealand (Twickenham).Number: 960
Caps: 1 (W:0, L:1)
Scoring: 0 Pts
Appearances: 1967:NZ

Peter Bernard GLOVER
Born: 25 September 1945 in York
Educated: De Aston School
Clubs: RAF (1), Bedford, Bath (2)
Position: Wing (3), Bench (3)
Debut: 7 Jan 1967 v Australia (Twickenham) Number: 950
Last game: 17 Apr 1971 v Presidents XV (Twickenham)
Caps: 3 (W:0, D:1, L:2)
Scoring: 0 Pts
Appearances: 1967:A, 1971:F,P

Reginald Edmund GODFRAY
Born: 10 May 1880 in St Helier, Jersey
Died: 4 February 1967 in Merton, London
Educated: Park House School, Victoria College
Clubs: Richmond (1)
Position: Centre (1)
Debut: 2 Dec 1905 v New Zealand (Crystal Palace). Number: 415
Caps: 1 (W:0, L:1)
Scoring: 0 Pts
Appearances: 1905:NZ

Herbert O GODWIN
Born: 21 December 1935 in Abergavenny, Wales
Died: January 2006 in Devon
Educated: Broadway SMS
Clubs: Standard, Coventry (11), Royal Leicestershire Regt, Army, Combined Services
Position: Hooker (11)
Debut: 28 Feb 1959 v France (Twickenham). Number: 885
Last game: 4 Nov 1967 v New Zealand (Twickenham)
Caps: 11 (W:2, D:2, L:7)
Scoring: 1T, 3 Pts
Appearances: 1959:F,S, 1963:S,NZ1,NZ2,A, 1964:NZ,I,F,S, 1967:NZ
Honours: Championship: 1963

Andrew Charles Thomas (Andy) GOMARSALL, MBE
Born: 24 July 1974 in Durham
Educated: Bedford School
Clubs: Oxford Brookes University, Wasps (6), Bath, Bedford (1), Gloucester (16), Worcester, Harlequins
Position: Scrum-half (16), Replacement (7), Bench (14)
Debut: 23 Nov 1996 v Italy (Twickenham) - 2T, 10 Pts.
Number: 1167
Last game: 27 Nov 2004 v Australia (Twickenham)
Caps: 23 (W:16, L:7)
Scoring: 6T, 2C, 34 Pts
Appearances: 1996:It,Ar, 1997:S,I,F,Ar2(r), 2000:It(r), 2002:Ar,SA(r), 2003:F,W(r),W,F(r),Geo(r),U, 2004:It,S,NZ1(r),NZ2,A,C,SA,A
Honours: RWC Winner: 2003. Championship: 2000, 2003

Andy Goode

Andrew James (Andy) GOODE

Born: 3 April 1980 in Coventry
Educated: King Henry VIII School, Bromsgrove School
Clubs: Leicester (9), Saracens
Position: Fly-half (3), Replacement (6), Bench (4)
Debut: 12 Mar 2005 (rep) v Italy (Twickenham) - 1C, 2 Pts. Number: 1263
Last game: 25 Nov 2006 v South Africa (Twickenham) - 3PG, 9 Pts
Caps: 9 (W:4, L:5)
Scoring: 7C, 10PG, 1DG, 47 Pts
Appearances: 2005:It(r),S(r), 2006:W(r),F(r),I,A1(r),A2,SA1(r),SA2

Anthony Lefroy Henniker GOTLEY

Born: 2 March 1887 in Tysoe
Died: May 1972 in Torbay
Educated: Tonbridge School
Clubs: Oxford University (2), Blackheath (4)
Position: Scrum-half (6)
Debut: 3 Mar 1910 v France (Parc des Princes). Number: 502
Last game: 18 Mar 1911 (capt) v Scotland (Twickenham)
Caps: 6 (W:4, L:2). As captain: 1 (W:1, L:0)
Scoring: 0 Pts
Appearances: 1910:F,S, 1911:W,F,I,S*
Honours: Championship: 1910

David GRAHAM

Born: June 1875 in Aspatria
Died: January 1962 in Carlisle
Educated: Aspatria HS
Clubs: Aspatria(1), Keswick, Rochdale, New Brighton
Position: Forward (1)
Debut: 5 Jan 1901 v Wales (Cardiff). Number: 358
Caps: 1 (W:0, L:1)
Scoring: 0 Pts
Appearances: 1901:W

Harry James GRAHAM

Born: Third quarter 1853 in Kingston
Died: Details unknown
Clubs: Wimbledon Hornets (4)
Position: Forward (4)
Debut: 15 Feb 1875 v Ireland (The Oval). Number: 59
Last game: 6 Mar 1876 v Scotland (The Oval)
Caps: 4 (W:3, D:1, L:0)
Scoring: 0 Pts
Appearances: 1875:I,S,I, 1876:S

John Duncan George GRAHAM

Born: Second quarter 1856
Died: Details unknown
Educated: Wellington College
Clubs: Wimbledon Hornets (1)
Position: Forward (1)
Debut: 13 Dec 1875 v Ireland (Dublin). Number: 73
Caps: 1 (W:1, L:0)
Scoring: 0 Pts
Appearances: 1875:I

Arthur GRAY

Born: 4 September 1917 in Leeds
Died: 25 August 1991 in Scarborough
Clubs: Otley (3), Wakefield Trinity RL
Position: Full-back (3)
Debut: 18 Jan 1947 v Wales (Cardiff) - 1C, 2 Pts. Number: 754
Last game: 15 Mar 1947 v Scotland (Twickenham)
Caps: 3 (W:2, L:1)
Scoring: 1C, 2 Pts
Appearances: 1947:W,I,S

Paul James GRAYSON, MBE

Born: 30 May 1971 in Chorley, Lancs
Educated: Parklands HS, Dr Tuson College
Clubs: Preston Grasshoppers, Waterloo, Northampton (32)
Position: Fly-half (24), Replacement (8), Bench (6)
Debut: 16 Dec 1995 v Samoa (Twickenham) - 1C, 5PG, 17 Pts. Number: 1163
Last game: 6 Mar 2004 v Ireland (Twickenham) - 1C, 2PG, 8 Pts
Caps: 32 (W:21, D:2, L:9)
Scoring: 2T, 78C, 72PG, 6DG, 400 Pts
Appearances: 1995:Sm, 1996:F,W,S,I, 1997:S,I,F,A(r),SA(r),NZ2, 1998:F,W,S,I,H,It,A, 1999:I,NZ(r),Tg,Fj(r),SA, 2003:S(r),I(r),F,F(r),Geo(r),U, 2004:It,S,I
Honours: RWC Winner: 2003. Championship: 1996, 2003

Paul Grayson

Will Green

John GREEN

Born: 17 September 1881 in Silsden
Died: 27 December 1968 in Wharfedale
Educated: Giggleswick School
Clubs: Skipton (8)
Position: Forward (8)
Debut: 11 Feb 1905 v Ireland (Cork). Number: 406
Last game: 16 Mar 1907 v Scotland (Blackheath)
Caps: 8 (W:3, D:1, L:4). As captain: 1 (W:0, L:1)
Scoring: 0 Pts
Appearances: 1905:I, 1906:S,F,SA, 1907:F,W,I*,S

Joseph Fletcher GREEN

Born: 28 April 1846 in West Ham
Died: 28 August 1923 in Leeds
Educated: Rugby School
Clubs: West Kent (1)
Position: Half-Back (1)
Debut: 27 Mar 1871 v Scotland (Raeburn Place). Number: 9
Caps: 1 (W:0, L:1)
Scoring: 0 Pts
Appearances: 1871:S

William Robert (Will) GREEN

Born: 25 October 1973 in Littlehampton
Educated: Eastbourne College
Clubs: Oxford Brookes University, Villagers (SA), Wasps (4), Leinster
Position: Prop (1), Replacement (3), Bench (2)
Debut: 15 Nov 1997 v Australia (Twickenham).Number: 1187
Last game: 23 Aug 2003 (rep) v Wales (Cardiff)
Caps: 4 (W:2, D:1, L:1)
Scoring: 0 Pts
Appearances: 1997:A, 1998:NZ1(r), 1999:US(r), 2003:W(r)

Phil Greening

Nick Greenstock

Philip Bradley Thomas (Phil) GREENING

Born: 3 October 1975 in Gloucester
Educated: Chosen Hill School, Oxstall's School, Gloucester College
Clubs: Spartans, Gloucester (5), Sale (11), Wasps (8)
Position: Hooker (17), Replacement (7), Bench (9)
Debut: 23 Nov 1996 (rep) v Italy (Twickenham).Number: 1172
Last game: 20 Oct 2001 v Ireland (Lansdowne Road)
Caps: 24 (W:16, L:8)
Scoring: 6T, 30 Pts. Discipline - Sin bins: 1
Appearances: 1996:It(r), 1997:W(r),Ar1, 1998:NZ1(r),NZ2(r), 1999:A(r),US,C,It(r),NZ(r),Tg,Fj,SA, 2000:I,F,W,It,S,SA1,SA2,A,SA, 2001:F,I
Honours: Championship: 2000, 2001

Nicholas James Jeremy (Nick) GREENSTOCK

Born: 3 November 1973 in Dubai, UAE
Educated: Sherborne School, Royal Holloway College
Clubs: Wasps (4), Harlequins, London Irish, Staines
Position: Centre (4)
Debut: 31 May 1997 v Argentina (Buenos Aires) - 1T, 5 Pts. Number: 1179
Last game: 29 Nov 1997 v South Africa (Twickenham) - 1T, 5 Pts
Caps: 4 (W:1, L:3)
Scoring: 2T, 10 Pts
Appearances: 1997:Ar1,Ar2,A,SA

John Henry GREENWELL

Born: Third quarter 1864 in Tynemouth
Died: 22 November 1943 in South Northumberland
Clubs: Rockcliff (2), Tynemouth
Position: Forward (2)
Debut: 7 Jan 1893 v Wales (Cardiff). Number: 252
Last game: 4 Feb 1893 v Ireland (Lansdowne Road)
Caps: 2 (W:1, L:1)
Scoring: 0 Pts
Appearances: 1893:W,I

John Eric (Jenny) GREENWOOD

Born: 23 July 1891 in Lewisham
Died: 23 July 1975 in Poole
Educated: Dulwich College
Clubs: Cambridge University (9), Old Alleynians, Leicester (4), Harlequins
Position: Forward (13)
Debut: 8 Apr 1912 v France (Parc des Princes).Number: 523
Last game: 20 Mar 1920 (capt) v Scotland (Twickenham) - 2C, 4 Pts
Caps: 13 (W:11, L:2). As captain: 4 (W:3, L:1)
Scoring: 12C, 2PG, 30 Pts
Appearances: 1912:F, 1913:SA,W,F,I,S, 1914:W,S,F, 1920:W*,F*,I*,S*
Honours: Grand Slam: 1913. Championship: 1914

John Richard Heaton (Dick) GREENWOOD

Born: 11 September 1940 in Macclesfield
Educated: Merchant Taylors' School
Clubs: Old Merchant Taylors', Crosby, Cambridge University, Waterloo (5), Coventry, Rugby Roma (IT), Lazio (IT)
Position: Flanker (5), Bench (2)
Debut: 12 Feb 1966 v Ireland (Twickenham) - 1T, 3 Pts. Number: 943
Last game: 8 Feb 1969 (capt) v Ireland (Lansdowne Road)
Caps: 5 (W:0, D:1, L:4). As captain: 1 (W:0, L:1)
Scoring: 1T, 3 Pts
Appearances: 1966:I,F,S, 1967:A, 1969:I*

William John Heaton (Will) GREENWOOD, MBE

Born: 20 October 1972 in Blackburn
Educated: Sedbergh School, Stonyhurst College
Clubs: Durham University, Preston Grasshoppers, Waterloo, Harlequins (40), Leicester (15)
Position: Centre (50), Replacement (5), Bench (3)
Debut: 15 Nov 1997 v Australia (Twickenham). Number: 1188
Last game: 27 Nov 2004 (rep) v Australia (Twickenham)
Caps: 55 (W:44, D:2, L:9)
Scoring: 31T, 155 Pts
Appearances: 1997:A,NZ1,SA,NZ2, 1998:F,W,S,I,H,It, 1999:C,It,Tg,Fj,SA, 2000:Ar(r),SA, 2001:W,It,S,F,I,A,R,SA, 2002:S,I,F,W,It,NZ,A,SA, 2003:F,W,It,S,I,NZ,A,F,Geo,SA,U(r),W,F,A, 2004:It,S,I,W,F,C(r),SA(r),A(r)
Honours: RWC Winner: 2003. Grand Slam: 2003.
Championship: 2001

The son of former England player and coach, Dick Greenwood, Will Greenwood quietly became one of the heroes of the 2003 World Cup winning team.

Playing in six of the seven matches, he was involved in all but one of England's tries, finishing joint top scorer with five.

His knack of scoring vital tries came to the aid of England on several occasions during the course of the tournament, not least his tries in tight games against Wales and South Africa. He scored on both occasions when England looked to be heading for defeat.

When not making crucial breaks he was working tirelessly in defence.

He played both inside and outside centre through his career but for superstitious reasons he always wore the

Will Greenwood

Danny Grewcock

No 13 jersey.

On one occasion when he didn't wear No 13, playing for the 1997 Lions, he was knocked unconscious.

Greenwood became part of the England set-up under Clive Woodward at the end of 1997, having joined Leicester from Harlequins in 1996, where the presence of Will Carling had severely limited his opportunities.

He also played for Preston Grasshoppers and Waterloo, returning to the Quins in 2000.

Thrown in against Australia and the All Blacks in 1997, he quickly developed a rapport with fellow centres Jeremy Guscott and then Mike Tindall. When Jonny Wilkinson joined the fray, England had the nucleus of a formidable defence, which would ultimately take them to World Cup victory.

Overlooked for the Six Nations in 1997, he was selected for that year's Lions tour, as the squad's one uncapped player, although injury prevented him making a Test appearance. He was also unlucky in 2001, but he finally made his Lions debut in 2005, replacing the injured captain Brian O'Driscoll.

A prolific try-scorer for England with 31 (only Rory Underwood has scored more tries for England), his clubs also benefited from his ability to spot gaps from midfield, and on his return to Harlequins in 2000, his match-winning try against Brive in the quarter-final of the European Shield was voted 'Try of the Season'. That season saw domestic disappointment in the final of the Pilkington Cup, losing to Newcastle Falcons. A winner's medal in the same competition with Leicester Tigers in 1997 is some consolation.

He was England's top try scorer in both the 2002 and 2003 Six Nations Championships, and the 2004 tournament saw him reach a couple of milestones. He was made England vice-captain under Lawrence Dallaglio and then earned his 50th cap against Ireland, playing in every England match.

Greenwood – who was educated at Stonyhurst College, and then Sedbergh School – won the last of his 55 England caps against Australia in 2004, and reluctantly retired from the game in 2006.

"Will has been a great servant to English rugby, both at club and international level," said England coach Andy Robinson. "His contribution to the 2003 World Cup-winning team was vital and will never be forgotten."

As England slipped down the world rankings in 2005 and 2006, Greenwood was one of the players England missed the most. His deft passing, eye for a gap, solid defence and his ability to read the game left England with far less midfield options.

He was awarded the MBE for his exploits in 2003 and now is regularly seen and heard as an analyst on Sky Sports and in the pages of The Daily Telegraph. He started his working life in the City and keeps those ties with corporate work for HSBC.

Walter GREG

Born: 14 February 1851 in Macclesfield
Died: 6 February 1906 in Assonam, Egypt
Educated: Marlborough School
Clubs: Marlborough Nomads, Manchester (2)
Position: Forward (2)
Debut: 13 Dec 1875 v Ireland (Dublin). Number: 74
Last game: 6 Mar 1876 v Scotland (The Oval)
Caps: 2 (W:2, L:0)
Scoring: 0 Pts
Appearances: 1875:I, 1876:S

Gordon George GREGORY

Born: 8 December 1907 in Taunton
Died: 4 December 1963 in Newton Abbot
Educated: Huish School
Clubs: Reading University, Taunton (3), Bath, Bristol (10)
Position: Hooker (9), Prop (4)
Debut: 14 Feb 1931 v Ireland (Twickenham). Number: 677
Last game: 17 Mar 1934 v Scotland (Twickenham)
Caps: 13 (W:6, L:7)
Scoring: 2C, 4 Pts
Appearances: 1931:I,S,F, 1932:SA,W,I,S, 1933:W,I,S, 1934:W,I,S
Honours: Championship: 1934

John Arthur (Jack) GREGORY

Born: 22 June 1923 in Bristol
Died: 16 December 2003 in Nailsea
Educated: Rydal School, St Andrew's College
Clubs: Dublin Wanderers, Clifton, Blackheath (1), Bristol, Army
Position: Wing (1)
Debut: 15 Jan 1949 v Wales (Cardiff). Number: 790
Caps: 1 (W:0, L:1)
Scoring: 0 Pts
Appearances: 1949:W

Daniel Jonathan (Danny) GREWCOCK, MBE

Born: 7 November 1972 in Coventry
Educated: Woodlands School, Crewe & Alsager College
Clubs: Manchester Metro University, Barkers Butts, Coventry (1), Saracens (23), Bath (45)
Position: Lock (51), Replacement (18), Bench (9)
Debut: 7 Jun 1997 v Argentina (Buenos Aires) - 1T, 5 Pts. Number: 1184
Last game: 24 Feb 2007 v Ireland (Croke Park)
Caps: 69 (W:44, L:25)
Scoring: 2T, 10 Pts. Discipline - Cautions: 1, Sin bins: 3, **Sent off:** 1
Appearances: 1997:Ar2,SA, 1998:W(r),S(r),I(r),A,NZ1,SA(r), 1999:S(r),A(r),US,C,It,NZ,Tg(r),SA, 2000:SA1,SA2,A,Ar,SA, 2001:W,It,S,I,A,R(r),SA, 2002:S(r),I(r),F(r),W,It,NZ,SA(r), 2003:F(r),W(r),It,S(r),I(r),W,F,U, 2004:It,S,W,F,NZ1,NZ2(r),C,SA,A, 2005:W,F,I,It,S,A,NZ, 2006:W,It,S,F,I(r),NZ,Ar, 2007:S,It,I
Honours: RWC Winner: 2003. Grand Slam: 2003. **Championship:** 2001

William Mitchell GRYLLS

Born: 9 January 1885 in Redruth
Died: 2 December 1962 in Wokingham
Educated: Haileybury & ISC
Clubs: RMC Sandhurst, Redruth (1), Indian Army, Army
Position: Lock (1)
Debut: 11 Feb 1905 v Ireland (Cork). Number: 407
Caps: 1 (W:0, L:1)
Scoring: 0 Pts
Appearances: 1905:I

Richard Heaton (Dickie) GUEST

Born: 12 March 1918 in Prescot
Educated: Cowley GS, St Helens School
Clubs: Liverpool University (1), Waterloo (12)
Position: Wing (13)
Debut: 21 Jan 1939 v Wales (Twickenham). Number: 746
Last game: 19 Mar 1949 v Scotland (Twickenham) - 1T, 3 Pts
Caps: 13 (W:7, D:1, L:5)
Scoring: 5T, 15 Pts
Appearances: 1939:W,I,S, 1947:W,I,S,F, 1948:A,W,I,S, 1949:F,S

Arthur George GUILLEMARD

Born: 18 December 1845 in Lewisham
Died: 7 August 1909 in Lewisham
Educated: Rugby School
Clubs: West Kent (2)
Position: Full-back (2)
Debut: 27 Mar 1871 v Scotland (Raeburn Place). Number: 10
Last game: 5 Feb 1872 v Scotland (The Oval)
Caps: 2 (W:1, L:1)
Scoring: 0 Pts
Appearances: 1871:S, 1872:S

Charles Henry Alexander GUMMER

Born: 20 November 1905
Died: 4 February 1974
Clubs: Plymouth Albion (1), Moseley, British Police
Position: No 8 (1)
Debut: 1 Apr 1929 v France (Stade Colombes) - 1T, 3 Pts. Number: 649
Caps: 1 (W:1, L:0)
Scoring: 1T, 3 Pts
Appearances: 1929:F

Charles Richard GUNNER

Born: 7 January 1853 in Bishops Waltham
Died: 4 February 1924 in Bishops Waltham
Educated: Marlborough School
Clubs: Marlborough Nomads (1)
Position: Three-quarter (1)
Debut: 13 Dec 1875 v Ireland (Dublin). Number: 75
Caps: 1 (W:1, L:0)
Scoring: 0 Pts
Appearances: 1875:I

Charles GURDON

Born: 3 December 1855 in Forehoe, Norfolk
Died: 26 June 1931 in London
Educated: Haileybury & ISC
Clubs: Cambridge University, Richmond (14)
Position: Forward (14)
Debut: 30 Jan 1880 v Ireland (Lansdowne Road). Number: 122
Last game: 13 Mar 1886 v Scotland (Raeburn Place)
Caps: 14 (W:10, D:3, L:1). As captain: 1 (W:0, D:1, L:0)
Scoring: 0 Pts
Appearances: 1880:I,S, 1881:I,W,S, 1882:I*,S, 1883:S, 1884:W,S, 1885:I, 1886:W,I,S
Honours: Championship: 1883, 1884

Edward Temple (Temple) GURDON

Born: 25 January 1854 in Barnham Broom, Norfolk
Died: 12 June 1929 in London
Educated: Haileybury & ISC
Clubs: Old Haileyburians (1), Cambridge University, Richmond (15)
Position: Forward (16)
Debut: 4 Mar 1878 v Scotland (The Oval). Number: 98
Last game: 13 Mar 1886 (capt) v Scotland (Raeburn Place)
Caps: 16 (W:12, D:3, L:1). As captain: 9 (W:8, D:1, L:0)
Scoring: 1T, 1 Pt
Appearances: 1878:S, 1879:I, 1880:S, 1881:I,W,S, 1882:S, 1883:W*,I*,S*, 1884:W*,I*,S*, 1885:W*,I*, 1886:S*
Honours: Championship: 1883 (capt), 1884 (capt)

Jeremy Clayton (Jerry) GUSCOTT, MBE

Born: 7 July 1965 in Bath
Educated: Ralph Allen CS
Clubs: Bath (65)
Position: Centre (62), Replacement (3), Bench (3)
Debut: 13 May 1989 v Romania (Bucharest) - 3T, 12 Pts. Number: 1133
Last game: 15 Oct 1999 v Tonga (Twickenham)- 2T, 10 Pts
Caps: 65 (W:51, L:14)
Scoring: 30T, 2DG, 143 Pts
Appearances: 1989:R,Fj, 1990:I,F,W,S,Ar, 1991:W,S,I,F,Fj,A,NZ,It,F,S,A, 1992:S,I,F,W,C,SA, 1993:F,W,S,I, 1994:R,C, 1995:I,F,W,S,Ar,It,A,NZ,F,SA,Sm, 1996:F,W,S,I,Ar, 1997:I(r),W(r), 1998:F,W,S,I,H,It,A,SA, 1999:S,I,F,A,US,C,It(r),NZ,Tg
Honours: Grand Slam: 1991, 1992, 1995. Championship: 1996

The "prince of centres", said World Cup-winning England coach, Sir Clive Woodward, and it is an apt description, given Guscott's magisterial presence on a rugby pitch.

Guscott was one of the finest centres of the modern era, and his record of 65 caps and 30 tries for England (when Guscott retired only only Rory Underwood had scored more) compares favourably with any rugby legend.

"Jerry epitomised the best of England rugby," Woodward said. "He was an intrinsic part of three Grand Slam-winning sides and three World Cup campaigns. He has been an invaluable support to younger players and an England centre to remember."

A supporter of Bath from the age of seven, he was part of the Bath team which dominated English rugby in the Nineties, helping to bring six league titles and six domestic cups to The Recreation Ground.

He made his debut as a teenager for Bath in 1984, before his call-up for the national team in 1989 against Romania. He rose to the occasion with a hat-trick of tries.

"He was one of the most gifted footballers England have ever had in their ranks," said former Bath and England coach Jack Rowell.

"When I saw how talented he was, I recommended to Twickenham that they fast-track him and fortunately they followed my advice."

Guscott's time with England saw him achieve the Triple Crown six times in eight seasons (including two Grand Slams), and he set, with Will Carling, the world record for most international appearances by a centre pairing: 45 matches.

Guscott was part of the 1991 England team which lost to Australia in the World Cup final, and was again involved in the 1995 campaign, when England were third.

His international career came to a premature end during the 1999 World Cup with a groin injury, but not before scoring a typically majestic length-of-field try against Tonga, earning a standing ovation at the end. He retired altogether a year later.

Guscott will go down in history as a Lions legend, after winning the 1997 series with a late drop goal against South Africa. He represented the Lions eight times, first on the winning tour to Australia in 1989 and four years later when the Lions lost in New Zealand.

Domestically he was part of a Bath team that ruled the roost in England and in 1998 he helped Bath become the first English team to lift the Heineken European Cup.

His career outside of rugby has seen him work as a labourer, PR man, fashion model, and television host, most famously as presenter of Gladiators in 1998. He is now a regular and articulate panelist for the BBC.

Jerry Guscott

Richard Hill

H-I

HAAG, Stephen Martin
HAIGH, Leonard
HALE, Peter Martin
HALL, Colin
HALL, John
HALL, Jonathan Peter
HALL, Norman MacLeod
HALLIDAY, Simon John
HAMERSLEY, Alfred St George
HAMILTON-HILL, Edward Alfred, OBE
HAMMETT, Ernest Dyer Galbraith
HAMMOND, Charles Edward Lucas
HANCOCK, Andrew William
HANCOCK, George Edward
HANCOCK, Patrick Sortain
HANCOCK, Philip Froude
HANCOCK, William Jack Henry
HANDFORD, Frank Gordon
HANDS, Reginald Harry Myburgh
HANLEY, Joseph
HANLEY, Steven Melvyn
HANNAFORD, Ronald Charles
HANVEY, Robert Jackson
HARDING, Ernest Harold
HARDING, Richard Mark
HARDING, Victor Sydney James
HARDWICK, Peter Fenton
HARDWICK, Robin John Kieren
HARDY, Evan Michael Pearce, OBE
HARE, William Henry, MBE
HARPER, Sir Charles Henry, KBE
HARRIMAN, Andrew Tuoyo
HARRIS, Stanley Wakefield, CBE
HARRIS, Thomas William Walter
HARRISON, Arthur Clifford
HARRISON, Arthur Leyland VC
HARRISON, Gilbert
HARRISON, Harold Cecil
HARRISON, Michael Edward
HARTLEY, Bernard Charles, OBE
HASKELL, James
HASLETT, Leslie Woods
HASTINGS, George William D
HAVELOCK, Harold
HAWCRIDGE, John Joseph
HAYWARD, Leslie William
HAZELL, Andrew Robert
HAZELL, David St George
HEALEY, Austin Sean
HEARN, Robert Daniel
HEATH, Arthur Howard
HEATON, John
HENDERSON, Alan Peter
HENDERSON, Sir Robert Samuel Findlay, KCMG
HEPPEL, Walter George
HERBERT, Alfred John
HESFORD, Robert
HESLOP, Nigel John
HETHERINGTON, James Gilbert George
HEWITT, Edwin Newbury
HEWITT, Walter William
HICKSON, John Lawrence
HIGGINS, Reginald
HIGNELL, Alastair James
HILL, Sir Basil Alexander, KBE
HILL, Richard Anthony, MBE
HILL, Richard John
HILLARD, Ronald Johnstone, CMG
HILLER, Robert
HIND, Alfred Ernest
HIND, Guy Reginald
HOBBS, Reginald Francis Arthur, CMG
HOBBS, Reginald Geoffrey Stirling, OBE
HODGES, Harold Augustus
HODGKINSON, Simon David
HODGSON, Charles Christopher
HODGSON, John McDonald
HODGSON, Stanley Arthur Murray
HOFMEYER, Murray Bernard
HOGARTH, Thomas Bradley
HOLFORD, Jonathan George
HOLLAND, David
HOLLIDAY, Thomas Edwin
HOLMES, Cyril Butler
HOLMES, Edgar
HOLMES, Walter Alan
HOLMES, William Barry
HOOK, William Gordon
HOOPER, Charles Alexander
HOPLEY, Damian Paul
HOPLEY, Frederick John Vanderby
HORAK, Michael John
HORDORN, Peter Cotton
HORLEY, Charles Henry
HORNBY, Albert Neilson
HORROCKS-TAYLOR, John Philip
HORSFALL, Edward Luke
HORTON, Anthony Lawrence
HORTON, John Philip
HORTON, Nigel Edgar
HOSEN, Roger Wills
HOSKING, Geoffrey Robert d'Aubrey
HOUGHTON, Samuel
HOWARD, Peter Dunsmore
HUBBARD, George Cairns
HUBBARD, John Cairns
HUDSON, Arthur
HUGHES, George Edgar
HULL, Paul Anthony
HULME, Frank Croft
HUNT, James Thomas
HUNT, Robert
HUNT, William Henry
HUNTER, Ian G
HUNTSMAN, Robert Paul
HURST, Andrew Charles Brunel
HUSKISSON, Thomas Frederick, MBE
HUTCHINSON, Frank
HUTCHINSON, James Ernest
HUTCHINSON, William Charles
HUTCHINSON, William Henry Heap
HUTH, Henry
HYDE, John Phillip
HYNES, William Bayard, CBE
HYSLOP, John Edgar Maxwell

IBBITSON, Ernest Denison
IMRIE, Henry Marshall
INGLIS, Rupert Edward
IRVIN, Samuel Howell
ISHERWOOD, Francis William Ramsbottom

Stephen Martin (Martin) HAAG

Born: 28 July 1965 in Chelmsford
Educated: Penwith VI Form College
Clubs: Bath (2), Bristol
Position: Lock (2)
Debut: 31 May 1997 v Argentina (Buenos Aires). Number: 1180
Last game: 7 Jun 1997 v Argentina (Buenos Aires)
Caps: 2 (W:1, L:1)
Scoring: 0 Pts
Appearances: 1997:Ar1,Ar2

Martin Haag

Leonard HAIGH

Born: 19 October 1880 in Prestwich
Died: Killed in action in 1916 in Woolwich
Educated: Sandringham House School
Clubs: Manchester (7)
Position: Prop (7)
Debut: 15 Jan 1910 v Wales (Twickenham). Number: 493
Last game: 18 Mar 1911 v Scotland (Twickenham)
Caps: 7 (W:4, D:1, L:2)
Scoring: 0 Pts
Appearances: 1910:W,I,S, 1911:W,F,I,S
Honours: Championship: 1910

Peter Martin HALE

Born: 12 August 1943 in Birmingham
Educated: Solihull GS
Clubs: Solihull, Moseley (3)
Position: Wing (3)
Debut: 20 Dec 1969 v South Africa (Twickenham). Number: 979
Last game: 28 Feb 1970 v Wales (Twickenham)
Caps: 3 (W:2, L:1)
Scoring: 0 Pts
Appearances: 1969:SA, 1970:I,W

Colin HALL

Born: Details unknown
Died: Details unknown
Clubs: Gloucester (2)
Position: Forward (2)
Debut: 9 Feb 1901 v Ireland (Lansdowne Road). Number: 365
Last game: 9 Mar 1901 v Scotland (Blackheath)
Caps: 2 (W:0, L:2)
Scoring: 0 Pts
Appearances: 1901:I,S

John HALL

Born: Details unknown
Died: Details unknown
Educated: Gateshead Institute
Clubs: North Durham (3), Hartlepool Rovers, Blackheath
Position: Forward (3)
Debut: 6 Jan 1894 v Wales (Birkenhead Park). Number: 263
Last game: 17 Mar 1894 v Scotland (Raeburn Place)
Caps: 3 (W:1, L:2)
Scoring: 0 Pts
Appearances: 1894:W,I,S

Jonathan Peter (Jon) HALL

Born: 15 March 1962 in Bath
Educated: Beechen Cliff School
Clubs: Oldfield Old Boys, Bath (21)
Position: Flanker (18), No 8 (2), Replacement (1), Bench (2)
Debut: 4 Feb 1984 (rep) v Scotland (Murrayfield). Number: 1082
Last game: 5 Feb 1994 v Scotland (Murrayfield)
Caps: 21 (W:7, D:1, L:13)
Scoring: 2T, 8 Pts
Appearances: 1984:S(r),I,F,SA1,SA2,A, 1985:R,F,S,I,W,NZ1,NZ2, 1986:W,S, 1987:I,F,W,S, 1990:Ar, 1994:S

Nim Hall

Norman MacLeod (Nim) HALL

Born: 2 August 1925 in Huddersfield
Died: 25 June 1972 in Paddington
Educated: Worksop College
Clubs: St Mary's Hospital (4), Royal Signals, Army, Huddersfield (2), Combined Services, Richmond (11)
Position: Fly-half (11), Full-back (6)
Debut: 18 Jan 1947 v Wales (Cardiff) - 1DG, 4 Pts. Number: 755
Last game: 12 Feb 1955 (capt) v Ireland (Lansdowne Road)
Caps: 17 (W:9, D:2, L:6). As captain: 13 (W:6, D:2, L:5)
Scoring: 8C, 4PG, 3DG, 39 Pts
Appearances: 1947:W,I,S,F, 1949:W*,I*, 1952:SA*,W*,S*,I*,F*, 1953:W*,I*,F*,S*, 1955:W*,I*
Honours: Championship: 1953 (capt)

Simon Halliday

Simon John HALLIDAY
Born: 13 July 1960 in Haverfordwest, Wales
Educated: Downside School
Clubs: Oxford University, Bath (16), Harlequins (7)
Position: Centre (14), Wing (8), Replacement (1), Bench (13)
Debut: 18 Jan 1986 v Wales (Twickenham). Number: 1111
Last game: 7 Mar 1992 v Wales (Twickenham)
Caps: 23 (W:17, D:1, L:5)
Scoring: 2T, 8 Pts
Appearances: 1986:W,S, 1987:S, 1988:S,I,I,A1,A, 1989:S,I,F,W,R,Fj(r), 1990:W,S, 1991:US,S,A, 1992:S,I,F,W
Honours: Grand Slam: 1992

Alfred St George HAMERSLEY
Born: 8 October 1848 in Great Haseley, Oxon
Died: 25 February 1929 in Bournemouth
Educated: Marlborough School
Clubs: Marlborough Nomads (4), Canterbury (NZ)
Position: Forward (4)
Debut: 27 Mar 1871 v Scotland (Raeburn Place). Number: 11
Last game: 23 Feb 1874 (capt) v Scotland (The Oval)
Caps: 4 (W:2, D:1, L:1). As captain: 1 (W:1, L:0)
Scoring: 1T, 1 Pt
Appearances: 1871:S, 1872:S, 1873:S, 1874:S*

Edward Alfred HAMILTON-HILL, OBE
Born: 22 November 1908
Died: 23 October 1979 in north Surrey
Educated: HMS Conway
Clubs: Royal Navy, Harlequins (3)
Position: Flanker (3)
Debut: 4 Jan 1936 v New Zealand (Twickenham). Number: 723
Last game: 8 Feb 1936 v Ireland (Lansdowne Road)
Caps: 3 (W:1, D:1, L:1)
Scoring: 0 Pts
Appearances: 1936:NZ,W,I

Ernest Dyer Galbraith HAMMETT
Born: 15 October 1891 in Radstock
Died: 23 June 1947 in Hove
Educated: Newport HS
Clubs: Newport (7), Cardiff, Blackheath (1)
Position: Centre (8)
Debut: 17 Jan 1920 v Wales (Swansea). Number: 547
Last game: 21 Jan 1922 v Wales (Cardiff)
Caps: 8 (W:6, L:2)
Scoring: 6C, 12 Pts
Appearances: 1920:W,F,S, 1921:W,I,S,F, 1922:W
Honours: Grand Slam: 1921

Charles Edward Lucas (Curly) HAMMOND
Born: 3 October 1879 in Pontefract
Died: 15 April 1963 in Ross
Educated: Bedford GS
Clubs: Oxford University, Harlequins (8)
Position: Forward (8)
Debut: 18 Mar 1905 v Scotland (Richmond).Number: 410
Last game: 8 Feb 1908 (capt) v Ireland (Richmond)
Caps: 8 (W:3, L:5). As captain: 1 (W:1, L:0)
Scoring: 0 Pts
Appearances: 1905:S,NZ, 1906:W,I,S,F, 1908:W,I*

Andrew William (Andy) HANCOCK
Born: 19 June 1939 in Dartford
Educated: Framlingham College
Clubs: London University, Sidcup, Cambridge, Northampton (3), Wasps
Position: Wing (3)
Debut: 27 Feb 1965 v France (Twickenham). Number: 935
Last game: 26 Feb 1966 v France (Stade Colombes)
Caps: 3 (W:1, D:1, L:1)
Scoring: 1T, 3 Pts
Appearances: 1965:F,S, 1966:F

George Edward HANCOCK

Born: 21 March 1912 in Wirral
Educated: Rock Ferry HS
Clubs: Birkenhead Park (3), RAF, Mount Hope (CA)
Position: Centre (3)
Debut: 21 Jan 1939 v Wales (Twickenham). Number: 747
Last game: 18 Mar 1939 v Scotland (Murrayfield)
Caps: 3 (W:2, L:1)
Scoring: 0 Pts
Appearances: 1939:W,I,S

Patrick Sortain HANCOCK

Born: 1883
Died: In Canada, details unknown
Educated: Dulwich College
Clubs: Leytonstone, Streatham, Richmond (3)
Position: Fly-half (3)
Debut: 9 Jan 1904 v Wales (Leicester). Number: 395
Last game: 19 Mar 1904 v Scotland (Inverleith)
Caps: 3 (W:1, D:1, L:1)
Scoring: 0 Pts
Appearances: 1904:W,I,S

Steve Hanley

Philip Froude (Froude) HANCOCK

Born: 29 August 1865 in Wellington, Somerset
Died: 16 October 1933 in Clifton
Clubs: Cambridge University, Wiveliscombe Blackheath (3)
Position: Forward (3)
Debut: 2 Jan 1886 v Wales (Blackheath). Number: 179
Last game: 15 Feb 1890 v Wales (Dewsbury)
Caps: 3 (W:2, L:1)
Scoring: 0 Pts
Appearances: 1886:W,I, 1890:W

William Jack Henry HANCOCK

Born: 26 September 1932 in Newport, Wales
Clubs: Army, Royal Electrical & Mechanical Engineers, Cross Keys, Newport (2), Salford RL
Position: Lock (2)
Debut: 22 Jan 1955 v Wales (Cardiff). Number: 850
Last game: 12 Feb 1955 v Ireland (Lansdowne Road)
Caps: 2 (W:0, D:1, L:1)
Scoring: 0 Pts
Appearances: 1955:W,I

Frank Gordon HANDFORD

Born: First quarter 1884 in Barton
Died: In South Africa, details unknown
Educated: The Leys School
Clubs: Manchester (4)
Position: Flanker (4)
Debut: 16 Jan 1909 v Wales (Cardiff). Number: 481
Last game: 20 Mar 1909 v Scotland (Richmond)
Caps: 4 (W:2, L:2)
Scoring: 0 Pts
Appearances: 1909:W,F,I,S

Reginald Harry Myburgh HANDS

Born: 26 July 1888 in Cape Town, South Africa
Died: Killed in action in 1918 in Boulogne, France
Educated: Diocesan College
Clubs: Oxford University (2), Manchester, Blackheath
Position: Forward (2)
Debut: 3 Mar 1910 v France (Parc des Princes). Number: 503
Last game: 19 Mar 1910 v Scotland (Inverleith)
Caps: 2 (W:2, L:0)
Scoring: 0 Pts
Appearances: 1910:F,S
Honours: Championship: 1910

Joseph (Jerry) HANLEY

Born: 14 September 1901
Died: January 1981 in Plymouth
Clubs: Civil Service, Plymouth Albion (7)
Position: Flanker (7)
Debut: 15 Jan 1927 v Wales (Twickenham). Number: 616
Last game: 17 Mar 1928 v Scotland (Twickenham) - 1T, 3 Pts
Caps: 7 (W:5, L:2)
Scoring: 1T, 3 Pts
Appearances: 1927:W,S,F, 1928:W,I,F,S
Honours: Grand Slam: 1928

Steven Melvyn (Steve) HANLEY
Born: 11 June 1979 in Whitehaven
Clubs: Aspatria, Sale (1)
Position: Wing (1)
Debut: 11 Apr 1999 v Wales (Wembley) - 1T, 5 Pts
Number: 1211
Caps: 1 (W:0, L:1)
Scoring: 1T, 5 Pts
Appearances: 1999:W

Ronald Charles HANNAFORD
Born: 19 October 1944 in Gloucester
Educated: Crypt GS
Clubs: Durham University, Cambridge University, Rosslyn Park, Bristol (3)
Position: No 8 (3), Bench (3)
Debut: 16 Jan 1971 v Wales (Cardiff) - 1T, 3 Pts. Number: 990
Last game: 27 Feb 1971 v France (Twickenham)
Caps: 3 (W:1, D:1, L:1)
Scoring: 1T, 3 Pts
Appearances: 1971:W,I,F

Robert Jackson (Bob) HANVEY
Born: 16 August 1899 in Wigton
Died: 17 October 1989 in Carlisle
Clubs: Aspatria (4)
Position: Prop (4)
Debut: 16 Jan 1926 v Wales (Cardiff). Number: 608
Last game: 20 Mar 1926 v Scotland (Twickenham)
Caps: 4 (W:1, D:1, L:2)
Scoring: 0 Pts
Appearances: 1926:W,I,F,S

Ernest Harold HARDING
Born: 22 May 1899 in Mile End
Died: 25 December 1980 in Liskeard, Cornwall
Clubs: Devonport Services (1), Royal Navy
Position: No 8 (1)
Debut: 14 Feb 1931 v Ireland (Twickenham).
Number: 678
Caps: 1 (W:0, L:1)
Scoring: 0 Pts
Appearances: 1931:I

Richard Mark HARDING
Born: 29 August 1953 in Bristol
Educated: Millfield School, Park GS
Clubs: Cambridge University, Bristol (12)
Position: Scrum-half (11), Replacement (1), Bench (7)
Debut: 5 Jan 1985 v Romania (Twickenham).
Number: 1102
Last game: 16 Jun 1988 (capt) v Fiji (Suva)
Caps: 12 (W:7, D:1, L:4). As captain: 1 (W:1, L:0)
Scoring: 1T, 4 Pts
Appearances: 1985:R,F,S, 1987:S,A,J,W, 1988:I(r),I,A1,A2,Fj*

Former Millfield School pupil, Richard Harding, is one of a line of post-war Bristol scrum-halves to represent England that stretches from Bill Redwood to Kyran Bracken and Shaun Perry. Quick, with a good pass, he has a couple of claims to rugby fame in that he was part of the team that first got the Twickenham crowd singing 'Swing Low Sweet Chariot' and was responsible for Alistair Hignell switching to play full-back.

Harding was the incumbent number nine at Cambridge University – where he did an MA in land economy – and Bristol, so Hignell was forced to change position to get a game and ended up playing there for England.

By the time Harding made his England debut, in the 22-15 win over Romania at Twickenham, he was already 31. He experienced a couple of strokes of fortune, for him, in Nigel Melville's injury and Richard Hill's suspension for the events in a torrid match in Cardiff against Wales in 1987.

These helped to accumulate a dozen caps at a time when England had a strong group of top notch scrum-halves.

He was preferred to Melville for the 1987 World Cup in Australia and New Zealand, and played in three games. These included the dismal quarter-final against Wales in Brisbane when he was outpaced by his opposite number, Robert Jones, for the clinching try, the defeat by Australia and the rout of Japan.

However, a year later, things went much better against the Irish. Melville went off with an ankle injury, Harding came on as replacement as England ran riot, with winger Chris Oti scoring a hat-trick and Harding revelling in the space that the Irish gave him as the crowd sang 'Swing Low', something England fans have been doing ever since.

Richard Harding

A month later he was in the England side that beat Ireland 21-10 in Dublin in a celebration match, and went on the summer tour down under, playing in two defeats by Australia and the 25-12 win over Fiji in Suva. That was his last international as Dewi Morris played in the entire 1989 Five Nations campaign.

These days Harding runs a highly successful estate agency that sells quality housing in the Bristol area and also has an office in Pall Mall, London where clients can buy property in the West Country.

Victor Sydney James HARDING
Born: 18 June 1932 in Southwark
Educated: St Marylebone GS
Clubs: Cambridge University, Army, Saracens (2), Sale (4), Harlequins, Edinburgh Wanderers
Position: Lock (6)
Debut: 25 Feb 1961 v France (Twickenham) - 1T, 3 Pts.
Number: 900
Last game: 17 Mar 1962 v Scotland (Murrayfield)
Caps: 6 (W:2, D:3, L:1)
Scoring: 1T, 3 Pts
Appearances: 1961:F,S, 1962:W,I,F,S

Rob Hardwick

Peter Fenton HARDWICK

Born: 15 May 1877 in Tynemouth
Died: 13 February 1924 in North Shields
Clubs: Percy Park (8)
Position: Forward (8)
Debut: 8 Feb 1902 v Ireland (Leicester). Number: 381
Last game: 19 Mar 1904 v Scotland (Inverleith)
Caps: 8 (W:3, D:1, L:4)
Scoring: 0 Pts
Appearances: 1902:I,S, 1903:W,I,S, 1904:W,I,S

Robin John Kieren (Rob) HARDWICK

Born: 29 March 1969 in Kenilworth
Educated: Coundon Court School, Coventry TC
Clubs: Coventry (1), La Rochelle (FR), London Irish, Birmingham
Position: Replacement Prop (1), Bench (3)
Debut: 23 Nov 1996 (rep) v Italy (Twickenham). Number: 1171
Caps: 1 (W:1, L:0)
Scoring: 0 Pts
Appearances: 1996:It(r)

Evan Michael Pearce HARDY, OBE

Born: 13 November 1927 in Meerut, India
Died: 13 January 1994 of Langport, Somerset
Educated: Ampleforth College
Clubs: Blackheath (3), Duke of Wellington's Regt, Army, Combined Services, Headingley
Position: Fly-half (3)
Debut: 10 Feb 1951 v Ireland (Lansdowne Road). Number: 821
Last game: 17 Mar 1951 v Scotland (Twickenham)
Caps: 3 (W:1, L:2)
Scoring: 0 Pts
Appearances: 1951:I,F,S

William Henry (Dusty) HARE, MBE

Born: 29 November 1952 in Newark
Educated: Magnus GS
Clubs: Newark, Nottingham (1), Leicester (24)
Position: Full-back (25), Bench (3)
Debut: 16 Mar 1974 v Wales (Twickenham). Number: 1024
Last game: 9 Jun 1984 v South Africa (Johannesburg) - 3PG, 9 Pts
Caps: 25 (W:11, D:2, L:12)
Scoring: 2T, 14C, 67PG, 1DG, 240 Pts
Appearances: 1974:W, 1978:F,NZ, 1979:NZ, 1980:I,F,W,S, 1981:W,S,Ar1,Ar2, 1982:F,W, 1983:F,W,S,I,NZ, 1984:S,I,F,W,SA1,SA2
Honours: Grand Slam: 1980

Dusty Hare was a farmer who first started playing rugby with Newark and Nottingham and then went on to play 394 matches for Leicester and win 25 England caps at full-back. A genius with the ball in hand, Hare's international debut was against Wales at Twickenham in 1974 and it was a vital day for England because it was their only win against Wales in 16 matches. Hare did not win his second cap until 1978 and his third came in 1980 when he played through the championship for the first time. He kicked three decisive penalties to win the game against Wales at Twickenham – in 1980 – and scored 10 points with the boot in the victory over Scotland, which clinched the Grand Slam. Hare joined Leicester in 1976 at a time when the club was enjoying some adventurous and visionary football under the guidance of coach Chalky White who encouraged the players to attack from anywhere on the pitch providing the options looked good. So Leicester were more than ready for the new targets of Cup and League success and Hare became part of the ever improving Leicester performances, starting with the Cup final in 1977. Leicester took risks but they gained the rewards as well.

Hare was in the Leicester side which came back from a world tour down under to win the league with the kind of football that opponents were unable to match, and the results flowed for the Tigers. Cup or League, it did not seem to matter to Leicester.

It was in a New Year's Eve match at Nuneaton that Hare broke the 7,000 points career mark with just 10 minutes to play on a day when he had been awarded an MBE. He retired from playing after the 1989 Cup final at Twickenham when Leicester lost to Bath. His career included England tours to Japan, Argentina, Canada and South Africa, and he was on the British and Irish Lions tour to New Zealand in 1983. He scored 7,191 points in top rugby with 240 for England and 88 for the Lions. He also fitted in first class cricket with Nottinghamshire and played junior tennis to a high level. He has been development co-ordinator at Leicester since 1994, and results continue to underline how progressive Leicester are no matter what the challenge. He says: "It's nice to see that some of the old players are still helping out at Tigers. I feel we are going back to the old-fashioned way of the club, the way it used to be, and everyone can see the importance now of running second team and junior sides."

Dusty Hare

Andy Harriman

Sir Charles Henry HARPER, KBE
Born: 24 February 1876 in Caistor
Died: 13 May 1950 in Central Devon
Educated: Blundell's School
Clubs: Oxford University (1), Blackheath, Exeter
Position: Forward (1)
Debut: 7 Jan 1899 v Wales (Swansea). Number: 331
Caps: 1 (W:0, L:1)
Scoring: 0 Pts
Appearances: 1899:W

Andrew Tuoyo (Andy) HARRIMAN
Born: 13 July 1964 in Lagos, Nigeria
Educated: Radley College
Clubs: Cambridge University, Harlequins (1)
Position: Wing (1)
Debut: 5 Nov 1988 v Australia (Twickenham). Number: 1129
Caps: 1 (W:1, L:0)
Scoring: 0 Pts
Appearances: 1988:A

Stanley Wakefield (Stan) HARRIS, CBE
Born: 13 December 1894 in Somerset East, South Africa
Died: 3 October 1973 in Kenilworth, South Africa
Educated: Bedford GS
Clubs: Blackheath (2), Pirates (SA), Kenya, Transvaal (SA)
Position: Wing (2)
Debut: 14 Feb 1920 v Ireland (Lansdowne Road). Number: 561
Last game: 20 Mar 1920 v Scotland (Twickenham) - 1T, 3 Pts
Caps: 2 (W:2, L:0)
Scoring: 1T, 3 Pts
Appearances: 1920:I,S

Thomas William Walter HARRIS
Born: Third quarter 1906 in Northampton
Died: 11 September 1958 in Northampton
Educated: Barry Road School
Clubs: Northampton (2)
Position: No 8 (2)
Debut: 16 Mar 1929 v Scotland (Murrayfield). Number: 643
Last game: 13 Feb 1932 v Ireland (Lansdowne Road)
Caps: 2 (W:1, L:1)
Scoring: 0 Pts
Appearances: 1929:S, 1932:I

Arthur Clifford (Cliff) HARRISON
Born: 10 May 1911 in Hartlepool
Died: 29 June 2003 in Durham
Clubs: Hartlepool Rovers (2)
Position: Wing (2)
Debut: 14 Feb 1931 v Ireland (Twickenham). Number: 679
Last game: 21 Mar 1931 v Scotland (Murrayfield)
Caps: 2 (W:0, L:2)
Scoring: 0 Pts
Appearances: 1931:I,S

Arthur Leyland HARRISON, VC
Born: 3 February 1886 in Torquay
Died: Killed in action in 1918 near Zeebrugge, Belgium
Educated: Dover College
Clubs: RNC Dartmouth, United Services, Royal Navy (2)
Position: Forward (2)
Debut: 14 Feb 1914 v Ireland (Twickenham). Number: 541
Last game: 13 Apr 1914 v France (Stade Colombes)
Caps: 2 (W:2, L:0)
Scoring: 0 Pts
Appearances: 1914:I,F
Honours: Championship: 1914

Gilbert (Gillie) HARRISON
Born: 13 June 1858 in Cottingham
Died: 9 November 1894 in Sculcoates
Educated: Cheltenham College
Clubs: Hull (7)
Position: Forward (7)
Debut: 5 Feb 1877 v Ireland (The Oval). Number: 88
Last game: 7 Feb 1885 v Ireland (Manchester)
Caps: 7 (W:5, D:1, L:1)
Scoring: 0 Pts
Appearances: 1877:I,S, 1879:S,I, 1880:S, 1885:W,I

Harold Cecil HARRISON
Born: 26 February 1889 in Solihull
Died: 26 March 1940 in Marylebone
Educated: King Edward's School
Clubs: RMA Woolwich, United Services, Royal Marines (1), Army, Royal Navy (3)
Position: Forward (4)
Debut: 20 Mar 1909 v Scotland (Richmond). Number: 491
Last game: 13 Apr 1914 v France (Stade Colombes)
Caps: 4 (W:3, L:1)
Scoring: 2C, 4 Pts
Appearances: 1909:S, 1914:I,S,F
Honours: Championship: 1914

Mike Harrison

Michael Edward (Mike) HARRISON

Born: 19 April 1956 in Barnsley
Educated: Queen Elizabeth GS
Clubs: Loughborough College, Wakefield (15)
Position: Wing (15)
Debut: 1 Jun 1985 v New Zealand (Christchurch) - 1T, 4 Pts. Number: 1108
Last game: 6 Feb 1988 (capt) v Wales (Twickenham)
Caps: 15 (W:4, L:11). As captain: 7 (W:3, L:4)
Scoring: 8T, 32 Pts
Appearances: 1985:NZ1,NZ2, 1986:S,I,F, 1987:I,F,W,S*,A*,J*,US*,W*, 1988:F*,W*

Wakefield wing Mike Harrison, who captained England in the inaugural World Cup in 1987, won the first of his 15 caps on the tour to New Zealand in 1985, which was led by Paul Dodge. England lost the Test matches 18-13 and 42-15 but Harrison made a name for himself. He was christened 'Burglar Bill', by scoring a breakaway try in each of the internationals and a local brewery even named a beer after him. He was awarded the national captaincy when scrum-half Richard Hill was one of four players suspended after a violent match against Wales in Cardiff in 1987 and marked his first game in charge with a try against the Scots in a 21-12 win at Twickenham before taking his team down under for the World Cup. On arrival in Australia Harrison apparently ordered his players out for a 'welcome' drink to get over the effects of the long flight – something that seems unthinkable these days. England's preparations were also hampered as squad members had to take holidays to train – Harrison was working for a building society – and they only trained together before the tournament at weekends.

Harrison scored five tries, including a hat-trick, in the group stages. This was a national World Cup record until Josh Lewsey scored five against Uruguay in 2003, as England put 60 points on Japan. But England were knocked out of the competition after an awful match, again against the Welsh, in Brisbane, which they lost 16-3. He later said: "We were not a bad side, we had one bad game and that cost us dear. All 15 players had an off day because on paper we should have easily won." Harrison won two more caps but his error against France in 1988 let in Laurent Rodriguez for the winning try, condemning England to defeat by a single point, and after a loss to Wales he was dropped from the side.

That was far from the end of rugby for the fitness fanatic Harrison however who continued to play, mostly in the centre for Wakefield Cougars in the Yorkshire leagues, well into his forties. His old club Wakefield, which also produced the 1980s centre Bryan Barley, was disbanded in 2004 when the financial struggle became too much.

Educated at Queen Elizabeth Grammar School, Wakefield, which also produced the World Cup winning centre Mike Tindall, Harrison has continued his career in the financial sector.

James Haskell

Bernard Charles (Jock) HARTLEY, OBE

Born: 16 March 1879 in Woodford
Died: 24 April 1960 in Chichester
Educated: Dulwich College
Clubs: Cambridge University, Blackheath (2)
Position: Forward (2)
Debut: 9 Mar 1901 v Scotland (Blackheath). Number: 369
Last game: 15 Mar 1902 v Scotland (Inverleith)
Caps: 2 (W:1, L:1)
Scoring: 0 Pts
Appearances: 1901:S, 1902:S

James HASKELL

Born: 2 April 1985 in Windsor
Educated: Wellington College
Clubs: Wasps (1)
Position: Flanker (1)
Debut: 17 Mar 2004 v Wales (Cardiff). Number: 1284
Caps: 1 (W:0, L:1)
Scoring: 0 Pts
Appearances: 2007:W

Leslie Woods HASLETT

Born: 5 June 1900 in Pontypool, Wales
Died: In Canada, details unknown
Educated: Cheltenham College
Clubs: RMA Woolwich, Blackheath, Birkenhead Park (2)
Position: Lock (2)
Debut: 13 Feb 1926 v Ireland (Lansdowne Road) - 1T, 3 Pts. Number: 612
Last game: 27 Feb 1926 v France (Twickenham)
Caps: 2 (W:1, L:1)
Scoring: 1T, 3 Pts
Appearances: 1926:I,F

George William D HASTINGS

Born: 7 November 1924 in Dursley
Clubs: Old Patesians, Gloucester (13)
Position: Prop (13)
Debut: 22 Jan 1955 v Wales (Cardiff). Number: 851
Last game: 15 Mar 1958 v Scotland (Murrayfield) - 1PG, 3 Pts
Caps: 13 (W:8, D:3, L:2)
Scoring: 1T, 1C, 2PG, 11 Pts
Appearances: 1955:W,I,F,S, 1957:W,I,F,S, 1958:W,A,I,F,S
Honours: Grand Slam: 1957. Championship: 1958

Harold HAVELOCK

Born: Details unknown
Died: Details unknown
Clubs: Hartlepool Rovers (3), West Hartlepool, Hull RL
Position: Flanker (3)
Debut: 1 Jan 1908 v France (Stade Colombes). Number: 454
Last game: 8 Feb 1908 v Ireland (Richmond)
Caps: 3 (W:2, L:1)
Scoring: 0 Pts
Appearances: 1908:F,W,I

Andy Hazell

John Joseph HAWCRIDGE
Born: Third quarter 1863 in Macclesfield
Died: 1 January 1905 in San Francisco, USA
Educated: Manningham Academy
Clubs: Manningham, Bradford (2)
Position: Three-quarter (2)
Debut: 3 Jan 1885 v Wales (Swansea) - 1T, 1 Pt. Number: 170
Last game: 7 Feb 1885 v Ireland (Manchester) - 1T, 1 Pt
Caps: 2 (W:2, L:0)
Scoring: 2T, 2 Pts
Appearances: 1885:W,I

Leslie William HAYWARD
Born: 17 May 1885 in Cheltenham
Died: Details unknown
Educated: Cheltenham GS
Clubs: Cheltenham (1)
Position: Centre (1)
Debut: 12 Feb 1910 v Ireland (Twickenham).Number: 499
Caps: 1 (W:0, D:1, L:0)
Scoring: 0 Pts
Appearances: 1910:I
Honours: Championship: 1910

Andrew Robert (Andy) HAZELL
Born: 25 April 1978 in Gloucester
Educated: Gloucester School
Clubs: Gloucester Old Boys, Gloucester (6)
Position: Flanker (2), Replacement (4), Bench (3)
Debut: 13 Nov 2004 v Canada (Twickenham). Number: 1256
Last game: 19 Mar 2005 (rep) v Scotland (Twickenham)
Caps: 6 (W:4, L:2)
Scoring: 1T, 5 Pts
Appearances: 2004:C,SA(r), 2005:W,F(r),It(r),S(r)

David St George HAZELL
Born: 23 April 1931 in Taunton
Educated: Taunton School
Clubs: Loughborough College, Leicester (4), Bristol
Position: Prop (4)
Debut: 22 Jan 1955 v Wales (Cardiff). Number: 852
Last game: 19 Mar 1955 v Scotland (Twickenham)-1PG,3 Pts
Caps: 4 (W:1, D:1, L:2)
Scoring: 3PG, 9 Pts
Appearances: 1955:W,I,F,S

Austin Sean HEALEY
Born: 26 October 1973 in Wallasey
Educated: St Anselm's College
Clubs: Birkenhead Park, Waterloo, Orrell, Leicester (51)
Position: Wing (31), Scrum-half (4), Fly-half (1), Full-back (1), Replacement (14), Bench (4)
Debut: 15 Feb 1997 (rep) v Ireland (Lansdowne Road). Number: 1175
Last game: 30 Aug 2003 v France (Marseille)
Caps: 51 (W:34, D:2, L:15)
Scoring: 15T, 75 Pts. Discipline - Sin bins: 1
Appearances: 1997:I(r),W,A(r),A(r),NZ1(r),SA(r),NZ2, 1998:F,W,S,I,A,NZ1,NZ2,H,It,A,SA(r), 1999:US,C,It,NZ,Tg,Fj,SA(r), 2000:I,F,W,It,S,SA1,SA2,A,SA(r), 2001:W(r),It,S,F,I(r),A,R,SA, 2002:S,I,F,W,It(r),NZ(r),A(r),SA(r), 2003:F
Honours: Championship: 2000, 2001

Robert Daniel (Bob) HEARN
Born: 12 August 1940 in Cheltenham
Educated: Cheltenham College
Clubs: Trinity College Dublin, Oxford University, Bedford (6)
Position: Centre (6)
Debut: 26 Feb 1966 v France (Stade Colombes). Number: 946
Last game: 15 Apr 1967 v Wales (Cardiff)
Caps: 6 (W:2, L:4)
Scoring: 0 Pts
Appearances: 1966:F,S, 1967:I,F,S,W

Arthur Howard HEATH
Born: 29 May 1856 in Newcastle-under-Lyme
Died: 24 April 1930 in Marylebone
Educated: Clifton College
Clubs: Oxford University (1)
Position: Full-back (1)
Debut: 6 Mar 1876 v Scotland (The Oval). Number: 80
Caps: 1 (W:1, L:0)
Scoring: 0 Pts
Appearances: 1876:S

John (Jack) HEATON
Born: 30 August 1912
Died: October 1998 in Dwyfor, Wales
Educated: Cowley GS
Clubs: Liverpool University (3), Nottingham, Waterloo (6)
Position: Centre (9)
Debut: 19 Jan 1935 v Wales (Twickenham). Number: 717
Last game: 19 Apr 1947 (capt) v France (Twickenham)
Caps: 9 (W:5, D:1, L:3). As captain: 2 (W:2, L:0)
Scoring: 4C, 3PG, 17 Pts
Appearances: 1935:W,I,S, 1939:W,I,S, 1947:I,S*,F*

Alan Peter HENDERSON
Born: 26 May 1920 in Kirkintilloch, Scotland
Educated: Taunton School
Clubs: Cambridge University (5), Edinburgh Wanderers (4)
Position: Hooker (9)
Debut: 18 Jan 1947 v Wales (Cardiff). Number: 756
Last game: 12 Feb 1949 v Ireland (Lansdowne Road)
Caps: 9 (W:3, L:6)
Scoring: 1T, 3 Pts
Appearances: 1947:W,I,S,F, 1948:I,S,F, 1949:W,I

Austin Healey

Sir Robert Samuel Findlay HENDERSON, KCMG

Born: 11 December 1858 in Calcutta, India
Died: 5 October 1924 in Millbank, London
Educated: Bedford GS, Fettes School
Clubs: Edinburgh University, Army Medical Service, Blackheath (5), St Mary's Hospital
Position: Forward (5)
Debut: 16 Dec 1882 v Wales (Swansea) - 1T, 1Pt. Number: 150
Last game: 3 Jan 1885 v Wales (Swansea)
Caps: 5 (W:5, L:0)
Scoring: 1T, 1 Pt
Appearances: 1883:W,S, 1884:W,S, 1885:W
Honours: Championship: 1883, 1884

Walter George HEPPEL

Born: First quarter 1877 in Axbridge
Died: 4 October 1939 in Reading
Clubs: Devonport Albion (1)
Position: Forward (1)
Debut: 14 Feb 1903 v Ireland (Lansdowne Road). Number: 389
Caps: 1 (W:0, L:1)
Scoring: 0 Pts
Appearances: 1903:I

Alfred John HERBERT

Born: 1 January 1933 in Stroud
Educated: Marling School
Clubs: Cambridge University, Wasps (6)
Position: Flanker (6)
Debut: 1 Mar 1958 v France (Stade Colombes). Number: 876
Last game: 21 Mar 1959 v Scotland (Twickenham)
Caps: 6 (W:2, D:3, L:1)
Scoring: 0 Pts
Appearances: 1958:F,S, 1959:W,I,F,S
Honours: Championship: 1958

Robert (Bob) HESFORD

Born: 26 March 1951 in Blackpool
Educated: Arnold School
Clubs: Durham University, Bristol (10)
Position: No 8 (7), Replacement (3), Bench (9)
Debut: 21 Feb 1981 (rep) v Scotland (Twickenham). Number: 1067
Last game: 20 Apr 1985 v Wales (Cardiff)
Caps: 10 (W:5, D:2, L:3)
Scoring: 0 Pts
Appearances: 1981:S(r), 1982:A,S,F(r), 1983:F(r), 1985:R,F,S,I,W

Nigel John HESLOP

Born: 4 December 1963 in West Hartlepool
Educated: Rainforth School
Clubs: Waterloo, Liverpool St Helens, Orrell (10),Oldham RL
Position: Wing (9), Replacement (1), Bench (5)
Debut: 28 Jul 1990 v Argentina (Buenos Aires).Number: 1137
Last game: 7 Mar 1992 (rep) v Wales (Twickenham)
Caps: 10 (W:9, L:1)
Scoring: 3T, 12 Pts
Appearances: 1990:Ar1,Ar2,Ar, 1991:W,S,I,F,US,F, 1992:W(r)
Honours: Grand Slam: 1991. Championship: 1992

James Gilbert George (Jim) HETHERINGTON
Born: 3 March 1932 in Brighton
Educated: Churcher's School
Clubs: Trojans, Cambridge University, Northampton (6)
Position: Full-back (6)
Debut: 1 Feb 1958 v Australia (Twickenham) - 1PG, 3 Pts. Number: 873
Last game: 21 Mar 1959 v Scotland (Twickenham)
Caps: 6 (W:3, D:2, L:1)
Scoring: 3PG, 9 Pts
Appearances: 1958:A,I, 1959:W,I,F,S
Honours: Championship: 1958

Edwin Newbury HEWITT
Born: 22 April 1924 in Coventry
Educated: Barker Butts School, Coventry TC
Clubs: Coventry (3)
Position: Full-back (3)
Debut: 20 Jan 1951 v Wales (Swansea) - 1C, 2 Pts. Number: 812
Last game: 24 Feb 1951 v France (Twickenham)
Caps: 3 (W:0, L:3)
Scoring: 1C, 2 Pts
Appearances: 1951:W,I,F

Nigel Heslop

Walter William HEWITT
Born: Third quarter 1854 in Greenwich
Died: Details unknown
Educated: Queen's House School
Clubs: Queen's House (4)
Position: Forward (4)
Debut: 5 Feb 1881 v Ireland (Manchester). Number: 133
Last game: 6 Feb 1882 v Ireland (Lansdowne Road)
Caps: 4 (W:2, D:2, L:0)
Scoring: 0 Pts
Appearances: 1881:I,W,S, 1882:I

John Lawrence HICKSON
Born: Third quarter 1862 in Wandsworth
Died: 4 August 1920 in Bradford
Clubs: Bingley, Bradford (6)
Position: Forward (6)
Debut: 8 Jan 1887 v Wales (Llanelli). Number: 189
Last game: 15 Mar 1890 v Ireland (Blackheath)
Caps: 6 (W:2, D:2, L:2). As captain:1 (W:1, L:0)
Scoring: 0 Pts
Appearances: 1887:W,I,S, 1890:W,S*,I

Reginald (Reg) HIGGINS
Born: 11 July 1930 in Widnes, Lancs
Died: Second quarter 1979 in Frodsham
Educated: Wade Deacon HS
Clubs: Leeds University, UAU, Royal Signals, Army, Combined Services, Liverpool (13)
Position: Flanker (13)
Debut: 16 Jan 1954 v Wales (Twickenham). Number: 838
Last game: 17 Jan 1959 v Wales (Cardiff)
Caps: 13 (W:8, D:1, L:4)
Scoring: 2T, 6 Pts
Appearances: 1954:W,NZ,I,S, 1955:W,I,F,S, 1957:W,I,F,S, 1959:W
Honours: Grand Slam: 1957

Alastair James HIGNELL
Born: 4 September 1955 in Ely, Cambs
Educated: Denstone College
Clubs: Cambridge University (5), Bristol (9)
Position: Full-back (14)
Debut: 31 May 1975 v Australia (Brisbane). Number: 1034
Last game: 17 Mar 1979 v Wales (Cardiff)
Caps: 14 (W:4, D:1, L:9)
Scoring: 3C, 14PG, 48 Pts
Appearances: 1975:A2, 1976:A,W,S,I, 1977:S,I,F,W, 1978:W, 1979:S,I,F,W

Sir Basil Alexander HILL, KBE
Born: 23 April 1880 in Broughty Ferry, Scotland
Died: 31 July 1960 in Coupar, Angus, Scotland
Educated: Newenheim School
Clubs: RNEC Keyham, Ordnance Services, Army, United Services, Blackheath (9)
Position: Forward (9)
Debut: 14 Feb 1903 v Ireland (Lansdowne Road). Number: 390
Last game: 12 Jan 1907 (capt) v Wales (Swansea)
Caps: 9 (W:2, D:2, L:5). As captain: 2 (W:1, L:1)
Scoring: 5C, 10 Pts
Appearances: 1903:I,S, 1904:W,I, 1905:W,NZ, 1906:SA, 1907:F*,W*

Alastair Hignell

Richard Anthony HILL, MBE
Born: 23 May 1973 in Dormansland, Surrey
Educated: Bishop Wordsworth School
Clubs: Brunel University, Salisbury, Saracens (71)
Position: Flanker (55), No 8 (13), Replacement (3)
Debut: 1 Feb 1997 v Scotland (Twickenham). Number: 1174
Last game: 26 Jun 2004 v Australia (Brisbane) - 1T, 5 Pts
Caps: 71 (W:50, D:2, L:19)
Scoring: 12T, 60 Pts
Appearances: 1997:S,I,F,W,A,A,NZ1,SA,NZ2, 1998:F,W,H(r),It(r),A,SA, 1999:S,I,F,W,A,US,C,It,NZ,Tg,Fj(r),SA, 2000:I,F,W,It,S,SA1,SA2,A,Ar,SA, 2001:W,It,S,F,I,A,SA, 2002:S,I,F,W,It,NZ,A,SA, 2003:F,W,It,S,I,NZ,A,F,Geo,F,A, 2004:It,S,I,W,F,NZ1,NZ2,A
Honours: RWC Winner: 2003. Grand Slam: 2003.
Championship: 2000, 2001

Richard Hill's influence within England's World Cup winning team of 2003 is demonstrated by the fact that he was the one player never dropped by England coach Sir Clive Woodward.

Hill did the majority of his most effective work away from the spotlight, notably on the blindside of the scrum but also at No 8 and openside.

Such was his importance to the team that when he was injured in the opening game of the 2003 World Cup there

Richard Anthony Hill

were fears England would not make it to the final stages without him. Fortunately for England he was available at exactly the right time, returning to take his place in the mighty back three alongside Lawrence Dallaglio and Neil Back. He quietly pocketed an MBE for his troubles.

England's Mr Dependable could play anywhere in the back row, and was equally effective in attack and defence, scoring 11 tries in his 71 internationals.

"I've dropped Back and Dallaglio, but I've never left Richard Hill out of my starting line-up because Richard Hill has never dropped off the pace," Woodward said.

"He's played fantastically well whether at 6, 8 or 7 and he's a brilliant footballer in a very competitive area."

And Lawrence Dallaglio added: "He was an unsung hero but he's shed that tag now and become one of the main men.

"He works at the coal-face, is very unfussy, has an incredible work-rate, gets through a lot of tackles and gets his hands on the ball. That's why he's so well respected."

Often referred to as the 'silent assassin' for his quiet but abrasive style, Hill entered the England scene from Saracens in 1997 against Scotland, as openside flanker ahead of Neil Back. Under Clive Woodward, eyes already on the prize, the forward line was completely reorganised to accommodate the talent at England's disposal and he moved to blindside flanker.

That same year he made the first of three successive Lions squads, winning two caps on the tour of South Africa.

But he failed to finish either of the 2001 or 2005 tours to Australia and New Zealand. Hill was taken out by a stray elbow in the second Test in Australia and injured his knee inside the first quarter of the trip to New Zealand.

Not even Hill would have made much difference to the scorelines in New Zealand but his absence in the final Test in Australia was a hugely significant factor in the Lions losing the decisive game.

Richard John HILL

Born: 4 May 1961 in Birmingham
Educated: Bishop Wordsworth School
Clubs: Exeter University, Salisbury, Bath (29)
Position: Scrum-half (26), Replacement (3), Bench (19)
Debut: 2 Jun 1984 v South Africa (Port Elizabeth).
Number: 1090
Last game: 2 Nov 1991 v Australia (Twickenham)
Caps: 29 (W:16, L:13). As captain: 3 (W:0, L:3)
Scoring: 2T, 8 Pts
Appearances: 1984:SA1,SA2, 1985:I(r),NZ2(r), 1986:F(r), 1987:I*,F*,W*,US, 1989:Fj, 1990:I,F,W,S,Ar1,Ar2,Ar, 1991:W,S,I,F,Fj,A,NZ,It,US,F,S,A
Honours: Grand Slam: 1991

England, without a Cardiff victory in 26 years, had been primed by a rousing pre-match team talk from Richard Hill, and within five minutes an all-out brawl broke out at a line-out. Several players were dropped for their roles in the scrap, including Hill.

He would spend the next two years in the international wilderness.

He returned against Fiji in 1989 a better player, and he played a key role in the 1990 Five Nations, scoring one spectacular try against, fittingly, Wales. Looking for the Grand Slam, England disappointingly lost 13-6 to the Scots.

There were no such slip-ups the following year, as England profited from a grittier, more pragmatic style of play, and Hill went on an unbroken run of 20 games, taking the Grand Slam.

The World Cup in 1991 saw them make the final, but a return to a more expansive approach didn't pay off as they were beaten 12-6 by Australia at Twickenham, and Hill's international career came to an end after 29 appearances, a record at the time for an England scrum-half.

In the 1993-94 season he helped Bath to the domestic 'Grand Slam', winning League and Cup, and also triumphing in the Middlesex 7s and Welsh National 7s. He crowned a brilliant career at Twickenham as Bath beat Leicester to claim the Pilkington Cup in front of 68,000 people, then a record for a club game.

It was inevitable that this naturally fit and energetic player would stay in the game, and he is currently head coach at Bristol, taking them to the top of the Guinness Premiership for large parts of the 2006-07 season, and marking himself as someone who is capable of taking charge of the national side one day.

Richard John Hill

Ronald Johnstone HILLARD, CMG

Born: 6 May 1903 in Durham
Died: 23 March 1971 in Weymouth
Educated: St Paul's School
Clubs: Oxford University (1), Old Pauline's
Position: Prop (1)
Debut: 3 Jan 1925 v New Zealand (Twickenham). Number: 596
Caps: 1 (W:0, L:1)
Scoring: 0 Pts
Appearances: 1925:NZ

Robert (Bob) HILLER

Born: 14 October 1942 in Woking
Educated: Bec School
Clubs: Birmingham University, Oxford University, Harlequins (19)
Position: Full-back (19)
Debut: 20 Jan 1968 v Wales (Twickenham) - 1C, 1PG, 5 Pts. Number: 964
Last game: 12 Feb 1972 (capt) v Ireland (Twickenham) - 1C, 2PG, 8 Pts
Caps: 19 (W:6, D:3, L:10). As captain: 7 (W:2, D:1, L:4)
Scoring: 3T, 12C, 33PG, 2DG, 138 Pts
Appearances: 1968:W,I,F,S, 1969:I,F,S,W,SA*, 1970:I*,W*,S*, 1971:I,F*,S,S,P, 1972:W*,I*

Bob Hiller had already made eight appearances for England at full-back when he was made captain for the first time for the match against South Africa at Twickenham in 1969.

The great difference for him was that he had four months to think about it because England chose a match squad that far ahead of the actual game.

The revolutionary long build-up was the idea of Don White of Northampton, England's first coach, and the 30-strong squad trained regularly, in contrast to previous matches when the team would have a run out on the eve of the match.

At those times matches between England and countries such as South Africa, New Zealand and Australia were much less frequent and the expectation for Hiller's team was high. At that time Hiller had not lost in an England shirt at Twickenham and that brief record was sustained as his team beat South Africa 11-8; Hiller kicking a penalty and converting one of the two tries scored by John Pullin and Peter Larter.

Hiller did not complete the match because he injured his right hip and had to come off injured for the first time, being replaced by Chris Wardlow.

Hiller had always been an outstanding sportsman throughout his education at Bec School and Birmingham and Oxford Universities, and won a Blue for cricket and rugby at Oxford. He moved on to Harlequins for his club rugby and first wore an England shirt on the tour to Canada in 1967. He broke into the England team in 1968 and played 19 times, scoring 138 points. These figures stood for 10 years and were finally broken by Dusty Hare of Leicester. Hiller scored three tries as well.

In 1971 England omitted Hiller from their first match against Wales at Cardiff but recalled him for the next five games which included a special match against Scotland and another against an Overseas team to mark the Centenary of the Rugby Football Union. Hiller scored in every match he played for England and in 1971 it was his three penalties against Ireland which provided England with their only win. Two more defeats at the start of 1972 led to Hiller's departure from the England team but there were many who thought he should have been retained.

Hiller was second choice full-back on two tours by the British and Irish Lions. In 1968 he understudied the tour captain Tom Kiernan of Ireland in South Africa and JPR Williams of Wales in New Zealand in 1971. Hiller still managed to score in each match he played in New Zealand – 110 points from 11 games.

Hiller was a stalwart of Surrey and any team he played for benefited from his sense of humour as well as the supply of points which came from one of the strongest kickers in the game. Hiller became president of Harlequins.

Bob Hiller

Alfred Ernest HIND
Born: 7 April 1878 in Preston
Died: 21 March 1947 in Oadby, Leicester
Educated: Uppingham School
Clubs: Cambridge University, Leicester (2), Nottingham
Position: Wing (2)
Debut: 2 Dec 1905 v New Zealand (Crystal Palace). Number: 416
Last game: 13 Jan 1906 v Wales (Richmond)
Caps: 2 (W:0, L:2)
Scoring: 0 Pts
Appearances: 1905:NZ, 1906:W

Guy Reginald HIND
Born: 4 April 1887 in Stoke-on-Trent
Died: 8 November 1970 in Newcastle-under-Lyne
Educated: Haileybury & ISC
Clubs: Guy's Hospital (2), Blackheath
Position: Prop (2)
Debut: 19 Mar 1910 v Scotland (Inverleith). Number: 470
Last game: 11 Feb 1911 v Ireland (Lansdowne Road)
Caps: 2 (W:1, L:1)
Scoring: 0 Pts
Appearances: 1910:S, 1911:I
Honours: Championship: 1910

Reginald Francis Arthur HOBBS, CMG
Born: 30 January 1878 in Leigh
Died: 10 July 1953 in Sutton Very, Wilts
Educated: Wellington College
Clubs: RMA Woolwich, Royal Engineers, Army, Blackheath (2)
Position: Forward (2)
Debut: 11 Mar 1899 v Scotland (Blackheath). Number: 336
Last game: 10 Jan 1903 v Wales (Swansea)
Caps: 2 (W:0, L:2)
Scoring: 0 Pts
Appearances: 1899:S, 1903:W

Reginald Geoffrey Stirling (Pooh) HOBBS, OBE
Born: 8 August 1908 in Elham
Died: Third quarter 1977 in Bromley, Kent
Educated: Wellington College
Clubs: RMA Woolwich, Royal Artillery, Army (1), Richmond (3)
Position: Lock (4)
Debut: 2 Jan 1932 v South Africa (Twickenham). Number: 687
Last game: 19 Mar 1932 v Scotland (Twickenham)
Caps: 4 (W:2, L:2)
Scoring: 0 Pts
Appearances: 1932:SA,W,I,S

Simon Hodgkinson

Harold Augustus HODGES
Born: 22 January 1886 in Mansfield Woodhouse
Died: Killed in action in 1918 near Mesnil, France
Educated: Sedbergh School
Clubs: Oxford University, Sorbonne (FR), Nottingham (2), Blackheath
Position: Prop (2)
Debut: 13 Jan 1906 v Wales (Richmond). Number: 422
Last game: 10 Feb 1906 v Ireland (Leicester)
Caps: 2 (W:0, L:2)
Scoring: 0 Pts
Appearances: 1906:W,I

Simon David HODGKINSON
Born: 15 December 1962 in Thornbury
Educated: Stamford School, Trent Poly
Clubs: Nottingham (14), Moseley
Position: Full-back (14), Bench (1)
Debut: 13 May 1989 v Romania (Bucharest) - 8C, 1PG, 19 Pts. Number: 1134
Last game: 11 Oct 1991 v United States (Twickenham) - 4C, 3PG, 17 Pts
Caps: 14 (W:12, L:2)
Scoring: 1T, 35C, 43PG, 203 Pts
Appearances: 1989:R,Fj, 1990:I,F,W,S,Ar1,Ar2,Ar, 1991:W,S,I,F,US
Honours: Grand Slam: 1991

Charles Christopher (Charlie) HODGSON
Born: 12 November 1980 in Halifax
Educated: Bradford GS
Clubs: Old Broadleians, Sale (29)
Position: Fly-half (23), Centre (2), Replacement (4), Bench (2)
Debut: 17 Nov 2001 v Romania (Twickenham) - 2T, 14C, 2PG, 44 Pts. Number: 1234
Last game: 18 Nov 2006 v South Africa (Twickenham) - 2PG, 6 Pts
Caps: 29 (W:17, L:12)
Scoring: 6T, 44C, 44PG, 3DG, 259 Pts
Appearances: 2001:R, 2002:S(r),I(r),It(r),Ar, 2003:F,W,It(r), 2004:NZ1,NZ2,A,C,SA,A, 2005:W,F,I,It,S,A,NZ,Sm, 2006:W,It,S,F,NZ,Ar,SA1
Honours: Championship: 2003

John McDonald HODGSON
Born: 13 February 1909 in Gosforth
Died: 21 April 1970
Clubs: Northern (7), Leicester
Position: Flanker (6), No 8 (1)
Debut: 2 Jan 1932 v South Africa (Twickenham). Number: 666
Last game: 8 Feb 1936 v Ireland (Lansdowne Road)
Caps: 7 (W:4, L:3)
Scoring: 0 Pts
Appearances: 1932:SA,W,I,S, 1934:W,I, 1936:I
Honours: Championship: 1934

Charlie Hodgson

Stanley Arthur Murray HODGSON
Born: 14 May 1928 in Durham
Clubs: Durham City (11)
Position: Hooker (11)
Debut: 16 Jan 1960 v Wales (Twickenham). Number: 887
Last game: 18 Jan 1964 v Wales (Twickenham)
Caps: 11 (W:4, D:4, L:3)
Scoring: 0 Pts
Appearances: 1960:W,I,F,S, 1961:SA,W, 1962:W,I,F,S, 1964:W

Murray Bernard HOFMEYER
Born: 9 December 1925 in Pretoria, South Africa
Died: 26 June 1990 in Johannesburg, South Africa
Educated: Pretoria HS
Clubs: Oxford University (3)
Position: Full-back (3)
Debut: 21 Jan 1950 v Wales (Twickenham) - 1C, 2 Pts. Number: 803
Last game: 18 Mar 1950 v Scotland (Murrayfield) - 1C, 1PG, 5 Pts
Caps: 3 (W:0, L:3)
Scoring: 2C, 1PG, 7 Pts
Appearances: 1950:W,F,S

Thomas Bradley HOGARTH
Born: First quarter 1878 in Hartlepool
Died: 1961
Clubs: Hartlepool Creelers, Hartlepool Rovers (1), West Hartlepool, Leicester, Gray's Athletic, Durham City
Position: Forward (1)
Debut: 22 Mar 1906 v France (Parc des Princes) - 1T, 3 Pts. Number: 435
Caps: 1 (W:1, L:0)
Scoring: 1T, 3 Pts
Appearances: 1906:F

Jonathan George (George) HOLFORD
Born: 1886
Died: Details unknown
Educated: Linden School
Clubs: Gloucester (2)
Position: Lock (2)
Debut: 17 Jan 1920 v Wales (Swansea). Number: 548
Last game: 31 Jan 1920 v France (Twickenham)
Caps: 2 (W:1, L:1)
Scoring: 0 Pts
Appearances: 1920:W,F

David (Dave) HOLLAND
Born: 1886 in Gloucester
Died: 7 March 1945 in Gloucester
Clubs: Devonport Albion (3), Gloucester, Oldham RL
Position: Forward (3)
Debut: 20 Jan 1912 v Wales (Twickenham). Number: 519
Last game: 16 Mar 1912 v Scotland (Inverleith) - 1T, 3 Pts
Caps: 3 (W:2, L:1)
Scoring: 1T, 3 Pts
Appearances: 1912:W,I,S

Thomas Edwin (Toff) HOLLIDAY
Born: 13 July 1898 in Wigton
Died: 19 July 1969 in Carlisle
Clubs: Aspatria (7), Oldham RL
Position: Full-back (7)
Debut: 17 Mar 1923 v Scotland (Inverleith). Number: 584
Last game: 20 Mar 1926 v Scotland (Twickenham)
Caps: 7 (W:4, D:1, L:2)
Scoring: 0 Pts
Appearances: 1923:S,F, 1925:I,S,F, 1926:F,S
Honours: Championship: 1923

Cyril Butler HOLMES
Born: 11 January 1915 in Bolton
Died: 21 June 1996
Educated: Wrekin College
Clubs: RMA Sandhurst, Manchester University, Manchester (3), Army
Position: Wing (3)
Debut: 15 Mar 1947 v Scotland (Twickenham) - 1T, 3 Pts. Number: 769
Last game: 29 Mar 1948 v France (Stade Colombes)
Caps: 3 (W:1, L:2)
Scoring: 1T, 3 Pts
Appearances: 1947:S, 1948:I,F

Edgar HOLMES
Born: 1863
Died: Details unknown
Clubs: Manningham (2)
Position: Forward (2)
Debut: 1 Mar 1890 v Scotland (Raeburn Place). Number: 219
Last game: 15 Mar 1890 v Ireland (Blackheath)
Caps: 2 (W:2, L:0)
Scoring: 0 Pts
Appearances: 1890:S,I

Walter Alan HOLMES
Born: 10 September 1925 in Nuneaton
Educated: Vicarage Street School
Clubs: Nuneaton (16)
Position: Prop (16)
Debut: 21 Jan 1950 v Wales (Twickenham). Number: 804
Last game: 21 Mar 1953 v Scotland (Twickenham)
Caps: 16 (W:8, D:1, L:7)
Scoring: 0 Pts
Appearances: 1950:W,I,F,S, 1951:W,I,F,S, 1952:SA,S,I,F, 1953:W,I,F,S
Honours: Championship: 1953

William Barry (Barry) HOLMES
Born: 6 January 1928 in Buenos Aires, Argentina
Died: 10 November 1949 in Salta, Argentina
Educated: St George's School
Clubs: Cambridge University (4), Richmond, Old Georgians (AR)
Position: Full-back (4)
Debut: 15 Jan 1949 v Wales (Cardiff). Number: 791
Last game: 19 Mar 1949 v Scotland (Twickenham)
Caps: 4 (W:2, L:2)
Scoring: 2C, 4 Pts
Appearances: 1949:W,I,F,S

Damian Hopley

William Gordon HOOK
Born: 21 December 1920 in Gloucester
Educated: Sir Thomas Rich's GS
Clubs: Gloucester (3)
Position: Full-back (3)
Debut: 17 Mar 1951 v Scotland (Twickenham) - 1C, 2 Pts. Number: 824
Last game: 19 Jan 1952 v Wales (Twickenham)
Caps: 3 (W:1, L:2)
Scoring: 1C, 2 Pts
Appearances: 1951:S, 1952:SA,W

Charles Alexander HOOPER
Born: 6 June 1869 in Stonehouse, Glos
Died: 16 September 1950 in Taplow, Bucks
Educated: Clifton College
Clubs: Cambridge University, Middlesex Wanderers (3), Gloucester
Position: Centre (3)
Debut: 6 Jan 1894 v Wales (Birkenhead Park). Number: 264
Last game: 17 Mar 1894 v Scotland (Raeburn Place)
Caps: 3 (W:1, L:2)
Scoring: 0 Pts
Appearances: 1894:W,I,S

Damian Paul HOPLEY
Born: 12 April 1970 in Lambeth, London
Educated: Harrow School
Clubs: Cambridge University, Wasps (3)
Position: Wing (2), Replacement (1), Bench (2)
Debut: 4 Jun 1995 (rep) v Samoa (Durban).Number: 1159
Last game: 16 Dec 1995 v Samoa (Twickenham)
Caps: 3 (W:2, L:1)
Scoring: 0 Pts
Appearances: 1995:Sm(r),SA,Sm

Damian Hopley only played three times for England but it is in his role as a revolutionary in the game that he will be remembered in rugby's history.

When the game turned professional in 1995 there was chaos all around. The RFU certainly had no idea how to make the new game of rugby union work and the major unions stumbled around in the first few years, a number of them unable to cope with the changes.

The rugby unions were the first with a voice because they were the ones to vote for the game to turn professional.

The clubs in England certainly had a voice as they drove the game forward but crucially the players were the silent majority.

Hopley changed that by setting up the first players' union in England – he is currently chief executive – and later going on to head up the worldwide body representing the players.

The players were in fact lucky to find a person of Hopley's calibre and commitment to lead the only body which represents their views.

Hopley's union (the PRA) have negotiated a series of concessions for the players including a deal that guaranteed they play a maximum of 32 matches each year.

An elite squad of 50 to 60 England players will be restricted to 32 matches a season, including a maximum of 10 internationals in a calendar year and eight in one season.

"We won the rugby World Cup in 2003 in spite of the system rather than because of it," said Hopley, who was a member of England's Sevens World Cup winning side in 1993.

"It just shows how lucky we were with the coincidence of a great group of players allied to a visionary coaching team. Since then, there had been a steady decline. In many ways, Robbo [Andy Robinson] was a victim of the system. We can't keep papering over the cracks. We've given lip service to the notion of involving the likes of ourselves in the decision-making process. It's about time that changed."

Frederick John Vanderby (John) HOPLEY

Born: 27 August 1883 in Grahamstown, South Africa
Died: 16 August 1951 in Marandellas, Rhodesia
Educated: Harrow School
Clubs: Rhodesia, Cambridge University, Blackheath (3), Villagers (SA)
Position: Flanker (3)
Debut: 5 Jan 1907 v France (Richmond). Number: 439
Last game: 8 Feb 1908 v Ireland (Richmond)
Caps: 3 (W:2, L:1)
Scoring: 0 Pts
Appearances: 1907:F,W, 1908:I

Michael John HORAK

Born: 3 June 1977 in Johannesburg, South Africa
Educated: Grey College
Clubs: Leicester, Bristol, Free State (SA), London Irish (1)
Position: Full-back (1)
Debut: 22 Jun 2002 v Argentina (Buenos Aires). Number: 1242
Caps: 1 (W:1, L:0)
Scoring: 0 Pts
Appearances: 2002:Ar

Peter Cotton HORDORN

Born: 13 May 1907 in Berkhampstead
Died: 22 June 1988 in Peterborough
Educated: Brighton College
Clubs: Oxford University, Newport, Blackheath (3), Gloucester (1)
Position: Flanker (3), No 8 (1)
Debut: 14 Feb 1931 v Ireland (Twickenham). Number: 680
Last game: 20 Jan 1934 v Wales (Cardiff)
Caps: 4 (W:1, L:3)
Scoring: 0 Pts
Appearances: 1931:I,S,F, 1934:W
Honours: Championship: 1934

Charles Henry HORLEY

Born: Third quarter 1860 in Pendlebury
Died: 10 May 1924 of Birkdale
Educated: Pendlebury Road School
Clubs: Swinton (1)
Position: Forward (1)
Debut: 7 Feb 1885 v Ireland (Manchester). Number: 175
Caps: 1 (W:1, L:0)
Scoring: 0 Pts
Appearances: 1885:I

Albert Neilson (Monkey) HORNBY

Born: 10 February 1847 in Blackburn
Died: 17 December 1925 in Parkfield, Nantwich
Educated: Harrow School
Clubs: Preston Grasshoppers (4), Manchester (5)
Position: Full-back (5), Three-quarter (4)
Debut: 5 Feb 1877 v Ireland (The Oval) - 1T, 1 Pt. Number: 89
Last game: 4 Mar 1882 (capt) v Scotland (Manchester)
Caps: 9 (W:4, D:3, L:2). As captain:1 (W:0, L:1)
Scoring: 1T, 1 Pt
Appearances: 1877:I,S, 1878:S,I, 1880:I, 1881:I,S, 1882:I,S*

Michael Horak

GHI

John Philip (Phil) HORROCKS-TAYLOR
Born: 27 October 1934 in Halifax
Educated: Heath GS
Clubs: Cambridge University (2), Halifax, Royal Signals, Wasps, Leicester (5), Middlesbrough (2)
Position: Fly-half (9), Bench (1)
Debut: 18 Jan 1958 v Wales (Twickenham). Number: 871
Last game: 18 Jan 1964 v Wales (Twickenham)
Caps: 9 (W:2, D:3, L:4)
Scoring: 1PG, 3 Pts
Appearances: 1958:W,A, 1961:S, 1962:S, 1963:NZ1,NZ2,A, 1964:NZ,W
Honours: Championship: 1958

Edward Luke HORSFALL
Born: 11 August 1917 in Huddersfield
Died: Second quarter 1981 in Bracknell
Educated: Giggleswick School
Clubs: Huddersfield, Bedford, Gloucester, Headingley, Harlequins (1), Cardiff, RAF, Combined Services
Position: Flanker (1)
Debut: 15 Jan 1949 v Wales (Cardiff). Number: 792
Caps: 1 (W:0, L:1)
Scoring: 0 Pts
Appearances: 1949:W

Anthony Lawrence (Tony) HORTON
Born: 13 July 1938 in Brentford
Educated: Stonyhurst College
Clubs: Royal Marines, Blackheath (7), Van der Stel (SA)
Position: Prop (7)
Debut: 16 Jan 1965 v Wales (Cardiff). Number: 928
Last game: 4 Nov 1967 v New Zealand (Twickenham)
Caps: 7 (W:1, D:1, L:5)
Scoring: 0 Pts
Appearances: 1965:W,I,F,S, 1966:F,S, 1967:NZ

John Philip HORTON
Born: 11 April 1951 in St Helens
Educated: Cowley GS, Didsbury College
Clubs: St Helens, Sale, Bath (13), Bristol
Position: Fly-half (13), Bench (7)
Debut: 4 Feb 1978 v Wales (Twickenham). Number: 1050
Last game: 9 Jun 1984 v South Africa (Johannesburg)
Caps: 13 (W:6, L:7)
Scoring: 4DG, 12 Pts
Appearances: 1978:W,S,I,NZ, 1980:I,F,W,S, 1981:W, 1983:S,I, 1984:SA1,SA2
Honours: Grand Slam: 1980

John Horton

Nigel Edgar HORTON
Born: 13 April 1948 in Birmingham
Educated: Wheelers Lane School
Clubs: King's Norton, Birmingham Police, Moseley (14), Toulouse (FR,6)
Position: Lock (20), Bench (2)
Debut: 8 Feb 1969 v Ireland (Lansdowne Road). Number: 974
Last game: 19 Jan 1980 v Ireland (Twickenham)
Caps: 20 (W:7, D:2, L:11)
Scoring: 1T, 4 Pts
Appearances: 1969:I,F,S,W, 1971:I,F,S, 1974:S, 1975:W, 1977:S,I,F,W, 1978:F,W, 1979:S,I,F,W, 1980:I
Honours: Championship: 1980

Roger Wills HOSEN
Born: 12 June 1933 in Helston, Cornwall
Died: 9 April 2005
Educated: Falmouth GS
Clubs: Loughborough College, Plymouth Albion, Wasps, Cheltenham, Northampton (5), Bristol (5)
Position: Full-back (8), Wing (2)
Debut: 25 May 1963 v New Zealand (Auckland) - 1C, 2PG, 8 Pts. Number: 917
Last game: 15 Apr 1967 v Wales (Cardiff) - 4PG, 12 Pts
Caps: 10 (W:3, L:7)
Scoring: 6C, 17PG, 63 Pts
Appearances: 1963:NZ1,NZ2,A, 1964:F,S, 1967:A,I,F,S,W

Geoffrey Robert d'Aubrey HOSKING
Born: 11 March 1922 in St Thomas
Educated: Cheltenham College
Clubs: Devonport Services (5), Royal Navy
Position: Lock (5)
Debut: 15 Jan 1949 v Wales (Cardiff). Number: 793
Last game: 21 Jan 1950 v Wales (Twickenham)
Caps: 5 (W:2, L:3)
Scoring: 1T, 3 Pts
Appearances: 1949:W,I,F,S, 1950:W

Samuel HOUGHTON
Born: 16 August 1870 in Runcorn
Died: 17 August 1920 in Runcorn
Clubs: Runcorn (1), Birkenhead Wanderers (1)
Position: Full-back (2)
Debut: 6 Feb 1892 v Ireland (Manchester). Number: 243
Last game: 4 Jan 1896 v Wales (Blackheath)
Caps: 2 (W:2, L:0)
Scoring: 0 Pts
Appearances: 1892:I, 1896:W
Honours: Championship: 1892

Peter Dunsmore HOWARD
Born: 20 December 1908 in Maidenhead
Died: 25 February 1965 in Lima, Peru
Educated: Mill Hill School
Clubs: Old Millhillians (8), Oxford University
Position: No 8 (7), Flanker (1)
Debut: 18 Jan 1930 v Wales (Cardiff). Number: 657
Last game: 6 Apr 1931 v France (Stade Colombes)
Caps: 8 (W:2, D:2, L:4). As captain:1 (W:0, L:1)
Scoring: 0 Pts
Appearances: 1930:W,I,F,S, 1931:W,I*,S,F
Honours: Championship: 1930

Nigel Horton

George Cairns (Scatter) HUBBARD
Born: 23 November 1867 in Benares, India
Died: 18 December 1931 of Eltham
Educated: Tonbridge School
Clubs: Blackheath (2)
Position: Three-quarter (2)
Debut: 2 Jan 1892 v Wales (Blackheath) - 1T, 2 Pts.
Number: 238
Last game: 6 Feb 1892 v Ireland (Manchester)
Caps: 2 (W:2, L:0)
Scoring: 1T, 2 Pts
Appearances: 1892:W,I
Honours: Championship: 1892

John Cairns HUBBARD
Born: 27 June 1902 in Woolwich
Died: 29 August 1997 in North Surrey
Educated: Tonbridge School
Clubs: Blackheath, Harlequins (1)
Position: Full-back (1)
Debut: 15 Mar 1930 v Scotland (Twickenham)
Number: 664
Caps: 1 (W:0, D:1, L:0)
Scoring: 0 Pts
Appearances: 1930:S
Honours: Championship: 1930

Arthur HUDSON
Born: 27 October 1882 in Gloucester
Died: 27 July 1973 in Gloucester
Clubs: Gloucester (8), Devonport, Harwich, Royal Navy, Combined Services
Position: Wing (7), Centre (1)
Debut: 13 Jan 1906 v Wales (Richmond) - 1T, 3 Pts.
Number: 423
Last game: 3 Mar 1910 v France (Parc des Princes) - 2T, 6 Pts
Caps: 8 (W:4, L:4)
Scoring: 9T, 27 Pts
Appearances: 1906:W,I,F, 1908:F,W,I,S, 1910:F
Honours: Championship: 1910

George Edgar HUGHES
Born: 24 February 1870 in Otley, Yorks
Died: 6 October 1947 in Walney-in-Barrow
Clubs: Barrow (1), Otley
Position: Forward (1)
Debut: 14 Mar 1896 v Scotland (Glasgow).
Number: 291
Caps: 1 (W:0, L:1)
Scoring: 0 Pts
Appearances: 1896:S

Paul Anthony HULL
Born: 17 May 1968 in Lambeth, London
Educated: Gordon BS
Clubs: Milton Keynes, Bristol (4)
Position: Full-back (4)
Debut: 4 Jun 1994 v South Africa (Pretoria).
Number: 1155
Last game: 10 Dec 1994 v Canada (Twickenham)
Caps: 4 (W:3, L:1)
Scoring: 0 Pts
Appearances: 1994:SA1,SA2,R,C

Paul Hull

Frank Croft (Frankie) HULME
Born: 31 August 1881 in Birkenhead
Died: Details unknown
Educated: Birkenhead Institute
Clubs: Birkenhead Park (4), Blackheath, Liverpool
Position: Half-Back (2), Fly-half (2)
Debut: 10 Jan 1903 v Wales (Swansea) Number: 386
Last game: 11 Feb 1905 v Ireland (Cork)
Caps: 4 (W:0, L:4)
Scoring: 0 Pts
Appearances: 1903:W,I, 1905:W,I

James Thomas HUNT
Born: Details unknown
Died: Details unknown
Clubs: Preston Grasshoppers, Manchester (3)
Position: Forward (3)
Debut: 6 Feb 1882 v Ireland (Lansdowne Road). Number: 143
Last game: 5 Jan 1884 v Wales (Leeds)
Caps: 3 (W:1, D:1, L:1)
Scoring: 0 Pts
Appearances: 1882:I,S, 1884:W
Honours: Championship: 1884

Robert HUNT
Born: 21 January 1856 in Preston
Died: 19 March 1913 in Blackburn
Educated: Preston GS
Clubs: Preston Grasshoppers, Manchester (4), Blackheath
Position: Three-quarter (4)
Debut: 30 Jan 1880 v Ireland (Lansdowne Road). Number: 123
Last game: 6 Feb 1882 v Ireland (Lansdowne Road) - 1T, 1 Pt
Caps: 4 (W:2, D:2, L:0)
Scoring: 2T, 1C, 1DG, 7 Pts
Appearances: 1880:I, 1881:W,S, 1882:I

William Henry HUNT
Born: 11 May 1854 in Preston
Died: 13 May 1904 in Manchester
Clubs: Preston Grasshoppers (3), Manchester (1)
Position: Forward (4)
Debut: 6 Mar 1876 v Scotland (The Oval). Number: 81
Last game: 11 Mar 1878 v Ireland (Lansdowne Road)
Caps: 4 (W:3, L:1)
Scoring: 0 Pts
Appearances: 1876:S, 1877:I,S, 1878:I

Ian G HUNTER
Born: 15 February 1969 in Harrow
Educated: Lake School
Clubs: Windermere, Carlisle, Nottingham, Northampton (7)
Position: Wing (6), Full-back (1), Bench (1)
Debut: 17 Oct 1992 v Canada (Wembley) - 2T, 10 Pts. Number: 1144
Last game: 22 Jun 1995 v France (Pretoria)
Caps: 7 (W:5, L:2)
Scoring: 3T, 15 Pts
Appearances: 1992:C, 1993:F,W, 1994:F,W, 1995:Sm,F

Robert Paul HUNTSMAN
Born: 5 May 1957 in Beverley
Educated: Hymers School, Bulmershe College
Clubs: Maidenhead, Headingley (2), Wasps
Position: Prop (2)
Debut: 1 Jun 1985 v New Zealand (Christchurch). Number: 1109
Last game: 8 Jun 1985 v New Zealand (Wellington)
Caps: 2 (W:0, L:2)
Scoring: 0 Pts
Appearances: 1985:NZ1,NZ2

Andrew Charles Brunel HURST
Born: 1 October 1935 in Cairo, Egypt
Educated: Dragon School
Clubs: Oxford University, Wasps (1)
Position: Wing (1)
Debut: 17 Mar 1962 v Scotland (Murrayfield). Number: 905
Caps: 1 (W:0, D:1, L:0)
Scoring: 0 Pts
Appearances: 1962:S

Thomas Frederick HUSKISSON, MBE
Born: 1 July 1914 in Richmond
Died: 25 April 2004
Educated: Merchant Taylors' School
Clubs: Old Merchant Taylors' (8), Army
Position: Lock (8)
Debut: 16 Jan 1937 v Wales (Twickenham). Number: 730
Last game: 18 Mar 1939 v Scotland (Murrayfield)
Caps: 8 (W:6, L:2)
Scoring: 0 Pts
Appearances: 1937:W,I,S, 1938:W,I, 1939:W,I,S
Honours: Championship: 1937

Frank HUTCHINSON
Born: 20 October 1885 in Wakefield
Died: 5 March 1960 in Leeds
Educated: Leeds GS
Clubs: Headingley (3)
Position: Fly-half (3)
Debut: 30 Jan 1909 v France (Leicester) - 1T, 3 Pts. Number: 485
Last game: 20 Mar 1909 v Scotland (Richmond)
Caps: 3 (W:2, L:1)
Scoring: 1T, 3 Pts
Appearances: 1909:F,I,S

James Ernest HUTCHINSON
Born: 1884
Died: Details unknown
Educated: Barnard Castle School
Clubs: Durham City (1)
Position: Wing (1)
Debut: 10 Feb 1906 v Ireland (Leicester). Number: 428
Caps: 1 (W:0, L:1)
Scoring: 0 Pts
Appearances: 1906:I

William Charles HUTCHINSON
Born: 1856
Died: 1880 in India
Educated: Christ's College
Clubs: Royal Indian Eng College (2)
Position: Half-Back (2)
Debut: 6 Mar 1876 v Scotland (The Oval). Number: 82
Last game: 5 Feb 1877 v Ireland (The Oval) - 2T, 2 Pts
Caps: 2 (W:2, L:0)
Scoring: 2T, 2 Pts
Appearances: 1876:S, 1877:I

William Henry Heap HUTCHINSON
Born: 31 October 1849 in Sculcoates
Died: 4 July 1929 in Beverley
Educated: Rugby School
Clubs: Hull (2)
Position: Forward (2)
Debut: 15 Feb 1875 v Ireland (The Oval). Number: 60
Last game: 13 Dec 1875 v Ireland (Dublin)
Caps: 2 (W:2, L:0)
Scoring: 0 Pts
Appearances: 1875:I,I

Ian Hunter

Henry HUTH
Born: 14 February 1856 in Huddersfield
Died: December 1929 in Kensington
Educated: London International College
Clubs: Huddersfield (1)
Position: Full-back (1)
Debut: 10 Mar 1879 v Scotland (Raeburn Place). Number: 111
Caps: 1 (W:0, D:1, L:0)
Scoring: 0 Pts
Appearances: 1879:S

John Phillip HYDE
Born: 8 June 1930 in Wellingborough
Educated: Wellingborough GS
Clubs: Northampton (2), Northamptonshire Regt, Army, Combined Services
Position: Wing (2)
Debut: 25 Feb 1950 v France (Stade Colombes).Number: 809
Last game: 18 Mar 1950 v Scotland (Murrayfield)
Caps: 2 (W:0, L:2)
Scoring: 0 Pts
Appearances: 1950:F,S

William Bayard HYNES, CBE
Born: Second quarter 1889 in Portsea
Died: 2 March 1968 in Chichester
Clubs: United Services (1), Royal Navy
Position: Lock (1)
Debut: 8 Apr 1912 v France (Parc des Princes). Number: 524
Caps: 1 (W:1, L:0)
Scoring: 0 Pts
Appearances: 1912:F

John Edgar Maxwell HYSLOP
Born: 31 March 1899 in Bristol
Died: 10 December 1990 in Sherborne
Educated: Wellington College
Clubs: Oxford University (3), Richmond
Position: Flanker (3)
Debut: 11 Feb 1922 v Ireland (Lansdowne Road) - 1T, 3 Pts. Number: 575
Last game: 18 Mar 1922 v Scotland (Twickenham)
Caps: 3 (W:2, D:1, L:0)
Scoring: 1T, 3 Pts
Appearances: 1922:I,F,S

Ernest Denison IBBITSON
Born: 1 February 1882 in Leeds
Died: c 1955 in Canada
Educated: Wesley College Sheffield
Clubs: Headingley (4)
Position: Lock (4)
Debut: 16 Jan 1909 v Wales (Cardiff). Number: 482
Last game: 20 Mar 1909 v Scotland (Richmond)
Caps: 4 (W:2, L:2)
Scoring: 0 Pts
Appearances: 1909:W,F,I,S

Henry Marshall IMRIE
Born: Third quarter 1877 in Durham
Died: 16 October 1938 in Middleton St George
Clubs: Durham City (2)
Position: Wing (2)
Debut: 2 Dec 1905 v New Zealand (Crystal Palace). Number: 417
Last game: 9 Feb 1907 v Ireland (Lansdowne Road) - 1T, 3 Pts
Caps: 2 (W:0, L:2)
Scoring: 1T, 3 Pts
Appearances: 1905:NZ, 1907:I

Rupert Edward INGLIS
Born: 17 May 1863 in St George's, Hanover Square
Died: Killed in action in 1916 in Ginchy, France
Educated: Rugby School
Clubs: Oxford University, Blackheath (3)
Position: Forward (3)
Debut: 2 Jan 1886 v Wales (Blackheath). Number: 180
Last game: 13 Mar 1886 v Scotland (Raeburn Place)
Caps: 3 (W:2, D:1, L:0)
Scoring: 0 Pts
Appearances: 1886:W,I,S

Samuel Howell IRVIN
Born: Third quarter 1880 in Hartlepool
Died: First quarter 1939 in Oldham
Clubs: Devonport Albion (1), Oldham RL
Position: Full-back (1)
Debut: 14 Jan 1905 v Wales (Cardiff). Number: 402
Caps: 1 (W:0, L:1)
Scoring: 0 Pts
Appearances: 1905:W

Francis William Ramsbottom ISHERWOOD
Born: 16 October 1852
Died: 30 April 1888 in Southsea
Educated: Rugby School
Clubs: Oxford University, Ravenscourt Park (1)
Position: Forward (1)
Debut: 5 Feb 1872 v Scotland (The Oval) - 1C, 2 Pts. Number: 28
Caps: 1 (W:1, L:0)
Scoring: 1C, 2 Pts
Appearances: 1872:S

J

Martin Johnson

JACKETT, Edward John
JACKSON, Allan Heslop
JACKSON, Barry K
JACKSON, Peter Barrie
JACKSON, Walter Jesse
JACOB, Frederick
JACOB, Herbert Percy
JACOB, Philip Gordon
JACOBS, Charles Ronald
JAGO, Raphael Anthony
JANION, Jeremy Paul Aubrey
JARMAN, John Wallace
JEAVONS, Nicholas Clive
JEEPS, Richard Eric Gautrey, CBE
JEFFERY, George Luxton
JENNINS, Christopher Robert
JEWITT, John Henry
JOHNS, William Alexander
JOHNSON, Martin Osborne, CBE
JOHNSTON, John Benedict
JOHNSTON, William Redpath
JONES, Arthur Vaughan
JONES, Christopher Michael
JONES, Frederick Archibald Leslie, CBE
JONES, Frederic Phelp
JONES, Herbert Arthur
JORDEN, Anthony Mervyn
JOWETT, Donald
JUDD, Philip Edward

Edward John (John) JACKETT
Born: 4 July 1878 in Falmouth
Died: 11 November 1935 in Middlesbrough
Clubs: Falmouth, Leicester (13), Devonport Albion, Transvaal (SA), De Beers (SA), Kimberley (SA), Dewsbury RL
Position: Full-back (13)
Debut: 2 Dec 1905 v New Zealand (Crystal Palace). Number: 418
Last game: 20 Mar 1909 v Scotland (Richmond)
Caps: 13 (W:4, D:1, L:8)
Scoring: 2C, 4 Pts
Appearances: 1905:NZ, 1906:W,I,S,F,SA, 1907:W,I,S, 1909:W,F,I,S

Allan Heslop JACKSON
Born: c 1856
Died: In Johannesburg, South Africa, details unknown
Clubs: Guy's Hospital (1), Blackheath (1)
Position: Half-Back (2)
Debut: 11 Mar 1878 v Ireland (Lansdowne Road). Number: 108
Last game: 30 Jan 1880 v Ireland (Lansdowne Road)
Caps: 2 (W:2, L:0)
Scoring: 0 Pts
Appearances: 1878:I, 1880:I

Barry K JACKSON
Born: 9 August 1937 in Manchester North
Clubs: Broughton Park (2)
Position: Prop (1), Replacement (1), Bench (3)
Debut: 21 Mar 1970 (rep) v Scotland (Murrayfield). Number: 986
Last game: 18 Apr 1970 v France (Stade Colombes)
Caps: 2 (W:0, L:2)
Scoring: 0 Pts
Appearances: 1970:S(r),F

Peter Barrie JACKSON
Born: 22 September 1930 in Birmingham
Died: 22 March 2004 in Solihull
Educated: King Edward VI School
Clubs: Old Edwardians, Coventry (20), Army
Position: Wing (20)
Debut: 21 Jan 1956 v Wales (Twickenham). Number: 863
Last game: 16 Mar 1963 v Scotland (Twickenham)
Caps: 20 (W:12, D:5, L:3)
Scoring: 6T, 18 Pts
Appearances: 1956:W,I,F, 1957:W,I,F,S, 1958:W,A,F,S, 1959:W,I,F,S, 1961:S, 1963:W,I,F,S
Honours: Grand Slam: 1957. Championship: 1958, 1963

Peter Jackson

Like many great players Peter Jackson – or Nijinsky as he was known - is remembered for one try in particular.

For Jackson – one of the greatest backs of the post-war generation – it came in 1958, at Twickenham, when the touring Australians were taking on England.

With the scores tied at 6-6 and England down to 14 men, due to injury, Jackson struck for one of the most memorable tries seen at Twickenham.

Taking the ball more than 60 yards out Jackson picked his way through the Australia defence to send Twickenham wild and hand the win to England.

Picking up the story in Rugby World Magazine, Donald Trelford explains the try with wonder.

"The ball came to Jackson on the right," Trelford recalls, "and what happened in the next 10 seconds is part of rugby legend.

"He had fought his way out of one tackle, stepped inside another, and was away down the touchline, eluding outstretched fingers with a negligent grace.

"Finally there was Terry Curley, the 13 and a half stone full-back, one foot firmly planted on the touchline, brow-beating Jackson to going inside.

"But then incredibly, impossibly, Jackson was round the outside and throwing himself in at the corner while Twickenham erupted!"

A year earlier Jackson had been a key member of one of England's most important teams, the Grand Slam winning side of 1957, which also won three Five Nations Championships.

Jackson may have been a legend in Europe but that fame became worldwide in 1959 when he was one of the stars of the Lions side that toured New Zealand.

On that trip Jackson scored 19 tries, a tally only bettered (by one try) by one of the most talented Irishmen ever to wear a Lions jersey, Tony O'Reilly.

One of Jackson's scores clinched the fourth Test 9-6 and like O'Reilly, Jackson endured some years in the international wilderness before being recalled for his final test in 1963, after missing the 1961 and 1962 campaigns.

Jackson's absence from the side was described by a contemporary writer as "a major cause of the decline of England as a major force".

The Daily Telegraph reported that "His sleight of foot enchanted the New Zealand crowds, who nicknamed him 'Pimpernel' ('they seek him here, they seek him there')."

Jackson was educated at King Edward VI School and attended his first England trial while still at the Old Edwardians club, although he made his name with Coventry, winning acclaim for his performance for a Midlands XV in 1951, that took on the South African tourists.

Jackson who played for the Army – during national service – was also captain of the Warwickshire side and with them won the County Championship seven times in eight seasons between 1958-65.

Jackson died in March 2004, aged 73, after a long illness.

A Coventry stalwart, he ran his own export packing company, becoming secretary, and subsequently president, of the club.

Walter Jesse JACKSON
Born: 16 March 1870 in Gloucester
Died: 1 December 1958 in Halifax
Clubs: Gloucester (1), Halifax
Position: Wing (1)
Debut: 17 Mar 1894 v Scotland (Raeburn Place). Number: 270
Caps: 1 (W:0, L:1)
Scoring: 0 Pts
Appearances: 1894:S

Frederick JACOB
Born: 4 January 1873 in Northbourne, Kent
Died: 1 September 1945 in Srinagar, India
Educated: Sandwich School
Clubs: Cambridge University (3), Gottingen University (GER), London University, Blackheath, Richmond (5), Cheltenham
Position: Forward (8)
Debut: 9 Jan 1897 v Wales (Newport). Number: 301
Last game: 4 Feb 1899 v Ireland (Lansdowne Road)
Caps: 8 (W:2, D:1, L:5)
Scoring: 0 Pts
Appearances: 1897:W,I,S, 1898:I,S,W, 1899:W,I

Herbert Percy JACOB
Born: 12 October 1902 in Elham
Died: 8 July 1996 in Myaree, Australia
Educated: Cranleigh School
Clubs: Oxford University (4), Blackheath (1)
Position: Wing (4), Centre (1)
Debut: 19 Jan 1924 v Wales (Swansea) - 1T, 3 Pts.
Number: 588
Last game: 22 Feb 1930 v France (Twickenham)
Caps: 5 (W:5, L:0)
Scoring: 4T, 12 Pts
Appearances: 1924:W,I,F,S, 1930:F
Honours: Grand Slam: 1924. Championship: 1930

Philip Gordon JACOB
Born: 14 May 1875 in Seoni, India
Died: Details unknown
Educated: Bedford GS
Clubs: Cambridge University, Blackheath (1)
Position: Scrum-half (1)
Debut: 5 Feb 1898 v Ireland (Richmond). Number: 313
Caps: 1 (W:0, L:1)
Scoring: 0 Pts
Appearances: 1898:I

Charles Ronald (Ron) JACOBS
Born: 28 October 1928 in Whittlesey, Cambs
Died: 10 November 2002
Educated: Oakham School
Clubs: Nottingham University, Northampton (29)
Position: Prop (29)
Debut: 21 Jan 1956 v Wales (Twickenham). Number: 864
Last game: 21 Mar 1964 (capt) v Scotland (Murrayfield)
Caps: 29 (W:14, D:5, L:10). As captain:2 (W:1, L:1)
Scoring: 0 Pts
Appearances: 1956:W,I,S,F, 1957:W,I,F,S, 1958:W,A,I,F,S, 1960:W,I,F,S, 1961:SA,W,I,F,S, 1963:NZ1,NZ2,A, 1964:W,I,F*,S*
Honours: Grand Slam: 1957. Championship: 1958

Nick Jeavons

Raphael Anthony JAGO
Born: 20 January 1882 in Chidcock, Dorset
Died: 1 March 1941 in Plymouth
Clubs: Devonport Albion (5)
Position: Scrum-half (5)
Debut: 13 Jan 1906 v Wales (Richmond). Number: 424
Last game: 9 Feb 1907 v Ireland (Lansdowne Road)
Caps: 5 (W:0, D:1, L:4)
Scoring: 1T, 3 Pts
Appearances: 1906:W,I,SA, 1907:W,I

Jeremy Paul Aubrey JANION
Born: 25 September 1946 in Bishop's Stortford
Educated: St Edmund's College
Clubs: Bedford (9), Richmond (3)
Position: Wing (7), Centre (5), Bench (2)
Debut: 16 Jan 1971 v Wales (Cardiff). Number: 991
Last game: 31 May 1975 v Australia (Brisbane)
Caps: 12 (W:3, D:1, L:8)
Scoring: 0 Pts
Appearances: 1971:W,I,F,S,S,P, 1972:W,S,SA, 1973:A, 1975:A1,A2

J K L

Dickie Jeeps

John Wallace (Wallace) JARMAN

Born: 15 July 1872 in Towcester
Died: September 1950 in Vancouver, Canada
Clubs: Merchant Venturers, Bristol (1)
Position: Forward (1)
Debut: 6 Jan 1900 v Wales (Gloucester). Number: 339
Caps: 1 (W:0, L:1)
Scoring: 0 Pts
Appearances: 1900:W

Nicholas Clive (Nick) JEAVONS

Born: 12 November 1957 in Calcutta, India
Educated: Wolverhampton GS, Tettenhall College, Wolverhampton Poly
Clubs: Moseley (14)
Position: Flanker (14)
Debut: 21 Feb 1981 v Scotland (Twickenham). Number: 1066
Last game: 19 Mar 1983 v Ireland (Lansdowne Road)
Caps: 14 (W:6, D:3, L:5)
Scoring: 1T, 4 Pts
Appearances: 1981:S,I,F,Ar1,Ar2, 1982:A,S,I,F,W, 1983:F,W,S,I

Richard Eric Gautrey (Dickie) JEEPS, CBE

Born: 25 November 1931 in Chesterton
Educated: Bedford Modern School
Clubs: Cambridge, Northampton (24)
Position: Scrum-half (24)
Debut: 21 Jan 1956 v Wales (Twickenham). Number: 859
Last game: 17 Mar 1962 (capt) v Scotland (Murrayfield)
Caps: 24 (W:13, D:6, L:5). As captain: 13 (W:5, D:4, L:4)
Scoring: 0 Pts
Appearances: 1956:W, 1957:W,I,F,S, 1958:W,A,I,F,S, 1959:I, 1960:W*,I*,F*,S*, 1961:SA*,W*,I*,F*,S*, 1962:W*,I*,F*,S*
Honours: Grand Slam: 1957. Championship: 1958

Dickie Jeeps is known as one of the greatest scrum-halves of his generation but one who incredibly made his name as a Lion before establishing himself in the England team.

Jeeps's chance to prove he could play at the highest level came in 1955 after he had been terrorising the opposition in Northampton colours for many years.

In Peter Jackson's Lions of England book we learn that it was Wales' peerless outside-half Cliff Morgan who played a key role in Jeeps's elevation straight to the Lions from Northampton.

Morgan had played against Jeeps in a club match for Cardiff in 1955 and he impressed the Welshman hugely.

"He was tough and knew the game," said Morgan. "I am convinced if his fellow Northampton player Don White had been in the party and working closely with him in the back row of the scrum, we'd have won the Test series."

His first Lions cap set a post-war record as he became only the second Englishman (after Bill Patterson) to play his first game of Test rugby as a Lion.

Jason Robinson played his first full game as a Lion in 2001 but unlike Jeeps had already played as a substitute for England.

Jeeps finally went on three Lions tours playing in 13 Tests; a record for an Englishman, with only three Tests a tour, that is unlikely to be beaten.

And with him starring in the famous red jersey the England selectors got the hint in 1956 selecting him for his first Red Rose cap against Wales, and he never looked back.

Jeeps was an all-round sportsman. A prolific cricketer, he played football for Cambridge City and even excelled as a speed skater.

"I wasn't the best player," Jeeps said modestly. "But I had the most determination."

Jeeps was made England captain for the 1959-60 Five Nations, only failing to pick up a Grand Slam because of a 3-3 draw with France.

He kept the captaincy for three seasons and 13 Test matches, before going on his last Lions tour in 1962, back to South Africa.

After his playing days were over Jeeps became the RFU's youngest president, climbing to the highest role in the land aged just 44.

George Luxton JEFFERY

Born: 1863
Died: 4 November 1937 in Stafford
Educated: St John's Wood School
Clubs: Blackheath (5), Cambridge University (1), Harlequins
Position: Forward (6)
Debut: 2 Jan 1886 v Wales (Blackheath).
Number: 181
Last game: 5 Mar 1887 v Scotland (Manchester) - 1T, 1 Pt
Caps: 6 (W:2, D:3, L:1)
Scoring: 1T, 1 Pt
Appearances: 1886:W,I,S, 1887:W,I,S

Christopher Robert JENNINS

Born: 5 February 1942 in Runcorn
Educated: Rydal School
Clubs: Liverpool University, Waterloo (3)
Position: Centre (3)
Debut: 7 Jan 1967 v Australia (Twickenham).
Number: 951
Last game: 25 Feb 1967 v France (Twickenham)
Caps: 3 (W:1, L:2)
Scoring: 0 Pts
Appearances: 1967:A,I,F

John Henry JEWITT

Born: Second quarter 1878 in Quebec, Co Durham
Died: Details unknown
Clubs: Hartlepool Rovers (1), Broughton Rangers RL
Position: Lock (1)
Debut: 11 Jan 1902 v Wales (Blackheath).
Number: 375
Caps: 1 (W:0, L:1)
Scoring: 0 Pts
Appearances: 1902:W

William Alexander JOHNS

Born: 1 February 1882 in Gloucester
Died: 10 March 1965 in Weston-super-Mare
Educated: Sir Thomas Rich's GS
Clubs: Gloucester (7)
Position: Forward (7)
Debut: 16 Jan 1909 v Wales (Cardiff).
Number: 483
Last game: 3 Mar 1910 v France (Parc des Princes)
Caps: 7 (W:4, D:1, L:2)
Scoring: 1T, 3 Pts
Appearances: 1909:W,F,I,S, 1910:W,I,F
Honours: Championship: 1910

Martin Johnson

Martin Osborne JOHNSON, CBE

Born: 9 March 1970 in Solihull
Educated: Robert Smyth School
Clubs: Wigston, Leicester (84), Tihoi (NZ), College Old Boys (NZ), King Country (NZ)
Position: Lock (82), Replacement (2)
Debut: 16 Jan 1993 v France (Twickenham).
Number: 1149
Last game: 22 Nov 2003 (capt) v Australia (Sydney)
Caps: 84 (W:67, D:2, L:15). As captain: 39 (W:34, L:5)
Scoring: 2T, 10 Pts. Discipline - Cautions: 3
Appearances: 1993:F,NZ, 1994:S,I,F,W,R,C, 1995:I,F,W,S,Ar,It,Sm,A,NZ,F,SA,Sm, 1996:F,W,S,I,It,Ar, 1997:S,I,F,W,A,NZ1,NZ2, 1998:F,W,S,I,H*,It*,A,SA, 1999:S,I,F,W,A*,US*,C*,It*,NZ*,Tg*,Fj*,SA*, 2000:SA1*,SA2*,A*,Ar*,SA*, 2001:W*,It*,S*,F*,SA*, 2002:S*,I*,F*,It(r),NZ*,A*,SA*, 2003:F*,W*,S*,I*,NZ*,A*,F*,Geo*,SA*,Sm*,U(r),W*,F*,A*
Honours: RWC Winner: 2003 (capt). Grand Slam: 1995, Championship: 1996, 2001 (capt), 2003 (capt)

When any history of English rugby is considered, the names Martin Osborne Johnson will be written across it in 10-foot high letters. He is quite simply the greatest English rugby player of all time.

Johnson, the softly spoken and modest second row from the Leicester Tigers won every domestic and European honour the game had to offer and on 22 November 2003 lifted the Rugby World Cup, as England became the first northern hemisphere side to win the trophy.

Historians will point to Jonny Wilkinson's drop goal winning that World Cup final against Australia – in Sydney – but everyone, including Wilkinson, knows it was Johnson's hand on the rudder that got England home.

"Johnno is simply a living legend," said Wilkinson in The Times after England lifted the Webb Ellis Cup.

"He is without doubt the greatest captain I've known and during that World Cup he was brilliant to work with.

"The moments Martin was at his best and most influential were in those final minutes before the start of a game.

"To see your captain like that makes you think 'God, am I

glad he's on my side'."

Before leading England to the World Cup win in 2003 he had been a central figure in their Grand Slam victory a few months earlier and was one of the prime reasons England were able to beat both Australia and New Zealand (on their own soil) in the run-up to the World Cup.

The 15-13 victory in New Zealand in the summer of 2003 was key in their World Cup triumph. It was a game in which the world saw Johnson in commanding form, especially as England's pack was reduced to six men at one point, with both Lawrence Dallaglio and Neil Back in the sin bin.

"You saw Martin Johnson at his absolute best in that 10-minute period," said former England and Lions coach, Sir Clive Woodward. "His leadership was just inspirational."

Johnson – who spent his late teens playing in New Zealand – burst onto the world stage back in New Zealand – for the 1993 Lions tour – but it was four years later when his name was etched into rugby's history.

Selected from the England ranks as the new Lions captain – by Ian McGeechan – Johnson led his side to a 2-1 series win over South Africa and four years later became the first man to lead the Lions on two successive tours.

Former Ireland captain, Keith Wood, who played with Johnson on Lions tours in 1997 and 2001 added: "As a leader he was second to none - the best captain I ever had. He would let his body and actions do all the talking.

"Martin was a nuisance to play against, but having played against him you understood how much of a benefit he was to your own side.

"He played on the edge and pushed everything to the limit so his team could win - but you would expect nothing less from your captain.

"He was the most influential skipper I've encountered and as a player he will go down as one of the all-time greats."

While captain of Leicester, Johnson delivered unprecedented success for the Tigers and it says much for his influence that the club went without a trophy for the three seasons after his retirement in the summer of 2005, before picking up the EDF Trophy in 2007.

While Johnson was captain he led Leicester to four successive Premiership titles from 1999, two domestic cups, and back-to-back Heineken Cup triumphs in 2001 and 2002.

"You can't underestimate the impact he's had on the game - for club, country and for The Lions," said Woodward.

"Johnno is an awesome individual, a world-class player and his leadership is outstanding."

Already the holder of the MBE, Johnson was made a CBE in the 2004 New Year honours. He was named the 1998-99 Allied Dunbar Premiership Player of the Season.

Martin Johnson

Ben Johnston

John Benedict (Ben) JOHNSTON
Born: 8 November 1978 in Clatterbridge
Clubs: New Brighton, Caldy, Saracens (2)
Position: Centre (1), Replacement (1)
Debut: 22 Jun 2002 v Argentina (Buenos Aires). Number: 1243
Last game: 9 Nov 2002 (rep) v New Zealand (Twickenham)
Caps: 2 (W:2, L:0)
Scoring: 0 Pts
Appearances: 2002:Ar,NZ(r)

William Redpath JOHNSTON
Born: 1887
Died: Details unknown
Educated: Colston's School
Clubs: Bristol (16), Gloucester
Position: Full-back (16)
Debut: 15 Jan 1910 v Wales (Twickenham). Number: 494
Last game: 13 Apr 1914 v France (Stade Colombes)
Caps: 16 (W:13, D:1, L:2)
Scoring: 0 Pts
Appearances: 1910:W,I,S, 1912:W,I,S,F, 1913:SA,W,F,I,S, 1914:W,I,S,F
Honours: Grand Slam: 1913, 1914. Championship: 1910

Arthur Vaughan JONES
Born: 25 September 1909 in Swansea, Wales
Clubs: United Services, Royal Artillery, Army (3)
Position: Flanker (3)
Debut: 13 Feb 1932 v Ireland (Lansdowne Road). Number: 695
Last game: 21 Jan 1933 v Wales (Twickenham)
Caps: 3 (W:2, L:1)
Scoring: 0 Pts
Appearances: 1932:I,S, 1933:W

Christopher Michael (Chris) JONES
Born: 24 June 1980 in Manchester
Educated: Stockport GS
Clubs: Sheffield Hallam University, Altrincham Kersal, Sale (10)
Position: Flanker (4), Lock (2), Replacement (4), Bench (3)
Debut: 15 Feb 2004 (rep) v Italy (Rome) - 1T, 5 Pts. Number: 1250
Last game: 25 Nov 2006 v South Africa (Twickenham)
Caps: 10 (W:4, L:6)
Scoring: 1T, 5 Pts
Appearances: 2004:It(r),S,I(r),W,NZ1, 2005:W, 2006:A1(r),A2,SA1(r),SA2

Frederick Archibald Leslie JONES, CBE
Born: 9 July 1874 in Fylde
Died: 24 January 1946 in Upton, Worcs
Educated: Hereford Cathedral School, Bromsgrove School
Clubs: Oxford University (2), Blackheath, Richmond
Position: Centre (2)
Debut: 5 Jan 1895 v Wales (Swansea) - 1T, 3 Pts. Number: 277
Last game: 2 Feb 1895 v Ireland (Lansdowne Road)
Caps: 2 (W:2, L:0)
Scoring: 1T, 3 Pts
Appearances: 1895:W,I

Chris Jones

J K L

Tony Jorden

Frederic Phelp JONES
Born: Second quarter 1871 in Birkenhead
Died: 14 August 1944 in Wirral
Educated: Wallasey GS
Clubs: New Brighton (1), Birkenhead Park
Position: Three-quarter (1)
Debut: 4 Mar 1893 v Scotland (Headingley). Number: 257
Caps: 1 (W:0, L:1)
Scoring: 0 Pts
Appearances: 1893:S

Herbert Arthur JONES
Born: 22 August 1918 in Landkey, Barnstaple
Died: 5 December 1998 in North Devon
Clubs: Barnstaple (3)
Position: Lock (3)
Debut: 21 Jan 1950 v Wales (Twickenham). Number: 805
Last game: 25 Feb 1950 v France (Stade Colombes)
Caps: 3 (W:1, L:2)
Scoring: 0 Pts
Appearances: 1950:W,I,F

Anthony Mervyn (Tony) JORDEN
Born: 28 January 1947 in Radlett, Herts
Educated: Monmouth School
Clubs: Cambridge University (1), Blackheath (4), Harlequins, Bedford (2)
Position: Full-back (7), Bench (7)
Debut: 18 Apr 1970 v France (Stade Colombes) - 2C, 1PG, 7 Pts. Number: 987
Last game: 15 Mar 1975 v Scotland (Twickenham)
Caps: 7 (W:3, D:1, L:3)
Scoring: 5C, 4PG, 22 Pts
Appearances: 1970:F, 1973:I,F,S, 1974:F, 1975:W,S

Donald JOWETT
Born: 4 December 1866 in Bradford
Died: 27 August 1908 in Heckmondwike
Clubs: Heckmondwike (6)
Position: Forward (6)
Debut: 16 Feb 1889 v New Zealand Natives (Blackheath). Number: 201
Last game: 7 Mar 1891 v Scotland (Richmond)
Caps: 6 (W:5, L:1)
Scoring: 1C, 2 Pts
Appearances: 1889:M, 1890:S,I, 1891:W,I,S

Philip Edward JUDD
Born: 8 April 1934 in Coventry
Educated: Broad Street School
Clubs: Coventry (22), RAF
Position: Prop (22)
Debut: 20 Jan 1962 v Wales (Twickenham). Number: 901
Last game: 4 Nov 1967 (capt) v New Zealand (Twickenham)
Caps: 22 (W:5, D:4, L:13). As captain: 5 (W:2, L:3)
Scoring: 0 Pts
Appearances: 1962:W,I,F,S, 1963:S,NZ1,NZ2,A, 1964:NZ, 1965:I,F,S, 1966:W,I,F,S, 1967:A,I*,F*,S*,W*,NZ*
Honours: Championship: 1963

K

KAY, Benedict James, MBE
KAYLL, Henry Edward
KEELING, John Hugh
KEEN, Brian Warwick
KEETON, George Haydn
KELLY, Geoffrey Arnold
KELLY, Thomas Stanley
KEMBLE, Arthur Twiss
KEMP, Dudley Thomas
KEMP, Thomas Arthur
KENDALL, Percy Dale
KENDREW, Sir Douglas Anthony, KCMG
KENNEDY, Robert Day
KENT, Charles Philip
KENT, Thomas
KERSHAW, Cecil Ashworth
KEWLEY, Edward
KEWNEY, Alfred Lionel, OBE
KEY, Alan, OBE
KEYWORTH, Mark
KILNER, Barron
KINDERSLEY, Richard Stephen
KING, Alexander David
KING, Ian
KING, John Abbott
KING, Quentin Eric Moffitt Ayres
KINGSTON, Peter
KITCHING, Alfred Everley
KITTERMASTER, Harold James
KNIGHT, Frederick P
KNIGHT, Peter Michael
KNOWLES, Edward
KNOWLES, Thomas Caldwell
KRIGE, Johannes Albertus

Alex King

Benedict James (Ben) KAY, MBE
Born: 14 December 1975 in Liverpool
Educated: Merchant Taylors' School
Clubs: Waterloo, Queensland University (AU), Leicester (45)
Position: Lock (40), Replacement (5), Bench (2)
Debut: 2 Jun 2001 v Canada (Markham). Number: 1223
Last game: 25 Nov 2006 (rep) v South Africa (Twickenham)
Caps: 45 (W:35, L:10)
Scoring: 2T, 10 Pts
Appearances: 2001:C1,C2,A,R,SA(r), 2002:S,I,F,W,It,Ar,NZ(r),A,SA, 2003:F,W,It,S,I,NZ,A,F,Geo,SA,Sm,W,F,A, 2004:It,S,I,W,F,C(r),SA(r), 2005:W,F,I,It,S, 2006:A2,NZ,Ar,SA1,SA2(r)
Honours: RWC Winner: 2003. Grand Slam: 2003

Henry Edward KAYLL
Born: 16 July 1855 in Sunderland
Died: 14 February 1910 in Vancouver, Canada
Educated: Richmond School
Clubs: Sunderland (1)
Position: Full-back (1)
Debut: 4 Mar 1878 v Scotland (The Oval). Number: 99
Caps: 1 (W:0, D:1, L:0)
Scoring: 0 Pts
Appearances: 1878:S

John Hugh KEELING
Born: 28 October 1925 in Cairo, Egypt
Clubs: Guy's Hospital (2), Rhodesia
Position: Hooker (2)
Debut: 3 Jan 1948 v Australia (Twickenham). Number: 776
Last game: 17 Jan 1948 v Wales (Twickenham)
Caps: 2 (W:0, D:1, L:1)
Scoring: 0 Pts
Appearances: 1948:A,W

Brian Warwick KEEN
Born: 1 June 1944 in Bury St Edmunds
Educated: Hardye's School
Clubs: Newcastle University (4), Northern, Moseley, Brazil
Position: Prop (4)
Debut: 20 Jan 1968 v Wales (Twickenham). Number: 965
Last game: 16 Mar 1968 v Scotland (Murrayfield)
Caps: 4 (W:1, D:2, L:1)
Scoring: 0 Pts
Appearances: 1968:W,I,F,S

George Haydn KEETON
Born: 13 October 1878 in Peterborough
Died: 7 January 1949 in Menton, France
Educated: Oakham School
Clubs: Cambridge University, Richmond (3), Leicester
Position: Hooker (3)
Debut: 9 Jan 1904 v Wales (Leicester). Number: 397
Last game: 19 Mar 1904 v Scotland (Inverleith)
Caps: 3 (W:1, D:1, L:1)
Scoring: 0 Pts
Appearances: 1904:W,I,S

Ben Kay

Geoffrey Arnold KELLY
Born: 9 February 1914 in Royston
Educated: The Perse School
Clubs: Letchworth, Bedford (4)
Position: Prop (4)
Debut: 18 Jan 1947 v Wales (Cardiff). Number: 757
Last game: 17 Jan 1948 v Wales (Twickenham)
Caps: 4 (W:2, D:1, L:1)
Scoring: 0 Pts
Appearances: 1947:W,I,S, 1948:W

Thomas Stanley KELLY
Born: Third quarter 1882 in Tiverton
Died: Details unknown
Educated: Blundell's School
Clubs: Exeter (12), London Devonians
Position: Lock (11), Prop (1)
Debut: 13 Jan 1906 v Wales (Richmond). Number: 425
Last game: 21 Mar 1908 v Scotland (Inverleith)
Caps: 12 (W:5, D:1, L:6). As captain: 1 (W:1, L:0)
Scoring: 0 Pts
Appearances: 1906:W,I,S,F,SA, 1907:F,W,I,S, 1908:F*,I,S

Arthur Twiss KEMBLE
Born: 3 February 1862 in Sebergham, Carlisle
Died: 13 March 1925 in Crawley Down, Sussex
Educated: Appleby GS
Clubs: Liverpool (3)
Position: Forward (3)
Debut: 3 Jan 1885 v Wales (Swansea). Number: 171
Last game: 5 Feb 1887 v Ireland (Lansdowne Road)
Caps: 3 (W:2, L:1)
Scoring: 0 Pts
Appearances: 1885:W,I, 1887:I

Dudley Thomas KEMP
Born: 18 January 1910 in Isle of Wight
Died: January 2003
Educated: King Edward VI School
Clubs: Blackheath (1)
Position: No 8 (1)
Debut: 19 Jan 1935 v Wales (Twickenham). Number: 718
Caps: 1 (W:0, D:1, L:0)
Scoring: 0 Pts
Appearances: 1935:W

Thomas Arthur (Tommy) KEMP
Born: 12 August 1915 in Bolton
Died: 26 November 2004
Educated: Denstone College
Clubs: Cambridge University (2), St Mary's Hospital (1), Richmond (2), Manchester, Army
Position: Fly-half (5)
Debut: 16 Jan 1937 v Wales (Twickenham). Number: 731
Last game: 17 Jan 1948 (capt) v Wales (Twickenham)
Caps: 5 (W:3, D:1, L:1). As captain: 1 (W:0, D:1, L:0)
Scoring: 0 Pts
Appearances: 1937:W,I, 1939:S, 1948:A,W*
Honours: Championship: 1937

Percy Dale (Toggie) KENDALL
Born: 21 August 1878 in Prescot
Died: Killed in action in 1915 in Ypres, Belgium
Educated: Elleray School New Brighton, Tonbridge School
Clubs: Cambridge University, Blackheath, Birkenhead Park (3)
Position: Scrum-half (3)
Debut: 9 Mar 1901 v Scotland (Blackheath). Number: 370
Last game: 21 Mar 1903 (capt) v Scotland (Richmond)
Caps: 3 (W:0, L:3). As captain: 1 (W:0, L:1)
Scoring: 0 Pts
Appearances: 1901:S, 1902:W, 1903:S*

Sir Douglas Anthony (Joe) KENDREW, KCMG
Born: 22 July 1910 in Barnstaple
Died: 28 February 1989 in Nottingham
Educated: Uppingham School
Clubs: Oxford University, Woodford (2), Paignton, City of Derry, Leicester (8), Leicestershire Regt, Army, Combined Services
Position: Prop (8), Hooker (1), No 8 (1)
Debut: 18 Jan 1930 v Wales (Cardiff). Number: 658
Last game: 8 Feb 1936 v Ireland (Lansdowne Road)
Caps: 10 (W:5, D:2, L:3). As captain: 2 (W:1, D:1, L:0)
Scoring: 1C, 2 Pts
Appearances: 1930:W,I, 1933:I,S, 1934:S, 1935:W*,I*, 1936:NZ,W,I
Honours: Championship: 1930, 1934

Robert Day KENNEDY
Born: 14 August 1925
Died: May 1979 in Rhodesia
Educated: Camborne School of Mines
Clubs: Rhodesia, Camborne School of Mines (3)
Position: Wing (3)
Debut: 12 Feb 1949 v Ireland (Lansdowne Road). Number: 797
Last game: 19 Mar 1949 v Scotland (Twickenham) - 1T, 3 Pts
Caps: 3 (W:2, L:1)
Scoring: 1T, 3 Pts
Appearances: 1949:I,F,S

Charles Philip KENT
Born: 4 August 1953 in Bridgwater
Died: 23 March 2005 in Dartmoor
Educated: Blundell's School
Clubs: Oxford University, Rosslyn Park (5)
Position: Centre (4), Replacement (1), Bench (3)
Debut: 15 Jan 1977 v Scotland (Twickenham) - 1T, 4 Pts. Number: 1045
Last game: 21 Jan 1978 (rep) v France (Parc des Princes)
Caps: 5 (W:2, L:3)
Scoring: 1T, 4 Pts
Appearances: 1977:S,I,F,W, 1978:F(r)

Thomas (Tom) KENT
Born: 19 June 1864 in Nottingham
Died: 29 January 1928
Clubs: Salford (6)
Position: Forward (6)
Debut: 3 Jan 1891 v Wales (Newport). Number: 226
Last game: 5 Mar 1892 v Scotland (Raeburn Place)
Caps: 6 (W:5, L:1)
Scoring: 0 Pts
Appearances: 1891:W,I,S, 1892:W,I,S
Honours: Championship: 1892

Cecil Ashworth KERSHAW
Born: 3 February 1895
Died: 1 November 1972 in Worthing
Educated: Wharfedale School
Clubs: RNC Osborne, RNC Dartmouth, United Services, Blackheath, Royal Navy (16)
Position: Scrum-half (16)
Debut: 17 Jan 1920 v Wales (Swansea). Number: 549
Last game: 2 Apr 1923 v France (Stade Colombes)
Caps: 16 (W:13, D:1, L:2)
Scoring: 2T, 6 Pts
Appearances: 1920:W,F,I,S, 1921:W,I,S,F, 1922:W,I,F,S, 1923:W,I,S,F
Honours: Grand Slam: 1921, 1923

Edward KEWLEY
Born: 20 June 1852 in Eton, Bucks
Died: 17 April 1940 in Winchester, Hants
Educated: Marlborough School
Clubs: Liverpool (7)
Position: Forward (7)
Debut: 23 Feb 1874 v Scotland (The Oval). Number: 52
Last game: 4 Mar 1878 (capt) v Scotland (The Oval)
Caps: 7 (W:4, D:2, L:1). As captain: 3 (W:1, D:1, L:1)
Scoring: 1T, 1 Pt
Appearances: 1874:S, 1875:S,I, 1876:S, 1877:I*,S*, 1878:S*

Alfred Lionel (Alf) KEWNEY, OBE
Born: 13 September 1882 in Tynemouth
Died: 16 December 1959 in Howden
Clubs: Rockcliff (4), Leicester (12)
Position: Forward (16)
Debut: 13 Jan 1906 v Wales (Richmond). Number: 426
Last game: 4 Jan 1913 v South Africa (Twickenham)
Caps: 16 (W:7, L:9)
Scoring: 2T, 6 Pts
Appearances: 1906:W,I,S,F, 1909:A,W,F,I,S, 1911:W,F,I,S, 1912:I,S, 1913:SA

Alan KEY, OBE
Born: 4 June 1908 in Amersham
Died: 2 July 1989 in Ploughley
Educated: Cranleigh School
Clubs: Old Cranleighans (2), Hon Artillery Company
Position: Scrum-half (2)
Debut: 8 Feb 1930 v Ireland (Lansdowne Road). Number: 662
Last game: 21 Jan 1933 v Wales (Twickenham)
Caps: 2 (W:0, L:2)
Scoring: 0 Pts
Appearances: 1930:I, 1933:W
Honours: Championship: 1930

J K L

Mark KEYWORTH
Born: 19 February 1948 in Bridgnorth
Educated: Ellesmere College, Cirencester Agricultural College
Clubs: Swansea (4), Aberystwyth
Position: Flanker (4), Bench (1)
Debut: 3 Jan 1976 v Australia (Twickenham).
Number: 1037
Last game: 6 Mar 1976 v Ireland (Twickenham)
Caps: 4 (W:1, L:3)
Scoring: 0 Pts
Appearances: 1976:A,W,S,I

Barron KILNER
Born: 11 October 1852 in Thornhill Leer
Died: 28 December 1922 in Wakefield
Clubs: Wakefield Trinity (1)
Position: Forward (1)
Debut: 30 Jan 1880 v Ireland (Lansdowne Road).
Number: 124
Caps: 1 (W:1, L:0)
Scoring: 0 Pts
Appearances: 1880:I

Richard Stephen KINDERSLEY
Born: 27 September 1858 in St Thomas, Devon
Died: 26 September 1932 in Beaminster, Dorset
Educated: Clifton College
Clubs: Oxford University (1), Exeter (2)
Position: Forward (3)
Debut: 16 Dec 1882 v Wales (Swansea).
Number: 151
Last game: 3 Jan 1885 v Wales (Swansea) - 1T, 1 Pt
Caps: 3 (W:3, L:0)
Scoring: 2T, 2 Pts
Appearances: 1883:W, 1884:S, 1885:W
Honours: Championship: 1883, 1884

Alexander David (Alex) KING
Born: 17 January 1975 in Brighton
Educated: Brighton College
Clubs: Bristol University, Rosslyn Park, Wasps (5)
Position: Fly-half (1), Replacement (4), Bench (10)
Debut: 7 Jun 1997 (rep) v Argentina (Buenos Aires) - 1T, 5 Pts. Number: 1186
Last game: 23 Aug 2003 v Wales (Cardiff) - 2C, 3PG, 1DG, 16 Pts
Caps: 5 (W:4, L:1)
Scoring: 1T, 3C, 3PG, 1DG, 23 Pts
Appearances: 1997:Ar2(r), 1998:SA(r), 2000:It(r), 2001:C2(r), 2003:W
Honours: Championship: 2000

Ian KING
Born: 5 May 1923 in Leyburn
Educated: Loretto School
Clubs: Harrogate (3)
Position: Full-back (3)
Debut: 16 Jan 1954 v Wales (Twickenham).
Number: 845
Last game: 13 Feb 1954 v Ireland (Twickenham) - 1C, 1PG, 5 Pts
Caps: 3 (W:2, L:1)
Scoring: 1C, 1PG, 5 Pts
Appearances: 1954:W,NZ,I

Alex King

John Abbott KING
Born: 21 August 1883 in Leeds
Died: Killed in action in 1916 in Guillemont, France
Educated: Giggleswick School
Clubs: Headingley (12)
Position: No 8 (12)
Debut: 21 Jan 1911 v Wales (Swansea). Number: 512
Last game: 15 Mar 1913 v Scotland (Twickenham)
Caps: 12 (W:8, L:4)
Scoring: 0 Pts
Appearances: 1911:W,F,I,S, 1912:W,I,S, 1913:SA,W,F,I,S
Honours: Grand Slam: 1913

Quentin Eric Moffitt Ayres KING
Born: 8 July 1895 in Bedford
Died: 30 October 1954 in Birmingham
Educated: St Edward's School
Clubs: Blackheath (1), Royal Artillery, Army
Position: Wing (1)
Debut: 19 Mar 1921 v Scotland (Inverleith) - 1T, 3 Pts.
Number: 568
Caps: 1 (W:1, L:0)
Scoring: 1T, 3 Pts
Appearances: 1921:S
Honours: Championship: 1921

Peter KINGSTON
Born: 24 July 1951 in Lydney
Educated: Lydney GS
Clubs: Moseley, Gloucester (5)
Position: Scrum-half (5), Bench (1)
Debut: 24 May 1975 v Australia (Sydney Cricket Ground).
Number: 1029
Last game: 17 Mar 1979 v Wales (Cardiff)
Caps: 5 (W:1, L:4)
Scoring: 0 Pts
Appearances: 1975:A1,A2, 1979:I,F,W

Alfred Everley KITCHING
Born: 6 May 1889 in Scarborough
Died: 17 March 1945 in Bulmer
Educated: Oundle School
Clubs: Cambridge University, Blackheath (1)
Position: Lock (1)
Debut: 8 Feb 1913 v Ireland (Lansdowne Road).
Number: 533
Caps: 1 (W:1, L:0)
Scoring: 0 Pts
Appearances: 1913:I
Honours: Championship: 1913

Peter Kingston

Harold James KITTERMASTER

Born: 7 January 1902 in Uppingham
Died: 28 March 1967 in Broughton, Scotland
Educated: Rugby School
Clubs: Oxford University (3), Harlequins (4)
Position: Fly-half (7)
Debut: 3 Jan 1925 v New Zealand (Twickenham) - 1T, 3 Pts. Number: 597
Last game: 20 Mar 1926 v Scotland (Twickenham)
Caps: 7 (W:2, D:2, L:3)
Scoring: 3T, 9 Pts
Appearances: 1925:NZ,W,I, 1926:W,I,F,S

Frederick P KNIGHT

Born: Details unknown
Died: Details unknown
Clubs: Devonport, Plymouth (1), Plymouth RL
Position: Flanker (1)
Debut: 9 Jan 1909 v Australia (Blackheath). Number: 476
Caps: 1 (W:0, L:1)
Scoring: 0 Pts
Appearances: 1909:A

Peter Michael KNIGHT

Born: 7 October 1947 in Bristol
Educated: Cathedral School
Clubs: Durham University, St Luke's College, Bristol (3)
Position: Full-back (2), Wing (1), Bench (1)
Debut: 26 Feb 1972 v France (Stade Colombes). Number: 1008
Last game: 3 Jun 1972 v South Africa (Johannesburg)
Caps: 3 (W:1, L:2)
Scoring: 0 Pts
Appearances: 1972:F,S,SA

Edward KNOWLES

Born: 1868 in Waberthwaite, Cumberland
Died: 29 June 1945 in Skipton
Clubs: Millom (2)
Position: Forward (2)
Debut: 14 Mar 1896 v Scotland (Glasgow). Number: 292
Last game: 13 Mar 1897 v Scotland (Manchester)
Caps: 2 (W:1, L:1)
Scoring: 0 Pts
Appearances: 1896:S, 1897:S

Thomas Caldwell (Tom) KNOWLES

Born: 6 May 1908 in West Bromwich
Died: 12 September 1985 in Birkenhead
Educated: Ampleforth College
Clubs: Birkenhead Park (1)
Position: Fly-half (1)
Debut: 21 Mar 1931 v Scotland (Murrayfield). Number: 681
Caps: 1 (W:0, L:1)
Scoring: 0 Pts
Appearances: 1931:S

Johannes Albertus (Jannie) KRIGE

Born: 6 June 1891 in Caledon, South Africa
Died: 27 September 1946 in Caledon, South Africa
Educated: Victoria College
Clubs: Guy's Hospital (1)
Position: Centre (1)
Debut: 17 Jan 1920 v Wales (Swansea). Number: 550
Caps: 1 (W:0, L:1)
Scoring: 0 Pts
Appearances: 1920:W

L

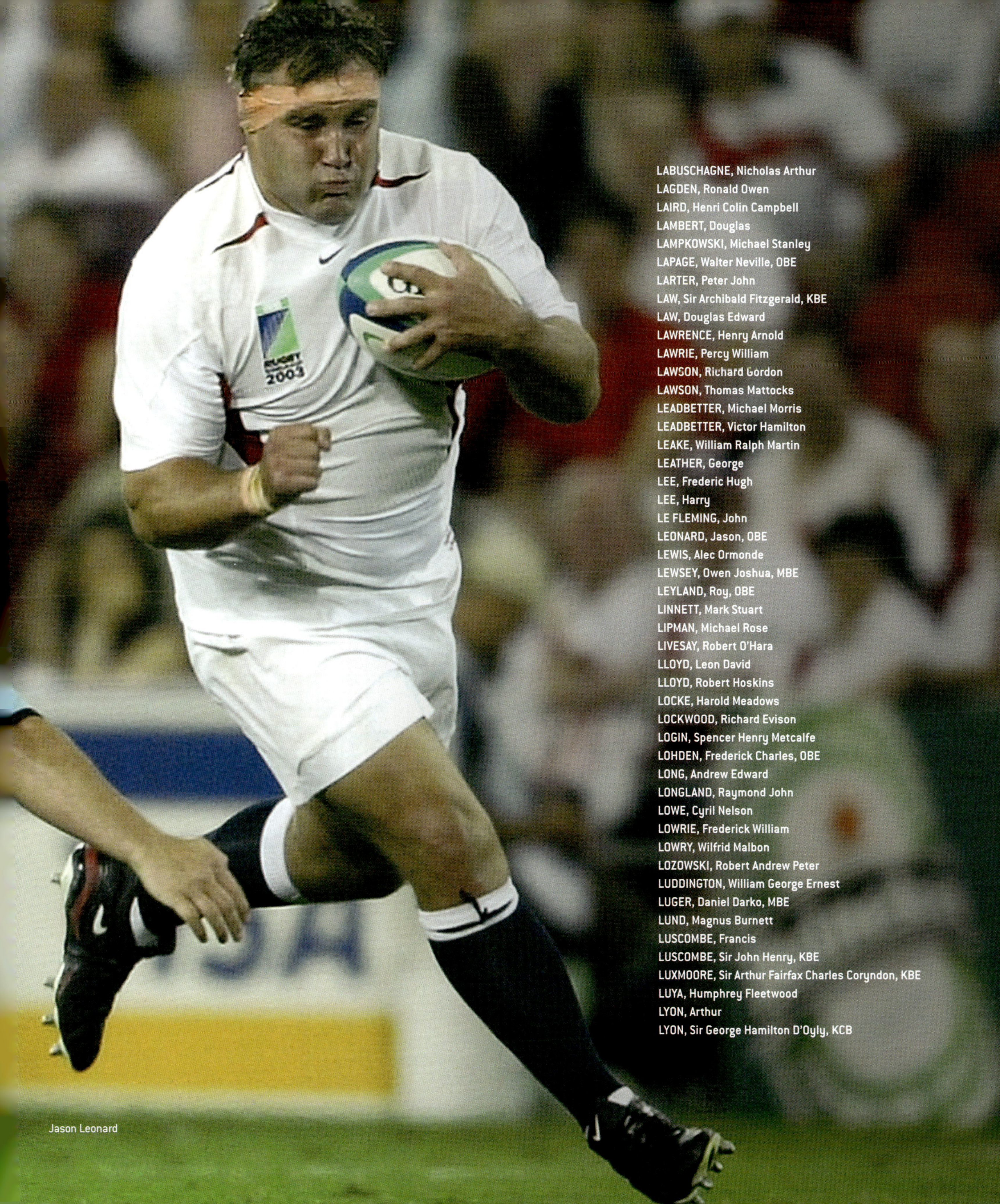

LABUSCHAGNE, Nicholas Arthur
LAGDEN, Ronald Owen
LAIRD, Henri Colin Campbell
LAMBERT, Douglas
LAMPKOWSKI, Michael Stanley
LAPAGE, Walter Neville, OBE
LARTER, Peter John
LAW, Sir Archibald Fitzgerald, KBE
LAW, Douglas Edward
LAWRENCE, Henry Arnold
LAWRIE, Percy William
LAWSON, Richard Gordon
LAWSON, Thomas Mattocks
LEADBETTER, Michael Morris
LEADBETTER, Victor Hamilton
LEAKE, William Ralph Martin
LEATHER, George
LEE, Frederic Hugh
LEE, Harry
LE FLEMING, John
LEONARD, Jason, OBE
LEWIS, Alec Ormonde
LEWSEY, Owen Joshua, MBE
LEYLAND, Roy, OBE
LINNETT, Mark Stuart
LIPMAN, Michael Rose
LIVESAY, Robert O'Hara
LLOYD, Leon David
LLOYD, Robert Hoskins
LOCKE, Harold Meadows
LOCKWOOD, Richard Evison
LOGIN, Spencer Henry Metcalfe
LOHDEN, Frederick Charles, OBE
LONG, Andrew Edward
LONGLAND, Raymond John
LOWE, Cyril Nelson
LOWRIE, Frederick William
LOWRY, Wilfrid Malbon
LOZOWSKI, Robert Andrew Peter
LUDDINGTON, William George Ernest
LUGER, Daniel Darko, MBE
LUND, Magnus Burnett
LUSCOMBE, Francis
LUSCOMBE, Sir John Henry, KBE
LUXMOORE, Sir Arthur Fairfax Charles Coryndon, KBE
LUYA, Humphrey Fleetwood
LYON, Arthur
LYON, Sir George Hamilton D'Oyly, KCB

Jason Leonard

Nicholas Arthur (Nick) LABUSCHAGNE
Born: 26 May 1931 in Durban, South Africa
Educated: Hilton College
Clubs: University of Cape Town (SA), Harlequins (1), Guy's Hospital (4)
Position: Hooker (5)
Debut: 17 Jan 1953 v Wales (Cardiff). Number: 833
Last game: 19 Mar 1955 v Scotland (Twickenham)
Caps: 5 (W:2, D:1, L:2)
Scoring: 0 Pts
Appearances: 1953:W, 1955:W,I,F,S
Honours: Championship: 1953

Ronald Owen LAGDEN
Born: 21 November 1889 in Maseru, Basutoland
Died: Killed in action in 1915 in Saint-Eloi, France
Educated: Mount Pellats School, Marlborough School
Clubs: Oxford University (1), Richmond
Position: No 8 (1)
Debut: 18 Mar 1911 v Scotland (Twickenham) - 2C, 4 Pts. Number: 516
Caps: 1 (W:1, L:0)
Scoring: 2C, 4 Pts
Appearances: 1911:S

Henri Colin Campbell (Colin) LAIRD
Born: 3 September 1908
Educated: Nautical College
Clubs: Harlequins (10)
Position: Fly-half (10)
Debut: 15 Jan 1927 v Wales (Twickenham). Number: 617
Last game: 9 Feb 1929 v Ireland (Twickenham)
Caps: 10 (W:8, L:2)
Scoring: 5T, 15 Pts
Appearances: 1927:W,I,S, 1928:A,W,I,F,S, 1929:W,I
Honours: Grand Slam: 1928
At 18 years and 152 days Henry Laird is the youngest player to have represented England

Douglas (Daniel) LAMBERT
Born: 4 October 1883 in Cranbrook
Died: Killed in action in 1915 in Loos, France
Educated: St Edward's School, Eastbourne College
Clubs: Harlequins (7)
Position: Wing (7)
Debut: 5 Jan 1907 v France (Richmond) - 5T, 15 Pts. Number: 440
Last game: 11 Feb 1911 v Ireland (Lansdowne Road)
Caps: 7 (W:3, L:4)
Scoring: 8T, 8C, 2PG, 46 Pts
Appearances: 1907:F, 1908:F,W,S, 1911:W,F,I

Michael Stanley (Mike) LAMPKOWSKI
Born: 4 January 1953 in Scunthorpe
Educated: St Bede's School
Clubs: Headingley (4), Wakefield Trinity RL
Position: Scrum-half (4)
Debut: 3 Jan 1976 v Australia (Twickenham) - 1T, 4 Pts.
Number: 1038
Last game: 6 Mar 1976 v Ireland (Twickenham)
Caps: 4 (W:1, L:3)
Scoring: 1T, 4 Pts
Appearances: 1976:A,W,S,I

Walter Neville LAPAGE, OBE
Born: 5 February 1883 in Nantwich
Died: 17 May 1939 in New Forest
Clubs: RNC Greenwich, United Services, Royal Navy (4)
Position: Centre (3), Wing (1)
Debut: 1 Jan 1908 v France (Stade Colombes) - 1T, 3 Pts. Number: 455
Last game: 21 Mar 1908 v Scotland (Inverleith)
Caps: 4 (W:2, L:2)
Scoring: 2T, 6 Pts
Appearances: 1908:F,W,I,S

Peter Larter

Peter John LARTER
Born: 7 September 1944 in Totnes
Educated: Churston Ferrers GS
Clubs: Northampton (24), RAF, Weston-super-Mare, Combined Services
Position: Lock (24), Bench (1)
Debut: 7 Jan 1967 v Australia (Twickenham). Number: 952
Last game: 20 Jan 1973 v Wales (Cardiff)
Caps: 24 (W:7, D:3, L:14)
Scoring: 1T, 1PG, 6 Pts
Appearances: 1967:A,NZ, 1968:W,I,F,S, 1969:I,F,S,W,SA, 1970:I,W,S,F, 1971:W,I,F,S,S,P, 1972:SA, 1973:NZ,W

Sir Archibald Fitzgerald LAW, KBE
Born: 1853
Died: 26 June 1921 in Wimborne
Educated: Wellington College
Clubs: Oxford University, Richmond (1)
Position: Forward (1)
Debut: 5 Mar 1877 v Scotland (Raeburn Place). Number: 93
Caps: 1 (W:0, L:1)
Scoring: 0 Pts
Appearances: 1877:S

Douglas Edward LAW
Born: 12 October 1902 in Huddersfield
Died: 13 July 1986 in Portsmouth
Educated: Birkenhead Institute
Clubs: Birkenhead Park (1)
Position: Prop (1)
Debut: 12 Feb 1927 v Ireland (Twickenham). Number: 622
Caps: 1 (W:1, L:0)
Scoring: 0 Pts
Appearances: 1927:I

Henry Arnold LAWRENCE
Born: 17 March 1848
Died: 16 April 1902 in Minchinhampton
Educated: Wellington College
Clubs: Richmond (4)
Position: Forward (4)
Debut: 3 Mar 1873 v Scotland (Glasgow). Number: 38
Last game: 8 Mar 1875 (capt) v Scotland (Raeburn Place)
Caps: 4 (W:2, D:2, L:0). As captain: 2 (W:1, D:1, L:0)
Scoring: 0 Pts
Appearances: 1873:S, 1874:S, 1875:I*,S*

Percy William LAWRIE
Born: 26 September 1888 in Lutterworth
Died: 27 December 1956 in Leicester
Educated: Wyggeston GS
Clubs: Stoneygate, Leicester (2)
Position: Wing (2)
Debut: 19 Mar 1910 v Scotland (Inverleith). Number: 507
Last game: 18 Mar 1911 v Scotland (Twickenham) - 1T, 3 Pts
Caps: 2 (W:2, L:0)
Scoring: 1T, 3 Pts
Appearances: 1910:S, 1911:S
Honours: Championship: 1910

Richard Gordon LAWSON
Born: 1 September 1901
Died: 3 January 1961 in Workington
Educated: St Bees School
Clubs: Workington (1)
Position: No 8 (1)
Debut: 14 Feb 1925 v Ireland (Twickenham). Number: 601
Caps: 1 (W:0, D:1, L:0)
Scoring: 0 Pts
Appearances: 1925:I

Thomas Mattocks LAWSON
Born: Third quarter 1900 in Cockermouth
Died: 21 October 1951 in Cockermouth
Educated: St Bees School
Clubs: Workington (2)
Position: No 8 (2)
Debut: 7 Jan 1928 v Australia (Twickenham). Number: 633
Last game: 21 Jan 1928 v Wales (Swansea)
Caps: 2 (W:2, L:0)
Scoring: 0 Pts
Appearances: 1928:A,W
Honours: Championship: 1928

Michael Morris (Mike) LEADBETTER
Born: 25 July 1946 in Southport
Clubs: Broughton Park (1), Rochdale Hornets RL
Position: Lock (1)
Debut: 18 Apr 1970 v France (Stade Colombes). Number: 988
Caps: 1 (W:0, L:1)
Scoring: 0 Pts
Appearances: 1970:F

Victor Hamilton (Vic) LEADBETTER
Born: First quarter 1930 in Kettering
Educated: Kettering GS
Clubs: Cambridge University, Edinburgh Wanderers (2)
Position: Lock (1), No 8 (1)
Debut: 20 Mar 1954 v Scotland (Murrayfield).Number: 846
Last game: 10 Apr 1954 v France (Stade Colombes)
Caps: 2 (W:1, L:1)
Scoring: 0 Pts
Appearances: 1954:S,F

William Ralph Martin LEAKE
Born: 21 December 1865 in Ceylon
Died: 14 November 1942 in south-west Surrey
Educated: Clifton College, Dulwich School
Clubs: Cambridge University, Old Alleynians, Harlequins (3)
Position: Half-Back (3)
Debut: 3 Jan 1891 v Wales (Newport). Number: 227
Last game: 7 Mar 1891 v Scotland (Richmond)
Caps: 3 (W:2, L:1)
Scoring: 0 Pts
Appearances: 1891:W,I,S

George (Jumbo) LEATHER
Born: 22 February 1881 in Leigh
Died: 2 January 1957 in Liverpool
Educated: Liverpool College
Clubs: Liverpool (1)
Position: Forward (1)
Debut: 9 Feb 1907 v Ireland (Lansdowne Road). Number: 446
Caps: 1 (W:0, L:1)
Scoring: 0 Pts
Appearances: 1907:I

Frederic Hugh LEE
Born: 14 September 1855 in Chelsea
Died: 6 February 1924 in Aberdeen, Scotland
Educated: Marlborough School
Clubs: Oxford University (2), Marlborough Nomads
Position: Forward (2)
Debut: 6 Mar 1876 v Scotland (The Oval) - 1T, 1 Pt. Number: 83
Last game: 5 Feb 1877 v Ireland (The Oval)
Caps: 2 (W:2, L:0)
Scoring: 1T, 1 Pt
Appearances: 1876:S, 1877:I

Mike Leadbetter

Harry LEE

Born: 8 December 1882 in Dewsbury
Died: 11 January 1933 in Leeds
Educated: Tettenhall College
Clubs: Cambridge University, Guy's Hospital, Blackheath (1)
Position: Full-back (1)
Debut: 5 Jan 1907 v France (Richmond). Number: 441
Caps: 1 (W:1, L:0)
Scoring: 0 Pts
Appearances: 1907:F

John LE FLEMING

Born: 23 October 1865 in Tonbridge
Died: 7 October 1942 in Montreux, Switzerland
Educated: Tonbridge School
Clubs: Cambridge University, Blackheath (1)
Position: Three-quarter (1)
Debut: 8 Jan 1887 v Wales (Llanelli). Number: 190
Caps: 1 (W:0, D:1, L:0)
Scoring: 0 Pts
Appearances: 1887:W

Jason LEONARD, OBE

Born: 14 August 1968 in Barking
Educated: Warren School
Clubs: Barking, Saracens (2), Harlequins (112)
Position: Prop (102), Replacement (12), Bench (7)
Debut: 28 Jul 1990 v Argentina (Buenos Aires). Number: 1138
Last game: 15 Feb 2004 (rep) v Italy (Rome)
Caps: 114 (W:86, D:2, L:26). As captain: 2 (W:2, L:0)
Scoring: 1T, 5 Pts. Discipline - Cautions: 1, Sin bins: 1
Appearances: 1990:Ar1,Ar2,Ar, 1991:W,S,I,F,Fj,A,NZ,It,US,F,S,A, 1992:S,I,F,W,C,SA, 1993:F,W,S,I,NZ, 1994:S,I,F,W,SA1,SA2,R,C, 1995:I,F,W,S,Ar,It,A,NZ,F,SA,Sm, 1996:F,W,S,I,It,Ar*, 1997:S,I,F,W,A,NZ1,SA,NZ2, 1998:F,W,S,I,H,It,A,SA, 1999:S,I,F,W,A,C(r),It,NZ,Fj,SA, 2000:I,F,W,It,S,SA1,SA2,A,Ar,SA, 2001:W,It,S,F,I,R, 2002:S(r),I(r),F(r),It(r),A,SA, 2003:F,S,I,NZ,W*,F(r),F(r),Geo(r),SA(r),Sm,U,W,F(r),A(r), 2004:It(r)
Honours: RWC Winner: 2003. Grand Slam: 1991, 1992, 1995. Championship: 1996, 2000, 2001, 2003

One of the former Essex carpenter's nicknames is 'Legend', and it's not hard to see why.

In a career that spanned the amateur and professional eras, Jason Leonard retired in 2004 as the world's most-capped player with 114 Test appearances for one team, a regular on the team sheet for 15 years and regarded as one of the game's finest props.

Fran Cotton, former Lions and England prop, believes he's the best ever:

"Jason is rugby's Sir Don Bradman. You're world class if you average over 50 in cricket. And then there was Bradman with his 99.94. It's the same with Leonard. He leaves every other prop trailing far behind. Nothing's impossible, but his mark looks like standing forever.

"He's been an outstanding player. But, more importantly, he's proved himself an outstanding man."

In one of the most physically-demanding positions in the game, Leonard became England's youngest ever prop at 21, making an immediate impact in a bruising show-down in Argentina in 1990.

After his baptism of fire he began a run of 40 straight England caps, taking in two Grand Slams in 1991 and 1992, with the lost World Cup final against Australia sandwiched disappointingly in-between.

Leonard started his club rugby at Barking before moving on to Saracens and then Harlequins in 1990, where he ended his career.

In 1993 he gained the first two of five Lions caps, and although the series was lost he won friends as 'song master' on the tour, and earned the nickname Fun Bus for his resemblance in the Lions red jersey to a London bus.

Following unsuccessful World Cups in 1995 and 1999, losing in the semi and quarter-final respectively, and after almost 10 years at the top, most would assume that his international career would be approaching a dignified denouement, but not this ultra-competitive powerhouse, and in 2003 he carved himself another small piece of rugby history.

A fourth Grand Slam under his not inconsiderably-sized belt, he then became the world's most capped player in a game against France (since overtaken by George Gregan) during England's triumphant World Cup campaign.

The appearance of Philippe Sella, the previous record-holder, in the dressing room to present him with a bottle of wine was evidence of his popularity amongst contemporaries.

No longer a regular by the time of the World Cup final, he came on during the crucial extra-time period to bring a steadying hand to an anxious scrum.

When he finally retired England coach Sir Clive Woodward led the tributes.

"Jason has been an outstanding ambassador for the game on and off the pitch. His contribution towards four Grand Slams and our World Cup win has been massive over the last 14 years," said Woodward.

"He will be sorely missed by his team-mates in the England squad, the coaches, management and of course the fans."

His 114 caps only brought one try, on the only occasion he actually captained England, against Argentina in 1996.

He was rewarded with an OBE.

Leonard retired in 2004 after helping Harlequins to Parker Pen Challenge Cup victory.

In another reference to Leonard's machine-like power and determination, a class 357 EMU train has the name-plate "Jason Leonard".

For England, 1990-2004 was most definitely the age of the train.

Alec Ormonde LEWIS

Born: 20 August 1920 in Brighton
Educated: Royal Masonic School
Clubs: Wells, Bath (10)
Position: Flanker (10)
Debut: 5 Jan 1952 v South Africa (Twickenham). Number: 827
Last game: 10 Apr 1954 v France (Stade Colombes)
Caps: 10 (W:6, D:1, L:3)
Scoring: 0 Pts
Appearances: 1952:SA,W,S,I,F, 1953:W,I,F,S, 1954:F
Honours: Championship: 1953

Jason Leonard

Josh Lewsey

Owen Joshua (Josh) LEWSEY, MBE

Born: 30 November 1976 in Bromley
Educated: Watford GS, Sanhurst
Clubs: Bristol University, Bristol (3), Wasps (43)
Position: Full-back (24), Wing (17), Fly-half (2), Centre (1), Replacement (2)
Debut: 20 Jun 1998 v New Zealand (Dunedin). Number: 1202
Last game: 24 Feb 2007 v Ireland (Croke Park)
Caps: 46 (W:27, L:19)
Scoring: 21T, 105 Pts
Appearances: 1998:NZ1,NZ2,SA, 2001:C1,C2,US, 2003:It,S,I,NZ,A,F,F(r),Geo,SA,U,F,A, 2004:It,S,I,W,F,NZ1,NZ2,A,C,SA,A, 2005:W,F,I,It,S,A,NZ,Sm, 2006:W,S,F,Ar(r),SA1,SA2, 2007:S,It,I
Honours: RWC Winner: 2003. Outright Championship: 2003

Josh Lewsey could have chosen Wales, but the Sandhurst-trained full-back picked his country of birth, England, to play his international rugby. His decision has brought dividends in the shape of a World Cup winner's medal in 2003 and an illustrious career wearing the red rose.

Chosen to tour the southern hemisphere in the summer of 2003, Lewsey cemented his place at full-back, as Jason Robinson moved to the wing. That trip will be forever remembered for his piledriving chest tackle on Australia's Mat Rogers in a 25-14 victory that paved the way for the World Cup campaign.

Rogers later acknowledged that trips to the beach had been more sedate since the tackle: "It ruined my surfing career. I can't lie on a surf board properly now because my rib sticks out," he said.

Lewsey used that summer success as a springboard into the World Cup, and became the first player to score a hat-trick of tries since Mike Harrison in 1987, as England destroyed Uruguay. He ended the game with five.

Lewsey made his name with Wasps after a brief period playing for Bristol whilst studying physiology and biochemistry at Bristol University.

When he started at university Wales were interested in the young full-back as his Welsh mum Mair revealed.

"A few coaches came to watch him but, after that, there was no interest shown in him whatsoever," his mother said. "I don't think he has a sense of what could have been – the opportunity wasn't there."

Lewsey's first taste of international rugby was a bitter one, as part of the England squad on the 'tour to hell' to the southern hemisphere in 1998, where an under-strength team were roundly thrashed.

Seeking some job security, he entered Sandhurst as a trainee officer, whilst continuing with his rugby, but in 1999 the two worlds collided.

During his first few weeks of training, Wasps made the Tetley's Bitter Cup Final against Northampton.

At Sandhurst, contact with the outside world during the first six weeks of training is not normally allowed, but he was given special dispensation. One catch: he had to finish his chores, cleaning of the latrines and all. Wasps won, but he missed the celebrations as he had to be back at Sandhurst by 8pm.

In 2002 he got his international career back on track, scoring twice against Italy in the Six Nations, winning the Hong Kong 7s with England, whilst also representing

England in that year's Commonwealth Games.

Lewsey was ever-present during the 2003 Grand Slam campaign in a year when he played the best rugby of his career. Solid in defence and a huge threat in attack.

His club career also flourished and he won three successive league titles between 2004 and 2006, with Wasps, also winning the Heineken Cup in 2004.

In 2005 further international recognition followed, touring New Zealand with the Lions, but an injury-interrupted 2006 Six Nations led him to take the summer off.

A self-confessed outdoor junkie – on one holiday he wrestled calves on a cowboy ranch in Arizona – he elected to go climbing in the Himalayas, reaching the base camp of K2.

He returned rejuvenated and helped Wasps win the Middlesex 7s for the first time since 1993, top-scoring in the tournament with 11 tries.

Michael Lipman

Roy (Bus) LEYLAND, OBE

Born: 6 March 1912 in Astley
Died: 4 January 1984 in Pewsey
Educated: Wigan GS
Clubs: Liverpool University, Wigan Old Boys, Waterloo (3), Leicester, Richmond, Army Education Corps, Army, Combined Services
Position: Wing (2), Centre (1)
Debut: 19 Jan 1935 v Wales (Twickenham).
Number: 719
Last game: 16 Mar 1935 v Scotland (Murrayfield)
Caps: 3 (W:1, D:1, L:1)
Scoring: 0 Pts
Appearances: 1935:W,I,S

Mark Stuart LINNETT

Born: 17 February 1963 in Rugby
Educated: Dunsmore CS
Clubs: Rugby, Moseley (1), Worcester, Birmingham
Position: Prop (1), Bench (4)
Debut: 4 Nov 1989 v Fiji (Twickenham) - 1T, 4 Pts.
Number: 1135
Caps: 1 (W:1, L:0)
Scoring: 1T, 4 Pts
Appearances: 1989:Fj

Michael Rose LIPMAN

Born: 16 January 1980 in London
Educated: St Joseph's College
Clubs: Bristol, Bath (3)
Position: Flanker (1), Replacement (2)
Debut: 19 Jun 2004 (rep) v New Zealand (Auckland).
Number: 1252
Last game: 17 Jun 2006 v Australia (Melbourne)
Caps: 3 (W:0, L:3)
Scoring: 0 Pts
Appearances: 2004:NZ2(r),A(r), 2006:A2

Robert O'Hara LIVESAY

Born: 27 June 1876 in Old Brompton, Gillingham
Died: 23 March 1946 in Magham Down, Sussex
Educated: Wellington College
Clubs: RMC Sandhurst, Queen's Royal West Surrey Regt, Blackheath (2), Army
Position: Fly-half (2)
Debut: 2 Apr 1898 v Wales (Blackheath).
Number: 325
Last game: 7 Jan 1899 v Wales (Swansea)
Caps: 2 (W:1, L:1)
Scoring: 0 Pts
Appearances: 1898:W, 1899:W

Leon David LLOYD

Born: 22 September 1977 in Coventry
Educated: Coundon Court School
Clubs: Barkers Butts, Leicester (5)
Position: Centre (2), Wing (1), Replacement (2)
Debut: 17 Jun 2000 (rep) v South Africa (Pretoria).
Number: 1220
Last game: 16 Jun 2001 v United States (San Francisco) - 2T, 10 Pts
Caps: 5 (W:4, L:1)
Scoring: 2T, 10 Pts
Appearances: 2000:SA1(r),SA2(r), 2001:C1,C2,US

Leon Lloyd

Andy Long

Robert Hoskins LLOYD
Born: 3 March 1943 in Plympton
Educated: Cheltenham College
Clubs: Clifton, Harlequins (5)
Position: Centre (5), Bench (3)
Debut: 4 Nov 1967 v New Zealand (Twickenham) - 2T, 6 Pts. Number: 961
Last game: 16 Mar 1968 v Scotland (Murrayfield)
Caps: 5 (W:1, D:2, L:2)
Scoring: 2T, 6 Pts
Appearances: 1967:NZ, 1968:W,I,F,S

Harold Meadows LOCKE
Born: First quarter 1898 in Birkenhead
Died: 23 March 1960 in Birmingham
Clubs: Birkenhead Park (12)
Position: Centre (12)
Debut: 17 Mar 1923 v Scotland (Inverleith). Number: 585
Last game: 19 Mar 1927 v Scotland (Murrayfield)
Caps: 12 (W:9, D:1, L:2)
Scoring: 1T, 3 Pts
Appearances: 1923:S,F, 1924:W,F,S, 1925:W,I,S,F, 1927:W,I,S
Honours: Championship: 1923, 1924

Richard Evison (Dicky) LOCKWOOD
Born: 11 November 1867 in Crigglestone
Died: 10 November 1915 in Leeds
Clubs: Dewsbury (4), Heckmondwike (10), Wakefield Trinity RL
Position: Three-quarter (12), Wing (2)
Debut: 8 Jan 1887 v Wales (Llanelli). Number: 191
Last game: 3 Feb 1894 (capt) v Ireland (Blackheath) - 1T, 3 Pts
Caps: 14 (W:8, D:2, L:4). As captain: 2 (W:1, L:1)
Scoring: 5T, 8C, 28 Pts
Appearances: 1887:W,I,S, 1889:M, 1891:W,I,S, 1892:W,I,S, 1893:W,I, 1894:W*,I*
Honours: Championship: 1892

Spencer Henry Metcalfe LOGIN
Born: 24 September 1851
Died: 22 January 1909 in Kingston
Educated: Wellington College
Clubs: Royal Naval College Dartmouth (1)
Position: Full-back (1)
Debut: 13 Dec 1875 v Ireland (Dublin). Number: 76
Caps: 1 (W:1, L:0)
Scoring: 0 Pts
Appearances: 1875:I

Frederick Charles LOHDEN, OBE
Born: 13 June 1871 in Hartlepool
Died: 13 April 1954 in Cheam
Educated: Durham School
Clubs: Hartlepool Rovers, Blackheath (1)
Position: Forward (1)
Debut: 7 Jan 1893 v Wales (Cardiff) - 1T, 2 Pts. Number: 253
Caps: 1 (W:0, L:1)
Scoring: 1T, 2 Pts
Appearances: 1893:W

Andrew Edward (Andy) LONG
Born: 2 September 1977 in Poole
Educated: St Peter's School
Clubs: Bournemouth, Bath (2), Munster, Rotherham, Newcastle
Position: Hooker (1), Replacement (1), Bench (2)
Debut: 15 Nov 1997 v Australia (Twickenham). Number: 1189
Last game: 16 Jun 2001 (rep) v United States (San Francisco)
Caps: 2 (W:1, D:1, L:0)
Scoring: 0 Pts
Appearances: 1997:A, 2001:US(r)

Cyril Lowe

Raymond John (Ray) LONGLAND

Born: 29 December 1908 in Lavendon
Died: 21 September 1975 in Aylesbury
Clubs: Olney, Buckingham, Bedford, RAF, Northampton (19), Combined Services
Position: Prop (19)
Debut: 19 Mar 1932 v Scotland (Twickenham). Number: 697
Last game: 19 Mar 1938 v Scotland (Twickenham)
Caps: 19 (W:11, D:2, L:6)
Scoring: 0 Pts
Appearances: 1932:S, 1933:W,S, 1934:W,I,S, 1935:W,I,S, 1936:NZ,W,I,S, 1937:W,I,S, 1938:W,I,S
Honours: Championship: 1934, 1937

Cyril Nelson LOWE

Born: 7 October 1891 in Holbeach, Lincs
Died: 6 February 1983 in mid-east Surrey
Educated: Dulwich College
Clubs: Cambridge University (9), Old Alleynians, Richmond, Blackheath (16), RAF
Position: Wing (25)
Debut: 4 Jan 1913 v South Africa (Twickenham). Number: 528
Last game: 2 Apr 1923 v France (Stade Colombes)
Caps: 25 (W:21, D:1, L:3)
Scoring: 18T, 1DG, 58 Pts
Appearances: 1913:SA,W,F,I,S, 1914:W,I,S,F, 1920:W,F,I,S, 1921:W,I,S,F, 1922:W,I,F,S, 1923:W,I,S,F
Honours: Grand Slam: 1913, 1914, 1921, 1923

Cyril Lowe

In an era when England will regularly play more than 10 Tests a year, records rarely stand for too long and few stretch back more than 20 years.

But one remarkable try-scoring record has stood the test of time, set by Cyril Lowe in the early part of the 20th century.

In the 1914 Five Nations Championship Lowe scored an incredible eight tries, a record not matched by any other Englishman as his country went on to record their second successive Grand Slam.

Lowe – who played for Blackheath – scored hat-tricks against both Scotland and France and his record of 18 tries in all stood until Rory Underwood overtook it, almost 70 years later, even though Lowe lost six years to the war.

In Five/Six Nations terms Lowe is still top of the tree, tied with Underwood, but ahead of anyone else just in Championship matches.

As Jason Woolgar explains in his excellent Official RFU History, Lowe was a hero in the First World War being awarded both the Distinguished Flying Cross and the Military Cross. Many historians believe the diminutive Lowe was also the inspiration for the fictional flyer, Biggles.

Between 1913 and 1925, Lowe – who was a triple Cambridge Blue – made 25 consecutive appearances which was a record for England, this run including all 16 games of England's four Grand Slams in that period.

Frederick William LOWRIE

Born: 1 March 1868 in Wakefield
Died: 9 August 1902 in Leeds
Educated: Wakefield College
Clubs: Wakefield Trinity (1), Batley (1)
Position: Forward (2)
Debut: 16 Feb 1889 v New Zealand Natives (Blackheath). Number: 202
Last game: 15 Feb 1890 v Wales (Dewsbury)
Caps: 2 (W:1, L:1)
Scoring: 0 Pts
Appearances: 1889:M, 1890:W

Wilfrid Malbon LOWRY
Born: 14 July 1900 in Birkenhead
Died: 4 July 1974 in Heswall
Educated: The Leys School
Clubs: Birkenhead Park (1), Waterloo
Position: Wing (1)
Debut: 31 Jan 1920 v France (Twickenham). Number: 557
Caps: 1 (W:1, L:0)
Scoring: 0 Pts
Appearances: 1920:F

Robert Andrew Peter (Rob) LOZOWSKI
Born: 18 November 1960 in Ealing
Educated: Gunnersbury School
Clubs: Old Gaytonians, Wasps (1)
Position: Centre (1)
Debut: 3 Nov 1984 v Australia (Twickenham). Number: 1097
Caps: 1 (W:0, L:1)
Scoring: 0 Pts
Appearances: 1984:A

William George Ernest LUDDINGTON
Born: 8 February 1894 in Farnham
Died: Killed in action in 1941 in the Mediterranean Sea
Clubs: Devonport Services (13), Royal Navy
Position: Prop (8), Lock (5)
Debut: 20 Jan 1923 v Wales (Twickenham). Number: 582
Last game: 16 Jan 1926 v Wales (Cardiff)
Caps: 13 (W:10, D:2, L:1)
Scoring: 5C, 1PG, 1GM, 16 Pts
Appearances: 1923:W,I,S,F, 1924:W,I,F,S, 1925:W,I,S,F, 1926:W
Honours: Grand Slam: 1923, 1924

Daniel Darko (Dan) LUGER, MBE
Born: 11 January 1975 in Chiswick
Educated: Latymer School
Clubs: Manchester University, Richmond, Orrell, Harlequins (20), Saracens (13), Perpignan (FR,5), Toulon (FR)
Position: Wing (32), Replacement (6), Bench (3)
Debut: 14 Nov 1998 v Netherlands (Huddersfield) - 1T, 5 Pts. Number: 1209
Last game: 9 Nov 2003 v Wales (Brisbane)
Caps: 38 (W:31, L:7)
Scoring: 24T, 120 Pts
Appearances: 1998:H,It,SA, 1999:S,I,F,W,A,US,C,It,NZ,Tg,Fj,SA, 2000:SA1,A,Ar,SA, 2001:W,I,A,R,SA, 2002:F(r),W,It, 2003:F,W,It,S(r),I(r),NZ(r),W,Geo(r),SA(r),U,W
Honours: RWC Winner: 2003. Grand Slam: 2003. Championship: 2001

Magnus Burnett LUND
Born: 25 June 1983 in Manchester
Educated: RGS Lancaster
Clubs: Sale (7)
Position: Flanker (4), Replacement (3)
Debut: 11 Jun 2006 v Australia (Sydney). Number: 1270
Last game: 24 Feb 2007 v Ireland (Croke Park)
Caps: 7 (W:2, L:5)
Scoring: 1T, 5 Pts
Appearances: 2006:A1,A2(r),NZ(r),Ar(r), 2007:S,It,I

Dan Luger

Magnus Lund

Francis LUSCOMBE
Born: Third quarter 1849 in Croydon
Died: 17 July 1926 in East Grinstead
Educated: Tonbridge School
Clubs: Gipsies (6)
Position: Forward (6)
Debut: 5 Feb 1872 v Scotland (The Oval). Number: 29
Last game: 6 Mar 1876 (capt) v Scotland (The Oval)
Caps: 6 (W:4, D:2, L:0). As captain: 2 (W:2, L:0)
Scoring: 0 Pts
Appearances: 1872:S, 1873:S, 1875:I,S,I*, 1876:S*

Sir John Henry LUSCOMBE KBE
Born: Second quarter 1848 in Lewisham
Died: 3 April 1937 in Worth, Sussex
Educated: Tonbridge School
Clubs: Gipsies (1)
Position: Forward (1)
Debut: 27 Mar 1871 v Scotland (Raeburn Place). Number: 12
Caps: 1 (W:0, L:1)
Scoring: 0 Pts
Appearances: 1871:S

Sir Arthur Fairfax Charles Coryndon LUXMOORE KBE
Born: 27 February 1876 in Hendon
Died: 25 September 1944 in Hammersmith, London
Educated: King's School
Clubs: Cambridge University, Richmond (2)
Position: Forward (2)
Debut: 10 Mar 1900 v Scotland (Inverleith). Number: 354
Last game: 5 Jan 1901 v Wales (Cardiff)
Caps: 2 (W:0, D:1, L:1)
Scoring: 0 Pts
Appearances: 1900:S, 1901:W

Humphrey Fleetwood LUYA
Born: 3 February 1918 in West Derby
Educated: Merchant Taylors' School
Clubs: Waterloo, Carlisle, Headingley (5)
Position: Lock (5)
Debut: 17 Jan 1948 v Wales (Twickenham). Number: 779
Last game: 15 Jan 1949 v Wales (Cardiff)
Caps: 5 (W:0, D:1, L:4)
Scoring: 0 Pts
Appearances: 1948:W,I,S,F, 1949:W

Arthur LYON
Born: 4 August 1851 in West Derby
Died: 4 December 1905 in New Zealand
Educated: Rugby School
Clubs: Liverpool (1)
Position: Full-back (1)
Debut: 27 Mar 1871 v Scotland (Raeburn Place). Number: 13
Caps: 1 (W:0, L:1)
Scoring: 0 Pts
Appearances: 1871:S

Sir George Hamilton D'Oyly LYON, KCB
Born: 3 October 1883 in Bankipore, India
Died: 19 August 1947 in Midhurst, Sussex
Educated: King's School, HMS Brittania
Clubs: United Services, Royal Navy (2)
Position: Full-back (2)
Debut: 21 Mar 1908 v Scotland (Inverleith). Number: 463
Last game: 9 Jan 1909 (capt) v Australia (Blackheath)
Caps: 2 (W:0, L:2). As captain: 1 (W:0, L:1)
Scoring: 0 Pts
Appearances: 1908:S, 1909:A*

M

MACILWAINE, Alfred Herbert
MACKIE, Osbert Gadesden
MACKINLAY, James Egan Harrison
MACLAREN, William
MACLENNAN, Roderick Ross Forrest
MADGE, Richard John Palmer
MALIR, Frank William Stewart
MALLETT, John Anthony H
MALLINDER, David James
MANGLES, Roland Henry, CMG
MANLEY, Donald Charles
MANN, William Edgar
MANTELL, Neil Dennington
MAPLETOFT, Mark Sterland
MARKENDALE, Ellis T
MARQUES, Reginald William David
MARQUIS, John Campbell
MARRIOTT, Charles John Bruce
MARRIOTT, Ernest Edward
MARRIOTT, Victor Robert
MARSDEN, George Herbert
MARSH, Henry
MARSH, James Holt
MARSHALL, Howard, OBE
MARSHALL, Murray Wyatt
MARSHALL, Robert Michall
MARTIN, Nicholas Owen
MARTIN, Ronald Christopher
MARTINDALE, Samuel Airey
MASSEY, Edward John
MATHER, Barrie-Jon
MATHIAS, John Lloyd
MATTERS, John Charles
MATTHEWS, John Robert Clive
MAUD, Philip, CBE
MAXWELL, Andrew William
MAYNARD, Alfred Frederic
McCANLIS, Maurice Alfred
McCARTHY, Neil
McFADYEAN, Colin William
McLEOD, Norman Frederick

MEARS, Lee Andrew
MEIKLE, Graham William Churchill
MEIKLE, Stephen Spencer Churchill
MELLISH, Frank Whitmore
MELVILLE, Nigel David
MERRIAM, Sir Laurence Pierce Brooke, KBE
MICHELL, Arthur Tompson
MIDDLETON, Bernard Boswell
MIDDLETON, John Alan, OBE
MILES, John Henry
MILLETT, Harry
MILLS, Frederick William
MILLS, Stephen Graham Ford
MILLS, William Alonzo
MILMAN, Dermot Lionel Kennedy
MILTON, Henry Cecil
MILTON, John Griffin
MILTON, Sir William Henry, KCVO
MITCHELL, Frank
MITCHELL, William Grant
MOBBS, Edgar Roberts
MOBERLY, William Octavius
MOODY, Lewis Walton, MBE
MOORE, Brian Christopher
MOORE, Edward James
MOORE, Norman Hope
MOORE, Sir Philip Brian Cecil, GCVO
MOORE, William Kenneth Thomas

MORDELL, Robert John
MORFITT, Samuel
MORGAN, James Rydiard
MORGAN, Oliver
MORGAN, William George Derek
MORLEY, Alan John, MBE
MORRIS, Alfred Drummond Warrington, CMG
MORRIS, Colin Dewi
MORRIS, Robert Jonathan S
MORRISON, Piercy Henderson
MORSE, Sydney
MORTIMER, William
MORTON, Harold James Storrs
MOSS, F
MULLINS, Andrew Richard
MYCOCK, Joseph S
MYERS, Edward
MYERS, Harry

Brian Moore

Alfred Herbert MACILWAINE
Born: 27 March 1889 in Sculcoates
Died: 1983 in South Africa
Educated: Clifton College
Clubs: United Services (4), Royal Artillery, Army (1), Hull & ER, Harlequins
Position: Prop (4), Lock (1)
Debut: 20 Jan 1912 v Wales (Twickenham). Number: 520
Last game: 14 Feb 1920 v Ireland (Lansdowne Road)
Caps: 5 (W:4, L:1)
Scoring: 0 Pts
Appearances: 1912:W,I,S,F, 1920:I

Osbert Gadesden MACKIE
Born: 23 August 1869 in Wakefield
Died: 25 January 1927 in Redcar, Yorks
Educated: Haileybury & ISC
Clubs: Cambridge University (2), Wakefield Trinity
Position: Centre (2)
Debut: 13 Mar 1897 v Scotland (Manchester). Number: 294
Last game: 5 Feb 1898 v Ireland (Richmond)
Caps: 2 (W:1, L:1)
Scoring: 0 Pts
Appearances: 1897:S, 1898:I

James Egan Harrison MACKINLAY
Born: 17 December 1850 in Guildford
Died: 1 July 1917 in Guisborough
Educated: Rugby School
Clubs: St George's Hospital (3)
Position: Forward (3)
Debut: 5 Feb 1872 v Scotland (The Oval). Number: 30
Last game: 15 Feb 1875 v Ireland (The Oval)
Caps: 3 (W:2, D:1, L:0)
Scoring: 0 Pts
Appearances: 1872:S, 1873:S, 1875:I

William MACLAREN
Born: Details unknown
Died: Details unknown
Clubs: Manchester (1)
Position: Three-quarter (1)
Debut: 27 Mar 1871 v Scotland (Raeburn Place). Number: 14
Caps: 1 (W:0, L:1)
Scoring: 0 Pts
Appearances: 1871:S

Roderick Ross Forrest MACLENNAN
Born: 23 December 1903 in Glasgow, Scotland
Died: 2 January 1986 in Nairn, Scotland
Educated: Merchant Taylors' School
Clubs: Old Merchant Taylors' (3), Headingley, London Scottish
Position: Prop (3)
Debut: 14 Feb 1925 v Ireland (Twickenham). Number: 602
Last game: 13 Apr 1925 v France (Stade Colombes)
Caps: 3 (W:1, D:1, L:1)
Scoring: 0 Pts
Appearances: 1925:I,S,F

John Mallett

Richard John Palmer MADGE
Born: 19 December 1914 in Exeter
Educated: Exeter School
Clubs: Exeter (4)
Position: Scrum-half (4)
Debut: 3 Jan 1948 v Australia (Twickenham). Number: 777
Last game: 20 Mar 1948 v Scotland (Murrayfield)
Caps: 4 (W:0, D:1, L:3)
Scoring: 0 Pts
Appearances: 1948:A,W,I,S

Frank William Stewart MALIR
Born: 4 August 1905 in India
Died: 22 January 1974 in Claro
Educated: Woodhouse Grove School, Heriot's School
Clubs: Otley (3)
Position: Centre (3)
Debut: 18 Jan 1930 v Wales (Cardiff). Number: 659
Last game: 15 Mar 1930 v Scotland (Twickenham)
Caps: 3 (W:1, D:1, L:1)
Scoring: 0 Pts
Appearances: 1930:W,I,S
Honours: Championship: 1930

John Anthony H MALLETT
Born: 28 May 1970 in Lincoln
Educated: Millfield School, West London Institute
Clubs: Bath (1)
Position: Replacement Prop (1), Bench (2)
Debut: 4 Jun 1995 (rep) v Samoa (Durban).
Number: 1158
Caps: 1 (W:1, L:0)
Scoring: 0 Pts
Appearances: 1995:Sm(r)

David James (Jim) MALLINDER
Born: 16 March 1966 in Halifax
Educated: Crossley School, Porter School, Carnegie College
Clubs: Old Crossleyans, Roundhay, Sale (2)
Position: Full-back (2)
Debut: 31 May 1997 v Argentina (Buenos Aires).
Number: 1181
Last game: 7 Jun 1997 v Argentina (Buenos Aires)
Caps: 2 (W:1, L:1)
Scoring: 0 Pts
Appearances: 1997:Ar1,Ar2

Roland Henry MANGLES, CMG
Born: 9 February 1874 in Guildford
Died: 29 September 1948 in Colchester
Educated: Marlborough School
Clubs: Richmond (2), Queen's Royal West Surrey Regt, Army
Position: Forward (2)
Debut: 9 Jan 1897 v Wales (Newport). Number: 302
Last game: 6 Feb 1897 v Ireland (Lansdowne Road)
Caps: 2 (W:0, L:2)
Scoring: 0 Pts
Appearances: 1897:W,I

Donald Charles (Dick) MANLEY
Born: 17 February 1932 in Exeter
Educated: Hele's School
Clubs: Exeter (4)
Position: Flanker (4)
Debut: 19 Jan 1963 v Wales (Cardiff).
Number: 912
Last game: 16 Mar 1963 v Scotland (Twickenham)
Caps: 4 (W:3, D:1, L:0)
Scoring: 0 Pts
Appearances: 1963:W,I,F,S
Honours: Championship: 1963

William Edgar MANN
Born: 19 January 1885 in Edmonton
Died: 14 February 1969 in Blyth
Educated: Marlborough School
Clubs: RMA Woolwich, United Services (3), Royal Artillery, Army
Position: Forward (3)
Debut: 21 Jan 1911 v Wales (Swansea).
Number: 513
Last game: 11 Feb 1911 v Ireland (Lansdowne Road)
Caps: 3 (W:1, L:2)
Scoring: 1T, 3 Pts
Appearances: 1911:W,F,I

Jim Mallinder

M N O

Mark Mapletoft

Ellis T MARKENDALE

Born: November 1856 in Salford
Died: Details unknown
Educated: Uppingham School
Clubs: Manchester Rangers (1)
Position: Forward (1)
Debut: 30 Jan 1880 v Ireland (Lansdowne Road) - 1T, 1 Pt. Number: 125
Caps: 1 (W:1, L:0)
Scoring: 1T, 1 Pt
Appearances: 1880:I

Reginald William David (David) MARQUES

Born: 9 December 1932 in St Margarets, Ware
Educated: Tonbridge School
Clubs: Cambridge University (13), Royal Engineers, Army, Combined Services, Harlequins (10)
Position: Lock (23)
Debut: 21 Jan 1956 v Wales (Twickenham). Number: 865
Last game: 21 Jan 1961 v Wales (Cardiff)
Caps: 23 (W:13, D:5, L:5)
Scoring: 1T, 3 Pts
Appearances: 1956:W,I,S,F, 1957:W,I,F,S, 1958:W,A,I,F,S, 1959:W,I,F,S, 1960:W,I,F,S, 1961:SA,W
Honours: Grand Slam: 1957. Championship: 1958

John Campbell MARQUIS

Born: First quarter 1876 in Birkenhead
Died: 28 January 1928 in Birkenhead
Clubs: Birkenhead Park (2)
Position: Scrum-half (2)
Debut: 3 Feb 1900 v Ireland (Richmond). Number: 353
Last game: 10 Mar 1900 v Scotland (Inverleith)
Caps: 2 (W:1, D:1, L:0)
Scoring: 0 Pts
Appearances: 1900:I,S

Charles John Bruce MARRIOTT

Born: 15 July 1861 in Rensham, Suffolk
Died: 25 December 1936 in Ipswich
Educated: Blackheath Prep School, Tonbridge School
Clubs: Cambridge University (2), Gipsies, Blackheath (5)
Position: Forward (7)
Debut: 5 Jan 1884 v Wales (Leeds). Number: 161
Last game: 5 Feb 1887 v Ireland (Lansdowne Road)
Caps: 7 (W:5, D:1, L:1). As captain: 2 (W:2, L:0)
Scoring: 0 Pts
Appearances: 1884:W,I,S, 1886:W*,I*,S, 1887:I
Honours: Championship: 1884

Neil Dennington MANTELL

Born: 13 October 1953 in Reigate
Educated: Reigate GS
Clubs: Rosslyn Park (1)
Position: Lock (1)
Debut: 24 May 1975 v Australia (Sydney Cricket Ground). Number: 1030
Caps: 1 (W:0, L:1)
Scoring: 0 Pts
Appearances: 1975:A1

Mark Sterland MAPLETOFT

Born: 25 December 1971 in Mansfield
Educated: Lawrence Sheriff School
Clubs: Loughborough University, Rugby, Gloucester (1), Saracens, Harlequins, London Irish
Position: Fly-half (1), Bench (1)
Debut: 7 Jun 1997 v Argentina (Buenos Aires) - 1PG, 3 Pts. Number: 1185
Caps: 1 (W:0, L:1)
Scoring: 1PG, 3 Pts
Appearances: 1997:Ar2

Ernest Edward MARRIOTT

Born: 15 January 1857 in Salford
Died: 1917
Educated: Rugby School
Clubs: Manchester (1)
Position: Forward (1)
Debut: 13 Dec 1875 v Ireland (Dublin). Number: 77
Caps: 1 (W:1, L:0)
Scoring: 0 Pts
Appearances: 1875:I

Chris Martin

Howard MARSHALL, OBE
Born: 20 December 1870 in Sunderland
Died: 9 October 1929 in Westminster
Educated: Elham School
Clubs: Barnard Castle, Cambridge University, Sunderland, St Bart's Hospital, Blackheath (1), London
Position: Half-Back (1)
Debut: 7 Jan 1893 v Wales (Cardiff) - 3T, 6 Pts. Number: 233
Caps: 1 (W:0, L:1)
Scoring: 3T, 6 Pts
Appearances: 1893:W

Murray Wyatt MARSHALL
Born: Third quarter 1852 in Guildford
Died: 28 July 1930 in Godalming
Educated: Wellington College
Clubs: Blackheath (10)
Position: Forward (10)
Debut: 3 Mar 1873 v Scotland (Glasgow). Number: 40
Last game: 11 Mar 1878 (capt) v Ireland (Lansdowne Road)
Caps: 10 (W:6, D:3, L:1). As captain: 1 (W:1, L:0)
Scoring: 0 Pts
Appearances: 1873:S, 1874:S, 1875:I,S,I, 1876:S, 1877:I,S, 1878:S,I*

Robert Michall MARSHALL
Born: 18 May 1917
Died: Killed in action in 1945
Educated: Giggleswick School
Clubs: Oxford University (5), Scarborough, Harlequins
Position: No 8 (3), Lock (2)
Debut: 12 Feb 1938 v Ireland (Lansdowne Road) - 1T, 3 Pts. Number: 740
Last game: 18 Mar 1939 v Scotland (Murrayfield)
Caps: 5 (W:3, L:2)
Scoring: 1T, 3 Pts
Appearances: 1938:I,S, 1939:W,I,S

Victor Robert MARRIOTT
Born: 29 January 1938 in Battersea
Educated: Balham GS
Clubs: Harlequins (4), Army, Combined Services
Position: Flanker (4)
Debut: 25 May 1963 v New Zealand (Auckland). Number: 918
Last game: 4 Jan 1964 v New Zealand (Twickenham)
Caps: 4 (W:0, L:4)
Scoring: 0 Pts
Appearances: 1963:NZ1,NZ2,A, 1964:NZ

George Herbert MARSDEN
Born: 16 October 1880 in Morley
Died: 7 July 1948 in Lytham St Annes
Clubs: Fylde, Morley (3), Bradford RL
Position: Fly-half (2), Scrum-half (1)
Debut: 6 Jan 1900 v Wales (Gloucester). Number: 348
Last game: 10 Mar 1900 v Scotland (Inverleith)
Caps: 3 (W:1, D:1, L:1)
Scoring: 0 Pts
Appearances: 1900:W,I,S

Henry MARSH
Born: 8 September 1850 in Ireland
Died: 25 April 1939 in Amersham
Educated: Rev Dr Stacpoole's School
Clubs: Royal Indian Eng College (1)
Position: Forward (1)
Debut: 3 Mar 1873 v Scotland (Glasgow). Number: 39
Caps: 1 (W:0, D:1, L:0)
Scoring: 0 Pts
Appearances: 1873:S

James Holt MARSH
Born: 1866
Died: 1 August 1928 in Leigh
Educated: Edinburgh Institute
Clubs: Swinton (1), Edinburgh Institute
Position: Three-quarter (1)
Debut: 6 Feb 1892 v Ireland (Manchester). Number: 244
Caps: 1 (W:1, L:0)
Scoring: 0 Pts
Appearances: 1892:I
Honours: Championship: 1892

Nicholas Owen MARTIN
Born: 26 June 1946 in Cambridge
Educated: The Perse School
Clubs: Cambridge University, Harlequins (1), Bedford
Position: Replacement Lock (1), Bench (1)
Debut: 26 Feb 1972 (rep) v France (Stade Colombes). Number: 1010
Caps: 1 (W:0, L:1)
Scoring: 0 Pts
Appearances: 1972:F(r)

Ronald Christopher (Chris) MARTIN
Born: 27 June 1961 in Truro
Educated: Penryn CS, Cornwall TC
Clubs: Bath University, Bath (4)
Position: Full-back (4), Bench (2)
Debut: 2 Feb 1985 v France (Twickenham). Number: 1106
Last game: 20 Apr 1985 v Wales (Cardiff)
Caps: 4 (W:1, D:1, L:2)
Scoring: 0 Pts
Appearances: 1985:F,S,I,W

Barrie-Jon Mather

Barrie-Jon MATHER
Born: 15 January 1973 in Wigan
Educated: Arnold School
Clubs: Castleford RL, Wigan RL, Sale (1), Kubota Spears (JP), Coventry
Position: Centre (1), Bench (1)
Debut: 11 Apr 1999 v Wales (Wembley).
Number: 1212
Caps: 1 (W:0, L:1)
Scoring: 0 Pts
Appearances: 1999:W

John Lloyd MATHIAS
Born: Third quarter 1878 in Cardigan, Wales
Died: 21 November 1940 in Bucklow
Clubs: Bristol (4)
Position: Lock (4)
Debut: 14 Jan 1905 v Wales (Cardiff).
Number: 403
Last game: 2 Dec 1905 v New Zealand (Crystal Palace)
Caps: 4 (W:0, L:4)
Scoring: 0 Pts
Appearances: 1905:W,I,S,NZ

John Charles MATTERS
Born: First quarter 1879 in Stoke Damerel
Died: 24 April 1949 in south-east Surrey
Clubs: Royal Naval Eng College Keyham (1)
Position: Wing (1)
Debut: 11 Mar 1899 v Scotland (Blackheath).
Number: 337
Caps: 1 (W:0, L:1)
Scoring: 0 Pts
Appearances: 1899:S

John Robert Clive MATTHEWS
Born: 14 June 1920 in Hastings
Died: 2 February 2004
Educated: Sutton Valence School
Clubs: Guy's Hospital, Royal Navy, Combined Services, Harlequins (10)
Position: Lock (10)
Debut: 26 Feb 1949 v France (Twickenham).
Number: 798
Last game: 5 Apr 1952 v France (Stade Colombes)
Caps: 10 (W:6, L:4)
Scoring: 0 Pts
Appearances: 1949:F,S, 1950:I,F,S, 1952:SA,W,S,I,F

Samuel Airey (Sam) MARTINDALE
Born: 5 May 1905 in Kendal
Died: 19 January 1986 in Kendal
Clubs: Kendal (1)
Position: Lock (1)
Debut: 1 Apr 1929 v France (Stade Colombes).
Number: 650
Caps: 1 (W:1, L:0)
Scoring: 0 Pts
Appearances: 1929:F

Edward John MASSEY
Born: 2 July 1900 in West Derby
Died: 30 April 1977 in Woking
Educated: Ampleforth College
Clubs: Liverpool, Leicester (3)
Position: Scrum-half (3)
Debut: 17 Jan 1925 v Wales (Twickenham). Number: 599
Last game: 21 Mar 1925 v Scotland (Murrayfield)
Caps: 3 (W:1, D:1, L:1)
Scoring: 0 Pts
Appearances: 1925:W,I,S

Philip MAUD, CBE
Born: 8 August 1870 in Sudbury
Died: 28 February 1947 in Chelsea
Educated: Leamington College
Clubs: RMA Woolwich, Royal Engineers, Blackheath (2)
Position: Forward (2)
Debut: 7 Jan 1893 v Wales (Cardiff).
Number: 254
Last game: 4 Feb 1893 v Ireland (Lansdowne Road)
Caps: 2 (W:1, L:1)
Scoring: 0 Pts
Appearances: 1893:W,I

Neil McCarthy

Lee Mears

Andrew William (Andy) MAXWELL

Born: 3 March 1951 in West Kirby
Educated: Caldy Grange GS
Clubs: New Brighton (1), Headingley (6)
Position: Centre (7)
Debut: 24 May 1975 v Australia (Sydney Cricket Ground). Number: 1031
Last game: 21 Jan 1978 v France (Parc des Princes)
Caps: 7 (W:1, L:6)
Scoring: 1T, 4 Pts
Appearances: 1975:A1, 1976:A,W,S,I,F, 1978:F

Alfred Frederic MAYNARD

Born: 23 March 1894 in Croydon
Died: Killed in action in 1916 in Beaumont Hamel
Educated: Seaford School, Durham School
Clubs: Cambridge University (3), Harlequins, Durham City
Position: Hooker (3)
Debut: 17 Jan 1914 v Wales (Twickenham). Number: 537
Last game: 21 Mar 1914 v Scotland (Inverleith)
Caps: 3 (W:3, L:0)
Scoring: 0 Pts
Appearances: 1914:W,I,S
Honours: Championship: 1914

Maurice Alfred McCANLIS

Born: 17 June 1906 in Quetta, India
Died: 27 September 1991 in Pershore, Worcs
Educated: Cranleigh School
Clubs: Oxford University, Old Cranleighians, Gloucester (2), Northampton
Position: Centre (2)
Debut: 17 Jan 1931 v Wales (Twickenham). Number: 672
Last game: 14 Feb 1931 v Ireland (Twickenham)
Caps: 2 (W:0, D:1, L:1)
Scoring: 0 Pts
Appearances: 1931:W,I

Neil McCARTHY

Born: 29 November 1974 in Slough
Educated: Leeds GS
Clubs: Bath, Bedford, Gloucester (3), Bristol, Orrell
Position: Replacement Hooker (3), Bench (7)
Debut: 6 Mar 1999 (rep) v Ireland (Lansdowne Road). Number: 1210
Last game: 18 Mar 2000 (rep) v Italy (Rome)
Caps: 3 (W:3, L:0)
Scoring: 0 Pts
Appearances: 1999:I(r),US(r), 2000:It(r)
Honours: Championship: 2000

Colin William McFADYEAN

Born: 11 March 1943 in Tavistock
Clubs: Loughborough College, UAU, Moseley (11)
Position: Centre (9), Wing (2)
Debut: 12 Feb 1966 v Ireland (Twickenham). Number: 944
Last game: 10 Feb 1968 (capt) v Ireland (Twickenham)
Caps: 11 (W:2, D:3, L:6). As captain: 2 (W:0, D:2, L:0)
Scoring: 4T, 1DG, 15 Pts
Appearances: 1966:I,F,S, 1967:A,I,F,S,W,NZ, 1968:W*,I*

Norman Frederick McLEOD

Born: 30 June 1856 in Madras, India
Died: 20 April 1921 in South Kensington, London
Educated: Clifton College
Clubs: Royal Indian Eng College (2)
Position: Forward (2)
Debut: 10 Mar 1879 v Scotland (Raeburn Place). Number: 112
Last game: 24 Mar 1879 v Ireland (The Oval)
Caps: 2 (W:1, D:1, L:0)
Scoring: 0 Pts
Appearances: 1879:S,I

Lee Andrew MEARS

Born: 5 March 1979 in Torquay
Educated: Colston's School, Paignton Community College
Clubs: Bath (14)
Position: Hooker (3), Replacement (11), Bench (2)
Debut: 26 Nov 2005 (rep) v Samoa (Twickenham). Number: 1267
Last game: 24 Feb 2007 (rep) v Ireland (Croke Park)
Caps: 14 (W:6, L:8)
Scoring: 0 Pts
Appearances:2005:Sm(r),2006:W(r),It(r),F(r),I,A1,A2(r), NZ(r),Ar(r),SA1(r),SA2, 2007:S(r),It(r),I(r)

M N O

Nigel Melville

Graham William Churchill MEIKLE
Born: 14 October 1911 in Waterloo
Died: 18 June 1981 in Whitehaven
Educated: St Bees School
Clubs: Cambridge University, Waterloo (3), Richmond, Leicester
Position: Wing (3)
Debut: 20 Jan 1934 v Wales (Cardiff) - 2T, 6 Pts. Number: 707
Last game: 17 Mar 1934 v Scotland (Twickenham) - 1T, 3 Pts
Caps: 3 (W:3, L:0)
Scoring: 4T, 12 Pts
Appearances: 1934:W,I,S
Honours: Championship: 1934

Stephen Spencer Churchill MEIKLE
Born: 6 July 1904
Died: 4 June 1960 in Liverpool
Educated: St Bees School
Clubs: Waterloo (1)
Position: Fly-half (1)
Debut: 16 Mar 1929 v Scotland (Murrayfield) - 1T, 3 Pts. Number: 644
Caps: 1 (W:0, L:1)
Scoring: 1T, 3 Pts
Appearances: 1929:S

Frank Whitmore MELLISH
Born: 26 March 1897 in Rondebosch, South Africa
Died: 21 August 1965 in Cape Town, South Africa
Educated: Wynberg BHS, Rondebosch HS, SA College School
Clubs: Cape Town, Villagers, Blackheath (6)
Position: Flanker (6)
Debut: 17 Jan 1920 v Wales (Swansea). Number: 551
Last game: 12 Feb 1921 v Ireland (Twickenham)
Caps: 6 (W:5, L:1)
Scoring: 1T, 3 Pts
Appearances: 1920:W,F,I,S, 1921:W,I
Honours: Championship: 1921

Nigel David MELVILLE
Born: 6 January 1961 in Leeds
Educated: Aireborough GS, NE London Poly
Clubs: Otley, Wakefield, Wasps (13)
Position: Scrum-half (13), Bench (9)
Debut: 3 Nov 1984 (capt) v Australia (Twickenham).
Number: 1098
Last game: 19 Mar 1988 (capt) v Ireland (Twickenham)
Caps: 13 (W:4, L:9). As captain: 7 (W:4, L:3)
Scoring: 0 Pts
Appearances: 1984:A*, 1985:I,W,NZ1,NZ2, 1986:W*,S*,I*,F*, 1988:F,W,S*,I*

Nigel Melville may have only won 13 caps in the 1980s but the man who went on to become the chief executive of USA Rugby is regarded by many as England's greatest scrum-half.

Making his name through the Divisional Championship Melville starred for the North, forcing his way into the England team for his debut against Australia at Twickenham in 1984.

In that match Melville became one of a select band of players to captain England on their debut.

An illustrious career lay in front of him but a series of

injuries including problems with his neck, shoulder, knee and ultimately his ankle, forced him to retire.

He made his name with Otley, Wakefield and Wasps, his premature departure from the game eventually sending him into coaching.

While at Wasps he coached the side to the first English title in the professional era, in 1996-97, and he took them to three domestic cup finals, winning two, before moving to Gloucester in 2002.

Melville delivered silverware – The Powergen Cup – for Gloucester in 2003 but it wasn't enough for him to keep his job in the long term. In that same season Gloucester dominated the domestic scene in England, finishing 15 points clear in the league at the end of the season, only to lose the title in the play-offs to Wasps.

"He was part of this club on one of our most memorable days, when we won the Powergen Cup at Twickenham, and I know that moment will be an everlasting memory for everyone," said Gloucester owner Tom Walkinshaw after Melville left the club in 2004.

He moved into the England structure in 2000, taking over the role as part-time manager of the England under-21 side.

In 2006 Melville was appointed chief executive officer and president of rugby operations for USA Rugby.

"This is a fantastic opportunity for anyone who loves rugby," he said. "I feel that everything I have done in the past has led me to this, and I am just really excited to get started."

Steve Mills

Sir Laurence Pierce Brooke MERRIAM KBE
Born: 28 January 1894 in Islington
Died: 27 July 1966 in London
Educated: St Paul's School
Clubs: Oxford University, Blackheath (2)
Position: Lock (2)
Debut: 17 Jan 1920 v Wales (Swansea). Number: 552
Last game: 31 Jan 1920 v France (Twickenham)
Caps: 2 (W:1, L:1)
Scoring: 0 Pts
Appearances: 1920:W,F

Arthur Tompson MICHELL
Born: 16 September 1852 in Headington
Died: 13 August 1923 in Headington
Educated: Rugby School
Clubs: Oxford University (3), Ravenscourt Park
Position: Half-Back (2), Three-quarter (1)
Debut: 15 Feb 1875 v Ireland (The Oval) - 1T, 1 Pt. Number: 61
Last game: 13 Dec 1875 v Ireland (Dublin)
Caps: 3 (W:2, D:1, L:0)
Scoring: 1T, 1 Pt
Appearances: 1875:I,S,I

Bernard Boswell MIDDLETON
Born: 25 December 1858 in Whitehaven
Died: 22 October 1947 in Bridge
Educated: Marlborough School
Clubs: Marlborough Nomads, Birkenhead Park (2)
Position: Forward (2)
Debut: 6 Feb 1882 v Ireland (Lansdowne Road). Number: 144
Last game: 5 Feb 1883 v Ireland (Manchester)
Caps: 2 (W:1, D:1, L:0)
Scoring: 0 Pts
Appearances: 1882:I, 1883:I
Honours: Championship: 1883

John Alan MIDDLETON, OBE
Born: 11 January 1894 in Ireland
Died: Details unknown
Educated: St Andrew's College
Clubs: Dublin Wanderers, Richmond (1), Royal Army Service Corps, Army
Position: Full-back (1)
Debut: 18 Mar 1922 v Scotland (Twickenham). Number: 578
Caps: 1 (W:1, L:0)
Scoring: 0 Pts
Appearances: 1922:S

John Henry (Jack) MILES
Born: 1879 in Grimsby
Died: 23 January 1953 in Sheffield
Educated: Medway Street School
Clubs: Medway Athletic, Stoneygate, Leicester (1), Northampton
Position: Wing (1)
Debut: 10 Jan 1903 v Wales (Swansea). Number: 387
Caps: 1 (W:0, L:1)
Scoring: 0 Pts
Appearances: 1903:W

Harry MILLETT
Born: 2 April 1892 in Islington
Died: 26 May 1974 in Wandsworth
Educated: University College School
Clubs: Guy's Hospital (1), Richmond, Harlequins
Position: Full-back (1)
Debut: 31 Jan 1920 v France (Twickenham). Number: 558
Caps: 1 (W:1, L:0)
Scoring: 0 Pts
Appearances: 1920:F

Frederick William MILLS
Born: 5 May 1849 in Chertsey
Died: 2 February 1904 in London
Educated: Marlborough School
Clubs: Marlborough Nomads (2), Bradford
Position: Full-back (2)
Debut: 5 Feb 1872 v Scotland (The Oval). Number: 31
Last game: 3 Mar 1873 v Scotland (Glasgow)
Caps: 2 (W:1, D:1, L:0)
Scoring: 0 Pts
Appearances: 1872:S, 1873:S

Stephen Graham Ford (Steve) MILLS
Born: 24 February 1951 in Cirencester
Clubs: Gloucester (5)
Position: Hooker (5), Bench (16)
Debut: 30 May 1981 v Argentina (Buenos Aires). Number: 1071
Last game: 3 Nov 1984 v Australia (Twickenham)
Caps: 5 (W:1, D:2, L:2)
Scoring: 0 Pts
Appearances: 1981:Ar1,Ar2, 1983:W, 1984:SA1,A

William Alonzo MILLS
Born: 2 February 1879 in Stoke Damerel
Died: Details unknown
Clubs: Devonport Albion (11)
Position: No 8 (11)
Debut: 13 Jan 1906 v Wales (Richmond). Number: 427
Last game: 18 Jan 1908 v Wales (Bristol)
Caps: 11 (W:4, D:1, L:6)
Scoring: 4T, 12 Pts
Appearances: 1906:W,I,S,F,SA, 1907:F,W,I,S, 1908:F,W

Dermot Lionel Kennedy MILMAN
Born: 24 October 1912 in Eltham, Kent
Died: 13 January 1990 in Warlingham, Surrey
Educated: Uppingham School, Bedford School
Clubs: Cambridge University, Bedford (4), Edinburgh Wanderers
Position: No 8 (4)
Debut: 16 Jan 1937 v Wales (Twickenham). Number: 732
Last game: 19 Mar 1938 v Scotland (Twickenham)
Caps: 4 (W:2, L:2)
Scoring: 0 Pts
Appearances: 1937:W, 1938:W,I,S
Honours: Championship: 1937

Henry Cecil (Cecil) MILTON
Born: 7 January 1884
Died: 29 December 1961 in Boscombe
Educated: Bedford GS
Clubs: Camborne School of Mines (1)
Position: Centre (1)
Debut: 10 Feb 1906 v Ireland (Leicester).
Number: 429
Caps: 1 (W:0, L:1)
Scoring: 0 Pts
Appearances: 1906:I

John Griffin (Jumbo) MILTON
Born: 1 May 1885 in South Africa
Died: 15 June 1915
Educated: Bedford GS
Clubs: Bedford GS (3), Camborne School of Mines (2)
Position: Forward (5)
Debut: 9 Jan 1904 v Wales (Leicester).
Number: 398
Last game: 9 Feb 1907 v Ireland (Lansdowne Road)
Caps: 5 (W:1, D:1, L:3)
Scoring: 0 Pts
Appearances: 1904:W,I,S, 1905:S, 1907:I

Sir William Henry MILTON, KCVO
Born: 3 December 1854 in Little Marlow, Bucks
Died: 6 March 1930 in Cannes, France
Educated: Marlborough School
Clubs: Marlborough Nomads (2)
Position: Half-Back (1), Three-quarter (1)
Debut: 23 Feb 1874 v Scotland (The Oval).
Number: 53
Last game: 15 Feb 1875 v Ireland (The Oval)
Caps: 2 (W:2, L:0)
Scoring: 0 Pts
Appearances: 1874:S, 1875:I

Frank MITCHELL
Born: 13 August 1872 in Market Weighton
Died: 11 October 1935 in Blackheath
Educated: St Peter's School
Clubs: Cambridge University (3), Blackheath (3)
Position: Forward (6)
Debut: 5 Jan 1895 v Wales (Swansea) - 1C, 2 Pts.
Number: 278
Last game: 14 Mar 1896 (capt) v Scotland (Glasgow)
Caps: 6 (W:3, L:3). As captain: 1 (W:0, L:1)
Scoring: 1T, 1C, 5 Pts
Appearances: 1895:W,I,S, 1896:W,I,S*

William Grant MITCHELL
Born: 23 May 1865
Died: 14 January 1905 in Vancouver, Canada
Educated: Bromsgrove School
Clubs: Cambridge University, Guy's Hospital, Richmond (7)
Position: Full-back (7)
Debut: 15 Feb 1890 v Wales (Dewsbury).
Number: 211
Last game: 4 Mar 1893 v Scotland (Headingley)
Caps: 7 (W:4, L:3)
Scoring: 0 Pts
Appearances: 1890:W,S,I, 1891:W,I,S, 1893:S

Lewis Moody

Edgar Roberts MOBBS
Born: 29 June 1882 in Northampton
Died: Killed in action in 1917 in Zillebeke, Belgium
Educated: Bedford Modern School
Clubs: Olney, Northampton (7)
Position: Wing (7)
Debut: 9 Jan 1909 v Australia (Blackheath) - 1T, 3 Pts.
Number: 477
Last game: 3 Mar 1910 (capt) v France (Parc des Princes)
Caps: 7 (W:3, D:1, L:3). As captain: 1 (W:1, L:0)
Scoring: 4T, 12 Pts
Appearances: 1909:A,W,F,I,S, 1910:I,F*
Honours: Championship: 1910 (capt)

William Octavius MOBERLY
Born: 14 November 1850 in Shoreham-by-Sea, Sussex
Died: 2 February 1914 in Pulurrian, Cornwall
Educated: Rugby School
Clubs: Oxford University, Clifton, Ravenscourt Park (1)
Position: Full-back (1)
Debut: 5 Feb 1872 v Scotland (The Oval).
Number: 32
Caps: 1 (W:1, L:0)
Scoring: 0 Pts
Appearances: 1872:S

Lewis Walton MOODY, MBE

Born: 12 June 1978 in Ascot
Educated: Oakham School
Clubs: Oakham, Bracknell, Leicester (44)
Position: Flanker (34), Replacement (10), Bench (1)
Debut: 2 Jun 2001 v Canada (Markham). Number: 1224
Last game: 25 Nov 2006 (rep) v South Africa (Twickenham)
Caps: 44 (W:31, L:13)
Scoring: 9T, 45 Pts. Discipline - Sin bins: 1, Sent off: 1
Appearances: 2001:C1,C2,US,I(r),R,SA(r), 2002:I(r),W,It,Ar,NZ,A,SA, 2003:F,W,F,F(r),Geo(r),SA,Sm(r),U,W,F(r),A(r), 2004:C,SA,A, 2005:F,I,It,S,A,NZ,Sm, 2006:W,It,S,F,I,A1,NZ,Ar,SA1(r),SA2(r)
Honours: RWC Winner: 2003. Championship: 2001, 2003

Brian Christopher MOORE

Born: 11 January 1962 in Birmingham
Educated: Crossley School, Porter School
Clubs: Nottingham University, Old Crossleyans, Nottingham (25), Harlequins (39), Richmond
Position: Hooker (63), Replacement (1), Bench (6)
Debut: 4 Apr 1987 v Scotland (Twickenham). Number: 1117
Last game: 22 Jun 1995 v France (Pretoria)
Caps: 64 (W:45, D:1, L:18)
Scoring: 1T, 4 Pts
Appearances: 1987:S,A,J,W, 1988:F,W,S,I,I,A1,A2,Fj,A, 1989:S,I,F,W,R,Fj, 1990:I,F,W,S,Ar1,Ar2, 1991:W,S,I,F,Fj,A,NZ,It,F,S,A, 1992:S,I,F,W,SA, 1993:F,W,S,I,NZ, 1994:S,I,F,W,SA1,SA2,R,C, 1995:I,F,W,S,Ar,It,Sm(r),A,NZ,F
Honours: Grand Slam: 1991, 1992, 1995

A trained solicitor and qualified manicurist, with a love for wine, opera and the classic French novel, Germinal, by Emile Zola, Brian Moore was an entirely different animal on the rugby field. Nicknamed 'pit bull', he was ferociously competitive, and played with a real passion for whichever team he was representing.

As a 16-year-old he was often the primary voice urging on team mates twice his age, leading by example.

His aggressive and combative attitude though, conceals the fact that he was arguably the most technically proficient English hooker of all time, eclipsing even Peter Wheeler, and keeping the equally adept Graham Dawe on the bench. He finished with 64 caps, then a record for an England forward.

The Harlequins man – who started his career at Nottingham, ending it at Richmond – took his chance against Scotland in the 1987 Five Nations when Dawe was suspended. He missed only four of England's next 68 games.

He brought his winner's attitude to the Lions squad in 1989, and after the 2-1 series win over Australia, he was famously spotted at Sydney Harbour Bridge the following morning still celebrating, doing aeroplane impressions.

His growing influence within the team was demonstrated in the last game of the 1990 Five Nations. Needing to beat Scotland for the Grand Slam, they missed out after Moore had successfully talked Will Carling into turning down a kickable penalty in favour of a pushover. England were repelled.

He got his revenge a year later with a victory over the Scots as England completed the Grand Slam, and then at the World Cup, beating Scotland 9-6 in the semi-final.

Brian Moore

The final ended in disappointment and a loss to Australia 12-6, and Moore pointed the finger of blame at both opponents and team mates, accusing David Campese of cynically preventing a try-scoring opportunity, and criticising England for adopting a running game rather than playing to their strengths – a superior pack. He was still voted Rugby World Player of the Year.

After another Grand Slam in 1992, Moore toured New Zealand with the Lions in 1993, continuing his tradition of entertaining cameos.

During the second Test in Wellington, as England prepared for a conversion following a try, a full can of beer was thrown onto the pitch. Moore picked it up and started to drink it before throwing it back to the New Zealand supporters. The Lions won the match after completely dominating a New Zealand pack containing his idol Sean Fitzpatrick, but lost the final match and the series.

Now an outspoken rugby commentator for the BBC and The Telegraph, he has written a wine column for The Sun, and, unsurprisingly, is a popular speaker on the after-dinner circuit.

Edward James MOORE

Born: 25 May 1862 in Dudley
Died: 7 March 1925 in Lewisham
Educated: Epsom College
Clubs: Oxford University (2), St Bart's Hospital, Blackheath
Position: Forward (2)
Debut: 5 Feb 1883 v Ireland (Manchester). Number: 157
Last game: 3 Mar 1883 v Scotland (Raeburn Place)
Caps: 2 (W:2, L:0)
Scoring: 0 Pts
Appearances: 1883:I,S
Honours: Championship: 1883

Norman Hope MOORE

Born: 1877 in Lewisham
Died: 8 March 1938 in Skipton
Clubs: Bristol (3)
Position: Forward (3)
Debut: 9 Jan 1904 v Wales (Leicester). Number: 399
Last game: 19 Mar 1904 v Scotland (Inverleith)
Caps: 3 (W:1, D:1, L:1)
Scoring: 2T, 6 Pts
Appearances: 1904:W,I,S

Sir Philip Brian Cecil MOORE, GCVO

Born: 6 April 1921
Educated: Cheltenham College, Dragon School
Clubs: Oxford University, Blackheath (1)
Position: No 8 (1)
Debut: 20 Jan 1951 v Wales (Swansea). Number: 813
Caps: 1 (W:0, L:1)
Scoring: 0 Pts
Appearances: 1951:W

William Kenneth Thomas (Bill) MOORE

Born: 24 February 1921 in Leicester
Died: 22 August 2002 in Leicester
Educated: Wyggeston GS
Clubs: Old Wyggestonians, Devonport Services, Royal Navy, Leicester (7)
Position: Scrum-half (7)
Debut: 18 Jan 1947 v Wales (Cardiff). Number: 758
Last game: 18 Mar 1950 v Scotland (Murrayfield)
Caps: 7 (W:4, L:3)
Scoring: 0 Pts
Appearances: 1947:W,I, 1949:F,S, 1950:I,F,S

Robert John (Bob) MORDELL

Born: 2 July 1950 in Twickenham
Educated: Thames Valley GS
Clubs: Wasps, Rosslyn Park (1), Oldham RL
Position: Flanker (1), Bench (2)
Debut: 4 Feb 1978 v Wales (Twickenham). Number: 1051
Caps: 1 (W:0, L:1)
Scoring: 0 Pts
Appearances: 1978:W

Bob Mordell

Samuel MORFITT

Born: First quarter 1869 in Kingston-upon-Hull
Died: 16 January 1954 in Kingston-upon-Hull
Clubs: West Hartlepool (6), Hull Kingston Rovers RL
Position: Wing (3), Centre (3)
Debut: 6 Jan 1894 v Wales (Birkenhead Park) - 1T, 3 Pts. Number: 265
Last game: 14 Mar 1896 v Scotland (Glasgow)
Caps: 6 (W:2, L:4)
Scoring: 3T, 9 Pts
Appearances: 1894:W,I,S, 1896:W,I,S

James Rydiard MORGAN

Born: 1890 in Cockermouth
Died: 29 April 1961 in Hawick, Scotland
Clubs: Hawick (1)
Position: Hooker (1)
Debut: 17 Jan 1920 v Wales (Swansea). Number: 553
Caps: 1 (W:0, L:1)
Scoring: 0 Pts
Appearances: 1920:W

Oliver (Olly) MORGAN

Born: 3 November 1985 in London
Educated: Millfield School
Clubs: Bracknell, Gloucester (2)
Position: Full-back (2)
Debut: 3 Feb 2007 v Scotland (Twickenham). Number: 1279
Last game: 24 Feb 2007 v Ireland (Croke Park)
Caps: 2 (W:1, L:1)
Scoring: 0 Pts
Appearances: 2007:S,I

Olly Morgan

William George Derek MORGAN
Born: 30 November 1935 in Newport, Monmouth, Wales
Educated: Lewis School
Clubs: Durham University, Medicals (9), UAU, Newbridge, Percy Park
Position: No 8 (9)
Debut: 16 Jan 1960 v Wales (Twickenham). Number: 888
Last game: 18 Mar 1961 v Scotland (Twickenham)
Caps: 9 (W:4, D:2, L:3)
Scoring: 0 Pts
Appearances: 1960:W,I,F,S, 1961:SA,W,I,F,S

Alan John MORLEY, MBE
Born: 25 June 1950 in Bristol
Educated: Colston's School
Clubs: Bristol (7)
Position: Wing (7), Bench (1)
Debut: 3 Jun 1972 v South Africa (Johannesburg) - 1T, 4 Pts. Number: 1013
Last game: 31 May 1975 v Australia (Brisbane)
Caps: 7 (W:2, L:5)
Scoring: 2T, 8 Pts
Appearances: 1972:SA, 1973:NZ,W,I, 1975:S,A1,A2

Alfred Drummond Warrington MORRIS, CMG
Born: 18 December 1883 in Richmond
Died: 24 March 1962 in Chelsea
Educated: Alverstoke School
Clubs: United Services, Royal Navy (3)
Position: Forward (3)
Debut: 9 Jan 1909 v Australia (Blackheath). Number: 478
Last game: 30 Jan 1909 v France (Leicester)
Caps: 3 (W:1, L:2)
Scoring: 0 Pts
Appearances: 1909:A,W,F

Dewi Morris

Colin (Dewi) MORRIS

Born: 9 February 1964 in Crickhowell, Wales
Educated: Brecon HS, Crewe & Alsager College
Clubs: Brecon, Winnington Park, Liverpool St Helens (5), Orrell (21), Sale
Position: Scrum-half (25), Replacement (1), Bench (20)
Debut: 5 Nov 1988 v Australia (Twickenham) - 1T, 4 Pts. Number: 1130
Last game: 22 Jun 1995 v France (Pretoria)
Caps: 26 (W:19, D:1, L:6)
Scoring: 5T, 21 Pts
Appearances: 1988:A, 1989:S,I,F,W, 1992:S,I,F,W,C,SA, 1993:F,W,S,I, 1994:F,W,SA1,SA2,R, 1995:S(r),Ar,Sm,A,NZ,F
Honours: Grand Slam: 1992. Championship: 1995

Robert Jonathan S (Robbie) MORRIS

Born: 20 February 1982 in Hertford
Clubs: Northampton (2), Newcastle
Position: Prop (2), Bench (2)
Debut: 22 Feb 2003 v Wales (Cardiff). Number: 1245
Last game: 9 Mar 2003 v Italy (Twickenham)
Caps: 2 (W:2, L:0)
Scoring: 0 Pts
Appearances: 2003:W,It
Honours: Championship: 2003

Piercy Henderson (Dolly) MORRISON

Born: 30 July 1868 in Guisborough
Died: 12 July 1936 in Newcastle-upon-Tyne
Educated: Loretto School
Clubs: Cambridge University (4), Northern
Position: Three-quarter (4)
Debut: 15 Feb 1890 v Wales (Dewsbury). Number: 212
Last game: 7 Feb 1891 v Ireland (Lansdowne Road)
Caps: 4 (W:3, L:1)
Scoring: 1T, 1 Pt
Appearances: 1890:W,S,I, 1891:I

Sydney MORSE

Born: 1 June 1854 in Birmingham
Died: 27 January 1929 in Kensington
Educated: Marlborough School
Clubs: Law Club (1), Marlborough Nomads (2)
Position: Half-Back (1), Full-back (1), Three-quarter (1)
Debut: 3 Mar 1873 v Scotland (Glasgow). Number: 41
Last game: 8 Mar 1875 v Scotland (Raeburn Place)
Caps: 3 (W:1, D:2, L:0)
Scoring: 0 Pts
Appearances: 1873:S, 1874:S, 1875:S

William MORTIMER

Born: 2 April 1874 in Warrington
Died: 31 October 1916 in Crowborough
Educated: Marlborough School
Clubs: Marlborough Nomads (1), Cambridge University, Blackheath
Position: Forward (1)
Debut: 7 Jan 1899 v Wales (Swansea). Number: 295
Caps: 1 (W:0, L:1)
Scoring: 0 Pts
Appearances: 1899:W

Robbie Morris

Andy Mullins

Harold James Storrs MORTON

Born: 31 January 1886 in Sheffield
Died: 3 January 1955 in Whitechapel
Educated: Uppingham School
Clubs: Cambridge University (2), London Hospital, United Hospitals, Blackheath (2)
Position: Prop (4)
Debut: 13 Feb 1909 v Ireland (Lansdowne Road). Number: 487
Last game: 12 Feb 1910 v Ireland (Twickenham)
Caps: 4 (W:2, D:1, L:1)
Scoring: 0 Pts
Appearances: 1909:I,S, 1910:W,I
Honours: Championship: 1910

F MOSS

Born: Details unknown
Died: Details unknown
Clubs: Broughton (3)
Position: Forward (3)
Debut: 3 Jan 1885 v Wales (Swansea). Number: 172
Last game: 2 Jan 1886 v Wales (Blackheath)
Caps: 3 (W:3, L:0)
Scoring: 0 Pts
Appearances: 1885:W,I, 1886:W

Andrew Richard (Andy) MULLINS

Born: 12 December 1964 in Eltham
Educated: Crockenhill School, Dulwich College
Clubs: Durham University, City University, Old Alleynians, Harlequins (1)
Position: Prop (1)
Debut: 4 Nov 1989 v Fiji (Twickenham). Number: 1136
Caps: 1 (W:1, L:0)
Scoring: 0 Pts
Appearances: 1989:Fj

Joseph S (Joe) MYCOCK

Born: 17 January 1916 in Bakewell
Educated: Giggleswick School
Clubs: Sale (5), Vale of Lune, Harlequins, RAF, Combined Services
Position: Lock (5)
Debut: 18 Jan 1947 (capt) v Wales (Cardiff). Number: 759
Last game: 3 Jan 1948 v Australia (Twickenham)
Caps: 5 (W:3, L:2). As captain: 2 (W:1, L:1)
Scoring: 0 Pts
Appearances: 1947:W*,I*,S,F, 1948:A

Edward MYERS

Born: 23 September 1895 in New York, USA
Died: 29 March 1956 in Bradford
Educated: Dollar Academy
Clubs: Leeds University, Headingley, Leicester, Bradford (18)
Position: Centre (12), Fly-half (6)
Debut: 14 Feb 1920 v Ireland (Lansdowne Road) - 1T, 3 Pts. Number: 562
Last game: 13 Apr 1925 v France (Stade Colombes)
Caps: 18 (W:15, D:1, L:2)
Scoring: 3T, 1DG, 13 Pts
Appearances: 1920:I,S, 1921:W,I, 1922:W,I,F,S, 1923:W,I,S,F, 1924:W,I,F,S, 1925:S,F
Honours: Grand Slam: 1923, 1924. Championship: 1921

Harry MYERS

Born: 3 February 1875 in Leeds
Died: 19 December 1906 in Keighley
Clubs: Keighley (1)
Position: Fly-half (1)
Debut: 5 Feb 1898 v Ireland (Richmond). Number: 314
Caps: 1 (W:0, L:1)
Scoring: 0 Pts
Appearances: 1898:I

N

NANSON, William Moore Bell
NASH, Edward Henry
NEALE, Bruce Alan
NEALE, Maurice Edward
NEAME, Stuart
NEARY, Anthony
NELMES, Barry George
NEWBOLD, Charles Joseph
NEWMAN, Sydney Charles
NEWTON, Andrew Winstanley
NEWTON, Philip Arthur
NICHOLAS, Philip Leach
NICHOLL, William
NICHOLSON, Basil Ellard
NICHOLSON, Edward Sealy
NICHOLSON, Elliot Tenint
NICHOLSON, Thomas
NINNES, Barry Francis
NOON, Jamie Darren
NORMAN, Douglas James
NORTH, Eustace Hebert
NORTHMORE, Samuel
NOVAK, Michael John
NOVIS, Anthony Leslie

Jamie Noon

William Moore Bell NANSON

Born: 12 December 1880 in Carlisle
Died: Killed in action in 1915 in El Krithia, Turkey
Educated: Lowther Street School
Clubs: Carlisle (2), Oldham RL
Position: Forward (2)
Debut: 5 Jan 1907 v France (Richmond) - 1T, 3 Pts. Number: 442
Last game: 12 Jan 1907 v Wales (Swansea)
Caps: 2 (W:1, L:1)
Scoring: 1T, 3 Pts
Appearances: 1907:F,W

Edward Henry NASH

Born: 20 December 1853 in Eton
Died: 18 September 1932 in Beaconsfield, Bucks
Educated: Rugby School
Clubs: Oxford University (1), Richmond
Position: Half-Back (1)
Debut: 15 Feb 1875 v Ireland (The Oval) - 1DG, 3 Pts. Number: 62
Caps: 1 (W:1, L:0)
Scoring: 1DG, 3 Pts
Appearances: 1875:I

Bruce Alan NEALE

Born: 15 September 1923 in Chelsea
Died: 28 January 1996 in Ipswich
Educated: Emanuel School
Clubs: Rosslyn Park (2), Royal Artillery, Army (1), Combined Services
Position: Lock (3)
Debut: 10 Feb 1951 v Ireland (Lansdowne Road). Number: 822
Last game: 17 Mar 1951 v Scotland (Twickenham)
Caps: 3 (W:1, L:2)
Scoring: 0 Pts
Appearances: 1951:I,F,S

Maurice Edward NEALE

Born: Second quarter 1886 in Thornbury
Died: 9 July 1967 in Bristol
Clubs: Blackheath (1)
Position: Centre (1)
Debut: 8 Apr 1912 v France (Parc des Princes). Number: 508
Caps: 1 (W:1, L:0)
Scoring: 0 Pts
Appearances: 1912:F

Tony Neary

Stuart NEAME

Born: 15 June 1856
Died: 16 November 1936 in Bromley, Kent
Educated: Cheltenham College
Clubs: Old Cheltonians (4), Blackheath
Position: Forward (4)
Debut: 10 Mar 1879 v Scotland (Raeburn Place).Number: 113
Last game: 28 Feb 1880 v Scotland (Manchester)
Caps: 4 (W:3, D:1, L:0)
Scoring: 0 Pts
Appearances: 1879:S,I, 1880:I,S

Anthony (Tony) NEARY

Born: 25 November 1948 in Manchester
Educated: De La Salle College
Clubs: Liverpool University, UAU, British University, Broughton Park (43)
Position: Flanker (42), Replacement (1), Bench (2)
Debut: 16 Jan 1971 v Wales (Cardiff). Number: 992
Last game: 15 Mar 1980 v Scotland (Murrayfield)
Caps: 43 (W:15, D:3, L:25). As captain: 7 (W:2, L:5)
Scoring: 5T, 19 Pts
Appearances: 1971:W,I,F,S,S,P, 1972:W,I,F,S,SA, 1973:NZ,W,I,F,S,NZ,A, 1974:S,I,F,W, 1975:I,F,W,S*,A1*, 1976:A*,W*,S*,I*,F*, 1977:I, 1978:F(r), 1979:S,I,F,W,NZ, 1980:I,F,W,S
Honours: Grand Slam: 1980

Tony Neary was the supreme English flanker of his generation and a lynchpin of Bill Beaumont's Grand Slam winning side of 1980. Fran Cotton, a colleague in the team that year, said he was "the complete openside and one of the very best in the world". Like Neil Back years later he supplemented his skills in the less glamorous aspects of a back rower's job with the ball-handling skills of a three-quarter. Neary scored several crucial tries for his country, not least one in England's 16-10 win over New Zealand in Auckland. The victory – in 1973 – was the only time England had won in the land of the Silver Fern until Martin Johnson's team did the trick in Wellington 30 years later. Later that same year Neary repeated the dose against the Australians at Twickenham in a 20-3 win that gave them wins over all three southern hemisphere giants in just over a year, something that the great Welsh teams of that era never managed.

Neary was picked for the triumphant 1974 British and Irish Lions tour to South Africa but was kept out of the Test team by Ireland's Fergus Slattery.

He got a Lions cap in Auckland in the final Test of Phil Bennett's tour of New Zealand three years later and was part of the North team that beat the All Blacks at Otley in 1979. This probably helped to ease the disappointment he felt in 1976 when he became the first player to skipper England to four defeats in the then Five

Nations and an unwanted Wooden Spoon but that fact should not reflect badly on the Broughton Park player as England were a shambles at the time. In 1975 he had captained England on their tour to Australia but had to pull out after the first Test with a rib injury.

Neary's form in the 1980 Five Nations would have made him an absolute certainty for a spot on Beaumont's Lions tour to South Africa but business commitments kept him out of the trip and it transpired that his last international was the Grand Slam clincher against Scotland at Murrayfield earlier that year which England won 30-18. At last he had something tangible to show for his undoubted talent.

Barry Nelmes

Also Neary's 43 caps in 1987 was a then record for an Englishman.

Sadly, Neary's life after rugby has been troubled. He was jailed for five years for fraud in 1998 and in 2003, living in London, he told The Sunday Times: "I don't follow rugby any more. I am just looking to get on with my life."

Barry George NELMES

Born: 17 April 1948 in Bristol
Died: 1 December 2006 in Cardiff, Wales
Educated: Portway SMS
Clubs: Bristol, Cardiff (6)
Position: Prop (6), Bench (6)
Debut: 24 May 1975 v Australia (Sydney Cricket Ground). Number: 1032
Last game: 25 Nov 1978 v New Zealand (Twickenham)
Caps: 6 (W:2, L:4)
Scoring: 1T, 4 Pts
Appearances: 1975:A1,A2, 1978:W,S,I,NZ

Charles Joseph NEWBOLD

Born: 12 January 1881 in Tunbridge Wells
Died: 26 October 1946 in Brentford
Educated: Uppingham School
Clubs: Cambridge University (3), Wanderers, Blackheath (3)
Position: Hooker (4), Forward (2)
Debut: 9 Jan 1904 v Wales (Leicester). Number: 400
Last game: 18 Mar 1905 v Scotland (Richmond)
Caps: 6 (W:1, D:1, L:4)
Scoring: 0 Pts
Appearances: 1904:W,I,S, 1905:W,I,S

Sydney Charles (Syd) NEWMAN

Born: 27 July 1919 in South Africa
Educated: Christian Bros College
Clubs: Witwatersrand University (SA), Oxford University (3)
Position: Full-back (3)
Debut: 19 Apr 1947 v France (Twickenham). Number: 773
Last game: 17 Jan 1948 v Wales (Twickenham) - 1PG, 3 Pts
Caps: 3 (W:1, D:1, L:1)
Scoring: 1PG, 3 Pts
Appearances: 1947:F, 1948:A,W

Andrew Winstanley NEWTON

Born: 12 September 1879
Died: 1944
Clubs: Blackheath (1), Royal Dublin Fusiliers, Army
Position: Wing (1)
Debut: 16 Mar 1907 v Scotland (Blackheath). Number: 449
Caps: 1 (W:0, L:1)
Scoring: 0 Pts
Appearances: 1907:S

Philip Arthur NEWTON

Born: 11 April 1860 in Brentford
Died: 25 December 1946 in New Forest
Educated: Blackheath Prep School
Clubs: Oxford University, Blackheath (1)
Position: Forward (1)
Debut: 4 Mar 1882 v Scotland (Manchester). Number: 146
Caps: 1 (W:0, L:1)
Scoring: 0 Pts
Appearances: 1882:S

M N O

Jamie Noon

Philip Leach NICHOLAS
Born: 30 May 1876 in Monmouth, Wales
Died: 31 January 1952 in Barnstaple
Educated: Monmouth School
Clubs: Oxford University, Exeter (1)
Position: Wing (1)
Debut: 11 Jan 1902 v Wales (Blackheath). Number: 376
Caps: 1 (W:0, L:1)
Scoring: 0 Pts
Appearances: 1902:W

William NICHOLL
Born: 30 October 1868 in Raistrick, Yorks
Died: 10 April 1922 in Brighouse
Clubs: Brighouse Rangers (2)
Position: Forward (2)
Debut: 2 Jan 1892 v Wales (Blackheath) - 1T, 2 Pts. Number: 239
Last game: 5 Mar 1892 v Scotland (Raeburn Place)
Caps: 2 (W:2, L:0)
Scoring: 1T, 2 Pts
Appearances: 1892:W,S
Honours: Championship: 1892

Basil Ellard NICHOLSON
Born: 1 January 1913 in Lewisham
Died: August 1985 in south-east Surrey
Educated: Whitgift School
Clubs: Old Whitgiftians, Harlequins (2)
Position: Centre (2)
Debut: 15 Jan 1938 v Wales (Cardiff). Number: 739
Last game: 12 Feb 1938 v Ireland (Lansdowne Road) - 1T, 3 Pts
Caps: 2 (W:1, L:1)
Scoring: 1T, 3 Pts
Appearances: 1938:W,I

Edward Sealy (Ernie) NICHOLSON
Born: 10 June 1912 in Long Ashton
Died: 16 March 1992 in Beccles
Educated: Marlborough School
Clubs: Oxford University (3), Guy's Hospital, Leicester (2), Blackheath
Position: Hooker (5)
Debut: 19 Jan 1935 v Wales (Twickenham). Number: 720
Last game: 18 Jan 1936 v Wales (Swansea)
Caps: 5 (W:2, D:2, L:1)
Scoring: 0 Pts
Appearances: 1935:W,I,S, 1936:NZ,W

Elliot Tenint NICHOLSON
Born: 13 December 1871 in West Derby
Died: 1 December 1953 in Wirral
Educated: Liverpool College
Clubs: Liverpool, Birkenhead Park (2)
Position: Wing (2)
Debut: 6 Jan 1900 v Wales (Gloucester) - 1T, 3 Pts. Number: 340
Last game: 3 Feb 1900 v Ireland (Richmond)
Caps: 2 (W:1, L:1)
Scoring: 1T, 3 Pts
Appearances: 1900:W,I

Thomas NICHOLSON
Born: Details unknown
Died: Details unknown
Clubs: Rockcliff (1)
Position: Three-quarter (1)
Debut: 4 Feb 1893 v Ireland (Lansdowne Road). Number: 256
Caps: 1 (W:1, L:0)
Scoring: 0 Pts
Appearances: 1893:I

Barry Francis NINNES
Born: 23 March 1948 in St Ives
Educated: Hayle GS, Camborne Technical College
Clubs: St Ives, Coventry (1)
Position: Lock (1)
Debut: 16 Jan 1971 v Wales (Cardiff). Number: 993
Caps: 1 (W:0, L:1)
Scoring: 0 Pts
Appearances: 1971:W

Jamie Darren NOON
Born: 9 May 1979 in Goole
Educated: Fyling Hall School
Clubs: Whitby, Newcastle (23)
Position: Centre (21), Replacement (2)
Debut: 2 Jun 2001 v Canada (Markham). Number: 1225
Last game: 25 Nov 2006 v South Africa (Twickenham)
Caps: 23 (W:10, L:13)
Scoring: 6T, 30 Pts
Appearances: 2001:C1,C2,US, 2003:W,F(r), 2005:W,F,I,It,S,A,NZ, 2006:W,It,S,F,I,A1(r),A2,NZ,Ar,SA1,SA2

Michael Novak

Douglas James (Doug) NORMAN
Born: 12 June 1897 in Leicester
Died: 27 December 1971 in Oadby, Leicester
Educated: Medway Street School
Clubs: Medway Athletic, Oadby, Leicester (2)
Position: Hooker (2)
Debut: 2 Jan 1932 v South Africa (Twickenham). Number: 688
Last game: 16 Jan 1932 v Wales (Swansea)
Caps: 2 (W:0, L:2)
Scoring: 0 Pts
Appearances: 1932:SA,W

Eustace Hebert NORTH
Born: 4 November 1868 in Lewisham
Died: 17 March 1942 in Wokingham
Educated: St Paul's School, Blackheath Prep School
Clubs: Oxford University (3), Blackheath
Position: Forward (3)
Debut: 3 Jan 1891 v Wales (Newport). Number: 228
Last game: 7 Mar 1891 v Scotland (Richmond)
Caps: 3 (W:2, L:1)
Scoring: 0 Pts
Appearances: 1891:W,I,S

Samuel NORTHMORE
Born: First quarter 1872 in Millom, Cumberland
Died: Details unknown
Clubs: Millom (1), Broughton Rangers RL
Position: Fly-half (1)
Debut: 6 Feb 1897 v Ireland (Lansdowne Road). Number: 307
Caps: 1 (W:0, L:1)
Scoring: 0 Pts
Appearances: 1897:I

Michael John NOVAK
Born: 27 September 1947 in Stratford-upon-Avon
Educated: Eastbourne College
Clubs: Eastbourne, Harlequins (3)
Position: Wing (3)
Debut: 28 Feb 1970 v Wales (Twickenham) - 1T, 3 Pts. Number: 984
Last game: 18 Apr 1970 v France (Stade Colombes)
Caps: 3 (W:0, L:3)
Scoring: 1T, 3 Pts
Appearances: 1970:W,S,F

Anthony Leslie (Tony) NOVIS
Born: 22 September 1906 in India
Died: 2 November 1997 in Cheltenham
Educated: Epsom College
Clubs: Oxford University, Leicestershire Regt, Army (2), Blackheath (5), Combined Services, Headingley
Position: Wing (5), Centre (2)
Debut: 16 Mar 1929 v Scotland (Murrayfield) - 1T, 3 Pts. Number: 645
Last game: 18 Mar 1933 (capt) v Scotland (Murrayfield)
Caps: 7 (W:4, L:3). As captain: 2 (W:1, L:1)
Scoring: 4T, 12 Pts
Appearances: 1929:S,F, 1930:W,I,F, 1933:I*,S*
Championship: 1930

M N O

O

OAKELEY, Francis Eckley
OAKES, Robert Frederick
OAKLEY, Lionel Frederick Lightborn
OBOLENSKY, Alexander
OJOMOH, Stephen Oziegbe
OLD, Alan Gerald Bernard
OLDHAM, William
OLVER, Christopher John
O'NEILL, Arthur
OPENSHAW, William Edward
ORWIN, John
OSBORNE, Richard Robinson
OSBORNE, Sidney Herbert
OTI, Christopher C
OUGHTRED, Bernard
OWEN, John Ernest
OWEN-SMITH, Harold Geoffrey Owen

Steve Ojomoh

Alexander Obolensky

Francis Eckley OAKELEY

Born: 5 February 1891 in Hereford
Died: Killed in action at sea in 1914
Educated: Hereford School, Eastman's School
Clubs: RNC Osborne, RNC Dartmouth, United Services, Royal Navy (4)
Position: Scrum-half (4)
Debut: 15 Mar 1913 v Scotland (Twickenham). Number: 534
Last game: 13 Apr 1914 v France (Stade Colombes)
Caps: 4 (W:4, L:0)
Scoring: 0 Pts
Appearances: 1913:S, 1914:I,S,F
Honours: Championship: 1913, 1914

Robert Frederick OAKES

Born: Third quarter 1872 in Hartlepool
Died: 22 October 1952 in Leeds
Clubs: Hartlepool Rovers (8), Headingley
Position: Forward (8)
Debut: 9 Jan 1897 v Wales (Newport). Number: 303
Last game: 11 Mar 1899 v Scotland (Blackheath)
Caps: 8 (W:2, D:1, L:5)
Scoring: 0 Pts
Appearances: 1897:W,I,S, 1898:I,S,W, 1899:W,S

Lionel Frederick Lightborn OAKLEY

Born: 24 January 1926 in Ramna, Dacca, India
Died: November 1981 in Bedford
Educated: Bedford School
Clubs: Bedford (1), Army
Position: Centre (1)
Debut: 20 Jan 1951 v Wales (Swansea). Number: 814
Caps: 1 (W:0, L:1)
Scoring: 0 Pts
Appearances: 1951:W

Alexander OBOLENSKY

Born: 17 February 1916 in St Petersburg, Russia
Died: Killed in action in 1940 in Martlesham Heath
Educated: Trent College
Clubs: Oxford University (4), Chesterfield, Rosslyn Park, Leicester
Position: Wing (4)
Debut: 4 Jan 1936 v New Zealand (Twickenham) - 2T, 6 Pts. Number: 724
Last game: 21 Mar 1936 v Scotland (Twickenham)
Caps: 4 (W:2, D:1, L:1)
Scoring: 2T, 6 Pts
Appearances: 1936:NZ,W,I,S

M N O

Making your debut in a Test match against the All Blacks is probably the dream of every schoolboy who has ever played rugby.

But to make your debut against New Zealand and score two tries in a victory has to put you amongst rugby's immortals.

Such was the feat completed by Prince Alexander Obolensky in 1936.

According to The Daily Telegraph the second one was one of the greatest ever seen at Twickenham: "From a scrum on England's 25-yard line, Gadney passed to the fly-half Peter Candler, who, two passes later, received it back from his inside-centre Peter Cranmer. Obolensky, seeing no way down his own right wing, had darted inwards and took an inside pass from Candler. Clasping the ball to his chest, and with his head back and his fair hair trailing behind, he bolted through a gap and sprinted 70 yards diagonally across the pitch to score in the left corner."

The son of Prince Serge Obolensky, Alexander and his family fled Russia after the Russian Revolution of 1917.

A graduate of Oxford University, where he won two Blues for rugby, Obolensky also played for Leicester and Rosslyn Park.

After starring for England Obolensky joined the RAF at the start of the Second World War and in 1940 was killed during a training exercise, on 29 March.

Steve Ojomoh

For many years, Bernard Gadney, his captain against New Zealand visited his grave on 29 March. "He was just a nice young chap," Gadney said. "It's what's in your heart that counts."

The Morning Post was fulsome in their praise of his performance against New Zealand, saying: "Runners we have seen before but never such a runner with such an innate idea of where to go and how to get there.

"His double swerve to gain his first try was remarkable enough but the extraordinary turn-in and diagonal right to left run which won him his second and which drew forth that great Twickenham rarity, a double roar of applause, will never be forgotten by anybody who saw it."

Stephen Oziegbe (Steve) OJOMOH

Born: 25 May 1970 in Benin City, Nigeria
Educated: West Buckland College
Clubs: West of England University, Rosslyn Park, Bath (12), Gloucester, Parma (IT), Newport
Position: No 8 (5), Flanker (4), Replacement (3), Bench (10)
Debut: 19 Feb 1994 v Ireland (Twickenham). Number: 1153
Last game: 20 Jun 1998 v New Zealand (Dunedin)
Caps: 12 (W:7, L:5)
Scoring: 0 Pts
Appearances: 1994:I,F,SA1(r),SA2,R, 1995:S(r),Ar,Sm,A(r),F, 1996:F, 1998:NZ1
Honours: Championship: 1995, 1996

Alan Gerald Bernard OLD

Born: 23 September 1945 in Middlesbrough
Educated: Acklam Hall GS, Queen Mary College
Clubs: London University, Durham University, Middlesbrough (9), Leicester (6), Sheffield (1), Morpeth
Position: Fly-half (16), Bench (14)
Debut: 15 Jan 1972 v Wales (Twickenham). Number: 1005
Last game: 21 Jan 1978 v France (Parc des Princes) - 2DG, 6 Pts
Caps: 16 (W:4, D:1, L:11)
Scoring: 1T, 8C, 23PG, 3DG, 98 Pts
Appearances: 1972:W,I,F,S,SA, 1973:NZ,A, 1974:S,I,F,W, 1975:I,A2, 1976:S,I, 1978:F

William OLDHAM

Born: 15 June 1887 in Coventry
Died: 27 April 1965 in Poole
Clubs: Coventry (2)
Position: Forward (2)
Debut: 21 Mar 1908 v Scotland (Inverleith).Number: 464
Last game: 9 Jan 1909 v Australia (Blackheath)
Caps: 2 (W:0, L:2)
Scoring: 0 Pts
Appearances: 1908:S, 1909:A

Christopher John OLVER

Born: 23 April 1961 in Manchester
Educated: Rossall School, Borough Road College
Clubs: Sandbach, Harlequins, Northampton (3)
Position: Hooker (3), Bench (31)
Debut: 3 Nov 1990 v Argentina (Twickenham). Number: 1141
Last game: 17 Oct 1992 v Canada (Wembley)
Caps: 3 (W:3, L:0)
Scoring: 0 Pts
Appearances: 1990:Ar, 1991:US, 1992:C

Arthur O'NEILL

Born: 1878 in Teignmouth
Died: 12 May 1954 in Brighton
Clubs: Teignmouth, Torquay Athletic (3), St Bart's Hospital
Position: Forward (3)
Debut: 5 Jan 1901 v Wales (Cardiff). Number: 359
Last game: 9 Mar 1901 v Scotland (Blackheath)
Caps: 3 (W:0, L:3)
Scoring: 0 Pts
Appearances: 1901:W,I,S

William Edward OPENSHAW

Born: 1851
Died: 7 February 1915 in Warrington
Educated: Harrow School
Clubs: Manchester (1)
Position: Half-Back (1)
Debut: 24 Mar 1879 v Ireland (The Oval). Number: 118
Caps: 1 (W:1, L:0)
Scoring: 0 Pts
Appearances: 1879:I

Christopher Olver

John Orwin

John ORWIN
Born: 20 March 1954 in Bradford
Educated: Buttershaw HS
Clubs: Gloucester (7), RAF, Bedford (7), Morley
Position: Lock (14)
Debut: 5 Jan 1985 v Romania (Twickenham). Number: 1103
Last game: 12 Jun 1988 (capt) v Australia (Sydney)
Caps: 14 (W:5, D:1, L:8). As captain: 3 (W:1, L:2)
Scoring: 0 Pts
Appearances: 1985:R,F,S,I,W,NZ1,NZ2, 1988:F,W,S,I,I*,A1*,A2*

Richard Robinson OSBORNE
Born: 20 May 1848 in Ashgill, Yorkshire
Died: 4 November 1926 in Rochdale
Educated: Hurstpierpoint College
Clubs: Manchester (1)
Position: Full-back (1)
Debut: 27 Mar 1871 v Scotland (Raeburn Place). Number: 15
Caps: 1 (W:0, L:1)
Scoring: 0 Pts
Appearances: 1871:S

Sidney Herbert OSBORNE
Born: 26 February 1880 in Camberwell
Died: 15 July 1939 in Hemel Hempstead
Educated: Fettes School
Clubs: Oxford University, Harlequins (1), St Bees
Position: Forward (1)
Debut: 18 Mar 1905 v Scotland (Richmond). Number: 411
Caps: 1 (W:0, L:1)
Scoring: 0 Pts
Appearances: 1905:S

Christopher (Chris) OTI
Born: 16 June 1965 in Paddington
Educated: Millfield School
Clubs: Durham University, Cambridge University (2), Nottingham, Wasps (11)
Position: Wing (13)
Debut: 5 Mar 1988 v Scotland (Murrayfield). Number: 1123
Last game: 8 Oct 1991 v Italy (Twickenham)
Caps: 13 (W:8, D:1, L:4)
Scoring: 8T, 32 Pts
Appearances: 1988:S,I, 1989:S,I,F,W,R, 1990:Ar1,Ar2, 1991:Fj,A,NZ,It

England's first black player for 80 years, Chris Oti, made his debut against Scotland at Murrayfield in 1988 and is credited as the man who inspired the most famous rugby song ever to be associated with the England team: Swing Low Sweet Chariot.

Oti scored a hat-trick for England in their 35-3 win over Ireland in 1988 – their 100th match against the Irish – and according to the RFU as Oti ran in his final try, a group from the Benedictine school Douai began singing the 150-year-old hymn, as they do for their first XV. The whole crowd joined in and it is now the England fans' anthem.

Chris Oti

Bernard OUGHTRED
Born: 22 August 1880 in Hartlepool
Died: 12 November 1949 in Barrow-in-Furness
Educated: West Hartlepool GS, King Edward's School
Clubs: Old Edwardians, Hartlepool Rovers (6), Hull & ER, Furness, Barrow
Position: Fly-half (4), Scrum-half (2)
Debut: 9 Mar 1901 v Scotland (Blackheath). Number: 371
Last game: 14 Feb 1903 (capt) v Ireland (Lansdowne Road)
Caps: 6 (W:2, L:4). As captain: 2 (W:0, L:2)
Scoring: 0 Pts
Appearances: 1901:S, 1902:W,I,S, 1903:W*,I*

John Ernest OWEN
Born: 21 September 1939 in Sutton Coldfield
Educated: Oundle School, Brocksfield HS
Clubs: Cambridge University, Blackheath, Moseley, Coventry (14)
Position: Lock (14)
Debut: 19 Jan 1963 v Wales (Cardiff) - 1T, 3 Pts. Number: 913
Last game: 4 Nov 1967 v New Zealand (Twickenham)
Caps: 14 (W:4, D:3, L:7)
Scoring: 1T, 3 Pts
Appearances: 1963:W,I,F,S,A, 1964:NZ, 1965:W,I,F,S, 1966:I,F,S, 1967:NZ
Honours: Championship: 1963

Harold Geoffrey Owen OWEN-SMITH
Born: 18 February 1909 in Rondebosch, South Africa
Died: 27 February 1990 in Rondebosch, South Africa
Educated: Diocesan College
Clubs: University of Cape Town, Oxford University (2), St Mary's Hospital (8)
Position: Full-back (10)
Debut: 20 Jan 1934 v Wales (Cardiff). Number: 708
Last game: 20 Mar 1937 (capt) v Scotland (Murrayfield)
Caps: 10 (W:8, D:1, L:1). As captain: 3 (W:3, L:0)
Scoring: 0 Pts
Appearances: 1934:W,I,S, 1936:NZ,W,I,S, 1937:W*,I*,S*
Honours: Championship: 1934, 1937 (capt)

John Owen

P

PAGE, John Jackson
PALLANT, John Noel
PALMER, Alexander Croydon, OBE
PALMER, Francis Hubert
PALMER, Godfrey Vaughan, CBE
PALMER, John Anthony
PALMER, Thomas
PARGETTER, Thomas Alfred
PARKER, Grahame Wilshaw, OBE
PARKER, Sydney
PARSONS, Ernest Ian
PARSONS, Michael James
PATTERSON, William Michael
PATTISSON, Richard Murrills
PAUL, Henry Rangi
PAUL, J E
PAYNE, Arthur Thomas
PAYNE, Colin Martin
PAYNE, John Henry
PAYNE, Timothy Adam N
PEARCE, Gary Stephen
PEARS, David
PEARSON, A W
PEART, Thomas George Anthony Hunter
PEASE, Frank Ernest
PENNY, Sidney Herbert
PENNY, William John
PERCIVAL, Rev Launcelot Jefferson, KCVO
PERITON, Harold Greaves
PERROTT, Edward Simcocks
PERRY, David Gordon
PERRY, Matthew Brendan
PERRY, Samuel Victor
PERRY, Shaun Andrew
PETERS, James
PHILLIPS, Charles
PHILLIPS, Malcolm Stanley
PICKERING, Arthur Stanley
PICKERING, Roger David Austin
PICKLES, Reginald Clarence Werrett
PIERCE, Richard
PILKINGTON, William Norman
PILLMAN, Charles Henry
PILLMAN, Robert Laurence
PINCH, John
PINCHING, William Wyatt
PITMAN, Sir Isaac James, KBE
PLUMMER, Kenneth Clive
POOLE, Francis Oswald
POOLE, Robert Watkins
POOL-JONES, Richard J
POPE, Edward Brian
PORTUS, Garnet Vere
POTTER, Stuart
POULTON, Ronald William
POWELL, David Lewes
PRATTEN, William Edgar
PREECE, Ivor
PREECE, Peter Stuart
PREEDY, Malcolm
PRENTICE, Frank Douglas
PRESCOTT, Robert Edward
PRESTON, Nicholas John
PRICE, Herbert Leo
PRICE, John
PRICE, P L A
PRICE, Thomas William
PROBYN, Jeffrey Alan
PROUT, Derek Henry
PULLIN, John Vivian
PURDY, Stanley John
PYKE, James
PYM, John Alfred

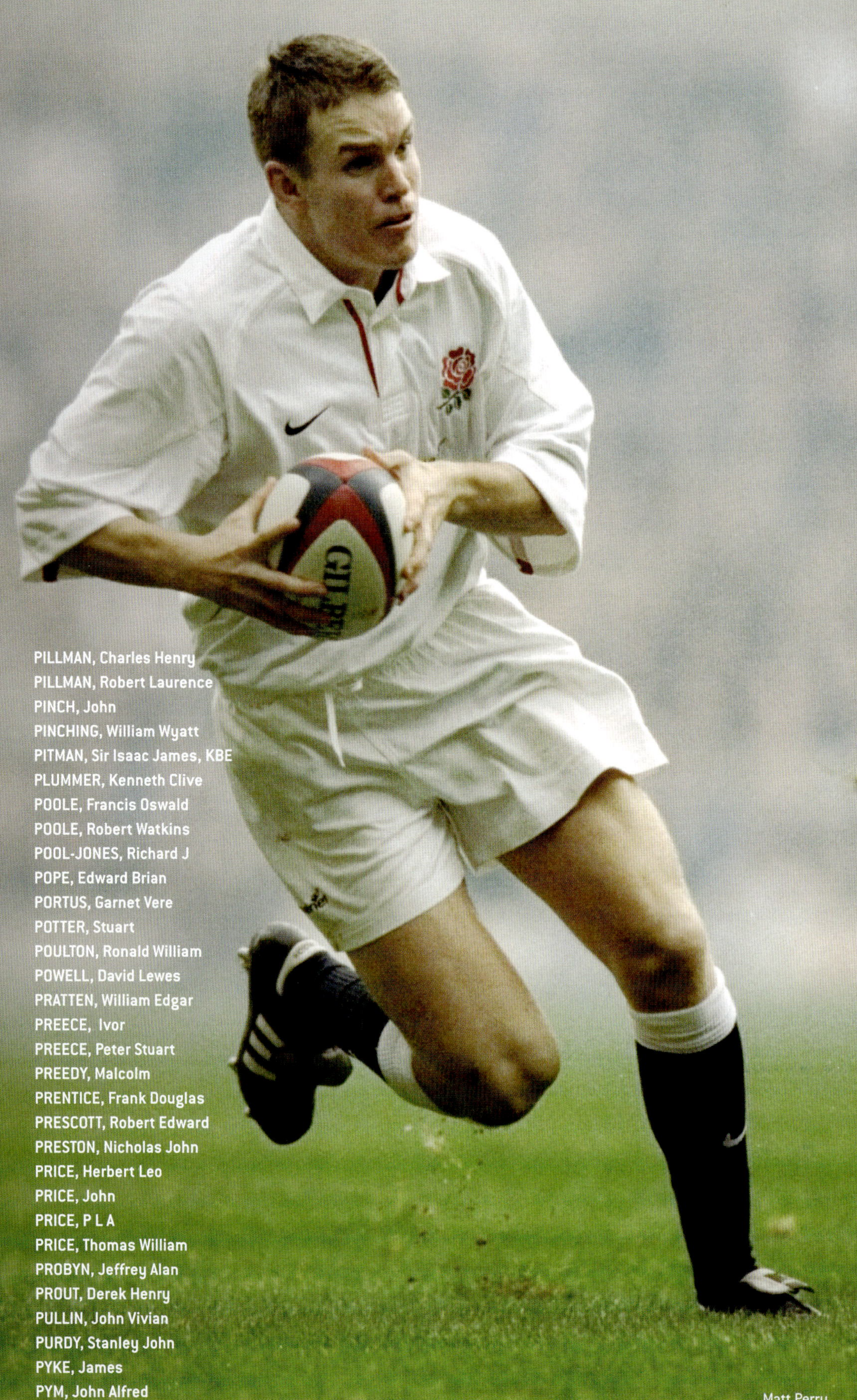

Matt Perry

John Jackson (Jacko) PAGE
Born: 16 April 1947 in Brighton
Educated: Cambridge HS
Clubs: Cambridge University, Bedford (4), Northampton (1) Position: Scrum-half (5), Bench (3)
Debut: 16 Jan 1971 v Wales (Cardiff). Number: 994
Last game: 15 Mar 1975 v Scotland (Twickenham)
Caps: 5 (W:2, D:1, L:2)
Scoring: 0 Pts
Appearances: 1971:W,I,F,S, 1975:S

John Noel PALLANT
Born: 24 December 1944 in Nottingham
Educated: High Pavement GS
Clubs: Loughborough College, UAU, Nottingham (3)
Position: No 8 (2), Lock (1)
Debut: 11 Feb 1967 v Ireland (Lansdowne Road). Number: 955
Last game: 18 Mar 1967 v Scotland (Twickenham)
Caps: 3 (W:2, L:1)
Scoring: 0 Pts
Appearances: 1967:I,F,S

Alexander Croydon PALMER, OBE
Born: 2 August 1887 in Dunedin, New Zealand
Died: 16 October 1963 in mid-east Surrey
Educated: Waitaki BHS (NZ)
Clubs: Otago University (NZ), London Hospital (2), Royal Army Medical Corps, Harlequins
Position: Wing (2)
Debut: 13 Feb 1909 v Ireland (Lansdowne Road) - 2T, 1C, 8 Pts. Number: 488
Last game: 20 Mar 1909 v Scotland (Richmond) - 1C, 2 Pts
Caps: 2 (W:1, L:1)
Scoring: 2T, 2C, 10 Pts
Appearances: 1909:I,S

Francis Hubert PALMER
Born: 6 August 1877 in Hereford
Died: Details unknown
Educated: Bedford GS
Clubs: Richmond (1)
Position: Wing (1)
Debut: 14 Jan 1905 v Wales (Cardiff). Number: 404
Caps: 1 (W:0, L:1)
Scoring: 0 Pts
Appearances: 1905:W

Godfrey Vaughan PALMER, CBE
Born: 21 February 1900 in Steyning
Died: 28 April 1972 in Chatham
Educated: Monmouth School
Clubs: RMC Sandhurst, Queen's Royal Regt, Army, North of Ireland, Cross Keys, Harlequins, Richmond (3), Combined Services
Position: Wing (3)
Debut: 11 Feb 1928 v Ireland (Lansdowne Road). Number: 634
Last game: 17 Mar 1928 v Scotland (Twickenham)
Caps: 3 (W:3, L:0)
Scoring: 2T, 6 Pts
Appearances: 1928:I,F,S
Honours: Championship: 1928

John Anthony PALMER
Born: 13 February 1957 in Malta
Educated: Prior Park School, St Mary's College
Clubs: Bath (3)
Position: Centre (2), Replacement (1), Bench (7)
Debut: 2 Jun 1984 v South Africa (Port Elizabeth). Number: 1091
Last game: 1 Mar 1986 (rep) v Ireland (Twickenham)
Caps: 3 (W:1, L:2)
Scoring: 0 Pts
Appearances: 1984:SA1,SA2, 1986:I(r)

Thomas (Tom) PALMER
Born: 27 March 1979 in London
Educated: Boroughmuir School, Otago BHS
Clubs: Leeds University, Barnet, Leeds (1), Wasps (5)
Position: Lock (2), Replacement (4), Bench (1)
Debut: 16 Jun 2001 (rep) v United States (San Francisco). Number: 1232
Last game: 24 Feb 2007 (rep) v Ireland (Croke Park)
Caps: 6 (W:3, L:3)
Scoring: 0 Pts
Appearances: 2001:US(r), 2006:Ar(r),SA1,SA2, 2007:It(r),I(r)

John Palmer

Tom Palmer

Thomas Alfred PARGETTER

Born: 21 July 1932 in Stratford
Educated: King Edward VI School
Clubs: Cambridge University, Moseley, Coventry (3)
Position: Lock (3)
Debut: 17 Mar 1962 v Scotland (Murrayfield). Number: 906
Last game: 25 May 1963 v New Zealand (Auckland)
Caps: 3 (W:1, D:1, L:1)
Scoring: 0 Pts
Appearances: 1962:S, 1963:F,NZ1
Honours: Championship: 1963

Grahame Wilshaw PARKER, OBE

Born: 11 February 1912 in Gloucester
Died: 11 November 1995 in Sidmouth
Educated: Crypt GS
Clubs: Cambridge University, Gloucester (1), Blackheath (1)
Position: Full-back (2)
Debut: 12 Feb 1938 v Ireland (Lansdowne Road) - 6C, 1PG, 15 Pts. Number: 741
Last game: 19 Mar 1938 v Scotland (Twickenham) - 3PG, 9 Pts
Caps: 2 (W:1, L:1)
Scoring: 6C, 4PG, 24 Pts
Appearances: 1938:I,S

Sydney PARKER

Born: 3 October 1853
Died: 21 May 1897 in Chelsea
Educated: Rugby School
Clubs: Liverpool (2)
Position: Forward (2)
Debut: 23 Feb 1874 v Scotland (The Oval). Number: 54
Last game: 8 Mar 1875 v Scotland (Raeburn Place)
Caps: 2 (W:1, D:1, L:0)
Scoring: 0 Pts
Appearances: 1874:S, 1875:S

Ernest Ian PARSONS

Born: 24 October 1912 in Christchurch, New Zealand
Died: Killed in action in 1940 in Turin, Italy
Educated: Christchurch BHS
Clubs: Canterbury University (NZ), RAF (1), Hull & ER
Position: Full-back (1)
Debut: 18 Mar 1939 v Scotland (Murrayfield). Number: 752
Caps: 1 (W:1, L:0)
Scoring: 0 Pts
Appearances: 1939:S

Michael James (Jim) PARSONS

Born: 13 March 1943 in Chipping Norton
Educated: King's School
Clubs: Oxford, Northampton (4)
Position: Lock (4)
Debut: 20 Jan 1968 v Wales (Twickenham). Number: 966
Last game: 16 Mar 1968 v Scotland (Murrayfield)
Caps: 4 (W:1, D:2, L:1)
Scoring: 0 Pts
Appearances: 1968:W,I,F,S

Henry Paul

William Michael (Bill) PATTERSON
Born: 11 April 1936 in Newcastle-upon-Tyne
Died: December 1998 in Sale
Educated: Stowe School, Sale GS
Clubs: Cambridge University, Sale (2), Wasps
Position: Centre (2)
Debut: 7 Jan 1961 v South Africa (Twickenham).Number: 886
Last game: 18 Mar 1961 v Scotland (Twickenham)
Caps: 2 (W:1, L:1)
Scoring: 0 Pts
Appearances: 1961:SA,S

Richard Murrills PATTISSON
Born: 5 August 1860 in Tonbridge
Died: 28 November 1948 in Cambridge
Educated: Tonbridge School
Clubs: Cambridge University (2), Gipsies, Blackheath
Position: Forward (2)
Debut: 5 Feb 1883 v Ireland (Manchester). Number: 158
Last game: 3 Mar 1883 v Scotland (Raeburn Place)
Caps: 2 (W:2, L:0)
Scoring: 0 Pts
Appearances: 1883:I,S
Honours: Championship: 1883

Henry Rangi PAUL
Born: 10 February 1974 in Tokoroa, New Zealand
Educated: Rutherford HS
Clubs: Ponsonby (NZ), Bradford RL, Bath, Gloucester (6), Harlequins RL
Position: Centre (3), Replacement (3), Bench (1)
Debut: 2 Mar 2002 (rep) v France (Stade de France). Number: 1238
Last game: 27 Nov 2004 v Australia (Twickenham)
Caps: 6 (W:4, L:2)
Scoring: 3C, 6 Pts
Appearances: 2002:F(r), 2004:It(r),S(r),C,SA,A

J E PAUL
Born: Details unknown
Died: Details unknown
Clubs: Royal Indian Eng College (1)
Position: Forward (1)
Debut: 8 Mar 1875 v Scotland (Raeburn Place). Number: 68
Caps: 1 (W:0, D:1, L:0)
Scoring: 0 Pts
Appearances: 1875:S

Arthur Thomas PAYNE
Born: 11 November 1907 in Bristol
Died: 6 June 1968 in Bristol
Clubs: Bristol (2)
Position: No 8 (2)
Debut: 9 Feb 1935 v Ireland (Twickenham). Number: 721
Last game: 16 Mar 1935 v Scotland (Murrayfield)
Caps: 2 (W:1, L:1)
Scoring: 0 Pts
Appearances: 1935:I,S

Colin Martin PAYNE
Born: 19 May 1937 in Edmonton
Died: March 2005
Educated: Sherborne School
Clubs: Oxford University, Harlequins (10), West of Scotland
Position: Lock (10)
Debut: 8 Feb 1964 v Ireland (Twickenham). Number: 924
Last game: 19 Mar 1966 v Scotland (Murrayfield)
Caps: 10 (W:2, D:2, L:6)
Scoring: 1T, 3 Pts
Appearances: 1964:I,F,S, 1965:I,F,S, 1966:W,I,F,S

Tim Payne

John Henry PAYNE

Born: 19 March 1858 in Broughton, Lancs
Died: 24 January 1942 in Victoria Park, Manchester
Educated: Cheltenham College, Manchester GS
Clubs: Cambridge University, Broughton Rangers (7)
Position: Half-Back (7)
Debut: 4 Mar 1882 v Scotland (Manchester). Number: 147
Last game: 7 Feb 1885 v Ireland (Manchester)
Caps: 7 (W:6, L:1)
Scoring: 1C, 2 Pts
Appearances: 1882:S, 1883:W,I,S, 1884:I, 1885:W,I
Honours: Championship: 1883, 1884

Timothy Adam N (Tim) PAYNE

Born: 29 April 1979 in Swindon
Clubs: Coventry, Bristol, Cardiff, Wasps (3)
Position: Prop (1), Replacement (2), Bench (1)
Debut: 26 Jun 2004 v Australia (Brisbane). Number: 1254
Last game: 17 Jun 2006 (rep) v Australia (Melbourne)
Caps: 3 (W:0, L:3)
Scoring: 0 Pts
Appearances: 2004:A, 2006:A1(r),A2(r)

Gary Stephen PEARCE

Born: 2 March 1956 in Dinton, Bucks
Educated: Mandeville County School
Clubs: Aylesbury, Northampton (36), Nottingham
Position: Prop (36), Bench (7)
Debut: 3 Feb 1979 v Scotland (Twickenham). Number: 1055
Last game: 11 Oct 1991 v United States (Twickenham)
Caps: 36 (W:12, D:5, L:19)
Scoring: 0 Pts
Appearances: 1979:S,I,F,W, 1981:Ar1,Ar2, 1982:A,S, 1983:F,W,S,I,NZ, 1984:S,SA2,A, 1985:R,F,S,I,W,NZ1,NZ2, 1986:W,S,I,F, 1987:I,F,W,S,A,US,W, 1988:Fj, 1991:US

David PEARS

Born: 6 December 1967 in Workington
Educated: Workington GS
Clubs: Aspatria, Sale, Harlequins (4), Camberley, Wharfedale, Worcester, Bracknell, Esher
Position: Fly-half (2), Full-back (1), Replacement (1), Bench (11)
Debut: 28 Jul 1990 v Argentina (Buenos Aires). Number: 1139
Last game: 5 Mar 1994 v France (Parc des Princes)
Caps: 4 (W:3, L:1)
Scoring: 0 Pts
Appearances: 1990:Ar1,Ar2, 1992:F(r), 1994:F
Honours: Championship: 1992

A W PEARSON

Born: 1854 in Australia
Died: In Australia, details unknown
Educated: Blackheath Prep School
Clubs: Guy's Hospital (2), Blackheath (5)
Position: Full-back (7)
Debut: 15 Feb 1875 v Ireland (The Oval) - 1C, 2 Pts. Number: 63
Last game: 11 Mar 1878 v Ireland (Lansdowne Road) - 2C, 4 Pts
Caps: 7 (W:4, D:2, L:1)
Scoring: 4C, 8 Pts
Appearances: 1875:I,S,I, 1876:S, 1877:S, 1878:S,I

David Pears

Sidney Herbert (Sid) PENNY
Born: 7 October 1875 in East End, London
Died: 23 May 1965 in Leicester
Educated: St Peter's School
Clubs: Granville, Belgrave St Peter's, Leicester (1)
Position: Forward (1)
Debut: 9 Jan 1909 v Australia (Blackheath). Number: 479
Caps: 1 (W:0, L:1)
Scoring: 0 Pts
Appearances: 1909:A

William John PENNY
Born: Third quarter 1856 in Langport
Died: 17 December 1904 at sea (SS Langdale)
Clubs: King's College Hospital (3), United Hospitals
Position: Full-back (3)
Debut: 11 Mar 1878 v Ireland (Lansdowne Road) - 1T, 1 Pt. Number: 109
Last game: 24 Mar 1879 v Ireland (The Oval)
Caps: 3 (W:2, D:1, L:0)
Scoring: 1T, 1 Pt
Appearances: 1878:I, 1879:S,I

Rev. Launcelot Jefferson PERCIVAL, KCVO
Born: 22 May 1869 in Clifton
Died: 22 June 1941 in Woking
Educated: Clifton College
Clubs: Oxford University (2), Rugby (1)
Position: Forward (3)
Debut: 7 Feb 1891 v Ireland (Lansdowne Road). Number: 231
Last game: 4 Mar 1893 v Scotland (Headingley)
Caps: 3 (W:2, L:1)
Scoring: 1T, 2 Pts
Appearances: 1891:I, 1892:I, 1893:S
Honours: Championship: 1892

Harold Greaves (Joe) PERITON
Born: 8 March 1901
Died: April 1980 in Westminster
Educated: Merchant Taylors' School
Clubs: Waterloo (21)
Position: Flanker (21)
Debut: 17 Jan 1925 v Wales (Twickenham). Number: 600
Last game: 15 Mar 1930 v Scotland (Twickenham)
Caps: 21 (W:12, D:2, L:7). As captain: 4 (W:2, L:2)
Scoring: 6T, 18 Pts
Appearances: 1925:W, 1926:W,I,F,S, 1927:W,I,S,F, 1928:A,I,F,S, 1929:W,I,S*,F*, 1930:W*,I*,F,S
Honours: Championship: 1928, 1930 (capt)

Thomas George Anthony Hunter PEART
Born: 10 September 1936 in Hartlepool
Died: 3 August 1988 in Darlington
Educated: Sedbergh School
Clubs: Blackheath, Army, Hartlepool Rovers (2)
Position: No 8 (2)
Debut: 22 Feb 1964 v France (Stade Colombes), Number: 925
Last game: 21 Mar 1964 v Scotland (Murrayfield)
Caps: 2 (W:1, L:1)
Scoring: 0 Pts
Appearances: 1964:F,S

Frank Ernest PEASE
Born: 17 January 1864 in Darlington
Died: 27 June 1957 in West Durham
Educated: Harrow School
Clubs: Darlington, Hartlepool Rovers (1)
Position: Forward (1)
Debut: 5 Feb 1887 v Ireland (Lansdowne Road) Number: 195
Caps: 1 (W:0, L:1)
Scoring: 0 Pts
Appearances: 1887:I

Edward Simcocks PERROTT
Born: 16 September 1851 in Llanfyllin, Wales
Died: 22 April 1915 in Llansantffraid, Wales
Educated: Cheltenham College
Clubs: Old Cheltonians (1)
Position: Forward (1)
Debut: 15 Feb 1875 v Ireland (The Oval). Number: 64
Caps: 1 (W:1, L:0)
Scoring: 0 Pts
Appearances: 1875:I

David Gordon PERRY

Born: 26 December 1937 in south-east Surrey
Educated: Clifton College
Clubs: Cambridge University, Harlequins, Bedford (15)
Position: No 8 (13), Lock (2)
Debut: 23 Feb 1963 v France (Twickenham). Number: 915
Last game: 26 Feb 1966 v France (Stade Colombes)
Caps: 15 (W:3, D:3, L:9). As captain: 4 (W:1, D:1, L:2)
Scoring: 2T, 6 Pts
Appearances: 1963:F,S,NZ1,NZ2,A, 1964:NZ,W,I, 1965:W*,I*,F*,S*, 1966:W,I,F
Honours: Championship: 1963

Matthew Brendan (Matt) PERRY

Born: 27 January 1977 in Bath
Educated: Millfield School
Clubs: Bath (36)
Position: Full-back (33), Centre (1), Replacement (2), Bench (6)
Debut: 15 Nov 1997 v Australia (Twickenham).Number: 1190
Last game: 7 Apr 2001 (rep) v France (Twickenham) - 1T, 5 Pts
Caps: 36 (W:21, D:2, L:13)
Scoring: 10T, 50 Pts
Appearances: 1997:A,NZ1,SA,NZ2, 1998:W,S,I,A,NZ1,NZ2,SA,H,It, 1998:A, 1999:I,F,W,A,US,C,It,NZ,Tg,Fj,SA, 2000:I,F,W,It,S,SA1,SA2,A,SA, 2001:W(r),F(r)
Honours: Outright Championship: 2000, 2001

Samuel Victor PERRY

Born: 16 July 1918 in Isle of Wight
Educated: King George V School
Clubs: Cambridge University (7), Waterloo
Position: Lock (7)
Debut: 18 Jan 1947 v Wales (Cardiff). Number: 760
Last game: 29 Mar 1948 v France (Stade Colombes)
Caps: 7 (W:1, D:1, L:5)
Scoring: 0 Pts
Appearances: 1947:W,I, 1948:A,W,I,S,F

Shaun Andrew PERRY

Born: 4 May 1978 in Wolverhampton
Educated: Park Hill HS
Clubs: Dudley Kingswinford, Coventry, Bristol (5)
Position: Scrum-half (2), Replacement (3), Bench (1)
Debut: 5 Nov 2006 v New Zealand (Twickenham) - 1T, 5 Pts. Number: 1275
Last game: 17 Mar 2007 v Wales (Cardiff)
Caps: 7 (W:2, L:5)
Scoring: 1T, 5 Pts
Appearances: 2006:NZ,Ar,SA1(r),SA2(r), 2007:I(r) F(r),W(r)

James PETERS

Born: 1 July 1879 in Salford
Died: March 1954 in Plymouth
Educated: Knowle School
Clubs: Plymouth (5), Barrow RL
Position: Fly-half (5)
Debut: 17 Mar 1906 v Scotland (Inverleith). Number: 433
Last game: 18 Jan 1908 v Wales (Bristol)
Caps: 5 (W:2, L:3)
Scoring: 2T, 6 Pts
Appearances: 1906:S,F, 1907:I,S, 1908:W

Matt Perry

The first black man to play rugby union for England, James Peters won five caps between 1906 and 1908.

The RFU were not, however, pioneers in race relations in those days and as Brendan Gallagher explained in The Daily Telegraph, Peters would have won many more caps had he been white.

As Gallagher spells out, Peters' international career was interrupted in 1906 when the South Africans arrived in England and Peters was absent from the Test match.

"Peters' 'sin' was to be born black and his exclusion from the match was probably the first, and still one of the most shocking, examples of racism in British sport.

"A black icon in America, where he is featured on a website commemorating 'heroes' in the fight for racial equality, Peters should have been playing in that Test in 1906 after a stunning performance in England's previous match, a 35-8 win over France in Paris."

But the Springboks who had already objected to Peters' presence in a game against Devon got their way and he wasn't seen at Crystal Palace for the Test match.

The "cleverest half-back in the kingdom bar none" and "a champion athlete" according to newspapers in the opening years of the 20th century, Peters was a star on the field.

The Yorkshire Post backed him, saying "his selection is by no means popular on racial grounds, though this should not prevail in sport".

Peters had already overcome so much to become the first outside-half in England.

His father – who was from the West Indies – worked in a circus until he was killed in a lion's cage, mauled to death, and young James was eventually placed in an orphanage in Southwark.

Work took him to Bristol where he established himself as one of England's best rugby players, Devon's county championship win in 1906 catapulting him into the national consciousness.

In 2003, the Museum of Rugby at Twickenham honoured Peters' career with an exhibition that chronicled his playing career.

It also charted his younger years as a circus bare-back rider who was raised in a orphanage before becoming "the best stand-off half-back" in the country.

The exhibition showed him captaining the home's cricket and rugby teams, excelling at athletics (he won the 100 yards, mile, long jump, high jump and walking races in 1894) and training as a printer and then a carpenter before his move to Bristol in 1898.

Peters played his club rugby in Bristol and Plymouth, and for Somerset and Devon.

Peters – quite rightly – finally became disillusioned with the union code, turning to rugby league in his thirties where he played for Barrow and St Helens, while working in the shipyards on the Cumbrian coast.

He returned to Plymouth and continued his trade as a carpenter until retirement. He died in the city at the age of 74, on March 26, 1954.

Charles PHILLIPS

Born: 14 August 1857
Died: 11 September 1940 in Westminster
Educated: Rugby School
Clubs: Oxford University (1), Birkenhead Park (2)
Position: Forward (3)
Debut: 28 Feb 1880 v Scotland (Manchester). Number: 130
Last game: 19 Mar 1881 v Scotland (Raeburn Place)
Caps: 3 (W:2, D:1, L:0)
Scoring: 0 Pts
Appearances: 1880:S, 1881:I,S

Malcolm Stanley PHILLIPS

Born: 3 March 1935 in Prestbury
Educated: Arnold School
Clubs: Oxford University (12), Fylde (13)
Position: Centre (23), Wing (2)
Debut: 1 Feb 1958 v Australia (Twickenham) - 1T, 3 Pts. Number: 874
Last game: 21 Mar 1964 v Scotland (Murrayfield)
Caps: 25 (W:11, D:6, L:8)
Scoring: 5T, 15 Pts
Appearances: 1958:A,I,F,S, 1959:W,I,F,S, 1960:W,I,F,S, 1961:W, 1963:W,I,F,S,NZ1,NZ2,A, 1964:NZ,W,I,F,S
Honours: Championship: 1958, 1963

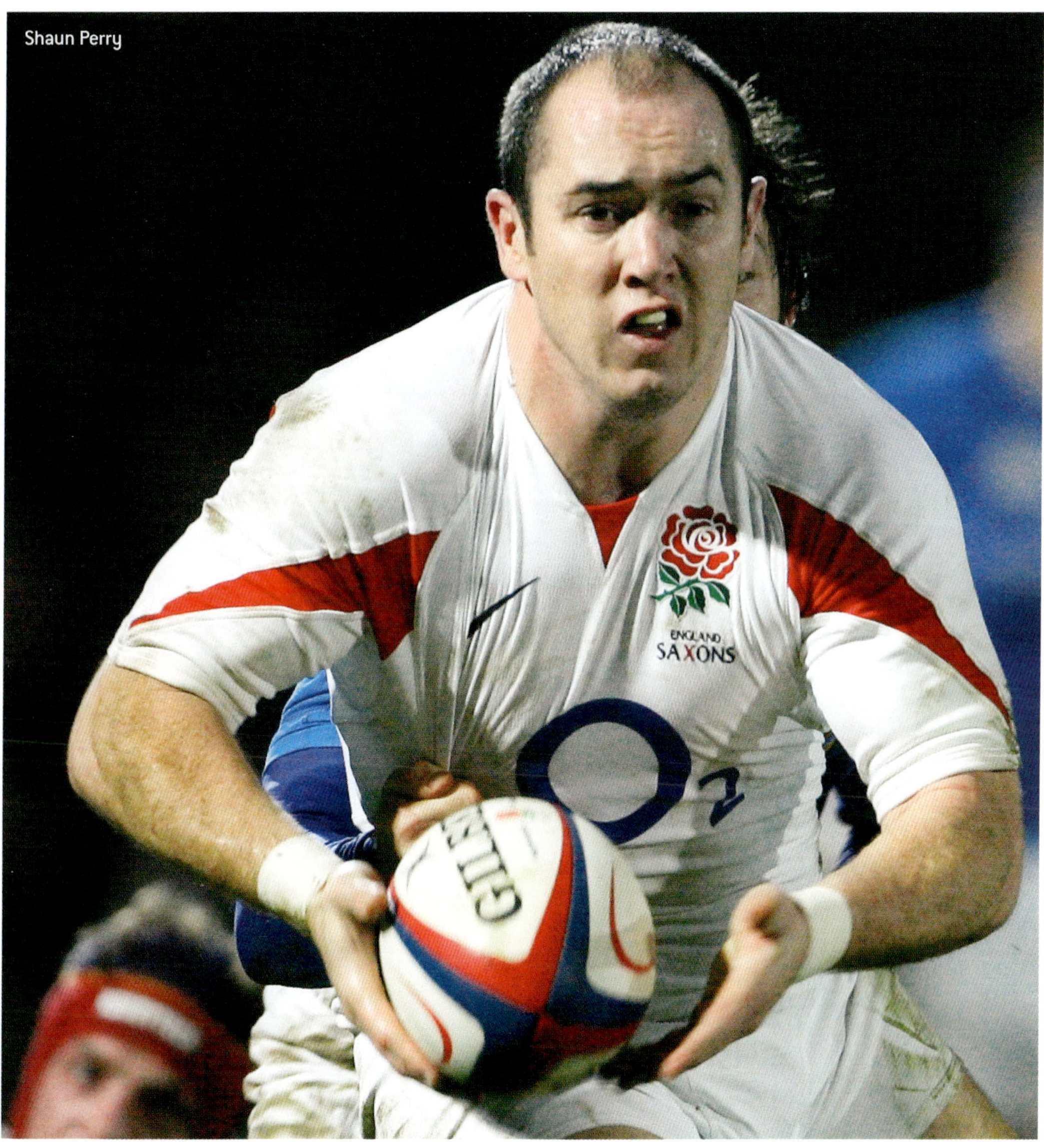
Shaun Perry

Arthur Stanley PICKERING
Born: 24 March 1885 in Dewsbury
Died: 17 February 1969 in York
Educated: Sedbergh School
Clubs: Harrogate (1), Headingley
Position: Centre (1)
Debut: 9 Feb 1907 v Ireland (Lansdowne Road) - 1PG, 3 Pts. Number: 447
Caps: 1 (W:0, L:1)
Scoring: 1PG, 3 Pts
Appearances: 1907:I

Roger David Austin PICKERING
Born: 15 June 1943 in Birmingham
Educated: Whitecliffe School
Clubs: Hull University, Bradford (6), Dax (FR)
Position: Scrum-half (6)
Debut: 11 Feb 1967 v Ireland (Lansdowne Road). Number: 956
Last game: 16 Mar 1968 v Scotland (Murrayfield)
Caps: 6 (W:3, L:3)
Scoring: 0 Pts
Appearances: 1967:I,F,S,W, 1968:F,S

Reginald Clarence Werrett PICKLES
Born: 11 December 1895 in Keynsham
Died: Details unknown
Clubs: Bristol (2)
Position: Full-back (2)
Debut: 11 Feb 1922 v Ireland (Lansdowne Road). Number: 576
Last game: 25 Feb 1922 v France (Twickenham)
Caps: 2 (W:1, D:1, L:0)
Scoring: 0 Pts
Appearances: 1922:I,F

Richard PIERCE
Born: 30 May 1874 in West Derby
Died: Details unknown
Educated: Charterhouse School
Clubs: Liverpool (2)
Position: Forward (2)
Debut: 5 Feb 1898 v Ireland (Richmond). Number: 315
Last game: 21 Mar 1903 v Scotland (Richmond)
Caps: 2 (W:0, L:2)
Scoring: 0 Pts
Appearances: 1898:I, 1903:S

William Norman PILKINGTON
Born: 26 July 1877 in Prescot
Died: 8 February 1935 in Prescot
Educated: Clifton College
Clubs: Cambridge University (1), St Helens Recreation, Blackheath
Position: Wing (1)
Debut: 12 Mar 1898 v Scotland (Edinburgh). Number: 318
Caps: 1 (W:0, D:1, L:0)
Scoring: 0 Pts
Appearances: 1898:S

Charles Henry (Cherry) PILLMAN
Born: 8 January 1890 in Bromley
Died: 13 November 1955 in Bromley
Educated: Tonbridge School
Clubs: Blackheath (18)
Position: Flanker (18)
Debut: 15 Jan 1910 v Wales (Twickenham). Number: 495
Last game: 21 Mar 1914 v Scotland (Inverleith)
Caps: 18 (W:14, D:1, L:3)
Scoring: 8T, 1C, 26 Pts
Appearances: 1910:W,I,F,S, 1911:W,F,I,S, 1912:W,F, 1913:SA,W,F,I,S, 1914:W,I,S
Honours: Grand Slam: 1913. Championship: 1910, 1914

English rugby is full of pioneers, full of men who defined the game of rugby union as we see it today. None more so than Charles 'Cherry' Pillman who did so much to define the role of the openside flanker at the start of the 20th century.

Pillman – who made his England debut in 1910 – was one of the first players to hunt down the outside-half as we see every openside flanker do in the modern game.

As John Griffiths explains in his book, British Lions: "At scrummages he created the custom of detaching himself quickly from the side of the pack when opponents heeled the ball. Possessed of amazing pace he then darted across the field to attack the fly-half before passing movements could be initiated. So successful was he with his methods that he quickly gained promotion to the England side, making his international bow, aged just 20."

Pillman – who played for Blackheath – was the star of the show on that Test debut when England ran out at Twickenham – for the first time – in 1910, masterminding England's first victory over Wales since 1898.

Pillman was at the centre of one of the most successful England teams in history, as the side went on to win the Home Nations Championship four times before the outbreak of the First World War.

He was a key figure in England's first Grand Slam of 1913, scoring 12 of his side's 50 points in victories over Wales, France, Ireland and Scotland.

Pillman went on to become one of the key players on the Lions tour to South Africa in 1910.

Although the series was lost 2-1 Pillman strode like a colossus over the second Test. He was instrumental in both Lions tries in the 8-3 victory and even converted the second.

Billy Millar was the Springbok captain that day and he remembered Pillman's influence saying; "My memories of his game seem to be only of Pillman's outstanding brilliance.

"I assert confidently that if ever a man can have won an international match through his own unorthodox and line-handed efforts, it can be said of the inspired black-haired Pillman."

Pillman's international career was ended by a broken leg as England beat Scotland on their way to their second successive Grand Slam in 1914.

Pillman was awarded the Military Cross in the First World War, returning to play for Blackheath. He died in 1955.

Robert Laurence PILLMAN
Born: 9 February 1893 in Sidcup
Died: Killed in action in 1916 in Armentieres, France
Educated: Merton Court School, Rugby School
Clubs: Blackheath (1)
Position: Flanker (1)
Debut: 13 Apr 1914 v France (Stade Colombes). Number: 542
Caps: 1 (W:1, L:0)
Scoring: 0 Pts
Appearances: 1914:F
Honours: Championship: 1914

John PINCH
Born: Third quarter 1870 in Lancaster
Died: 1946 in Lancaster
Clubs: Lancaster (3)
Position: Forward (3)
Debut: 4 Jan 1896 v Wales (Blackheath). Number: 285
Last game: 13 Mar 1897 v Scotland (Manchester)
Caps: 3 (W:2, L:1)
Scoring: 0 Pts
Appearances: 1896:W,I, 1897:S

William Wyatt (Nipper) PINCHING
Born: 24 March 1851 in Gravesend
Died: 16 August 1878 at sea (SS Eldorado)
Educated: King's College, Cheltenham College
Clubs: Guy's Hospital (1)
Position: Forward (1)
Debut: 5 Feb 1872 v Scotland (The Oval). Number: 33
Caps: 1 (W:1, L:0)
Scoring: 0 Pts
Appearances: 1872:S

Sir Isaac James PITMAN, KBE
Born: 14 August 1901 in Kensington
Died: 1 September 1985 in Chelsea
Educated: Summer Fields School, Eton School
Clubs: Oxford University (1), Harlequins
Position: Wing (1)
Debut: 18 Mar 1922 v Scotland (Twickenham). Number: 579
Caps: 1 (W:1, L:0)
Scoring: 0 Pts
Appearances: 1922:S

Kenneth Clive PLUMMER
Born: 17 January 1947 in Falmouth
Clubs: Bristol (4)
Position: Wing (4)
Debut: 12 Apr 1969 v Wales (Cardiff). Number: 977
Last game: 20 Mar 1976 v France (Parc des Princes)
Caps: 4 (W:0, L:4)
Scoring: 0 Pts
Appearances: 1969:W, 1976:S,I,F

Francis Oswald POOLE
Born: 17 December 1870 in Houghton
Died: 22 May 1949 in Newcastle-under-Lyme
Educated: Cheltenham College
Clubs: Oxford University (3), Gloucester, Sunderland
Position: Forward (3)
Debut: 5 Jan 1895 v Wales (Swansea). Number: 279
Last game: 9 Mar 1895 v Scotland (Richmond)
Caps: 3 (W:2, L:1)
Scoring: 0 Pts
Appearances: 1895:W,I,S

Robert Watkins POOLE
Born: 4 November 1874 in Hartlepool
Died: c 1930
Educated: Hartlepool School
Clubs: Hartlepool Rovers (1), Broughton Rangers RL
Position: Full-back (1)
Debut: 14 Mar 1896 v Scotland (Glasgow). Number: 293
Caps: 1 (W:0, L:1)
Scoring: 0 Pts
Appearances: 1896:S

Richard Pool-Jones

Stuart Potter

Richard J POOL-JONES
Born: 22 October 1969 in London
Educated: King's School
Clubs: Cambridge University, Biarritz (FR), Wasps, Stade Francais (FR,1)
Position: Flanker (1)
Debut: 6 Jun 1998 v Australia (Brisbane). Number: 1197
Caps: 1 (W:0, L:1)
Scoring: 0 Pts
Appearances: 1998:A

Edward Brian POPE
Born: 29 June 1911 in Barnet
Educated: Uppingham School
Clubs: Cambridge University, Blackheath (3)
Position: Scrum-half (3)
Debut: 17 Jan 1931 v Wales (Twickenham). Number: 673
Last game: 6 Apr 1931 v France (Stade Colombes)
Caps: 3 (W:0, D:1, L:2)
Scoring: 0 Pts
Appearances: 1931:W,S,F

Garnet Vere PORTUS
Born: 7 June 1883 in Morpeth, NSW, Australia
Died: 15 June 1954 in Australia
Educated: Maitland HS
Clubs: Sydney University, Oxford University, Blackheath (2)
Position: Fly-half (2)
Debut: 1 Jan 1908 v France (Stade Colombes) - 1T, 3 Pts. Number: 456
Last game: 8 Feb 1908 v Ireland (Richmond)
Caps: 2 (W:2, L:0)
Scoring: 1T, 3 Pts
Appearances: 1908:F,I

Stuart POTTER
Born: 11 November 1967 in Lichfield
Educated: Lichfield Priory Grange School
Clubs: Lichfield, Nottingham, Leicester (1), Rugby
Position: Replacement Centre (1)
Debut: 6 Jun 1998 (rep) v Australia (Brisbane). Number: 1200
Caps: 1 (W:0, L:1)
Scoring: 0 Pts
Appearances: 1998:A(r)

Ronald William (Ronnie) POULTON
Born: 12 September 1889 in Headington
Died: Killed in action in 1915 in Ploegsteert, Belgium
Educated: Dragon School, Rugby School
Clubs: Harlequins (9), Oxford University (4), Liverpool (4)
Position: Centre (16), Wing (1)
Debut: 30 Jan 1909 v France (Leicester). Number: 486
Last game: 13 Apr 1914 (capt) v France (Stade Colombes) - 4T, 12 Pts
Caps: 17 (W:14, L:3). As captain: 4 (W:4, L:0)
Scoring: 8T, 1DG, 28 Pts
Appearances: 1909:F,I,S, 1910:W, 1911:S, 1912:W,I,S, 1913:SA,W,F,I,S, 1914:W*,I*,S*,F*
Honours: Grand Slam: 1913, 1914 (capt). Championship: 1910

The Jonny Wilkinson/Brian O'Driscoll of his day, and then some more Beckham, Flintoff, Gower in one, was how Frank Keating, the eminent rugby writer described Ronnie Poulton-Palmer, the dashing young man who lit up English rugby before the First World War.

Poulton was one of 111 rugby internationals killed in the First World War, one year after leading England to their second successive Grand Slam in 1914.

In that 1914 campaign captain Poulton was in superb form, scoring four tries in the final game, a 39-13 hammering of France, still a record for an Englishman in the Championship.

Keating, The Guardian and Rugby World's writer remembers the effect Poulton-Palmer's death had.

"Any schoolboy of a certain age who had an elderly sportsmaster who valued role models will know by heart 05 05 15 as the day that, at 12.20 am, Lt Ronnie Poulton-Palmer, of the 4th Royal Berkshires, was dispatched by a single sniper's bullet at Ploegsteert Wood, Belgium," Keating recalls.

"He died without speaking. He was 25. In England's last rugger match, only 13 months before in Paris, he had scored four tries. As an Oxford fresher he'd scored five tries against Cambridge, still a record."

P Q R

Ronnie Poulton

Born in Headington in September 1889, Poulton-Palmer was heir to Huntley & Palmers' biscuit millions, loved by people of every class and age.

After his death, his commanding officer, Captain Crutwell wrote to his family saying: "When I went round his old company as they stood to, at dawn, almost every man was crying."

He was known as Ronnie Poulton until 1914 when Palmer was added to his name, an addition, according to The Daily Telegraph, which came about after he became a beneficiary in his uncle's will, G W Palmer of the Huntley & Palmer biscuit-making business.

Of Ronnie Poulton-Palmer, it once was written: "The wondrous Poulton, the fleet and flaxen, a golden-haired Apollo who stood as a symbol of the heart of England."

David Lewes (Piggy) POWELL

Born: 17 May 1942 in Rugby
Educated: Daventry GS
Clubs: Rugby, Northampton (11)
Position: Prop (11)
Debut: 15 Jan 1966 v Wales (Twickenham). Number: 937
Last game: 27 Mar 1971 v Scotland (Murrayfield)
Caps: 11 (W:3, D:2, L:6)
Scoring: 0 Pts
Appearances: 1966:W,I, 1969:I,F,S,W, 1971:W,I,F,S,S

William Edgar PRATTEN

Born: 29 May 1907 in Lewisham
Died: Third quarter 1969 in Thanet
Educated: Marlborough School
Clubs: Blackheath (2), Sidcup
Position: Lock (2)
Debut: 19 Mar 1927 v Scotland (Murrayfield). Number: 623
Last game: 2 Apr 1927 v France (Stade Colombes)
Caps: 2 (W:0, L:2)
Scoring: 0 Pts
Appearances: 1927:S,F

Ivor PREECE

Born: 15 December 1920 in Coventry
Died: 14 March 1987 in Coventry
Clubs: Coventry (12)
Position: Fly-half (10), Centre (2)
Debut: 14 Feb 1948 v Ireland (Twickenham). Number: 780
Last game: 24 Feb 1951 v France (Twickenham)
Caps: 12 (W:3, L:9). As captain: 6 (W:3, L:3)
Scoring: 1DG, 3 Pts
Appearances: 1948:I,S,F, 1949:F*,S*, 1950:W*,I*,F*,S*, 1951:W,I,F

Peter Stuart PREECE

Born: 15 November 1949 in Meriden
Educated: King Henry VIII School
Clubs: Coventry (12)
Position: Centre (11), Replacement (1)
Debut: 3 Jun 1972 v South Africa (Johannesburg). Number: 1014
Last game: 17 Jan 1976 (rep) v Wales (Twickenham)
Caps: 12 (W:4, L:8)
Scoring: 0 Pts
Appearances: 1972:SA, 1973:NZ,W,I,F,S,NZ, 1975:I,F,W,A2, 1976:W(r)

Malcolm PREEDY

Born: 15 September 1960 in Gloucester
Educated: Hucclecote Secondary School
Clubs: Gloucester (1)
Position: Prop (1)
Debut: 2 Jun 1984 v South Africa (Port Elizabeth). Number: 1092
Caps: 1 (W:0, L:1)
Scoring: 0 Pts
Appearances: 1984:SA1

Frank Douglas (Doug) PRENTICE

Born: Third quarter 1898 in Leicester
Died: 3 October 1962 in Paddington
Educated: Wyggeston GS
Clubs: Westleigh, Leicester (3)
Position: No 8 (3)
Debut: 11 Feb 1928 v Ireland (Lansdowne Road).Number: 635
Last game: 17 Mar 1928 v Scotland (Twickenham)
Caps: 3 (W:3, L:0)
Scoring: 0 Pts
Appearances: 1928:I,F,S
Honours: Championship: 1928

Robert Edward (Robin) PRESCOTT

Born: 5 April 1913 in Paddington
Died: 18 May 1975 in Dartmouth
Educated: Wells House Prep School, Marlborough School
Clubs: Oxford University, Harlequins (6), Army, Combined Services, Guildford
Position: Prop (6)
Debut: 16 Jan 1937 v Wales (Twickenham). Number: 733
Last game: 18 Mar 1939 v Scotland (Murrayfield)
Caps: 6 (W:5, L:1)
Scoring: 1T, 3 Pts
Appearances: 1937:W,I, 1938:I, 1939:W,I,S
Honours: Championship: 1937

Nicholas John (Nick) PRESTON

Born: 5 April 1958 in Prestwich
Educated: RGS Lancaster
Clubs: Nottingham University, Richmond (3)
Position: Centre (3), Bench (5)
Debut: 24 Nov 1979 v New Zealand (Twickenham). Number: 1060
Last game: 2 Feb 1980 v France (Parc des Princes) - 1T, 4 Pts
Caps: 3 (W:2, L:1)
Scoring: 1T, 4 Pts
Appearances: 1979:NZ, 1980:I,F
Honours: Championship: 1980

Herbert Leo PRICE

Born: 21 June 1899 in Sutton, Surrey
Died: 18 July 1943 in Victoria Park, Manchester
Educated: Bishop's Stortford School
Clubs: Oxford University (2), Leicester (2), Harlequins
Position: Flanker (4)
Debut: 11 Feb 1922 v Ireland (Lansdowne Road).Number: 577
Last game: 10 Feb 1923 v Ireland (Leicester) - 1T, 3 Pts
Caps: 4 (W:4, L:0)
Scoring: 2T, 6 Pts
Appearances: 1922:I,S, 1923:W,I
Honours: Championship: 1923

John PRICE

Born: 1938
Clubs: Coventry (1)
Position: Lock (1)
Debut: 11 Feb 1961 v Ireland (Lansdowne Road). Number: 897
Caps: 1 (W:0, L:1)
Scoring: 0 Pts
Appearances: 1961:I

P L A PRICE

Born: Details unknown
Died: Details unknown
Clubs: Royal Indian Eng College (3)
Position: Half-Back (3)
Debut: 5 Feb 1877 v Ireland (The Oval). Number: 90
Last game: 4 Mar 1878 v Scotland (The Oval)
Caps: 3 (W:1, D:1, L:1)
Scoring: 0 Pts
Appearances: 1877:I,S, 1878:S

Thomas William PRICE

Born: 26 July 1914
Died: 11 July 1991 in Gloucester
Educated: St Mark's School
Clubs: Gloucester (2), Cheltenham (4)
Position: Prop (6)
Debut: 20 Mar 1948 v Scotland (Murrayfield). Number: 782
Last game: 19 Mar 1949 v Scotland (Twickenham)
Caps: 6 (W:2, L:4)
Scoring: 0 Pts
Appearances: 1948:S,F, 1949:W,I,F,S

Robin Prescott

Jeffrey Alan (Jeff) PROBYN

Born: 27 April 1956 in Bethnal Green
Educated: Nautical College
Clubs: Old Albanians, Streatham-Croydon, Richmond, Wasps (32), Askeans (5), Bedford, Barking, Bristol
Position: Prop (36), Replacement (1), Bench (6)
Debut: 16 Jan 1988 v France (Parc des Princes). Number: 1121
Last game: 20 Mar 1993 v Ireland (Lansdowne Road)
Caps: 37 (W:25, D:1, L:11)
Scoring: 3T, 12 Pts
Appearances: 1988:F,W,S,I,I,A1,A2,A, 1989:S,I,R(r), 1990:I,F,W,S,Ar1,Ar2,Ar, 1991:W,S,I,F,Fj,A,NZ,It,F,S,A, 1992:S,I,F,W, 1993:F,W,S,I
Honours: Grand Slam: 1991, 1992

For a player who was willing to join a Saracens squad at 44, having to wait until 31 for his first taste of international recognition will have come relatively easily to Jeff Probyn.

Despite not playing a part in the inaugural World Cup of 1987, even though he was selected for the squad, his patience was rewarded with a debut against France in the following year's Five Nations, establishing himself as the country's best tighthead, playing 37 of England's next 44 games.

During the Grand Slam-winning year of 1991 the Wasps and Askeans prop anchored the England pack, following disappointment the previous year when they lost the final game to Scotland, and missed out on the Slam. This may have been at the back of his mind during the 1991 rematch when he went head-to-head with David Sole in an entertaining cameo, as England overwhelmed the Scots 21-12 with a Nigel Heslop try, and a conversion and five penalties from the boot of Simon Hodgkinson.

The 1991 Slam was tempered with World Cup Final defeat at the hands of Australia, but domestic domination continued with another successful Five Nations clean sweep in 1992.

Jeff Probyn

Probyn suffered disappointment with the British and Irish Lions, twice missing out on selection at his peak, although he did make a World XV tour of South Africa in 1989. He retired from the big stage in 1993 after being the only member of England's pack to be omitted from the Lions squad.

He became a member of the Rugby Football Union (RFU) committee, before leaving to pursue a career in the media. Tough talking as well as tough tackling, he has spoken out on various issues, including cross-code transfers, and has even co-presented The Rugby Show with Rhodri Williams on talkSPORT radio.

He is also a founder member – alongside Brian Moore and Paul Rendall – of the mildly hedonistic Front Row Union Club, confessing to passions ranging from cabinet-making and Italian arias to pickled eggs and obscure Eighties synth duo Blancmange.

"Jeff, warts and all, is still the best scrummager in England on the tight head and when he goes that will be the turning point for changing our game," according to Dick Best, the former England and Lions coach.

Derek Henry PROUT

Born: 10 November 1942 in Launceston
Died: 27 July 2005
Educated: Redruth Technical School
Clubs: Launceston, Redruth, Loughborough College, UAU, Northampton (2)
Position: Wing (2)
Debut: 20 Jan 1968 v Wales (Twickenham). Number: 967
Last game: 10 Feb 1968 v Ireland (Twickenham)
Caps: 2 (W:0, D:2, L:0)
Scoring: 0 Pts
Appearances: 1968:W,I

John Vivian PULLIN

Born: 1 November 1941 in Aust, Thornbury
Educated: Thornbury GS, Cirencester Agricultural College
Clubs: Bristol Saracens, Bristol (42)
Position: Hooker (41), Replacement (1), Bench (4)
Debut: 15 Jan 1966 v Wales (Twickenham). Number: 938
Last game: 20 Mar 1976 v France (Parc des Princes)
Caps: 42 (W:13, D:4, L:25). As captain: 13 (W:6, D:1, L:6)
Scoring: 1T, 3 Pts
Appearances: 1966:W, 1968:W,I,F,S, 1969:I,F,S,W,SA, 1970:I,W,S,F, 1971:W,I,F,S,S,P, 1972:W,I,F,S,SA*, 1973:NZ*,W*,I*,F*,S*,NZ*,A*, 1974:S*,I*,F*,W*, 1975:I,W(r),S,A1,A2*, 1976:F

Victories for any England captain over one of the three major southern hemisphere countries of New Zealand, Australia and South Africa are rare enough. But wins over all three – under one captain – is the stuff of legends.

Martin Johnson of course was an England captain to complete the hat-trick but more than 20 years before, Bristol hooker John Pullin was the first England skipper to do the same.

Pullin achieved his treble in less than 18 months, starting with an 18-9 victory over the Springboks at Ellis Park.

New Zealand followed – in Auckland – and at Twickenham the final member of the holy trinity fell.

Pullin was joined in all three victories by fly-half Alan Old and forwards Stack Stevens, Chris Ralston, John Watkins, Andy Ripley and Tony Neary.

John Pullin

The win in New Zealand was perhaps the most significant as no England team had won in the land of the long white cloud before.

"We lulled them into a false sense of security!" said Pullin. "Their forwards weren't quite as good as they thought they were."

Pullin finally captained his country 13 times and his record of 42 caps at hooker for England was a record and it took until 1993 for Brian Moore to set a new standard.

Pullin wasn't just an England hero as he starred for the immortal 1971 Lions – also going on the 1968 tour – and was the only Englishman to figure in the most famous try in the history of rugby: the one for the Barbarians that stunned the All Blacks in 1973.

"THAT" try, started by Phil Bennett and finished with a dive by Gareth Edwards, swept up the left touchline, the ball going through the hands of Pullin, John Dawes, Tommy David and Derek Quinnell.

Pullin was also the man to utter one of rugby's immortal quotes: "We may not be much good, but at least we turn up."

The England skipper was forced into that line of self-deprecation in 1973 after the troubles in Ireland had wrecked the Five Nations Championship.

Wales and Scotland had cancelled their games at Lansdowne Road but England travelled and although they were beaten it was a gesture that ensures the English rugby team and their supporters always receive a hearty welcome in Dublin.

"I decided fairly much straight away that I was going," Pullin recalled. "I didn't want a reserve hooker getting in. I had never come off in an England game and I suppose I wanted to keep that record."

A farmer, born in Aust, in the West country, Pullin made his name in the impressive Bristol side of the 1960s, winning his first cap in 1966 and in his 13 matches as skipper he won six, drew one, lost six.

Stanley John PURDY

Born: 6 February 1936 in Rugby
Educated: Lawrence Sheriff School
Clubs: Nottingham University, UAU, Rugby (1), Army, Combined Services, Fylde
Position: Flanker (1)
Debut: 17 Mar 1962 v Scotland (Murrayfield).
Number: 907
Caps: 1 (W:0, D:1, L:0)
Scoring: 0 Pts
Appearances: 1962:S

James PYKE

Born: 8 February 1866 in St Helens
Died: 17 May 1941 in St Helens
Clubs: St Helens Recreation (1)
Position: Forward (1)
Debut: 2 Jan 1892 v Wales (Blackheath).
Number: 240
Caps: 1 (W:1, L:0)
Scoring: 0 Pts
Appearances: 1892:W
Honours: Championship: 1892

John Alfred PYM

Born: 25 March 1891 in Kingston
Died: 9 February 1969 in Auckland, New Zealand
Educated: Cheltenham College
Clubs: RMA Woolwich, Royal Artillery, Army, Blackheath (4)
Position: Scrum-half (4)
Debut: 20 Jan 1912 v Wales (Twickenham) - 1T, 3 Pts.
Number: 521
Last game: 8 Apr 1912 v France (Parc des Princes)
Caps: 4 (W:3, L:1)
Scoring: 1T, 3 Pts
Appearances: 1912:W,I,S,F

Q-R

QUINN, James Patrick

RAFTER, Michael
RALSTON, Christopher Wayne
RAMSDEN, Harold Edward
RANSON, John Matthew
RAPHAEL, John Edward
RAVENSCROFT, John
RAVENSCROFT, Stephen Charles Wood
RAWLINSON, William Cecil Welsh
REDFERN, Stephen Paul
REDMAN, Nigel Charles
REDMOND, Gerald Francis
REDWOOD, Brian William
REES, David Llewellyn
REES, Gary William
REES, Tom
REEVE, James Stanley Roope
REGAN, Martin
REGAN, Mark Peter, MBE
RENDALL, Paul Anthony George
REW, Henry
REYNOLDS, Frank Jeffrey
REYNOLDS, Shirley
RHODES, John
RICHARDS, Dean, MBE
RICHARDS, Edward Ernest
RICHARDS, Joseph
RICHARDS, Peter Charles
RICHARDS, Stephen Brookhouse
RICHARDSON, James Vere
RICHARDSON, William Ryder
RICKARDS, Cyril Henry
RIMMER, Gordon
RIMMER, Laurance Ivor
RIPLEY, Andrew George
RISMAN, Augustus Beverley Walter
RITSON, John Anthony Sydney, OBE
ROBBINS, Graham Leslie
ROBBINS, Peter George Derek
ROBERTS, Alan Dixon
ROBERTS, Ernest William, OBE
ROBERTS, Geoffrey Dorling, OBE
ROBERTS, James
ROBERTS, Reginald Sidney
ROBERTS, Samuel
ROBERTS, Victor George
ROBERTSHAW, Albert Rawson
ROBINSON, Arthur
ROBINSON, Ernest Frederick
ROBINSON, George Carmichael
ROBINSON, Jason Thorpe, MBE
ROBINSON, John James
ROBINSON, Richard Andrew, OBE
ROBSON, Alan
ROBSON, Matthew
RODBER, Timothy Andrew Keith
ROGERS, Derek Prior, OBE
ROGERS, John Henry
ROGERS, Walter Lacy Yea
ROLLITT, David Malcolm
RONCORONI, Anthony Dominic Sebastian
ROSE, William Marcus Henderson
ROSSBOROUGH, Peter Alec
ROSSER, David William Albert
ROTHERHAM, Alan
ROTHERHAM, Arthur
ROUGHLEY, David F K
ROWELL, Robert Errington
ROWLEY, Arthur James
ROWLEY, Hugh Campbell
ROWNTREE, Christopher Graham
ROYDS, Sir Percy Molyneux Rawson, KBE
ROYLE, A V
RUDD, Edward Lawrence
RUSSELL, Richard Forbes
RUTHERFORD, Donald
RYALLS, Henry John
RYAN, Dean
RYAN, Peter Henry

Jason Robinson

James Patrick (Pat) QUINN
Born: 19 February 1930 in Widnes, Lancs
Died: 18 January 1986 in Leicester
Educated: Wade Deacon HS, Sheffield Training College, Carnegie College
Clubs: Army, New Brighton (5), Harrogate
Position: Centre (5)
Debut: 16 Jan 1954 v Wales (Twickenham). Number: 840
Last game: 10 Apr 1954 v France (Stade Colombes)
Caps: 5 (W:3, L:2)
Scoring: 0 Pts
Appearances: 1954:W,NZ,I,S,F

Michael (Mike) RAFTER
Born: 31 March 1952 in Bristol
Educated: St Brendan's College
Clubs: St Luke's University, Bristol (17)
Position: Flanker (16), Replacement (1), Bench (2)
Debut: 15 Jan 1977 v Scotland (Twickenham). Number: 1046
Last game: 6 Jun 1981 v Argentina (Buenos Aires)
Caps: 17 (W:6, D:2, L:9)
Scoring: 0 Pts
Appearances: 1977:S,F,W, 1978:F,W,S,I,NZ, 1979:S,I,F,W,NZ, 1980:W(r), 1981:W,Ar1,Ar2
Honours: Championship: 1980

Christopher Wayne RALSTON
Born: 25 May 1944 in Hendon
Educated: King William's School
Clubs: Richmond (22)
Position: Lock (22)
Debut: 27 Mar 1971 v Scotland (Murrayfield). Number: 999
Last game: 15 Mar 1975 v Scotland (Twickenham)
Caps: 22 (W:7, D:1, L:14)
Scoring: 1T, 4 Pts
Appearances: 1971:S,P, 1972:W,I,F,S,SA, 1973:NZ,W,I,F,S,NZ,A, 1974:S,I,F,W, 1975:I,F,W,S

Harold Edward RAMSDEN
Born: Third quarter 1873 in Keighley
Died: Details unknown
Clubs: Bingley (2)
Position: Forward (2)
Debut: 12 Mar 1898 v Scotland (Edinburgh). Number: 319
Last game: 2 Apr 1898 v Wales (Blackheath)
Caps: 2 (W:1, D:1, L:0)
Scoring: 0 Pts
Appearances: 1898:S,W

John Matthew RANSON
Born: 26 July 1938 in Durham
Clubs: Birmingham University, Durham City, Rosslyn Park (7), Headingley, Selby
Position: Wing (7)
Debut: 25 May 1963 v New Zealand (Auckland) - 1T, 3 Pts. Number: 919
Last game: 21 Mar 1964 v Scotland (Murrayfield)
Caps: 7 (W:1, D:1, L:5)
Scoring: 2T, 6 Pts
Appearances: 1963:NZ1,NZ2,A, 1964:W,I,F,S

Steve Ravenscroft

John Edward RAPHAEL
Born: 30 April 1882 in Brussels, Belgium
Died: Killed in action in 1917 in Remy, Belgium
Educated: Merchant Taylors' School
Clubs: Oxford University (5), Old Merchant Taylor's (4)
Position: Centre (6), Wing (2), Five-Eighth (1)
Debut: 11 Jan 1902 v Wales (Blackheath). Number: 377
Last game: 22 Mar 1906 v France (Parc des Princes)
Caps: 9 (W:4, L:5)
Scoring: 1T, 3 Pts
Appearances: 1902:W,I,S, 1905:W,S,NZ, 1906:W,S,F

John RAVENSCROFT
Born: 11 June 1856 in Wirral
Died: 20 August 1902 of Buenos Aires, Argentina
Educated: Rugby School
Clubs: Oxford University, Birkenhead Park (1)
Position: Forward (1)
Debut: 5 Feb 1881 v Ireland (Manchester). Number: 134
Caps: 1 (W:1, L:0)
Scoring: 0 Pts
Appearances: 1881:I

Stephen Charles Wood (Steve) RAVENSCROFT
Born: 2 November 1970 in Bradford
Educated: Bedford GS
Clubs: Saracens (2), London Welsh
Position: Centre (1), Replacement (1), Bench (1)
Debut: 6 Jun 1998 v Australia (Brisbane). Number: 1198
Last game: 27 Jun 1998 (rep) v New Zealand (Auckland)
Caps: 2 (W:0, L:2)
Scoring: 0 Pts
Appearances: 1998:A,NZ2(r)

William Cecil Welsh RAWLINSON
Born: 17 December 1855
Died: 14 February 1898 in Northampton
Educated: Clifton College
Clubs: RMC Sandhurst, Lincolnshire Regt, Blackheath (1)
Position: Forward (1)
Debut: 6 Mar 1876 v Scotland (The Oval). Number: 84
Caps: 1 (W:1, L:0)
Scoring: 0 Pts
Appearances: 1876:S

Stephen Paul (Steve) REDFERN
Born: 26 October 1957 in Leicester
Educated: Coalville GS
Clubs: Coalville, Leicester (1), Sheffield RL, Leicester Cobblers RL
Position: Replacement Prop (1), Bench (1)
Debut: 18 Feb 1984 (rep) v Ireland (Twickenham).
Number: 1085
Caps: 1 (W:1, L:0)
Scoring: 0 Pts
Appearances: 1984:I(r)

Nigel Redman

P Q R

Nigel Charles REDMAN

Born: 16 August 1964 in Cardiff, Wales
Educated: Priory CS, South Bristol Technical College
Clubs: Weston-super-Mare, Bath (20)
Position: Lock (19), Replacement (1), Bench (1)
Debut: 3 Nov 1984 v Australia (Twickenham). Number: 1099
Last game: 12 Jul 1997 v Australia (Sydney Football Stadium)
Caps: 20 (W:12, L:8)
Scoring: 1T, 4 Pts
Appearances: 1984:A, 1986:S(r), 1987:I,S,A,J,W, 1988:Fj, 1990:Ar1,Ar2, 1991:Fj,It,US, 1993:NZ, 1994:F,W,SA1,SA2,1997:Ar1,A

Gerald Francis REDMOND

Born: 23 March 1943 in Weston
Educated: Weston-super-Mare GS, St Luke's School
Clubs: Cambridge University (1), Bedford, St Luke's College, Weston-super-Mare, Bristol
Position: No 8 (1), Bench (1)
Debut: 18 Apr 1970 v France (Stade Colombes). Number: 989
Caps: 1 (W:0, L:1)
Scoring: 0 Pts
Appearances: 1970:F

David Rees

Brian William REDWOOD

Born: 6 February 1939 in Bristol
Educated: Bristol GS
Clubs: Exeter University, Oxford University, Bristol (2)
Position: Scrum-half (2)
Debut: 20 Jan 1968 v Wales (Twickenham) - 1T, 3 Pts. Number: 968
Last game: 10 Feb 1968 v Ireland (Twickenham)
Caps: 2 (W:0, D:2, L:0)
Scoring: 1T, 3 Pts
Appearances: 1968:W,I

David Llewellyn REES

Born: 15 October 1974 in Kingston-upon-Thames
Educated: Gosforth HS, RGS Newcastle
Clubs: Manchester Metro University, Northern, Sale (11), Bristol, Leeds, Newbury
Position: Wing (10), Replacement (1)
Debut: 15 Nov 1997 v Australia (Twickenham).Number: 1191
Last game: 26 Jun 1999 v Australia (Sydney)
Caps: 11 (W:5, D:2, L:4)
Scoring: 3T, 15 Pts
Appearances: 1997:A,NZ1,SA,NZ2, 1998:F,W,SA(r), 1999:S,I,F,A

Gary William REES

Born: 2 May 1960 in Long Eaton, Derbyshire
Educated: Trent Poly
Clubs: Nottingham (23)
Position: Flanker (17), Replacement (6), Bench (9)
Debut: 9 Jun 1984 (rep) v South Africa (Johannesburg). Number: 1094
Last game: 11 Oct 1991 v United States (Twickenham)
Caps: 23 (W:13, L:10)
Scoring: 2T, 8 Pts
Appearances: 1984:SA2(r),A, 1986:I,F, 1987:F,W,S,A,J,US,W, 1988:S(r),I,I,A1,A2,Fj, 1989:W(r),R(r),Fj(r), 1990:Ar(r), 1991:Fj,US

Tom REES

Born: 11 September 1984 in London
Educated: Harriet Costello School, RGS High Wycombe
Clubs: Wasps (3)
Position: Replacement Flanker (3)
Debut: 3 Feb 2007 (rep) v Scotland (Twickenham). Number: 1280
Last game: 24 Feb 2007 (rep) v Ireland (Croke Park)
Caps: 3 (W:2, L:1)
Scoring: 0 Pts
Appearances: 2007:S(r),It(r),I(r)

James Stanley Roope (Jim) REEVE

Born: 12 September 1908 in Kensington
Died: 6 November 1936 in East Harling, Norfolk
Educated: Rugby School
Clubs: Cambridge University, Harlequins (8)
Position: Wing (8)
Debut: 1 Apr 1929 v France (Stade Colombes).Number: 651
Last game: 21 Mar 1931 v Scotland (Murrayfield) - 2T, 6 Pts
Caps: 8 (W:3, D:2, L:3)
Scoring: 5T, 15 Pts
Appearances: 1929:F, 1930:W,I,F,S, 1931:W,I,S
Honours: Championship: 1930

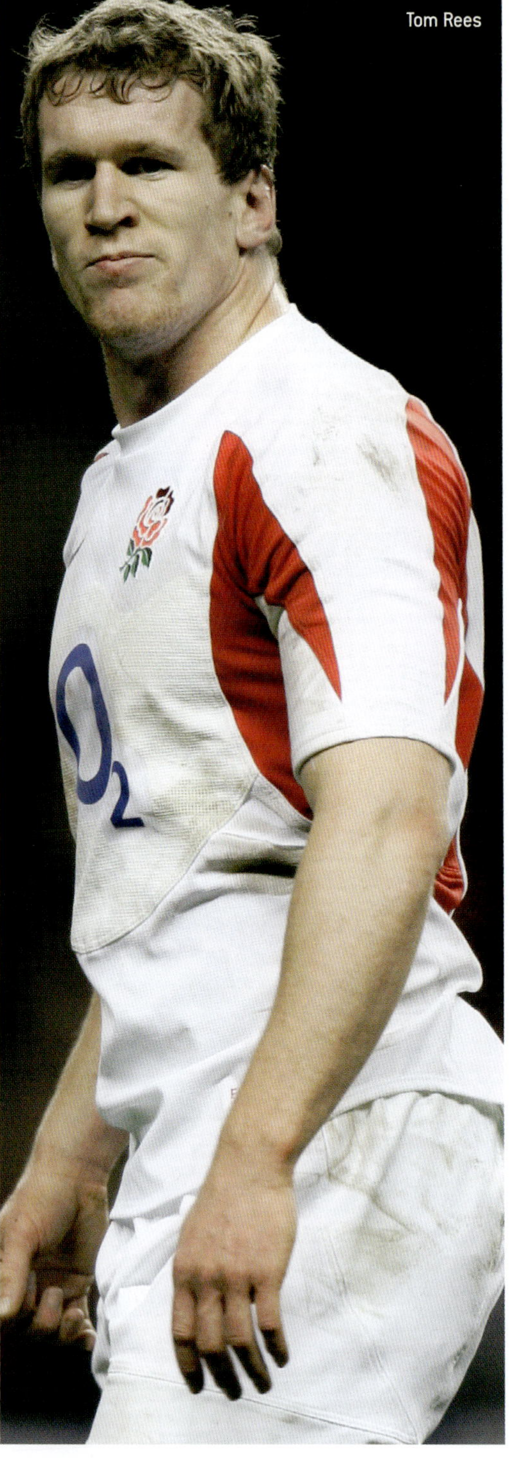
Tom Rees

Martin REGAN

Born: 24 September 1929 in St Helens
Educated: West Park GS, St Mary's College
Clubs: St Helens, Liverpool (12), Blackheath
Position: Fly-half (12)
Debut: 17 Jan 1953 v Wales (Cardiff). Number: 834
Last game: 14 Apr 1956 v France (Stade Colombes)
Caps: 12 (W:8, D:1, L:3)
Scoring: 1T, 3 Pts
Appearances: 1953:W,I,F,S, 1954:W,NZ,I,S,F, 1956:I,S,F
Honours: Championship: 1953

Mark Regan

Mark Peter (Ronnie) REGAN, MBE

Born: 28 January 1972 in Bristol
Educated: St Brendan's School
Clubs: Keynsham, St Bernadette's Old Boys, Bristol (13), Bath (10), Leeds (10)
Position: Hooker (20), Replacement (13), Bench (16)
Debut: 18 Nov 1995 v South Africa (Twickenham). Number: 1160
Last game: 26 Jun 2004 v Australia (Brisbane)
Caps: 33 (W:22, D:1, L:10)
Scoring: 3T, 15 Pts
Appearances: 1995:SA,Sm, 1996:F,W,S,I,It,Ar, 1997:S,I,F,W,A,NZ2(r), 1998:F, 2000:SA1(r),A(r),Ar,SA(r), 2001:It(r),S(r),C2(r),R, 2003:F(r),It(r),W,Geo(r),Sm, 2004:It(r),I(r),NZ1(r),NZ2,A
Honours: RWC Winner: 2003. Championship: 1996, 2001, 2003

Mark 'Ronnie' Regan is one of the true characters of the modern game, making the transition from the amateur to the professional era with ease.

He made his England debut just after the game had become 'open' in 1995, making his name as an uncompromising hooker in the Bristol front row.

Brian Moore's retirement after the 1995 World Cup allowed Regan to move into the England team and while he was a squad member in 2003 when England won the World Cup he failed to make the matchday 22.

After that 1995 debut he kept his place for the next two Five Nations championships, and after moving to local rivals Bath, he was selected for the 1997 Lions tour to South Africa.

During that tour he developed an intense rivalry with Keith Wood, and managed to force his way into the team for the final Test.

Loss of form, however, saw him lose his place with England, despite playing a major role in Bath's Heineken Cup victory in 1998, and he missed out on the 1999 World Cup.

Determination has always been a strong part of his game, and having shed a stone he began the 1999-2000 season a much-improved player, and was voted Bath's forward of the year.

Despite this, England coach Clive Woodward preferred to look elsewhere and left him on the bench for most of that season's Six Nations.

A switch to Leeds Tykes in 2002 saw his international career take an upturn and he worked his way back into the England picture in the 2003 Six Nations and World Cup warm-up games.

In the opening game of the World Cup, he wrote a little bit of history by becoming the first ever Leeds Tykes player to score a try for England, but his opportunities thereafter were limited by the presence of Steve Thompson.

International retirement followed the World Cup triumph, along with an MBE, and he returned to give his all at club level where he remained a crowd favourite.

In 2004 he left for Leeds and in 2005, after securing a Powergen Cup medal, he rejoined Bristol on their return to the Premiership, helping them into the Premiership top four in 2006-07.

Paul Anthony George RENDALL

Born: 18 February 1954 in London
Educated: St Joseph's School
Clubs: Slough, Wasps (27), Askeans (1)
Position: Prop (27), Replacement (1), Bench (23)
Debut: 17 Mar 1984 v Wales (Twickenham). Number: 1087
Last game: 8 Oct 1991 (rep) v Italy (Twickenham)
Caps: 28 (W:14, D:1, L:13)
Scoring: 0 Pts
Appearances: 1984:W,SA2, 1986:W,S, 1987:I,F,S,A,J,W, 1988:F,W,S,I,I,A1,A2,A, 1989:S,I,F,W,R, 1990:I,F,W,S, 1991:It(r)

Prop Paul 'The Judge' Rendall, a legend at Wasps, took his time to break through into the international team and did not make his Test debut until he was 30, packing down against the Welsh in the 1984 defeat at Twickenham. He also represented Buckinghamshire, Middlesex, London, The Barbarians, Askeans and a World XV on tour, amongst others, in a distinguished career.

Dick Greenwood picked him for the summer tour of South Africa – in 1984 – and Rendall played in the second Test in Johannesburg which England lost 35-9. He was absent for the next season, played against Wales and Scotland in 1986 and by the time the inaugural World Cup came around in 1987, Rendall was firmly established in the international side although it was not a campaign that England players and fans will remember with any fondness.

However England's failure to get further than the quarter-finals in Australia prompted a radical rethink with manager Geoff Cooke putting an emphasis on fitness and testing, something that saw Rendall hit the gym and play nine times for his country in 1988. This included a win, 28-19, against the touring Australians at Twickenham which signalled the start of the Will Carling era. It was also during this year that he was joined in the England scrum by his Wasps colleague, Jeff Probyn, like Rendall another late developer.

Rendall played in the famous Grand Slam decider against Scotland in 1990, which England blew dramatically, but was coming under pressure for his place. He was left behind for England's summer tour to Argentina – in 1990 – which saw the emergence of Jason Leonard who would eventually replace him in the England team.

Rendall made his final international appearance as a replacement in England's 1991 World Cup pool match against Italy. In his autobiography Leonard claimed that: "Rendall taught me everything I know about propping and drinking. The older he got the better he got – the ultimate tourist."

After retirement Rendall, whose nickname comes from his role in mock courts on England tours, coached in lower level rugby with stints at Bracknell, Slough and Rugby Lions. He had particular success as director of rugby at Bracknell, a post he took in 1992, where he oversaw a series of promotions culminating in a place in National One in 2001-02. That was as good as it got for Bracknell who were relegated that year and Rendall departed to be replaced by Bob Crooks.

Henry REW

Born: 11 November 1906 in Exeter
Died: Killed in action in 1940 in El Alamein, Libya
Educated: Exeter School
Clubs: Royal Tank Regt, Army (3), Blackheath (4), Exeter (3)
Position: Prop (10)
Debut: 16 Mar 1929 v Scotland (Murrayfield). Number: 646
Last game: 17 Mar 1934 v Scotland (Twickenham)
Caps: 10 (W:5, D:2, L:3)
Scoring: 0 Pts
Appearances: 1929:S,F, 1930:F,S, 1931:W,S,F, 1934:W,I,S
Honours: Championship: 1930, 1934

Frank Jeffrey (Jeff) REYNOLDS

Born: 2 January 1916 in Canton, China
Died: 29 July 1996 in Somerset West, South Africa
Educated: Cranleigh School
Clubs: Duke of Wellington's Regt, Army (1), Old Cranleighans (2), RMC Sandhurst, Blackheath
Position: Fly-half (3)
Debut: 20 Mar 1937 v Scotland (Murrayfield). Number: 736
Last game: 19 Mar 1938 v Scotland (Twickenham) - 1DG, 4 Pts
Caps: 3 (W:2, L:1)
Scoring: 1T, 1DG, 7 Pts
Appearances: 1937:S, 1938:I,S
Honours: Championship: 1937

Dean Richards

Shirley REYNOLDS

Born: 1874 in Lahore, India
Died: 9 January 1946 in Epsom
Educated: Christ's Hospital School
Clubs: Richmond (4)
Position: Forward (4)
Debut: 6 Jan 1900 v Wales (Gloucester). Number: 349
Last game: 9 Feb 1901 v Ireland (Lansdowne Road)
Caps: 4 (W:1, D:1, L:2)
Scoring: 0 Pts
Appearances: 1900:W,I,S, 1901:I

John RHODES

Born: Third quarter 1869 in Pontefract
Died: 22 May 1925 in Sculcoates
Clubs: Castleford (3), Hull KR RL
Position: Forward (3)
Debut: 4 Jan 1896 v Wales (Blackheath). Number: 286
Last game: 14 Mar 1896 v Scotland (Glasgow)
Caps: 3 (W:1, L:2)
Scoring: 0 Pts
Appearances: 1896:W,I,S

Dean RICHARDS, MBE

Born: 11 July 1963 in Nuneaton
Educated: John Cleveland College
Clubs: Roanne (FR), Leicester (48)
Position: No 8 (46), Replacement (2), Bench (7)
Debut: 1 Mar 1986 v Ireland (Twickenham) - 2T, 8 Pts. Number: 1114
Last game: 16 Mar 1996 v Ireland (Twickenham)
Caps: 48 (W:35, D:1, L:12)
Scoring: 6T, 24 Pts
Appearances: 1986:I,F, 1987:S,A,J,US,W, 1988:F,W,S,I,A1,A2,Fj,A, 1989:S,I,F,W,R, 1990:Ar, 1991:W,S,I,F,Fj,A,NZ,It,US, 1992:S(r),F,W,C, 1993:NZ, 1994:W,SA1,C, 1995:I,F,W,S,Sm,A,NZ, 1996:F(r),S,I
Honours: Grand Slam: 1991, 1995. Championship: 1992, 1996

Deano to both team-mates and supporters, Dean Richards was the archetypal team player from the old school. A ramshackled demeanour concealed an ability to take games by the scruff of the neck with his brilliant plays at close quarters, doing whatever it took to pull his team back into contention.

Discarded several times by seemingly more adventurous coaches, he was always recalled to provide the platform from which England could attack. It is no coincidence he was on the losing side only four times in his last 29 internationals.

Richards made his debut for England against Ireland in 1986, scoring two tries in a 25-20 win, and he made the 1987 World Cup squad, though still considered a fringe player. He played four times during that campaign and the following season he made his position permanent.

On the back of his progress for England he toured Australia with the Lions in 1989, winning the series and forming a formidable back-row partnership with Mike Teague and Finlay Calder.

Injury interrupted his career several times, and 1990 was a wipe-out, but the following year he joined up with Teague once again, and, with Peter Winterbottom, formed another highly effective unit to secure the Grand Slam and take England to the quarter-finals of the World Cup.

However, a tactical rethink saw him replaced by Mickey Skinner, and he played no further part as England lost to Australia in the final.

He returned to England's Grand Slam-winning forward line in 1992, but was once again the victim of a tactical overhaul the next year, this time Jack Rowell feeling his particular abilities weren't needed in a disappointing Five Nations for England.

His talents were still appreciated by that year's Lions, travelling to New Zealand and earning three further caps.

He returned once more to the 1995 Grand Slam-winning team, and captained Leicester to the Courage League Championship.

In that same year (1995) he became only the second Tigers forward to score 100 tries for the club.

His contribution for Leicester was never in doubt and, alongside Neil Back and John Wells, he drove the Tigers to the Heineken Cup final in 1997. He played his last game in an England shirt in 1996, before switching to coaching.

He had been part of two English title wins as a player for Leicester in 1988 and 1995.

Back-to-back Heineken Cups and four successive Premiership titles followed as a coach – not bad for a man regarded by some as a dinosaur during his playing days.

He ended a 24-year association with Leicester for a new challenge with Grenoble in 2004. He had played for Roanne in France before his Leicester heyday.

Peter Richards

Richards left Grenoble to take over at NEC Harlequins after their relegation in 2005. He took them straight back up and into seventh in their first season (2006-07) back in the top flight.

Edward Ernest RICHARDS

Born: 11 March 1905 in East Stonehouse
Died: 9 June 1982 in Plymouth
Clubs: Penryn, Plymouth Albion (2), London Highfield RL
Position: Scrum-half (2)
Debut: 16 Mar 1929 v Scotland (Murrayfield). Number: 647
Last game: 1 Apr 1929 v France (Stade Colombes)
Caps: 2 (W:1, L:1)
Scoring: 0 Pts
Appearances: 1929:S,F

Joseph RICHARDS

Born: Details unknown
Died: Details unknown
Clubs: Bradford (3)
Position: Forward (3)
Debut: 3 Jan 1891 v Wales (Newport). Number: 229
Last game: 7 Mar 1891 v Scotland (Richmond)
Caps: 3 (W:2, L:1)
Scoring: 0 Pts
Appearances: 1891:W,I,S

Peter Charles RICHARDS

Born: 10 March 1978 in Portsmouth
Educated: Lord Wandsworth College
Clubs: London Irish, Harlequins, Treviso (IT), Bristol, Wasps, Gloucester (6)
Position: Scrum-half (4), Replacement (2), Bench (2)
Debut: 11 Jun 2006 v Australia (Sydney). Number: 1271
Last game: 25 Nov 2006 v South Africa (Twickenham)
Caps: 6 (W:1, L:5)
Scoring: 0 Pts
Appearances: 2006:A1,A2,NZ(r),Ar(r),SA1,SA2

Stephen Brookhouse RICHARDS

Born: 28 August 1941 in West Kirby
Educated: Clifton College
Clubs: Oxford University, Richmond (9), Bristol, Sheffield
Position: Hooker (9)
Debut: 16 Jan 1965 v Wales (Cardiff). Number: 929
Last game: 15 Apr 1967 v Wales (Cardiff)
Caps: 9 (W:3, D:1, L:5)
Scoring: 0 Pts
Appearances: 1965:W,I,F,S, 1967:A,I,F,S,W

James Vere RICHARDSON

Born: 16 December 1903 in Prenton, Cheshire
Died: 1 May 1995 in Padstowe
Educated: Uppingham School
Clubs: Oxford University, Birkenhead Park (5), Richmond
Position: Centre (5)
Debut: 7 Jan 1928 v Australia (Twickenham) - 3C, 6 Pts. Number: 630
Last game: 17 Mar 1928 v Scotland (Twickenham)
Caps: 5 (W:5, L:0)
Scoring: 1T, 8C, 1DG, 23 Pts
Appearances: 1928:A,W,I,F,S
Honours: Grand Slam: 1928

William Ryder (Ryder) RICHARDSON

Born: Third quarter 1861 in Chorlton
Died: 30 July 1920 in Dover
Educated: Manchester GS
Clubs: Oxford University, Manchester (1)
Position: Half-Back (1)
Debut: 5 Feb 1881 v Ireland (Manchester). Number: 135
Caps: 1 (W:1, L:0)
Scoring: 0 Pts
Appearances: 1881:I

Cyril Henry RICKARDS

Born: 11 January 1854
Died: 25 February 1920 in Thanet
Educated: Rugby School, Cheltenham College
Clubs: RMA Woodwich, Royal Artillery, Gipsies (1)
Position: Forward (1)
Debut: 3 Mar 1873 v Scotland (Glasgow). Number: 42
Caps: 1 (W:0, D:1, L:0)
Scoring: 0 Pts
Appearances: 1873:S

Gordon RIMMER

Born: 28 February 1925 in Southport
Educated: King George V School
Clubs: Waterloo (12)
Position: Scrum-half (12)
Debut: 15 Jan 1949 v Wales (Cardiff). Number: 794
Last game: 20 Mar 1954 v Scotland (Murrayfield)
Caps: 12 (W:3, L:9)
Scoring: 0 Pts
Appearances: 1949:W,I, 1950:W, 1951:W,I,F, 1952:SA,W, 1954:W,NZ,I,S

Laurance Ivor RIMMER

Born: 31 May 1935 in Liverpool South
Educated: Birkenhead Institute
Clubs: Oxford University, Old Birkonians, Bath (5)
Position: Flanker (5)
Debut: 7 Jan 1961 v South Africa (Twickenham). Number: 894
Last game: 18 Mar 1961 v Scotland (Twickenham)
Caps: 5 (W:1, D:1, L:3)
Scoring: 0 Pts
Appearances: 1961:SA,W,I,F,S

Andy Ripley

Andy Ripley

Andrew George (Andy) RIPLEY

Born: 1 December 1947 in South Liverpool
Educated: Greenway Comp School Bristol
Clubs: University of East Anglia, Rosslyn Park (24), Brescia (IT)
Position: No 8 (24), Bench (8)
Debut: 15 Jan 1972 v Wales (Twickenham). Number: 1006
Last game: 21 Feb 1976 v Scotland (Murrayfield)
Caps: 24 (W:8, D:1, L:15)
Scoring: 2T, 8 Pts
Appearances: 1972:W,I,F,S,SA, 1973:NZ,W,I,F,S,NZ,A, 1974:S,I,F,W, 1975:I,F,S,A1,A2, 1976:A,W,S

Andy Ripley played No 8 for Rosslyn Park and England between 1972 and 1976, and will always be remembered for his Corinthian, swashbuckling style.

A big man at 6'5", 'Rippers' was renowned for his deceptively laid-back approach but he was unmistakably a winner.

"He is one of the most cherished figures in the rugby world," explained Mick Cleary The Daily Telegraph's rugby correspondent in 2005.

"He's one of Britain's sporting icons and a mass of contradictions. Ripley fired imaginations because he was something that English rugby was not supposed to be – maverick, unrestrained, dangerous. He ought to have been French, with his long stride and musketeer's bandana."

He made his England debut in 1972 against Wales. He played in an England team considered to be rather ordinary – they lost seven games in a row at one point – but they had their moments.

Two years later, Ripley was the outstanding player as England beat a Welsh team that included Gareth Edwards and Phil Bennett. He scored a decisive try as England won for the first time in 11 years.

That year (1974) he also joined the British and Irish Lions tour to South Africa.

Considering it was the Lions' Seventies heyday, this was a huge achievement, and proof that behind the good-natured exterior beat the heart of a real player.

Ripley was a natural all-round athlete and competitor. A qualified yachtsman, he also ran the 400 metres in the UK athletics championship, and was World Veteran indoor rowing champion. His indoor rowing ability will have come in handy in 1981 as he pitted his physical wits against fellow sportsmen in the TV show Superstars, finishing as runner-up to rugby league star Keith Fielding in the 1981 series final.

In 1981, Ripley captained the Barbarians in the Hong Kong 7s, and they overcame a talented Australian side including the Ella brothers and Brendan Moon to take the title – the first British-based team to win the competition.

Since 2005, Ripley has battled with prostate cancer, and is very active with the Prostate Cancer Charity raising awareness and breaking down barriers. Despite, or because of, this, he continues to test himself physically and in 2007 was training for the next world indoor rowing championships.

Bev Risman

Augustus Beverley Walter (Bev) RISMAN

Born: 23 November 1937 in Salford
Educated: Cockermouth GS
Clubs: Manchester University (4), Loughborough College (4), UAU
Position: Fly-half (6), Centre (2)
Debut: 17 Jan 1959 v Wales (Cardiff). Number: 879
Last game: 25 Feb 1961 v France (Twickenham)
Caps: 8 (W:1, D:3, L:4)
Scoring: 1C, 2PG, 8 Pts
Appearances: 1959:W,I,F,S, 1961:SA,W,I,F

John Anthony Sydney RITSON, OBE
Born: 18 August 1887 in Chester-le-Street
Died: 16 October 1957 in Guildford
Educated: Uppingham School
Clubs: Durham University, Edinburgh University Northern (8)
Position: Forward (8)
Debut: 3 Mar 1910 v France (Parc des Princes). Number: 469
Last game: 15 Mar 1913 v Scotland (Twickenham)
Caps: 8 (W:7, L:1)
Scoring: 2T, 6 Pts
Appearances: 1910:F,S, 1912:F, 1913:SA,W,F,I,S
Honours: Grand Slam: 1913. Championship: 1910

Graham Leslie ROBBINS
Born: 24 September 1956 in Sutton Coldfield
Educated: Fairfax HS
Clubs: Coventry (2), Rugby
Position: No 8 (2)
Debut: 18 Jan 1986 v Wales (Twickenham). Number: 1112
Last game: 15 Feb 1986 v Scotland (Murrayfield)
Caps: 2 (W:1, L:1)
Scoring: 0 Pts
Appearances: 1986:W,S

Peter George Derek ROBBINS
Born: 21 September 1933 in Coventry
Died: 25 March 1987 in Edgbaston
Educated: Bishop Vesey GS
Clubs: Oxford University (12), Moseley (6), Coventry (1)
Position: Flanker (19)
Debut: 21 Jan 1956 v Wales (Twickenham). Number: 866
Last game: 17 Mar 1962 v Scotland (Murrayfield)
Caps: 19 (W:11, D:4, L:4)
Scoring: 0 Pts
Appearances: 1956:W,I,S,F, 1957:W,I,F,S, 1958:W,A,I,S, 1960:W,I,F,S, 1961:SA,W, 1962:S
Honours: Grand Slam: 1957. Championship: 1958

Alan Dixon ROBERTS
Born: First quarter 1888 in Newcastle-upon-Tyne
Died: 1 September 1940 in East Anglesey
Educated: Durham School
Clubs: Cambridge University, Northern (8)
Position: Wing (8)
Debut: 21 Jan 1911 v Wales (Swansea) - 1T, 3 Pts. Number: 514
Last game: 14 Feb 1914 v Ireland (Twickenham) - 1T, 3 Pts
Caps: 8 (W:5, L:3)
Scoring: 5T, 15 Pts
Appearances: 1911:W,F,I,S, 1912:I,S,F, 1914:I
Honours: Championship: 1914

Ernest William ROBERTS, OBE
Born: 14 November 1878 in Lowestoft
Died: 19 November 1933 in Manchester
Educated: Merchant Taylors' School
Clubs: Royal Naval Eng College Keyham (6), RNC Dartmouth, Royal Navy
Position: Forward (6)
Debut: 5 Jan 1901 v Wales (Cardiff). Number: 360
Last game: 16 Mar 1907 (capt) v Scotland (Blackheath)
Caps: 6 (W:0, L:6). As captain: 1 (W:0, L:1)
Scoring: 0 Pts
Appearances: 1901:W,I, 1905:NZ, 1906:W,I, 1907:S*

Geoffrey Dorling (Khaki) ROBERTS, OBE
Born: 27 August 1886 in Exeter
Died: 7 March 1967 in Southwark
Educated: Rugby School
Clubs: Oxford University, Harlequins (3), Exeter
Position: Forward (3)
Debut: 16 Mar 1907 v Scotland (Blackheath). Number: 450
Last game: 18 Jan 1908 v Wales (Bristol) - 1C, 2 Pts
Caps: 3 (W:1, L:2)
Scoring: 3C, 6 Pts
Appearances: 1907:S, 1908:F,W

James ROBERTS
Born: 25 June 1932
Educated: Mill Hill School
Clubs: Cambridge University, Old Millhillians (9), Sale (9)
Position: Wing (18)
Debut: 16 Jan 1960 v Wales (Twickenham) - 2T, 6 Pts. Number: 889
Last game: 4 Jan 1964 v New Zealand (Twickenham)
Caps: 18 (W:8, D:5, L:5)
Scoring: 6T, 18 Pts
Appearances: 1960:W,I,F,S, 1961:SA,W,I,F,S, 1962:W,I,F,S, 1963:W,I,F,S, 1964:NZ
Honours: Championship: 1963

Peter Robbins

Reginald Sidney ROBERTS
Born: 4 December 1911 in Coventry
Died: May 1992 in Coventry
Clubs: Coventry (1), Huddersfield RL
Position: Hooker (1)
Debut: 13 Feb 1932 v Ireland (Lansdowne Road). Number: 696
Caps: 1 (W:1, L:0)
Scoring: 0 Pts
Appearances: 1932:I

Samuel (Sam) ROBERTS
Born: Details unknown
Died: Details unknown
Clubs: Swinton (2)
Position: Full-back (2)
Debut: 8 Jan 1887 v Wales (Llanelli). Number: 192
Last game: 5 Feb 1887 v Ireland (Lansdowne Road)
Caps: 2 (W:0, D:1, L:1)
Scoring: 0 Pts
Appearances: 1887:W,I

Victor George (Vic) ROBERTS
Born: 6 August 1924 in Penryn
Died: 14 March 2004 in Horsham
Educated: Falmouth GS
Clubs: Penryn (16), Swansea, Harlequins
Position: Flanker (16)
Debut: 19 Apr 1947 v France (Twickenham) - 1T, 3 Pts. Number: 774
Last game: 14 Apr 1956 v France (Stade Colombes)
Caps: 16 (W:7, L:9). As captain: 1 (W:0, L:1)
Scoring: 2T, 6 Pts
Appearances: 1947:F, 1949:W,I,F,S, 1950:I,F,S, 1951:W*,I,F,S, 1956:W,I,S,F

Albert Rawson (Rawson) ROBERTSHAW
Born: Third quarter 1861 in Bradford
Died: 17 November 1920 in Bradford
Clubs: Bradford (5)
Position: Three-quarter (5)
Debut: 2 Jan 1886 v Wales (Blackheath). Number: 182
Last game: 5 Mar 1887 v Scotland (Manchester)
Caps: 5 (W:2, D:3, L:0)
Scoring: 0 Pts
Appearances: 1886:W,I,S, 1887:W,S

Arthur ROBINSON
Born: 8 November 1865 in Darlington
Died: 9 April 1948 in Scone, Perth, Scotland
Educated: Cheltenham College
Clubs: Cambridge University, Hartlepool Rovers, Blackheath (4)
Position: Forward (4)
Debut: 16 Feb 1889 v New Zealand Natives (Blackheath). Number: 203
Last game: 15 Mar 1890 v Ireland (Blackheath)
Caps: 4 (W:3, L:1)
Scoring: 0 Pts
Appearances: 1889:M, 1890:W,S,I

Ernest Frederick (Ernie) ROBINSON

Born: 17 January 1929
Died: 2 July 1993 in Coventry
Clubs: Coventry (4)
Position: Hooker (4)
Debut: 20 Mar 1954 v Scotland (Murrayfield). Number: 847
Last game: 18 Mar 1961 v Scotland (Twickenham)
Caps: 4 (W:2, D:1, L:1)
Scoring: 0 Pts
Appearances: 1954:S, 1961:I,F,S

George Carmichael (Tot) ROBINSON

Born: Second quarter 1876 in Gateshead
Died: 29 May 1940 in Penrith, Cumberland
Educated: Dame Allan's School
Clubs: Gosforth, Percy Park (8), Blackheath
Position: Wing (8)
Debut: 6 Feb 1897 v Ireland (Lansdowne Road) - 1T, 3 Pts. Number: 308
Last game: 9 Mar 1901 v Scotland (Blackheath) - 1T, 3 Pts
Caps: 8 (W:2, D:1, L:5)
Scoring: 8T, 24 Pts
Appearances: 1897:I,S, 1898:I, 1899:W, 1900:I,S, 1901:I,S

Jason Thorpe ROBINSON, MBE

Born: 30 July 1974 in Leeds
Educated: Matthew Murray HS
Clubs: Hunslet RL, Leeds RL, Wigan RL, Bath, Sale (41)
Position: Full-back (23), Wing (11), Centre (3), Replacement (4)
Debut: 17 Feb 2001 (rep) v Italy (Twickenham). Number: 1221
Last game: 10 Feb 2007 v Italy (Twickenham) - 1T, 5 Pts
Caps: 41 (W:33, L:8). As captain: 6 (W:2, L:4)
Scoring: 25T, 125 Pts. Discipline - Sin bins: 1
Appearances: 2001:It(r),S(r),F(r),I,A,R,SA, 2002:S,I,F,It,NZ,A,SA, 2003:F,W,S,I,NZ,A,F,Geo,SA,Sm,U(r),W,F,A, 2004:It,S,I,W,F,C*,SA*,A*, 2005:W*,F*,I*, 2007:S,It
Honours: RWC Winner: 2003. Outright Championship: 2001, 2003

When Rugby union turned professional in 1995 it was inevitable that players would join the 15-a-side code from rugby league.

Many came but few succeeded, the biggest success being the former Wigan legend, Jason Robinson.

A devastating finisher, Robinson was England's only try scorer in the 2003 World Cup Final, cancelling out Lote Tuqiri's opener for the Australians. But that wasn't Robinson's only record in the union game as he became the first former rugby league player to captain England.

Robinson was also the first black player to lead England and coach Andy Robinson who handed him the honour said: "Jason is an outstanding member of the England team who has led by example for the three years he has been playing international rugby union.

"He has an exceptional record not only in this sport but also in rugby league, earning him the respect of the whole squad.

"Jason touched hearts with the way he played and that goes for the players and coaches as well as the spectators.

Jason Robinson

Andy Robinson

"He set England alight on the training pitch as well as in the games."

Born in Leeds, Robinson had a record-breaking career in rugby league with the all-conquering Wigan side. Nicknamed Billy Whizz he was an integral member of the Great Britain rugby league side, completing a rare double when he played for union's British and Irish Lions in 2001, before he made a start for England!

He played in 296 league games, scoring 171 tries for Wigan before making a temporary switch in 1996, in a loan deal at Bath. The move to union became permanent in 2000 when he signed for Sale Sharks.

In 2005 he made his second Lions tour – to New Zealand – but retired from international rugby in September of that year, a season in which he led Sale to the first English title in their history.

Robinson was coaxed out of retirement in 2007 by new England coach Brian Ashton, scoring two tries in his first game back, against Scotland.

"Jason knows what it takes to be at the top of the world game in professional sport," said Ashton.

"Apart from being a fantastic rugby player, he has outstanding values as a person which will be important to the England team in the coming year."

Robinson's sojourn into the England team didn't last long though as at the end of the 2006-07 season he announced his retirement from the club game, only with the intention to play for England until the end of the 2007 World Cup.

In typical Robinson style he celebrated his final game for Sale with a try 10 seconds from the end of their final game of the season – against Bath – to win the match!

Following this he was named by Ashton as captain of England's summer tour to South Africa.

John James ROBINSON

Born: 28 June 1872 in Burton-upon-Trent
Died: 3 January 1959 in Headingley, Leeds
Educated: Appleby GS
Clubs: Cambridge University (1), Headingley (3), Burton
Position: Forward (4)
Debut: 4 Mar 1893 v Scotland (Headingley). Number: 258
Last game: 15 Mar 1902 v Scotland (Inverleith)
Caps: 4 (W:2, L:2)
Scoring: 1T, 3 Pts
Appearances: 1893:S, 1902:W,I,S

Richard Andrew (Andy) ROBINSON, OBE

Born: 3 April 1964 in Taunton
Educated: Richard Huish School
Clubs: Loughborough College, Taunton, Bath (8)
Position: Flanker (8), Bench (2)
Debut: 12 Jun 1988 v Australia (Sydney). Number: 1127
Last game: 18 Nov 1995 v South Africa (Twickenham)
Caps: 8 (W:4, D:1, L:3)
Scoring: 1T, 4 Pts
Appearances: 1988:A2,Fj,A, 1989:S,I,F,W, 1995:SA

Andy Robinson completed a rare double in 2004, joining an elite band of people to play for England and then go on to be in sole charge of coaching them.

Robinson's reign as forwards coach under Sir Clive Woodward was however far more successful than his two-year reign as head coach.

With Woodward in charge and Robinson – who won eight caps as a player – as his second in command, England won the 2003 Grand Slam and the World Cup.

But when Woodward – and a number of key England players – left in the wake of the World Cup win, Robinson struggled, losing 13 of the 22 games in which he was in sole charge.

The absence of players like Martin Johnson, Jonny Wilkinson, Neil Back, Jason Leonard and Will Greenwood certainly hampered Robinson and made comparisons with Woodward's time in charge invidious.

Robinson's exit from the role as head coach followed a desperate 2006 when he lost seven games on the trot, including a defeat at Twickenham to Argentina.

The former Bath flanker enjoyed sensational success as a club player leading Bath to a league and cup double in his first season as captain, in 1992.

He made his England debut – as a player – in 1988 and was selected for the 1989 British and Irish Lions tour of Australia, failing to make the Test team.

Ironically he took over as Bath coach in 1997 when Brian Ashton resigned; the same man replacing him as England coach almost 10 years later.

Unlike with England, Robinson made an immediate impact as Bath coach lifting the Heineken Cup in 1998.

Two years after coaching Bath to Europe's biggest crown he was taken by Woodward into the England set-up where he was named forwards coach, becoming one of the key figures in England's success in the subsequent years.

Robinson was also an assistant coach on both the 2001 and 2005 Lions tours.

"Robbo is passionate and emotional about the game but tactically and technically there is no-one to rival him in this country," said his former Bath colleague Jon Callard.

"He is the guy at the coal-face and that in-depth knowledge is invaluable.

"What Robbo did at Bath was a revelation. He brought a technical dimension that was missing from the previous coaches."

Robinson couldn't bring the same success to England though and was axed as England slipped from first in the world in 2003 to seventh by the end of 2006.

New elite rugby director Rob Andrew said: "Andy played a significant part in England's Grand Slam, unbeaten tour to Australia and New Zealand and RWC success in 2003.

"He also recorded excellent wins against Australia, South Africa and Wales during his tenure as head coach and was always totally committed to the role."

Alan ROBSON

Born: Details unknown
Died: Details unknown
Clubs: Northern (5)
Position: Hooker (5)
Debut: 19 Jan 1924 v Wales (Swansea). Number: 589
Last game: 16 Jan 1926 v Wales (Cardiff)
Caps: 5 (W:4, D:1, L:0)
Scoring: 0 Pts
Appearances: 1924:W,I,F,S, 1926:W
Honours: Grand Slam: 1924

Matthew ROBSON

Born: 16 December 1908 in Bellingham
Died: 30 November 1983 in Edinburgh, Scotland
Educated: George Heriot's School
Clubs: Oxford University (4), Heriot's FP, Blackheath
Position: Centre (4)
Debut: 18 Jan 1930 v Wales (Cardiff). Number: 660
Last game: 15 Mar 1930 v Scotland (Twickenham)
Caps: 4 (W:2, D:1, L:1)
Scoring: 1T, 3 Pts
Appearances: 1930:W,I,F,S
Honours: Championship: 1930

Timothy Andrew Keith (Tim) RODBER

Born: 2 July 1969 in Richmond, Yorks
Educated: Churcher's School, Oxford Poly
Clubs: Oxford Old Boys, Petersfield, Green Howards, Army, Northampton (44)
Position: Flanker (22), Lock (7), No 8 (7), Replacement (8), Bench (8)
Debut: 18 Jan 1992 v Scotland (Murrayfield). Number: 1143
Last game: 20 Oct 1999 (rep) v Fiji (Twickenham)
Caps: 44 (W:33, L:11)
Scoring: 5T, 25 Pts
Appearances: 1992:S,I, 1993:NZ, 1994:I,F,W,SA1,SA2,R,C, 1995:I,F,W,S,Ar,It,Sm(r),A,NZ,F,SA,Sm, 1996:W,S(r),I(r),It,Ar, 1997:S,I,F,W,A, 1998:H(r),It(r),A,SA, 1999:S,I,F,W,A,US(r),NZ(r),Fj(r)
Honours: Grand Slam: 1995. Championship: 1992, 1996

Tim Rodber

England profited during the 1990s from a surplus of talented forwards and the Green Howards army officer, Tim Rodber, began his England career at No 8, before the arrival of Lawrence Dallaglio. Moving to blindside flanker, he played a key role in the 1995 Grand Slam and World Cup season.

Rodber joined Northampton Saints where he would remain for the entirety of his career, and made his England debut five years later in the 1992 Five Nations contest with Scotland.

A powerful player with quick hands, he played alongside Matt Dawson and Dallaglio in England's triumph at the 1993 World Cup 7s, and was an ever-present for England throughout 1994, playing 12 games. He did however manage to get himself sent off for fighting against Eastern Province during the tour to South Africa, only the second England player to ever claim this dubious honour.

He claims this was officially his worst moment in rugby.

After his pivotal work in the 1995 Grand Slam season, and along England's route to a World Cup semi-final, he was unlucky to be in and out of the team the following year, more through an erratic selection policy than any loss of form. British Army officers are made of stern stuff though, and he bounced back to play in every Five Nations game of 1997, and earned two caps for the British and Irish Lions as they beat South Africa.

Injury blighted his chances under Clive Woodward, missing his first 12 games, but he returned to England action for one last Five Nations in 1999, where he shouldered up alongside Martin Johnson to considerable effect. He signed off with one last showdown with the Welsh.

He was Saints captain from 1994-99, under Ian McGeechan's management, without great success, but ended his career on a high in 2000.

Having experienced the bitter taste of defeat two weeks earlier in the Tetley's Bitter Cup final, losing to Wasps, there was a sting in the season's tail.

In front of 64,000 people at Twickenham, and a world-wide audience of 60 million, he helped his injured captain, Pat Lam, lift the Heineken Cup, as Northampton beat Munster 9-8 in a nail-biting finale.He retired at the end of the following season.

Derek Prior (Budge) ROGERS, OBE

Born: 20 June 1939 in Bedford
Educated: Bedford School
Clubs: City University, Bedford (34)
Position: Flanker (34)
Debut: 11 Feb 1961 v Ireland (Lansdowne Road) - 1T, 3 Pts. Number: 898
Last game: 12 Apr 1969 (capt) v Wales (Cardiff)
Caps: 34 (W:10, D:6, L:18). As captain: 7 (W:2, D:1, L:4)
Scoring: 3T, 9 Pts
Appearances: 1961:I,F,S, 1962:W,I,F, 1963:W,I,F,S,NZ1,NZ2,A, 1964:NZ,W,I,F,S, 1965:W,I,F,S, 1966:W*,I*,F*,S*, 1967:A,S,W,NZ, 1969:I,F*,S*,W*
Honours: Championship: 1963

Budge Rogers

Budge Rogers was a tireless flanker who broke into the England side in 1962 against Ireland in Dublin and when he finished his international career he had won 34 caps, a record at the time. When he made his 31st appearance he equalled the previous record which was established by the legendary Lord Wakefield of Kendal in 1927.

Rogers first made an impact as a player at Bedford School and was a natural to join the Bedford club which enjoyed one of its most successful periods during the 1960s when Rogers was a fast rising back-row forward. Rogers won an England squad place for the first time in 1961 and toured South Africa with the British and Irish Lions the following year.

His team-mate David Perry also played alongside him for England and captained the side in 1965. Rogers took over as England captain in 1966 but three defeats and a draw against Ireland sent the side to the bottom of the championship table. England failed to score in Paris where Rogers was one of three players affected by injury.

Rogers maintained a high level of consistency in his performances, no matter where he played, and was always on or near the ball. He trained hard, recognising that fitness was a great factor in his position. Apart from his contribution to Bedford and England he also captained the Barbarians and in 1966-67 led East Midlands in the county championship.

At the start of the Seventies Bedford were judged the best side in England and Wales. In 1975, captained by Rogers, they beat Rosslyn Park 28-12 in the final of the English club knock-out competition before a gate of more than 17,000 at Twickenham.

Rogers always looked destined to have a considerable part in rugby once he gave up playing. He managed the England under-23 squad to Canada in 1977. Next he led an England tour to the Far East, with two Tests in Japan and two more in Colombo.

Rogers moved on to become chairman of the England selectors and finally he had the highest office in the English game when he became president of the Rugby Football Union. He was awarded an OBE for his services to rugby.

John Henry ROGERS

Born: First quarter 1867 in Aston
Died: 30 March 1922 in Birmingham
Educated: Bromsgrove School
Clubs: Moseley Woodstock, Moseley (4)
Position: Forward (4)
Debut: 15 Feb 1890 v Wales (Dewsbury). Number: 213
Last game: 7 Mar 1891 v Scotland (Richmond)
Caps: 4 (W:2, L:2)
Scoring: 1T, 1 Pt
Appearances: 1890:W,S,I, 1891:S

Walter Lacy Yea ROGERS

Born: 20 September 1878 in Pewsey, Wilts
Died: 10 February 1948 in Kensington
Educated: Rugby School
Clubs: Oxford University, Royal Artillery, Army, Blackheath (2)
Position: Forward (2)
Debut: 14 Jan 1905 v Wales (Cardiff). Number: 405
Last game: 11 Feb 1905 v Ireland (Cork)
Caps: 2 (W:0, L:2)
Scoring: 0 Pts
Appearances: 1905:W,I

David Malcolm ROLLITT

Born: 24 March 1943 in Wombwell, Barnsley
Educated: Barnsley GS
Clubs: Bristol University, Loughborough College, UAU, Bristol (11), Wakefield, Richmond
Position: No 8 (6), Flanker (5), Bench (1)
Debut: 11 Feb 1967 v Ireland (Lansdowne Road).Number: 957
Last game: 31 May 1975 v Australia (Brisbane)
Caps: 11 (W:5, L:6)
Scoring: 1T, 3 Pts
Appearances: 1967:I,F,S,W, 1969:I,F,S,W, 1975:S,A1,A2

Anthony Dominic Sebastian RONCORONI

Born: 16 March 1909 in Hendon
Died: 20 July 1953 in Bognor Regis
Educated: Rossall School
Clubs: West Herts (3), Richmond
Position: Lock (3)
Debut: 21 Jan 1933 v Wales (Twickenham). Number: 700
Last game: 18 Mar 1933 v Scotland (Murrayfield)
Caps: 3 (W:1, L:2)
Scoring: 0 Pts
Appearances: 1933:W,I,S

William Marcus Henderson (Marcus) ROSE

Born: 12 January 1957 in Loughborough
Educated: Loughborough GS
Clubs: Durham University, Leicester, Cambridge University (5), Coventry, Harlequins (5)
Position: Full-back (10), Bench (5)
Debut: 7 Mar 1981 v Ireland (Lansdowne Road) - 1T, 1C, 6 Pts. Number: 1068
Last game: 23 May 1987 v Australia (Sydney)
Caps: 10 (W:3, D:1, L:6)
Scoring: 2T, 4C, 22PG, 82 Pts
Appearances: 1981:I,F, 1982:A,S,I, 1987:I,F,W,S,A

Marcus Rose

Peter Alec ROSSBOROUGH

Born: 30 June 1948 in Coventry
Educated: King Henry VIII School
Clubs: Durham University, UAU, British University, Coventry (7)
Position: Full-back (7), Bench (1)
Debut: 16 Jan 1971 v Wales (Cardiff) - 1PG, 3 Pts. Number: 995
Last game: 1 Feb 1975 v France (Twickenham) - 1T, 4PG, 16 Pts
Caps: 7 (W:2, L:5)
Scoring: 1T, 3C, 7PG, 1DG, 34 Pts
Appearances: 1971:W, 1973:NZ,A, 1974:S,I, 1975:I,F

David William Albert ROSSER

Born: 27 March 1938 in Portsmouth
Educated: Rochdale GS
Clubs: Cambridge University (4), Manchester, Army, Wasps (1), London Welsh
Position: Centre (5)
Debut: 16 Jan 1965 v Wales (Cardiff). Number: 930
Last game: 15 Jan 1966 v Wales (Twickenham)
Caps: 5 (W:1, D:1, L:3)
Scoring: 0 Pts
Appearances: 1965:W,I,F,S, 1966:W

Alan ROTHERHAM

Born: 31 July 1862
Died: 30 August 1898 in Marylebone
Educated: Uppingham School
Clubs: Oxford University (6), Coventry, Richmond (6)
Position: Half-Back (12)
Debut: 16 Dec 1882 v Wales (Swansea). Number: 152
Last game: 5 Mar 1887 (capt) v Scotland (Manchester)
Caps: 12 (W:8, D:3, L:1). As captain: 3 (W:0, D:2, L:1)
Scoring: 2T, 2 Pts
Appearances: 1883:W,S, 1884:W,S, 1885:W,I, 1886:W,I,S, 1887:W*,I*,S*
Honours: Championship: 1883, 1884

Arthur ROTHERHAM

Born: 27 May 1869 in Coventry
Died: 3 March 1946 in Hambledon, Surrey
Educated: Uppingham School
Clubs: Cambridge University, St Thomas's Hospital, Middlesex Wanderers, Richmond (5), Coventry
Position: Scrum-half (5)
Debut: 12 Mar 1898 v Scotland (Edinburgh). Number: 320
Last game: 11 Mar 1899 (capt) v Scotland (Blackheath)
Caps: 5 (W:1, D:1, L:3). As captain: 3 (W:0, L:3)
Scoring: 0 Pts
Appearances: 1898:S,W, 1899:W*,I*,S*

David F K ROUGHLEY

Born: 10 December 1946 in Warrington
Educated: Beaumont Street School
Clubs: Liverpool (3)
Position: Centre (3), Bench (1)
Debut: 17 Nov 1973 v Australia (Twickenham). Number: 1022
Last game: 16 Feb 1974 v Ireland (Twickenham)
Caps: 3 (W:1, L:2)
Scoring: 0 Pts
Appearances: 1973:A, 1974:S,I

Robert Errington (Bob) ROWELL

Born: 29 August 1939 in Lorbridge
Educated: Wymondham College
Clubs: Hull University, Loughborough College, Leicester (2), Fylde, Waterloo
Position: Lock (2)
Debut: 18 Jan 1964 v Wales (Twickenham). Number: 922
Last game: 16 Jan 1965 v Wales (Cardiff)
Caps: 2 (W:0, D:1, L:1)
Scoring: 0 Pts
Appearances: 1964:W, 1965:W

Arthur James ROWLEY

Born: 1908 in Coventry
Died: 11 April 1995
Clubs: Coventry (1)
Position: No 8 (1)
Debut: 2 Jan 1932 v South Africa (Twickenham). Number: 689
Caps: 1 (W:0, L:1)
Scoring: 0 Pts
Appearances: 1932:SA

Hugh Campbell ROWLEY

Born: March 1854 in Charlton
Died: Details unknown
Educated: Manchester GS
Clubs: Bowdon & Lymm, Manchester (9)
Position: Forward (7), Half-Back (2)
Debut: 10 Mar 1879 v Scotland (Raeburn Place). Number: 114
Last game: 4 Mar 1882 v Scotland (Manchester)
Caps: 9 (W:5, D:3, L:1)
Scoring: 3T, 3 Pts
Appearances: 1879:S,I, 1880:I,S, 1881:I,W,S, 1882:I,S

Graham Rowntree

Christopher Graham (Graham) ROWNTREE

Born: 18 April 1971 in Stockton-on-Tees
Educated: John Cleveland College
Clubs: Nuneaton, Leicester (54)
Position: Prop (47), Replacement (7), Bench (25)
Debut: 18 Mar 1995 (rep) v Scotland (Twickenham). Number: 1156
Last game: 17 Jun 2006 v Australia (Melbourne)
Caps: 54 (W:38, L:16)
Scoring: 0 Pts
Appearances: 1995:S(r),It,Sm,Sm, 1996:F,W,S,I,It,Ar, 1997:S,I,F,W,A, 1998:A,NZ1,NZ2,SA,H(r),It(r), 1999:US,C,It(r),Tg,Fj(r), 2001:C1,C2,US,I(r),A,R,SA, 2002:S,I,F,W,It, 2003:F(r),W,It,S,I,NZ,F, 2004:C,SA,A, 2005:W,F,I,It, 2006:A1,A2
Honours: Grand Slam: 2003. Championship: 1995, 1996, 2001

How Graham Rowntree missed out on being a World Cup winner only England coach Sir Clive Woodward will know,

Graham Rowntree

but he can count himself as the unluckiest player in the land when it came to selection for the 30-man squad that finally lifted the Webb Ellis Cup in 2003.

A legend at the Leicester Tigers, winning the European Cup in 2001 against Stade Francais will always be one of his favourite memories, along with the 15-13 defeat of New Zealand in Wellington in 2003.

Rowntree's role in that pivotal win in New Zealand – England's first since 1973 – is often forgotten. England's scrum was reduced to six men after the sin-binning of Lawrence Dallagio and Neil Back but Rowntree was a key reason why they held firm in the face of adversity, making Woodward's decision to leave him at home for the World Cup, only two months later, all the more inexplicable.

One of the game's gentlemen off the pitch he made his England debut as a replacement for Jason Leonard against Scotland in the 1995 Grand Slam season.

Despite his heartache in missing out in 2003, Rowntree refused to go quietly from the England scene. Even after his 2003 World Cup disappointment he kept coming back, winning the last of his caps on England's 2006 trip to Australia, where they lost both games.

Rowntree went on British and Irish Lions tours in 1997 and 2005, winning his first cap in the second Test of his second tour to New Zealand.

Rowntree was a member of the famous ABC Club at Leicester, along with Richard Cockerill and Darren Garforth.

The club was so called after the letters worn on the players' backs, a tradition at Leicester until the English Premiership outlawed it.

He joined the Leicester Tigers aged just 16 from Nuneaton, appearing for England at Under-16 and Under-18, before going on to enjoy a glittering career.

His Leicester honours were numerous, starting with the 1993 cup final, where he was the youngest player in the side.

After that final appearance he was part of five English championship-winning sides, three domestic cup finals and three Heineken Cup finals.

An amateur player in the days of his first final he worked as an insurance broker before becoming a professional rugby player.

Rowntree captained his beloved Tigers on his 398th and last game in their colours in 2007 when they played Argentina in a friendly at Welford Road, before starting life as the club's assistant forwards coach.

He also became only the second player from any club to make 200 appearances in the English top division and was the first Leicester player to receive the ERC Elite award for appearing in 50 Heineken Cup games.

Sir Percy Molyneux Rawson ROYDS, KBE

Born: Second quarter 1874 in Rochdale
Died: 25 March 1955 in Marylebone
Educated: Eastmans Naval School
Clubs: RNC Greenwich, United Services, Royal Navy, Blackheath (3)
Position: Centre (3)
Debut: 12 Mar 1898 v Scotland (Edinburgh) - 1T, 3 Pts.
Number: 321
Last game: 7 Jan 1899 v Wales (Swansea)
Caps: 3 (W:1, D:1, L:1)
Scoring: 1T, 3 Pts
Appearances: 1898:S,W, 1899:W

Dean Ryan

Peter Ryan

A V (Artie) ROYLE
Born: Details unknown
Died: Details unknown
Clubs: Broughton Rangers (1)
Position: Full-back (1)
Debut: 16 Feb 1889 v New Zealand Natives (Blackheath). Number: 204
Caps: 1 (W:1, L:0)
Scoring: 0 Pts
Appearances: 1889:M

Edward Lawrence (Ted) RUDD
Born: 28 September 1944 in Aigburth, Liverpool
Educated: St Edward's College
Clubs: Oxford University (3), Liverpool (3)
Position: Wing (6)
Debut: 16 Jan 1965 v Wales (Cardiff). Number: 931
Last game: 19 Mar 1966 v Scotland (Murrayfield)
Caps: 6 (W:0, D:2, L:4)
Scoring: 0 Pts
Appearances: 1965:W,I,S, 1966:W,I,S

Richard Forbes RUSSELL
Born: 5 April 1879 in Bingham
Died: 30 May 1960 in Lezayre, Isle of Man
Educated: St Peter's School
Clubs: Cambridge University, Leicester (1), Castleford, Cork
Position: Forward (1)
Debut: 2 Dec 1905 v New Zealand (Crystal Palace). Number: 419
Caps: 1 (W:0, L:1)
Scoring: 0 Pts
Appearances: 1905:NZ

Donald (Don) RUTHERFORD
Born: 22 September 1937 in Tynemouth
Educated: Tynemouth HS, St Luke's College
Clubs: Percy Park (5), Preston Grasshoppers, Wasps, Gloucester (9)
Position: Full-back (14)
Debut: 16 Jan 1960 v Wales (Twickenham) - 1C, 2PG, 8 Pts. Number: 890
Last game: 4 Nov 1967 v New Zealand (Twickenham) - 1C, 2 Pts
Caps: 14 (W:4, D:3, L:7)
Scoring: 6C, 8PG, 36 Pts
Appearances: 1960:W,I,F,S, 1961:SA, 1965:W,I,F,S, 1966:W,I,F,S, 1967:NZ

Henry John RYALLS
Born: 12 December 1858 in Wirral
Died: 17 October 1949 in Birkenhead
Educated: Birkenhead Institute
Clubs: New Brighton (2)
Position: Forward (2)
Debut: 3 Jan 1885 v Wales (Swansea) - 1T, 1 Pt. Number: 173
Last game: 7 Feb 1885 v Ireland (Manchester)
Caps: 2 (W:2, L:0)
Scoring: 1T, 1 Pt
Appearances: 1885:W,I

Dean RYAN
Born: 22 June 1966 in Tuxford
Clubs: Newark, Saracens, Wasps (3), Newcastle (1), Bristol
Position: No 8 (3), Flanker (1), Bench (2)
Debut: 28 Jul 1990 v Argentina (Buenos Aires) - 1T, 4 Pts. Number: 1140
Last game: 22 Mar 1998 v Scotland (Murrayfield)
Caps: 4 (W:3, L:1)
Scoring: 1T, 4 Pts
Appearances: 1990:Ar1,Ar2, 1992:C, 1998:S

Peter Henry RYAN
Born: 1 October 1930 in Bucklow
Educated: Harrow School
Clubs: Cambridge University, Richmond (2)
Position: Flanker (2)
Debut: 22 Jan 1955 v Wales (Cardiff). Number: 853
Last game: 12 Feb 1955 v Ireland (Lansdowne Road)
Caps: 2 (W:0, D:1, L:1)
Scoring: 0 Pts
Appearances: 1955:W,I

Tim Stimpson

S

SACKEY, Paul Henry
SADLER, Edward Harry
SAGAR, John Warburton
SALMON, James Lionel Broome
SAMPLE, Charles Hubert, OBE
SAMPSON, Paul Christian
SANDERS, Donald Louis G
SANDERS, Frank Warren
SANDERSON, Alexander
SANDERSON, Patrick Harold
SANDFORD, Joseph Ruscombe Poole
SANGWIN, Roger Dennis
SARGENT, Gordon Alan Frank
SAVAGE, Keith Frederick
SAWYER, Charles Montague
SAXBY, Leslie Eric
SCARBROUGH, Daniel Graham R
SCHOFIELD, John Wood
SCHOLFIELD, John Arthur
SCHWARZ, Reginald Oscar
SCORFIELD, Edward Scafe
SCOTT, Charles Tillard
SCOTT, Edward Keith
SCOTT, Frank Sholl
SCOTT, Harry
SCOTT, John Phillip
SCOTT, John Stanley Marshall
SCOTT, Mason Thompson
SCOTT, William Martin
SEDDON, Robert L
SELLAR, Kenneth Anderson
SEVER, Harry Sedgwick
SHACKLETON, Ian Roger
SHARP, Richard Adrian William, OBE
SHAW, Cecil Hamilton
SHAW, Frederick
SHAW, James Fraser
SHAW, Simon Dalton, MBE
SHEASBY, Christopher Mark Andrew
SHEPPARD, Austin
SHERIDAN, Andrew John
SHERRARD, Charles William
SHERRIFF, George Albert
SHEWRING, Harry Edward
SHOOTER, John Henry
SHUTTLEWORTH, Dennis William, OBE
SIBREE, Herbert John Hyde
SILK, Nicholas
SIMMS, Kevin Gerard
SIMPSON, Colin Peter
SIMPSON, Paul Donald
SIMPSON, Thomas
SIMPSON-DANIEL, James David
SIMS, David
SKINNER, Michael Gordon
SLADEN, Geoffrey Mainwaring
SLEIGHTHOLME, Jonathan Mark
SLEMEN, Michael Anthony Charles
SLOCOCK, Lancelot Andrew Noel
SLOW, Charles Frederick
SMALL, Harold Dudley
SMALLWOOD, Alastair McNaughton
SMART, Colin Edward
SMART, Sidney Edward John
SMEDDLE, Robert William
SMITH, Charles Albert
SMITH, Dyne Fenton
SMITH, Gerald Walter Gordon
SMITH, John Vincent
SMITH, Keith
SMITH, Michael John Knight, OBE
SMITH, Oliver James
SMITH, Ronald Cove
SMITH, Simon Timothy
SMITH, Stephen James
SMITH, Stephen Rider
SMITH, Trellevyn Harvey
SOANE, Frank
SOBEY, Wilfred Henry
SOLOMON, Bertie
SPARKS, Robert Henry Ware
SPEED, Henry
SPENCE, William Frederick
SPENCER, Jeremy
SPENCER, John Sothern
SPONG, Roger Spencer
SPOONER, Reginald Herbert
SPRINGMANN, Herman Heinrich
SPURLING, Aubrey
SPURLING, Norman
SQUIRES, Peter John
STAFFORD, Richard Calvert
STAFFORD, William Francis Howard
STANBURY, Edward
STANDING, G
STANGER-LEATHES, Christopher Francis
STARK, Kendrick James
STARKS, Anthony
STARMER-SMITH, Nigel Christopher
START, Sydney Philp
STEEDS, John Harold
STEELE-BODGER, Michael Roland, CBE
STEINTHAL, Francis Eric
STEPHENSON, Michael
STEVENS, Claude Brian
STEVENS, Matthew J H
STILL, Ernest Robert
STIMPSON, Tim Richard George
STIRLING, Robert Victor
STODDART, Andrew Ernest
STODDART, Wilfred Bowring
STOKES, Frederic
STOKES, Lennard
STONE, Francis le Strange
STOOP, Adrian Dura
STOOP, Frederick MacFarlane
STOUT, Frank Moxon
STOUT, Percy Wyfold, OBE
STRETTLE, David
STRINGER, Nicholas Courtenay
STRONG, Edward Linwood
STURNHAM, Ben
SUMMERSCALE, George Edward
SUTCLIFFE, John William
SWARBRICK, David William
SWAYNE, Deneys Harald
SWAYNE, John Walter Rocke
SWIFT, Anthony Hugh
SYDDALL, James Paul
SYKES, Alexander Richard V
SYKES, Frank Douglas
SYKES, Patrick William
SYRETT, Ronald Edward

Paul Sackey

Paul Henry SACKEY
Born: 8 November 1979 in London
Educated: John Fisher School
Clubs: Bedford, London Irish, Wasps (2)
Position: Wing (2)
Debut: 5 Nov 2006 v New Zealand (Twickenham). Number: 1276
Last game: 11 Nov 2006 v Argentina (Twickenham) - 1T, 5 Pts
Caps: 2 (W:0, L:2)
Scoring: 1T, 5 Pts
Appearances: 2006:NZ,Ar

Edward Harry SADLER
Born: 8 May 1910 in Colchester
Died: 26 December 1992 in Surbiton
Clubs: Royal Signals, Army (2), Oldham RL
Position: Flanker (2)
Debut: 11 Feb 1933 v Ireland (Twickenham) - 1T, 3 Pts. Number: 701
Last game: 18 Mar 1933 v Scotland (Murrayfield)
Caps: 2 (W:1, L:1)
Scoring: 1T, 3 Pts
Appearances: 1933:I,S

Jamie Salmon

John Warburton SAGAR
Born: 6 December 1878 in Easington
Died: 10 January 1941 in Bournemouth
Educated: Durham School
Clubs: Cambridge University (2), Castleford
Position: Full-back (2)
Debut: 5 Jan 1901 v Wales (Cardiff). Number: 361
Last game: 9 Feb 1901 v Ireland (Lansdowne Road)
Caps: 2 (W:0, L:2)
Scoring: 0 Pts
Appearances: 1901:W,I

James Lionel Broome (Jamie) SALMON
Born: 16 October 1959 in Hong Kong
Educated: Wellington College
Clubs: Wellington College, Blackheath, Wellington (NZ), Harlequins (12)
Position: Centre (12)
Debut: 1 Jun 1985 v New Zealand (Christchurch). Number: 1110
Last game: 8 Jun 1987 v Wales (Brisbane)
Caps: 12 (W:4, L:8)
Scoring: 1T, 4 Pts
Appearances: 1985:NZ1,NZ2, 1986:W,S, 1987:I,F,W,S,A,J,US,W

The only man to play international rugby for both England and New Zealand, Jamie Salmon holds a record that can no longer be equalled.

Hong Kong-born Salmon emigrated to New Zealand, played for Wellington and was capped three times for the All Blacks in 1981, before heading to England and wearing the Red Rose 12 times, including appearances in the 1987 World Cup.

But the International Rugby Board outlawed anyone from matching Salmon, ruling that players can now only play for one country, at Test level, in their careers.

"Obviously an unhealthy situation had developed," Salmon said. "In my day the switches were few and far between but people were desperately searching around for grandparents so they can qualify for another country.

"Argentina have had a particular problem with losing players to Italy. I think the new rules are pretty reasonable and will help the South Sea Islanders particularly."

Once back in England, Salmon carved out a career with Harlequins on the field as a centre and off it as the club's manager before starting a career in the media that saw him on ITV's commentary team at the World Cup.

Paul Sampson

Charles Hubert SAMPLE, OBE

Born: 22 November 1862 in Castle Ward
Died: 2 June 1938 in Corbridge
Educated: Edinburgh Academy
Clubs: Cambridge University (3)
Position: Full-back (3)
Debut: 4 Feb 1884 v Ireland (Lansdowne Road) - 1C, 2 Pts. Number: 165
Last game: 13 Mar 1886 v Scotland (Raeburn Place)
Caps: 3 (W:2, D:1, L:0)
Scoring: 1C, 2 Pts
Appearances: 1884:I, 1885:I, 1886:S
Honours: Championship: 1884

Paul Christian SAMPSON

Born: 12 July 1977 in Wakefield
Educated: Woodhouse Grove School
Clubs: Wasps (3), Bath, Worcester, Blackheath, London Welsh
Position: Wing (3)
Debut: 4 Jul 1998 v South Africa (Cape Town).Number: 1208
Last game: 9 Jun 2001 v Canada (Burnaby)
Caps: 3 (W:2, L:1)
Scoring: 0 Pts
Appearances: 1998:SA, 2001:C1,C2

Donald Louis G (Sandy) SANDERS

Born: 6 September 1924 in Fulham
Clubs: Ipswich YMCA, Harlequins (9)
Position: Prop (9)
Debut: 16 Jan 1954 v Wales (Twickenham). Number: 841
Last game: 14 Apr 1956 v France (Stade Colombes)
Caps: 9 (W:5, L:4)
Scoring: 0 Pts
Appearances: 1954:W,NZ,I,S,F, 1956:W,I,S,F

Frank Warren SANDERS

Born: 24 January 1893 in Newton Abbot
Died: 22 June 1953 in Plymouth
Clubs: Plymouth Albion (3)
Position: Hooker (3)
Debut: 10 Feb 1923 v Ireland (Leicester). Number: 583
Last game: 2 Apr 1923 v France (Stade Colombes)
Caps: 3 (W:3, L:0)
Scoring: 0 Pts
Appearances: 1923:I,S,F
Honours: Championship: 1923

Alex Sanderson

Pat Sanderson

Alexander (Alex) SANDERSON
Born: 7 October 1979 in Chester
Educated: Kirkham GS
Clubs: Sale (5), Saracens
Position: Flanker (1), No 8 (1), Replacement (3), Bench (1)
Debut: 17 Nov 2001 (rep) v Romania (Twickenham) - 1T, 5 Pts. Number: 1235
Last game: 30 Aug 2003 v France (Marseille)
Caps: 5 (W:4, L:1)
Scoring: 1T, 5 Pts
Appearances: 2001:R(r), 2002:Ar, 2003:It(r),W(r),F
Honours: Championship: 2003

Patrick Harold (Pat) SANDERSON
Born: 6 September 1977 in Chester
Educated: Kirkham GS, Bury GS
Clubs: Littleborough, Sale (3), Harlequins (3), Worcester (9)
Position: Flanker (8), No 8 (4), Replacement (3)
Debut: 20 Jun 1998 v New Zealand (Dunedin). Number: 1203
Last game: 25 Nov 2006 v South Africa (Twickenham)
Caps: 15 (W:6, L:9). As captain: 2 (W:0, L:2)
Scoring: 1T, 5 Pts
Appearances: 1998:NZ1,NZ2,SA, 2001:C1(r),C2(r),US(r), 2005:A,NZ,Sm, 2006:A1*,A2*,NZ,Ar,SA1,SA2

Joseph Ruscombe Poole SANDFORD
Born: 5 March 1881
Died: 29 July 1916 in Khartoum, Sudan
Educated: All Hallows School, Marlborough College
Clubs: Oxford University, Marlborough Nomads (1)
Position: Centre (1)
Debut: 10 Feb 1906 v Ireland (Leicester). Number: 430
Caps: 1 (W:0, L:1)
Scoring: 0 Pts
Appearances: 1906:I

Roger Dennis SANGWIN
Born: 2 December 1937 in Holderness
Educated: Sedbergh School
Clubs: Hull & ER (2)
Position: Centre (2
Debut: 4 Jan 1964 v New Zealand (Twickenham). Number: 920
Last game: 18 Jan 1964 v Wales (Twickenham)
Caps: 2 (W:0, D:1, L:1)
Scoring: 0 Pts
Appearances: 1964:NZ,W

Gordon Alan Frank SARGENT
Born: 18 October 1949 in Gloucester
Educated: Lydney GS
Clubs: Gloucester (1)
Position: Replacement Prop (1), Bench (5)
Debut: 7 Mar 1981 (rep) v Ireland (Lansdowne Road). Number: 1069
Caps: 1 (W:1, L:0)
Scoring: 0 Pts
Appearances: 1981:I(r)

Keith Frederick SAVAGE
Born: 24 August 1940 in Warwick
Educated: Leamington College
Clubs: Loughborough College, Northampton (13), Harlequins
Position: Wing (13)
Debut: 15 Jan 1966 v Wales (Twickenham). Number: 939
Last game: 16 Mar 1968 v Scotland (Murrayfield)
Caps: 13 (W:3, D:2, L:8)
Scoring: 1T, 3 Pts
Appearances:1966:W,I,F,S, 1967:A,I,F,S,W,NZ, 1968:W,F,S

Dan Scarbrough

Charles Montague SAWYER
Born: 20 March 1856 in Rusholme, Manchester
Died: 30 March 1921 in Ormskirk, Lancs
Clubs: Broughton Wasps, Broughton (2)
Position: Three-quarter (2)
Debut: 28 Feb 1880 v Scotland (Manchester).Number: 131
Last game: 5 Feb 1881 v Ireland (Manchester) - 1T, 1 Pt
Caps: 2 (W:2, L:0)
Scoring: 1T, 1 Pt
Appearances: 1880:S, 1881:I

Leslie Eric SAXBY
Born: 19 May 1900 in Bradfield
Died: 26 August 1956 in High Flats, Natal, South Africa
Educated: Reading School
Clubs: Gloucester (2)
Position: Flanker (2)
Debut: 2 Jan 1932 v South Africa (Twickenham).
Number: 690
Last game: 16 Jan 1932 v Wales (Swansea)
Caps: 2 (W:0, L:2)
Scoring: 0 Pts
Appearances: 1932:SA,W

Daniel Graham R (Dan) SCARBROUGH
Born: 16 February 1978 in Bingley
Educated: Bradford GS
Clubs: Wakefield, Leeds (1), Saracens
Position: Full-back (1)
Debut: 23 Aug 2003 v Wales (Cardiff).
Number: 1249
Caps: 1 (W:1, L:0)
Scoring: 0 Pts
Appearances: 2003:W

John Wood SCHOFIELD
Born: Second quarter 1858 in Barton
Died: 3 May 1931 in Bucklow
Educated: Uppingham School
Clubs: Manchester Rangers (1)
Position: Forward (1)
Debut: 30 Jan 1880 v Ireland (Lansdowne Road).
Number: 126
Caps: 1 (W:1, L:0)
Scoring: 0 Pts
Appearances: 1880:I

John Arthur SCHOLFIELD
Born: 6 April 1888 in Fylde
Died: 14 September 1967 in Barnstaple
Educated: Sedbergh School
Clubs: Cambridge University (1), Manchester, Preston Grasshoppers, Harlequins
Position: Centre (1)
Debut: 21 Jan 1911 v Wales (Swansea) - 1T, 3 Pts.
Number: 515
Caps: 1 (W:0, L:1)
Scoring: 1T, 3 Pts
Appearances: 1911:W

Reginald Oscar SCHWARZ
Born: 4 May 1875 in Lee, Lewisham
Died: Killed in action in 1918 in Etaples, France
Educated: St Paul's School
Clubs: Cambridge University, Richmond (3)
Position: Fly-half (3)
Debut: 11 Mar 1899 v Scotland (Blackheath).
Number: 338
Last game: 9 Feb 1901 v Ireland (Lansdowne Road)
Caps: 3 (W:0, L:3)
Scoring: 0 Pts
Appearances: 1899:S, 1901:W,I

Edward Scafe SCORFIELD
Born: March/April 1882 in Tynemouth
Died: 1966 in Australia
Educated: RGS Newcastle
Clubs: Percy Park (1)
Position: Lock (1)
Debut: 3 Mar 1910 v France (Parc des Princes).
Number: 504
Caps: 1 (W:1, L:0)
Scoring: 0 Pts
Appearances: 1910:F
Honours: Championship: 1910

Charles Tillard SCOTT
Born: 26 August 1877 in Kingston
Died: 6 November 1965 in Market Harborough
Educated: Tonbridge School, Cheltenham College
Clubs: Cambridge University (2), London Hospital, Blackheath (2)
Position: Forward (4)
Debut: 6 Jan 1900 v Wales (Gloucester). Number: 350
Last game: 9 Feb 1901 v Ireland (Lansdowne Road)
Caps: 4 (W:1, L:3)
Scoring: 0 Pts
Appearances: 1900:W,I, 1901:W,I

Edward Keith SCOTT
Born: 14 June 1918 in Truro, Cornwall
Died: 3 June 1995 in Truro
Educated: Clifton College
Clubs: Oxford University, St Mary's Hospital (1), Redruth (4), Harlequins
Position: Centre (5)
Debut: 18 Jan 1947 v Wales (Cardiff). Number: 761
Last game: 20 Mar 1948 (capt) v Scotland (Murrayfield)
Caps: 5 (W:1, D:1, L:3). As captain: 3 (W:0, L:3)
Scoring: 0 Pts
Appearances: 1947:W, 1948:A*,W,I*,S*

Frank Sholl SCOTT

Born: 9 January 1886 in Perth, Australia
Died: 4 February 1952 in Truro
Educated: Epsom College
Clubs: Bristol (1), Gloucester
Position: Wing (1)
Debut: 12 Jan 1907 v Wales (Swansea). Number: 445
Caps: 1 (W:0, L:1)
Scoring: 0 Pts
Appearances: 1907:W

Harry SCOTT

Born: 7 November 1926 in Batley, Yorks
Educated: Stretford Junior Tech, Salford TC
Clubs: Eccles, United Services, Manchester (1)
Position: Full-back (1)
Debut: 26 Feb 1955 v France (Twickenham). Number: 856
Caps: 1 (W:0, L:1)
Scoring: 0 Pts
Appearances: 1955:F

John Phillip SCOTT

Born: 28 September 1954 in Exeter
Educated: Hele's School, St Luke's College
Clubs: Exeter, Rosslyn Park (4), Cardiff (30)
Position: No 8 (30), Lock (3), Replacement (1)
Debut: 21 Jan 1978 v France (Parc des Princes). Number: 1048
Last game: 9 Jun 1984 (capt) v South Africa (Johannesburg)
Caps: 34 (W:14, D:3, L:17). As captain: 4 (W:0, L:4)
Scoring: 1T, 4 Pts
Appearances: 1978:F,W,S,I,NZ, 1979:S(r),I,F,W,NZ, 1980:I,F,W,S, 1981:W,S,I,F,Ar1,Ar2, 1982:I,F,W, 1983:F,W,S*,I*,NZ, 1984:S,I,F,W,SA1*,SA2*
Honours: Grand Slam: 1980

John Scott managed to perform the difficult trick of being a popular English rugby player in Wales in the early 1980s thanks to his association with the Cardiff club which he captained to five Welsh Cup wins between 1981 and 1987. He still lives in the Principality and provides a trenchant rugby column for one of the region's papers, The South Wales Echo.

Scott, who could play at No 8 or in the second row, went to St Luke's College, Exeter, which churned out England internationals in that era. His representative career began with Devon at the age of 17, and he was the youngest forward ever to play in an England trial.

He played for the under-23s in 1975, becoming captain two years later before converting to No 8 in 1978 and winning his first four caps in that position, before being recalled as a second row to play the All Blacks that year.

In 1979 Scott played in England's 10-9 defeat by the All Blacks, which was seen as a letdown at the time as the North, fielding several internationals, had beaten the tourists the week before, and Scott received some harsh criticism in the press. Despite the barbs Scott was retained at No 8 for the 1980 Five Nations campaign when he scored a pushover try in England's opening 24-9 win over Ireland, which supplemented scores by Steve Smith and Mike Slemen, although he was criticised by some for his celebrations of his try.

Wins in Paris and Murrayfield plus the brutal 9-8 win over Wales at Twickenham gave England the Grand Slam which saw 10 Englishmen make the trip to South Africa with the British and Irish Lions but Scott was not amongst them.

Scott took over the England captaincy from Steve Smith in 1983, losing the final two games of the championship, and the job, but he was part of the side that beat the All Blacks 15-9 at Twickenham in November 1983, making up for the disappointment of four years previously.

England managed one win in 1984 and once hooker Peter Wheeler declared he was going to opt out of the tour to South Africa, Scott was reinstated as captain. Two heavy defeats, 33-15 and 35-9, left him with an international captaincy record of played four, lost four. That was curtains for Scott as far as Test rugby was concerned but he continued to play for Cardiff where he is something of a local hero.

John Scott

John Stanley Marshall SCOTT

Born: 23 January 1935
Educated: Radley College, Leas School
Clubs: Oxford University (1), Birkenhead Park, Harlequins, Negri Sembilan (Malaya)
Position: Full-back (1)
Debut: 1 Mar 1958 v France (Stade Colombes). Number: 877
Caps: 1 (W:1, L:0)
Scoring: 0 Pts
Appearances: 1958:F
Honours: Championship: 1958

Mason Thompson SCOTT

Born: 20 December 1865 in Newcastle-upon-Tyne
Died: 1 June 1916 in Carlisle
Educated: Craigmount School Edinburgh
Clubs: Cambridge University (1), Northern (2), Blackheath
Position: Half-Back (3)
Debut: 5 Feb 1887 v Ireland (Lansdowne Road). Number: 196
Last game: 15 Mar 1890 v Ireland (Blackheath)
Caps: 3 (W:2, L:1)
Scoring: 0 Pts
Appearances: 1887:I, 1890:S,I

William Martin SCOTT

Born: 27 March 1870 in Gateshead
Died: 26 February 1944 in Horsham, Sussex
Educated: Craigmount School
Clubs: Cambridge University (1), Blackheath, Northern
Position: Half-Back (1)
Debut: 16 Feb 1889 v New Zealand Natives (Blackheath). Number: 205
Caps: 1 (W:1, L:0)
Scoring: 0 Pts
Appearances: 1889:M

Robert L (Bob) SEDDON

Born: 1860 in Yorkshire
Died: 15 August 1888 in West Maitland, Australia
Clubs: Broughton Rangers (3)
Position: Forward (3)
Debut: 8 Jan 1887 v Wales (Llanelli). Number: 193
Last game: 5 Mar 1887 v Scotland (Manchester)
Caps: 3 (W:0, D:2, L:1)
Scoring: 0 Pts
Appearances: 1887:W,I,S

Kenneth Anderson (Monkey) SELLAR

Born: 11 August 1906 in Lewisham
Died: 15 May 1989 in Cape Town, South Africa
Clubs: RNC Dartmouth, RNC Greenwich, United Services, Combined Services, Royal Navy (7), Blackheath
Position: Full-back (7)
Debut: 15 Jan 1927 v Wales (Twickenham). Number: 618
Last game: 25 Feb 1928 v France (Twickenham)
Caps: 7 (W:6, L:1)
Scoring: 0 Pts
Appearances: 1927:W,I,S, 1928:A,W,I,F
Honours: Championship: 1928

Harry Sedgwick (Hal) SEVER

Born: 3 March 1910 in Bucklow
Died: June 2005
Educated: Shrewsbury School
Clubs: Sale (10)
Position: Wing (10)
Debut: 4 Jan 1936 v New Zealand (Twickenham) - 1T, 3 Pts. Number: 725
Last game: 19 Mar 1938 v Scotland (Twickenham)
Caps: 10 (W:6, D:1, L:3)
Scoring: 5T, 1DG, 19 Pts
Appearances: 1936:NZ,W,I,S, 1937:W,I,S, 1938:W,I,S
Honours: Championship: 1937

Most People believe England had just one special wing – Prince Obolensky – on duty when they first beat the All Blacks in 1936.

But closer examination of England in that era shows another exemplary performer, who made his debut that day.

The game is of course remembered as "Obolensky's Match" as he scored two tries but few remember England scored one other try on that famous day, coming from Sale's Hal Sever.

Sever – in a career curtailed by the Second World War – won 10 caps, making a try-scoring debut in that famous game against the All Blacks.

Educated at Shrewsbury School, Sever – an exceptional wing of his age – was an impressive, all-round sportsman, also playing rugby for Cheshire and the Barbarians.

Sever went on to be a crucial member of England's Triple Crown-winning side of 1937 and when he died in June 2005 he was – at 95 – the oldest surviving England international.

In the 1937 series he scored in each game, converting a drop goal in the win over Wales and scoring a memorable try in the 9-8 win over Ireland, another following in the 6-3 victory over the Scots.

Sever's last game – in 1938 – was also memorable because taking on the Scots he played in the first game to be televised by the BBC.

After the war he became a North Western Counties selector and in his business life rose to managing director of the Refuge Assurance.

"The most impressive wing of the Thirties was H.S. Sever," according to (WJT Collins) in his book Rugby Recollections.

"He played in all of the games (Triple Crown) of 1936-37-38 and won the admiration of comrades and opponents. A magnificent runner, fast and strong, he was very difficult to tackle. A fine kicker, a dropper of goals, great in defence, he was one of England's greatest wings."

RFU president Malcolm Phillips said: "On behalf of the RFU I am sorry to hear of Hal's death. He was a fantastic player and his place in English rugby history is guaranteed."

Hal Sever with Jonny Wilkinson

Ian Roger SHACKLETON

Born: 17 June 1948 in Shipley, Yorks
Educated: Bradford GS
Clubs: Cambridge University, Harrogate (4), Bradford, Richmond
Position: Fly-half (4), Bench (1)
Debut: 20 Dec 1969 v South Africa (Twickenham). Number: 980
Last game: 21 Mar 1970 v Scotland (Murrayfield)
Caps: 4 (W:2, L:2)
Scoring: 1T, 3 Pts
Appearances: 1969:SA, 1970:I,W,S

Richard Adrian William SHARP, OBE

Born: 9 September 1938 in Mysore, India
Educated: Montpelier School, Blundell's School
Clubs: Oxford University (9), Redruth, Royal Navy, Royal Marines, Wasps (4), Bristol (1)
Position: Fly-half (14)
Debut: 16 Jan 1960 v Wales (Twickenham). Number: 891
Last game: 7 Jan 1967 (capt) v Australia (Twickenham)
Caps: 14 (W:7, D:4, L:3). As captain: 5 (W:3, D:1, L:1)
Scoring: 2T, 4C, 1PG, 3DG, 26 Pts
Appearances: 1960:W,I,F,S, 1961:I,F, 1962:W,I,F, 1963:W*,I*,F*,S*, 1967:A*
Honours: Championship: 1963 (capt)

Richard Sharp was at his home in Cornwall when he was summoned to Twickenham to join the England squad for the first match of the 1960 championship against Wales. He had already been at the ground the previous month to play for Oxford in the Varsity Match and suddenly he was back to make his international debut against Wales as replacement for the injured Bev Risman.

Sharp's career encompassed a variety of clubs from Oxford University to Wasps and Redruth and he also played for the Royal Navy, when he was doing his national service, and for Cornwall.

Sharp was of leggy and willowy build, one of seven new caps, and there was little doubt that Wales fancied their chances of containing Sharp and blunting England's attack at the same time. Instead Sharp had a wonderful debut. England won 14-6, scoring two tries through their wing Jim Roberts, and Sharp was at the heart of so many good things in England's biggest win over Wales since 1921.

Sharp played out the season as England gained a Triple Crown and drew with France in Paris, depriving the French of a first Grand Slam. But for England fans the fair-haired Sharp was both a magnet and an inspiration. Risman started the 1961 championship but Sharp played in the matches against Ireland and France. In 1962 Sharp also played against Ireland and France and was also in the team which drew 0-0 with Wales at Twickenham.

Every quality player in Britain and Ireland knew that the summer of 1962 meant the chance to tour South Africa with the British and Irish Lions, and Sharp was duly one of those selected. The tours in those days were long haul and very demanding and Sharp was chosen for the Lions when he was at the height of his game. But he was to miss out on an early chance of becoming a great Test player for the Lions because on the eve of the first international he broke his cheekbone when he was tackled high against Northern Transvaal in Pretoria.

So Sharp missed the first two Tests and when he returned for the final two Tests he did not have the impact which had been anticipated pre-tour.

Richard Sharp

In 1963 Sharp played what proved to be his final Championship. He played in all four matches, taking over the captaincy for the opening victory at Cardiff and going on from there to be champions. Sharp had a sensational end to his championship appearances when he scored a try against Scotland at Twickenham with an attack which began 50 yards out and included a dummy scissors and a dummy on the way to the try line. Sharp's farewell to England was against Australia in 1967.

Sharp taught at Sherborne in the 1960s but returned to Cornwall in 1968 to work for English China Clay.

Simon Shaw

Cecil Hamilton SHAW

Born: 1 August 1879 in Wolverhampton
Died: 13 November 1964 in Wolverhampton
Educated: Sedbergh School
Clubs: Moseley (6)
Position: Forward (6)
Debut: 17 Mar 1906 v Scotland (Inverleith). Number: 434
Last game: 16 Mar 1907 v Scotland (Blackheath)
Caps: 6 (W:2, D:1, L:3)
Scoring: 0 Pts
Appearances: 1906:S,SA, 1907:F,W,I,S

Frederick SHAW

Born: Details unknown
Died: Details unknown
Clubs: Cleckheaton (1)
Position: Forward (1)
Debut: 5 Feb 1898 v Ireland (Richmond). Number: 316
Caps: 1 (W:0, L:1)
Scoring: 0 Pts
Appearances: 1898:I

James Fraser SHAW

Born: 2 January 1878 in Burton-upon-Trent
Died: 23 July 1941 in Bromley
Educated: King William's School
Clubs: Royal Naval Eng College Keyham (2)
Position: Forward (2)
Debut: 12 Mar 1898 v Scotland (Edinburgh). Number: 322
Last game: 2 Apr 1898 v Wales (Blackheath)
Caps: 2 (W:1, D:1, L:0)
Scoring: 0 Pts
Appearances: 1898:S,W

Simon Dalton SHAW, MBE
Born: 1 September 1973 in Nairobi, Kenya
Educated: St Peter's School, Godalming VI Form College
Clubs: Pirates (NZ), Cranleigh, Bristol (6), Wasps (28)
Position: Lock (20), Replacement (14), Bench (1)
Debut: 23 Nov 1996 v Italy (Twickenham). Number: 1168
Last game: 18 Mar 2006 v Ireland (Twickenham)
Caps: 34 (W:21, L:13)
Scoring: 2T, 10 Pts. Discipline - Sin bins: 2, Sent off: 1
Appearances: 1996:It,Ar, 1997:S,I,F,W,A,SA(r), 2000:I,F,W,It,S,SA1(r),SA2(r), 2001:C1(r),C2,US,I, 2003:It(r),W,F(r),F(r), 2004:It(r),S(r),NZ1,NZ2,A, 2005:Sm(r), 2006:W(r),It(r),S(r),F(r),I
Honours: Championship: 2000, 2001, 2003

Chris Sheasby

Christopher Mark Andrew (Chris) SHEASBY
Born: 30 November 1966 in Windsor
Educated: Radley College
Clubs: London University, Cambridge University, Harlequins, Wasps (7), London Irish
Position: No 8 (2), Replacement (5)
Debut: 23 Nov 1996 v Italy (Twickenham) - 1T, 5 Pts.
Number: 1169
Last game: 6 Dec 1997 (rep) v New Zealand (Twickenham)
Caps: 7 (W:4, D:1, L:2)
Scoring: 1T, 5 Pts
Appearances: 1996:It,Ar, 1997:W(r),Ar1(r),Ar2(r),SA(r),NZ2(r)

Austin SHEPPARD
Born: 1 May 1950 in Bristol
Clubs: Bristol (2)
Position: Prop (1), Replacement (1), Bench (4)
Debut: 17 Jan 1981 (rep) v Wales (Cardiff). Number: 1064
Last game: 20 Apr 1985 v Wales (Cardiff)
Caps: 2 (W:0, L:2)
Scoring: 0 Pts
Appearances: 1981:W(r), 1985:W

Andrew John SHERIDAN
Born: 1 November 1979 in Bromley
Educated: Dulwich College
Clubs: Richmond, Bristol, Sale (11)
Position: Prop (9), Replacement (2), Bench (3)
Debut: 13 Nov 2004 (rep) v Canada (Twickenham). Number: 1257
Last game: 18 Nov 2006 v South Africa (Twickenham)
Caps: 11 (W:6, L:5)
Scoring: 0 Pts
Appearances: 2004:C(r), 2005:A,NZ,Sm, 2006:W,It,S,F(r),I,NZ,SA1

Charles William SHERRARD
Born: 25 December 1849 in London
Died: 1921
Educated: Rugby School
Clubs: Blackheath (1), Royal Engineers (1), Army
Position: Forward (2)
Debut: 27 Mar 1871 v Scotland (Raeburn Place). Number: 16
Last game: 5 Feb 1872 v Scotland (The Oval)
Caps: 2 (W:1, L:1)
Scoring: 0 Pts
Appearances: 1871:S, 1872:S

Andrew Sheridan

S
T

George Albert SHERRIFF
Born: 29 May 1937 in Stepney
Clubs: Saracens (3)
Position: No 8 (3)
Debut: 19 Mar 1966 v Scotland (Murrayfield). Number: 947
Last game: 4 Nov 1967 v New Zealand (Twickenham)
Caps: 3 (W:0, L:3)
Scoring: 0 Pts
Appearances: 1966:S, 1967:A,NZ

Harry Edward SHEWRING
Born: 26 April 1881 in Keynsham, Somerset
Died: 27 November 1960 in Keynsham, Somerset
Educated: Colston's School
Clubs: Bristol (10)
Position: Centre (10)
Debut: 11 Feb 1905 v Ireland (Cork). Number: 408
Last game: 16 Mar 1907 v Scotland (Blackheath)
Caps: 10 (W:3, D:1, L:6)
Scoring: 1T, 3 Pts
Appearances: 1905:I,NZ, 1906:W,S,F,SA, 1907:F,W,I,S

John Henry SHOOTER
Born: 25 March 1874 in Nottingham
Died: 13 August 1922 in Leeds
Clubs: Morley (4), Hunslet RL
Position: Forward (4)
Debut: 4 Feb 1899 v Ireland (Lansdowne Road). Number: 334
Last game: 10 Mar 1900 v Scotland (Inverleith)
Caps: 4 (W:1, D:1, L:2)
Scoring: 0 Pts
Appearances: 1899:I,S, 1900:I,S

Dennis William SHUTTLEWORTH, OBE
Born: 22 July 1928 in Leeds
Died: 2 April 2001
Educated: Roundhay School
Clubs: Blackheath (1), Headingley (1), RMA Sandhurst, Halifax, Duke of Wellington's Regt, Army, Combined Services
Position: Scrum-half (2)
Debut: 17 Mar 1951 v Scotland (Twickenham). Number: 825
Last game: 21 Mar 1953 v Scotland (Twickenham)
Caps: 2 (W:2, L:0)
Scoring: 0 Pts
Appearances: 1951:S, 1953:S
Honours: Championship: 1953

Herbert John Hyde SIBREE
Born: 9 May 1885 in Antananarivo, Madagascar
Died: 20 August 1962 in Ticehurst, Sussex
Educated: Eltham College
Clubs: Harlequins (3)
Position: Scrum-half (3)
Debut: 1 Jan 1908 v France (Stade Colombes). Number: 457
Last game: 20 Mar 1909 v Scotland (Richmond)
Caps: 3 (W:2, L:1)
Scoring: 0 Pts
Appearances: 1908:F, 1909:I,S

James Simpson-Daniel

Nicholas SILK
Born: 26 May 1941 in Lewes
Educated: Lewes GS
Clubs: Oxford University, Harlequins (4), St Thomas's Hospital, British University
Position: Flanker (4)
Debut: 16 Jan 1965 v Wales (Cardiff). Number: 932
Last game: 20 Mar 1965 v Scotland (Twickenham)
Caps: 4 (W:1, D:1, L:2)
Scoring: 0 Pts
Appearances: 1965:W,I,F,S

Kevin Gerard SIMMS
Born: 25 December 1964 in Prescot
Educated: West Park GS
Clubs: Cambridge University, Liverpool (7), Wasps (8), Liverpool St Helens
Position: Centre (15)
Debut: 5 Jan 1985 v Romania (Twickenham). Number: 1104
Last game: 6 Feb 1988 v Wales (Twickenham)
Caps: 15 (W:4, D:1, L:10)
Scoring: 1T, 4 Pts
Appearances: 1985:R,F,S,I,W, 1986:I,F, 1987:I,F,W,A,J,W, 1988:F,W

Colin Peter SIMPSON
Born: 21 September 1942 in Ipswich
Educated: Ipswich School
Clubs: RMA Sandhurst, Royal Anglian Regt, Army, Combined Services, Harlequins (1)
Position: Wing (1)
Debut: 16 Jan 1965 v Wales (Cardiff). Number: 933
Caps: 1 (W:0, L:1)
Scoring: 0 Pts
Appearances: 1965:W

Paul Donald SIMPSON
Born: 7 June 1958 in Leeds
Educated: Newcastle Poly
Clubs: Gosforth, Bath (3)
Position: Flanker (2), No 8 (1), Bench (3)
Debut: 19 Nov 1983 v New Zealand (Twickenham). Number: 1080
Last game: 7 Feb 1987 v Ireland (Lansdowne Road)
Caps: 3 (W:1, L:2)
Scoring: 0 Pts
Appearances: 1983:NZ, 1984:S, 1987:I

Dave Sims

Mickey Skinner

Thomas SIMPSON
Born: 8 August 1881 in Newcastle-upon-Tyne
Died: 25 June 1956 in Northumberland
Clubs: Rockcliff (11)
Position: Wing (11)
Debut: 15 Mar 1902 v Scotland (Inverleith). Number: 382
Last game: 30 Jan 1909 v France (Leicester) - 1T, 3 Pts
Caps: 11 (W:4, D:1, L:6)
Scoring: 3T, 9 Pts
Appearances: 1902:S, 1903:W,I,S, 1904:I,S, 1905:I,S, 1906:S,SA, 1909:F

James David SIMPSON-DANIEL
Born: 30 May 1982 in Stockton-on-Tees
Educated: Sedbergh School
Clubs: Gloucester (9)
Position: Wing (5), Centre (1), Replacement (3), Bench (3)
Debut: 9 Nov 2002 v New Zealand (Twickenham). Number: 1244
Last game: 11 Feb 2006 (rep) v Italy (Rome) - 1T, 5 Pts
Caps: 9 (W:7, L:2)
Scoring: 2T, 10 Pts
Appearances: 2002:NZ,A, 2003:W(r),It,W, 2004:I(r),NZ1, 2005:Sm, 2006:It(r)
Honours: Championship: 2003

David (Dave) SIMS
Born: 22 November 1969 in Gloucester
Educated: Churchdown School Gloucester
Clubs: Longlevens, Sunnybank (AU), Gloucester (3), Worcester, Bedford, Exeter
Position: Lock (2), Replacement (1), Bench (1)
Debut: 20 Jun 1998 (rep) v New Zealand (Dunedin).
Number: 1205
Last game: 4 Jul 1998 v South Africa (Cape Town)
Caps: 3 (W:0, L:3)
Scoring: 0 Pts
Appearances: 1998:NZ1(r),NZ2,SA

Michael Gordon (Mickey) SKINNER
Born: 26 November 1958 in Newcastle-upon-Tyne
Educated: Walbottle GS
Clubs: Blaydon, Blackheath, Harlequins (21)
Position: Flanker (20), Replacement (1), Bench (8)
Debut: 16 Jan 1988 v France (Parc des Princes). Number: 1122
Last game: 7 Mar 1992 v Wales (Twickenham) - 1T, 4 Pts
Caps: 21 (W:16, L:5)
Scoring: 3T, 12 Pts
Appearances: 1988:F,W,S,I,I, 1989:Fj, 1990:I,F,W,S,Ar1,Ar2, 1991:Fj(r),US,F,S,A, 1992:S,I,F,W
Honours: Grand Slam: 1992

Geoffrey Mainwaring SLADEN
Born: 3 August 1904 in Reigate
Clubs: RNC Dartmouth, United Services, Royal Navy (3)
Position: Centre (3)
Debut: 19 Jan 1929 v Wales (Twickenham). Number: 638
Last game: 16 Mar 1929 v Scotland (Murrayfield)
Caps: 3 (W:1, L:2)
Scoring: 0 Pts
Appearances: 1929:W,I,S

Jon Sleightholme

Jonathan Mark (Jon) SLEIGHTHOLME

Born: 5 August 1972 in Malton, Yorks
Educated: Whitgift School, Chester College
Clubs: Grimsby, Hull Ionians, Wakefield, Bath (12), Northampton
Position: Wing (12), Bench (1)
Debut: 20 Jan 1996 v France (Parc des Princes). Number: 1164
Last game: 7 Jun 1997 v Argentina (Buenos Aires)
Caps: 12 (W:9, L:3)
Scoring: 4T, 20 Pts
Appearances: 1996:F,W,S,I,It,Ar, 1997:S,I,F,W,Ar1,Ar2
Honours: Championship: 1996

Michael Anthony Charles (Mike) SLEMEN

Born: 11 May 1951 in Liverpool
Educated: St Edmund's College
Clubs: St Luke's University, Liverpool (31)
Position: Wing (31)
Debut: 6 Mar 1976 v Ireland (Twickenham). Number: 1042
Last game: 4 Feb 1984 v Scotland (Murrayfield)
Caps: 31 (W:15, D:2, L:14)
Scoring: 8T, 32 Pts
Appearances: 1976:I,F, 1977:S,I,F,W, 1978:F,W,S,I,NZ, 1979:S,I,F,W,NZ, 1980:I,F,W,S, 1981:W,S,I,F, 1982:A,S,I,F,W, 1983:NZ, 1984:S
Honours: Grand Slam: 1980

Mike Slemen

Mike Slemen, like most Liverpool youngsters, was a soccer fan at first, and claims he was more interested in the round ball game until he was 18, but once he concentrated on rugby union he developed into one of the finest wings England has ever produced. A fast and direct runner, whose hero unsurprisingly was Gerald Davies, Slemen had a good footballing brain and overtook Peter Squires as England's most capped winger in 1983 when he won his 30th cap. He eventually finished with 31, won between 1976 and 1984.

Slemen had a brilliant reading of the game, was a top-notch cover defender and some observers say that he could have made it as a fly-half.

Slemen represented Devon whilst a student at St Luke's College, Exeter, and played for the England under-23 against Tonga in 1974.

Playing for Liverpool, now Liverpool St Helens, Slemen was, and remains, a teacher at Old Merchant Taylor's School, Crosby, and was first capped in England's 13-12 win over Ireland in 1976. Next up were the Welsh who steam rollered England 30-9, though Slemen played a full part in England's improvement over the next few years that culminated in the Grand Slam for Bill Beaumont's team.

He scored the first of eight international tries against Scotland in 1977 as England failed to win the championship but all that came right in 1980 when Slemen scored in the wins over Ireland and the Slam-clinching win over the Scots at Murrayfield. Interestingly that was Slemen's 20th cap and the first international he played in where both wingers scored. His partner, John Carleton, got a hat-trick that day, which probably sums up some of England's rugby in the 1970s perfectly.

Slemen was a British and Irish Lion that summer and although he had to return home after the first Test he still had time to score one of the best tries of the decade, against a South African Invitation XV in Potchefstroom, when he was on hand to finish a move that involved more than 30 passes and took two minutes and 47 seconds to complete. Even the partisan Afrikaaners in the stands applauded. Slemen continued playing for an underachieving England side but was involved just once, for the win over New Zealand, in 1983. His last cap was against Scotland in 1984 after which the young Rory Underwood, who would win nearly three times as many caps, got the nod.

Lancelot Andrew Noel (Andrew) SLOCOCK

Born: 25 December 1886 in Stratford
Died: Killed in action in 1916 in Guillemont, France
Educated: Marlborough School
Clubs: Liverpool (8)
Position: Forward (8)
Debut: 5 Jan 1907 v France (Richmond) - 1T, 3 Pts. Number: 443
Last game: 21 Mar 1908 (capt) v Scotland (Inverleith) - 1T, 3 Pts
Caps: 8 (W:3, L:5). As captain: 1 (W:0, L:1)
Scoring: 3T, 9 Pts
Appearances: 1907:F,W,I,S, 1908:F,W,I,S*

Charles Frederick SLOW

Born: Second quarter 1911 in Northampton
Died: 15 April 1939 in Stony Stratford
Clubs: Northampton, Leicester (1), Stony Stratford
Position: Fly-half (1)
Debut: 17 Mar 1934 v Scotland (Twickenham). Number: 711
Caps: 1 (W:1, L:0)
Scoring: 0 Pts
Appearances: 1934:S
Honours: Championship: 1934

Harold Dudley (Harry) SMALL

Born: 7 January 1922 in South Africa
Educated: Dundee HS
Clubs: Witwatersrand University (SA), Oxford University (4)
Position: Flanker (4)
Debut: 21 Jan 1950 v Wales (Twickenham). Number: 806
Last game: 18 Mar 1950 v Scotland (Murrayfield)
Caps: 4 (W:1, L:3)
Scoring: 0 Pts
Appearances: 1950:W,I,F,S

Alastair McNaughton SMALLWOOD
Born: 18 November 1892 in Alloa, Scotland
Died: 9 June 1985 in Uppingham
Educated: RGS Newcastle
Clubs: Cambridge University (2), Gosforth Nomads, Leicester (12)
Position: Wing (10), Centre (4)
Debut: 31 Jan 1920 v France (Twickenham). Number: 559
Last game: 21 Mar 1925 v Scotland (Murrayfield)
Caps: 14 (W:12, D:1, L:1)
Scoring: 7T, 1DG, 25 Pts
Appearances: 1920:F,I, 1921:W,I,S,F, 1922:I,S, 1923:W,I,S,F, 1925:I,S
Honours: Grand Slam: 1921, 1923

Colin Edward SMART
Born: 5 March 1950 in Highbury
Educated: Skinner's School, Cardiff College
Clubs: Newport (17)
Position: Prop (17)
Debut: 3 Mar 1979 v France (Twickenham). Number: 1057
Last game: 19 Mar 1983 v Ireland (Lansdowne Road)
Caps: 17 (W:7, D:3, L:7)
Scoring: 0 Pts
Appearances: 1979:F,W,NZ, 1981:S,I,F,Ar1,Ar2, 1982:A,S,I,F,W, 1983:F,W,S,I

Sidney Edward John SMART
Born: First quarter 1888 in Gloucester
Died: 25 January 1969 in Gloucester
Educated: Deacon's School
Clubs: Gloucester (12)
Position: No 8 (12)
Debut: 4 Jan 1913 v South Africa (Twickenham). Number: 529
Last game: 20 Mar 1920 v Scotland (Twickenham)
Caps: 12 (W:10, L:2)
Scoring: 0 Pts
Appearances: 1913:SA,W,F,I,S, 1914:W,I,S,F, 1920:W,I,S
Honours: Grand Slam: 1913, 1914

Robert William SMEDDLE
Born: 14 July 1908 in Leeds
Died: 15 December 1987 in Newcastle-upon-Tyne
Educated: Durham School
Clubs: Cambridge University (4), Durham City, Blackheath
Position: Wing (4)
Debut: 19 Jan 1929 v Wales (Twickenham). Number: 639
Last game: 6 Apr 1931 v France (Stade Colombes) - 1T, 3 Pts
Caps: 4 (W:1, L:3)
Scoring: 2T, 6 Pts
Appearances: 1929:W,I,S, 1931:F

Charles Albert (Whacker) SMITH
Born: 18 July 1878 in Gloucester
Died: 20 January 1940
Clubs: Gloucester (1)
Position: Wing (1)
Debut: 5 Jan 1901 v Wales (Cardiff). Number: 362
Caps: 1 (W:0, L:1)
Scoring: 0 Pts
Appearances: 1901:W

Dyne Fenton SMITH
Born: 21 July 1890 in Brighton
Died: 28 August 1969 in Lambeth
Educated: Sherborne School
Clubs: Richmond (2)
Position: Lock (2)
Debut: 15 Jan 1910 v Wales (Twickenham). Number: 496
Last game: 12 Feb 1910 v Ireland (Twickenham)
Caps: 2 (W:1, D:1, L:0)
Scoring: 0 Pts
Appearances: 1910:W,I
Honours: Championship: 1910

Gerald Walter Gordon SMITH
Born: 14 February 1877 in Southampton
Died: 23 January 1911 in Carbis Bay
Educated: Camborne School of Mines
Clubs: Redruth, Blackheath (3)
Position: Centre (3)
Debut: 6 Jan 1900 v Wales (Gloucester). Number: 351
Last game: 10 Mar 1900 v Scotland (Inverleith)
Caps: 3 (W:1, D:1, L:1)
Scoring: 1T, 1DG, 7 Pts
Appearances: 1900:W,I,S

Colin Smart

S T

Ollie Smith

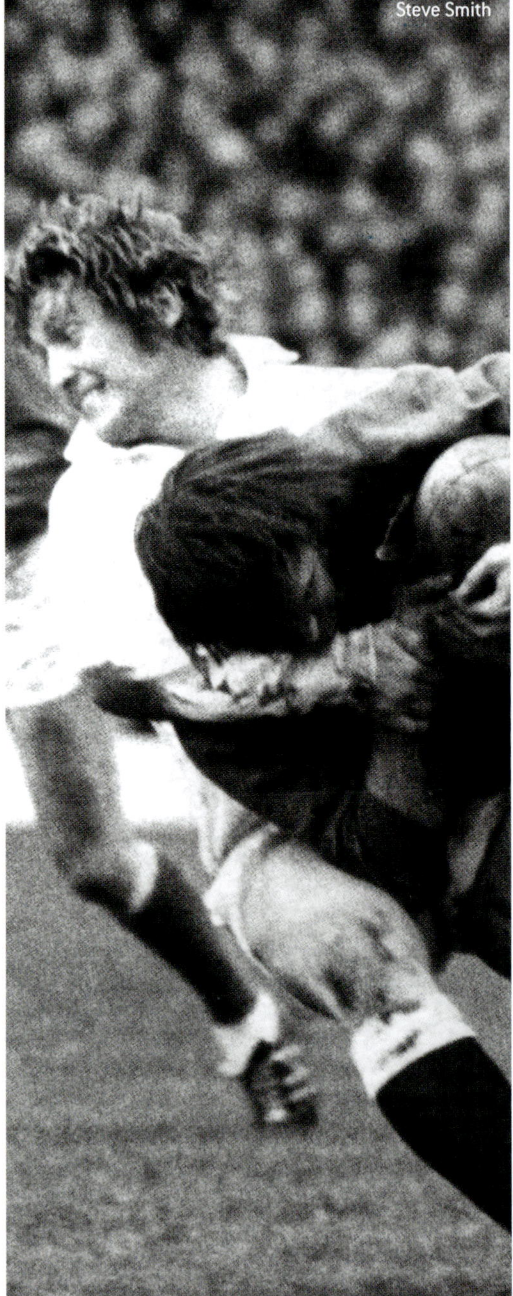
Steve Smith

John Vincent SMITH
Born: 23 May 1926 in Stroud
Educated: Marling School
Clubs: Cambridge University (4), Stroud, Rosslyn Park, Army
Position: Wing (4)
Debut: 21 Jan 1950 v Wales (Twickenham) - 1T, 3 Pts. Number: 807
Last game: 18 Mar 1950 v Scotland (Murrayfield) - 2T, 6 Pts
Caps: 4 (W:1, L:3)
Scoring: 4T, 12 Pts
Appearances: 1950:W,I,F,S

Keith SMITH
Born: 19 November 1952 in Leeds
Died: 2 June 2006 in Leeds
Educated: Cross Green School
Clubs: Roundhay (4), Wakefield Trinity RL
Position: Centre (4), Bench (1)
Debut: 2 Mar 1974 v France (Parc des Princes).Number: 1023
Last game: 15 Mar 1975 v Scotland (Twickenham)
Caps: 4 (W:2, D:1, L:1)
Scoring: 0 Pts
Appearances: 1974:F,W, 1975:W,S

Michael John Knight (Mike) SMITH, OBE
Born: 30 June 1933 in Westcotes, Leicester
Educated: Stamford School
Clubs: Oxford University (1), Hinckley, Leicester
Position: Fly-half (1)
Debut: 21 Jan 1956 v Wales (Twickenham). Number: 867
Caps: 1 (W:0, L:1)
Scoring: 0 Pts
Appearances: 1956:W

Oliver James (Ollie) SMITH
Born: 14 August 1982 in Leicester
Educated: John Cleveland College
Clubs: Loughborough University, Old Bosworthians, Market Bosworth, Leicester (5)
Position: Centre (1), Replacement (4), Bench (1)
Debut: 9 Mar 2003 (rep) v Italy (Twickenham). Number: 1246
Last game: 19 Mar 2005 (rep) v Scotland (Twickenham)
Caps: 5 (W:4, L:1)
Scoring: 0 Pts
Appearances: 2003:It(r),W(r),F, 2005:It(r),S(r)
Honours: Championship: 2003

Ronald Cove (Ron) SMITH
Born: 26 November 1899 in Edmonton
Died: 9 March 1988 in Brighton
Educated: Merchant Taylors' School
Clubs: Cambridge University (5), Old Merchant Taylors' (22), King's College Hospital (2), London University
Position: Lock (29)
Debut: 19 Mar 1921 v Scotland (Inverleith). Number: 569
Last game: 9 Feb 1929 (capt) v Ireland (Twickenham)
Caps: 29 (W:22, D:2, L:5). As captain: 7 (W:6, L:1)
Scoring: 1T, 3 Pts
Appearances: 1921:S,F, 1922:I,F,S, 1923:W,I,S,F, 1924:W,I,F,S, 1925:NZ,W,I,S,F, 1927:W,I,S,F, 1928:A*,W*,I*,F*,S*, 1929:W*,I*
Honours: Grand Slam: 1923, 1924, 1928 (capt).
Championship: 1921

Simon Timothy SMITH
Born: 29 April 1960 in Baldock
Educated: King Edward VII School
Clubs: Lancaster University, Cambridge University, Lichfield, Fylde, Wasps (9), Rosslyn Park
Position: Wing (9)
Debut: 5 Jan 1985 v Romania (Twickenham) - 1T, 4 Pts. Number: 1105
Last game: 15 Feb 1986 v Scotland (Murrayfield)
Caps: 9 (W:3, D:1, L:5)
Scoring: 3T, 12 Pts
Appearances: 1985:R,F,S,I,W,NZ1,NZ2, 1986:W,S

Stephen James (Steve) SMITH
Born: 22 July 1951 in Stockport
Educated: King's School
Clubs: Loughborough College, Sale (28)
Position: Scrum-half (26), Replacement (2), Bench (14)
Debut: 10 Feb 1973 v Ireland (Lansdowne Road). Number: 1018
Last game: 5 Mar 1983 v Scotland (Twickenham)
Caps: 28 (W:13, D:4, L:11). As captain: 5 (W:2, D:1, L:2)
Scoring: 2T, 8 Pts
Appearances: 1973:I,F,S,A, 1974:I,F, 1975:W(r), 1976:F, 1977:F(r), 1979:NZ, 1980:I,F,W,S, 1981:W,S,I,F,Ar1,Ar2, 1982:A,S,I*,F*,W*, 1983:F*,W*,S
Honours: Grand Slam: 1980

Stephen Rider SMITH
Born: 21 October 1934 in India
Educated: Eltham College
Clubs: Cambridge University (3), Aldershot Services, Richmond (1), Blackheath (1), India
Position: Scrum-half (5)
Debut: 17 Jan 1959 v Wales (Cardiff). Number: 880
Last game: 21 Mar 1964 v Scotland (Murrayfield)
Caps: 5 (W:1, D:2, L:2)
Scoring: 0 Pts
Appearances: 1959:W,F,S, 1964:F,S

Trellevyn Harvey (Trevor) SMITH
Born: 3 April 1920 in Bedford
Clubs: Northampton (1)
Position: Hooker (1)
Debut: 20 Jan 1951 v Wales (Swansea). Number: 815
Caps: 1 (W:0, L:1)
Scoring: 0 Pts
Appearances: 1951:W

Frank (Buster) SOANE
Born: 12 September 1865 in Bath
Died: 1 April 1932 in Bath
Educated: Clifton House School
Clubs: Oldfield Park, Bath (4)
Position: Forward (4)
Debut: 4 Mar 1893 v Scotland (Headingley). Number: 259
Last game: 17 Mar 1894 v Scotland (Raeburn Place)
Caps: 4 (W:1, L:3)
Scoring: 0 Pts
Appearances: 1893:S, 1894:W,I,S

Wilfred Henry (Wilf) SOBEY
Born: 1 April 1905
Died: 27 February 1988
Educated: Mill Hill School
Clubs: Cambridge University, Old Millhillians (5)
Position: Scrum-half (5)
Debut: 18 Jan 1930 v Wales (Cardiff). Number: 661
Last game: 16 Jan 1932 v Wales (Swansea)
Caps: 5 (W:2, D:1, L:2)
Scoring: 0 Pts
Appearances: 1930:W,F,S, 1932:SA,W
Honours: Championship: 1930

Bertie (Barney) SOLOMON
Born: 8 March 1885 in Redruth
Died: 30 June 1961 in Redruth
Clubs: Treleigh Rangers, Redruth (1)
Position: Centre (1)
Debut: 15 Jan 1910 v Wales (Twickenham) - 1T, 3 Pts. Number: 497
Caps: 1 (W:1, L:0)
Scoring: 1T, 3 Pts
Appearances: 1910:W
Honours: Championship: 1910

Robert Henry Ware SPARKS
Born: 19 February 1899 in East Stonehouse
Died: August 1984 in Cheltenham
Clubs: Plymouth Albion (9), Civil Service
Position: Prop (9)
Debut: 11 Feb 1928 v Ireland (Lansdowne Road). Number: 629
Last game: 6 Apr 1931 v France (Stade Colombes)
Caps: 9 (W:4, L:5)
Scoring: 0 Pts
Appearances: 1928:I,F,S, 1929:W,I,S, 1931:I,S,F
Honours: Championship: 1928

Henry (Harry) SPEED
Born: 19 August 1871 in Castleford
Died: 3 July 1937 in Pontefract
Clubs: Castleford (4)
Position: Forward (4)
Debut: 6 Jan 1894 v Wales (Birkenhead Park). Number: 266
Last game: 14 Mar 1896 v Scotland (Glasgow)
Caps: 4 (W:1, L:3)
Scoring: 0 Pts
Appearances: 1894:W,I,S, 1896:S

Stephen Smith

ST

John Spencer

William Frederick SPENCE
Born: Second quarter 1867 in Birkenhead
Died: Details unknown
Educated: Fettes School
Clubs: Birkenhead Park (1)
Position: Half-Back (1)
Debut: 15 Mar 1890 v Ireland (Blackheath). Number: 221
Caps: 1 (W:1, L:0)
Scoring: 0 Pts
Appearances: 1890:I

Jeremy SPENCER
Born: 27 June 1939
Clubs: Harlequins (1), St Jean-de-Luz (FR)
Position: Scrum-half (1)
Debut: 15 Jan 1966 v Wales (Twickenham). Number: 940
Caps: 1 (W:0, L:1)
Scoring: 0 Pts
Appearances: 1966:W

John Sothern SPENCER
Born: 10 August 1947 in Staincliffe
Educated: Cressbrook School, Sedbergh School
Clubs: Cambridge University (1), Headingley (13), Wharfedale
Position: Centre (14)
Debut: 8 Feb 1969 v Ireland (Lansdowne Road). Number: 975
Last game: 17 Apr 1971 (capt) v Presidents XV (Twickenham)
Caps: 14 (W:5, L:9). As captain: 4 (W:1, L:3)
Scoring: 2T, 6 Pts
Appearances: 1969:I,F,S,W,SA, 1970:I,W,S,F, 1971:W,I*,S*,S*,P*

Roger Spencer SPONG
Born: 23 October 1906 in Barnet
Died: 27 March 1980 in south-west Surrey
Educated: Mill Hill School
Clubs: Old Millhillians (8)
Position: Fly-half (8)
Debut: 1 Apr 1929 v France (Stade Colombes). Number: 652
Last game: 16 Jan 1932 v Wales (Swansea)
Caps: 8 (W:3, D:1, L:4)
Scoring: 0 Pts
Appearances: 1929:F, 1930:W,I,F,S, 1931:F, 1932:SA,W
Honours: Championship: 1930

Reginald Herbert SPOONER
Born: 21 October 1880 in Litherland, Lancs
Died: 2 October 1961 in Lincoln
Educated: Marlborough School
Clubs: Marlborough Nomads, Liverpool (1)
Position: Centre (1)
Debut: 10 Jan 1903 v Wales (Swansea). Number: 388
Caps: 1 (W:0, L:1)
Scoring: 0 Pts
Appearances: 1903:W

Herman Heinrich (Henry) SPRINGMANN
Born: Second quarter 1859 in West Derby
Died: 17 October 1936 in Aled
Educated: Craigmount School
Clubs: Liverpool (2)
Position: Forward (2)
Debut: 10 Mar 1879 v Scotland (Raeburn Place). Number: 115
Last game: 5 Mar 1887 v Scotland (Manchester)
Caps: 2 (W:0, D:2, L:0)
Scoring: 0 Pts
Appearances: 1879:S, 1887:S

Aubrey SPURLING
Born: 19 July 1856 in Camberwell
Died: 26 March 1945 in Maidstone
Educated: Blackheath Prep School
Clubs: Blackheath (1)
Position: Forward (1)
Debut: 6 Feb 1882 v Ireland (Lansdowne Road). Number: 145
Caps: 1 (W:0, D:1, L:0)
Scoring: 0 Pts
Appearances: 1882:I

Norman SPURLING
Born: 15 February 1864 in Blackheath
Died: 20 July 1919
Educated: Blackheath Prep School
Clubs: Blackheath (3)
Position: Forward (3)
Debut: 6 Feb 1886 v Ireland (Lansdowne Road). Number: 184
Last game: 8 Jan 1887 v Wales (Llanelli)
Caps: 3 (W:1, D:2, L:0)
Scoring: 0 Pts
Appearances: 1886:I,S, 1887:W

Peter John SQUIRES
Born: 4 August 1951 in Ripon, Yorks
Educated: Ripon GS, St John's College
Clubs: Harrogate (29)
Position: Wing (29)
Debut: 24 Feb 1973 v France (Twickenham). Number: 1021
Last game: 17 Mar 1979 v Wales (Cardiff)
Caps: 29 (W:12, D:2, L:15)
Scoring: 6T, 24 Pts
Appearances: 1973:F,S,NZ,A, 1974:S,I,F,W, 1975:I,F,W,S,A1,A2, 1976:A,W, 1977:S,I,F,W, 1978:F,W,S,I,NZ, 1979:S,I,F,W

Richard Calvert (Dick) STAFFORD
Born: 23 July 1893 in Bedford
Died: 1 December 1912 in Bedford
Educated: Bedford Modern School
Clubs: Bedford (4)
Position: Prop (4)
Debut: 20 Jan 1912 v Wales (Twickenham). Number: 522
Last game: 8 Apr 1912 v France (Parc des Princes)
Caps: 4 (W:3, L:1)
Scoring: 0 Pts
Appearances: 1912:W,I,S,F

William Francis Howard STAFFORD
Born: 19 December 1854
Died: 8 August 1942 in Wokingham
Educated: Wellington College
Clubs: RMA Sandhurst, Royal Engineers (1), Army
Position: Forward (1)
Debut: 23 Feb 1874 v Scotland (The Oval). Number: 55
Caps: 1 (W:1, L:0)
Scoring: 0 Pts
Appearances: 1874:S

Edward STANBURY

Born: Third quarter 1897 in Plympton
Died: 1 May 1968 in Plympton
Clubs: Plymouth Albion (16)
Position: Flanker (16)
Debut: 16 Jan 1926 v Wales (Cardiff). Number: 609
Last game: 1 Apr 1929 v France (Stade Colombes) - 2C, 4 Pts
Caps: 16 (W:9, D:1, L:6)
Scoring: 5C, 1PG, 13 Pts
Appearances: 1926:W,I,S, 1927:W,I,S,F, 1928:A,W,I,F,S, 1929:W,I,S,F
Honours: Grand Slam: 1928

G STANDING

Born: Details unknown
Died: Details unknown
Clubs: Blackheath (2)
Position: Forward (2)
Debut: 16 Dec 1882 v Wales (Swansea). Number: 153
Last game: 5 Feb 1883 v Ireland (Manchester)
Caps: 2 (W:2, L:0)
Scoring: 0 Pts
Appearances: 1883:W,I
Honours: Championship: 1883

Christopher Francis STANGER-LEATHES

Born: 9 May 1881 in Kensington
Died: 27 February 1966 in Gosforth
Educated: Sherborne School
Clubs: Northern (1)
Position: Full-back (1)
Debut: 11 Feb 1905 v Ireland (Cork). Number: 401
Caps: 1 (W:0, L:1)
Scoring: 0 Pts
Appearances: 1905:I

Kendrick James STARK

Born: 18 August 1904 in Edmonton
Died: 27 March 1988 in Horsham
Educated: Dulwich College
Clubs: Old Alleynians (9), Hon Artillery Company
Position: Prop (9)
Debut: 15 Jan 1927 v Wales (Twickenham). Number: 619
Last game: 17 Mar 1928 v Scotland (Twickenham)
Caps: 9 (W:7, L:2)
Scoring: 1C, 1PG, 5 Pts
Appearances: 1927:W,I,S,F, 1928:A,W,I,F,S
Honours: Grand Slam: 1928

Anthony STARKS

Born: 11 August 1873 in Castleford
Died: January 1952 in Kingston-upon-Hull
Clubs: Castleford (2), Hull KR RL
Position: Forward (2)
Debut: 4 Jan 1896 v Wales (Blackheath). Number: 287
Last game: 1 Feb 1896 v Ireland (Leeds)
Caps: 2 (W:1, L:1)
Scoring: 0 Pts
Appearances: 1896:W,I

Nigel Christopher STARMER-SMITH

Born: 25 December 1944 in Cheltenham
Educated: Magdalen School
Clubs: Oxford University, Harlequins (7)
Position: Scrum-half (7), Bench (3)
Debut: 20 Dec 1969 v South Africa (Twickenham). Number: 981
Last game: 17 Apr 1971 v Presidents XV (Twickenham)
Caps: 7 (W:2, L:5)
Scoring: 0 Pts
Appearances: 1969:SA, 1970:I,W,S,F, 1971:S,P

Sydney Philp START

Born: 17 May 1879 in Salford
Died: 14 December 1969 in Maidstone
Educated: Manchester GS
Clubs: RNEC Keyham, United Services (1), Royal Navy
Position: Scrum-half (1)
Debut: 16 Mar 1907 v Scotland (Blackheath). Number: 451
Caps: 1 (W:0, L:1)
Scoring: 0 Pts
Appearances: 1907:S

Nigel Starmer-Smith

Micky Steele-Bodger

John Harold STEEDS

Born: 27 September 1916 in Edmonton
Educated: St Edward's School
Clubs: Cambridge University, Middlesex Hospital (2), Saracens (3)
Position: Hooker (5)
Debut: 26 Feb 1949 v France (Twickenham). Number: 799
Last game: 18 Mar 1950 v Scotland (Murrayfield)
Caps: 5 (W:3, L:2)
Scoring: 0 Pts
Appearances: 1949:F,S, 1950:I,F,S

Michael Roland (Micky) STEELE-BODGER, CBE

Born: 4 September 1925 in Tamworth
Educated: Rugby School
Clubs: Cambridge University (4), Edinburgh University (5), Harlequins, Moseley
Position: Flanker (9)
Debut: 18 Jan 1947 v Wales (Cardiff). Number: 762
Last game: 29 Mar 1948 v France (Stade Colombes)
Caps: 9 (W:3, D:1, L:5)
Scoring: 0 Pts
Appearances: 1947:W,I,S,F, 1948:A,W,I,S,F

Francis Eric STEINTHAL

Born: 21 November 1886 in Bradford
Died: In USA, details unknown
Educated: Bradford GS
Clubs: Oxford University, Ilkley (2)
Position: Centre (2)
Debut: 18 Jan 1913 v Wales (Cardiff). Number: 530
Last game: 25 Jan 1913 v France (Twickenham)
Caps: 2 (W:2, L:0)
Scoring: 0 Pts
Appearances: 1913:W,F
Honours: Championship: 1913

Michael Stephenson

Michael STEPHENSON

Born: 28 September 1980 in Tynemouth
Educated: Durham School
Clubs: Durham City, Newcastle (3), Bath
Position: Wing (3)
Debut: 2 Jun 2001 v Canada (Markham). Number: 1226
Last game: 16 Jun 2001 v United States (San Francisco)
Caps: 3 (W:3, L:0)
Scoring: 0 Pts
Appearances: 2001:C1,C2,US

Claude Brian (Stack) STEVENS

Born: 2 June 1940 in Godolphin, Cornwall
Educated: Leedstown HS, Cornwall TC
Clubs: Penzance & Newlyn (20), Harlequins (5)
Position: Prop (25), Bench (2)
Debut: 20 Dec 1969 v South Africa (Twickenham). Number: 982
Last game: 15 Mar 1975 v Scotland (Twickenham)
Caps: 25 (W:9, D:1, L:15)
Scoring: 2T, 8 Pts
Appearances: 1969:SA, 1970:I,W,S, 1971:P, 1972:W,I,F,S,SA, 1973:NZ,W,I,F,S,NZ,A, 1974:S,I,F,W, 1975:I,F,W,S

Brian 'Stack' Stevens is a legendary figure in Cornwall for whom he was capped 83 times, between 1959 and 1976, in addition to propping the English scrummage 25 times and providing inspiration for young Cornish props such as Trevor Woodman to take up the sport.

A farmer, and fiercely proud Cornishman, Stevens is president of the Cornwall Commonwealth Games Association that is aiming to get Cornish athletes to compete in the games, in Delhi, in 2010 under the black and white flag of St Piran.

Stevens played more than 500 games for Penzance & Newlyn, although he did have a brief spell at Harlequins to boost his international prospects in the 1970s.

He was another late maturing prop, like Paul Rendall and Jeff Probyn, although in the late 1960s playing your club rugby in Cornwall was possibly not the best way to attract the attention of the international selectors.

However Stevens forced his way in for the 1969 match against South Africa at Twickenham, which England won 11-9, and won three caps in the 1971 season although he missed out on being picked for the British and Irish Lions tour to New Zealand.

Injuries to Sandy Carmichael and Ray McLoughlin meant that Stevens was called out as cover and he ended up playing six provincial matches although he did not make the Test team. According to some reports he struggled to get used to the New Zealand conditions but off the field took a deep interest in the methods of the New Zealand farmers.

He would return to New Zealand in 1973 when his try, along with scores for Tony Neary and Peter Squires, helped England turn the rugby world on its head by beating the All Blacks 16-10 in Auckland. He also helped John Pullin's side beat South Africa, 18-9, in Johannesburg in 1972. In that match Stevens had to go off injured and England were reduced to seven-man scrums for 20 minutes. Once the Cornishman returned England started to take control of the game and ground out a famous win. His last game for England was against Scotland in 1975 when England squeaked home by a point.

Legend has it that England's first dietician was appalled at Stevens' daily intake of Cornish pasties and he was once almost dropped from the national side for refusing to wear a sponsored tracksuit. "Unlike some, I don't suffer from cold leg," he is alleged to have said.

Matthew J H (Matt) STEVENS

Born: 1 October 1982 in Durban, South Africa
Educated: Kearsney College
Clubs: Bath (10)
Position: Prop (7), Replacement (3), Bench (2)
Debut: 12 Jun 2004 (rep) v New Zealand (Dunedin). Number: 1251
Last game: 12 Mar 2006 v France (Stade de France)
Caps: 10 (W:5, L:5)
Scoring: 0 Pts
Appearances: 2004:NZ1(r),NZ2(r), 2005:I,It,S,NZ(r),Sm, 2006:W,It,F

Ernest Robert STILL

Born: 14 July 1852 in Epsom
Died: 23 November 1931 in Epsom
Educated: Rugby School
Clubs: Oxford University, Ravenscourt Park (1)
Position: Forward (1)
Debut: 3 Mar 1873 v Scotland (Glasgow). Number: 43
Caps: 1 (W:0, D:1, L:0)
Scoring: 0 Pts
Appearances: 1873:S

Tim Richard George STIMPSON

Born: 10 September 1973 in Liverpool
Educated: Silcoates School
Clubs: Durham University, Wakefield, West Hartlepool, Newcastle (7), Leicester (12), Perpignan (FR), Leeds, Nuneaton, Nottingham
Position: Full-back (7), Wing (3), Replacement (9), Bench (3)
Debut: 23 Nov 1996 v Italy (Twickenham). Number: 1170
Last game: 23 Nov 2002 (rep) v South Africa (Twickenham) - 2C, 4 Pts
Caps: 19 (W:11, D:1, L:7)
Scoring: 2T, 5C, 5PG, 35 Pts
Appearances: 1996:It, 1997:S,I,F,W,A,NZ2(r), 1998:A,NZ1,NZ2(r),SA(r), 1999:US(r),C(r), 2000:SA1, 2001:C1(r),C2(r), 2002:W(r),Ar,SA(r)

Robert Victor (Bob) STIRLING

Born: 4 September 1919 in Lichfield
Died: 15 January 1991 in Halton
Educated: Nether Edge GS
Clubs: Aylestone St James, RAF, Combined Services, Leicester (13), Wasps (5)
Position: Prop (18)
Debut: 20 Jan 1951 v Wales (Swansea). Number: 816
Last game: 10 Apr 1954 (capt) v France (Stade Colombes)
Caps: 18 (W:10, D:1, L:7). As captain: 5 (W:3, L:2)
Scoring: 1T, 3 Pts
Appearances: 1951:W,I,F,S, 1952:SA,W,S,I,F, 1953:W,I,F,S, 1954:W*,NZ*,I*,S*,F*
Honours: Championship: 1953

Matt Stevens

Tim Stimpson

ST

Andrew Ernest (Drewy) STODDART

Born: 11 March 1863 in Westoe, South Shields
Died: 4 April 1915 in St John's Wood, London
Educated: St John's Wood School
Clubs: Harlequins, Blackheath (10)
Position: Three-quarter (10)
Debut: 3 Jan 1885 v Wales (Swansea). Number: 174
Last game: 4 Mar 1893 (capt) v Scotland (Headingley)
Caps: 10 (W:6, D:1, L:3). As captain: 4 (W:1, L:3)
Scoring: 2T, 1C, 1GM, 8 Pts
Appearances: 1885:W,I, 1886:W,I,S, 1889:M, 1890:W*,I*, 1893:W*,S*

Wilfred Bowring STODDART

Born: 27 April 1871 in West Derby, Liverpool
Died: 8 January 1935 in Grassendale, Liverpool
Educated: Royal Liverpool Institute
Clubs: Liverpool (3)
Position: Forward (3)
Debut: 9 Jan 1897 v Wales (Newport). Number: 304
Last game: 13 Mar 1897 v Scotland (Manchester)
Caps: 3 (W:1, L:2)
Scoring: 0 Pts
Appearances: 1897:W,I,S

Frederic STOKES

Born: 12 July 1850 in Greenwich
Died: 7 February 1929 in Inhurst House, Berks
Educated: Rugby School
Clubs: Blackheath (3)
Position: Forward (3)
Debut: 27 Mar 1871 (capt) v Scotland (Raeburn Place). Number: 17
Last game: 3 Mar 1873 (capt) v Scotland (Glasgow)
Caps: 3 (W:1, D:1, L:1). As captain: 3 (W:1, D:1, L:1)
Scoring: 0 Pts
Appearances: 1871:S*, 1872:S*, 1873:S*

Lennard STOKES

Born: 12 February 1856 in Greenwich
Died: 3 May 1933 in Upton, Hants
Educated: Sydney College
Clubs: Blackheath (12)
Position: Three-quarter (10), Full-back (2)
Debut: 15 Feb 1875 v Ireland (The Oval). Number: 65
Last game: 19 Mar 1881 (capt) v Scotland (Raeburn Place) - 1DG, 3 Pts
Caps: 12 (W:8, D:3, L:1). As captain: 5 (W:4, D:1, L:0)
Scoring: 17C, 2DG, 40 Pts
Appearances: 1875:I, 1876:S, 1877:I,S, 1878:S, 1879:S,I, 1880:I*,S*, 1881:I*,W*,S*

Francis le Strange STONE

Born: Third quarter 1886 in Lewisham
Died: 7 October 1938 in Westminster, London
Educated: Harrow School
Clubs: Blackheath (1)
Position: No 8 (1)
Debut: 13 Apr 1914 v France (Stade Colombes). Number: 543
Caps: 1 (W:1, L:0)
Scoring: 0 Pts
Appearances: 1914:F
Honours: Championship: 1914

Adrian Dura STOOP

Born: 27 March 1883 in Kensington
Died: 27 November 1957 in Aldershot
Educated: Rugby School, Dover School
Clubs: Oxford University (1), Harlequins (14)
Position: Fly-half (13), Scrum-half (2)
Debut: 18 Mar 1905 v Scotland (Richmond). Number: 412
Last game: 16 Mar 1912 v Scotland (Inverleith)
Caps: 15 (W:8, D:2, L:5). As captain: 2 (W:1, D:1, L:0)
Scoring: 2T, 6 Pts
Appearances: 1905:S, 1906:S,F,SA, 1907:F,W, 1910:W*,I*,S, 1911:W,F,I,S, 1912:W,S
Honours: Championship: 1910 (capt)

Many English rugby players defined the game we see today, none more so than Adrian Stoop who is credited with revolutionising back play – in his performances with Harlequins and England – at the turn of the 21st century.

Stoop, a former Rugby School pupil, redefined the role of the outside-half, paving the way for players like Jonny Wilkinson and Dan Carter to run the game from the No 10 shirt in the modern era.

Described by The Sunday Telegraph as "the father of modern rugby," Stoop led England to victory against Wales, in the first international match to be staged at Twickenham in 1910.

Stoop also had the honour of scoring the first international try at Twickenham, crossing the line within seconds of the start of the match.

His younger brother Frederick later joined him in the England team, and they enjoyed a 14-5 win over Scotland in 1910 that brought England's first Championship for 18 years.

The game against Wales in 1910 was the first of two matches as England captain for the half-Dutch outside-half who won 15 caps for England and played 182 times for Harlequins.

The Harlequins Ground in south-west London was named the Stoop Memorial Ground in his honour, a name the club changed to the Twickenham Stoop in 2005.

A critically acclaimed book – The Story of Adrian Stoop by Ian Cooper – was published in 2005.

According to a review of the book in The Independent: "Stoop is credited with pretty well inventing the modern game, including the concept of half-backs, the crazy notion of fitness training, analysis of opponents and the practising of moves."

The Sunday Times adds on Stoop's influence: "Adrian Stoop transformed the game. He made the stand-off half an attacking pivot and would run from any position. His approach was typified by the try he launched for England against Wales, the Triple Crown holders, in 1910, catching the kick-off and running out of defence.

Adrian Stoop (right)

Wales never recovered."

Stoop – who died in 1957 – became the president of the Harlequins from 1920 to 1949, and also president of the Rugby Football Union.

Frederick MacFarlane (Tim) STOOP
Born: 17 September 1888 in Kensington
Died: 24 November 1972 in south-west Surrey
Educated: Rugby School
Clubs: Harlequins (4)
Position: Centre (4)
Debut: 19 Mar 1910 v Scotland (Inverleith). Number: 509
Last game: 4 Jan 1913 v South Africa (Twickenham)
Caps: 4 (W:2, L:2)
Scoring: 0 Pts
Appearances: 1910:S, 1911:F,I, 1913:SA
Honours: Championship: 1910

Frank Moxon STOUT
Born: 21 February 1877 in Gloucester
Died: 30 May 1926 in Storrington, Sussex
Clubs: Gloucester (7), Richmond (7)
Position: Forward (14)
Debut: 9 Jan 1897 v Wales (Newport). Number: 305
Last game: 18 Mar 1905 (capt) v Scotland (Richmond)
Caps: 14 (W:2, D:2, L:10). As captain: 4 (W:0, D:1, L:3)
Scoring: 1T, 1C, 5 Pts
Appearances: 1897:W,I, 1898:I,S,W, 1899:I,S, 1903:S, 1904:W*,I,S, 1905:W*,I*,S*

Percy Wyfold STOUT, OBE
Born: 20 November 1875 in Gloucester
Died: 9 October 1937 in Marylebone
Educated: Crypt GS
Clubs: Gloucester (5), Richmond, Bristol
Position: Centre (3), Wing (2)
Debut: 12 Mar 1898 v Scotland (Edinburgh). Number: 323
Last game: 11 Mar 1899 v Scotland (Blackheath)
Caps: 5 (W:1, D:1, L:3)
Scoring: 1T, 3 Pts
Appearances: 1898:S,W, 1899:W,I,S

David STRETTLE
Born: 23 July 1983 in Warrington
Educated: Lymm HS
Clubs: Rotherham, Harlequins (1)
Position: Wing (1)
Debut: 24 Feb 2007 v Ireland (Croke Park) - 1T, 5 Pts. Number: 1282
Caps: 1 (W:0, L:1)
Scoring: 1T, 5 Pts
Appearances: 2007:I

Nicholas Courtenay STRINGER
Born: 4 October 1960 in Harrow
Clubs: Wasps (5)
Position: Full-back (2), Replacement (3), Bench (9)
Debut: 2 Jan 1982 (rep) v Australia (Twickenham). Number: 1074
Last game: 5 Jan 1985 v Romania (Twickenham)
Caps: 5 (W:3, L:2)
Scoring: 0 Pts
Appearances: 1982:A(r), 1983:NZ(r), 1984:SA1(r),A, 1985:R

Edward Linwood STRONG
Born: December 1861 in Axbridge
Died: 20 March 1945 in Barisal, India
Educated: Edinburgh Academy
Clubs: Oxford University (3), Bath
Position: Forward (3)
Debut: 5 Jan 1884 v Wales (Leeds). Number: 162
Last game: 1 Mar 1884 v Scotland (Blackheath)
Caps: 3 (W:3, L:0)
Scoring: 0 Pts
Appearances: 1884:W,I,S
Honours: Championship: 1884

Ben STURNHAM
Born: 6 March 1974 in St Albans
Clubs: St Albans, Saracens (3), Bath, Bristol
Position: Flanker (1), Replacement (2), Bench (1)
Debut: 6 Jun 1998 v Australia (Brisbane).Number: 1199
Last game: 27 Jun 1998 (rep) v New Zealand (Auckland)
Caps: 3 (W:0, L:3)
Scoring: 0 Pts
Appearances: 1998:A,NZ1(r),NZ2(r)

George Edward SUMMERSCALE
Born: Third quarter 1879 in Durham
Died: 31 December 1936 in Durham
Clubs: Durham City (1)
Position: Forward (1)
Debut: 2 Dec 1905 v New Zealand (Crystal Palace). Number: 420
Caps: 1 (W:0, L:1)
Scoring: 0 Pts
Appearances: 1905:NZ

John William SUTCLIFFE
Born: 14 April 1868 in Shibden, near Halifax
Died: 7 July 1947 in Bradford
Educated: Bradford St Thomas's School
Clubs: Bradford, Heckmondwike (1)
Position: Three-quarter (1)
Debut: 16 Feb 1889 v New Zealand Natives (Blackheath) - 1T, 1C, 3 Pts. Number: 206
Caps: 1 (W:1, L:0)
Scoring: 1T, 1C, 3 Pts
Appearances: 1889:M

David Strettle

ST

Ben Sturnham

Tony Swift

David William SWARBRICK
Born: 17 January 1927 in Tynemouth
Educated: Kingswood School
Clubs: Oxford University (6), Blackheath
Position: Wing (6)
Debut: 18 Jan 1947 v Wales (Cardiff). Number: 763
Last game: 12 Feb 1949 v Ireland (Lansdowne Road)
Caps: 6 (W:2, D:1, L:3)
Scoring: 0 Pts
Appearances: 1947:W,I,F, 1948:A,W, 1949:I

Deneys Harald SWAYNE
Born: 23 November 1909
Died: 9 September 1990 in Mendip
Educated: Bromsgrove School
Clubs: Oxford University (1), St George's Hospital, Harlequins
Position: Flanker (1)
Debut: 17 Jan 1931 v Wales (Twickenham). Number: 674
Caps: 1 (W:0, D:1, L:0)
Scoring: 0 Pts
Appearances: 1931:W

John Walter Rocke SWAYNE
Born: 27 May 1906
Died: June 1987 in Sedgemoor
Educated: Bromsgrove School
Clubs: Bridgwater & Albion (1), Harlequins
Position: No 8 (1)
Debut: 19 Jan 1929 v Wales (Twickenham). Number: 640
Caps: 1 (W:1, L:0)
Scoring: 0 Pts
Appearances: 1929:W

Anthony Hugh (Tony) SWIFT
Born: 24 May 1959 in Preston
Educated: Hutton GS
Clubs: UWIST, Swansea (6), Bath
Position: Wing (6)
Debut: 30 May 1981 v Argentina (Buenos Aires). Number: 1072
Last game: 9 Jun 1984 v South Africa (Johannesburg)
Caps: 6 (W:1, D:2, L:3)
Scoring: 0 Pts
Appearances: 1981:Ar1,Ar2, 1983:F,W,S, 1984:SA2

James Paul (Jamie) SYDDALL
Born: 7 March 1956 in Barton
Educated: De La Salle College
Clubs: Waterloo (2)
Position: Lock (2)
Debut: 6 Feb 1982 v Ireland (Twickenham). Number: 1075
Last game: 3 Nov 1984 v Australia (Twickenham)
Caps: 2 (W:0, L:2)
Scoring: 0 Pts
Appearances: 1982:I, 1984:A

Alexander Richard V SYKES
Born: Details unknown
Died: Details unknown
Educated: Birkenhead Institute
Clubs: Liverpool University, Blackheath (1)
Position: Forward (1)
Debut: 13 Apr 1914 v France (Stade Colombes).Number: 544
Caps: 1 (W:1, L:0)
Scoring: 0 Pts
Appearances: 1914:F
Honours: Championship: 1914

Frank Douglas SYKES
Born: 9 December 1927 in Batley, Yorks
Educated: St Paul's College
Clubs: Huddersfield, Northampton (4), Boston (US)
Position: Wing (4)
Debut: 26 Feb 1955 v France (Twickenham). Number: 857
Last game: 4 Jun 1963 v Australia (Sydney Sports Ground)
Caps: 4 (W:1, L:3)
Scoring: 1T, 3 Pts
Appearances: 1955:F,S, 1963:NZ2,A

Patrick William SYKES
Born: 3 March 1925 in Vancouver, Canada
Educated: St John's School
Clubs: Cambridge University, Wasps (7), RAF, Combined Services, Plymouth
Position: Scrum-half (7)
Debut: 29 Mar 1948 v France (Stade Colombes). Number: 785
Last game: 28 Feb 1953 v France (Twickenham)
Caps: 7 (W:5, D:1, L:1)
Scoring: 0 Pts
Appearances: 1948:F, 1952:S,I,F, 1953:W,I,F
Honours: Championship: 1953

Ronald Edward SYRETT
Born: 5 January 1931 in Amersham
Educated: RGS High Wycombe
Clubs: Wasps (11), RAF
Position: Flanker (11)
Debut: 18 Jan 1958 v Wales (Twickenham). Number: 872
Last game: 24 Feb 1962 v France (Stade Colombes)
Caps: 11 (W:7, D:3, L:1)
Scoring: 1T, 3 Pts
Appearances: 1958:W,A,I,F, 1960:W,I,F,S, 1962:W,I,F
Honours: Championship: 1958

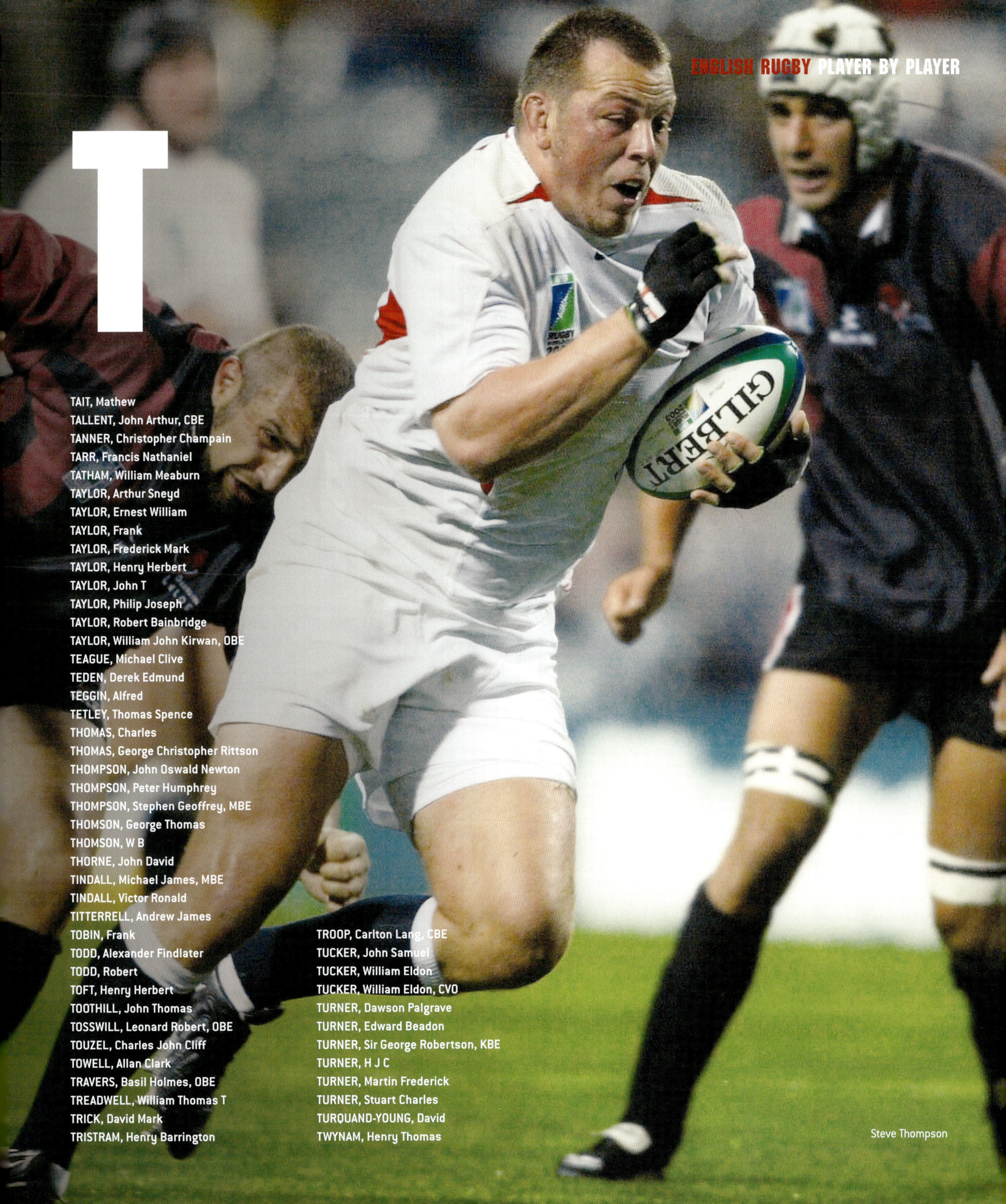

T

TAIT, Mathew
TALLENT, John Arthur, CBE
TANNER, Christopher Champain
TARR, Francis Nathaniel
TATHAM, William Meaburn
TAYLOR, Arthur Sneyd
TAYLOR, Ernest William
TAYLOR, Frank
TAYLOR, Frederick Mark
TAYLOR, Henry Herbert
TAYLOR, John T
TAYLOR, Philip Joseph
TAYLOR, Robert Bainbridge
TAYLOR, William John Kirwan, OBE
TEAGUE, Michael Clive
TEDEN, Derek Edmund
TEGGIN, Alfred
TETLEY, Thomas Spence
THOMAS, Charles
THOMAS, George Christopher Rittson
THOMPSON, John Oswald Newton
THOMPSON, Peter Humphrey
THOMPSON, Stephen Geoffrey, MBE
THOMSON, George Thomas
THOMSON, W B
THORNE, John David
TINDALL, Michael James, MBE
TINDALL, Victor Ronald
TITTERRELL, Andrew James
TOBIN, Frank
TODD, Alexander Findlater
TODD, Robert
TOFT, Henry Herbert
TOOTHILL, John Thomas
TOSSWILL, Leonard Robert, OBE
TOUZEL, Charles John Cliff
TOWELL, Allan Clark
TRAVERS, Basil Holmes, OBE
TREADWELL, William Thomas T
TRICK, David Mark
TRISTRAM, Henry Barrington
TROOP, Carlton Lang, CBE
TUCKER, John Samuel
TUCKER, William Eldon
TUCKER, William Eldon, CVO
TURNER, Dawson Palgrave
TURNER, Edward Beadon
TURNER, Sir George Robertson, KBE
TURNER, H J C
TURNER, Martin Frederick
TURNER, Stuart Charles
TURQUAND-YOUNG, David
TWYNAM, Henry Thomas

Steve Thompson

Mathew TAIT
Born: 6 February 1986 in Shotley Bridge
Educated: Barnard Castle School
Clubs: Newcastle (7)
Position: Centre (4), Wing (1), Replacement (2), Bench (1)
Debut: 5 Feb 2005 v Wales (Cardiff). Number: 1260
Last game: 24 Feb 2007 (rep) v Ireland (Croke Park)
Caps: 7 (W:2, L:5)
Scoring: 0 Pts
Appearances: 2005:W, 2006:A1,A2,SA1,SA2, 2007:It(r),I(r)

John Arthur TALLENT, CBE
Born: 8 March 1911 in Bromley
Died: 14 April 2004 in Hampshire
Educated: Sherborne School
Clubs: Cambridge University (4), Blackheath (1)
Position: Centre (4), Fly-half (1)
Debut: 21 Mar 1931 v Scotland (Murrayfield) - 2T, 6 Pts. Number: 682
Last game: 9 Feb 1935 v Ireland (Twickenham)
Caps: 5 (W:1, L:4)
Scoring: 3T, 9 Pts
Appearances: 1931:S,F, 1932:SA,W, 1935:I

Christopher Champain TANNER
Born: 24 June 1908 in Cheltenham
Died: Killed in action in 1941 in Crete
Educated: Cheltenham College
Clubs: Cambridge University (1), Richmond, Gloucester (4)
Position: Wing (5)
Debut: 15 Mar 1930 v Scotland (Twickenham). Number: 665
Last game: 19 Mar 1932 v Scotland (Twickenham) - 1T, 3 Pts
Caps: 5 (W:2, D:1, L:2)
Scoring: 1T, 3 Pts
Appearances: 1930:S, 1932:SA,W,I,S
Honours: Championship: 1930

Francis Nathaniel (Frank) TARR
Born: 14 August 1887 in Belper
Died: Killed in action in 1915 in Ypres, Belgium
Educated: Stoneygate School, Uppingham School
Clubs: Oxford University (3), Leicester (1), Headingley, Richmond
Position: Centre (4)
Debut: 9 Jan 1909 v Australia (Blackheath). Number: 480
Last game: 15 Mar 1913 v Scotland (Twickenham)
Caps: 4 (W:2, L:2)
Scoring: 2T, 6 Pts
Appearances: 1909:A,W,F, 1913:S
Honours: Championship: 1913

William Meaburn TATHAM
Born: 30 July 1862 in Walsingham
Died: 18 October 1938 in Don Valley
Educated: Marlborough School
Clubs: Marlborough Nomads, Oxford University (7)
Position: Forward (7)
Debut: 4 Mar 1882 v Scotland (Manchester). Number: 148
Last game: 1 Mar 1884 v Scotland (Blackheath)
Caps: 7 (W:6, L:1)
Scoring: 1T, 1 Pt
Appearances: 1882:S, 1883:W,I,S, 1884:W,I,S
Honours: Championship: 1883, 1884

Mathew Tait

Arthur Sneyd TAYLOR
Born: 7 December 1859 in Greenwich
Died: 7 April 1921 in Surbiton
Educated: Merchant Taylors' School
Clubs: Cambridge University, Guy's Hospital, Blackheath (4)
Position: Full-back (4)
Debut: 16 Dec 1882 v Wales (Swansea). Number: 154
Last game: 6 Feb 1886 v Ireland (Lansdowne Road)
Caps: 4 (W:4, L:0)
Scoring: 0 Pts
Appearances: 1883:W,I, 1886:W,I
Honours: Championship: 1883

Ernest William TAYLOR
Born: 20 February 1869 in Newcastle-upon-Tyne
Died: Details unknown
Clubs: Rockcliff (14)
Position: Half-Back (7), Scrum-half (6), Fly-half (1)
Debut: 6 Feb 1892 v Ireland (Manchester). Number: 245
Last game: 4 Feb 1899 v Ireland (Lansdowne Road)
Caps: 14 (W:7, L:7). As captain: 6 (W:2, L:4)
Scoring: 2T, 3C, 1GM, 15 Pts
Appearances: 1892:I, 1893:I, 1894:W,I,S*, 1895:W,I,S, 1896:W*,I*, 1897:W*,I*,S*, 1899:I
Honours: Championship: 1892

Frank (Sos) TAYLOR
Born: 4 May 1890 in Leicester
Died: 22 September 1956 in Leicester
Educated: Medway Street School
Clubs: Medway Old Boys, Medway Athletic, Leicester (2)
Position: Prop (2)
Debut: 31 Jan 1920 v France (Twickenham). Number: 560
Last game: 14 Feb 1920 v Ireland (Lansdowne Road)
Caps: 2 (W:2, L:0)
Scoring: 0 Pts
Appearances: 1920:F,I

Frederick Mark (Tim) TAYLOR
Born: 18 March 1888 in Leicester
Died: 2 March 1966 in Evington, Leicester
Educated: Medway Street School
Clubs: Medway Old Boys, Medway Athletic, Leicester (1)
Position: Fly-half (1)
Debut: 17 Jan 1914 v Wales (Twickenham). Number: 538
Caps: 1 (W:1, L:0)
Scoring: 0 Pts
Appearances: 1914:W
Honours: Championship: 1914

Henry Herbert TAYLOR
Born: 21 September 1858 in Greenwich
Died: 25 May 1942 in Steyning
Educated: Merchant Taylors' School
Clubs: St George's Hospital (2), Blackheath (3)
Position: Half-Back (5)
Debut: 10 Mar 1879 v Scotland (Raeburn Place). Number: 116
Last game: 4 Mar 1882 v Scotland (Manchester)
Caps: 5 (W:3, D:1, L:1)
Scoring: 6T, 6 Pts
Appearances: 1879:S, 1880:S, 1881:I,W, 1882:S

John T TAYLOR
Born: 26 May 1876
Died: 8 September 1951 in Ashington
Clubs: Castleford (3), West Hartlepool (8)
Position: Centre (10), Full-back (1)
Debut: 6 Feb 1897 v Ireland (Lansdowne Road). Number: 309
Last game: 18 Mar 1905 v Scotland (Richmond)
Caps: 11 (W:3, L:8). As captain: 1 (W:0, L:1)
Scoring: 1T, 1C, 5 Pts
Appearances: 1897:I, 1899:I, 1900:I, 1901:W*,I, 1902:W,I,S, 1903:W,I, 1905:S

Philip Joseph (Noddy) TAYLOR
Born: 6 June 1931 in Wakefield
Clubs: Wakefield, Army, Blackheath, Loughborough College, Northampton (6)
Position: No 8 (6)
Debut: 22 Jan 1955 v Wales (Cardiff). Number: 854
Last game: 17 Mar 1962 v Scotland (Murrayfield)
Caps: 6 (W:1, D:3, L:2)
Scoring: 0 Pts
Appearances: 1955:W,I, 1962:W,I,F,S

Mike Teague

Robert Bainbridge (Bob) TAYLOR
Born: 30 April 1942 in Northampton
Educated: Northampton GS, King Alfred's School
Clubs: Northampton (16)
Position: Flanker (10), No 8 (6), Bench (1)
Debut: 15 Jan 1966 v Wales (Twickenham). Number: 941
Last game: 27 Mar 1971 v Scotland (Murrayfield)
Caps: 16 (W:6, L:10). As captain: 1 (W:0, L:1)
Scoring: 2T, 6 Pts
Appearances: 1966:W, 1967:I,F,S,W,NZ, 1969:F,S,W,SA, 1970:I,W,S,F*, 1971:S,S

William John Kirwan TAYLOR, OBE
Born: 29 June 1905 in Sutton, Surrey
Died: 28 August 1994 in Lausanne, Switzerland
Educated: Epsom College
Clubs: Cambridge University, Blackheath (5)
Position: Wing (5)
Debut: 7 Jan 1928 v Australia (Twickenham) - 1T, 3 Pts. Number: 631
Last game: 17 Mar 1928 v Scotland (Twickenham)
Caps: 5 (W:5, L:0)
Scoring: 2T, 6 Pts
Appearances: 1928:A,W,I,F,S
Honours: Grand Slam: 1928

Michael Clive (Mike) TEAGUE
Born: 8 October 1959 in Gloucester
Educated: Churchdown School
Clubs: Gloucester Old Boys, Gloucester (22), Cardiff, Moseley (5)
Position: Flanker (18), No 8 (8), Replacement (1), Bench (5)
Debut: 2 Feb 1985 (rep) v France (Twickenham). Number: 1107
Last game: 20 Mar 1993 v Ireland (Lansdowne Road)
Caps: 27 (W:16, D:2, L:9)
Scoring: 3T, 12 Pts
Appearances: 1985:F(r),NZ1,NZ2, 1989:S,I,F,W,R, 1990:F,W,S, 1991:W,S,I,F,Fj,A,NZ,It,F,S,A, 1992:SA, 1993:F,W,S,I
Honours: Grand Slam: 1991

Another in the seemingly endless conveyor belt of rugged, no-nonsense West Country forwards, Mike Teague played for Gloucester and Moseley, and was a key member of the England back row, alongside Peter Winterbottom and Dean Richards, that drove them to the Grand Slam and the final of the World Cup in 1991. Unfortunately, the backs couldn't capitalise on the heroic work of the forwards, and they lost to Australia 12-6.

After suffering the disappointment of missing the Grand Slam in the final match of the 1990 Five Nations to Scotland, the team was fired up for the first match of the 1991 campaign against Wales. Determined not to miss out again, and seeking their first victory at Cardiff Arms Park since 1963, they set about the Welsh.

The back row was in particularly belligerent mood, and it was fitting that Teague scored the only try of the game, driven over by Dean Richards and co.

Better known as Iron Mike, Teague made his England debut in 1985 against France, and played against the All Blacks that summer, but it would be another four years before he pulled on the England jersey again.

Denied the Five Nations title by Wales in 1989, he still

Mike Teague

impressed enough to earn a call-up to the British and Irish Lions squad to tour Australia. After missing the first Test defeat (The Lions' heaviest against Australia), he came in for the final two Tests, where his performances were so influential that not only did they win those games, and the series 2-1, but also he was voted player of the series.

Teague made his final bow for England against Ireland in 1993, but made that year's Lions tour of New Zealand, coming in for the final Test and the team's only win.

He is one of the few men to hold a 100% win record with the Lions.

"Players like Mike believe that they are the best whether they are in or out of the international team. They have the burning commitment and a desire to be the best. Other players who do not have that belief sometimes fade away after temporary impact," said England coach Geoff Cooke.

England captain Phil Vickery added: "Teaguey is a legend and a top bloke and if I could come away with the compliments and honours that he had in his playing days then, as a rugby player, I couldn't ask for anything more."

A stalwart with Gloucester through the 1980s, he coined the phrase "ain't got time to bleed!" Teague played in two cup finals with Gloucester. They shared the first with Moseley in 1982 but lost to Bath 46-8 in 1990, the most one-sided contest in Twickenham's cup history.

Derek Edmund TEDEN

Born: 19 July 1916 in Edmonton
Died: Killed in action in 1940 in the Friesian Islands
Educated: Taunton School
Clubs: Richmond (3)
Position: Prop (3)
Debut: 21 Jan 1939 v Wales (Twickenham) - 1T, 3 Pts. Number: 748
Last game: 18 Mar 1939 v Scotland (Murrayfield)
Caps: 3 (W:2, L:1)
Scoring: 1T, 3 Pts
Appearances: 1939:W,I,S

Alfred TEGGIN

Born: 22 October 1860 in Broughton, Lancs
Died: 23 July 1941 in Cleveleys, Blackpool
Clubs: Broughton Rangers (6)
Position: Forward (6)
Debut: 4 Feb 1884 v Ireland (Lansdowne Road). Number: 166
Last game: 5 Mar 1887 v Scotland (Manchester)
Caps: 6 (W:3, D:2, L:1)
Scoring: 1T, 1 Pt
Appearances: 1884:I, 1885:W, 1886:I,S, 1887:I,S
Honours: Championship: 1884

Thomas Spence TETLEY

Born: Second quarter 1856 in Bradford
Died: 15 August 1924 in Wharfedale
Clubs: Bradford (1)
Position: Three-quarter (1)
Debut: 6 Mar 1876 v Scotland (The Oval). Number: 85
Caps: 1 (W:1, L:0)
Scoring: 0 Pts
Appearances: 1876:S

Charles THOMAS

Born: 1875
Died: 1935
Clubs: Barnstaple (4)
Position: Forward (4)
Debut: 5 Jan 1895 v Wales (Swansea). Number: 280
Last game: 4 Feb 1899 v Ireland (Lansdowne Road)
Caps: 4 (W:2, L:2)
Scoring: 1T, 3 Pts
Appearances: 1895:W,I,S, 1899:I

George Christopher Rittson THOMAS

Born: 18 December 1926 in Cardiff, Wales
Educated: Dragon School, Sherborne School
Clubs: Oxford University (3)
Position: Flanker (3)
Debut: 20 Jan 1951 v Wales (Swansea) - 1T, 3 Pts. Number: 817
Last game: 24 Feb 1951 v France (Twickenham)
Caps: 3 (W:0, L:3)
Scoring: 1T, 3 Pts
Appearances: 1951:W,I,F

Steve Thompson

John Oswald Newton THOMPSON

Born: 2 December 1920 in Paddington
Died: 3 April 1974 near Luderitz, S W Africa
Educated: Diocesan College
Clubs: University of Cape Town, Oxford University (2)
Position: Scrum-half (2)
Debut: 15 Mar 1947 v Scotland (Twickenham). Number: 770
Last game: 19 Apr 1947 v France (Twickenham)
Caps: 2 (W:2, L:0)
Scoring: 0 Pts
Appearances: 1947:S,F

Peter Humphrey THOMPSON

Born: 18 January 1929 in Scarborough
Educated: Leeds GS
Clubs: Headingley (13), Waterloo (4)
Position: Wing (17)
Debut: 21 Jan 1956 v Wales (Twickenham). Number: 868
Last game: 21 Mar 1959 v Scotland (Twickenham)
Caps: 17 (W:10, D:4, L:3)
Scoring: 5T, 15 Pts
Appearances: 1956:W,I,S,F, 1957:W,I,F,S, 1958:W,A,I,F,S, 1959:W,I,F,S
Honours: Grand Slam: 1957. Championship: 1958

Stephen Geoffrey (Steve) THOMPSON, MBE

Born: 15 July 1978 in Hemel Hempstead
Educated: Northampton BHS
Clubs: Old Scouts, Northampton (47)
Position: Hooker (43), Replacement (4), Bench (1)
Debut: 2 Feb 2002 v Scotland (Murrayfield). Number: 1236
Last game: 18 Mar 2006 (rep) v Ireland (Twickenham)
Caps: 47 (W:33, L:14)
Scoring: 3T, 15 Pts
Appearances: 2002:S,I,F,W,It,Ar,NZ,A,SA, 2003:F,W,It,S,I,NZ,A,F(r),F,Geo,SA,Sm(r),W,F,A, 2004:It,S,I,W,F,NZ1,A(r),C,SA,A, 2005:W,F,I,It,S,A,NZ,Sm, 2006:W,It,S,F,I(r)
Honours: RWC Winner: 2003. Grand Slam: 2003

Steve Thompson

George Thomas THOMSON
Born: 1857
Died: 31 October 1899 in Sydney, Australia
Educated: Heath GS
Clubs: Halifax (9)
Position: Forward (9)
Debut: 4 Mar 1878 v Scotland (The Oval). Number: 100
Last game: 7 Feb 1885 v Ireland (Manchester)
Caps: 9 (W:6, D:2, L:1)
Scoring: 1T, 1 Pt
Appearances: 1878:S, 1882:I,S, 1883:W,I,S, 1884:I,S, 1885:I
Honours: Championship: 1883, 1884

W B THOMSON
Born: 1871 in Matabeleland, S Rhodesia
Died: Details unknown
Educated: Bedford Modern School
Clubs: Blackheath (4)
Position: Centre (3), Full-back (1)
Debut: 2 Jan 1892 v Wales (Blackheath). Number: 241
Last game: 9 Mar 1895 v Scotland (Richmond)
Caps: 4 (W:3, L:1)
Scoring: 1T, 3 Pts
Appearances: 1892:W, 1895:W,I,S
Honours: Championship: 1892

Mike Tindall

John David THORNE
Born: 1 January 1934 in Bristol
Educated: Speedwell Secondary School
Clubs: Bristol (3)
Position: Hooker (3)
Debut: 19 Jan 1963 v Wales (Cardiff). Number: 914
Last game: 23 Feb 1963 v France (Twickenham)
Caps: 3 (W:2, D:1, L:0)
Scoring: 0 Pts
Appearances: 1963:W,I,F
Honours: Championship: 1963

Michael James (Mike) TINDALL, MBE
Born: 18 October 1978 in Wakefield
Educated: Queen Elizabeth GS
Clubs: Bath (41), Gloucester (11)
Position: Centre (48), Replacement (4), Bench (1)
Debut: 5 Feb 2000 v Ireland (Twickenham) - 1T, 5 Pts. Number: 1216
Last game: 24 Feb 2007 v Ireland (Croke Park)
Caps: 52 (W:38, L:14)
Scoring: 12T, 2C, 64 Pts
Appearances: 2000:I,F,W,It,S,SA1,SA2,A,Ar,SA, 2001:W(r),R,SA(r), 2002:S,I,F,W,It,NZ,A,SA, 2003:It,S,I,NZ,A,F,Geo,SA,Sm,W,F(r),A, 2004:W,F,NZ1,NZ2,A,C,SA,A, 2005:A,NZ,Sm, 2006:W,It,S,F,I(r), 2007:S,It,I
Honours: RWC Winner: 2003. Outright Championship: 2000, 2001, 2003

Victor Ronald TINDALL
Born: 1 August 1928 in Kingsclere
Educated: Wallasey GS
Clubs: Liverpool University (4), Richmond, RAF, Combined Services
Position: Wing (4)
Debut: 20 Jan 1951 v Wales (Swansea). Number: 818
Last game: 17 Mar 1951 v Scotland (Twickenham)
Caps: 4 (W:1, L:3)
Scoring: 0 Pts
Appearances: 1951:W,I,F,S

Andrew James (Andy) TITTERRELL
Born: 10 January 1981 in Dartford
Educated: Sevenoaks School
Clubs: Saracens, Waterloo, Sale (4)
Position: Replacement Hooker (4), Bench (5)
Debut: 19 Jun 2004 (rep) v New Zealand (Auckland). Number: 1253
Last game: 19 Mar 2005 (rep) v Scotland (Twickenham)
Caps: 4 (W:3, L:1)
Scoring: 0 Pts
Appearances: 2004:NZ2(r),C(r), 2005:It(r),S(r)

Frank TOBIN
Born: 23 September 1849 in Liverpool
Died: 6 February 1927 in Liverpool
Educated: Rugby School
Clubs: Cambridge University, Liverpool (1)
Position: Half-Back (1)
Debut: 27 Mar 1871 v Scotland (Raeburn Place). Number: 18
Caps: 1 (W:0, L:1)
Scoring: 0 Pts
Appearances: 1871:S

Andy Titterrell

Henry Herbert (Herbert) TOFT
Born: 2 October 1909 in Salford
Died: 7 July 1987 in Chichester
Educated: Manchester GS
Clubs: Manchester University, Waterloo (10), RAF, Combined Services
Position: Hooker (10)
Debut: 21 Mar 1936 v Scotland (Twickenham). Number: 727
Last game: 18 Mar 1939 (capt) v Scotland (Murrayfield)
Caps: 10 (W:7, L:3). As captain: 4 (W:2, L:2)
Scoring: 0 Pts
Appearances: 1936:S, 1937:W,I,S, 1938:W,I,S*, 1939:W*,I*,S*
Honours: Championship: 1937

John Thomas TOOTHILL
Born: Second quarter 1866 in Bradford
Died: 29 June 1947 in Bradford
Clubs: Manningham, Bradford (12)
Position: Forward (12)
Debut: 1 Mar 1890 v Scotland (Raeburn Place). Number: 220
Last game: 3 Feb 1894 v Ireland (Blackheath)
Caps: 12 (W:9, L:3)
Scoring: 1T, 1 Pt
Appearances: 1890:S,I, 1891:W,I, 1892:W,I,S, 1893:W,I,S, 1894:W,I
Honours: Championship: 1892

Leonard Robert TOSSWILL, OBE
Born: 12 January 1880 in Exeter
Died: 3 October 1932 in Roehampton, Surrey
Educated: Marlborough School
Clubs: Marlborough Nomads, St Bart's Hospital, Exeter (3)
Position: Forward (3)
Debut: 11 Jan 1902 v Wales (Blackheath). Number: 378
Last game: 15 Mar 1902 v Scotland (Inverleith)
Caps: 3 (W:2, L:1)
Scoring: 0 Pts
Appearances: 1902:W,I,S

Charles John Cliff TOUZEL
Born: Second quarter 1855 in Wirral, Cheshire
Died: 24 August 1899 in Stroud
Educated: Wellington College
Clubs: Cambridge University (2), Blackheath, Liverpool
Position: Forward (2)
Debut: 5 Feb 1877 v Ireland (The Oval). Number: 91
Last game: 5 Mar 1877 v Scotland (Raeburn Place)
Caps: 2 (W:1, L:1)
Scoring: 0 Pts
Appearances: 1877:I,S

Alexander Findlater TODD
Born: 20 September 1873 in Lewisham
Died: Killed in action in 1915 in Poperinghe, Belgium
Educated: Mill Hill School
Clubs: Cambridge University, Blackheath (2)
Position: Forward (2)
Debut: 3 Feb 1900 v Ireland (Richmond). Number: 296
Last game: 10 Mar 1900 v Scotland (Inverleith)
Caps: 2 (W:1, D:1, L:0)
Scoring: 0 Pts
Appearances: 1900:I,S

Robert TODD
Born: April 1847 in Bury
Died: 9 February 1927 in Stockport
Educated: Allesley College
Clubs: Manchester (1)
Position: Forward (1)
Debut: 5 Mar 1877 v Scotland (Raeburn Place).
Number: 94
Caps: 1 (W:0, L:1)
Scoring: 0 Pts
Appearances: 1877:S

Allan Clark TOWELL
Born: Second quarter 1925 in Middlesbrough
Educated: Middlesbrough College
Clubs: Loughborough College, Middlesbrough, Leicester (1), Bedford (1)
Position: Centre (2)
Debut: 29 Mar 1948 v France (Stade Colombes). Number: 786
Last game: 17 Mar 1951 v Scotland (Twickenham)
Caps: 2 (W:1, L:1)
Scoring: 0 Pts
Appearances: 1948:F, 1951:S

Basil Holmes (Jaika) TRAVERS, OBE
Born: 7 July 1919 in Waverley, Sydney, Australia
Died: 18 December 1998 in Sydney, Australia
Educated: Sydney C of E GS
Clubs: Sydney University (AU), Oxford University (4), Harlequins (2), New South Wales (AU)
Position: Flanker (4), No 8 (2)
Debut: 18 Jan 1947 v Wales (Cardiff). Number: 764
Last game: 19 Mar 1949 v Scotland (Twickenham) - 2C, 4 Pts
Caps: 6 (W:3, D:1, L:2)
Scoring: 2C, 4 Pts
Appearances: 1947:W,I, 1948:A,W, 1949:F,S

William Thomas TREADWELL
Born: 13 March 1939 in Brentford
Educated: St Benedict's School
Clubs: Guy's Hospital, Wasps (3)
Position: Hooker (3)
Debut: 12 Feb 1966 v Ireland (Twickenham). Number: 945
Last game: 19 Mar 1966 v Scotland (Murrayfield)
Caps: 3 (W:0, D:1, L:2)
Scoring: 0 Pts
Appearances: 1966:I,F,S

David Mark TRICK
Born: 26 October 1960 in Dartford
Educated: Bryanston School
Clubs: Plymouth Albion, Tavistock, Bath (2)
Position: Wing (2)
Debut: 19 Mar 1983 v Ireland (Lansdowne Road). Number: 1078
Last game: 2 Jun 1984 v South Africa (Port Elizabeth)
Caps: 2 (W:0, L:2)
Scoring: 0 Pts
Appearances: 1983:I, 1984:SA1

Henry Barrington TRISTRAM
Born: 5 September 1861 in Greatham, Durham
Died: 1 October 1946 in St Helier, Jersey
Educated: Loretto School, Winchester School
Clubs: Oxford University (4), Richmond (1), Durham City, Newton Abbot, Durham University
Position: Full-back (5)
Debut: 3 Mar 1883 v Scotland (Raeburn Place). Number: 159
Last game: 5 Mar 1887 v Scotland (Manchester)
Caps: 5 (W:4, D:1, L:0)
Scoring: 0 Pts
Appearances: 1883:S, 1884:W,S, 1885:W, 1887:S
Honours: Championship: 1883, 1884

Carlton Lang TROOP, CBE
Born: 10 June 1910 in Malton
Died: 2 June 1992 in Rye
Educated: St Peter's School
Clubs: RMC Sandhurst, Devonport Services, Richmond, Aldershot Services, Duke of Wellington's Regt, Army (2)
Position: No 8 (2)
Debut: 11 Feb 1933 v Ireland (Twickenham). Number: 702
Last game: 18 Mar 1933 v Scotland (Murrayfield)
Caps: 2 (W:1, L:1)
Scoring: 0 Pts
Appearances: 1933:I,S

John Samuel (Sam) TUCKER
Born: 1 June 1895 in Bristol
Died: 4 January 1973 in Bristol
Educated: St Nicholas & St Leonard CS
Clubs: Bristol (27), Army
Position: Hooker (27)
Debut: 21 Jan 1922 v Wales (Cardiff). Number: 572
Last game: 17 Jan 1931 (capt) v Wales (Twickenham)
Caps: 27 (W:14, D:4, L:9). As captain: 3 (W:1, D:2, L:0)
Scoring: 2T, 6 Pts
Appearances: 1922:W, 1925:NZ,W,I,S,F, 1926:W,I,F,S, 1927:W,I,S,F, 1928:A,W,I,F,S, 1929:W,I,F, 1930:W,I,F*,S*, 1931:W*
Honours: Grand Slam: 1928. Championship: 1930 (capt)

David Trick

Stuart Turner

William Eldon TUCKER
Born: 17 August 1872 in Bermuda
Died: 18 October 1953
Educated: Trinity College Port Hope (CA)
Clubs: Cambridge University (5), St George's Hospital, Blackheath
Position: Forward (5)
Debut: 6 Jan 1894 v Wales (Birkenhead Park). Number: 267
Last game: 9 Mar 1895 v Scotland (Richmond)
Caps: 5 (W:3, L:2)
Scoring: 0 Pts
Appearances: 1894:W,I, 1895:W,I,S

William Eldon (Bill) TUCKER, CVO
Born: 6 August 1903 in Bermuda
Died: 4 August 1991 in Bermuda
Educated: Sherborne School
Clubs: Cambridge University (1), St George's Hospital, Blackheath (2), TA
Position: No 8 (3)
Debut: 13 Feb 1926 v Ireland (Lansdowne Road). Number: 613
Last game: 8 Feb 1930 v Ireland (Lansdowne Road)
Caps: 3 (W:1, L:2)
Scoring: 0 Pts
Appearances: 1926:I, 1930:W,I
Honours: Championship: 1930

Dawson Palgrave TURNER
Born: 15 December 1846
Died: 25 February 1909 in Tunbridge Wells
Educated: Rugby School
Clubs: Richmond (6)
Position: Forward (6)
Debut: 27 Mar 1871 v Scotland (Raeburn Place). Number: 19
Last game: 8 Mar 1875 v Scotland (Raeburn Place)
Caps: 6 (W:3, D:2, L:1)
Scoring: 0 Pts
Appearances: 1871:S, 1872:S, 1873:S, 1874:S, 1875:I,S

Edward Beadon TURNER
Born: September 1854 in Epping
Died: 30 June 1931 in Paddington
Educated: Uppingham School
Clubs: St George's Hospital (3)
Position: Forward (3)
Debut: 13 Dec 1875 v Ireland (Dublin). Number: 78
Last game: 11 Mar 1878 v Ireland (Lansdowne Road) - 1T, 1 Pt
Caps: 3 (W:3, L:0)
Scoring: 1T, 1 Pt
Appearances: 1875:I, 1877:I, 1878:I

Sir George Robertson TURNER, KBE
Born: 22 October 1855
Died: 7 April 1941 in Hove
Educated: Uppingham School
Clubs: St George's Hospital (1)
Position: Forward (1)
Debut: 6 Mar 1876 v Scotland (The Oval). Number: 86
Caps: 1 (W:1, L:0)
Scoring: 0 Pts
Appearances: 1876:S

H J C TURNER
Born: Details unknown
Died: Details unknown
Clubs: Manchester (1)
Position: Forward (1)
Debut: 27 Mar 1871 v Scotland (Raeburn Place). Number: 20
Caps: 1 (W:0, L:1)
Scoring: 0 Pts
Appearances: 1871:S

Martin Frederick TURNER
Born: 1 August 1921 in Croydon
Educated: Whitgift School
Clubs: Cambridge University, Blackheath (2)
Position: Wing (2)
Debut: 20 Mar 1948 v Scotland (Murrayfield). Number: 783
Last game: 29 Mar 1948 v France (Stade Colombes)
Caps: 2 (W:0, L:2)
Scoring: 0 Pts
Appearances: 1948:S,F

Stuart Charles TURNER
Born: 22 April 1972 in Southport
Clubs: Waterloo, Orrell, Worcester, Rotherham, Sale (1)
Position: Replacement Prop (1)
Debut: 17 Mar 2004 (rep) v Wales (Cardiff). Number: 1285
Caps: 1 (W:0, L:1)
Scoring: 0 Pts
Appearances: 2007:W

David TURQUAND-YOUNG
Born: 1904
Clubs: Richmond (5), Royal Tank Regt, Army
Position: Lock (5)
Debut: 7 Jan 1928 v Australia (Twickenham). Number: 632
Last game: 1 Apr 1929 v France (Stade Colombes)
Caps: 5 (W:3, L:2)
Scoring: 0 Pts
Appearances: 1928:A,W, 1929:I,S,F
Honours: Championship: 1928

Henry Thomas TWYNAM
Born: First quarter 1853 in Winchester
Died: 19 May 1899 in Kensington
Educated: Sherborne School
Clubs: Richmond (8)
Position: Half-Back (8)
Debut: 24 Mar 1879 v Ireland (The Oval) - 1T, 1 Pt. Number: 119
Last game: 1 Mar 1884 v Scotland (Blackheath)
Caps: 8 (W:7, D:1, L:0)
Scoring: 4T, 4 Pts
Appearances: 1879:I, 1880:I, 1881:W, 1882:I, 1883:I, 1884:W,I,S
Honours: Championship: 1883, 1884

U-V

UBOGU, Victor Eriakpo
UNDERWOOD, Adrian Martin
UNDERWOOD, Rory, MBE
UNDERWOOD, Tony
UNWIN, Ernest James
UNWIN, Geoffrey Thomas
UREN, Richard
UTTLEY, Roger Miles, OBE

VALENTINE, James
VANDERSPAR, Charles Henry Richard
VAN GISBERGEN, Mark
VAN RYNEVELD, Clive Berrange
VARLEY, Henry
VARNDELL , Thomas William
VASSALL, Henry
VASSALL, Henry Holland
VAUGHAN, Douglas Brian
VERELST, Courteney Lee
VERNON, George Frederick
VICKERY, George
VICKERY, Philip John, MBE
VIVYAN, Elliott John
VOYCE, Anthony Thomas, OBE
VOYCE, Thomas Michael Dunstan
VYVYAN, Hugh Donnithorne

Rory Underwood

Victor Ubogu

Victor Eriakpo UBOGU

Born: 8 September 1964 in Lagos, Nigeria
Educated: West Buckland College
Clubs: Oxford University, Moseley, Richmond, Bath (24)
Position: Prop (21), Replacement (3), Bench (12)
Debut: 17 Oct 1992 v Canada (Wembley). Number: 1145
Last game: 26 Jun 1999 (rep) v Australia (Sydney)
Caps: 24 (W:17, L:7)
Scoring: 1T, 5 Pts
Appearances: 1992:C,SA, 1993:NZ, 1994:S,I,F,W,SA1,SA2,R,C, 1995:I,F,W,S,Ar,Sm,A,NZ,F,SA, 1999:F(r),W(r),A(r)
Honours: Grand Slam: 1995

The first black man to play in the forwards for England, Victor Ubogu was an uncompromising prop who always played the game with a broad smile on his face.

Born in Nigeria he learned his rugby at West Buckland School and later at Oxford University, making his England debut in 1992 and enjoying a seven-year Test career.

Ubogu went from solid club player at Moseley and Richmond to a man of international repute at Bath, where he won the Heineken Cup in 1998.

He was never the archetypal prop. Varsity-educated, meticulously groomed and driving a canary yellow Lotus Esprit sports car aren't normally on the CV of those who play at the coalface.

But Ubogu was as unconventional as they come, hitting his best form on the tighthead in England's 1995 Grand Slam team and scoring his one Test try, against Wales in that same season.

"The days are gone when props just had to put their head down in the scrum and push," explained former Bath and England prop Gareth Chilcott in The Guardian. "The game has changed and all players from one to fifteen have to tackle, run, handle the ball and play an expansive role. Victor has always been happy with the ball in his hand but now he has worked hard on his scrummaging he is becoming one of the best."

Ubogu now owns a travel company offering trips to sporting events and corporate hospitality.

Adrian Martin UNDERWOOD

Born: 19 July 1940 in Kidderminster
Educated: King Charles I School, St Luke's College
Clubs: Northampton (4), Exeter (1)
Position: Wing (4), Centre (1)
Debut: 20 Jan 1962 v Wales (Twickenham). Number: 902
Last game: 8 Feb 1964 v Ireland (Twickenham)
Caps: 5 (W:1, D:2, L:2)
Scoring: 0 Pts
Appearances: 1962:W,I,F,S, 1964:I

Rory UNDERWOOD, MBE

Born: 19 June 1963 in Middlesbrough
Educated: Barnard Castle School
Clubs: Leicester (85), RAF, Bedford
Position: Wing (85), Bench (1)
Debut: 18 Feb 1984 v Ireland (Twickenham). Number: 1084
Last game: 16 Mar 1996 v Ireland (Twickenham)
Caps: 85 (W:55, D:2, L:28).
Scoring: 49T, 210 Pts
Appearances: 1984:I,F,W,A, 1985:R,F,S,I,W, 1986:W,I,F, 1987:I,F,W,S,A,J,W, 1988:F,W,S,I,I,A1,A2,Fj,A, 1989:S,I,F,W,R,Fj, 1990:I,F,W,S,Ar, 1991:W,S,I,F,Fj,A,NZ,It,US,F,S,A, 1992:S,I,F,W,SA, 1993:F,W,S,I,NZ, 1994:S, I,F,W,SA1,SA2,R,C, 1995:I,F,W,S,Ar,It,Sm,A,NZ,F,SA,Sm, 1996:F,W,S,I
Honours: Grand Slam: 1991, 1992, 1995.
Championship: 1996

This dashing winger from the Leicester Tigers – Rory Underwood – really could fly. A trained RAF fighter pilot, once clear he was almost impossible to catch, and he still holds the record for most tries for England: 49 in 85 appearances, and third only to all-time record try scorer Japan's Daisuke Ohata and Australia's David Campese.

The first England player to win 50 caps, Underwood was a contemporary of Rob Andrew at Barnard Castle School, playing at Student, under-23, Colts and England B levels on his way to a first full cap at the tender age of 20.

A great coach could have ironed out his rough edges and unleashed the finished article, but his blistering pace was often enough to conjure a try from a half chance, and his ability to feint inside and out at top speed over the final few metres sent shivers down the spines of the most organised back lines.

He first appeared in the uninspired England team of the mid-Eighties, making his debut against Ireland in 1984. He struggled to make an impact, and although he scored his first try in only his second game, he scored only once more in his first three seasons for England.

It wasn't until the arrival of Geoff Cooke as England coach that his international career took off.

He scored five tries against Fiji in 1989, equalling an 82-year-old record for the number of tries scored in a match, and secured a berth in the Lions squad to tour Australia, scoring four times in eight games as the Lions won 2-1.

Underwood also made an impression on the World Cup history books, scoring 11 tries in 15 World Cup games, only to be rewarded with a runners-up medal in 1991, coming

Rory Underwood

within a controversial fingertip of a match-altering try, and disappointment as a losing semi-finalist in 1995.

Underwood – who lived in Malaysia until he was 14 – made up for these failures with Grand Slams in 1991, 1992 and 1995. In 1996 he completed 10 years of Five Nations tournaments without missing a match.

Lining-up alongside his brother Tony in 1992 they became the first brothers to represent England for 55 years.

He toured again with the Lions in 1993. Despite losing the series 2-1, he scored a superb try in the second Test – the Lions' biggest ever victory over the All Blacks. Going past John Kirwan, his brother memorably said it was "like watching a Porsche going past a Lada."

At club level, Underwood achieved success with Leicester, helping them win the championship in 1988 and 1995, the Pilkington Cup in 1993 and make the 1997 Heineken Cup final, having retired from the international scene the season before.

After working as a pilot, Underwood is now a management consultant and occasional model for the RAF's new clothing range.

Tony Underwood

Tony UNDERWOOD

Born: 17 February 1969 in Ipoh, Malaysia
Educated: Barnard Castle School
Clubs: Cambridge University, Leicester (20), Newcastle (7)
Position: Wing (27), Bench (1)
Debut: 17 Oct 1992 v Canada (Wembley). Number: 1146
Last game: 5 Dec 1998 v South Africa (Twickenham)
Caps: 27 (W:21, L:6)
Scoring: 13T, 65 Pts
Appearances: 1992:C,SA, 1993:S,I,NZ, 1994:S,I,W,SA1,SA2,R,C, 1995:I,F,W,S,Ar,It,A,NZ, 1996:Ar, 1997:S,I,F,W, 1998:A,SA
Honours: Grand Slam: 1995

Ernest James (Jimmy) UNWIN

Born: 18 September 1912 in Birdbrook, Essex
Died: 23 November 2003
Educated: Haileybury & ISC
Clubs: RMC Sandhurst, Middlesex Regt, Army (1), Rosslyn Park (3)
Position: Wing (4)
Debut: 20 Mar 1937 v Scotland (Murrayfield) - 1T, 3 Pts. Number: 737
Last game: 19 Mar 1938 v Scotland (Twickenham) - 1T, 3 Pts
Caps: 4 (W:2, L:2)
Scoring: 3T, 9 Pts
Appearances: 1937:S, 1938:W,I,S
Honours: Championship: 1937

Geoffrey Thomas UNWIN

Born: 1 June 1874 in Ecclesall Bay
Died: 12 February 1948 in Hemel Hempstead
Educated: Marlborough School
Clubs: Oxford University, Moseley, Blackheath (1), Cheltenham, Derby
Position: Fly-half (1)
Debut: 12 Mar 1898 v Scotland (Edinburgh). Number: 324
Caps: 1 (W:0, D:1, L:0)
Scoring: 0 Pts
Appearances: 1898:S

Richard UREN

Born: 26 February 1926 in Wirral
Clubs: Waterloo (4)
Position: Full-back (4)
Debut: 14 Feb 1948 v Ireland (Twickenham) - 2C, 4 Pts. Number: 781
Last game: 11 Feb 1950 v Ireland (Twickenham)
Caps: 4 (W:1, L:3)
Scoring: 2C, 1PG, 7 Pts
Appearances: 1948:I,S,F, 1950:I

Roger Miles UTTLEY, OBE

Born: 11 September 1949 in Blackpool
Educated: Blackpool GS, Northumberland College
Clubs: Gosforth (19), Wasps (4)
Position: Lock (11), No 8 (7), Flanker (5), Bench (1)
Debut: 10 Feb 1973 v Ireland (Lansdowne Road). Number: 1019
Last game: 15 Mar 1980 v Scotland (Murrayfield)
Caps: 23 (W:12, D:2, L:9). As captain: 5 (W:2, D:1, L:2)
Scoring: 2T, 8 Pts
Appearances: 1973:I,F,S,NZ,A, 1974:I,F,W, 1975:F,W,S,A1,A2, 1977:S*,I*,F*,W*, 1978:NZ, 1979:S*, 1980:I,F,W,S
Honours: Grand Slam: 1980

James VALENTINE

Born: 29 July 1866 in Salford
Died: 25 July 1904 in Barmouth
Educated: Brindley Heath School
Clubs: Swinton (4)
Position: Centre (3), Three-quarter (1)
Debut: 15 Feb 1890 v Wales (Dewsbury). Number: 214
Last game: 14 Mar 1896 v Scotland (Glasgow)
Caps: 4 (W:1, L:3)
Scoring: 1C, 2 Pts
Appearances: 1890:W, 1896:W,I,S

Charles Henry Richard VANDERSPAR
Born: 1852
Died: 9 April 1877 in Colombo, Ceylon
Educated: Wellington College
Clubs: Richmond (1)
Position: Full-back (1)
Debut: 3 Mar 1873 v Scotland (Glasgow). Number: 44
Caps: 1 (W:0, D:1, L:0)
Scoring: 0 Pts
Appearances: 1873:S

Mark VAN GISBERGEN
Born: 30 June 1977 in New Zealand
Clubs: Waikato (NZ), Wasps (1)
Position: Replacement Full-back (1), Bench (3)
Debut: 12 Nov 2005 (rep) v Australia (Twickenham). Number: 1264
Caps: 1 (W:1, L:0)
Scoring: 0 Pts
Appearances: 2005:A(r)

Roger Uttley

Clive Berrange VAN RYNEVELD
Born: 19 March 1928 in Cape Town, South Africa
Educated: Diocesan College
Clubs: University of Cape Town (SA), Oxford University (4)
Position: Centre (4)
Debut: 15 Jan 1949 v Wales (Cardiff). Number: 795
Last game: 19 Mar 1949 v Scotland (Twickenham) - 2T, 6 Pts
Caps: 4 (W:2, L:2)
Scoring: 3T, 9 Pts
Appearances: 1949:W,I,F,S

Mark Van Gisbergen

Henry (Harry) VARLEY
Born: 25 November 1867 in Cleckheaton, Yorks
Died: 21 November 1915 in Oldham
Clubs: Liversedge (1)
Position: Scrum-half (1)
Debut: 5 Mar 1892 v Scotland (Raeburn Place). Number: 248
Caps: 1 (W:1, L:0)
Scoring: 0 Pts
Appearances: 1892:S
Honours: Championship: 1892

Thomas William (Tom) VARNDELL
Born: 16 September 1985 in Ashford
Educated: Oakham School
Clubs: Leicester (3), Bedford
Position: Wing (2), Replacement (1)
Debut: 26 Nov 2005 (rep) v Samoa (Twickenham) - 1T, 5 Pts. Number: 1268
Last game: 17 Jun 2006 v Australia (Melbourne) - 1T, 5 Pts
Caps: 3 (W:1, L:2)
Scoring: 2T, 10 Pts
Appearances: 2005:Sm(r), 2006:A1,A2

Tom Varndell

Henry (Harry) VASSALL
Born: 22 October 1860 in Tadcaster
Died: 5 January 1926 of Repton
Educated: Marlborough School
Clubs: Oxford University (4), Marlborough Nomads, Blackheath (1)
Position: Forward (5)
Debut: 19 Feb 1881 v Wales (Blackheath) - 3T, 3 Pts. Number: 137
Last game: 16 Dec 1882 v Wales (Swansea)
Caps: 5 (W:2, D:2, L:1)
Scoring: 3T, 3 Pts
Appearances: 1881:W,S, 1882:I,S, 1883:W
Honours: Championship: 1883

Henry Holland (Jumbo) VASSALL
Born: 23 March 1887 in Torrington, Devon
Died: 8 October 1949 in Bridgwater
Educated: Bedford GS
Clubs: Oxford University (1), Blackheath
Position: Centre (1)
Debut: 8 Feb 1908 v Ireland (Richmond). Number: 461
Caps: 1 (W:1, L:0)
Scoring: 0 Pts
Appearances: 1908:I

Douglas Brian VAUGHAN

Born: 15 July 1925 in Wrexham, Wales
Died: 19 April 1977 in Isle of Man
Educated: Luton School
Clubs: Cambridge University, Royal Navy, Devonport Services (4), Headingley (4), Harlequins, United Services
Position: No 8 (6), Flanker (2)
Debut: 3 Jan 1948 v Australia (Twickenham). Number: 778
Last game: 21 Jan 1950 v Wales (Twickenham)
Caps: 8 (W:2, D:1, L:5)
Scoring: 0 Pts
Appearances: 1948:A,W,I,S, 1949:I,F,S, 1950:W

Courteney Lee VERELST

Born: 16 November 1855 in Wirral
Died: 9 January 1890 in Ceylon
Educated: Charterhouse School
Clubs: Liverpool (2)
Position: Forward (2)
Debut: 13 Dec 1875 v Ireland (Dublin). Number: 79
Last game: 11 Mar 1878 v Ireland (Lansdowne Road)
Caps: 2 (W:2, L:0)
Scoring: 0 Pts
Appearances: 1875:I, 1878:I

George Frederick VERNON

Born: 20 June 1856 in Marylebone, London
Died: 10 August 1902 in Elmina, Gold Coast
Educated: Rugby School
Clubs: Blackheath (5)
Position: Forward (5)
Debut: 4 Mar 1878 v Scotland (The Oval). Number: 101
Last game: 5 Feb 1881 v Ireland (Manchester)
Caps: 5 (W:4, D:1, L:0)
Scoring: 0 Pts
Appearances: 1878:S,I, 1880:I,S, 1881:I

George VICKERY

Born: 25 May 1879 in Chard
Died: June 1970 in Neath, Wales
Clubs: Aberavon, Bath (1)
Position: Forward (1)
Debut: 11 Feb 1905 v Ireland (Cork). Number: 409
Caps: 1 (W:0, L:1)
Scoring: 0 Pts
Appearances: 1905:I

Philip John (Phil) VICKERY, MBE

Born: 14 March 1976 in Barnstaple
Educated: Budehaven School
Clubs: Bude, Gloucester (47), Wasps (3)
Position: Prop (46), Replacement (6), Bench (1)
Debut: 21 Feb 1998 v Wales (Twickenham). Number: 1193
Last game: 24 Feb 2007 (capt) v Ireland (Croke Park)
Caps: 52 (W:37, L:15). As captain: 5 (W:4, L:1)
Scoring: 2T, 10 Pts. Discipline - Cautions: 1
Appearances: 1998:W,A,NZ1,NZ2,SA, 1999:US,C,It,NZ,Tg,SA, 2000:I,F,W,S,A,Ar(r),SA(r), 2001:W,It,S,A,SA, 2002:I,F,Ar*,NZ,A,SA, 2003:NZ(r),A,Geo,SA,Sm(r),U*,W,F,A, 2004:It,S,I,W,F, 2005:W(r),F,A,NZ, 2006:SA1(r),SA2, 2007:S*,It*,I*
Honours: RWC Winner: 2003. Championship: 2000, 2001

Phil Vickery

For someone whose nickname is The Raging Bull, has an oriental tattoo which translates as "I'll fight you to the death", and comes in at over 19 stone, it's no surprise that Phil Vickery became an essential part of the England pack.

The complete modern prop, he allies great scrummaging technique and destructive tackling with deft ball-handling skills.

A typically no-nonsense Cornishman, his career has been regularly disrupted by injury, but being as strong as an ox, and with a will to match, he has made numerous comebacks and was named England captain for the 2007 RBS Six Nations.

His progress through the ranks of English rugby was remarkable even by modern standards. He made his England debut against Wales in 1998, after just 34 games for Gloucester, and only 81 days after his first England A cap, playing a part in the 1999 World Cup campaign.

On the back of this he muscled himself into the Lions squad, making three appearances on the 2001 tour of Australia.

He enhanced his growing stature in the England squad leading the tour to Argentina in 2002, and, with many top players rested, they emerged as victors.

Vickery recovered from a back injury that kept him out of the 2003 Grand Slam series to re-establish his partnership with club colleague Trevor Woodman, playing in all seven World Cup games as they became world champions.

That campaign also saw him score his first try for his country, touching down in the third game against the Samoans, when England were struggling in a World Cup pool match.

When Brian Ashton was named England coach for the 2007 Six Nations one of his first actions was to name Vickery as his captain, although injury prevented him playing a full part in the Championship.

In his life after rugby he has his own sports clothing company to fall back on, or he can call on his training as a qualified artificial inseminator, gained during his time on his parents' farm.

Elliott John VIVYAN

Born: 6 January 1879 in Stoke Damerel
Died: 3 December 1935 in Wirral
Educated: Stoke School
Clubs: Devonport Albion (4)
Position: Wing (3), Centre (1)
Debut: 5 Jan 1901 v Wales (Cardiff). Number: 363
Last game: 19 Mar 1904 v Scotland (Inverleith) - 1T, 3 Pts
Caps: 4 (W:1, D:1, L:2)
Scoring: 3T, 2C, 13 Pts
Appearances: 1901:W, 1904:W,I,S

Anthony Thomas (Tom) VOYCE, OBE

Born: 18 May 1897 in Gloucester
Died: 22 January 1980 in Gloucester
Clubs: Gloucester (27), Cheltenham, Richmond, Blackheath, Army
Position: Flanker (27)
Debut: 14 Feb 1920 v Ireland (Lansdowne Road). Number: 563
Last game: 20 Mar 1926 v Scotland (Twickenham) - 1T, 3 Pts
Caps: 27 (W:19, D:3, L:5)
Scoring: 5T, 15 Pts
Appearances: 1920:I,S, 1921:W,I,S,F, 1922:W,I,F,S, 1923:W,I,S,F, 1924:W,I,F,S, 1925:NZ,W,I,S,F, 1926:W,I,F,S
Honours: Grand Slam: 1921, 1923, 1924

Another post-First World War pioneer, Tom Voyce was a key member of England's Grand Slam-winning sides of 1921, 1923 and 1924, almost mirroring the side's titles in the 1990s.

Following his debut in 1920, Voyce – who followed the great Cherry Pillman into the team – became a player England could not do without. Voyce – who played at lock or in the back row – finally played in 27 consecutive internationals, before his last in 1926.

He became something of a talisman for England as they only lost once in his first 18 Tests.

In the Gloucester Rugby Hall of Fame they reveal that Wavell Wakefield, the England captain of that time, described Voyce as "a wonderful inspiration to any side".

Wakefield added: "Tom had the personality and mental competitive outlook that makes up a great player, and he was a shining example to others in that he was determined to put something back into the game for all the pleasure he had out of it."

On the British and Irish Lions trip to South Africa in 1924 Voyce showed his versatility by playing in the backs.

Voyce was a great Gloucester stalwart, finally becoming president of the RFU in 1960 and being awarded the OBE two years later.

His great-nephew, also called Tom Voyce, made his England debut – on the wing – in 2001.

Tom Michael Voyce

Thomas Michael Dunstan (Tom) VOYCE

Born: 5 January 1981 in Truro
Educated: Penair School, King's College
Clubs: Bath (1), Wasps (8)
Position: Wing (4), Full-back (2), Replacement (3), Bench (1)
Debut: 16 Jun 2001 (rep) v United States (San Francisco). Number: 1233
Last game: 11 Jun 2006 v Australia (Sydney)
Caps: 9 (W:4, L:5)
Scoring: 3T, 15 Pts
Appearances: 2001:US(r), 2004:NZ2,A, 2005:Sm, 2006:W(r),It,F(r),I,A1

Hugh Donnithorne VYVYAN

Born: 8 September 1976 in Guildford
Educated: Downside School
Clubs: Newcastle University, Northern, Villagers (SA), Newcastle, Saracens (1)
Position: Replacement Back-row (1), Bench (1)
Debut: 13 Nov 2004 (rep) v Canada (Twickenham) - 1T, 5 Pts. Number: 1258
Caps: 1 (W:1, L:0)
Scoring: 1T, 5 Pts
Appearances: 2004:C(r)

Hugh Vyvyan

U V

W-Y

WACKETT, John Arthur Sibley
WADE, Sir Charles Gregory, KCMG
WADE, Michael Richard
WAKEFIELD, Sir William Wavell, KCB
WALDER, David John Hume
WALKER, Sir George Augustus, KCB
WALKER, Henry W
WALKER, Roger
WALLENS, John Noel Stanley
WALSHE, Nicholas Patrick James
WALTON, Ernest John
WALTON, William
WARD, George
WARD, Herbert
WARD, James Ibotson
WARD, John William
WARD, Sir Lancelot Edward Barrington, KCVO
WARDLOW, Christopher Story
WARFIELD, Peter John
WARR, Antony Lawley
WATERS, Fraser Henry Hamilton
WATKINS, John Arthur
WATKINS, John Kingdon, CBE
WATSON, Fischer Burges, CBE
WATSON, James Henry Digby
WATT, David Edward James
WEBB, Charles Samuel Henry
WEBB, James William George
WEBB, Jonathan Mark
WEBB, Rodney Edward
WEBB, St Lawrence Hugh
WEBSTER, Jan Godfrey
WEDGE, Thomas Grenfell
WEIGHILL, Robert Harold George
WELLS, Cyril Mowbray
WEST, Bryan Ronald
WEST, Dorian Edward, MBE
WEST, Richard John
WESTON, Henry Thomas Franklin
WESTON, Lionel Edward
WESTON, Michael Philip
WESTON, William Henry
WHEATLEY, Arthur A
WHEATLEY, Harold F
WHEELER, Peter John
WHITE, Colin
WHITE, Donald Frederick
WHITE, Julian Martin, MBE
WHITE-COOPER, William Robert Steven
WHITELEY, Eric Cyprian Perry
WHITELEY, W
WHITLEY, Herbert
WICKES, Richard Henry Hamilton
WIGGLESWORTH, Henry John
WIGHTMAN, Brian John
WILKINS, Dennis Thomas
WILKINSON, Edgar
WILKINSON, Harry
WILKINSON, Harry James
WILKINSON, Jonathan Peter, OBE
WILKINSON, P
WILKINSON, Robert Michael
WILLCOCKS, T J
WILLCOX, John Graham
WILLIAM-POWLETT, Sir Peveril Barton Reiby Wallop, KCB
WILLIAMS, Christopher Gareth
WILLIAMS, Cyril Stoate
WILLIAMS, John Edward
WILLIAMS, John Michael
WILLIAMS, Peter Nicholas
WILLIAMS, Samuel George
WILLIAMS, Samuel Horatio
WILLIAMSON, Rupert Henry
WILSON, Arthur James
WILSON, Charles Edward
WILSON, Charles Plumpton
WILSON, Dyson Stayt
WILSON, Guy Sumerfield
WILSON, Kenneth James
WILSON, Roger Parker
WILSON, Walter Carandini, CBE
WINN, Christopher Elliott
WINTERBOTTOM, Peter James, MBE
WINTLE, Trevor Clifford
WODEHOUSE, Norman Atherton
WOOD, Albert
WOOD, Alfred Ernest
WOOD, George William
WOOD, Martyn Benjamin
WOOD, Robert
WOOD, Robert Dudley
WOODGATE, Elliott Edward
WOODHEAD, Ernest
WOODMAN, Trevor James, MBE
WOODRUFF, Charles Garfield
WOODS, Samuel Moses James
WOODS, Thomas
WOODS, Thomas
WOODWARD, Sir Clive Ronald, KBE
WOODWARD, John Edward
WOOLDRIDGE, Charles Sylvester
WORDSWORTH, Alan John
WORSLEY, Joseph Paul Richard, MBE
WORSLEY, Michael Anthony
WORTON, Joseph Bute
WRENCH, Frederick David Bryan
WRIGHT, Cyril Carne Glenton
WRIGHT, Frank Thurlow
WRIGHT, Ian Douglas
WRIGHT, James Frost
WRIGHT, John Cecil
WRIGHT, Thomas Peter
WRIGHT, William Henry George
WYATT, Derek Murray

YARRANTON, Peter George
YATES, Kevin Peter
YIEND, William
YOUNG, Arthur Tudor
YOUNG, John Robert Chester
YOUNG, Malcolm
YOUNG, Peter Dalton
YOUNGS, Nicholas Gerald

Jonny Wilkinson

John Arthur Sibley WACKETT

Born: 27 September 1930 in Hatfield
Clubs: Welwyn GC, Rosslyn Park (2)
Position: Hooker (2)
Debut: 17 Jan 1959 v Wales (Cardiff). Number: 881
Last game: 14 Feb 1959 v Ireland (Lansdowne Road)
Caps: 2 (W:1, L:1)
Scoring: 0 Pts
Appearances: 1959:W,I

Sir Charles Gregory (Gregory) WADE, KCMG

Born: 26 January 1863 in Singleton, NSW, Australia
Died: 26 September 1922 in Potts Point, NSW, Australia
Educated: King's School, All Saint's College
Clubs: Oxford University, Richmond (2), New South Wales (AU)
Position: Three-quarter (8)
Debut: 16 Dec 1882 v Wales (Swansea) - 3T, 3 Pts. Number: 155
Last game: 6 Feb 1886 v Ireland (Lansdowne Road)
Caps: 8 (W:8, L:0)
Scoring: 7T, 7 Pts
Appearances: 1883:W,I,S, 1884:W,S, 1885:W, 1886:W,I
Honours: Championship: 1883, 1884

Michael Richard WADE

Born: 13 September 1937 in Leicester
Educated: Wyggeston GS
Clubs: Oadby, Old Wyggestonians, Cambridge University, RAF, Leicester (3), Stade Bordelais UC (FR)
Position: Centre (3)
Debut: 20 Jan 1962 v Wales (Twickenham). Number: 903
Last game: 24 Feb 1962 v France (Stade Colombes)
Caps: 3 (W:1, D:1, L:1)
Scoring: 1T, 3 Pts
Appearances: 1962:W,I,F

Sir William Wavell (Wavell) WAKEFIELD KBE

Born: 10 March 1898 in Beckenham
Died: 12 August 1983 in Kendal
Educated: Craig Prep School, Sedbergh School
Clubs: Harlequins (21), Cambridge University (6), RAF, Leicester (4), Furness
Position: Flanker (21), No 8 (10)
Debut: 17 Jan 1920 v Wales (Swansea). Number: 554
Last game: 2 Apr 1927 v France (Stade Colombes)
Caps: 31 (W:20, D:3, L:8). As captain: 13 (W:7, D:2, L:4)
Scoring: 6T, 18 Pts
Appearances: 1920:W,F,I,S, 1921:W,I,S,F, 1922:W,I,F,S, 1923:W,I,S,F, 1924:W*,I*,F*,S*, 1925:NZ*,W*,I*,S*,F*, 1926:W*,I*,F*,S*, 1927:S,F
Honours: Grand Slam: 1921, 1923, 1924 (capt)

Once the legendary Wavell Wakefield was selected in the England team there was simply no shifting him and he played in 29 consecutive Tests in the 1920s.

And these 29 Tests – at flanker and No 8 – brought three Grand Slams and one Five Nations championship as England ruled the roost in Europe.

Wakefield – who played for Harlequins – went on to play for England 31 times, a then record that stood for 42 years as the rest of the nation's rugby players stood in his wake.

A member of the Royal Flying Corps in the First World War, Wakers, as he was affectionately known, was an accomplished all-round sportsman.

He played cricket for the MCC and was the RAF champion at the 440 yards, finally settling for a life in rugby.

He set a record for captaining England 13 times, a mark that stood until Bill Beaumont overtook it in the 1980s.

Wakefield was elected into the Rugby Hall of Fame in 1999, the citation describing the huge effect he'd had on the game.

"Wavell Wakefield, or to be more accurate, Lord Wakefield of Kendal, bestrode more than half a century of rugby development not just in England but rugby worldwide," the Hall of Fame explained.

"He revolutionised the function of the pack who, until he came on the scene, were extremely static, concentrating almost entirely on set-piece.

"He developed forward play in the loose and came up with defensive systems for the forwards, including the use of a fast openside flanker putting pressure on the opposition fly-half from set-piece."

Wakefield wasn't content to dominate on the field. He became a Conservative Member of Parliament for Swindon in 1935 and he was knighted in 1944. After serving in the Second World War he went on to become president of the RFU and the president of his club, Harlequins.

David John Hume (Dave) WALDER

Born: 7 May 1978 in Newcastle
Educated: Oundle School
Clubs: Durham University, Northern, Newcastle (4), Wasps
Position: Fly-half (3), Replacement (1), Bench (3)
Debut: 2 Jun 2001 v Canada (Markham) - 1C, 2 Pts. Number: 1227
Last game: 23 Aug 2003 (rep) v Wales (Cardiff) - 1C, 2 Pts
Caps: 4 (W:4, L:0)
Scoring: 2T, 11C, 3PG, 41 Pts
Appearances: 2001:C1,C2,US, 2003:W(r)

Dave Walder

Sir George Augustus (Gus) WALKER, KCB
Born: 24 August 1912 in Garforth
Died: 11 December 1986 in King's Lynn
Educated: St Bees School
Clubs: Cambridge University, Blackheath (2)
Position: Fly-half (2)
Debut: 21 Jan 1939 v Wales (Twickenham). Number: 749
Last game: 11 Feb 1939 v Ireland (Twickenham)
Caps: 2 (W:1, L:1)
Scoring: 0 Pts
Appearances: 1939:W,I

Henry W (Harry) WALKER
Born: Second quarter 1915 in Aston
Clubs: Coventry (9)
Position: Prop (9)
Debut: 18 Jan 1947 v Wales (Cardiff). Number: 765
Last game: 29 Mar 1948 v France (Stade Colombes)
Caps: 9 (W:3, D:1, L:5)
Scoring: 0 Pts
Appearances: 1947:W,I,S,F, 1948:A,W,I,S,F

Nick Walshe

Roger WALKER
Born: 18 September 1846 in Bury
Died: 11 November 1919 in Reading
Educated: Rossall School
Clubs: Manchester (5)
Position: Forward (5)
Debut: 23 Feb 1874 v Scotland (The Oval). Number: 56
Last game: 28 Feb 1880 v Scotland (Manchester)
Caps: 5 (W:4, D:1, L:0)
Scoring: 0 Pts
Appearances: 1874:S, 1875:I, 1876:S, 1879:S, 1880:S

John Noel Stanley WALLENS
Born: 25 December 1901 in Birkenhead
Died: Details unknown
Clubs: Waterloo (1)
Position: Full-back (1)
Debut: 2 Apr 1927 v France (Stade Colombes). Number: 627
Caps: 1 (W:0, L:1)
Scoring: 0 Pts
Appearances: 1927:F

Nicholas Patrick James (Nick) WALSHE
Born: 1 November 1974 in Chiswick
Educated: Worth Abbey School
Clubs: Kingston University, Rosslyn Park, Harlequins, Saracens, Sale, Bath (2)
Position: Replacement Scrum-half (2), Bench (2)
Debut: 11 Jun 2006 (rep) v Australia (Sydney). Number: 1273
Last game: 17 Jun 2006 (rep) v Australia (Melbourne)
Caps: 2 (W:0, L:2)
Scoring: 0 Pts
Appearances: 2006:A1(r),A2(r)

Ernest John (Katie) WALTON
Born: November 1879 in York
Died: 8 April 1947 of Waterford, Ireland
Educated: St Peter's School
Clubs: Castleford (2), Oxford University (2)
Position: Scrum-half (4)
Debut: 5 Jan 1901 v Wales (Cardiff). Number: 364
Last game: 15 Mar 1902 v Scotland (Inverleith)
Caps: 4 (W:2, L:2)
Scoring: 0 Pts
Appearances: 1901:W,I, 1902:I,S

William WALTON
Born: 23 September 1874
Died: 1 June 1940 in Wakefield
Clubs: Castleford (1), Wakefield Trinity RL
Position: Forward (1)
Debut: 17 Mar 1894 v Scotland (Raeburn Place). Number: 271
Caps: 1 (W:0, L:1)
Scoring: 0 Pts
Appearances: 1894:S

George WARD
Born: 19 March 1885
Died: 1963 in Leicester
Clubs: Belgrave, Leicester (6)
Position: No 8 (6)
Debut: 18 Jan 1913 v Wales (Cardiff).
Number: 531
Last game: 21 Mar 1914 v Scotland (Inverleith)
Caps: 6 (W:6, L:0)
Scoring: 0 Pts
Appearances: 1913:W,F,S, 1914:W,I,S
Honours: Championship: 1913, 1914

Herbert WARD
Born: 1873 in Bradford
Died: 18 February 1955 in Wharfedale
Clubs: Bradford (1)
Position: Full-back (1)
Debut: 5 Jan 1895 v Wales (Swansea).
Number: 281
Caps: 1 (W:1, L:0)
Scoring: 0 Pts
Appearances: 1895:W

James Ibotson WARD
Born: 24 April 1858 in Staines
Died: 28 September 1924 in Marylebone
Educated: Tonbridge School
Clubs: Gipsies, Richmond (2)
Position: Forward (2)
Debut: 5 Feb 1881 v Ireland (Manchester).
Number: 136
Last game: 6 Feb 1882 v Ireland (Lansdowne Road)
Caps: 2 (W:1, D:1, L:0)
Scoring: 0 Pts
Appearances: 1881:I, 1882:I

John William WARD
Born: 29 January 1873 in Castleford
Died: 30 April 1939 in Hemsworth
Clubs: Castleford (3)
Position: Forward (3)
Debut: 4 Jan 1896 v Wales (Blackheath).
Number: 288
Last game: 14 Mar 1896 v Scotland (Glasgow)
Caps: 3 (W:1, L:2)
Scoring: 0 Pts
Appearances: 1896:W,I,S

Sir Lancelot Edward Barrington WARD, KCVO
Born: 4 July 1884 in Droitwich
Died: 17 November 1953 in Bury St Edmunds
Educated: Bromsgrove School, Westminster School
Clubs: Edinburgh University (4), Oxford University
Position: No 8 (4)
Debut: 15 Jan 1910 v Wales (Twickenham).
Number: 498
Last game: 19 Mar 1910 v Scotland (Inverleith)
Caps: 4 (W:3, D:1, L:0)
Scoring: 0 Pts
Appearances: 1910:W,I,F,S
Honours: Championship: 1910

Christopher Story WARDLOW
Born: 12 July 1942 in Carlisle
Educated: Creighton School
Clubs: Carlisle (1), Northampton (5)
Position: Centre (5), Replacement (1), Bench (4)
Debut: 20 Dec 1969 (rep) v South Africa (Twickenham).
Number: 983
Last game: 27 Mar 1971 v Scotland (Murrayfield)
Caps: 6 (W:2, D:1, L:3)
Scoring: 0 Pts
Appearances: 1969:SA(r), 1971:W,I,F,S,S

Peter John WARFIELD
Born: 1 April 1951 in Waddington, Lincs
Educated: Haileybury & ISC
Clubs: Durham University, Rosslyn Park (3), Cambridge University (3)
Position: Centre (6), Bench (1)
Debut: 6 Jan 1973 v New Zealand (Twickenham).
Number: 1017
Last game: 15 Mar 1975 v Scotland (Twickenham)
Caps: 6 (W:1, L:5)
Scoring: 0 Pts
Appearances: 1973:NZ,W,I, 1975:I,F,S

Peter Warfield

Antony Lawley (Tim) WARR
Born: 15 May 1913 in Selly Oak, Birmingham
Died: 29 January 1995 of Kingston St Mary
Educated: Bromsgrove School
Clubs: Oxford University (2), Weston-super-Mare, Moseley, Harlequins, Wakefield, Gloucester, Richmond
Position: Wing (2)
Debut: 20 Jan 1934 v Wales (Cardiff) - 1T, 3 Pts.
Number: 709
Last game: 10 Feb 1934 v Ireland (Lansdowne Road)
Caps: 2 (W:2, L:0)
Scoring: 1T, 3 Pts
Appearances: 1934:W,I
Honours: Championship: 1934

Fraser Waters

John Watkins

Fraser Henry Hamilton WATERS
Born: 31 March 1976 in Cape Town, South Africa
Educated: Bishop's College, Harrow School
Clubs: Bath, Bristol, Wasps (3)
Position: Centre (1), Replacement (2)
Debut: 16 Jun 2001 v United States (San Francisco). Number: 1230
Last game: 26 Jun 2004 (rep) v Australia (Brisbane)
Caps: 3 (W:1, L:2)
Scoring: 0 Pts
Appearances: 2001:US, 2004:NZ2(r),A(r)

John Arthur WATKINS
Born: 28 November 1945 in Gloucester
Educated: Linden School
Clubs: Gloucester (7)
Position: Flanker (7), Bench (6)
Debut: 3 Jun 1972 v South Africa (Johannesburg). Number: 1015
Last game: 15 Feb 1975 v Wales (Cardiff)
Caps: 7 (W:3, L:4)
Scoring: 0 Pts
Appearances: 1972:SA, 1973:NZ,W,NZ,A, 1975:F,W

John Kingdon WATKINS, CBE
Born: 24 February 1913 in Taunton
Died: 13 May 1970 in St Marylebone
Educated: Epsom College
Clubs: Devonport Services, United Services, Royal Navy (3), Combined Services
Position: Flanker (3)
Debut: 21 Jan 1939 v Wales (Twickenham). Number: 750
Last game: 18 Mar 1939 v Scotland (Murrayfield)
Caps: 3 (W:2, L:1)
Scoring: 0 Pts
Appearances: 1939:W,I,S

Fischer Burges WATSON, CBE
Born: September 1884 in Portsea
Died: 14 August 1960 in Chichester
Educated: Ashdown House School, Forest Row School, HMS Brittania
Clubs: United Services, Royal Navy (2)
Position: Forward (2)
Debut: 21 Mar 1908 v Scotland (Inverleith). Number: 465
Last game: 20 Mar 1909 v Scotland (Richmond) - 1T, 3 Pts
Caps: 2 (W:0, L:2)
Scoring: 1T, 3 Pts
Appearances: 1908:S, 1909:S

James Henry Digby (Bungy) WATSON
Born: 31 August 1890 in Portsea
Died: Killed in action at sea in 1914
Educated: King's School
Clubs: Edinburgh University, Blackheath (3), London Hospitals
Position: Centre (2), Wing (1)
Debut: 17 Jan 1914 v Wales (Twickenham). Number: 539
Last game: 13 Apr 1914 v France (Stade Colombes) - 1T, 3 Pts
Caps: 3 (W:3, L:0)
Scoring: 1T, 3 Pts
Appearances: 1914:W,S,F
Honours: Championship: 1914

David Edward James WATT
Born: 5 July 1938 in Bristol
Educated: Kingsdown Secondary School, Bristol Cathedral School
Clubs: Bristol (4)
Position: Lock (4)
Debut: 11 Feb 1967 v Ireland (Lansdowne Road). Number: 958
Last game: 15 Apr 1967 v Wales (Cardiff)
Caps: 4 (W:2, L:2)
Scoring: 0 Pts
Appearances: 1967:I,F,S,W

Charles Samuel Henry WEBB
Born: Third quarter 1902 in Plymouth
Died: 28 October 1961 in Plymouth
Clubs: Devonport Services (8), Royal Navy (4)
Position: Lock (11), Prop (1)
Debut: 2 Jan 1932 v South Africa (Twickenham). Number: 691
Last game: 21 Mar 1936 v Scotland (Twickenham)
Caps: 12 (W:5, D:1, L:6)
Scoring: 0 Pts
Appearances: 1932:SA,W,I,S, 1933:W,I,S, 1935:S, 1936:NZ,W,I,S

James William George WEBB
Born: 17 October 1900 in Upton, near Northampton
Died: Details unknown
Clubs: Northampton (3)
Position: No 8 (3)
Debut: 27 Feb 1926 v France (Twickenham). Number: 614
Last game: 16 Mar 1929 v Scotland (Murrayfield)
Caps: 3 (W:1, L:2)
Scoring: 1T, 3 Pts
Appearances: 1926:F,S, 1929:S

Jonathan Mark (Jon) WEBB
Born: 24 August 1963 in Ealing
Educated: RGS Newcastle, Royal College of Surgeons
Clubs: Bristol University, Northern, Bristol (16), Bath (17)
Position: Full-back (32), Replacement (1), Bench (9)
Debut: 23 May 1987 (rep) v Australia (Sydney) - 1C, 2 Pts. Number: 1119
Last game: 20 Mar 1993 v Ireland (Lansdowne Road) - 1PG, 3 Pts
Caps: 33 (W:20, D:1, L:12)
Scoring: 4T, 41C, 66PG, 296 Pts
Appearances: 1987:A(r),J,US,W, 1988:F,W,S,I,I,A1,A2,A, 1989:S,I,F,W, 1991:Fj,A,NZ,It,F,S,A, 1992:S,I,F,W,C,SA, 1993:F,W,S,I
Honours: Grand Slam: 1992

Jon Webb

W Y

Jan Webster

Rodney Edward WEBB

Born: 18 August 1943 in Newbold-on-Avon
Educated: Newbold Grange HS
Clubs: Coventry (12)
Position: Wing (12), Bench (1)
Debut: 18 Mar 1967 v Scotland (Twickenham) - 1T, 3 Pts. Number: 959
Last game: 26 Feb 1972 v France (Stade Colombes)
Caps: 12 (W:4, D:1, L:7)
Scoring: 2T, 6 Pts
Appearances: 1967:S,W,NZ, 1968:I,F,S, 1969:I,F,S,W, 1972:I,F

St Lawrence Hugh (Larry) WEBB

Born: 7 March 1931 in Melbourne, Australia
Died: 30 May 1978 at sea
Educated: St George's School, Willesden TC
Clubs: Bedford (4), Aldershot Services, Blackheath, Royal Engineers, Position: Prop (4)
Debut: 17 Jan 1959 v Wales (Cardiff). Number: 882
Last game: 21 Mar 1959 v Scotland (Twickenham)
Caps: 4 (W:1, D:2, L:1)
Scoring: 0 Pts
Appearances: 1959:W,I,F,S

Jan Godfrey WEBSTER

Born: 24 August 1946 in Southport
Educated: Queen Mary's School, City of Birmingham College
Clubs: Walsall, Moseley (11)
Position: Scrum-half (11), Bench (9)
Debut: 15 Jan 1972 v Wales (Twickenham). Number: 1007
Last game: 15 Feb 1975 v Wales (Cardiff)
Caps: 11 (W:3, L:8)
Scoring: 0 Pts
Appearances: 1972:W,I,SA, 1973:NZ,W,NZ, 1974:S,W, 1975:I,F,W

Thomas Grenfell WEDGE

Born: Third quarter 1881 in Penzance
Died: 11 December 1964 in St Ives
Clubs: St Ives (2)
Position: Scrum-half (2)
Debut: 5 Jan 1907 v France (Richmond). Number: 444
Last game: 16 Jan 1909 v Wales (Cardiff)
Caps: 2 (W:1, L:1)
Scoring: 0 Pts
Appearances: 1907:F, 1909:W

Robert Harold George (Bob) WEIGHILL

Born: 9 September 1920 in Kings Norton
Died: 27 October 2000 in Halton
Educated: Wirral GS
Clubs: Birkenhead Park, Waterloo, RAF, Harlequins (4), Leicester
Position: No 8 (4)
Debut: 15 Mar 1947 v Scotland (Twickenham). Number: 771
Last game: 29 Mar 1948 (capt) v France (Stade Colombes)
Caps: 4 (W:2, L:2). As captain: 1 (W:0, L:1)
Scoring: 0 Pts
Appearances: 1947:S,F, 1948:S,F*

Cyril Mowbray WELLS

Born: 21 March 1871 in St Pancras, London
Died: 22 August 1963 in St John's Wood, London
Educated: Dulwich College
Clubs: Cambridge University (1), Harlequins (5)
Position: Half-Back (5), Scrum-half (1)
Debut: 4 Mar 1893 v Scotland (Headingley). Number: 260
Last game: 13 Mar 1897 v Scotland (Manchester)
Caps: 6 (W:2, L:4)
Scoring: 0 Pts
Appearances: 1893:S, 1894:W,S, 1896:S, 1897:W,S

Bryan Ronald WEST

Born: 7 June 1948 in Northampton
Educated: Northampton GS
Clubs: Loughborough College (4), Northampton (4), Wakefield Trinity RL
Position: Flanker (8), Bench (1)
Debut: 20 Jan 1968 v Wales (Twickenham). Number: 969
Last game: 21 Mar 1970 v Scotland (Murrayfield)
Caps: 8 (W:3, D:2, L:3)
Scoring: 0 Pts
Appearances: 1968:W,I,F,S, 1969:SA, 1970:I,W,S

Dorian Edward WEST, MBE

Born: 5 October 1967 in Wrexham, Wales
Educated: Ashby GS
Clubs: Nottingham, Leicester (21)
Position: Hooker (10), Replacement (11), Bench (9)
Debut: 7 Feb 1998 (rep) v France (Stade de France). Number: 1192
Last game: 16 Nov 2003 (rep) v France (Sydney)
Caps: 21 (W:17, L:4). As captain: 1 (W:0, L:1)
Scoring: 3T, 15 Pts
Appearances: 1998:F(r),S(r), 2000:Ar(r), 2001:W,It,S,F(r),C1,C2,US,I(r),A,SA, 2002:F(r),W(r),It(r), 2003:W(r),F*,F(r),U,F(r)
Honours: RWC Winner: 2003. Championship: 2001

Dorian West

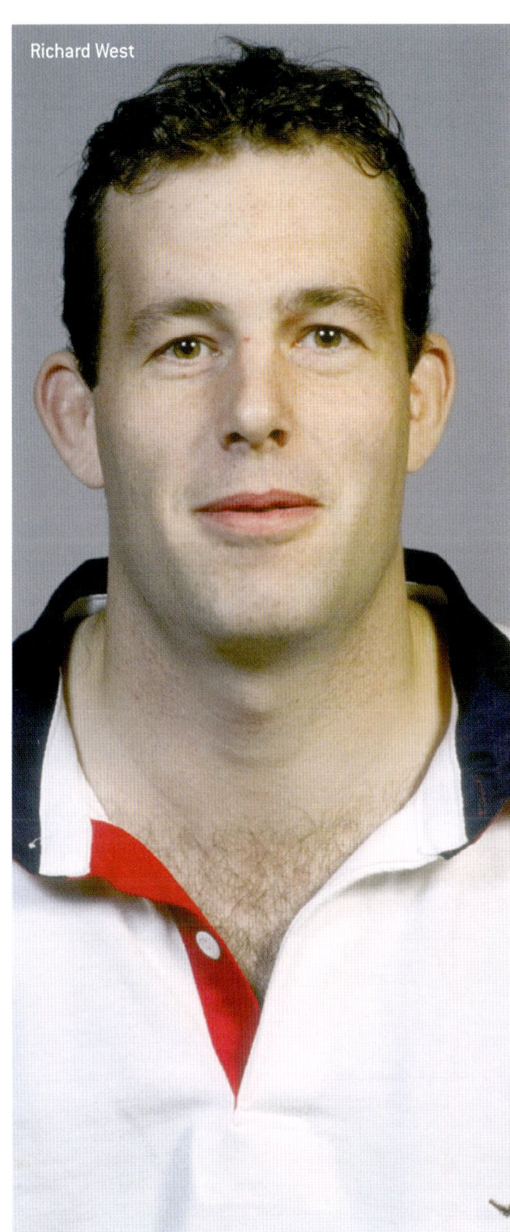
Richard West

Richard John WEST
Born: 20 March 1971 in Hereford
Educated: Old Swinford School
Clubs: Richmond, Gloucester (1)
Position: Lock (1)
Debut: 4 Jun 1995 v Samoa (Durban). Number: 1157
Caps: 1 (W:1, L:0)
Scoring: 0 Pts
Appearances: 1995:Sm

Henry Thomas Franklin WESTON
Born: 9 July 1869 in Potterspury
Died: 9 April 1955 in Towcester
Clubs: Northampton (1)
Position: Forward (1)
Debut: 9 Mar 1901 v Scotland (Blackheath). Number: 372
Caps: 1 (W:0, L:1)
Scoring: 0 Pts
Appearances: 1901:S

Lionel Edward WESTON
Born: 22 February 1947 in Much Wenlock
Educated: Bedford Modern School
Clubs: Loughborough College, West of Scotland (2), Rosslyn Park
Position: Scrum-half (2), Bench (2)
Debut: 26 Feb 1972 v France (Stade Colombes). Number: 1009
Last game: 18 Mar 1972 v Scotland (Murrayfield)
Caps: 2 (W:0, L:2)
Scoring: 0 Pts
Appearances: 1972:F,S

Michael Philip (Mike) WESTON
Born: 21 August 1938 in Durham
Educated: Durham School
Clubs: Richmond (12), Durham City (17)
Position: Centre (24), Fly-half (5)
Debut: 16 Jan 1960 v Wales (Twickenham). Number: 892
Last game: 16 Mar 1968 (capt) v Scotland (Murrayfield)
Caps: 29 (W:11, D:6, L:12). As captain: 5 (W:1, L:4)
Scoring: 1T, 1DG, 6 Pts
Appearances: 1960:W,I,F,S, 1961:SA,W,I,F,S, 1962:W,I,F, 1963:W,I,F,S,NZ1*,NZ2*,A*, 1964:NZ,W,I,F,S, 1965:F,S, 1966:S, 1968:F*,S*
Honours: Championship: 1963

William Henry WESTON
Born: 21 December 1904 in Potterspury
Died: 5 January 1987 in Towcester
Educated: Oakham School
Clubs: Northampton (16)
Position: Flanker (16)
Debut: 11 Feb 1933 v Ireland (Twickenham). Number: 703
Last game: 19 Mar 1938 v Scotland (Twickenham)
Caps: 16 (W:10, D:2, L:4)
Scoring: 0 Pts
Appearances: 1933:I,S, 1934:I,S, 1935:W,I,S, 1936:NZ,W,S, 1937:W,I,S, 1938:W,I,S
Honours: Championship: 1934, 1937

Arthur A WHEATLEY
Born: 6 December 1908 in Coventry
Died: 4 February 1993 in Weston
Educated: South Street School Coventry
Clubs: Coventry (5)
Position: Lock (5)
Debut: 16 Jan 1937 v Wales (Twickenham). Number: 734
Last game: 19 Mar 1938 v Scotland (Twickenham)
Caps: 5 (W:3, L:2)
Scoring: 0 Pts
Appearances: 1937:W,I,S, 1938:W,S
Honours: Championship: 1937

Harold F WHEATLEY
Born: 25 December 1912 in Coventry
Clubs: Coventry (7)
Position: Prop (4), Lock (3)
Debut: 8 Feb 1936 v Ireland (Lansdowne Road). Number: 726
Last game: 18 Mar 1939 v Scotland (Murrayfield)
Caps: 7 (W:3, L:4)
Scoring: 0 Pts
Appearances: 1936:I, 1937:S, 1938:W,S, 1939:W,I,S
Honours: Championship: 1937

Peter John WHEELER
Born: 26 November 1948 in South Norwood
Educated: Brockley County School
Clubs: Old Brockleians, Leicester (41)
Position: Hooker (41), Bench (6)
Debut: 1 Feb 1975 v France (Twickenham). Number: 1026
Last game: 17 Mar 1984 (capt) v Wales (Twickenham)
Caps: 41 (W:17, D:2, L:22). As captain: 5 (W:2, L:3)
Scoring: 0 Pts
Appearances: 1975:F,W, 1976:A,W,S,I, 1977:S,I,F,W, 1978:F,W,S,I,NZ, 1979:S,I,F,W,NZ, 1980:I,F,W,S, 1981:W,S,I,F,1982:A,S,I,F,W, 1983:F,S,I,NZ*, 1984:S*,I*,F*,W*
Honours: Grand Slam: 1980

Peter Wheeler was arguably England's greatest hooker, with superb technique at set pieces and a rare attacking vision.

An outspoken commentator on the administration of the game, he also had a vision for its future, and was a leading advocate for its professionalisation.

Wheeler made his first appearance in a Leicester jersey in 1969, and his England debut came in 1975 against France, after waiting patiently on the bench. Although he suffered a bad neck injury in only his second England

Peter Wheeler

W
Y

game, putting him out for the rest of that season, he became a regular in the front row the following season, providing a world class attacking platform on 41 occasions until his retirement in 1984.

The international world had an early taste of his abilities as England overpowered the Australians at Twickenham in 1976.

Wheeler's ball-winning skills and irresistible harassing of his opposite number, alongside captain Tony Neary, laid the foundations for an emphatic victory.

He joined the Lions tour of New Zealand in 1977 where he played in the second Test. A rare win in Christchurch allowed him to keep his place, and he appeared in 13 of the 26 matches on that trip.

He had been put on standby for the 1974 Lions trip to South Africa, even before he had played for England.

Between 1979 and 1981 he captained Leicester, leading them to a hat-trick of John Player Cups, but his finest hour as an England player was his role in England's Grand Slam-winning season of 1980.

Wheeler – who played 349 times for Leicester – continued as first-choice hooker on the subsequent Lions tour of South Africa, where he played in all four Tests and earned rave reviews, despite the Lions losing the series.

The following year he was a member of the Barbarians squad that won Hong Kong Sevens.

Run-ins with the game's administration meant he had to wait before claiming the England captaincy, but in late 1983 he finally took the reins, duly inspiring England to a rare victory over the All Blacks.

He retired following the 1984 Five Nations, as England's third most-capped player, but continued to play an active role in revolutionising rugby union from the part-time sport it once was to its current professional level.

He observed the changes that were taking place at Leicester during the late Seventies, and continued his work off the field, where he rose to the position of the club's chief executive.

Colin WHITE

Born: 31 March 1947 in Newcastle-upon-Tyne
Clubs: Gosforth (4)
Position: Prop (4), Bench (1)
Debut: 19 Nov 1983 v New Zealand (Twickenham).
Number: 1081
Last game: 3 Mar 1984 v France (Parc des Princes)
Caps: 4 (W:2, L:2)
Scoring: 0 Pts
Appearances: 1983:NZ, 1984:S,I,F

Donald Frederick (Don) WHITE

Born: 16 January 1926 in East Barton, Northants
Educated: Wellingborough GS
Clubs: Northampton (14), Northamptonshire Regt, Army, Combined Services
Position: Flanker (14)
Debut: 18 Jan 1947 v Wales (Cardiff) - 1T, 3 Pts.
Number: 766
Last game: 21 Mar 1953 v Scotland (Twickenham)
Caps: 14 (W:8, D:1, L:5)
Scoring: 2T, 6 Pts
Appearances: 1947:W,I,S, 1948:I,F, 1951:S, 1952:SA,W,S,I,F, 1953:W,I,S
Honours: Championship: 1953

Julian Martin WHITE, MBE

Born: 14 May 1973 in Plymouth
Clubs: Okehampton, Plymouth Albion, Dannevirke (NZ), Crusaders (NZ), Bridgend, Saracens (8), Bristol (6), Leicester (28)
Bridgend, Saracens (8), Bristol (6), Leicester (28)
Position: Prop (33), Replacement (9), Bench (1)
Debut: 17 Jun 2000 v South Africa (Pretoria).
Number: 1218
Last game: 24 Feb 2007 (rep) v Ireland (Croke Park)
Caps: 42 (W:24, L:18)
Scoring: 0 Pts. Discipline - Sin bins: 2
Appearances: 2000:SA1,SA2,Ar,SA, 2001:F,C1,C2,US,I,R(r), 2002:S,W,It, 2003:F,W,F,F,Sm,U(r), 2004:W(r),F(r),NZ1,NZ2,A,C,SA,A, 2005:W, 2006:W(r),It(r),S,F,I,A1,A2,NZ,Ar,SA1,SA2, 2007:S(r),It(r),I(r)
Honours: RWC Winner: 2003. Outright Championship: 2001, 2003

Julian White

William Robert Steven (Steve) WHITE-COOPER

Born: 15 July 1974 in Cape Town, South Africa
Clubs: Harlequins (2)
Position: Flanker (2)
Debut: 9 Jun 2001 v Canada (Burnaby).
Number: 1228
Last game: 16 Jun 2001 v United States (San Francisco)
Caps: 2 (W:2, L:0)
Scoring: 0 Pts
Appearances: 2001:C2,US

Eric Cyprian Perry WHITELEY

Born: 20 July 1904 in Croydon
Died: 16 March 1973 in Surrey
Educated: Dulwich College
Clubs: Old Alleynians (2), Hon Artillery Company
Position: Full-back (2)
Debut: 21 Mar 1931 v Scotland (Murrayfield).
Number: 683
Last game: 6 Apr 1931 v France (Stade Colombes)
Caps: 2 (W:0, L:2)
Scoring: 0 Pts
Appearances: 1931:S,F

W WHITELEY

Born: 1871
Died: Details unknown
Clubs: Bramley (1)
Position: Forward (1)
Debut: 4 Jan 1896 v Wales (Blackheath).
Number: 289
Caps: 1 (W:1, L:0)
Scoring: 0 Pts
Appearances: 1896:W

Herbert WHITLEY

Born: 26 August 1903 in Morpeth
Died: 1975 in Central Cleveland
Educated: Durham School
Clubs: Northern (1)
Position: Scrum-half (1)
Debut: 19 Jan 1929 v Wales (Twickenham).
Number: 593
Caps: 1 (W:1, L:0)
Scoring: 0 Pts
Appearances: 1929:W

Richard Henry Hamilton WICKES

Born: 31 December 1901 in Uxbridge
Died: 2 June 1963 of Surbiton
Educated: Bilton Grange School, Wellington College
Clubs: Cambridge University, Harlequins (10)
Position: Wing (10)
Debut: 9 Feb 1924 v Ireland (Belfast) - 1T, 3 Pts.
Number: 592
Last game: 15 Jan 1927 v Wales (Twickenham)
Caps: 10 (W:4, D:2, L:4)
Scoring: 4T, 12 Pts
Appearances: 1924:I, 1925:NZ,W,I,S,F, 1926:W,I,S, 1927:W
Honours: Championship: 1924

Steve White-Cooper

Henry John WIGGLESWORTH
Born: Third quarter 1860 in Doncaster
Died: 3 March 1925 in Hunslet
Clubs: Thornes (1)
Position: Three-quarter (1)
Debut: 4 Feb 1884 v Ireland (Lansdowne Road). Number: 167
Caps: 1 (W:1, L:0)
Scoring: 0 Pts
Appearances: 1884:I
Honours: Championship: 1884

Brian John WIGHTMAN
Born: 23 September 1936 in Birmingham
Died: 29 November 1999 in New Zealand
Educated: King Edward's School
Clubs: Old Edwardians, Loughborough College, UAU, Moseley (1), Coventry (4), Rosslyn Park
Position: No 8 (5)
Debut: 17 Jan 1959 v Wales (Cardiff). Number: 883
Last game: 4 Jun 1963 v Australia (Sydney Sports Ground)
Caps: 5 (W:1, D:1, L:3)
Scoring: 0 Pts
Appearances: 1959:W, 1963:W,I,NZ2,A
Honours: Championship: 1963

Dennis Thomas (Squire) WILKINS
Born: 26 December 1924 in Leeds
Clubs: United Services, Roundhay (4), Royal Navy (9), Combined Services
Position: Lock (13)
Debut: 20 Jan 1951 v Wales (Swansea). Number: 819
Last game: 21 Mar 1953 v Scotland (Twickenham)
Caps: 13 (W:7, D:1, L:5)
Scoring: 0 Pts
Appearances: 1951:W,I,F,S, 1952:SA,W,S,I,F, 1953:W,I,F,S
Honours: Championship: 1953

Edgar WILKINSON
Born: 1863 in Bradford
Died: 27 August 1896 in Bradford
Clubs: Bradford (5)
Position: Forward (5)
Debut: 2 Jan 1886 v Wales (Blackheath) - 1T, 1 Pt. Number: 183
Last game: 5 Mar 1887 v Scotland (Manchester)
Caps: 5 (W:2, D:3, L:0)
Scoring: 2T, 2 Pts
Appearances: 1886:W,I,S, 1887:W,S

Harry WILKINSON
Born: 22 March 1903 in Halifax
Died: 1 October 1988 in Hastings, New Zealand
Educated: Tettenhall College
Clubs: Halifax (4)
Position: Flanker (4)
Debut: 19 Jan 1929 v Wales (Twickenham) - 2T, 6 Pts. Number: 641
Last game: 22 Feb 1930 v France (Twickenham)
Caps: 4 (W:2, L:2)
Scoring: 2T, 6 Pts
Appearances: 1929:W,I,S, 1930:F
Honours: Championship: 1930

Harry James WILKINSON
Born: Second quarter 1864 in Halifax
Died: 7 June 1942 in Halifax
Clubs: Halifax (1)
Position: Forward (1)
Debut: 16 Feb 1889 v New Zealand Natives (Blackheath). Number: 207
Caps: 1 (W:1, L:0)
Scoring: 0 Pts
Appearances: 1889:M

Jonathan Peter (Jonny) WILKINSON, OBE
Born: 25 May 1979 in Frimley
Educated: Lord Wandsworth College
Clubs: Farnham, Newcastle (55)
Position: Fly-half (49), Centre (4), Replacement (2), Bench (3)
Debut: 4 Apr 1998 (rep) v Ireland (Twickenham). Number: 1194
Last game: 24 Feb 2007 v Ireland (Croke Park) - 1C, 2PG, 8 Pts
Caps: 55 (W:45, L:10). As captain: 1 (W:1, L:0)
Scoring: 6T, 126C, 173PG, 22DG, 867 Pts
Appearances: 1998:I(r),A,NZ1, 1999:S,I,F,W,A,US,C,It,NZ,Fj,SA(r), 2000:I,F,W,It,S,SA2,A,Ar,SA, 2001:W,It,S,F,I,A,SA, 2002:S,I,F,W,It,NZ,A,SA, 2003:F,W,It*,S,I,NZ,A,F,Geo,SA,Sm,W,F,A, 2007:S,It,I
Honours: RWC Winner: 2003. Grand Slam: 2003. Championship: 2000, 2001

The greatest fly-half of his generation, Jonny Wilkinson's name entered English rugby folklore with a drop goal in the dying seconds of extra time in the 2003 World Cup Final in Sydney against Australia, that handed England The Webb Ellis Cup.

His knack for match-changing moments of genius comes straight from the pages of a Boy's Own annual, and his dedication to the sport is second to none. His dad jokes that only Christmas Day tends to interfere with his training regime.

Wilkinson was of course ensured his place as a legend in England rugby long before that drop goal sailed through the posts.

His prolific ability with the boot ensured that record after record went to the lad from Frimley and that winning kick was merely the latest feat in an incredible career.

Destined for greatness from a very early age Wilkinson made his England debut aged just 18.

In his short career, and despite a freakish series of

Jonny Wilkinson

injuries, he has quickly acquired a habit for collecting headlines and passing milestones.

In 2006 he had already scored more than double the number of points of any other Englishman. No player had scored more conversions or penalties in Tests for England and his record of 89 points in one Six Nations championship in 2001 is a record.

The British public voted him BBC Sports Personality of the Year in 2003 following his World Cup exploits, and he became the youngest ever union player to receive a New Year's Honour in 2002.

England captain Martin Johnson paid tribute to Wilkinson after his ice-cool kick to win the World Cup in 2003.

"I can't say enough about the team, because we had the lead and we lost it but we came back. And I can't say enough about Wilko at the end," said Johnson.

"There is a lot of pressure on him and he gets built up to a degree where people expect superhuman stuff from him and most of the stuff he does is verging on that.

"To call him a kicker doesn't do him justice because the work he puts in on the field and in all aspects of his game is fantastic.

"He is a very special player, a very special person.

"Jonny is a lot more famous than me. I think he will probably captain England one day if he wants to, if he chooses to. I am sure he will be given that option one day."

Johnson was right, Wilkinson was given the job of captaining England in 2004, when Andy Robinson took over from Sir Clive Woodward.

But a succession of morale-sapping injuries prevented Wilkinson from playing for England between the 2003 World Cup and the 2007 RBS Six Nations.

He did play international rugby in that period, being selected by Woodward for the first and second Tests on the British and Irish Lions tour to New Zealand in 2005, injury excluding him from the third and final match against the All Blacks.

Woodward added: "He's a wonderful player and I just think he's getting better and better."

Born to break records, Wilkinson has already taken over from his club mentor, Rob Andrew, as England's all-time highest points scorer with his brutally accurate dead ball kicking, and he was only the third kicker to win the Zurich Golden Boot for scoring over 1,000 points for his only club, Newcastle Falcons.

"Leading England out at Twickenham is something I used to dream of doing when I was 10 or 11 playing mini-rugby," he has said, and he duly achieved this against Italy in 2004 when Martin Johnson was unavailable.

After his injury nightmare Wilkinson triumphantly returned to the England fray in 2007, making an immediate impact with 27 points in his first game back against Scotland, continuing his inexorable progress to becoming the highest points scorer in Test history.

Natural modesty, however, would prevent him from claiming a spot in any all-time 15, no doubt deferring to boyhood heroes Jonathan Davies, Grant Fox and Rob Andrew.

P WILKINSON

Born: Details unknown
Died: Details unknown
Clubs: Law Club (1)
Position: Half-Back (1)
Debut: 5 Feb 1872 v Scotland (The Oval). Number: 34
Caps: 1 (W:1, L:0)
Scoring: 0 Pts
Appearances: 1872:S

Robert Michael (Bob) WILKINSON

Born: 25 July 1951 in Luton
Educated: St Albans School
Clubs: Cambridge University, Bedford (6)
Position: Lock (6), Bench (1)
Debut: 31 May 1975 v Australia (Brisbane). Number: 1035
Last game: 20 Mar 1976 v France (Parc des Princes)
Caps: 6 (W:1, L:5)
Scoring: 0 Pts
Appearances: 1975:A2, 1976:A,W,S,I,F

T J WILLCOCKS
Born: Details unknown
Died: Details unknown
Clubs: Buckfastleigh, Plymouth Albion (1)
Position: Forward (1)
Debut: 11 Jan 1902 v Wales (Blackheath). Number: 379
Caps: 1 (W:0, L:1)
Scoring: 0 Pts
Appearances: 1902:W

John Graham WILLCOX
Born: 16 February 1937 in Sutton Coldfield
Educated: Ratcliffe College, RMA Sandhurst
Clubs: Oxford University (10), RMA Sandhurst, Fylde, Army, Harlequins (6), Paris University Club (FR), Headingley, Malton
Position: Full-back (16)
Debut: 11 Feb 1961 v Ireland (Lansdowne Road). Number: 899
Last game: 21 Mar 1964 v Scotland (Murrayfield)
Caps: 16 (W:6, D:5, L:5). As captain: 3 (W:0, D:1, L:2)
Scoring: 4C, 3PG, 17 Pts
Appearances: 1961:I,F,S, 1962:W,I,F,S, 1963:W,I,F,S, 1964:NZ*,W*,I*,F,S
Honours: Championship: 1963

Sir Peveril Barton Reiby Wallop WILLIAM-POWLETT, KCB
Born: 5 March 1898 in Abergavenny, Wales
Died: 10 November 1985 in Honiton
Educated: Cordwalles School
Clubs: RNC Osborne, RNC Dartmouth, United Services (1), Blackheath, Wanderers, Royal Navy
Position: Prop (1)
Debut: 18 Mar 1922 v Scotland (Twickenham). Number: 580
Caps: 1 (W:1, L:0)
Scoring: 0 Pts
Appearances: 1922:S

Christopher Gareth WILLIAMS
Born: 21 December 1950
Educated: Lydney GS
Clubs: Gloucester (1), RAF
Position: Fly-half (1)
Debut: 20 Mar 1976 v France (Parc des Princes).Number: 1043
Caps: 1 (W:0, L:1)
Scoring: 0 Pts
Appearances: 1976:F

Cyril Stoate WILLIAMS
Born: 17 November 1887 in Stroud
Died: Details unknown
Educated: Mill Hill School, Truro College
Clubs: Manchester University, Manchester (1)
Position: Full-back (1)
Debut: 3 Mar 1910 v France (Parc des Princes). Number: 505
Caps: 1 (W:1, L:0)
Scoring: 0 Pts
Appearances: 1910:F
Honours: Championship: 1910

John Edward WILLIAMS
Born: 31 January 1932 in Leeds North
Educated: Mill Hill School
Clubs: Old Millhillians (8), Army, Headingley, Harlequins, Sale (1)
Position: Scrum-half (9)
Debut: 10 Apr 1954 v France (Stade Colombes). Number: 848
Last game: 16 Jan 1965 v Wales (Cardiff)
Caps: 9 (W:3, D:1, L:5)
Scoring: 1T, 3 Pts
Appearances: 1954:F, 1955:W,I,F,S, 1956:I,S,F, 1965:W

John Michael WILLIAMS
Born: 24 August 1927 in Penzance
Died: 6 September 2000 in Budock
Educated: Rugby School
Clubs: Cambridge University, Penzance & Newlyn (2), Richmond
Position: Centre (2)
Debut: 10 Feb 1951 v Ireland (Lansdowne Road). Number: 823
Last game: 17 Mar 1951 v Scotland (Twickenham)
Caps: 2 (W:1, L:1)
Scoring: 0 Pts
Appearances: 1951:I,S

Peter Nicholas WILLIAMS
Born: 14 December 1958 in Wigan
Educated: Upholland GS, Chester College
Clubs: Orrell (4), Salford RL
Position: Fly-half (4), Bench (1)
Debut: 4 Apr 1987 v Scotland (Twickenham). Number: 1118
Last game: 8 Jun 1987 v Wales (Brisbane)
Caps: 4 (W:2, L:2)
Scoring: 0 Pts
Appearances: 1987:S,A,J,W

Samuel George WILLIAMS
Born: 14 May 1880 in Stoke Damerel
Died: 19 March 1955 in Plymouth
Clubs: Devonport Albion (7)
Position: Forward (7)
Debut: 11 Jan 1902 v Wales (Blackheath). Number: 380
Last game: 16 Mar 1907 v Scotland (Blackheath)
Caps: 7 (W:2, L:5)
Scoring: 2T, 6 Pts
Appearances: 1902:W,I,S, 1903:I,S, 1907:I,S

Samuel Horatio WILLIAMS
Born: 2 November 1885 in Rogerston
Died: 30 April 1936 at sea
Educated: Newport Intermediate School
Clubs: Newport (4)
Position: Full-back (4)
Debut: 21 Jan 1911 v Wales (Swansea). Number: 510
Last game: 18 Mar 1911 v Scotland (Twickenham)
Caps: 4 (W:2, L:2)
Scoring: 0 Pts
Appearances: 1911:W,F,I,S

Rupert Henry WILLIAMSON
Born: 22 November 1886 in South Africa
Died: 16 March 1946
Educated: St Andrew's School
Clubs: Oxford University (5), Blackheath
Position: Scrum-half (5)
Debut: 18 Jan 1908 v Wales (Bristol) - 1T, 3 Pts. Number: 460
Last game: 30 Jan 1909 v France (Leicester)
Caps: 5 (W:2, L:3)
Scoring: 2T, 6 Pts
Appearances: 1908:W,I,S, 1909:A,F

Arthur James WILSON
Born: 29 December 1886 in Newcastle-upon-Tyne
Died: Killed in action in 1917 in Flanders, Belgium
Educated: Glenalmond Academy
Clubs: Camborne School of Mines (1), Camborne
Position: Forward (1)
Debut: 13 Feb 1909 v Ireland (Lansdowne Road). Number: 489
Caps: 1 (W:1, L:0)
Scoring: 0 Pts
Appearances: 1909:I

Charles Edward WILSON
Born: 2 June 1871 in Fermoy, Co Cork, Ireland
Died: Killed in action in 1914 in Soissons, France
Educated: Dover College
Clubs: Blackheath (1), Queen's Regt, Army
Position: Forward (1)
Debut: 5 Feb 1898 v Ireland (Richmond). Number: 317
Caps: 1 (W:0, L:1)
Scoring: 0 Pts
Appearances: 1898:I

Charles Plumpton WILSON
Born: 12 May 1859 in Roydon, Norfolk
Died: 9 March 1938 in East Dereham, Norfolk
Educated: Uppingham School, Marlborough College
Clubs: Cambridge University (1), Marlborough Nomads
Position: Forward (1)
Debut: 19 Feb 1881 v Wales (Blackheath). Number: 138
Caps: 1 (W:1, L:0)
Scoring: 0 Pts
Appearances: 1881:W

Dyson Stayt (Tug) WILSON
Born: 7 October 1926 in Wilderness, South Africa
Educated: King Edward VII School, Rydal School
Clubs: Harlequins (1), Metropolitan Police (7), Rhodesia
Position: Flanker (8)
Debut: 28 Feb 1953 v France (Twickenham). Number: 836
Last game: 19 Mar 1955 v Scotland (Twickenham)
Caps: 8 (W:5, L:3)
Scoring: 4T, 12 Pts
Appearances: 1953:F, 1954:W,NZ,I,S,F, 1955:F,S
Honours: Championship: 1953

Guy Sumerfield WILSON

Born: 30 August 1907 in Leigh
Died: 8 July 1979 in Lancaster
Clubs: Tyldesley (2), Manchester, Birkenhead Park
Position: Wing (2)
Debut: 19 Jan 1929 v Wales (Twickenham) - 1C, 2 Pts. Number: 642
Last game: 9 Feb 1929 v Ireland (Twickenham) - 1C, 2 Pts
Caps: 2 (W:1, L:1)
Scoring: 2C, 4 Pts
Appearances: 1929:W,I

Kenneth James (Tug) WILSON

Born: 25 November 1938 in Newark
Died: 1 December 1993 in Oldham
Educated: King's GS
Clubs: Cheltenham, Gloucester (1), RAF, Combined Services, Oldham RL
Position: Prop (1)
Debut: 23 Feb 1963 v France (Twickenham). Number: 916
Caps: 1 (W:1, L:0)
Scoring: 0 Pts
Appearances: 1963:F
Honours: Championship: 1963

Roger Parker WILSON

Born: 13 May 1870 in West Derby
Died: 12 December 1943 in Southport
Clubs: Liverpool University, Liverpool Old Boys (3), St Bart's Hospital
Position: Forward (3)
Debut: 3 Jan 1891 v Wales (Newport). Number: 230
Last game: 7 Mar 1891 v Scotland (Richmond)
Caps: 3 (W:2, L:1)
Scoring: 2T, 2 Pts
Appearances: 1891:W,I,S

Walter Carandini WILSON, CBE

Born: 22 June 1885
Died: 12 April 1968 in Brighton
Educated: Tonbridge School
Clubs: Leicestershire Regt, United Services, Army, Richmond (2)
Position: Wing (2)
Debut: 9 Feb 1907 v Ireland (Lansdowne Road). Number: 448
Last game: 16 Mar 1907 v Scotland (Blackheath)
Caps: 2 (W:0, L:2)
Scoring: 0 Pts
Appearances: 1907:I,S

Christopher Elliott WINN

Born: 13 November 1926 in Beckenham
Educated: King's College
Clubs: Oxford University, Rosslyn Park (8)
Position: Wing (8)
Debut: 5 Jan 1952 v South Africa (Twickenham) - 1T, 3 Pts. Number: 828
Last game: 10 Apr 1954 v France (Stade Colombes)
Caps: 8 (W:5, L:3)
Scoring: 3T, 9 Pts
Appearances: 1952:SA,W,S,I,F, 1954:W,S,F

Peter Winterbottom

Peter James WINTERBOTTOM MBE

Born: 31 May 1960 in Horsforth, Leeds
Educated: Rossall School, Seale-Hayne Agricultural College
Clubs: Fleetwood, Exeter, Headingley (29), Hawke's Bay (NZ), Meralomas (CA), Harlequins (29)
Position: Flanker (58), Bench (1)
Debut: 2 Jan 1982 v Australia (Twickenham).Number: 1073
Last game: 20 Mar 1993 v Ireland (Lansdowne Road)
Caps: 58 (W:31, D:2, L:25).
Scoring: 3T, 13 Pts
Appearances: 1982:A,S,I,F,W, 1983:F,W,S,I,NZ, 1984:S,F,W,SA1,SA2, 1986:W,S,I,F, 1987:I,F,W,A,J,US,W, 1988:F,W,S,1989:R,Fj, 1990:I,F,W,S,Ar1,Ar2,Ar, 1991:W,S,I,F,A,NZ,It,F,S,A, 1992:S,I,F,W,C,SA, 1993:F,W,S,I
Honours: Grand Slam: 1991, 1992

Peter Winterbottom or Winters to his friends – started his rugby career as a farmer, playing No 8 for Lancashire schools and England colts, but he ended it as one of the most respected openside flankers in the world and an international financier.

After switching to flanker with England B in 1981, he made his England debut a year later in a historical victory over Australia at Twickenham, alongside another impressive debutante, the young Erica Roe whose 'talents' were also obvious from the start.

A season playing in New Zealand for Hawke's Bay helped Winterbottom to hone his handling skills, and he garnered early comparisons with legendary French flanker Jean-Pierre Rives with his flair and his striking blond hair, which earned him the nickname 'The Straw Man'.

Rives had uniquely extravagant skills, but Winterbottom – the first English forward to win 50 caps – played with more physical vigour, his tackling particularly impressive.

The Pit Bull himself, Brian Moore, described him as the hardest man he ever met.

The year after his England debut he toured New Zealand with the Lions, playing in all four Tests. Despite losing the series, Winterbottom was voted one of New Zealand's players of 1983 for his performances.

England underachieved throughout the 1980s, but Winterbottom maintained a reputation as one of England's most consistent performers.

The World Cup disappointment of 1987, however, remains a low point and he vowed never again to repeat the experience.

The following year he moved from his hometown club of Headingley in Leeds to Harlequins where he captained them in three Pilkington Cup Finals, winning against Northampton in 1991.

The start of the 1990s saw England's fortunes improve under the leadership of coach Geoff Cooke and captain Will Carling, and Winterbottom was an ever present in the Grand Slams of 1991 and 1992.

Losing out to Australia in the 1991 World Cup final was his one disappointment.

Winterbottom – who was honoured with the MBE in 1994 – retired from the international stage in 1993, still recognised as one of the best flankers in the world, having thrived on the tough circuits of New Zealand and South African rugby, and holding off the persistent claims of future England coach Andy Robinson.

His last international game was on the 1993 Lions tour and on arrival back home Peter Jackson The Daily Mail's rugby correspondent said: "What a way to finish. A 2-1 points verdict over Michael Jones, six years his junior, will be still talked about in 50 years time."

Winterbottom definitely jumped a long time before he was pushed adding: "One reason I am retiring after the last Test is I don't want to hang on too long. I don't want to wait to be dropped. I've always wanted to go out at the top."

Trevor Clifford WINTLE
Born: 10 January 1940 in Forest of Dean
Educated: Lydney GS
Clubs: Cambridge University, Rosslyn Park, St Mary's Hospital, Northampton (5)
Position: Scrum-half (5)
Debut: 19 Mar 1966 v Scotland (Murrayfield). Number: 948
Last game: 12 Apr 1969 v Wales (Cardiff)
Caps: 5 (W:2, L:3)
Scoring: 0 Pts
Appearances: 1966:S, 1969:I,F,S,W

Norman Atherton WODEHOUSE
Born: 18 May 1887 in Basford, Nottingham
Died: Killed in action at sea in 1941
Educated: HMS Brittania College
Clubs: United Services (9), Royal Navy (5)
Position: Forward (14)
Debut: 3 Mar 1910 v France (Parc des Princes). Number: 506
Last game: 15 Mar 1913 (capt) v Scotland (Twickenham)
Caps: 14 (W:10, L:4). As captain: 6 (W:5, L:1)
Scoring: 2T, 6 Pts
Appearances: 1910:F, 1911:W,F,I,S, 1912:W,I,S,F*, 1913:SA*,W*,F*,I*,S*
Honours: Grand Slam: 1913 (capt). Championship: 1910

Albert WOOD
Born: Details unknown
Died: In Australia, details unknown
Clubs: Halifax (1)
Position: Forward (1)
Debut: 4 Feb 1884 v Ireland (Lansdowne Road). Number: 168
Caps: 1 (W:1, L:0)
Scoring: 0 Pts
Appearances: 1884:I
Honours: Championship: 1884

Alfred Ernest WOOD
Born: 27 November 1883 in Wolverhampton
Died: 15 February 1963 in Oldham
Educated: Liverpool College
Clubs: Oxford University, Gloucester (3), Cheltenham, Oldham RL
Position: Full-back (3)
Debut: 1 Jan 1908 v France (Stade Colombes). Number: 458
Last game: 8 Feb 1908 v Ireland (Richmond) - 2C, 4 Pts
Caps: 3 (W:2, L:1)
Scoring: 4C, 8 Pts
Appearances: 1908:F,W,I

George William (Pedlar) WOOD
Born: 5 February 1886 in Leicester
Died: 12 June 1969 in Leicester
Educated: Melbourne Road School
Clubs: Melbourne Road Old Boys, Leicester (1), Nottingham, Nuneaton
Position: Scrum-half (1)
Debut: 17 Jan 1914 v Wales (Twickenham). Number: 540
Caps: 1 (W:1, L:0)
Scoring: 0 Pts
Appearances: 1914:W
Honours: Championship: 1914

Martyn Benjamin WOOD
Born: 25 April 1977 in Harrogate
Educated: Harrogate GS
Clubs: Wasps (2), Bath
Position: Replacement Scrum-half (2), Bench (2)
Debut: 9 Jun 2001 (rep) v Canada (Burnaby) - 1T, 5 Pts. Number: 1229
Last game: 16 Jun 2001 (rep) v United States (San Francisco)
Caps: 2 (W:2, L:0)
Scoring: 1T, 5 Pts
Appearances: 2001:C2(r),US(r)

Robert WOOD
Born: 1873
Died: Details unknown
Clubs: Liversedge (1)
Position: Half-Back (1)
Debut: 3 Feb 1894 v Ireland (Blackheath). Number: 268
Caps: 1 (W:0, L:1)
Scoring: 0 Pts
Appearances: 1894:I

Robert Dudley WOOD
Born: First quarter 1873 in West Derby
Died: Details unknown
Clubs: Liverpool Old Boys (3)
Position: Forward (3)
Debut: 9 Feb 1901 v Ireland (Lansdowne Road). Number: 366
Last game: 14 Feb 1903 v Ireland (Lansdowne Road)
Caps: 3 (W:0, L:3)
Scoring: 0 Pts
Appearances: 1901:I, 1903:W,I

Elliott Edward WOODGATE
Born: 21 January 1922 in Totnes
Died: January 2000 in Newport, Wales
Educated: Dartmouth SMS
Clubs: Kingswear, Paignton (1)
Position: Prop (1)
Debut: 19 Jan 1952 v Wales (Twickenham). Number: 830
Caps: 1 (W:0, L:1)
Scoring: 0 Pts
Appearances: 1952:W

Ernest (Ernie) WOODHEAD
Born: 2 February 1857 in Huddersfield
Died: 10 June 1944 in Huddersfield
Educated: Huddersfield College
Clubs: Edinburgh University, Dublin University, Huddersfield (1)
Position: Forward (1)
Debut: 30 Jan 1880 v Ireland (Lansdowne Road). Number: 127
Caps: 1 (W:1, L:0)
Scoring: 0 Pts
Appearances: 1880:I

Martyn Wood

Trevor James WOODMAN, MBE
Born: 4 August 1976 in Plymouth
Educated: Liskeard School
Clubs: Bath, Plymouth Albion, Bath, Gloucester (22), Sale
Position: Prop (14), Replacement (8), Bench (5)
Debut: 21 Aug 1999 (rep) v United States (Twickenham). Number: 1213
Last game: 19 Jun 2004 v New Zealand (Auckland)
Caps: 22 (W:18, L:4)
Scoring: 0 Pts
Appearances: 1999:US(r), 2000:I(r),It(r), 2001:W(r),It(r), 2002:NZ, 2003:S(r),I(r),A,F,Geo,SA,W(r),F,A, 2004:It,S,I,W,F,NZ1,NZ2
Honours: RWC Winner: 2003. Championship: 2000, 2001, 2003

Charles Garfield (Peter) WOODRUFF
Born: 30 October 1920 in Newport, Wales
Educated: Newport HS
Clubs: Civil Service, Harlequins (4), Cheltenham
Position: Wing (4)
Debut: 20 Jan 1951 v Wales (Swansea). Number: 820
Last game: 17 Mar 1951 v Scotland (Twickenham)
Caps: 4 (W:1, L:3)
Scoring: 0 Pts
Appearances: 1951:W,I,F,S

Trevor Woodman

Samuel Moses James WOODS
Born: 14 April 1867 in Ashfield, NSW, Australia
Died: 30 April 1931 in Taunton
Educated: Sydney GS, Brighton College
Clubs: Cambridge University (6), Wellington (4), Blackheath, Bridgwater & Albion (3)
Position: Forward (13)
Debut: 15 Feb 1890 v Wales (Dewsbury). Number: 215
Last game: 9 Mar 1895 (capt) v Scotland (Richmond)
Caps: 13 (W:9, L:4). As captain: 5 (W:4, L:1)
Scoring: 1T, 1C, 6 Pts
Appearances: 1890:W,S,I, 1891:W,I,S, 1892:I*,S, 1893:W,I*, 1895:W*,I*,S*
Honours: Championship: 1892 (capt)

Thomas (Tommy) WOODS
Born: 9 February 1883 in Bridgwater
Died: 12 April 1955 in Rochdale
Clubs: Bridgwater & Albion (1), Rochdale Hornets RL
Position: Forward (1)
Debut: 21 Mar 1908 v Scotland (Inverleith). Number: 466
Caps: 1 (W:0, L:1)
Scoring: 0 Pts
Appearances: 1908:S

Thomas (Tom) WOODS
Born: First quarter 1890 in Pontypool, Wales
Died: Details unknown
Clubs: Royal Navy (1), Devonport Services (3), United Services, Newbridge, Pontypool (1), Wigan RL
Position: Forward (5)
Debut: 20 Mar 1920 v Scotland (Twickenham). Number: 565
Last game: 28 Mar 1921 v France (Stade Colombes)
Caps: 5 (W:5, L:0)
Scoring: 1T, 3 Pts
Appearances: 1920:S, 1921:W,I,S,F
Honours: Grand Slam: 1921

Sir Clive Ronald WOODWARD, KBE
Born: 6 January 1956 in Ely, Cambs
Educated: HMS Conway
Clubs: Harlequins, Loughborough College, Leicester (21), Manly (AU)
Position: Centre (20), Replacement (1), Bench (2)
Debut: 19 Jan 1980 (rep) v Ireland (Twickenham). Number: 1062
Last game: 17 Mar 1984 v Wales (Twickenham)
Caps: 21 (W:12, D:2, L:7)
Scoring: 4T, 16 Pts
Appearances: 1980:I(r),F,W,S, 1981:W,S,I,F,Ar1,Ar2, 1982:A,S,I,F,W, 1983:I,NZ, 1984:S,I,F,W
Honours: Grand Slam: 1980

Saturday 22 November 2003 is the date that Clive Woodward became a household name. Not as the elegant and influential centre who became an integral part of the England Grand Slam-winning team of 1980, but as the mastermind who revolutionised English rugby coaching, taking it into the professional era and culminating in the capture of the World Cup, and a subsequent knighthood.

His 2003 World Cup triumph was based on practices pioneered in the southern hemisphere, surrounding himself with a team of experts in each area of the game, ensuring that every part of the game was examined in

Clive Woodward

detail, and that England were the best-prepared for any situation. They even brought along their own chef and lawyer and his mantra was for the team to do 100 things one per cent better. The reward for Woodward's total rugby preparation couldn't have tasted sweeter.

He made his England debut in 1980 as a replacement against Ireland, impressing with his pace, and proving to be as much a creator as scorer, with one or two tricks up his sleeve, including a crowd-pleasing sidestep.

Woodward – who played his club rugby for Harlequins and Leicester – made the starting line-up for the next match against France, and perhaps his finest moment of that Grand Slam-winning season came against Scotland with two tries.

"He not only had speed but guile," explained Bill Beaumont, his England captain in 1980.

"But above everything else he was a beautifully balanced runner. He ran at opponents, then just when you thought he was sure to be downed, he produced a breath-taking sidestep and left his man for dead."

Woodward's intelligent playing skills led to inclusion in the 1980 Lions tour of South Africa, where he played in two Tests but missed out on the fourth Test victory.

The 1981 campaign proved to be a less successful season for England, but Woodward was selected to lead the Barbarians in the Hong Kong Sevens tournament, where they became the first northern hemisphere side to win it.

The 1982 season stood out for one fantastic solo try in another disappointing Five Nations championship, and 1983 was all but written off with a broken leg.

His final appearance against Wales in 1984 was at the relatively tender age of 28, after which he moved to Australia, playing alongside the legendary Ella brothers for Manly and taking his first steps in the business world.

Woodward couldn't keep away from English rugby for too long though and returned in the 1990s, with a pouchful of ideas, to coach Henley, London Irish and Bath, before taking on the task of transforming the England scene in 1997, replacing Jack Rowell.

Things didn't go smoothly at first as England lost successive Grand Slams they should have won in 1999, 2000 and 2001, finally pulling off Woodward's only Six Nations clean sweep in 2003.

That 2003 side went on to beat both New Zealand and Australia in their own backyards and the rest is history.

Even though he had a contract until 2007, Woodward (now Sir Clive) left the RFU in 2004 to devote his energies to coaching the British and Irish Lions, and to move into football.

Heading up the Lions tour was his last job in rugby and it was a disaster as the side lost by a record margin.

He tried to return to rugby in 2006, applying for the elite rugby director role at the RFU, which went to Rob Andrew.

Ever the revolutionary, and determined to put his money where his mouth was, Woodward decided to test his ideas in the world of football, joining Southampton as director of coaching.

Unfortunately, his mind was more open than many of his new colleagues and after a difficult year he switched to become director of elite performance at the British Olympic Association, where he is building towards the 2012 Olympics.

John Edward WOODWARD

Born: 17 April 1931 in High Wycombe
Educated: RGS High Wycombe
Clubs: RAF, Wasps (15)
Position: Wing (15)
Debut: 5 Jan 1952 v South Africa (Twickenham). Number: 829
Last game: 17 Mar 1956 v Scotland (Murrayfield)
Caps: 15 (W:8, D:2, L:5)
Scoring: 6T, 1PG, 21 Pts
Appearances: 1952:SA,W,S, 1953:W,I,F,S, 1954:W,NZ,I,S,F, 1955:W,I, 1956:S
Honours: Championship: 1953

Charles Sylvester WOOLDRIDGE

Born: 31 December 1858 in Winchester
Died: 19 February 1941 in Winchester
Educated: Winchester College
Clubs: Oxford University (3), Blackheath (4)
Position: Forward (7)
Debut: 16 Dec 1882 v Wales (Swansea). Number: 156
Last game: 7 Feb 1885 v Ireland (Manchester)
Caps: 7 (W:7, L:0)
Scoring: 0 Pts
Appearances: 1883:W,I,S, 1884:W,I,S, 1885:I
Honours: Championship: 1883, 1884

Joe Worsley

Alan John (Nellie) WORDSWORTH
Born: 9 November 1953 in Thornton Heath
Educated: Whitgift School
Clubs: Cambridge University (1), Harlequins
Position: Replacement Fly-half (1)
Debut: 24 May 1975 (rep) v Australia (Sydney Cricket Ground). Number: 1033
Caps: 1 (W:0, L:1)
Scoring: 0 Pts
Appearances: 1975:A1(r)

Joseph Paul Richard (Joe) WORSLEY, MBE
Born: 14 June 1977 in Redbridge, Hants
Educated: Hitchin BS
Clubs: Welwyn GC, Wasps (55)
Position: Flanker (26), No 8 (12), Replacement (17), Bench (4)
Debut: 15 Oct 1999 v Tonga (Twickenham). Number: 1214
Last game: 24 Feb 2007 v Ireland (Croke Park)
Caps: 55 (W:36, L:19)
Scoring: 9T, 45 Pts. Discipline - Sin bins: 1
Appearances: 1999:Tg,Fj, 2000:It(r),S(r),SA1(r),SA2(r), 2001:It(r),S(r),F(r),C1,C2,US,A,R,SA, 2002:S,I,F,W(r),Ar, 2003:W(r),It,S(r),I(r),NZ(r),A(r),W,SA(r),Sm,U, 2004:It,I,W(r),F,NZ1(r),NZ2,A,SA,A, 2005:W,F,I,It,S, 2006:W,It,S,F,I,A1(r),A2,SA1,SA2, 2007:S,I
Honours: RWC Winner: 2003. Outright Championship: 2000, 2001, 2003

Michael Anthony (Mike) WORSLEY
Born: 1 December 1976 in Warrington
Educated: St Ambrose College
Clubs: West Park, Orrell, Bristol, London Irish (1), Harlequins (2)
Position: Replacement Prop (3), Bench (1)
Debut: 9 Mar 2003 (rep) v Italy (Twickenham). Number: 1247
Last game: 19 Mar 2005 (rep) v Scotland (Twickenham)
Caps: 3 (W:2, L:1)
Scoring: 0 Pts
Appearances: 2003:It(r), 2004:A(r), 2005:S(r)
Honours: Championship: 2003

Joseph Bute (John) WORTON
Born: 31 March 1901 in Fulham
Died: 14 January 1991 in south-west Surrey
Educated: Haileybury & ISC
Clubs: RMC Sandhurst, Harlequins (2), Middlesex Regt, Army, Combined Services
Position: Scrum-half (2)
Debut: 16 Jan 1926 v Wales (Cardiff). Number: 610
Last game: 15 Jan 1927 v Wales (Twickenham)
Caps: 2 (W:1, D:1, L:0)
Scoring: 0 Pts
Appearances: 1926:W, 1927:W

Frederick David Bryan WRENCH
Born: 27 November 1936 in Northwich
Educated: Sandbach School
Clubs: Leeds University, Winnington Park, Wilmslow, UAU, Cambridge University, Harlequins (2), Wolfhounds
Position: Prop (2)
Debut: 22 Feb 1964 v France (Stade Colombes). Number: 926
Last game: 21 Mar 1964 v Scotland (Murrayfield)
Caps: 2 (W:1, L:1)
Scoring: 0 Pts
Appearances: 1964:F,S

Cyril Carne Glenton WRIGHT
Born: 7 March 1887 in Oporto, Portugal
Died: 15 September 1960 in Hampstead,London
Educated: Tonbridge School
Clubs: Cambridge University (2), Blackheath
Position: Centre (2)
Debut: 13 Feb 1909 v Ireland (Lansdowne Road). Number: 490
Last game: 20 Mar 1909 v Scotland (Richmond)
Caps: 2 (W:1, L:1)
Scoring: 0 Pts
Appearances: 1909:I,S

Frank Thurlow WRIGHT
Born: 2 July 1862 in Leigh
Died: 30 April 1934 in Marseilles, France
Clubs: Edinburgh Academicals, Manchester (1)
Position: Half-Back (1)
Debut: 19 Mar 1881 v Scotland (Raeburn Place). Number: 139
Caps: 1 (W:0, D:1, L:0)
Scoring: 0 Pts
Appearances: 1881:S

Ian Douglas WRIGHT
Born: 24 December 1945 in Croydon
Died: 2000
Educated: Felixtowe GS, Worthing HS, St Luke's College
Clubs: Rosslyn Park, Northampton (4)
Position: Fly-half (3), Replacement (1), Bench (3)
Debut: 16 Jan 1971 v Wales (Cardiff). Number: 996
Last game: 20 Mar 1971 (rep) v Scotland (Twickenham)
Caps: 4 (W:1, D:1, L:2)
Scoring: 0 Pts
Appearances: 1971:W,I,F,S(r)

James Frost WRIGHT
Born: 1 April 1863 in Bramham, Yorks
Died: 4 October 1932 in Blackpool
Clubs: Idle, Bradford (1)
Position: Half-Back (1)
Debut: 15 Feb 1890 v Wales (Dewsbury). Number: 216
Caps: 1 (W:0, L:1)
Scoring: 0 Pts
Appearances: 1890:W

John Cecil WRIGHT
Born: 6 August 1910
Educated: Sedbergh School
Clubs: Crewe, Nantwich, Metropolitan Police (1), British Police, Newport
Position: Lock (1)
Debut: 20 Jan 1934 v Wales (Cardiff). Number: 710
Caps: 1 (W:1, L:0)
Scoring: 0 Pts
Appearances: 1934:W
Honours: Championship: 1934

Thomas Peter (Peter) WRIGHT
Born: 28 February 1931 in Glanford
Died: 22 April 2002 in Devizes
Educated: Judd School
Clubs: Tonbridge, Blackheath (13), Penarth, Cowbridge, Devizes
Position: Prop (13)
Debut: 16 Jan 1960 v Wales (Twickenham). Number: 893
Last game: 17 Mar 1962 v Scotland (Murrayfield)
Caps: 13 (W:5, D:4, L:4)
Scoring: 0 Pts
Appearances: 1960:W,I,F,S, 1961:SA,W,I,F,S, 1962:W,I,F,S

William Henry George (Jock) WRIGHT
Born: 6 June 1889 in Plymouth
Died: Details unknown
Clubs: Plymouth Albion (2)
Position: Prop (2)
Debut: 17 Jan 1920 v Wales (Swansea). Number: 555
Last game: 31 Jan 1920 v France (Twickenham)
Caps: 2 (W:1, L:1)
Scoring: 0 Pts
Appearances: 1920:W,F

Derek Murray WYATT
Born: 4 December 1949 in Woolwich
Educated: RGS Colchester
Clubs: Oxford University, Bedford (1)
Position: Replacement Wing (1), Bench (1)
Debut: 21 Feb 1976 (rep) v Scotland (Murrayfield). Number: 1040
Caps: 1 (W:0, L:1)
Scoring: 0 Pts
Appearances: 1976:S(r)

Peter George YARRANTON
Born: 30 September 1924 in Acton
Died: 1 June 2003 in West London
Educated: Willesden Technical College
Clubs: Wasps (5), RAF, Combined Services
Position: Lock (5)
Debut: 16 Jan 1954 v Wales (Twickenham). Number: 842
Last game: 19 Mar 1955 v Scotland (Twickenham)
Caps: 5 (W:3, L:2)
Scoring: 0 Pts
Appearances: 1954:W,NZ,I, 1955:F,S

Kevin Peter YATES
Born: 6 November 1972 in Medicine Hat, Canada
Educated: John Bentley School
Clubs: Chippenham, Bath (2), Wellington (NZ), Hurricanes (NZ), Sale, Saracens
Position: Prop (2), Bench (2)
Debut: 31 May 1997 v Argentina (Buenos Aires). Number: 1182
Last game: 7 Jun 1997 v Argentina (Buenos Aires)
Caps: 2 (W:1, L:1)
Scoring: 0 Pts
Appearances: 1997:Ar1,Ar2

William YIEND
Born: Third quarter 1861 in Winchcombe
Died: 22 January 1939 in Cheltenham
Clubs: Leicester Victoria, Hartlepool Rovers (6), Gloucester, Leicester, Keighley, Peterborough
Position: Forward (6)
Debut: 16 Feb 1889 v New Zealand Natives (Blackheath). Number: 208
Last game: 4 Mar 1893 v Scotland (Headingley)
Caps: 6 (W:5, L:1)
Scoring: 0 Pts
Appearances: 1889:M, 1892:W,I,S, 1893:I,S
Honours: Championship: 1892

Arthur Tudor YOUNG
Born: 14 October 1901 in Darjeeling, India
Died: 26 February 1933 in Bareilly, India
Educated: Tonbridge School
Clubs: Cambridge University (6), Blackheath (12), Royal Tank Regt, Army
Position: Scrum-half (18)
Debut: 19 Jan 1924 v Wales (Swansea). Number: 590
Last game: 9 Feb 1929 v Ireland (Twickenham)
Caps: 18 (W:12, L:6)
Scoring: 2T, 6 Pts
Appearances: 1924:W,I,F,S, 1925:NZ,F, 1926:I,F,S, 1927:I,S,F, 1928:A,W,I,F,S, 1929:I
Honours: Grand Slam: 1924, 1928

John Robert Chester YOUNG
Born: 6 September 1937 in Chester
Educated: Bishop Vesey GS
Clubs: Oxford University (1), Harlequins (8)
Position: Wing (9)
Debut: 8 Feb 1958 v Ireland (Twickenham). Number: 875
Last game: 25 Feb 1961 v France (Twickenham)
Caps: 9 (W:4, D:2, L:3)
Scoring: 2T, 6 Pts
Appearances: 1958:I, 1960:W,I,F,S, 1961:SA,W,I,F
Honours: Championship: 1958

Malcolm YOUNG
Born: 4 January 1946 in Mickley, Northumberland
Educated: Queen Elizabeth GS
Clubs: Cambridge University, Gosforth (10)
Position: Scrum-half (10), Bench (8)
Debut: 15 Jan 1977 v Scotland (Twickenham) - 1T, 4 Pts. Number: 1047
Last game: 3 Feb 1979 v Scotland (Twickenham)
Caps: 10 (W:4, D:1, L:5)
Scoring: 1T, 4C, 1PG, 15 Pts
Appearances: 1977:S,I,F,W, 1978:F,W,S,I,NZ, 1979:S

Peter Dalton YOUNG
Born: 9 November 1927 in Bristol
Died: 23 May 2002
Educated: Clifton College
Clubs: Cambridge University, Clifton, Rosslyn Park, Wanderers (9)
Position: Lock (9)
Debut: 16 Jan 1954 v Wales (Twickenham). Number: 843
Last game: 19 Mar 1955 (capt) v Scotland (Twickenham)
Caps: 9 (W:4, D:1, L:4). As captain: 2 (W:1, L:1)
Scoring: 1T, 3 Pts
Appearances: 1954:W,NZ,I,S,F, 1955:W,I,F*,S*

Nicholas Gerald (Nick) YOUNGS
Born: 15 December 1959 in West Runton
Educated: Cawston College, Gresham's School, Shuttleworth Agricultural College
Clubs: Bedford, Leicester (6)
Position: Scrum-half (6), Bench (5)
Debut: 19 Mar 1983 v Ireland (Lansdowne Road). Number: 1079
Last game: 17 Mar 1984 v Wales (Twickenham)
Caps: 6 (W:2, L:4)
Scoring: 0 Pts
Appearances: 1983:I,NZ, 1984:S,I,F,W

ACKNOWLEDGEMENTS

During the course of writing this book the team involved have accessed a large number of newspapers, magazines, including the pages of Rugby World Magazine, books and on-line resources, including BBC Sport on-line, all of which we have attempted to credit where they have been used. A number of excellent books, though, have been a huge source of help and I would like to acknowledge and recommend them to you:

The Daily Telegraph Chronicle of Rugby *(Guinness)*
Lions of England by Peter Jackson *(Mainstream)*
Thomas Clem, The History of the British Lions *(Mainstream)*
Spink, Alex, The Save & Prosper Rugby Union Who's Who *(Collins Willow)*
Griffiths, John British Lions *(Crowood)*
Farmer, Stuart, The Official England Rugby Miscellany *(Vision Sports)*
Gate, Robert, Rugby League Fact Book *(Guinness 1991)*
Godwin, Terry, The Complete Who's Who of International Rugby *(Blandford Press 1987)*
Griffiths, John, The Book of English International Rugby 1871-1982 *(Collins Willow 1982)*
Griffiths, John, The Phoenix Book of International Rugby Records *(Phoenix 1987)*
Griffiths, John, The Five Nations Championship 1947-93 *(Methuen 1993)*
Griffiths, John, 100 years of England Schools' Rugby *(RFU 2003)*
Maule, Raymond, The Complete Who's Who of England Rugby Union Internationals *(Breedon Books 1992)*
Morgan, Paul & Griffiths, John, IRB World Rugby Yearbook 2007 *(VSP 2006)*
New Zealand Rugby Almanacks 1936-2006
Pacitti, Paolo & Volpe, Francesco, Rugby 2006 *(Edigrafital 2006)*
Playfair Rugby Football Annuals 1948-49 to 1972-73
Rothmans Rugby Union Yearbooks 1972 to 1999-2000
Rothmans Rugby League Yearbooks 1981-82 to 1999
South African Rugby Annuals 1999-2006
Stansfield, Dan, The Who, When & Where of English International Rugby since 1947 *(Stansfield Publishing 1997)*
Test Rugby Lists *(Five Mile Press Australia 1999)*
Woolgar, Jason, England: The Official Rugby Football Union History *(Virgin Books 2004)*

The pictures in this book were provided courtesy of the following:

GETTY IMAGES, 101 Bayham Street, London NW1 0AG www.gettyimages.com

Colorsport, www.colorsport.co.uk

Design and Artwork by Newleaf Design & Media

Series Editor Vanessa Gardner

Proofread by Jane Pamenter

Creative Director Kevin Gardner